ORACLE®

Oracle Press™

Oracle9i Application Server Portal Handbook

D1404801

Oracle Press™

Oracle9*i* Application Server Portal Handbook

Steve Vandivier
Kelly Cox

McGraw-Hill/Osborne

New York Chicago San Francisco
Lisbon London Madrid Mexico City Milan
New Delhi San Juan Seoul Singapore Sydney Toronto

McGraw-Hill/Osborne
2600 Tenth Street
Berkeley, California 94710
U.S.A.

To arrange bulk purchase discounts for sales promotions, premiums, or fund-raisers, please contact McGraw-Hill/Osborne at the above address. For information on translations or book distributors outside the U.S.A., please see the International Contact Information page immediately following the index of this book.

Oracle9*i* Application Server Portal Handbook

Book p/n 0-07-213007-5 and CDs p/ns 0-07-213006-7; 0-07-219584-3; 0007-219585-1 parts of
ISBN 0-07-222249-2

Publisher Brandon A. Nordin	**Copy Editor** Dennis Weaver
Vice President & Associate Publisher Scott Rogers	**Proofreader** Cheryl Abel
Acquisitions Editor Jeremy Judson	**Indexer** Valerie Perry
Project Editor Elizabeth Seymour	**Computer Designers** George Toma Charbak & Elizabeth Jang
Acquisitions Coordinator Athena Honore	**Illustrators** Michael Mueller & Lyssa Wald
Technical Editor Leslie Tierstein	**Series Design** Damore Johann Design, Inc.

This book was composed with Corel VENTURA™ Publisher.

To Ginger Ormiston Kenworthy, wife of Jim Kenworthy and mother of Beth and Billy, who died in the destruction of the World Trade Center with so many others on September 11, 2001.
—*Steve Vandivier*

To Cory
—*Kelly Cox*

About the Authors

Steve Vandivier is the President and CEO of AVANCO International, Inc., a Certified Oracle Solutions Provider specializing in business intelligence, data warehousing, business process improvement, relational database design, and Web-based Portal application development. A 1979 graduate of the University of Virginia and President of the Mid-Atlantic Association of Oracle Professionals (MAOP), he has served many large and middle tier commercial clients as a software analyst, developer, and project manager, designing and developing large scale management, financial, and decision support systems for use on the Web. He is a member of the Oracle Business Intelligence and Portal Customer Advisory Boards (CAB), a select group of international consultants that offers feedback and advice to Oracle's Product Development Division. He is a sought-after speaker who has presented numerous times at Oracle's Open World, the IOUG-A Live!, the Oracle Development Tools Users Group, the South East Oracle Users Conference, and ECO. He is a member of the Board of Directors for the Virginia Chamber of Commerce. His firm of fifty software specialists, based in Mclean, Virginia was recognized by the Virginia Chamber of Commerce as being among the fastest growing private businesses in the state for four of the last five years.

Kelly McDonald Cox is an independent consultant specializing in the Oracle database and tools, based in the Washington D.C. area. In addition to her client work, she writes and teaches courses on the Oracle database and application server for Learning Tree International, has been a speaker at several Oracle conferences, and is a member of the International Oracle Users Group (IOUG) Portal SIG and Web steering committees. One of these days, she'll have the time to put up her own Web site.

Contents at a Glance

Contents

PART I
Getting Started

Foreword

The Internet is redefining the way businesses operate and the way enterprises communicate with their employees, customers and partners. Software, designed for the Internet, has enabled businesses to dramatically reduce expenses. In fact, using our own E-Business Suite, Oracle saved over $1B in one year. Enterprises are more responsive and agile as a result of better communications between employees, customers and partners.

Timely and accurate information is more critical than ever for users to get their job done. Database applications deliver this business-critical information to the users. Using the Internet, database applications that were traditionally accessible only within the enterprise are now accessible beyond the enterprise. Virtual enterprises, integrating suppliers, partners and customers, are now being realized by the new generation of Internet-enabled database applications. These virtual enterprises significantly increase the number of users that require access to the business-critical information stored in the database. As a result, the applications to access these databases must be high performance, available all the time, and easy to access.

Finding the right information at the right time is more challenging than ever given the wealth of information. On the Internet, users utilize Internet Portals such as Yahoo! to find public information. Users can personalize and simplify their view by including only the information they want in the portal. Within an enterprise, users require not only this public information but also corporate information from multiple intranet sites and database applications. Navigating between these sites and applications is often very cumbersome and time consuming. An Enterprise Portal simplifies the user's experience by aggregating the public, Internet information with the corporate, intranet information on a single page. An Enterprise Portal speeds the user's search by including only the information relevant to the user's job role. Enterprise Portal frameworks are now an essential component of the e-business software infrastructure to simplify access to all this information.

Oracle is the world's largest supplier of e-business software. 98 of the Fortune 100 use Oracle for e-business. Oracle uniquely offers a complete and integrated Internet platform including the Oracle9i database, application server and tools.

Oracle offers complete and integrated suites for developing e-business software, Internet Developer Suite, and deploying e-business software, Oracle9i Application Server. Developers can now productively build database applications that deliver complete functionality including transaction processing, business intelligence and, most importantly, enterprise portals. Internet Developer Suite includes a complete set of business intelligence tools that can quickly and easily answer any question about any business. Oracle Business Intelligence tools include the award-winning Oracle Discoverer for ad hoc query and analysis, Oracle Reports for high-fidelity database publishing, Business Intelligence Beans for developing analytical applications, and Oracle Warehouse Builder for designing and developing data warehouses. Internet Developer Suite includes a complete set of application development tools to productively develop transaction-processing applications. Oracle Application Development tools include the productive, model-based development tools, Designer and Forms Developer, and the flexible, component-based Java development tool, JDeveloper. Oracle tools automate application development and reduce both the labor and the time required to deliver database applications. Better yet, by reducing the error-prone manual coding process, Oracle tools dramatically improve the overall quality of applications.

Oracle9i Portal, an integral component of the Internet Developer Suite and Oracle9i Application Server, provides the most productive, functional, scalable and cost-effective Enterprise Portal framework on the market.

Using only a standard web browser, developers can quickly build Enterprise Portals without writing any code. They can even develop self-service web sites and database application components without writing even a single line of code. In fact, developers can easily assemble Enterprise Portals using pre-built information and application components.

Enterprise Portals must integrate with both existing and new applications. Oracle9i Portal components, called portlets, allow developers to integrate any existing or new application. Using Internet Developer Suite and the Portal Development Kit (PDK), developers can productively build and deliver portlets. As an example, any component developed using Oracle Discoverer or Oracle Reports is automatically available as a portlet. As members of the Oracle Portal Partner Initiative (OPPI), several vendors are delivering information and application portlets. High quality business content, such as business news and stock quote services, as well as application functionality, such as collaboration and advanced search services, is now available from the OPPI members. Developers can include these pre-built portlets to quickly deliver a complete Enterprise Portal.

Can a single Enterprise Portal address the needs of all the users?

To address the individual needs of all users, Oracle9i Portal framework provides role-based personalization and a sophisticated security model. Oracle9i Portal automatically personalizes the content based on the role of the user. As a result, users get the relevant information and only the information they are authorized to get. Users are more productive as they are not inundated with too much information. The security model offers the convenience of the single sign-on facility so users no longer have to remember multiple passwords. Users log in once to Oracle9i Portal and have access to all the authorized web sites and applications. Now, users can simply and quickly find all the relevant information and applications they need to get their job done.

An Enterprise Portal must be accessible from anywhere. The built-in mobile feature in Oracle9i Portal allows users to access the content from mobile devices such as Palm Pilot and WAP-enabled phones. In other words, to mobile-enable a portal requires no additional effort by developers. Users can now access the portal from a desktop computer as well as a variety of mobile devices.

Oracle9i Portal delivers unparalleled scalability and performance by leveraging the unique features of the Oracle9i Database and Oracle9i Application Server. In fact, Oracle developed an Enterprise Portal, My Oracle (http://my.oracle.com), as the home page for all employees, customers, and partners. Leveraging the Oracle9i platform, My Oracle delivers personalized content to one of the largest online business communities on the Internet.

To dramatically lower the cost of ownership and time to market, Oracle9i Portal is the first Enterprise Portal framework to also be available as a hosted developer service. By simply registering at Oracle Portal Online (http://portal.oracle.com), developers can start utilizing the Oracle9i Portal functionality in just a few minutes. Developers no longer have to install any software on their computer to start developing and deploying Enterprise Portals. Moreover, by providing a hosted service, Oracle eliminates customer's hardware and software infrastructure costs, dramatically lowering the total cost of ownership.

Simply put, Oracle9i Portal provides the most productive, functional, scalable and cost-effective Enterprise Portal framework on the market.

The authors of this book understand the power of the Oracle9i Portal framework and its integral role in the e-business software infrastructure. Steve and Kelly offer the Oracle developer community a valuable resource—a reference for developing powerful Enterprise Portals using all the techniques they have mastered in their extensive experience with the Oracle9i Portal product and their participation in the Oracle Portal and Business Intelligence Customer Advisory Boards. This book includes an exploration of the features and use of all the key elements of Oracle9i Portal to help save you time and effort.

Oracle9i Portal, along with the information contained in this book, will enable you to deliver the Enterprise Portal to serve as the home page for your e-business in record time.

—Sohaib Abbasi
Senior Vice President
Development & Education
Oracle Corporation

Acknowledgments

There are many highs and lows that accompany the writing of a book. Writing is a labor of love and pain mixed together, not for the feint of heart. Books are not written in a vacuum and the world goes on even as a new work begins to take shape. The Portal product has gone through at least seven iterations since this project began— from its WebDB roots to Portal Beta, to Portal Pre-Production, to Portal versions 3.06, 3.07, 3.08, and now 3.09. This is an excellent product but it was a distinct challenge to keep up with the enhancements to the software over the last months as it continued to improve.

In January, I broke my shoulder while skiing with my family.I continued to write while my arm was immobilized in a sling for six weeks. I thought writing with one hand would be my authoring low point but there were others. Of course, September 11 is etched in everyone's head. That one day has had such an impact on our collective perspective and in the way we all look at the world in which we live. Out of a terrible experience, we have grown together as a nation, as neighbors, as brothers and sisters, as family. It has really been an awesome thing to see our country, and the world community, unite together in such a supportive way. And through it all, the work on book went on.

One of my most memorable days writing was a beautiful summer day when I wanted to play outside with my kids. I couldn't because I had a chapter to produce. My younger daughter, Abby, came in from playing and asked me to go outside with her. Reluctantly, I told her I couldn't. Sensing I was feeling down, she asked, "How is the book comin', Dad?" in the most positive voice she could muster. I told her things were OK but I was getting a little discouraged and I really didn't want to be inside writing on such a beautiful day. She responded with great seriousness. "Dad, you know what you need to do? You need to be like The Little Engine That Could." I sat her in my lap and said, "OK, tell me what you mean by that."

"Well, to finish this book and to do a good job you just need to say "I think I can, I think I can, I think I can.' And you know what? Before long you will be able to say,

'I know I can, I know I can, I know I can' and then writing the book will be easy!" With that, she gave me a kiss and went outside to play. Shortly afterward, my older daughter, Allie, came inside, hugged me and said, "Dad, I know you are working hard, and I don't want to disturb you, but I just wanted to tell you I love you very much and you are doing a good job."

That day taught me a lot about life, about the importance of fighting hard to finish tasks even when it gets discouraging. More significantly, I saw firsthand the value of family and the unconditional faith and love that are embodied in your children. I feel nothing else could be more important or would offer more to make life worth living. So to my wife, Amy, and my two daughters, Allie and Abby: Thank you so much for your patience and your abiding love.

I want to thank my co-author Kelly Cox for her tremendous contribution to this book. It would not be the book that it is without her hard work, dedication, and technical skill and abilities. Our technical editor, Leslie Tierstein, was absolutely awesome and supported the technical editing process with a perfect mix of encouragement and tough love when the writing was not up to the standards she knew we could produce. Thanks, too, to Ross Doll, Athena Honore, Elizabeth Seymour, and Dennis Weaver of McGraw-Hill/Osborne for their great work in editing, fitting all the pieces together, and hustling us up for our deadlines. I would particularly like to thank Jeremy Judson of McGraw-Hill/Osborne, who had the patience of a saint and a supportive professional approach to this project that made working hard for him a pleasure, not a job or a duty. I would like to thank my wonderful mother who served as a surrogate project manager for Jeremy by frequently prodding me to meet my deadlines and "to get that book done." Thanks, too, to my father and sister who are always supportive of me, no matter what I am doing.

In the professional community I want to acknowledge Marlene Theriault, an accomplished technical author, software professional, our MAOP DBA SIG chair, and a good friend who supported me with great advise and friendly chats at the local Starbucks down the street. I particularly appreciate the help and support provided by Paul Encarnacion of Oracle Corporation, a first-class person and professional who always seems to find time to support clients and his fellow peers despite an extremely demanding workload. Others at Oracle that supported this book include Harry Wong, Patanjali Venkatacharya, John Boyle, Sanjay Khanna, Jay Daugherty, Bill Lankenau, and Todd Vendor. Thanks to my friends at Your Conference Connection and ODTUG, Kathleen McCasland and Larissa Skipper, for checking in with me frequently and offering moral support.

I wish to thank everyone at my company, AVANCO International for supporting me through this process. There were so many times I should have been supporting managers, projects, proposal efforts, or administration and I was working on the book instead. I sincerely appreciate everyone for stepping it up a notch so I could accomplish this. Particularly I want to thank Salima Benelmouffok and Anissa Stevens for their writing contributions. Finally, to all of my family, friends, and neighbors too numerous to mention: You are all wonderful and your caring gives me the incentive and confidence to try to be a better person.

—*Steve Vandivier*

When I first learned of WebDB and what it could do for my then-clients at the United States Postal Service, I was eager to get my hands on the product and learn more. Since then, there have been many people at Oracle who have helped to that end—especially Akila Kumar, Barry Hiern, Hong-Wei Lu, Todd Vender, Patanjali Venkatacharya, Sanjay Singh, Marc Risney, and Paul Encarnacion. Special thanks go to Harry Wong for his ongoing willingness to help, and for his work with the IOUG Portal SIG. In addition, big kudos go to the Portal group at Oracle Support, for its quick and complete responses to my many requests for assistance.

Volunteering with the IOUG has provided so many opportunities to learn and expand my professional horizons. Thanks to Ann Kilhoffer-Reichert, Gaimil Villareal, Eashwar Iyer, Yipeng Chen, Hanming Tu, and all the volunteers who tested our initial WebDB prototype site for managing technical content. Greg Grimes, Harold Fennell, Earl Schaffer, Elizabeth Reardon, Julie Ferry, Rebecca Stoner and Lisa Elliot are to be commended for their efforts in creating and managing the WebDB (now Portal) SIG; Greg especially for sharing his insights with me and with the broader community. It was Peter Koletzke, at times guru, coach, mentor, and cheerleader, who encouraged me to write about Portal and reviewed some of my initial work on the subject. Thanks for everything, Peter.

The instructors, students, and staff of Learning Tree International have contributed significantly to this book, by sharing their questions, solutions, and methods. Particularly noteworthy are Kent Hinckley, for his patient advice and insistence on accuracy; Dag Hoftun-Knutsen, with his brilliant techniques and "SQL Acrobatics"; Garry Chan, for venturing to produce a course on an early release of Oracle Web Server; and student Anita Kapoor, for suggesting the cross-tab report portlet. I've learned a lot from you all.

The real work was done by those people who put this book together and got it to the book stores. Elizabeth Seymour, ever-patient Project Editor; Athena Honore, task mistress extraordinaire; and Jeremy Judson, Acquisitions Editor, were among those who actually managed to get a book out of us. Dennis Weaver had the arduous task of sorting out Portal's Creative Capitalization and our periodic reinventing of style conventions. Leslie Tierstein's rigorous tech editing managed to help me find the writer in this programmer.

I wouldn't have gotten through this without the patient support of my family, friends and neighbors, who always seemed to know when to ask about the book and when not to mention it. Going back a few years, I owe a debt of gratitude to Henry Jacobs, who introduced me to Oracle, and Steve Jepsen, now at Oracle, who gave me my first one-hour briefing on how it all works. I owe my foundation in management information systems to the brilliant teaching and research of the faculty at the Massachusetts Institute of Technology's Sloan School of Management, most memorably Rich Wang, Tom Allen, and Tom Malone.

And of course, there's little Cory who, at age five, is blessed with compassion, patience, and an understanding of the world that never ceases to amaze me. Whenever I mentioned that I had "good news" for him, he would ask, "Is the book done?" Now he gets his Mommy back.

—Kelly Cox

Introduction

eveloping corporate portals can be a daunting task for any organization. Oracle 9iAS Portal simplifies the job considerably, by providing a framework upon which you will build and expand. The key to success with a Portal project is to understand the framework and the places where you can exert the most leverage to make it do what you want it to do. Beyond offering an exploration of the product itself, this book will endeavor to teach you concepts of portal development and organization, Web development and administration, and practical relational database development and administration. After reading this book, you will understand:

- The concept of an enterprise information portal

- A methodology for developing your own corporate portal

- How to choose the appropriate Portal feature to meet your requirements

- Techniques to make your organization's resources available and searchable

- Oracle 9iAS Portal customization and extensions

- Portal architecture and administration

About this Book

The *Oracle 9iAS Portal Handbook* addresses the needs of corporate IT professionals, managers, knowledge workers, and line-of-business professionals from large and small corporations who are seeking to easily deliver and leverage enterprise information for competitive gain.

The book will concentrate on a methodology for creating a portal from the ground up following a rapid application development (RAD) process. An understanding of Oracle8i and PL/SQL coding techniques is helpful for this intermediate-level book, but is not required. We attempt to explain any complexities in the code in comments and notes, but a good SQL or PL/SQL reference may prove handy.

We assume that readers have a basic understanding of relational concepts and database management systems. The reader should also have practical software development experience, either in a Web-based or client-server environment. Intermediate or expert Oracle developers will be able to learn Portal concepts quickly, and more novice readers will pick up solid development practices and principals of Portal development and Internet architecture.

This book offers a concise example-based presentation of how to use Oracle Portal to organize structured information and unstructured content within your company and deliver it directly to the individuals in your organization that need it. Included with this book is a copy of Oracle 9i Application Server for Windows NT. Download a copy of the Oracle8i database, follow Chapter 2 to install Oracle 9iAS, and you will be ready to develop a working enterprise information portal using all of Oracle Portal's many features. The book is organized in a cookbook format with hands-on tutorials and exercises based on practical examples that will simplify the process of developing an enterprise portal.

Portal has been something of a moving target over the last few years, as Oracle has continued to improve the product and add new features. We started this book when the current release was 3.0.7.6.2, wrote most of it on version 3.0.8, and performed final edits and testing against version 3.0.9. The book is targeted at the 3.0.9 release, and we strongly recommend this version for any production development. Most of the code and techniques in the book will work against 3.0.8, but we made a few changes in response to improvements in the 3.0.9 release that are not available in 3.0.8. Subsequent patches may also affect what we provide for you here. Please check the Oracle Press Web site for updates and tips on how to deal with version differences.

How to Use this Book

For each topic in this book, we first offer a general explanation of the available features and options, and follow that with a detailed exercise that illustrates those features and additional techniques. We use illustrations to show you what the screens look like, but the book is best read in front of a browser window logged into a Portal session, so you can follow along and experiment as you go. While you don't have to do the exercises to learn from this book, many of your questions about how to implement advanced features will be answered by a thorough review of the techniques shown.

To do the exercises, you will need to download a zip file from the Oracle Press Web site (www.oraclepress.com), extract it, and run the scripts as directed in "readme" files contained within. These scripts build supporting tables, data, procedures, and functions that are referenced in the exercises. Most of the code shown in the book is provided in text form to save you some typing, and all of the components you will build have been exported using the Portal export utility and saved in the appropriate chapter directory. Two bonus chapters, and related content, are available for download from the same Oracle Press URL address.

Throughout the book, you will be following tutorials and exercises that will involve some coding using Structured Query Language (SQL) and PL/SQL. SQL (pronounced "sequel") is a standard interface language that allows programmers, database administrators (DBAs), and end users to interface with a relational database, in our case Oracle8i. Programmers and end users can SELECT, UPDATE, INSERT, and DELETE records from the database. DBAs can use SQL commands to CREATE, ALTER, and DROP database objects such as tables or views, create users and grant them roles and privileges to access database information, and tune the database system. PL/SQL adds procedural constructs and many of the features of a full-fledged programming language.

If you have limited experience with the Oracle database and its structures, we highly recommend reading *Oracle DBA 101* (Oracle Press, 2000) written by Marlene Theriault, Rachel Carmichael, and James Vescusi. Important relational concepts that we will not delve into in the *Oracle 9iAS Portal Handbook* are covered clearly and concisely in their book.

Make sure you also check out the Oracle Technology Web site for the latest information and technical data about Oracle Portal. You may register for OTN at http://technet.oracle.com/register/oraclepress_nt.

Conventions

SQL and PL/SQL code is not case sensitive but, for readability, we try to follow certain standards and conventions that are generally acknowledged in the industry. Commands, reserved words, datatypes, and Oracle package names are coded in UPPERCASE. All other references, including table and column names, views, variables, and user-defined procedures and functions, are typically coded in lowercase. We use blank lines and indented statements throughout the code to suggest the intended logic flow, and add comments where necessary for documentation purposes. For more information about how to code SQL and PL/SQL, read *Oracle PL/SQL Tips and Techniques* (Oracle Press, 1999), written by Joe Trezzo, Brad Brown, and Rich Niemiec.

The following code is a simple example of the documented code that will be used throughout the book:

```
--Program empsalrv.sql
--Created: 7-31-2001
--Developer: Steve Vandivier
/*
Description:  This code selects the department name, city, employee
name, hire -date, salary, commission, and total salary for employees of
the company and produces a salary review notification report for the HR
department by department, city and hiredate.
```

```
*/
SELECT    dept.dname, dept.loc, emp.ename, emp.hiredate,
          SUM(emp.sal), SUM(emp.comm), (SUM(emp.sal))+(SUM(emp.comm))
FROM      SCOTT.dept, SCOTT.emp
WHERE     dept.deptno = emp.deptno
GROUP BY  dept.dname, dept.loc, emp.hiredate;
```

Now that we have been properly introduced, let's get started!

PART

I

Getting Started

CHAPTER
1

Overview of
Enterprise
Information Portals

S cience fiction and movie writers have shown a fascination over the years with the concept of transporting individuals to a different dimension in space and time using a device commonly referred to as a portal. Portals have transported people to another dimension in *Star Trek*, forward in time in the H.G. Wells classic *The Time Machine*, to another world in *Alice In Wonderland*, and back to the Middle Ages in Michael Crichton's book, *Timeline*. It's fascinating to think that we could use a portal to go back in time and do historical research on location. It is, of course, impossible to do. Or is it?

We may not physically be able to go back in time, but with the Internet, we have the next best thing: an entire world where, with the click of a mouse, we can mentally transport ourselves to the Middle Ages, to Hollywood for a movie premiere, overseas for the news from Europe, or into space to witness the discovery of a new solar system. This amalgamation of interconnected computer networks we call the World Wide Web is indeed a vast world full of wonder and unlimited information.

We can harness and effectively utilize this great power and possibility by using Internet portals. Internet portals such as Lycos, Excite, Netscape, and Yahoo have been on the scene for some time. These Web sites use sophisticated search engines that allow us to hunt for desired topics on the Web, and use our search results to transport ourselves again and again to myriad new worlds on the Internet.

It is important for modern businesses to have the same ability to transport to the information they need to stay competitive. Enterprise information portals (EIPs) are gateways to corporate information delivered in a context that is tailored to today's corporate knowledge workers. This book will focus on how businesses can leverage the power of the Internet, the Oracle 9*i* relational database, and Oracle Portal to organize and access information and use it to create strategic competitive advantages and corporate gain.

Technology Convergence

Everyone is aware of the predominance of the Internet and what a huge role it plays in industrialized society today. The amazing thing is how fast it has become a part of our popular culture, not to mention our business culture. It took 35 years for radios to penetrate over 50 million households worldwide. Television took 13 years to reach the same number of people. The Internet entered the lives of 50 million individuals four years after it was introduced. An astounding seven people gain access to the Internet every second, and it is available in nearly every country in the world. The Internet had more users in its first five years than the telephone had in its first 30 years.

Entire industries are refocusing and reinventing themselves around Internet technology. The reasons for this are many and varied. A few years ago at any major Oracle technical show or press conference, you would have heard Oracle's CEO Larry Ellison espouse the Network Computer (NC) during his keynote address, with enthusiastic backing from his good friend and fellow CEO, Scott McNealy of Sun Microsystems. The NC was a computer that would be designed and built solely to allow users to access the Internet and run programs over the Net. It was a good concept and, as with many concepts that Larry promotes, it was visionary and slightly ahead of its time. The business results of those early NC announcements have been mixed at best, but of great benefit to the IT community.

The NC never made noticeable inroads in the traditional PC market. The personal computer industry reacted quickly to the introduction of the NC and cut its prices drastically in reaction to a plausible business concept that had some teeth. I believe we have Larry Ellison to thank for substantially reducing the cost of corporate PC buys over the last few years. These kinds of announcements also forced Bill Gates to reinvent Microsoft around the Internet. To understand why Internet computing is so important, we need to understand that it really is a historical convergence of many technologies. Without consistent research and breakthroughs in the areas of networks, software, databases, hardware, and telecommunications, there would be no such thing as Internet computing.

History of Internet Computing

What was the reason for proposing the NC and why is Internet computing so important? To understand this, it is important to understand how the computer industry has evolved over the last 20 years. In the early 1980s, the industry was very mainframe centric. The data for any business or government entity resided in one place: on a powerful mainframe computer. IBM—"Big Blue"—dominated the market with its powerful mainframes. Cray Systems offered supercomputers that took up entire rooms and offered incredible power for scientific applications that required millions of calculations per second. Desktop PCs had barely been invented and midrange computers ("minicomputers") were not in widespread use in corporate America.

A major problem at the time was that interfacing with these goliaths was an antiquated and clunky process. In 1980 the computer technology field was centered on punch card "technology." Punched computer cards were the primary way to interface with the mainframes used at most large corporations. Programmers keyed in their COBOL source code on punched cards or later used "dumb-terminals," as shown in Figure 1-1, that created electronic files directly on midrange computers that could generate punched card decks of code for consumption on the mainframe.

It was an all-day process to feed the cards into the mainframe and get a compiled printout back, only to find an error that needed to be fixed. "Dimpled and hanging chad" ruled the day, frequently causing production run problems. It was a common occurrence to drop a huge deck of punch cards on the floor and incur the wrath of the lead developer on a project. Clunky electronic sorters could put the program back together again, but problems like these required a better way to do business.

The personal computer came on the business scene in a big way in 1981 when IBM introduced the IBM PC and Bill Gates introduced the DOS operating system. Until then, personal computers were designed for games and for people pursuing technical hobbies—but not for businesses. The first modems, 300-baud dinosaurs, offered direct access to remote computers over a phone line. Work was still predominantly mainframe centric, but programs like dBase, Word, VisiCalc, Excel, Lotus, and eventually Oracle, began appearing on the scene designed for the desktop. We didn't know it at that time, but PC ownership and proliferation were the resolution of many problems— seemingly lower cost of ownership, control over information, and a better user interface—and also the beginning of bigger problems.

During the 1980s and early 1990s, MS Windows was introduced and programs designed to store information on the desktop continued to proliferate. Then came the advent and popularity of client/server computing in the late 1980s and more prevalently into the early 1990s. Client/server computing was truly the result of a lot of different technologies coming together, particularly networks and their telecommunications infrastructure.

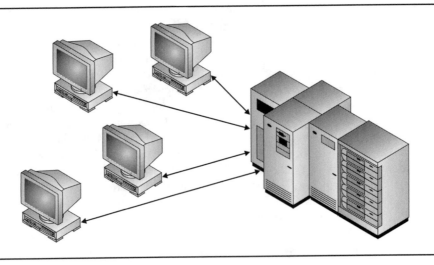

FIGURE 1-1. *"Dumb terminals" connected to a mainframe computer*

Networks

The concept of networks was introduced in the 1970s by the Department of Defense with its initial backbone network known as the Advanced Research Projects Agency Network (ARPANET). The first ARPANET was a prototype proof of concept that connected four computers and later was rolled out to provide networked connections to over 50 DoD clients, agencies, colleges, universities, and research institutions involved in military research projects. ARPANET was designed to establish a networked communications link between DoD clients, agencies, universities and other research facilities.

It can truly be thought of as the precursor to the Internet of today. File Transfer Protocol (FTP), Internet Protocol (IP) addresses, Telnet, and email were all introduced with ARPANET. ARPANET enhanced the ability of individuals to share data and information between mainframe computer systems, a huge breakthrough in computing technology. As a DoD network, ARPANET was proprietary and seldom used outside of the military realm.

As the personal computer was introduced, and as more research was applied to the early versions of connected networks, new standards and structures were introduced to enhance network sophistication. The invention of network interface cards (NICs) for PCs and greater standardization of network protocols, including Transmission Control Protocol (TCP), coupled with the IP address protocol and more efficient packet switching to speed data access led to a greater commercialization of the network. Businesses and organizations began to purchase NICs to install in their office PCs so that printers, files, and computers could be shared as depicted in Figure 1-2.

This information and hardware sharing led to tremendous initial cost savings for organizations, because they could cut down on the cost of equipment and resources. Initially these networks were somewhat slow and cumbersome. Network lines snaked throughout offices everywhere connecting computers and printers. Eventually networks became faster and more efficient—and they became much, much bigger and more wide-ranging, leading to wide area networks (WANs) that connected companies and organizations nationwide and worldwide.

The World Wide Web project was born in the late 1980s as a centralized Web site developed by Tim Berners-Lee, Director of the CERN Particle Physics Lab in Switzerland. Simply put, it offered easy access to network information on a much wider scale. In order to get to the "Web," as the site was known then, you needed to perform a Telnet link to the CERN particle physics lab computers at address nxoc01.cern.ch in Switzerland. After you waited…and waited… and waited to get in to a computer across the Atlantic, you encountered some opening remarks from the World Wide Web project and you were offered a number of hypertext links embedded in the initial document.

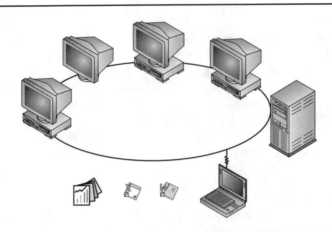

FIGURE 1-2. *Networks allow organizations to share resources and applications*

Although it was cumbersome, the World Wide Web became a very popular site for research and quickly gained popular acceptance. In the United States, the Internet grew out of the academic community where an ARPANET clone for universities, the National Science Foundation Network (NSFNET), took root in the mid-1980s. NSFNET slowly grew in popularity inside, and later outside, of the academia as a research and communications tool, and eventually joined forces with DARPANET (Defense Advanced Research Projects Agency Network, renamed from ARPANET) and other fledgling networks to became known simply as the Internet.

When the Internet was opened up commercially in the mid-1990s for Internet service providers (ISPs), the Internet phenomenon got underway. Corporations and individuals began signing up for Internet services so that they could tap into the Internet for research and to communicate via e-mail. Today, e-mail messages outstrip private mail by a staggering ten to one margin. The Internet is phenomenal, but it didn't reach its current level of popularity until some major advances in software were realized.

Internet Access Software

In the beginning, Internet surfing was not at all user friendly and quite restrictive. Gopher was a commonly used Internet navigator that offered a text-oriented, menu-driven Web "surfing" user interface that, when combined with an understanding of UNIX commands, allowed end users to find information on the Internet. Gopher allowed a limited search service, but it did not allow users to truly browse the Internet; you really needed to know where you were going in order to use it effectively.

Hypertext was a term coined in the mid-1960s by Ted Nelson, who wanted to find a nonhierarchical way to browse through information for a project he devised and code-named Xanadu. Nelson's dream was to make his Xanadu hypertext library framework the universal method for performing concise Internet searches using concepts he coined like the "docuverse," "xanalogical storage," and other esoteric abstractions. *Wired* magazine calls the 30-year-long Xanadu project the "longest running vaporware project in the history of computing." Despite the criticism, Nelson's hypertext allowed keywords to be linked to one another in a way that offered text searches in more of a relational manner based on interrelated meanings. Graphics, video, and sound could be linked to hypertext to offer hypermedia as well.

Hypertext was the precursor to Hypertext Markup Language (HTML) and the WWW project was, of course, the beginning of what we know today as the World Wide Web. The WWW site offered a much easier way to perform research on the Web then Gopher. The problem with the WWW site was that everything was hypertext oriented and many searches ended up at dead ends where there was no going back. There were so many hypertext links in some cases, and searches were so flat and far-reaching, that research was not productive because too much disparate information was revealed.

The most important advance for the Internet was the development of a graphical Web browser named Mosaic by Marc Andreeson, a college student at the University of Illinois at Champaign-Urbana, working at the National Center for Supercomputing (NCSA). Mosaic was multimedia based and combined the best of hyperlink searches, sophisticated search engines, and embedded graphics and sound. The Web was transformed immediately forever. Mosaic offered much of what the Netscape and Internet Explorer Browsers of today offer including:

- The ability to key in a specific URL address in the document Location URL: search field

- The ability to view MPEG movie images

- Hypertext links to Web sites on the Internet

- The ability to move forward and back on the browser with the click of a button

- Personalizing the Web experience by allowing annotation of Web sites for future reference

- The ability to change fonts and colors on Web pages for more dramatic effect

- The ability to combine text and graphics within documents on a page

Upon graduation, Andreeson co-founded Netscape using the concepts of the Mosaic browser as the foundation for his Netscape Navigator, and within a few years the Web started to gain some of its status as the popular cultural icon it has become today. Today Netscape Communicator and Microsoft's Internet Explorer are the most popular browser tools offered worldwide; they both provide unlimited access to the power of the Internet.

Database Computing

At the same time that Internet software was evolving, database computing was using the new network architectures to provide advances in the way information is stored, accessed, and utilized. We all know that databases are software repositories capable of storing large amounts of data and information. In the 1980s, hierarchical network databases such as IBM's IDMS and Honeywell's IDS2 were prevalent. As depicted in Figure 1-3, hierarchical databases work with a parent-child tree structure dictating the way in which records are retrieved.

As the example indicates, you would first retrieve project records subordinate to a specific work category of interest. To do that you must first prime a key, in this case work type, with the type of work you are interested in. Then you can peruse the projects that are linked to the category chosen until a specific project or projects are found. After finding the correct project, you can then look for all the project financial information by a date range or other metric that in turn is chained to the new project record retrieved.

In this manner you can walk down through various chains of records until the record or records you want to retrieve for update or for reporting are found. Inserting

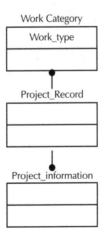

FIGURE 1-3. *A hierarchical database requires navigating many records to retrieve data*

a new record into the chain is done by identifying the search order for the record and then storing the new record with all of the requisite links that are required to identify the pecking order of the record for future update or reporting. As you can see, this method works fine, but it is very cumbersome to walk all of the chains required to find an individual record.

12 Rules of RDBMS

In the late 70's and early 80's, hierarchical database computing gave way to relational database technology. Before 1970, the most advanced databases were hierarchical in nature. In a series of articles written in the 1970s, Dr. Edgar Codd presented a new type of database that was relational in nature, not hierarchical. Codd's theories were fairly radical at the time and theorists and engineers were skeptical of his work. In 1985, Codd wrote his guidelines for a relational database management system (RDBMS) in the form of his famous 12 rules for *ComputerWorld Magazine*. They were as follows:

1. Data should be presented to the user in table form.

2. Every data element should be accessible without ambiguity.

3. A field should be allowed to remain empty for future use.

4. The description of a database should be accessible to the user.

5. A database must support a clearly defined language to define the database, view the definition, manipulate the data, and restrict data values to maintain database integrity.

6. Data should be able to be changed through any view available to the user.

7. All records in a file must be able to be added, deleted, or changed with a single command.

8. Changes in how data is stored or retrieved should not affect how the user accesses the data.

9. The user's view of the data should be unaffected by its actual form in files.

10. Constraints on user input should exist to maintain data integrity.

11. A database design should allow for distribution of data over several computer sites.

12. Data fields that affect the organization of the database cannot be changed.

Many companies jumped into the market with relational database product offerings at about the same time but Oracle is generally recognized as the first commercial relational database company. Other companies to follow included Ingres, Informix, Sybase, IBM, and Microsoft, but none had the marketing clout and aggressiveness that Oracle possessed. Today, Oracle is the second largest software company in the world. It dominates the relational database market with a 50- percent share of the worldwide market. It is a fact that none of these companies, including Oracle, have implemented a 100-percent purely relational database as envisioned by Dr. Codd. It is also quite true that they all have the capability to store and retrieve information in a relational nature and they all follow most of Codd's 12 RDBMS rules in some manner.

Single-Tier Architecture

Oracle's first relational databases were single-tier applications that executed entirely on a mainframe computer. Users logged onto the mainframe using terminals and wrote C or Cobol code to manipulate, update, store, and retrieve data. The interface in the early versions of Oracle was through a set of code called Pro*C or Pro*Cobol that used Structured Query Language (SQL) extensions to allow the compiled language to interface with the database using SQL commands. SQL could be used to update records, retrieve them, create new records, create tables and other database structures, and generally interface with the database software.

One of the early advantages of the Oracle database over its competitors was that it was portable across many vendor platforms and operating systems. Today Oracle basically runs on any platform, from a PC running Windows 98 or 2000 to a large HP or Sun computer running the HP-UX or Solaris operating system (UNIX versions devised by HP and Sun, respectively). Oracle is also extremely scaleable— any organization can start out with a small database running on Windows NT on a PC and expand it until it reaches a virtually unlimited size on a different platform. The same database can grow and be moved very easily.

Client Server (Multitier Architecture)

In the 1980s, client/server networks were introduced and Oracle became the first company to introduce a client/server version of its database in 1987. The client/server model allows many types of operating systems, including Novell's Netware, Microsoft's Windows, and various flavors of UNIX and other mainframe and PC-based operating systems, to seamlessly coexist on the network and be accessible to the end user.

Oracle can reside on a Windows NT Compaq server as depicted in Figure 1-4 or on a large Sun Server running Solaris, and all hardware and OS systems can coexist on the same network. Applications can be distributed so that the end user can issue a query to find the latest information about a specific subject and the query will be directed to the Compaq database server or the Sun Server, or both, to get the answer.

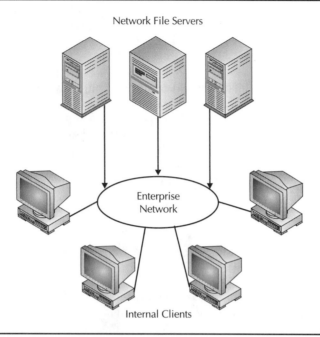

Network File Servers

Enterprise Network

Internal Clients

FIGURE 1-4. *A client/server network system*

The user never needs to know where the data resides. Client/server systems originated in a two-tier architecture where the client PC and the user interface represent one tier of the application and the database server represents the other.

All application logic runs on the client machine and the database delivers the requested information. The network sends and receives information and requests back and forth between the PC and the server. Client/server computing layers complicated network architecture on top of a complex relational database architecture. Needless to say, with this kind of complexity supporting an application, it is often difficult to pin down the source of performance problems. Poorly written application code, insufficient network capacity, or database tuning or design issues can be the source of a slow system. More to the point, it frequently takes a database administrator, a network engineer, and a senior application developer working together to pin down performance problems in the client/server environment.

Internet Computing (Thin-Client Architecture)

With the advent of client/server computing, mainframes began a steady decline and many large mainframe computer manufacturers went out of business. The PC ruled, and it seemed that everything would continue to charge along in a desktop Microsoft-centered world—until corporations around the world began to realize that computing on the desktop was getting out of hand.

What were these organizations discovering that was so insidious and such a problem? First of all, everyone needed a PC on their desktop to do anything and they needed Windows on the PC to do it. This was ultimately a very expensive proposition, because PCs were expensive to network and maintain and they required expert technicians to maintain the working environment throughout the enterprise since computing wasn't centralized anymore. The Windows operating system offered a development standard to work and program on, but it was very complicated—especially in a networked environment.

Strategic enterprise applications residing in a client/server environment became like an expensive car with too many widgets and computer controls. They were nice when they worked but failed more often than not and were a technician's nightmare to diagnose and maintain. Software configuration management, including version control and deployment, and maintenance of code, became a CIO's worst nightmare as large corporations tried to maintain mission-critical applications that were spread out on desktops throughout the enterprise. Data was no longer on one mainframe. It was on countless servers throughout the organization, and there was a lot of redundancy and duplication of effort going on in the database world. But then came the Internet and a new way to access information and data.

Web-based thin-client architecture is typically a three-tier system where the database server still exists as the final tier as shown in Figure 1-5. The first tier belongs to the client interface, where the only true requirement is that the end-user machine has a Java-enabled Web browser installed. The middle tier consists of an HTTP application server and an application layer that is specific to the application being executed by the end user. The application server provides the point of entry for the end user from the Internet or intranet to the application they want to run on the Web. The user simply accesses the application server by typing the proper URL from the desktop browser directly or from a link on the corporate home page. The application server then acts as a broker establishing a link between the application software on the application server and the final tier of the system, the database server.

Oracle establishes the connection between the database server and the application server using Net8, a software component that comes with the Oracle 9i database. Net8 provides the ability for a machine to connect and communicate to an Oracle database across a network. We will be using Oracle Portal in a thin-client architecture both to perform our development activities and to run the application. A thin-client architecture eliminates many of the headaches and hidden costs of client/server systems, including software configuration management, PC configuration and setup on the network, and software maintenance and deployment.

In many ways thin-client computing is a throwback to a simpler time. Users simply need a "dumb terminal" to access an application, and that is really all they

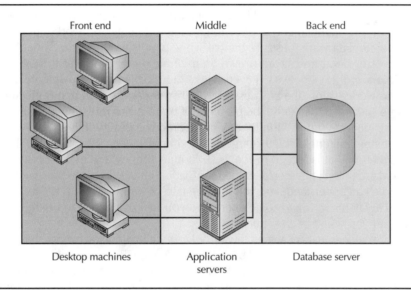

Front end	Middle	Back end
Desktop machines	Application servers	Database server

FIGURE 1-5.   *Thin-client three-tier architecture*

need to understand. Web applications and browsers are very intuitive, and there is usually very little training required for the user to become productive. From the developer point of view, there is one place to deploy applications and that is on the application server. Lastly, the database can still be distributed across many database servers within the enterprise, but the connection to those database servers is maintained and handled from one place, the application server. All of this is much simpler to control and to understand, and it requires fewer corporate resources and specialists to maintain it.

Business Intelligence and Knowledge Management

The previous discussion has shown how historical advances in networks, software, and hardware have converged to form the basis for Internet computing. But what about the data we have collected during that time? The greatest problem of all—that still requires a great deal of work—is the many islands of information that have accumulated on individual desktops and network servers throughout corporations everywhere in the world from the 1980s and 1990s.

Today, data is everywhere. Excel spreadsheets are on the CFO's desk. Strategic corporate documents are on the CEO's laptop. Lists of key clients are stored on the secretaries' electronic Rolodex files. Employee data is in the Oracle database on the HR department stand-alone NT network, and strategic corporate information is stored on the financial ERP application on the midrange Sun workstation and in the corporate data warehouse. Technical white papers written by members of R&D or engineering departments are strewn on multiple servers and PCs throughout corporations worldwide. Data is everywhere, and locked in that disparate data is the knowledge about the business and about the competition that is the key to corporate success. Ultimately, the problem of finding and integrating all that data is a very expensive proposition for any corporation to deal with and resolve.

In the new millennium, 20 years after the introduction of the IBM PC, data (and the information that is locked inside) is still found everywhere in most organizations. Find the data, unlock the secrets of the information embedded in it, present it in a way that people can understand, and you can use it to powerful strategic advantage. Leave it locked away on an island somewhere and you will be the first to be thrown off the island, and you won't be the "Survivor."

Two disciplines that are geared toward solving the information overload problem are knowledge management (KM) and business intelligence (BI). Knowledge management is the act of gathering, organizing, understanding, sharing, and reusing the knowledge that has been gained inside of an organization. This can include competitive information, but more often than not it is procedural in nature and relates to communication within the organization about internal organizational objectives.

Knowledge management is collaborative and seeks to promote knowledge of one's job responsibilities as well as to promote organizational objectives and goals by disseminating information about corporate best practices. Examples of knowledge management include published IT web development standards, corporate accounting procedures, and the company employee manual. Various tools can be used to promote knowledge management, including, as we will see, Oracle Portal.

Executive information systems (EIS), decision support, data mining, operational data stores, multidimensional online analytical processing (MOLAP), relational online analytical processing (ROLAP), and now business intelligence—all terms that are a little confusing for those of us that are trying to keep up with the growing information revolution and its terminology. There is a movement within industry to capture data from our legacy systems and transform all that data into information that can be proactively used to improve business and business processes.

It is becoming increasingly important to use data as a strategic weapon in order to keep market share, build market share, or, in the case of government, do more with less. Business intelligence tools such as Oracle's Discoverer, Reports, Express Objects, and Express Analyzer create a proactive reporting environment that allows retrieval of enterprise information quickly, by function, and in an appropriate manner to answer the business questions at hand.

Business intelligence is a strategic approach to using information that can lead to informed business decisions and tactical corporate advantages over business competitors. Business intelligence applications provide a mechanism for gathering and analyzing internal and external information and that can lead to business process improvement or reengineering. Improvement can come in the form of understanding customers better, leading to better and more targeted selling opportunities. Identifying breakdowns in internal accounting controls can lead to real cost savings. In many ways, BI is similar to KM, but it is more proactive and goes beyond a best practices approach to actually identifying and solving problems and providing measurable return on investment (ROI).

Software products such as Oracle Discoverer, a Web-based database browser that allows ad hoc reporting and graphical representations of corporate trends are typical of a BI tool. Data mining products, such as Oracle's Darwin, allow quantification and identification of hard-to-find trends or data anomalies and are also frequently used in a BI environment. BI tools can identify cases of fraud in an insurance company that can lead to huge savings for the company when the fraud is uncovered and the perpetrators are caught. In many cases, BI tools are used in conjunction with a data warehouse.

The corporate data warehouse integrates disparate corporate islands of information and draws data together in a single database source. This typically involves drawing together structured information resident in one or more enterprise systems. But what is the display mechanism for unstructured data such as Word or HTML documents? How is information best displayed to the end user on the Internet? How is structured and unstructured information gathered together in one place so that users do not have to move in and out of various systems and user interfaces to find the information they want?

We have Internet computing to solve the historical software and hardware technical architecture problems we have discussed. We have data warehousing and business intelligence applications to solve the information island problem. What we didn't have until now is a way to bring these new technologies home and put them all under one roof. This unifying technology is the enterprise information portal.

Enterprise Information Portals

Enterprise information portals (EIPs) offer a solution to the dilemma that is posed by the need to unlock the power of internally and externally stored corporate information.

Defining an EIP

A starting point for a definition of an enterprise information portal is as follows:

Web applications that provide a single point of entry for corporations to identify and unlock structured and unstructured information from many sources, both inside and outside the enterprise, in order to tap into the corporate knowledge base and make better, more informed business decisions.

In their capacity as the gateway to enterprise information needs, portals are often thought of and defined as a corporate dashboard. In this definition, the enterprise portal is the single point of entry to the entire enterprise, including enterprise resource planning (ERP) applications, business intelligence systems, knowledge management and workflow, e-mail, and any other mission-critical application. Users log into the portal with a single user name and password and immediately have access to anything in the company that applies to their business function.

The dashboard concept is indeed one of Oracle's visions for Oracle Portal. All products from the BI tool suite from Oracle Discoverer 3i and Express, to Developer, to Oracle Applications have been engineered to ensure easy single source access from the Oracle Portal product in order to provide this capability.

Although corporate information portals have been around for a while, until recently they did not truly deliver. Before products like Oracle Portal came along, companies developed corporate intranets that served up information to users. It was a labor-intensive process to put an intranet Web site together and not a collaborative process. Intranets were often built department by department so that information gathered and displayed from one department to the next was often redundant. Reorganization of the intranet Web site information was required from time to time because links were often broken or information became dated. In order for the CEO to perform an enterprise search, it was often necessary to log in and out of intranets by department to find required information—and then it was nearly impossible to put it all together.

Search engines could not delve into all enterprise information assets across departments, so the islands of information within a company remained intact. The problem wasn't that an organization wanted to preserve departmental fiefdoms or that information wasn't considered a corporate asset. It was more that the products used to create the corporate intranet knowledge base were inadequate. Intranet applications also didn't easily integrate the corporate data warehouse or business intelligence tool suite into the intranet information set.

Most of all, the traditional corporate intranet didn't offer the opportunity to enhance individuals' work roles by personalizing information they needed to do their jobs. Everyone was offered everything, and nothing available was truly role-based within the organization. Intranets actually did the opposite of what they were intended to do. They created more islands of information, not fewer.

In contrast, enterprise information portal tools provide three types of processing under one umbrella:

■ Business Intelligence and decision support

■ Collaborative support by department and corporate wide to support job function

■ Knowledge management facilities to improve best practices

By unifying these disciplines under one roof, enterprise information portals offer the promise that has been lacking in corporate computing since the computer revolution began. A number of other characteristics define an enterprise information portal. These include:

- Integration of informational access from a wide variety of sources, including structured data sets and unstructured content

- Organization of information in a way that is easy for users to browse and search

- Organization and assembly of information for the user in a highly personalized way that coincides with job function and personal preference

- Storage and retrieval of information in a distributed manner that is location neutral to the end user

- A secure way to update and retrieve corporate information using enforced role-based security

- A method for automated categorization of new types of information so those items can be identified and cross-referenced with other like items

Oracle Portal offers all of these features and many more.

A Brief History of Oracle Portal

Oracle Portal is a cornerstone Web development product in Oracle Corporation's Internet e-business strategy. Oracle Portal's user-friendly development environment facilitates Web site creation, application development, and content creation and management by allowing developers and end users to rapidly create business intelligence portals that include forms, reports, graphics, and workflow applications tailored to the end user. Oracle Portal offers true knowledge management within the enterprise by unifying business processes and applications as shown in Figure 1-6.

Oracle Portal started out as an internal Oracle product that was developed by senior Oracle developers, led by Mike Hitchwa, at a client site (Princeton University). This programmer development aid was transformed into WebDB 1.0.

WebDB was originally designed to be a database-driven collaborative development tool that offered rapidly engineered HTML Web applications that were easy to build and easy to change. The WebDB product offered a site builder function that created and built Web sites to house applications. The focus for WebDB was almost exclusively as a development tool for Web-based applications that interface with the Oracle database. WebDB allowed developers to build menus, forms, reports, charts, organization hierarchies, and calendars as well as offering the ability to build Web frames and customized HTML pages. Previous versions of the product also offered utilities and monitoring tools to enable ongoing maintenance of the deployed WebDB application.

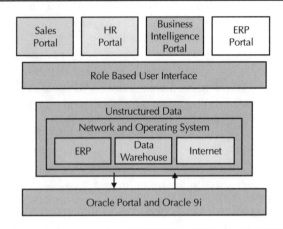

FIGURE 1-6. *Oracle Portal provides unified access to information*

Oracle Portal 3.0 offers a radical shift in functionality and form from its WebDB roots. Simple forms, reports, graphics and workflow applications are still easily generated using a slightly modified wizards-based user interface. The added focus now is on offering all the capability and ease of use of the WebDB product with a primary focus that meets all the characteristics of a true portal product as described above. New features include:

- Portal development facilities to create organized entry points on one Web page for multiple applications and data stores within an organization

- A portlet application programming interface (API) and development framework

- Personalized portal pages that allow customization of portal pages for individuals based on personal preferences and needs

- Single sign-on and enhanced security

- A modified user interface for form, chart, report, and calendar development

- Enhancements to the Portal build functions that include portlet registration

- Enterprise search capability that includes external non-portal Web sites

There are many ways that Oracle Portal utilizes the power of the Oracle database, as we shall see.

Oracle Portal Architecture

The Oracle Portal user interface facilitates a collaborative and disciplined framework for teams to develop and administer the content area (portal administrators), perform DBA functions (DBAs), or develop applications (portal developers). The portal administrator can assign roles to users or groups so that they can collaboratively contribute content and help administer a site. The portal administrator or DBA also creates content consumers (users) with assigned user roles based on their job function. In this way, the architecture of Oracle Portal offers a personalized Web experience for any end user based on their role and requirements within the organization.

Oracle Portal is built around Oracle's role-based security to facilitate collaborative development by role or group, a central tenet of any Web portal product and almost by nature the root definition of an enterprise portal. Oracle *roles* are exactly what the name implies—they are permissions granted by the DBA that allow a database user to have certain access, abilities, and permissions to work with the database in some capacity. End users that work in the Human Resources (HR) department will be assigned an HR role within Oracle Portal tied to the HR role in the Oracle 9*i* database. In this case, only HR employees will be able to access salary information and other sensitive data via the HR portal (see Figure 1-6).

Similarly, sales staff will be able to see their own commission status by using the Sales portal and Sales database role, but this information will be off-limits to others in the organization. In this way, Oracle Portal utilizes the Oracle role-based security to enforce personalization and functional standardization from within the Portal application.

As we will see in the next chapter on installation, Oracle Portal is primarily a set of PL/SQL procedures stored in the database. *PL/SQL* is Oracle's procedural language extension to the ANSI-standard SQL that comes with any relational database and allows update and manipulation of data in the database. PL/SQL adds loop functionality and other exception processing capabilities that are not easily done in SQL. PL/SQL has the added capability of being compiled and stored in the database, allowing code to execute very quickly and easily.

These database-stored procedures are almost a necessity for Web-based applications where keeping code resident in the database saves a great deal of bandwidth on the network. There is less interaction between the client application, the application server, and the database using stored PL/SQL procedures, and correspondingly fewer bits streaming back and forth across the network lines. The Oracle Portal product is primarily implemented using stored PL/SQL procedures and thus is very fast and efficient.

As you will see in the next chapter, when Portal is first installed, five end-user default accounts are created:

■ **portal30**   An account created to handle database administration (DBA) and interface duties, including creating and managing schemas, and other database objects.

- **portal30_admin**   An account created for the portal administrator to grant permissions to users, set up Portal roles, and grant authority to create and implement content and applications.

- **portal30_sso**   The account that maintains all interaction with the login server for single sign-on.

- **portal30_public**   The account that all users log into when they first bring up the initial Portal page and before they are authenticated to work within the Portal product.

- **portal30_sso_public**   The account used during initial sign-on to Oracle Portal; it provides interaction with the login server application.

We will discuss all of these accounts and their uses in later chapters.

A critical component in the Oracle Portal architecture is mod_plsql for Apache, a set of procedures that interprets user requests and identifies PL/SQL procedures in the database to fulfill the request and deliver the appropriate response. When a request is made from a working Oracle Portal application to the database for information, it is performed through the end user's Web browser to the database within a URL command line.

The URL is constructed by Portal and passed to the Oracle database via Apache using Common Gateway Interface (CGI) parameters. The URL CGI command uses the Data Access Descriptor (DAD) function of the Apache HTTP server to identify the PL/SQL procedure within the database to be run and provide the intended report or content back to the client. The DAD contains information on the Apache iAS server that provides the method to connect to the database and retrieve information.

As an example, a PL/SQL procedure may be invoked to run a form or chart from the database. A URL will be constructed in the location or address bar of the browser and passed via mod_plsql to the database where the appropriate procedure will be invoked and executed, as shown in Figure 1-7. Once executed the output response is sent back to the Web browser for the end user and the completed form or chart will be displayed.

It is important to understand some definitions of terms within Oracle Portal to fully understand the architecture and properly work within the tool. Oracle Portal is itself a portal that facilitates development of enterprise information portals. The Oracle Portal is made up of *portal pages* that are designed and developed within Oracle Portal to conform to a common style, color theme, look, and feel.

A portal page is just a page on your Web site that is developed in Oracle Portal and invoked by the user through their Web browser. Portal pages can be broken down into *regions* as displayed in Figure 1-8. One or more regions are laid out on the portal page canvas in whatever design method is appropriate and these regions are then populated with *portlets,* PL/SQL procedures, search engines, forms, reports, or Java

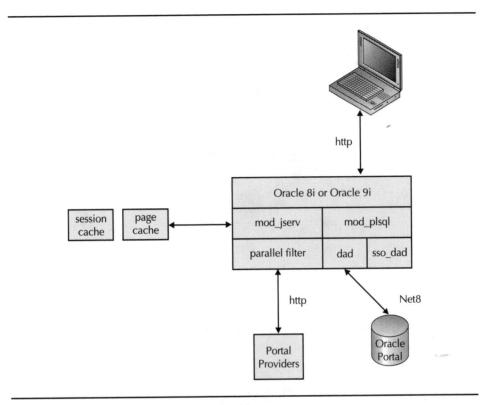

FIGURE I-7.   *A critical Oracle Portal component is the mod_plsql package*

procedures that serve up HTML code from the application server and data from the database.

Portlet applications or procedures must be defined within the Oracle Portal tool and registered to a *portlet provider* API in order to use them. At execution time, Oracle Portal uses the registration information stored in the Oracle 9*i* database to facilitate communication between the portlet application located in a region of a portal page with whatever procedure or function the portlet application was programmed to provide. It then renders the application functionality back to the end user via the portal server.

Portlets can be made up of procedures, applications, or functions including forms, graphs, reports, search engines, links to other web sites, or corporate data warehouse ad hoc query tools. Portlets are added to a region using a page customization feature that allows the portal administrator or other authorized user to add portlets to a page from a list of portlet providers and associated portlets available to that user.

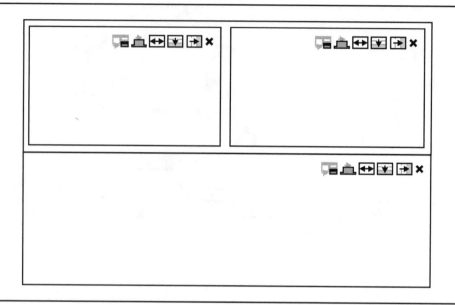

FIGURE 1-8. *Portal pages are segmented into regions that each run portlet applications*

The power of Oracle Portal is realized by registering and grouping portlets by business function in a focused way on a portal page. Tabs can be added for each line in the business to allow a personalized and focused approach to data management, even down to and including calendar and scheduling tabs for personal portal page use.

Web content, including documents, URL links, PL/SQL code, images, and other items are grouped together to form a *content area*. Oracle Portal organizes the structure of content on a Web site into *folders*. Folders contain one or more links, search features, PL/SQL calls, or Oracle Portal applications, each defined as an *item* in the folder. Folders can be grouped, sorted, and linked to assure that like items and content are grouped together. Items added to a file are defined with attributes, including file type, name and description of the item, expiration date of the content, and other metadata definitions. These attributes facilitate cross-referencing of items, allow classification grouping, role-based assignment, and a solid infrastructure to build the enterprise information portal.

Another component of the Oracle Portal architecture is the Apache Jserve Parallel Filter Servlet feature, depicted in Figure 1-7. When a page is requested, the Parallel Filter makes a call to the page engine in the database to request and invoke instructions on how the page should be laid out. In order to comply with the request, the database page engine determines which portlet providers and associated applications are included on the page and makes calls to their initialization routines,

...ssing user context information for the current user session. When the page engine
...to the Parallel Filter with the proper requested page layout, it also supplies the
...el Filter with session information that was generated by the portlet provider(s).
...e Parallel Filter can also obtain page layout information when a page layout is
...ly cached in memory. We will see later that Oracle Portal caching is an important
...rmance enhancement option for those Web pages where content stays relatively
...in nature. Caching output in memory saves users from recurring calls to the
...ase for the same information, and results in a much more efficient working
...l system.

hapter Summary

...s chapter has provided the context and historical necessity for enterprise information
portals. We have seen how portals offer the promise of unifying all of an organization's
information assets under a single presentation umbrella, including structured
information in the corporate data warehouse, business intelligence applications,
and unstructured content. We have had a quick overview of the history and new
features of Oracle Portal. Now let's install Oracle Portal and get a real look at
what Oracle Portal is all about.

CHAPTER
2

Getting Started
with Oracle Portal

I n order to effectively use this book, you will need to install the Oracle 9i Application Server (9iAS) CDs that include Oracle Portal, the Oracle HTTP Apache server, Oracle Wireless (formerly Portal-to-Go), and Oracle Enterprise Manager on your computer using the Oracle Portal trial CDs that are included with this book. In order to install Oracle Portal, the Oracle8i Enterprise Edition relational database management system must be installed on a machine on the network or on the same machine you will install Portal. Oracle8i may be ordered from the Oracle Store, downloaded (www.oracle.com) on a trial basis, or you may purchase the Oracle8i Starter Kit from Oracle Press that contains a trial version of Oracle8i and tutorials and information concerning its use. This chapter will show you how to install Oracle Portal and how to download and install the tables and database information you will need to complete the tutorials that you will be using to work through the exercises in this book.

Preliminary Housekeeping Tasks

You will need to install Oracle8i on the host server machine before you install the Oracle 9i Application Server (iAS) including Oracle Portal and Portal-to-Go. In order to take advantage of all of the tutorials within this book, you should select the Oracle8i Enterprise Edition database "typical" install that includes installation and configuration of the Oracle interMedia document search engine. Refer to the Oracle8i documentation for more information about installing and configuring this option. We will be using interMedia in conjunction with the portal development effort later in the book.

You will need to ensure that your computer system meets the minimum requirements required to install Oracle8i and 9iAS, including Oracle Portal. This install of Oracle 9iAS will focus on a typical install of Oracle Portal. Please refer to the documentation and release notes that come with the 9iAS product if you have any problems with the install. The Oracle 9iAS software automatically installs more than one product, including Oracle Portal, the product we will be focusing on in this book. It is not necessary to install Oracle 9iAS and the Oracle version 8.1.6 or above database on the same computer. If you install the database on a separate computer, you must be able to connect to it across the network and you should test this before you attempt to install the Oracle 9iAS software.

You must install the Oracle 9iAS software on a computer that runs the Windows NT Server or Windows NT Workstation operating system with service pack 5.0 or above or a computer that runs the Sun Microsystems Solaris 2.6 UNIX operating system or above. The following are the system requirements for installing and running Oracle8i and Oracle Portal on a Windows NT Server:

System Element	Requirement
Operating system	Windows NT Workstation or Server using service pack (SP) 3 or higher (SP 6 recommended); Windows 2000, or Solaris 2.6
Memory (RAM)	256MB minimum (512MB+ recommended)
NT page file	800MB minimum
Disk space	650MB required for a Minimal Edition install of Oracle Portal; additional space will be required for the database install
Web browser	Netscape Navigator 4.0.8, Netscape Communicator 4.76, or Internet Explorer 4.0.1 (SP1) or 5.0.1 (or higher)

The Universal Installer

Starting with the introduction of Oracle8i, all Oracle products now use the Oracle Universal Installer. The installer is Java based and has the same look and feel on all Oracle platforms, including Windows NT and Sun Solaris. As the name implies, the installer installs new Oracle software on any supported platform and will also deinstall products from that same computer. Always use the installer to add or delete Oracle products from your computer. Never delete directories or files manually, or you might not be able to deinstall the software. If you do need to deinstall any Oracle software manually, it is important to make sure the Windows NT registry is properly updated to ensure all elements of the Oracle software are properly removed. Let the Oracle deinstall option remove software where possible.

Oracle8i and Oracle9i Application Server Install Requirements

Oracle 9iAS can be installed on a single machine or within a two- or three-tier architecture. Before installing the 9iAS product, you must have installed the Oracle8i database, release 8.1.6.2.0 or higher (8.1.7 or higher preferred), on a server machine on your network or on a single NT or other machine. In order to install the Oracle database on Windows NT or Windows 2000, you must have administrator privileges on the machine where you are installing the database. The installation process will install all Oracle database software and create one preconfigured database for you.

When installing the database, you have the option on the Database Identification page of the install procedure to type the "global name" assigned to name the database and the Oracle System Identifier (SID). The SID is a unique name that identifies your database instance on the network. An instance represents the utilized memory and processes that define a single and unique operational occurrence of the

Oracle engine. You should make note of the names you assign in the two database identification fields during the database installation, as they will be used later when you install Oracle Portal. For the purposes of these exercises, we have named the Global Database Name `or8i.com` and the SID `or8i`.

Once you have created the Oracle8i preconfigured database, you will need to perform some basic tasks before you get started with the install of Oracle Portal 9iAS.

Exercise 2.1: Deinstalling the Oracle HTTP Server (Apache)

The Oracle HTTP Server (Apache) is installed in both the Oracle database home directory and in the Oracle 9iAS home directory. It is not necessary to have two versions of the Oracle HTTP Server running and you should drop the version installed on the Oracle database home directory. Deinstall it using the following procedures:

1. Choose Start | Settings | Control Panel.

2. Double-click on Services to display the Services Panel.

3. Scroll down to OracleOR8iHTTPServer and highlight this service.

4. Double-click and bring up the Service dialog box.

5. Click on Manual Startup Type and click OK.

6. Choose Start | Shutdown.

7. Click Restart The Computer?

8. Start the Oracle8i Enterprise Edition Universal Installer.

9. Click Deinstall Products on the Welcome page.

10. Click the plus sign next to the OraHome81 to expand and view the database products.

11. Click the check box in front of Oracle HTTP Server 1.3.12.0.1a (or later version).

12. Choose Remove... at the bottom of the Inventory page.

13. Click Close after the HTTP Server has been removed and exit the Oracle Universal Installer.

Oracle 8i DBA Duties

NOTE
This book will not delve into DBA duties unless it is absolutely imperative to the install or operation of Oracle Portal.

The first step required to prepare for the Oracle 9iAS install is to increase the amount of physical space available to Oracle Portal. Oracle stores database objects in "tablespaces," which are logically defined areas within the Oracle database to which are assigned actual physical data files that will hold database information and procedures. The USERS tablespace will hold the Oracle Portal data and procedures you will work with. The SYSTEM tablespace holds database objects that are used for controlling the database and performing DBA duties and also controls sorting functions and other application and database control procedures. The USERS tablespace will be used to store information and objects that will be accessed by your Portal application. In addition, the TEMP tablespace will be used in the install process and may be used to temporarily hold the results of complex database queries as they are formatted and sorted by Oracle Portal.

The second DBA duty will be to change some entries in the initialization file that contains the parameters to optimize the database for a particular usage or environment.

To perform both of these tasks, you will need to know the passwords to two Oracle accounts that are automatically created when an Oracle database is created. When you first install Oracle on your machine, the SYSTEM user is installed with the password of MANAGER. The SYS user comes with the password CHANGE_ON_INSTALL. It is a good idea to change both passwords to something that is more familiar to you, and not known to everyone else, in order to administer the database and install Oracle Portal.

It is important to modify the initialization file that contains all of the parameters that control the operation of your Oracle8i database. The name of this file is always `init.ora`. The `init.ora` file will be found under the `admin` directory where you installed the Oracle8i database. In the case of the sample install in the book, Oracle home is on the logical E: drive on Windows NT Workstation under the `ORACLE` directory.

A few parameters in particular need to be set: `MAX_ENABLED_ROLES`, `OPEN_CURSORS`, `SHARED_POOL_SIZE`, `LARGE_POOL_SIZE`, and `JAVA_POOL_SIZE`. `MAX_ENABLED_ROLES` controls the number of user roles that are allowed. Oracle extensively uses role-based security to control which users can manage and control database content. You can also use role-based security within applications that you will develop to control who has access to database objects and information.

Oracle allocates system memory dedicated to the Oracle database and its applications for certain functions using the pool size parameters. `SHARED_POOL_SIZE` allocates memory to shared procedures that include SQL code, packages, and procedures that are kept in memory and reused. In this manner, frequently used Oracle SQL procedures are executed much more quickly in memory using the shared pool memory cache. `JAVA_POOL_SIZE` is used to compile and execute Java procedures and code in the database. Java procedures typically require a great deal of memory and this parameter should be set relatively high. `LARGE_POOL_SIZE` augments the `SHARED_POOL_SIZE` memory allocation pool and defines the memory allocation for large complex SQL commands. We will double the default large pool space allocation.

OPEN_CURSORS controls how many cursors are available for use by PL/SQL code that is stored in the database and that controls the majority of Oracle Portal's actions. Cursors control the results of a PL/SQL statement that selects more than one row from the database so that the result set can be read and manipulated one row at a time. Cursors allow data to be manipulated and allow exception processing on results so that PL/SQL code can be written in a more procedural manner. Let's go to our first exercise to change these database parameters and get the database prepared to install Oracle Portal.

Exercise 2.2: Preparing the Database for the Oracle Portal Install

Oracle offers several ways to change user passwords and to increase the amount of file space allocated to a tablespace. For example, experienced Oracle DBAs might prefer to use DBA Studio for this task. DBA Studio should be used to allocate space and we will also use the utility SQL*Plus that is installed with every Oracle database and with Oracle Portal. SQL*Plus allows you to interactively work with the database. If you log on to the system under an ID that has DBA role privileges (such as SYSTEM or SYS), you will be able to create tables, create users, change database configurations and parameters, add space to the database, and otherwise control the function and capabilities of the database system as an administrator using SQL*Plus.

We will first log on to SQL*Plus, change the password for SYS, and modify the database to include more space for the Portal install.

Choose Start | Programs | Oracle - OraHome81 | Application Development | SQL Plus

After SQL*Plus starts, a Log On dialog box will appear on your screen and allow you to log on to the Oracle8*i* database. You will log on to the database with the User Name SYSTEM and a Password of MANAGER with full DBA authority, as shown in the illustration.

If all goes well, you will see the following dialog response back under the SQL*Plus canvas that indicates you are logged into the database properly:

```
SQL*Plus: Release 8.1.7.0.0 - Production on Sun March 4 10:05:05 2000
(c) Copyright 2000 Oracle Corporation. All rights reserved.
Connected to:
```

```
Oracle8i Enterprise Edition Release 8.1.7.0.0 - Production
With the Partitioning option
JServer Release 8.1.7.0.0 - Production
SQL>
```

The cursor will be blinking and awaiting your response. Type the following command to change the user name SYS password from CHANGE_ON_INSTALL to a password of SYS:

```
SQL> alter user sys identified by sys;
User altered.
```

You will now be able to log onto the SYS account using a password of SYS, which is easier to work with for the time being. If you use a different password, make sure you remember the password you typed. Next, type the following and hit RETURN after typing the semicolon to see how much free space you have in each tablespace.

```
select tablespace_name, sum(bytes)/(1024*1024) Megs
from dba_free_space
group by tablespace_name;
```

You will see a report that looks like the following:

```
TABLESPACE_NAME                        MEGS

------------------------------- ----------

DRSYS                           16.1796875

INDX                            19.9921875

RBS                             41.9921875

SYSTEM                          143.546875

TEMP                            59.9921875

TOOLS                            9.9921875

USERS                           66.859375

7 rows selected
```

This report shows each tablespace in the database and the amount of free space still remaining in the tablespace. In the case of the USERS and TEMP tablespaces above, 66MB and almost 60MB of space are available, respectively—not enough to install Oracle Portal. Oracle and Oracle Portal also need additional freespace in the SYSTEM tablespace—100MB or more is recommended. Almost 143MB is already available, so we don't need to change this allocation. Oracle Portal will need 250MB of free space minimum in the USERS tablespace and 100MB in the TEMP tablespace. Let's allocate some physical disk space to both of these tablespaces so that we can install Oracle Portal successfully. You do this by creating a data file of the appropriate size, located on a disk file system where there is sufficient space, and adding that data file to the tablespace. The names of such data files usually follow the standards set by the initial Oracle installation. You may invoke the Oracle DBA Studio utility to add data files and space. You may invoke DBA Studio in the following manner:

 1. Choose Start | Programs | Oracle-ORAHome81 | Database Administration | DBA Studio.

 2. Find the Oracle database and click the plus sign to connect to the database.

 3. Type SYSTEM in the Username field and MANAGER in the Password field.

 4. Find the USERS tablespace under the Storage icon and highlight it.

 5. Next to the size field type 250MB and click Apply.

 6. Increase the TEMP tablespace to 100MB.

 7. Choose File from the menu and choose Exit to close out DBA Studio.

Consult the Oracle DBA Users Guide if you have any problems adding data files and additional space to the USERS and TEMP tablespace using DBA Studio.

After you have altered the tablespaces to add the requisite space, rerun the SQL*Plus script above. We should now see the USERS tablespace at 250MB of space and the TEMP tablespace should show 100MB of space available.

Next, we will change the parameters for the init.ora file to conform to what is needed to install and run Oracle Portal. You must stop the database instance and then restart it in order for the Oracle database to recognize any changes made to the initialization or other parameter files. Get into the Windows Notepad and complete the following steps:

 1. Choose Start | Programs | Accessories | Notepad.

 2. Click on File | Open.

 3. Navigate to your Oracle home directory and change the file type at the bottom of the search box to All Files from Text Documents (*.txt).

 4. Navigate to Oracle | Admin | Or8i | Pfile, where Or8i is the database name. You should see the init.ora file—select it for edit.

 5. Find and edit the following lines or add them to the end of the file:

```
open_cursors = 75

max_enabled_roles = 30
```

```
compatible = 8.1.0

shared_pool_size = 80000000

large_pool_size = 1228800

java_pool_size = 30000000
```

6. Click on File | Save.

7. Exit from Notepad.

8. Choose Start | Settings | Control Panel.

9. Double-click on Services to display the Services Panel.

10. Scroll down to OracleServiceOR8i and highlight this service.

11. Stop the database from running by clicking the Stop button.

12. Restart the database by clicking the Start button.

13. Close the Control Panel.

NOTE
*Oracle Portal requires a minimum OPEN_CURSORS
= 50 and minimum of MAX_ENABLED_ROLES =
25 to run, but it is a good practice to bump those
numbers up a little as Oracle's minimums in their
documentation are truly that, minimums!*

You need to write down a couple of things before you continue with this install.
First, remember the password for the SYS account. You changed the password for the
purposes of these exercises to SYS. When you are done with these exercises, change
it again to something a little tougher for a hacker to crack!

Secondly, you will need to know the hostname of the computer where you installed
the Oracle8i database. On Windows NT, if you aren't sure, go to the DOS command
prompt of the machine where the database is installed and type hostname. The
computer will respond with the hostname. Write it down. The hostname should be
in lowercase and/or numbers with no underscores or special characters in the name.
If you are installing everything on one stand-alone machine such as a laptop for
demonstration purposes, you can substitute the synonym localhost for the actual
name of the host machine. To be safe, always use the actual hostname of the computer.

Lastly, you will need to remember a connect string for the remote or local Oracle
database that you are connecting into. The connect string will provide a convenient
shorthand location name that Oracle applications use to find the database and server
on the network. We will discuss how to create the network connect string name a
little later in this chapter- here we are using or8i. We will connect into the database
using that name later in our exercises.

Now you are finished with your preliminary DBA duties. While you are surely not a certified DBA, you have successfully prepared the server and database to install Oracle Portal!

Installing Oracle 9iAS including Oracle Portal

In order to install Oracle Portal on Windows NT, you need to have administrator privileges. If you are not sure what operating system privileges you have, contact your system administrator to get the proper operating system logon ID privileges. On Windows NT, you need to install from an ID that belongs to the Administrators group. To find out whether you have those privileges on Windows NT, you can check your ID listed in the User Manager utility under Programs | Administrative Tools (Common).

> **NOTE**
> *This chapter discusses installing Oracle Portal on NT. For details on installing Oracle Portal on Solaris, please consult the Oracle Portal Release Notes.*

The following exercises will walk you through the process of installing Oracle 9iAS. The "Oracle HTTP server only" or "Minimal Edition" installation options will install all the features Oracle Portal requires and will involve less user input to the process. You will be installing the PL/SQL procedures and code that are stored in the Oracle8i Enterprise Edition database as well as utilities, images, required support files, single sign-on applets, and program code that will be resident under the Oracle iSuites home directory. The PL/SQL code routines in the database and the data and executable files on the application server work together to execute Oracle Portal in a development and production environment. You will also be installing and configuring the Oracle HTTP server that serves as the portal Web request broker. The Oracle HTTP server is actually the Apache HTTP server that is bundled together with Oracle Portal in the Oracle 9iAS CDs included with this book.

Now let's get started!

Exercise 2.3: Starting the Oracle iAS Install Using the Oracle Universal Installer

Take the 90-day trial CDs included with this book and place disk 1 in the CD ROM drive on the computer you are installing the software on or on any CD ROM drive on a network drive that has been mapped as a local drive and is accessible from your computer.

When you install the CD, it should automatically execute using the Autorun install feature. If it doesn't, use the following instructions to start the Universal Installer and begin the Oracle Portal Installation process, as shown in Figure 2-1.

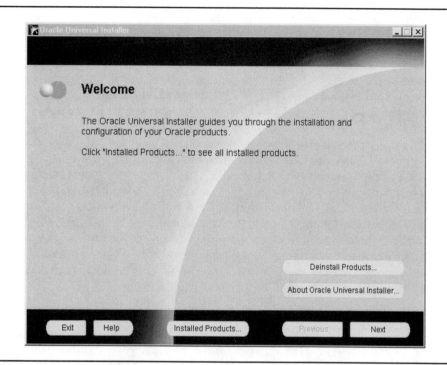

FIGURE 2-1. *The Oracle Universal Installer Welcome page*

1. Choose Start | Run.

2. Enter the CD ROM drive letter and directory path in the open field as follows:

   `Drive letter:\Disk1\install\win32\setup.exe.`
   Alternatively, you may go through MS Explorer to find the `setup.exe`
   file under the same directory structure on the CD ROM.

3. Click OK to start the setup utility and the Oracle Universal Installer.

NOTE
On Solaris, you may start the Oracle
Universal Installer (OUI) by going to
the proper drive and typing the following:
`Drive Letter:/portal30/disk1/`
`install/solaris/runInstaller.`

Exercise 2.4: Installing the Oracle Portal Software
The Oracle Universal Installer will walk you through the process of installing the
Portal software. You will first see an Installation Overview option. Click Yes on

the screen if you wish to have additional documentation available to you during the installation process. From the Welcome page of the Universal Installer, click Next to proceed to the Installation Types menu. Choose Minimal Edition, which will install the Oracle 9iAS Portal, 9iAS Wireless, Oracle Enterprise Manager, and the Oracle HTTP Server. Click Next to proceed to the Destination Oracle Home and Oracle Home Name window, as shown in Figure 2-2. There, you will be presented with a default Home name and the Home location to install the Oracle 9iAS file from the CD ROM.

The default destination offered when you first come to this page is the iSuites Oracle home—a different Oracle home than the Oracle8i database is installed in. If you are using Oracle version 8.1.6, or 8.1.7 you *must* accept the Oracle iSuites home destination path that is offered or you will possibly corrupt your existing Oracle database and the install will not be successful. Increasingly, particularly with Web-based products, tools such as Oracle 9iAS and Portal must be installed in a separate Oracle home directory due to Oracle software version conflicts that may arise.

In order to specify a separate Oracle home for Oracle Portal, you should accept the iSuites Oracle home name offered. If you choose your own name for Portal, the Oracle home name can be up to 16 characters long, consisting of alphanumeric

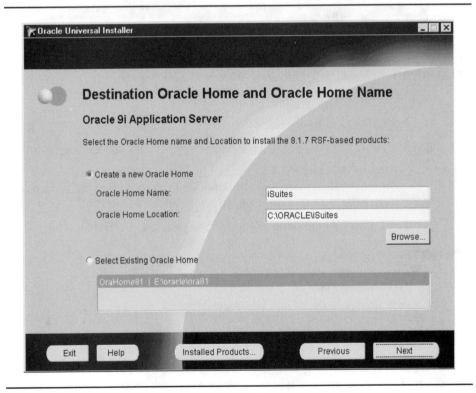

FIGURE 2-2. *The Destination Oracle Home window identifies the Oracle home and its file location*

characters and underscores only. Do not use dashes, periods, semicolons, or any other special character if you do decide to change the default Oracle home location. If you accept the default, iSuites will be the Oracle 9iAS home name.

Next you must define the Oracle home location for the iSuites Oracle home. Make sure you have the 650MB of disk space required on the drive that is offered and accept the default if there is enough space. If there is not enough space, click the Browse button and go to a separate directory and choose (or create) a name under a directory path of your choice. If you are satisfied with the directory path you have chosen or the one that was offered to you, click Next.

NOTE
The Installer will create the new Oracle home directory if it doesn't exist already.

You will see the Installation Types window dialog box next, as shown in Figure 2-3. Choose the Minimal Edition option to install the minimum configuration required for the exercises in this book. Click Next to proceed.

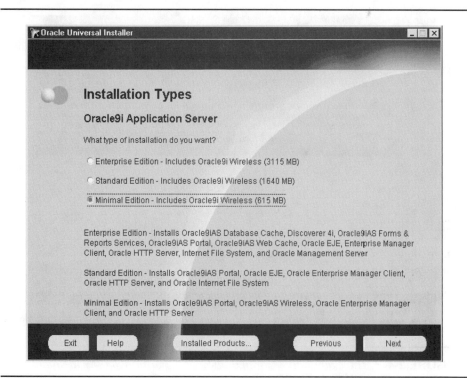

FIGURE 2-3.   *The Installation Types window of the Oracle 9iAS install*

The Component Configuration and Startup screen, as shown in Figure 2-4, will identify the optional products that will be installed as part of the installation. If you choose not to install any products listed, you will have to configure the product separately after the software is fully installed. Accept the defaults listed and click Next. Your machine will reboot at this point to create the file structure and set the registry for the rest of the install. After rebooting, you will proceed to the Apache Listener Configuration dialog box.

Apache Listener Configuration
The Apache server must be configured to allow a proper connection to the Oracle database. The first screen that comes up is the Database Access Descriptor (DAD) page for the Oracle Portal. In order to configure the server listener for Oracle Portal, you must specify the Oracle Portal DAD Name, the Portal Schema Name, and the TNS Connect String that defines how the Apache server connects to the database across the network. The Apache server listener has been customized to provide a built-in gateway to the Oracle database to efficiently execute PL/SQL database

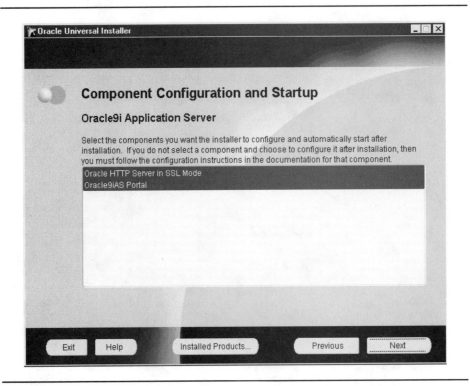

FIGURE 2-4. *The Component Configuration and Startup window identifies optional install components*

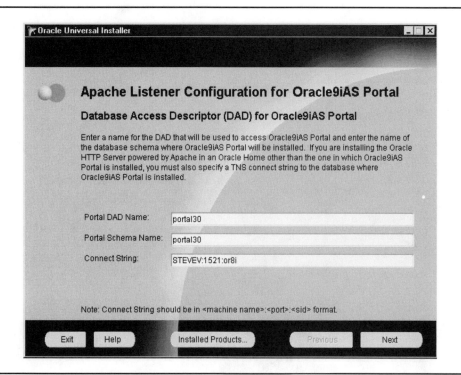

FIGURE 2-5. *Configure the Apache Data Access Descriptor for Oracle Portal*

procedures and applications in Oracle Portal. By defining the DAD name, database schema name, and TNS connect string, the Apache Web server is configured to recognize where the Portal content areas are located, including the PL/SQL procedures that drive the product. When installed, there will be a user with the name specified by the DAD that has full DBA and administrator privileges within Oracle Portal.

When the Portal DAD Configuration screen first comes up, the default Oracle Portal DAD name and schema name will be Portal30. Accept these names unless they are just too plain and basic for you. I always accept the defaults unless I know for a fact that the default doesn't work. No sense in tempting fate! You will need to put in a TNS connect string in the <hostname>:<port>:<sid> format. As an example, type <hostname>:1521:OR8i in the TNS Connect String field, as shown in Figure 2-5. Remember what you have typed because you will need it later when you actually create the connect string using the Net8 Configuration Assistant.

Click on Next and you will come to the Apache Listener Configuration screen for the login server DAD connection. The login server governs the single sign-on (SSO) access that is a key feature of Oracle Portal. Single sign-on allows the end user to

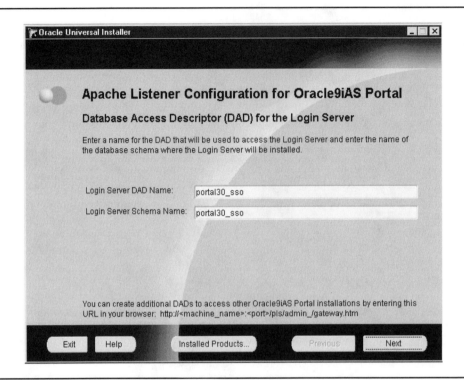

FIGURE 2-6. *Configure the Data Access Descriptor for the login server single sign-on*

sign onto Web database applications one time within Oracle Portal and then access any Portal registered application without requiring the user to sign on to each application separately. In this window, again accept the default Login Server DAD Name and Login Server Schema Name as shown in Figure 2-6, and click Next.

You should now see the Wireless Edition repository information screen. Oracle Wireless Edition, alternatively known as Portal-to-Go, is the wireless version of the Oracle Portal product. Oracle Wireless Edition is installed by default with the 9iAS software, whether you will use it or not. Future releases of Oracle Portal will likely merge some of the functionality of Oracle Wireless Edition into Oracle Portal.

On the Wireless Edition repository information screen, key in the name of your host computer in the Hostname field. If you are installing it all on your own computer, you may type `localhost` as the host computer name. In the Port field type `1521` if you are on a Windows NT or Windows 2000 computer, or `1526` if working with a UNIX machine. Next, type the SID name that we have been using—in our case `or8i`—as depicted in Figure 2-7.

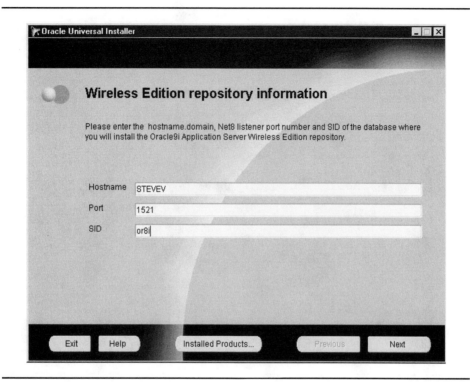

FIGURE 2-7. *Enter the Wireless Edition hostname, port, and SID*

The next window you will see is the Wireless Edition schema information. This information will be used to create an Oracle user name that will be the owner of the tables and repository information that will drive the Wireless Edition application. Type in a user name in the Username field. We used P2G. Type a password that you will remember. We used P2G, the same name as the user name so that it would be easy to remember. You may change that password later by following the example we used to change the SYS password in Exercise 2-2. Type this information in as depicted in Figure 2-8 and click on Next to proceed to the next install window.

Lastly we need to type in the SYSTEM password for the database to enable the installation of the system files for the Wireless Edition application. The default password for any Oracle database is MANAGER. Unless you or your DBA changed that password, type in MANAGER now as shown in Figure 2-9.

Finally, a summary window will appear that reflects the software that will be installed. Click Install and, while you are waiting for the software to install, don't run anything else on your computer. The installation is a complicated process that creates

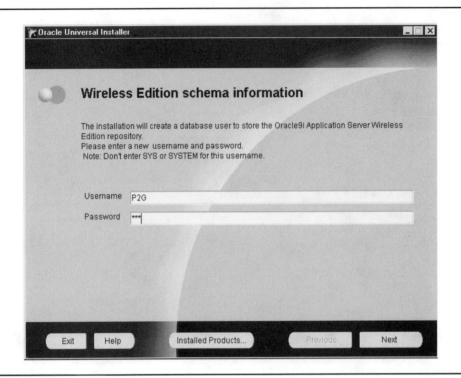

FIGURE 2-8. *Wireless Edition schema information window*

numerous components, including those components that comprise Oracle Portal: JDBC drivers that allow Oracle Portal to use Java to access the Oracle database, network protocols, and application server components. It may take up to 45 minutes to install all of this software, so while you are waiting let's get prepared for the network configuration we will need to perform in the next step.

The Net8 Configuration Assistant

Net8 is a piece of communications software that allows connection between a client and the Oracle database. The software acts essentially as a broker or middleman between the client request and the database response. When a client queries information using SQL from their Web browser to the Oracle database on the network, the Net8 software is configured with the Apache HTTP server to know where the database is located for the requested data. The request is handed off through the HTTP server to the Apache server listener that is configured to work with Net8 to pass the request onto the database using the Net8 protocol. Net8 is a multilayered component that can be configured to handle various network protocols such as TCP/IP, IPX/SPX (Novell), DECnet, and others.

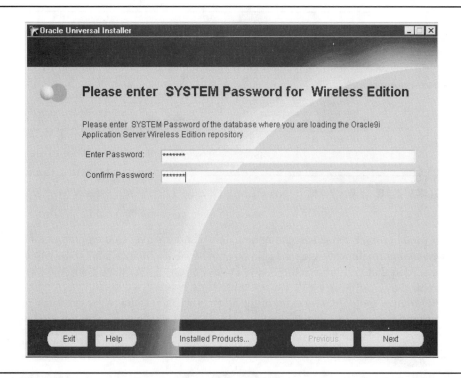

FIGURE 2-9.   *Enter the system password for the Wireless Edition repository*

On the application layer, Net8 uses the Transparent Network Substrate (TNS) application programming interface (API) as a middle ground to translate, send, and receive SQL requests between the client and the database host. When a request is made of the database via the browser and through the Apache server, Net8 performs a "handshake" with the database server and hands the translated request to the database server. The server receives the request, processes it, and passes the response back to the client via Net8 and the Apache server, as depicted in Figure 2-10.

A TNS connect string name and configuration are requirements when connecting to a database server that is located under a separate Oracle home from the product being installed. You will need to create a TNS connect string that has the same name as what you entered in the Portal and PORTAL_SSO DAD Configuration window so that when you log in through the Application server, you will connect to the database.

If the software install has completed, you now have the Oracle Portal files installed on the application server and you are ready to install the Portal database packages and procedures into the Oracle8i database. First, you will need to be able to use the Net8 configuration assistant to create the `tnsnames.ora` file that will support

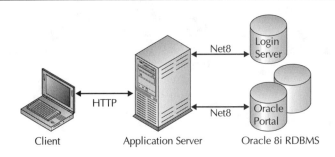

FIGURE 2-10. *The Net8 handshake that allows clients and servers to interact on the network*

your Portal connection across the network or via your server to the database. If all has proceeded normally with your install, you should see a Configuration Tools window on your screen that will launch the Net8 Configuration Assistant, shown in Figure 2-11.

You may configure Net8 via the wizard or check the "Perform typical configuration" box at the bottom of the Welcome page to have the configuration performed for you. Choose this option. The Configuration Assistant will identify the

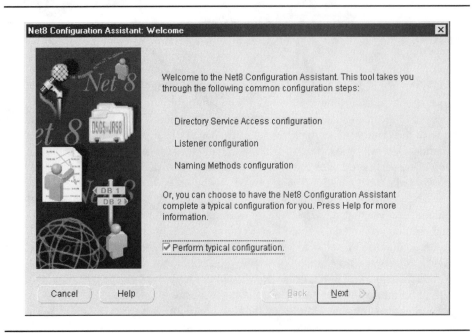

FIGURE 2-11. *The Net8 Configuration Assistant Welcome window*

proper configuration and path to the database and test the connection using the SCOTT userid and TIGER password that comes preinstalled with demo tables and data with every Oracle database. Assuming the test is successful, the `tnsnames.ora` file, located in the Portal `ORACLE_HOME/NETWORK/ADMIN` directory, will look something like this:

```
# TNSNAMES.ORA Network Configuration File:
 #D:\Oracle\Ora81\network\admin\tnsnames.ora
# Generated by Oracle configuration tools
EXTPROC_CONNECTION_DATA.EXYZ.COM =
   (DESCRIPTION =
     (ADDRESS_LIST =
       (ADDRESS = (PROTOCOL = IPC)(KEY = EXTPROC0)))
     (CONNECT_DATA = (SID = PLSExtProc)
       (PRESENTATION = RO)))

OR8I.EXYZ.COM =
   (DESCRIPTION =
     (ADDRESS_LIST =
       (ADDRESS = (PROTOCOL = TCP)(HOST = [your computer host name])(PORT = 1521)))
     (CONNECT_DATA =(SERVICE_NAME = or8i.com)))
```

If the test connection to the database succeeds, the install process will automatically continue to the next step. Let's go to the next step, installing the Oracle Portal packages and procedures into the database.

Configuring the Portal with the Oracle Portal Configuration Assistant

You have finished the process of installing the Portal file structures and you have completed configuring the Portal software to "talk" to the database using Net8. Now we will install all of the PL/SQL packages and procedures that drive Oracle Portal from within the database. The Portal Configuration Assistant will read Java procedures, PL/SQL, SQL, documentation, and other database items from the install CD and store them in the database.

At this point in the install you should see a window entitled "Oracle Configuration Assistant" that looks like Figure 2-12. The two options available allow you to install or deinstall the Oracle Portal and Oracle Portal SSO schema and associated tables and data in the database. Upon completion, you will be able to log into these two schemas from a Web browser to work within Oracle Portal. Choose Install Oracle Portal and the Login Server (the Apache HTTP login server) and click Next.

On the next screen, Step 2 of 6: Database Authentication, you need to remember your SYS password and the connection information you wrote down earlier. As mentioned previously, the SYS password for a freshly installed Oracle database is CHANGE_ON_INSTALL. However, we changed it earlier to SYS, so type that password in now. The connection information includes the name of the host computer that the Oracle8i database is installed on and the port number and SID of the database. On Windows NT, the port number is typically set to 1521 by default and under Solaris it is set to 1526. The SID of your database is whatever you named it when you originally

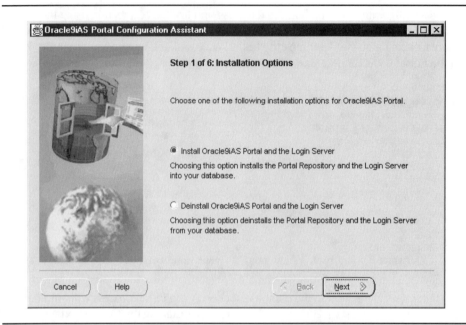

FIGURE 2-12. *The Oracle Portal Configuration Assistant installs the Portal and SSO schemas*

installed your database—we called it or8i earlier. If you are unsure of what you named it, you can check the init.ora file on the database server machine located under the Oracle8i ORACLE_HOME directory at Oracle/ADMIN/OR8i/PFILE/ INIT.ORA. Open it with MS Notepad and check for the INSTANCE_NAME parameter that will indicate the instance name. Your responses on this window should look much like the responses indicated in Figure 2-13. Click Next and move on to step 3.

The next window, Step 3 of 6: Oracle Portal Schema, gives the schema name and Data Access Descriptor for the Oracle Portal software. The DAD is comprised of the configuration information that the Apache Web server uses to connect to the Oracle database, Portal PL/SQL procedures, and gateways to meet HTTP calls from end users to fulfill Web page requests. Unless you have a strong preference to the contrary, accept the default choices for the Oracle Portal Schema and Oracle Portal DAD entries. The default entry is portal30. Your screen should look like Figure 2-14.

The next window, Step 4 of 6: Single Sign-On (SSO) Schema, identifies the schema and DAD for the single sign-on mechanism for Oracle Portal. Single sign-on is a key feature of Oracle Portal enabling end users to securely log onto the database once within Oracle Portal with a single userid and password and use that one userid and password to access all Oracle applications and products registered and accessed within Oracle Portal. Accept the default SSO Schema and SSO DAD names on this window. The default entry for these two names is PORTAL30_SSO as shown in Figure 2-15.

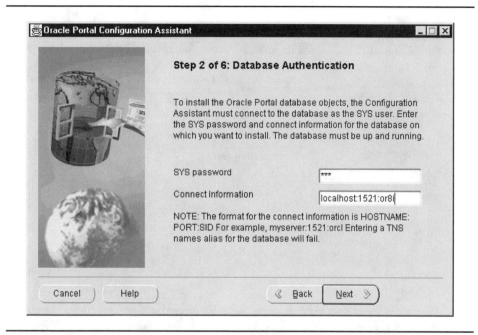

FIGURE 2-13. *The Database Authentication screen collects database connection information*

The next screen allows you to specify which tablespaces to use to store the Portal objects. The default, document, and logging tablespace entries on the Step 5 of 6: Tablespace Options screen should indicate USERS on this window, as shown in Figure 2-16. The temporary tablespace entry should show TEMP. If any of these windows default to SYSTEM, you should switch them to another tablespace by clicking on the arrow next to the tablespace name and changing the tablespace area from the drop-down menu.

The default tablespace, USERS, is used to store the majority of the Oracle database objects necessary to run Oracle Portal and should have a minimum of 250MB of space available at this point. The TEMP temporary tablespace is used in the installation of the product and to perform sorting operations and to reduce overhead when Portal performs various management operations.

The document tablespace is where all content for a Portal Web site is stored. It should be large enough to hold all documents, links, and other content that will go into the Portal site. It should initially be sized for growth and preferably have the AUTOEXTEND option on so that as more and more content is added to the site, the tablespace can grow with the site with minimal DBA interaction required. This is particularly important for small companies that don't have the luxury of hiring a DBA to monitor tablespace usage. As the tablespace grows, Oracle allocates segments of

FIGURE 2-14. *The Oracle Portal Schema window names the Portal and DAD object repository*

space to the initial tablespace measured and valued in units known as "extents." Too many extents can result in an inefficient database. If you or a DBA can monitor the database and add space when needed, then do not use the autoextend option because it tends to result in a system that is less efficient due to the number of extents and files that accumulate over time assigned to the tablespace. We will discuss how to manage extents and monitor and maintain an efficient Portal database in Chapter 12, where we discuss maintaining the Portal site.

The logging tablespace is the tablespace where statistics are collected related to the creation and usage of an Oracle Portal site. The logging tablespace includes information about the users and developers who have logged into Portal, the machine and browser that is used for each Portal access session, and various Portal DBA parameters, including storage and allocation to users of the system, memory allocation, object creation dates, and Portal version control statistics.

Make sure that if you use the USERS tablespace for the default, document, and logging Portal tablespace that there is at least 250MB of free space available in the USERS Oracle tablespace or that the AUTOEXTEND option is on for that tablespace. This will allow for growth and ensure that the Portal install procedure will not terminate

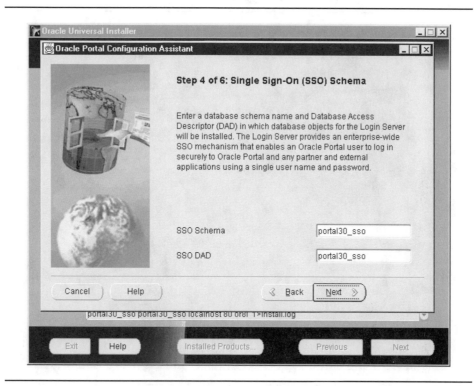

FIGURE 2-15.   *The Single Sign-On window names the SSO schema and DAD object repository*

abnormally due to lack of space. If you followed the instructions for sizing tablespaces earlier in this chapter, you should have plenty of space. The Tablespace Options window should look like the screen in Figure 2-16. If it does, click Next and let's proceed to the final installation procedures.

The Apache server has been enhanced for Oracle Portal to include an HTTP server module named mod_plsql that facilitates calls to Oracle Portal's PL/SQL services in the Oracle8i database. The mod_plsql module provides tight integration and security between Apache, Oracle Portal, and the database, and improves the interaction and performance of PL/SQL programs invoked via Web requests. At this point in the install, the Configuration Wizard will detect that a version of the mod_plsql PL/SQL Web Toolkit package was initially installed when you installed your Oracle8i database. It is a good idea to overwrite the existing packages at this point to ensure that you have the latest PL/SQL Toolkit that is compatible with Oracle Portal. Click Yes to install the Oracle Portal version of the PL/SQL Web Toolkit in the database, as shown in Figure 2-17, and proceed.

The last step in the process will install all of the packages and procedures that make up Oracle Portal, using the installation parameters you just defined. It will take

FIGURE 2-16. *The Tablespace Options window defines where to store Portal objects in the database*

about an hour for all of the packages to load into the database. Again, don't use the machine while this procedure is active because memory contention or other conflicts could arise. When the process is finished, you should see a window that shows that the installation was successful, as shown in Figure 2-18. You can check the installation log on the Portal's `Oracle_Home` location at `<Oracle_Home>/assistants/opca/install.log` to ensure that no errors were encountered.

Troubleshooting the Oracle Portal Install

If the installation routine encountered any errors, look through the `install.log` file and note the errors that are indicated. If any messages identify a possible space problem in any Oracle tablespace or lack of rollback segments, you will need to deinstall the Portal software, increase the size of the tablespace in question using the procedure we went through at the beginning of the chapter, and reinstall the software. To deinstall the Oracle Portal software, use the following procedure to delete the Portal and SSO schemas and DADs:

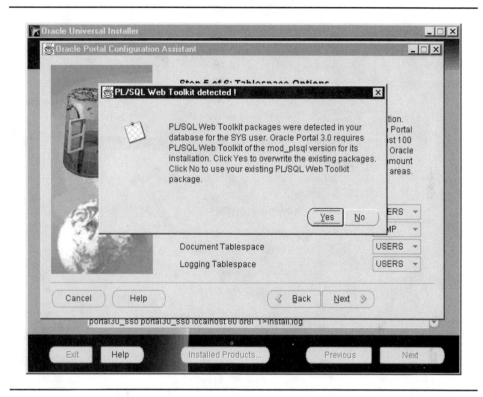

FIGURE 2-17. *Answer Yes to overwrite the PL/SQL Web Toolkit packages*

1. Choose Start | Programs | Oracle - OraHome8P | Oracle Portal 3.0 Configuration Assistant.

2. Choose Deinstall Oracle Portal or the login server.

3. Choose Deinstall Oracle Portal on the next screen to delete the Portal schema and DAD.

4. Type in the SYS password and the login connection information.

5. Choose Deinstall Login Server after Oracle Portal is deleted and repeat step 4.

After the schemas and DADs are deleted, you should be able to increase your tablespace size if that was the source of the problem. Then, start the Configuration Assistant from the Program Menu as we did in step 1 of the deinstall procedure for the Portal and SSO schemas and reinstall the software PL/SQL packages using the six-step configuration procedure described in the section entitled Configuring the Portal with the Oracle Portal Configuration Assistant.

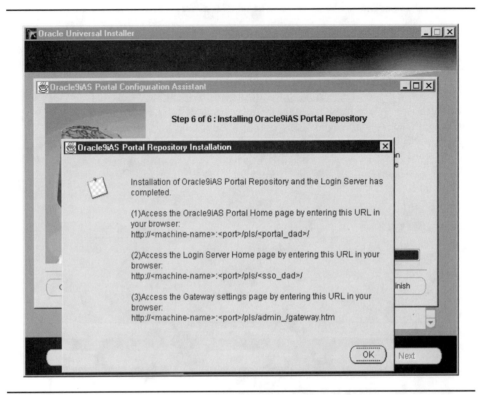

FIGURE 2-18. *Congratulations, you have just successfully installed Oracle Portal!*

If you had errors installing files on the application server at the beginning of the Oracle 9iAS install, then you should first print and work through the Oracle 9iAS Portal Troubleshooting Guide found at http://technet.oracle.com/products/iportal/ htdocs/portal_troubleshooting.htm. This guide is a step-by-step process to debug a nonfunctioning portal to identify specific problems that may be occurring to prevent the Portal software from executing. Work through all of the tips offered as they apply to your problems, paying particular attention to the diagnostic utilities and the ssodatan scripts. These scripts can be found in the `<iSuites Home>/portal30/ admin/plsql` directory. The diagnostic utilities script attempts to connect to the portal and identify specific problems with key components of the software in the event of a failure to execute any one element of the software. The ssodatan script will generally handle many login problems associated with an incorrect install. In particular, if you are getting a WC-41439 error when trying to log in to the portal, this script should fix the problem. This particular error indicates that in logging into the database through the Apache server using mod_plsql, your DAD configuration is incorrect or that there is a problem with mod_plsql. At the DOS prompt, type ssodatan and hit the ENTER key to get instructions for executing the script in the proper format.

If you have tried everything in the troubleshooting guide, try to deinstall the PL/SQL procedures and use the Universal Installer to Deinstall Oracle 9iAS completely and start again from scratch. Make sure you only deinstall Oracle 9iAS, and not the Oracle database as well. You cannot remove portions of the iAS software—it is an all or nothing deinstall procedure. If you had problems installing files, it might have been because you were low on disk space or memory, or had other applications open. You may also be short of virtual swap space on your NT machine; 600 is recommended. Add more virtual space, if necessary. Free up disk space or choose another drive to install the software on, reboot the computer, and shut down all programs other than the Oracle database that might be running. Then try it again from the beginning.

If you need some additional assistance, you might want to try logging into Oracle's Technical Network for Oracle Portal at http://technet.oracle.com/products/iportal or http://technet.oracle.com/products/ias/. You may also be able to navigate to Oracle support at http://www.oracle.com/support/products and look for a support thread for Oracle 9iAS and the individual products found in the 9i Application Server.

Support Files for Oracle Portal Hands-On Tutorials

To perform the exercises in this book, you will need to have tables and Web site content that have been specifically created for these exercises. You will be developing forms, reports, graphs, and charts that utilize the data from these Oracle tables. In addition, documents and content can be used to show the rich combination of structured and unstructured information that Oracle Portal can control and present to an end user. You will typically work with this content from within the Oracle Portal product, but you need to install the tables and their associated data on your computer before you can work through these exercises.

The CD ROM that accompanies this book contains the Oracle 9iAS product only, but does not contain the sample files and tables that accompany this book. You may download those files by going to the URL http://www.oraclepressbooks.com/ and selecting the Free Code link for this book. The file is a self-extracting zip file. Download the file to a temporary directory such as C:\portalhandbook. Find the file using the Windows NT Explorer and execute it by double-clicking the file. The file will extract and create sub-directories of Web content, SQL, and database tables for use throughout the book.

The `root` directory contains a `readme.doc` file to coach you on the proper way to install and work with the downloaded support files and the latest information on Oracle 9iAS and Oracle Portal.

- `Tables` contains an executable to create and load data into tables in your Oracle8i database

- `SQL` directories will contain SQL and PL/SQL scripts you can use throughout the book to save yourself some typing.

- `Content` directories will contain Oracle Web content that you will use to enhance the Portal Web site you will develop throughout this book.

- Documents are Word, HTML, PowerPoint, and other documents you will use to support the Web site with unstructured content that can be organized and accessed using Oracle Portal and interMedia.

NOTE
You will be instructed in the `readme.doc` file what files and tables you will be using for each chapter and how to use them. If you are unable to finish a chapter or exercise in one sitting, you should be able to stop and save your work in most cases. If you can't, you will be informed in advance and you can quit and drop back to where you started an exercise and start again. We will try to keep each exercise short and sweet so you won't have to drop back.

Now that we have installed Oracle Portal and the Oracle Portal support files, let's move on to the next chapter, log on to the Portal home page, kick the tires, see what it looks like, and create a quick portal application. By the way, your manager has gotten a little impatient that it has taken a couple of hours to install the software. We need to show some quick results!

CHAPTER
3

Getting Around in
Oracle Portal

e can now sign on to Oracle Portal and get our first look at the user interface (UI) and major features of the product. We'll start with a brief tour of some of the features accessible from the Portal home page, including facilities that administrators may find useful for setting up user accounts, creating applications and content areas, and administering database schemas. To set up our working environment, we'll concentrate on the Portal home page and the Portal Navigator, tools that provides the functionality to build working Web portal applications that integrate diverse components such as content, forms, reports, and charts. We will have our first meeting with eXYZ corporate management (a fictitious organization) and understand what the company does and what they are expecting from the portal we build. Last, we will build a Portal page to impress the boss; get a head start on the project, and buy some time so we can define requirements in the next chapter and develop our Web portal design.

A Walk Through Oracle Portal

Oracle Portal has an intuitive user interface that facilitates collaborative Web development. The development environment is itself set up as a portal and you will essentially be using a Portal platform to develop your enterprise portals. Teams of developers, content providers, and database administrators will be working collaboratively to create forms, reports, and charts, establish content within their business area, or create and manage database tables and the completed working Portal site. Application components will be developed, content identified, and database structures created that will result in working Portal pages, designed to provide a high-level view or entry point into the applications and content you will develop for use by your end users. The entire process is iterative and, like working with any Web site, the job of creating and managing it never really ends. Let's get started by finding the Portal Welcome Page as shown in Figure 3-1, take a look at Portal's features, and get a feel for how we will proceed with this project.

Exercise 3.1: Logging on to Oracle Portal
Oracle Portal is accessed through a Java-enabled Web browser as defined in the System Requirements in Chapter 2. The latest versions of both Netscape and Internet Explorer are certified by Oracle to work seamlessly with Portal. To log on to Oracle Portal, follow these steps:

1. Bring up your Web browser.

2. Under the URL address or location window, type
   `http://<hostname>:<port>/pls/portal30/portal30.home`

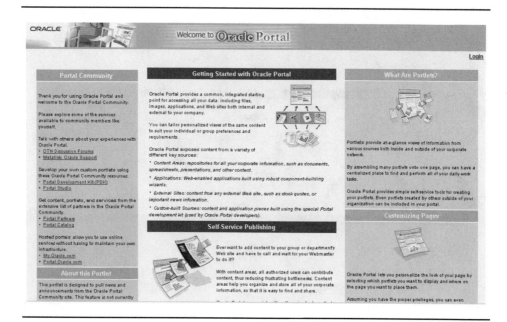

FIGURE 3-1.   *The Oracle Portal URL and initial login screen*

(where the hostname is the server name or IP address of the machine where the Oracle 9iAS Apache application server is installed on the network and port is the port number from the install. The default port is 7777.) The address for our stand-alone install is `http://localhost:<port>/pls/portal30/portal30.home`.

3. Click the Login link in the upper right of the screen. The Single Sign-On login screen will appear, as in Figure 3-2.

4. Type PORTAL30 in the User Name field and PORTAL30 in the Password field of the Single Sign-On screen, or use the username and password that you supplied during the installation process.

5. Click the Login button.

The Oracle Portal Home Page

You are now logged in as the Oracle Portal owner with full rights and permissions to do anything within Oracle Portal. From the Portal home page, you have at your disposal all of the development tools you need to create Portal Web sites. You will notice immediately that the central Portal page is broken into distinct sections

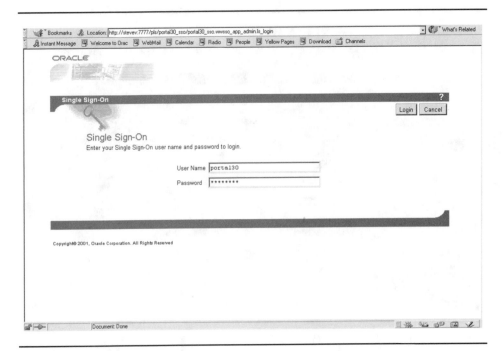

FIGURE 3-2. *The Oracle Portal Single Sign-On screen*

known as *regions.* Each of these sections contains one or more *portlets,* or applications, that guide some part of the process of building, administering, or maintaining a Portal content area or Web site. There are four main tabs across the top of the right hand region of the page: Build, Administer, Administer Database, and Monitor. Each of these provides separate application functions that may be utilized by different people within your organization based upon the makeup of the Portal development team and their respective individual skill sets.

Build, Administer, and Monitor the Portal

Look at the four tabbed working environments on the Portal home page: Build, Administer, Administer Database, and Monitor. Each of these tabs contains portlets that support specific administration and build processes. As you can see in Figure 3-3, the Build page is the starting point for creating pages, content areas, and applications. Later in this chapter, we will create a new page to see how easy it is to build Portal pages. Also, later in this chapter we will create a default page style and layout for eXYZ Corporation and utilize that format on our Portal site to give all of our pages a distinctive look and feel. In Chapter 5 we will begin the process of creating applications and then in Chapter 6 we will build a content area from the ground up.

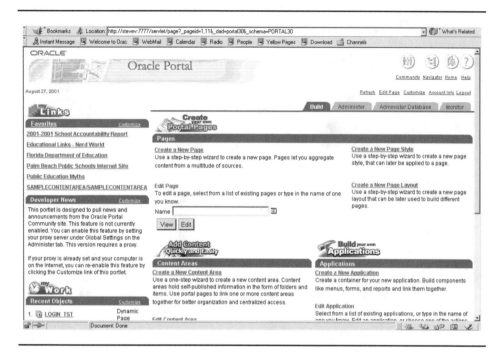

FIGURE 3-3. *The Build tab provides the mechanism to create pages, content, and applications*

You will use the Build tab extensively at the beginning of your development effort to create the infrastructure that will contain Web content and application components including Portal forms, reports, charts, and calendars. You will use the Build tab to create and name descriptive containers that will house Portal pages and page styles, content areas, and database applications.

The Administer tab, shown in Figure 3-4, allows the Portal administrator to register individuals as Portal users, assign them to role-based groups, edit and create new Portal privileges and profiles, alter system settings, provide IDs and descriptive information to create and modify unique portlet providers, and create links to other Portal sites. The Services portlet provides the ability to adjust the Apache listener gateway and improve throughput to the Portal application once it is deployed. The Provider portlet facilitates initial setup and editing of new portlet providers that allow you to create entirely custom applications and deploy them to the Portal interface. You may administer remote applications from other Portal sites in your company or across the Internet using the Node portlet. Outside Portal nodes may be identified and specified using the Nodes portlet to seamlessly integrate multiple Portal sites into one.

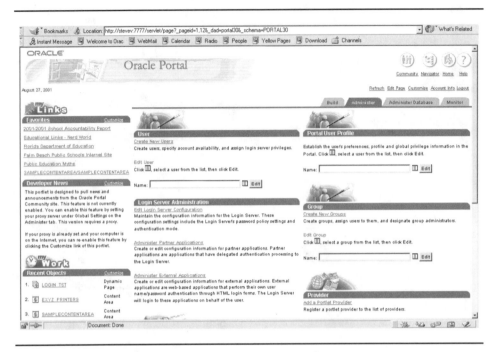

FIGURE 3-4. *The Administer tab provides user setup and system tuning utilities*

At the beginning of a project, the Portal administrator will register all members of the project team and assign them to a specific group as a Developer, DBA, Portlet Publisher, or Authenticated User of the system. Each of these default groups has separate privileges that are apparent when the user logs into Portal and they see only the development functions that they are privileged to see. For instance, an individual assigned only as a Developer will see all of the Portal tabs that we have just discussed but will find no reports or development functions listed under the Administer Database or Monitor tab. We will discuss users, groups, and privileges in more detail when we register our team within Portal to begin our project and assign them to groups.

The Administer Database tab, shown in Figure 3-5, provides database access and edit forms, utilities, reports, and charts that assist in monitoring database activities and functions. These include many reports that are staples for any DBA and that provide handy views of database configuration settings as well as memory usage and space utilization. These reports can supplement or replace those provided by Oracle Enterprise Manager (OEM) or other database monitoring and administration tools but have the added benefit of being available from any Internet accessible workstation.

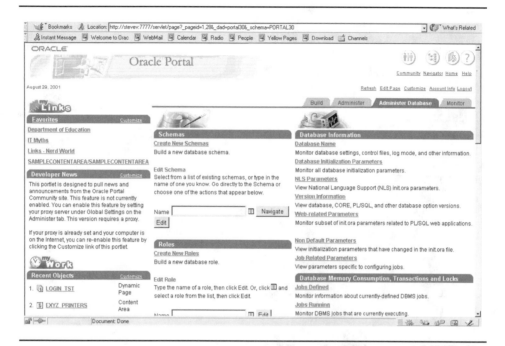

FIGURE 3-5. *The Database Administer tab provides helpful utilities and reports for the DBA*

The Monitor tab provides reports, charts, and responses to frequently asked questions that may arise during the monitoring of an active Portal site as seen in Figure 3-6. A Portal administrator can use these features to determine how to use the Oracle Portal caching and tuning mechanisms, to enhance system performance, and to get an idea of the most frequently used areas of the site.

The Portal Navigator

An interface that developers will find handy is the *Navigator.* You will be using the Navigator to move around in Portal and to work with Portal pages, content areas, applications, and database objects. In fact, the Navigator may be, by far, the most frequently used link for doing development within Portal. All of the functions on the Build tab are also available in the Navigator. You will find it is much easier to continue development beyond the initial setup stage using the Navigator.

The Navigator is used to locate the Portal object or type of object you are interested in working with. Your ability to see or edit objects within the Navigator will be directly related to the privileges the Portal administrator has assigned to you as a user. All objects that are displayed in the Oracle Portal Navigator are sorted

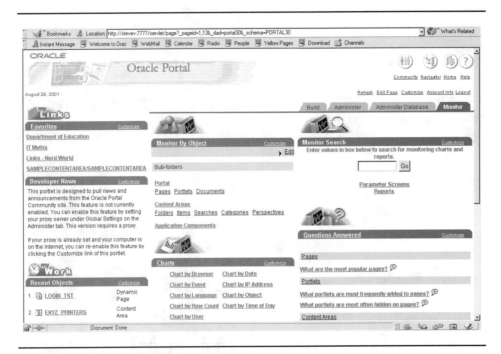

FIGURE 3-6. *The Monitor tab is used to monitor the performance of the deployed Portal site*

and displayed the same way, regardless of the object type. Each type of object (Pages, Content Areas, Applications, and Database Objects) is displayed in a hierarchical fashion, starting from a high-level list so that individual items may be more easily found and manipulated. Clicking on any of the objects on a Navigator page takes you to the next level, listing the objects contained within the parent object. To help you keep your place in the hierarchy, a path is displayed above the list of objects, tracking each traversed level. You may create a new object or object container using the link(s) displayed beside the Create New: text at the top of the page. Each Navigator tab has a Find field at the top of the screen that can be especially helpful in locating an object as the Portal site grows to hundreds of components.

Table 3-1 shows the display name and the descriptive criteria for each display column on all Navigator tabs.

The Pages Tab

Click on the Navigator icon to take a look at the Oracle Portal Navigator window displaying the Pages tab, as shown in Figure 3-7. The Pages tab displays all information about the Page objects in the Portal Repository. The Pages tab displays the Type, Name, Actions, Owner, and Modified columns, with an up and down arrow after each column name. Clicking on one of the arrows sorts the objects in ascending or descending order based on the data within the corresponding column.

Name	Description
Type	Describes each of the items in the list of available objects for a specific tab and level.
Name	Descriptive name for individual objects, such as pages, content, applications, or database objects.
Actions	The action that can be taken by the user to work with an object based on the user's privileges. This can include creating, editing, deleting, viewing, granting access, or exporting an object.
Owner	The owner or creator of an object.
Modified	The date that the object was modified.

TABLE 3-1. *Navigator Display Fields*

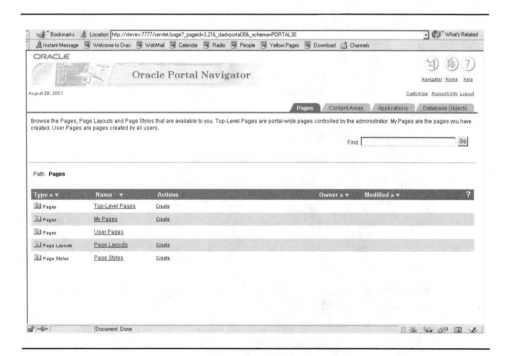

FIGURE 3-7. *The Portal Navigator Pages tab displays a list of Page, Layout, and Style objects*

Sorting can be especially helpful in locating an object when the Portal site contains many objects worked on by many developers.

A page is the interface that the end users see when they interact with the Web portal to access an application, view content, or search for a document. Page objects come in three basic types:

- **Top-Level Pages**   Created and controlled by the Portal administrator and used by anyone accessing the Portal site

- **My Pages**   Pages that you have created

- **User Pages** Other Portal users have created these and given you access to them

Page layouts and page style containers are also shown in the Pages window of the Oracle Portal Navigator. Page layouts depict the row and column subdivisions, or regions of a page, and how portlets are arranged within those regions. Page styles allow the Portal administrator or designated individual to create color themes, fonts, sizes, and styles for all elements of the Portal page, including headers, links, tabs, banners, and text.

Click on the Top-Level Pages link and you can see how the page hierarchy works, as shown in Figure 3-8. You will notice the Top-Level Pages container has become part of the path that is listed, and now two pages that are in the Top-Level Pages object container are listed. In this case, the Oracle Portal home page and the Oracle Portal Navigator page that we are currently browsing are listed in the Top-Level Pages container. Both pages are owned by the Portal30 master account. As the owner of both pages, Portal30 can perform the following Actions on these pages:

- **Edit**   Control the layout of regions on a page and the configuration and content that is displayed to the end user

- **Customize**   Control the layout of regions and page content for yourself only

- **Delete**   Delete a page from the Portal Repository

- **Copy**   Copy a specified page to My Pages and rename it. All permissions and grants are copied to the new page.

- **Create SubPage**   Create pages that are subordinately linked to the parent page

- **Reset Default**   Reset the default home page back to the Oracle Portal home page if another page was made the default

- **Make Default**   Make the selected page the default home page for the user. The home page appears in bold type on the Pages tab

- **Remove from Top-Level**   Changes the Page from Top-Level status to My Page

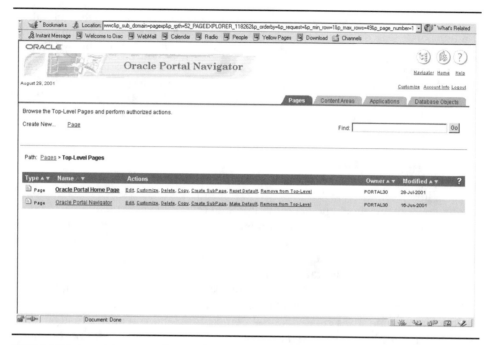

FIGURE 3-8. *The pages hierarchy of objects shows the relationship of page type to pages*

Go back from the top-level pages in the Navigator to the root pages directory by clicking on Pages in the Path field. In addition to top-level pages, you'll see User Pages listed. These are pages developed by other users. Administrators will see all pages under this link. The developer who created the page will have the page listed under his or her own My Pages area. After a developer has granted privileges to you, the same page will be listed under your User Pages directory. All pages are listed by name based on the name the user gave to the page in conjunction with the name of the user that has created it. You must know the page creator's name in order to identify and search for a page. You may also search for the page using the Find box at the top of the screen.

Be careful about offering delete privileges to another user because once a page is deleted, it is no longer in the Portal Repository and cannot be recovered. Edit privileges allow the grantee the ability to edit the page and save it under a new name that will not affect the original page that was granted. In this manner, if someone working on the Sales tab grants a nicely formatted page layout and style to the Human Resources branch of an organization, the HR branch can use that same page layout and style in their branch and keep a uniform look and feel within the company while still maintaining the identity of the HR department in the actual final page rendering on the Portal site.

The Find search mechanism appears on the right side of the Page tab and allows for a detailed search of the portal for a page that matches the criteria of the search. The search will find all pages that contain some or all of the text that the user enters in the data entry field. Try keying in `style` and click Go. You should see all of the default page styles available for use in Portal. Type `design` in the Find text entry field to retrieve the style for Design-Time Pages Page Style. The Find search capability is very useful when your portal gets larger, and is very useful to find user pages sent to you by others.

The Content Areas Tab

A *content area* is an object container that holds and categorizes Web content including images, links, text, documents, and even PL/SQL or Java programs. All content upload, formatting, organization, and access grants are controlled via content areas. Content areas are made up of *Folders* that are arranged in a hierarchical parent/child relationship much like the Windows file folder structure. You may organize content areas and folders in any logical manner that makes sense for your organization.

If you are building a Portal site using content areas, you will get a stand-alone home page built into each content area. This page can serve as the main interface for many types of Web implementations. Change the colors and fonts of the content area with the same styles created for the Portal pages, and you have a ready-made site. Add or remove elements from the navigation bar to meet the needs of your users, and change the terminology and/or icons to make the site part of the corporate culture. We will discuss various methods for designing content areas and organizing folders in Chapter 4, and we will develop content areas in Chapter 6.

Click on the Content Areas tab within the Oracle Portal Navigator. You will see the content areas that come with the initial installation of the Portal product, as seen in Figure 3-9.

The first content area you will see is the Monitor tab. The Monitor content area provides the organization and structure for the many component items used to produce the portlets on the Monitor tab of the Oracle home page. In other words, the Monitor content area is a container for the application code needed to monitor the Portal system. We can go to the Monitor tab of the home page, click on one of the links, and execute the code that resides in the Monitor Content container. Three other default content areas come with Portal:

- Portlet Repository

- Sample Content Area

- Oracle Portal Online Help

The *Portlet Repository* contains all of the portlets available to your Portal site, organized by provider. *Portlet providers* are applications, content areas, or external

FIGURE 3-9. *The Content Areas tab of the Oracle Portal Navigator*

providers that are developed or configured within Portal. In a distributed environment with multiple nodes or instances of Portal on separate machines, remote node portlet providers and portlets are also registered in the Portlet Repository.

The Sample Content Area comes as a default template container ready for you to rename and add in new content. The Online Help content area holds all of the Oracle documentation that comes with Portal, including the Quick Tour, Task Help, and Tips and Troubleshooting.

NOTE
Content areas are easy to edit and customize. You can add your own online help including development standards, code examples and workarounds, project methodologies that you may want to follow, developer and content administrator checklists, and other internally developed help support to the default Oracle Portal Online Help content area if you wish.

The Shared Objects link is not really a true content area but it contains objects that are shared across multiple content areas. Among these shared objects are the Personal Folders that allow end users to store their own private content. Perspectives, categories, navigation bars, styles, and custom types can be shared across multiple content areas to promote reuse of common objects.

To see how Oracle Portal shares objects, click on the Contents link next to the Shared Objects entry listed under Actions. Then click on Categories and then General to see all of the objects that are shared between multiple content areas in the General category. While in this Content Area view, click on the Content Area Map entry to see a different view of the content areas available to you. Expand the Monitor folder tab by clicking on the plus sign (+) and the Monitor by Object subfolder and the Content Areas folder to see all folders and subfolders, as shown in Figure 3-10. Click on the Home icon and then the Navigator icon to go back to the Navigator. On the Path: Content Areas > Shared Objects > Categories line, click on the Content Areas link at the beginning of the string to go back to the root Content Areas directory.

FIGURE 3-10. *The Content Area Map screen*

Assuming the maximum privileges are granted, the user will be able to perform various actions, including the following:

- **Contents**   Create or edit folders, categories, navigation bars, perspectives, styles, and custom types

- **Edit Properties**   Edit the content area properties, including sizing, languages that are configured and available for content, and access privileges

- **Delete**   Delete the content area

- **Edit Root Folder**   Edit the properties of the base folder, including the name, style, images, navigation bar, and access privileges

- **Copy Root Folder**   Copy the root folder to a new name and location

Three basic elements make up the content area application development environment: the navigation bar, the banner, and the folder area. We viewed the folder structure when we looked at the content area map. The navigation bar facilitates navigation within the content area, assists with searches for specific content, and links to related content. The banner displays the title for the content area page and the date it was last changed.

It is important for you to understand how these three components work together in order to develop and maintain content areas. Let's look at these content area elements in more detail:

1. Click on the Monitor link under the Content Area Name column.

2. You are now in the content area home page.

3. Click the Edit Folder link in the upper right-hand corner to display the content area, as seen in Figure 3-11.

4. The blue area on the left side of the screen is the navigation bar.

5. Note the Monitor Folder Area. It has subfolders named Monitor by Object and Monitor by Event, and they contain their own subfolders.

6. Place the cursor over the + sign next to Chart by Object. Don't click on it, but note from the bubble help that it is a Category within the Monitor folder.

7. Note the banner at the top that identifies this page as the Navigator and Folder areas for the Monitor content areas. Note the edit properties and icons and the last date changed for the content area.

8. Click on the View Folder link and return to the Navigator root areas directory.

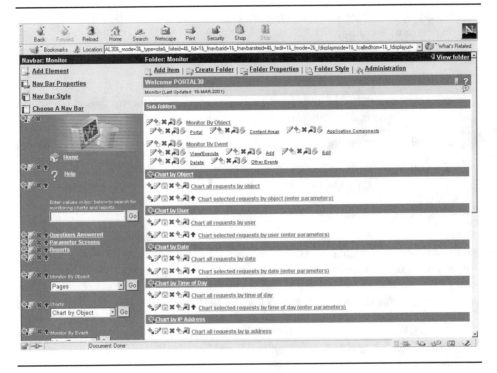

FIGURE 3-11. *The content area includes the navigation bar, banner, and folder area*

Just like the Pages tab, the Content Area tab has a Find tool that allows users to search for a specific content area name and display all objects that meet the search criteria. As is true for all Navigator tabs, the results may be sorted in ascending or descending order using the sort arrows next to the display fields.

The Applications Tab

Applications within Portal interface with the Oracle database to provide fully functional Web-based application systems. Developers can create applications from the Applications tab from scratch or modify and reuse an existing application. Developers do not need extensive knowledge of SQL programming to create applications. A wizards-based user interface allows the developer to point and click to select the required tables and columns to create applications as database procedures stored in the database. When an application component is invoked, the corresponding procedure is executed on the server. The results of the SQL query it performs are wrapped in HTML and JavaScript using the fonts and colors chosen in the development session and the full results are displayed within the user's browser.

Table 3-2 lists the many kinds of application components that can be built using Oracle Portal and shows the chapters in this book where you can learn how to build and customize them.

Component	Topic	Chapter
Forms	Master-detail forms, forms based on tables or views, forms based on procedures	Chapter 7
Reports	Query by example, reports from Query Wizard, reports from SQL Query	Chapter 8
Charts	Charts from Query Wizard, charts from SQL Query	Chapter 9
Calendar	Personal or enterprise calendars for scheduling	Chapter 9
Dynamic page	Embed your own SQL and PL/SQL code within HTML to finely control applications	Chapter 10
Hierarchy	Produce hierarchy reports based on parent/child database relationships	Chapter 9
Menu	HTML pages that provide hypertext links to other menus or application components	Chapter 10
Frame driver	A master-detail page with two frames, one that drives the results of the other	Chapter 10
Link	A link that ties one application together with another by a particular field	Chapters 8–11
List of values	Used within all components to assist with data entry	Chapters 7–11
XML components	Components that facilitate display of XML pages within Portal	Chapter 10
URL	Component that allows display of internal or external URLs	Chapter 10

TABLE 3-2. *Oracle Components Discussed in the Oracle 9iAS Portal Handbook*

Explore the Applications tab of the Oracle Portal Navigator. You will see in Figure 3-12 that the default install of Oracle Portal has an EXAMPLE_APP, PEOPLE_APP, PORTAL_APP, TASK_APP, and Shared Components. Click on EXAMPLE_APP to show its contents. The EXAMPLE_APP includes every type of component listed in Table 3-2 using tables installed and owned by the Portal30 user. The PEOPLE_APP uses the demonstration tables to produce a few employee- oriented reports, hierarchies, and forms. The PORTAL_APP is an empty template container ready to house components created by the development team. The TASK_APP contains sample applications that are work and task oriented and can be reused for that kind of functionality. Last, Shared Components isn't really an application, but a container for colors, fonts, images, JavaScripts, and ready-to-use templates that can be incorporated into any application component to enhance its look and feel.

FIGURE 3-12. *The Oracle Portal Navigator Application tab*

Portal developers can perform various actions on application components, including

- Manage
- Run
- Edit
- Delete
- Grant access

Granting access is worth discussing in some additional depth. Application access privileges define the actions you can perform on an application and the components owned by it. By default, you are granted the highest level of access, Manage, on any application you create yourself. With Manage privileges, not only can you perform actions on the application and create components within it, but also you can grant access privileges to other Portal developers, or delete the application. Application-level privileges potentially apply to all components in an application. Any component built in an application by default inherits privileges from the application. For example, after MY_CHART is created in MY_APP, any Oracle Portal developers with Edit or higher access privileges on MY_APP can edit MY_CHART. There is an override feature, so that users with the Manage privilege on the application can set different access levels on individual components within the application. The power of the application components is that they can be reused and shared to enforce a common development standard across the organization.

Database Objects

Oracle Portal is a tool stored in and driven by the Oracle relational database. The data you use within your company is stored in tables in an Oracle database. The Portal application, and all its functionality, is stored in the database. Security and the intelligence to connect to other applications and Web URLs will be stored in the database. So, it is very important to understand the relationship between Portal and the database(s) it is connected to, and to have the tools to do that. Portal must reside in the Oracle 8i or 9i database to function properly, but it can connect to the data stored in prior versions of Oracle that may be housed on other computers on your network. The mechanism to easily view database objects and to work with them is available under the Database Objects tab of the Oracle Portal Navigator. The Database Objects tab offers a very simple way to navigate through the tables, view and update data, and work with database objects that you will be using and accessing with the application components that you will develop.

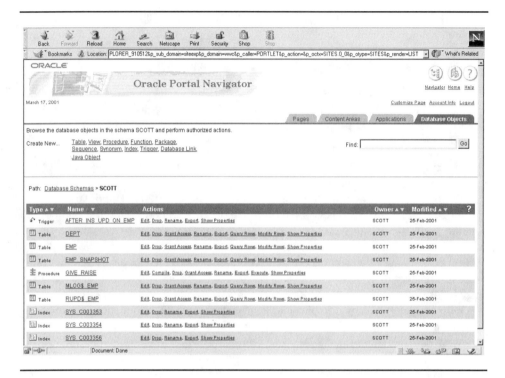

FIGURE 3-13. *The Oracle Portal Navigator Database Objects tab*

Click on the Database Objects tab in the Portal Navigator. Since you are logged in as the Portal administrator with full system-level database permissions, you can see all of the schemas in the Oracle8i database that you are connected to. If you have permissions to other database tables via database links, you will see the schemas in all of the databases you are attached to including remote databases. Scroll down to the SCOTT schema and click on the SCOTT schema name or on the Open link to see the objects that SCOTT owns, as seen in Figure 3-13.

Portal users will have varying levels of access to database objects. The DBA will have full access to all database objects. Developers may have full access to objects or not depending on the roles and privileges that the Portal administrator or DBA gives them. You will create DBA and Developer accounts in Chapter 5, and then you will have the DBA assign database permissions to the development team. The Portal30 user's role as the DBA allows full access on all of the database objects to do some or all of the following operations:

■ **Edit** At the schema level, allows password and default tablespace changes; at the schema objects level allows edit of column names and column characteristics and constraints

- **Drop**   At the schema level, allows the schema to be dropped, including all objects in the schema; at the schema objects level, allows individual schema objects to be dropped, including tables, indexes, views, and triggers

- **Grant Access**   At the schema level, allows specific Portal users or groups to have access to the entire schema and all objects; at the schema object level, allows Portal users to be granted access to individual objects

- **Rename**   Allows an individual object within a schema to be renamed

- **Export**   Allows export of an object

- **Query Rows**   Queries specific table objects for information

- **Modify Rows**   Allows INSERT, UPDATE, and DELETE operations on tables from within the Portal interface

- **Show Properties**   Displays the definition and structure of a specific schema object

As in the other Portal Navigator screens, you may use the Find search mechanism to find schemas or objects. If you are unsure of the name of the object or schema, you may use a portion of the name and use the % wildcard and click Go to find what you are looking for. It may widen your search a bit and allow you to find what you need.

NOTE
The wildcard % sign can be used on any keyword search within Portal or generally within Oracle using SQL*Plus or other tool to find something when you are unsure of the exact name. You may use it at the front or back, or surrounding the text or numeric string you are searching for.

Kickoff Meeting with eXYZ Management

In addition to familiarizing ourselves with the development environment, we have to understand the problem we will be solving with our portal application. Our mythical eXYZ Corporation, started in 1984 as a one-person operation that sold gift baskets out of a garage in Northern Virginia, is now a world-class online purveyor of goods and services. The company uses many older disparate applications internally to manage and monitor much of its payroll, sales, and accounting functions.

The company president, John Dahlman, is concerned that eXYZ must do more with less in order to stay competitive in the current marketplace. He has turned to his CIO, Linda Carter, to work on a plan to integrate enterprise systems and focus IT development efforts. Ms. Carter has recommended the use of an Enterprise Information Portal to accomplish that goal. Her plan is to use the customer and competitive information that the company has accumulated as a strategic advantage over the competition. She has found that the company has done a good job of collecting information but a poor job of organizing that information and disseminating it to the people that need it.

Ms. Carter has discussed problems and goals with each of the business unit managers within the company including Management, Human Resources, Sales and Marketing, and Finance. She has heard about Oracle Portal and its ability to unify a company's information sources and provide information from one source to individuals based on job function. To quote her from the management meeting, "That sounds exactly like the kind of tool we need here at eXYZ." She would like to see a demonstration of what the tool could accomplish. After a successful demonstration of a prototype application, she would like to work with the development team to define goals for the system, evaluate short- and long-term requirements based on current business problems, define the project scope, and design and build the system.

Creating and Editing Users

The first job that the Portal 30 owner must complete after installing Portal is to create Portal user accounts. Groups should be created first so that user privileges can be understood within the context of overall Portal privileges for the enterprise. Users can then be assigned to groups in bulk as opposed to on an individual basis. Out of the box, Portal provides groups that contain sufficient privileges for the entire development team. These include DBA, Portal administration, Portal development, and Portlet publishers.

All potential users of the Portal site and contributors to the site must be created as Portal users. Creating a Portal user is a task performed by a DBA or developer who was previously assigned Portal_administrator privileges or with privileges to access the *login server* from the Portal_SSO account. The Login Server is the facility of Oracle Portal that registers and enforces the *Single Sign-On (SSO)* mechanism for Oracle Portal users to log in securely to Oracle Portal. A single sign-on user account is what the user logs into Portal with to access applications with their single-user name and password. The user does not have to remember multiple user names and passwords for individual applications after they have gained successful entry into the Portal.

Login server administrators can create single sign-on user accounts using the login server or the Users portlet on the Administer tab of the Oracle Portal home page. Anyone that has All Users/Create privileges in the Administration Privileges section of the Group or User privileges tab can also create another user. It is a good idea to designate one person and a backup per line of the business to create users for their section. Let's create a new user for the portal.

Exercise 3.2: Create and Edit a New User from the Administer Tab

1. Go back to the Portal home page (by clicking the Home link) and select the Administer tab. From the Administer tab, click on the Create New Users link.

2. In the User Name field, type PATM as shown in Figure 3-14.

3. Enter a Password for the user name—for now also make it the same as the user name, PATM. You can change the password later.

4. In the Confirm Password field, enter the same temporary password.

5. In the E-Mail Address field, enter: patm@exyz.com.

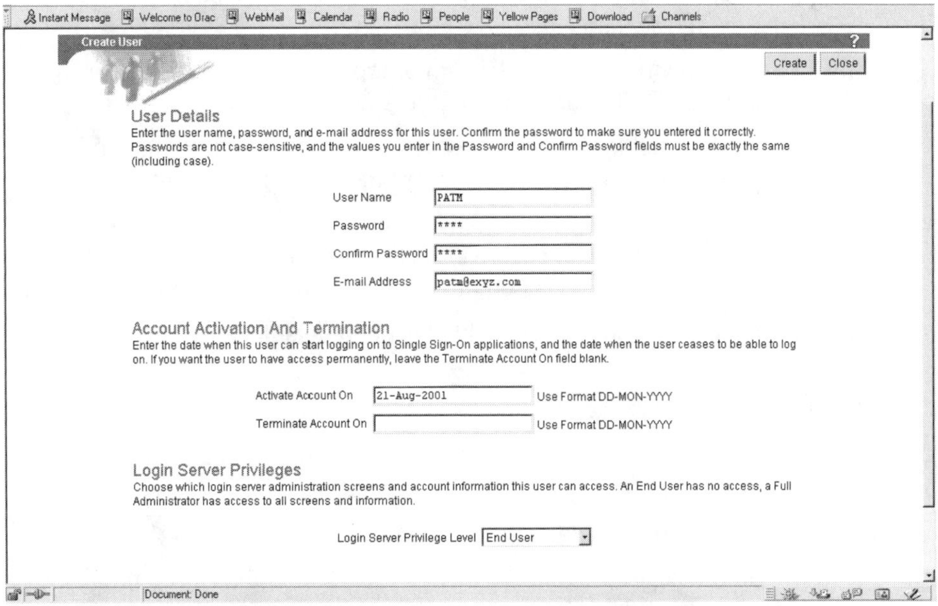

FIGURE 3-14.   *The user name and field definitions in the Create New Users dialog box*

6. In the Account Activation and Termination section, accept today's date for the date of activation in DD-MON-YYYY format and leave the termination field blank so that it will stay open indefinitely.

7. Choose End User for the Login Server Privilege level. The DBA and Portal administrator will support the login server.

8. Go back to the top of the page and click on Create.

9. You should see your user name, PATM, as a link at the top of the page—click on it to edit it.

10. Optionally fill in the Personal Detail information at the top of the page.

11. Check the box to Allow User to Log On. This will allow the user to connect to the Portal login server and develop and/or contribute new content. Not checking this box will only allow the user to see pages marked Public and prevents the user from logging into the portal.

12. Choose PORTAL_DEVELOPERS and PORTLET_PUBLISHERS for Group Membership.

13. Leave the Database Schema as Portal30_Public.

14. Fill in Organizational Details and include a picture if you have a bitmap or other image available.

15. Click the Apply button at the bottom or top of the page and then move to the Preferences Tab at the top of the page.

16. Leave all Personal Preferences checked to display user information in the company directory and to create a personal folder to store information.

17. Click on PORTAL_DEVELOPERS as the Default Group. Group preferences such as the default home page will be the user preference unless an individual preference is chosen; then, that overrides the group preference.

18. Leave the Default Home Page field blank and default to the Group Preference just chosen.

19. Click Apply and proceed to the Contact Info tab.

20. Key in contact information for the user's telephone numbers, office address, and home address.

21. Click Apply and proceed to the Privileges tab.

22. Leave all privileges as None for now and default to the Group privileges assigned via the PORTAL_DEVELOPERS group. The Privileges page contains all of the same privileges and choices as the Group Privileges page.

23. Click OK and exit.

Go to the Administer tab and edit user PATM and grant additional page, content area, and applications privileges by editing the settings as follows:

- All Pages   Manage
- All Layouts   Manage
- All Styles   Create
- All Content Areas   Create
- All Applications   Manage

The individual user privileges for PATM should be as shown in Figure 3-15. Log back in as PATM and see how the new privileges have modified the development environment. PATM is the lead developer and will be assembling pages, so applications privileges and page privileges should be set as high as possible to the Manage access privilege level so that PATM can manage the access privileges of the development team. We have a qualified content administrator and DBA on staff so

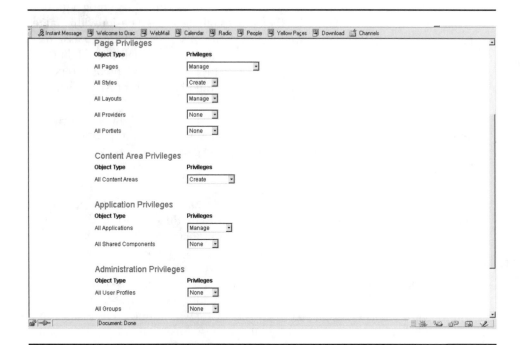

FIGURE 3-15.   *The Create New Users dialog box controls personal privilege grants*

from the standpoint of content and database administration, only view privileges are necessary for PATM. Schema View privileges come with the PORTAL_DEVELOPERS group privilege so we just need to provide a few individual privileges for PATM.

Granting Developer Access Privileges

Granting access privileges within Portal can be among the most complex issues to understand. In Chapters 4 and 5 we will talk in more general terms about how privileges can interrelate and how to afford access to the Portal development and user environment to members of your organization. From a developer's point of view, nothing can happen before database schema privileges are granted. Portal is a database application, so everything starts with the database when it comes to assigning user and group privileges and database access grants. We created the PATM user and assigned PATM to the PORTAL_DEVELOPERS group earlier, and now we will show how to ensure that PATM has the right privileges to create applications and reference the tables within the CORP_SITE schema.

If there is a requirement for a backup DBA at eXYZ, it might be a good idea to go back and give PATM Manage authority for all schemas and event logs, using the Access Privileges tab. All privileges that you wish to give to your development team can be given using the specific User Access Privileges tab or by assigning a group privilege to users using the Edit User Preferences tab. It is much easier with a large group to ensure that your group privileges are properly specified and to assign additional privileges to specific individuals using the Privileges tab of the Edit Portal User Profile link. Offer the Manage privilege for a function to only one or two people within a group. Everyone else within the group should have lesser privileges that default to the group privilege.

Let's spend some time now setting up a good working environment under the PATM account. Log in as PATM, since you will be doing most work under a specific account, not as the Portal owner. Examine the left side of the page.

My Links—Favorites

My Links is a personalized list of your favorite links to other Web sites, applications, or places within the corporate intranet where you might want to readily obtain information or quickly find a favorite application or procedure. The Favorites portlet, with its My Links image above the header, is a personalized list of your favorite links to other Web sites, applications, or places within your own corporate intranet where you might want to readily obtain information. You can create groups of favorite links to ensure that your links are organized according to function and need. The links you establish here will only be displayed when you log on with your own user name. No one else will share these. It is easy to establish these links with a few clicks of the mouse. Let's go ahead and establish one now for the PATM account.

Exercise 3.3: Establishing a Personalized Web Link

In this exercise we will establish a link to the Osborne/McGraw-Hill Oracle Press Web site so that we can download the tables and documents we will need to work on the exercises throughout this book. Make sure you are hooked up to the Internet either directly or via a dial-up connection before you try this exercise.

1. Click on the Favorites link. The Navigate Favorites Page will be displayed, Click on Create Favorite.

2. You will see the Add Favorite page shown in Figure 3-16. Type `Oracle Press` in the Name field, http://www.osborne.com/oracle/index.html in the URL field, and `Osborne/McGraw-Hill Oracle Press Web Site` in the Description field. Click Create. Your link is created and the Create Link page is cleared.

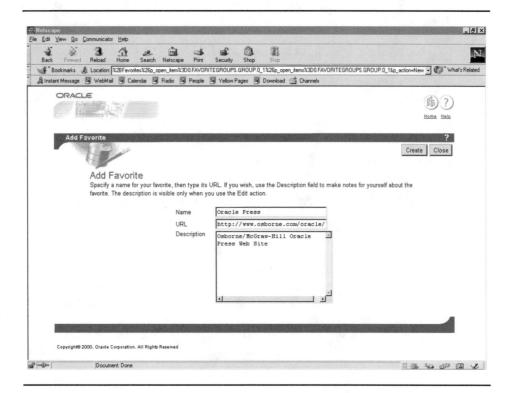

FIGURE 3-16. *The Add Favorites page allows you to easily add favorite Web links*

3. Click Close and click on Home in the Navigate Favorites page.

4. Oracle Press should be on the list of Favorite links. (Click on the Refresh button if it's not.)

5. Click the link and see if it works! You should now be on the Oracle Press home page.

6. Click Back on your browser and you will be right back to your Oracle Portal home page.

You will also notice a Customize link next to the Favorites link. The Customize feature allows each Portal user to personalize the look and feel of their own Portal pages without affecting the look and feel of the same Web pages for another individual. Let's see how it works.

Exercise 3.4: Using the Customize Feature to Edit the Favorites Portlet Settings

1. Click the Customize link on the Favorites tab.

2. On the Edit Favorites Portlet Settings page (see Figure 3-17), change the banner to say My Favorites.

3. Click on the drop-down list arrow in the Show field and note the options are Hierarchy and Flat List. Leave the option as Hierarchy.

4. Note that the Display field has an option for displaying All Favorites or limiting the list to the last number of Favorites.

5. Click OK and note that the banner has changed to My Favorites.

My Work—Recent Objects

My Work automatically stores your latest objects and development efforts for the Portal content area, page, or application you are working on. When you finish working on an object, a link to the object will appear within the My Work region under the Recent Objects tab. This is a convenient way to reaccess or view the properties of objects that you are developing.

There is a Customize link for customizing the appearance of the My Work section, just as there is for customizing the My Links area.

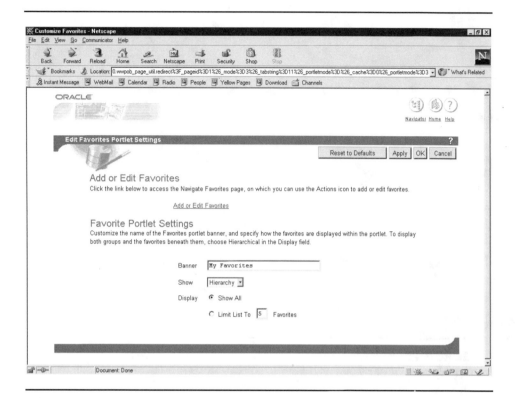

FIGURE 3-17. *The Customize Favorites function allows customized display of My Favorites links*

Exercise 3.5: Customizing the Recent Objects Portlet

1. Click the Customize link on the Recent Objects portlet.

2. Within the Edit Recent Objects Portlet Settings page (see Figure 3-18), change the Display field to Limit List To 8 Recent Objects (from the default of 5).

3. Check the Object Image check box and the Numbered List check box under Display.

4. Click OK.

5. Click the Refresh link in the upper-right corner of the home page if you don't see a change.

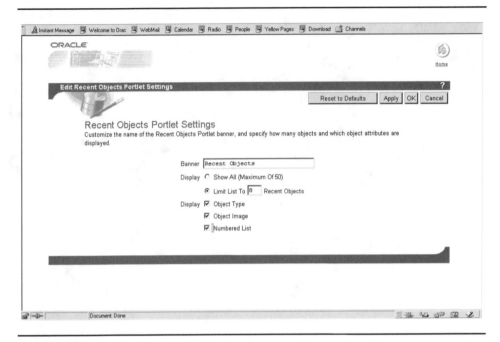

FIGURE 3-18. *The Edit Recent Objects Portlet Settings page modifies the display of the My Work portlet*

Notice the new look of the information displayed in the Recent Objects portlet. The portlet now displays icons and number information for the My Work section for PATM, the current user. For other users, the display for My Work - Recent Objects would remain unchanged. This ability to personalize your own Web environment is an important characteristic of an Enterprise Information Portal and something that is easily accomplished in Oracle Portal.

On the Web—External Applications
External applications such as Hotmail, E*Trade, and other Internet-based applications can be customized within the External Applications window to automatically execute and sign onto the application from within Oracle Portal. If you have a Hotmail or Yahoo account, for instance, you can connect to the Internet and check e-mail from within your Portal application without signing on each time with your Hotmail or Yahoo userid and password.

NOTE
If you don't have a Hotmail account, it is easy to set one up. Go to http://www.msn.com/ and click on the Hotmail link to establish a Hotmail account. There are other e-mail providers on the Web, but this exercise will illustrate connection to Hotmail. We will see how to set up and connect to external applications in Chapter 12.

You can use the External Applications portlet Customize function to provide the user name and password automatically whenever you connect to an external application from within Portal. Make sure you are still connected to the Internet and let's see how it works.

Exercise 3.6: Customizing External Applications

1. Click on Customize on the External Applications tab.

2. Check the box to Display Hotmail and click on the Edit icon (pencil).

3. Enter your Hotmail User Name/ID and Password on the Edit External Application Login Information page, as shown in Figure 3-19.

4. Click OK.

5. Click the Hotmail link next to the Edit icon to test out the connection.

6. You should automatically be logged into your Hotmail account and see your e-mail. If there is a problem, you may not be connected to the Internet or the external application information may be incorrect for Hotmail. You may fix the external configuration in the Administer tab, Login Server Administration function. (Chapter 12 covers the Login Server Administration function.)

7. Exit from Hotmail and return to the Customize External Applications page.

8. Click OK to return to the Portal home page.

You should see a link to Hotmail under the Web External Applications tab of the Portal home page.

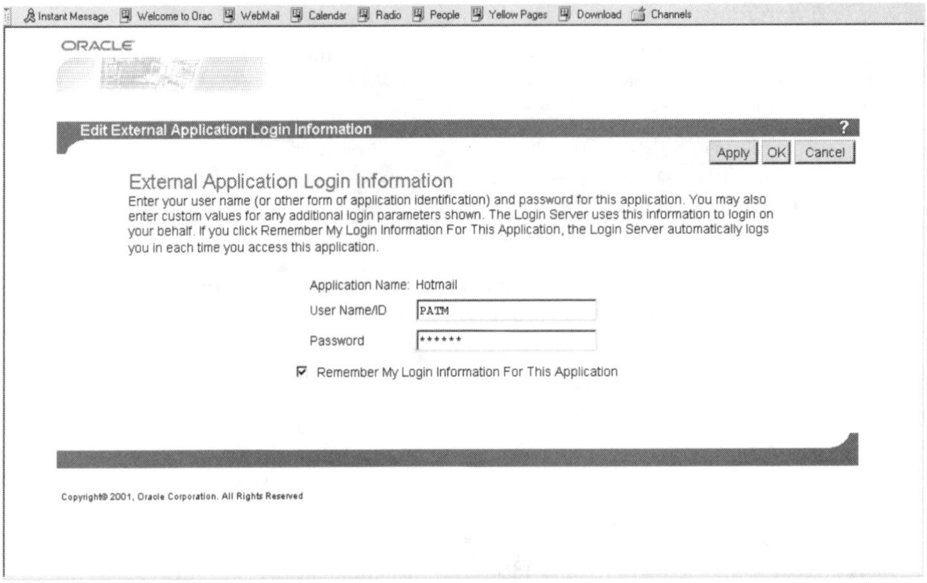

FIGURE 3-19. *Use the External Application Login screen to facilitate application integration*

Oracle Portal Shortcut Icons

The Navigator, Home, and Help icons and corresponding shortcut links are found in the upper right of your screen, as seen in Figure 3-20. These shortcuts are available on all of the design tabs that the user has access to. Each of these icons or links

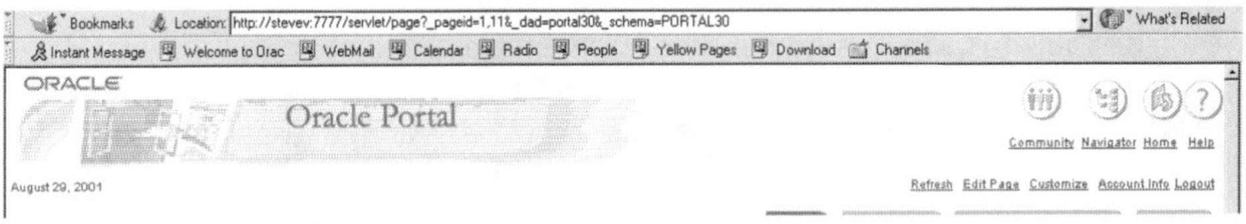

FIGURE 3-20. *The Oracle Portal shortcut icons provide standard navigation shortcuts*

gives the user the ability to navigate through Portal to the development environment required for the task at hand. The standard icons available are as follows:

- **Community**   Provides a link to the Oracle Technology Network Portal Community home page for Oracle 9iAS developers

- **Navigator**   Provides access to all Oracle Portal objects

- **Home**   Brings the user back to the Oracle Portal home development tabs

- **Help**   Provides tutorials and the online help system

Other useful links also appear on the Portal home page. These include

- **Refresh**   Recalls all content for a Portal page from the database and refreshes the information displayed on a Portal page

- **Edit Page**   Allows full control over a page, including access control and style changes for others

- **Customize**   Allows the user to customize the look, feel, and display of a Portal page without affecting the page's appearance to others

- **Account_Info**   Allows users to modify their personal Portal account information and passwords

- **Logout**   Allows users to log out and disconnect from a Portal session

We will look at the Edit Page and Customize links after we create our central Portal page, but let's look at the other links now.

The Home and Help Icons

The Home icon allows you to go directly to your default or specified home page at any time while you are working within Portal. The default home for the Portal administrator is the Portal home page. You may override that option at any time by accessing the Account Info link and changing the default home page. You will have the option to do that later in this chapter.

Help comes from many directions within Oracle Portal. In the upper right-hand corner of your screen you will see a question mark. Click on the Help icon; another browser window is opened with the Help screen. As you will remember from our previous section, the Help system is a content area that is focused on the Help function of Oracle Portal.

The navigation bar on the left supports the navigation and search of the Oracle Portal Help files, as seen in Figure 3-21. The Search field can be used to perform

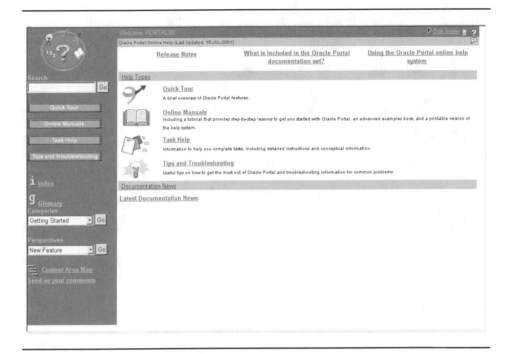

FIGURE 3-21. *The Help screen is a content area that appears as a separate browser window*

detailed searches of documents, including "fuzzy" searches of material that is related to your search request. You may also explicitly jump to a category that is related to a task you are trying to accomplish or choose a perspective for content related to your job function. This is often the easiest way to find the help topic you are searching for. There are navigation elements to support the Quick Tour, Online Manuals, Task Help, and Tips and Troubleshooting on the navigation bar and in the main page area. The Quick Tour and Task Help are particularly good. Task Help provides step-by-step instructions for Portal setup for each Portal Developer role that is useful for getting started, particularly for the Portal administrator. The Latest Documentation News link provides the latest in news about Oracle Portal, including Release Notes and error messages obtained directly from the Oracle Technology Network Web site.

Just below the banner of the Help content area are three links that provide a direct link to release notes, information about the Portal documentation set, and support on how to use the Portal Help system. Click on the Help Types link on the brown border field just above the Quick Tour and notice that the upper right-hand corner link has changed from Edit Folder to Edit Category. Also note that there are two types of subcategories now: Oracle Portal Online Help and Online Manuals.

Throughout the system, you will note a question mark on the far right side of the Oracle banner that is seen at the top of most Portal pages. If you are still in the Help system, you should see it next to the Edit Folder or Edit Category link. By clicking the question mark on the banner for various pages, you will get page-level help that is context sensitive for the actual function you are performing at that time. If you click on the help icon in the Category or Folder banner, a new Help window appears with detailed help for the functions on the current screen. This Help function is extremely supportive and is provided on nearly every page in the Portal development environment. You may provide similar context-sensitive help for your end users in the portal applications you develop. When you are done, close the Help window.

Refresh Page

Another important link is *Refresh Page.* As the name implies, this link will go back to the database and recall and regenerate all elements of a Portal page on your screen. Although a reload or refresh is common on any browser, the Refresh Page option within Portal is critical because of the caching features of Oracle Portal.

Oracle caches Portal pages or portions of Portal pages in memory to ensure that Portal pages are rendered quickly and efficiently with no loss of information. As you develop content areas, applications, and pages, you will notice that there are options within the Create or Edit Wizards to apply caching to various objects. This caching works with the various Portal objects to enable them to be stored in memory and/or disk store to speed retrieval from the browser.

In general, if an application or item does not change frequently, it is a good candidate for caching. Content that changes frequently or applications that access data that changes on a frequent basis are probably not good candidates. Cached content is rendered from a temporary disk store and not from the database when it is accessed for the second (and subsequent) time by anyone. For some types of content, such as pages, this means that there will be no call to the database to access the page (or part of the page). In this case whatever is cached on disk will be displayed on the user's screen even if the object has been updated (and its display changed) since it was originally displayed in the browser.

The Refresh Page option overrides the caching characteristics of a page or item and refreshes the entire page directly from the database and not from memory. Whenever you see Refresh Page, you can be assured that you will get the most up-to-date information and display that your Portal site has to offer. We will discuss caching in more detail throughout the book and in the Chapter 12 section on tuning.

Customize

The *Customize* function allows you to change the page format that you are working on and personalize it for your own preferences. Any changes you make using the

Customize link are visible only when accessing it under your own account. We will look at the Customize link after we have created the eXYZ home page.

Account Info

The *Account Info* function allows users to key in useful information about themselves that can be shared by members of the Portal development team during the development process and then by all members of the organization after the portal is deployed. If you click on the Account Info link, you will see a form that looks like Figure 3-22.

Log in to the PORTAL30 administrator account and click on the Account Info link. Key in your own personal information on the pages for each of the three tabs: Main, Preferences, and Contact Info. On the Preferences tab, make sure that your date of birth is in the right format and that you check Display Information In Directory. You can make your default group PORTAL_ADMINISTRATORS and your default home page the Oracle Portal home page, but this is already your default so it is not

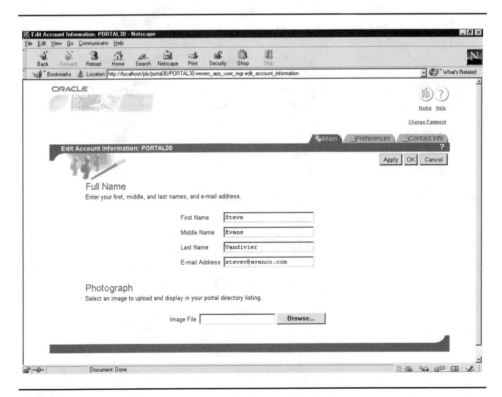

FIGURE 3-22. *Use the Account Info link to update your personal information and preferences*

necessary to fill anything in here. If you have any problems, click on the page-level Help question mark for assistance. Click Apply as you go on each Account Info page or type in all information and click OK when you are finished.

Logout

You may log out from Portal at any time by clicking on the Logout link in the upper right-hand corner of any Portal page. Logout disconnects your session from the Portal login server and sends you back to the Portal Welcome screen. At this point you can click Login to log back into the system, or exit from your browser.

Building a Portal Home Page

Portal sites can be built using content areas or Portal pages, or both. Content areas meet many of the organizational and functional needs identified in the early chapters of this book. Application components can be incorporated into both Portal pages and content areas, and both interfaces can incorporate custom code requirements. Both interfaces use the same styles that you'll develop to standardize the look and feel of the site.

If your application requires a central "dashboard" that allows users to view and access disparate functions on the same page, then it is a likely candidate for a Portal page. If your needs are more aligned with searchable content set up in the standard left-navigation/right-display format, you may find that the default home page for a content area meets the requirement without modification. A major advantage of Oracle Portal is that you don't have to give up functionality if you choose one path or the other. Content area folders can display as portlets in the Portal page, so you essentially have the best of all worlds.

Portal Page Anatomy

Portals introduce some new terms and concepts that require clarification. First, what exactly is a Portal page? To the end user, a Portal page is simply a single HTML page with a few distinguishing characteristics. To be considered a portal, it must have subdivisions, known as *portlets*, which display different kinds of content. This content can come from the site that delivers the page or from other sites, known as *portlet providers*. The portlets are arranged in *regions*, which help control the vertical or horizontal positioning of the portlets on the page. Regions are initially created by specifying the number and size of columns in the page *layout*.

A page always has a *style* that specifies the fonts and colors for each type of text or region on the page. When the amount of information to be displayed exceeds the available screen size, additional room is created with the addition of *tab pages*. If used, tab pages are indicated by active tabs near the top of the screen. When the user clicks on a tab, the content of the region is replaced with the content assigned to that tab page. Finally, in the Oracle Portal implementation, each portal page has a *banner* across the top of the screen that supports graphics, a welcome message, and customizable navigation buttons. Figure 3-23 illustrates these concepts.

To produce the portal, you need to create a page and, optionally, one or more layouts and one or more styles. The number of layouts and styles you create depends on the extent to which you will allow end users to customize the page. You have the ability as the page designer to restrict or allow end-user customization of styles, portlets displayed, banner, and page layout. Users with the permission to edit the page essentially become page designers, but you may wish to allow personal customization as well. One way to allow personalization while maintaining required components is to allow customization of one tab within the Portal page, but not the others. In portal terminology, this page would be known as a "My" tab. If you wish to allow the users to change the appearance of the site, you can create several styles for them to choose from or give them the privilege to create their own styles. As we build the page, we will show where to set up each of these permissions.

Every page requires a style, and unless you plan to use the provided default styles, you will need to create styles. Styles allow you to create a corporate standard look and feel across any Portal pages you develop. Add the company logo or a site-specific graphic, set the colors to coordinate nicely with this and other graphics,

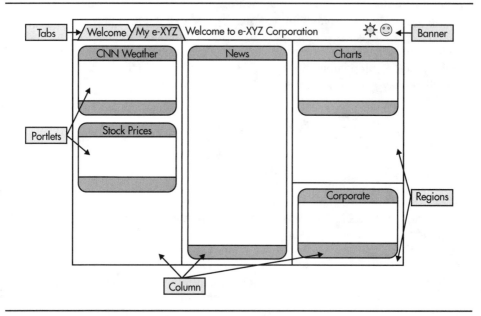

FIGURE 3-23. *The elements of a Portal page*

and the design work is done. A style administrator can work independently of developers to ensure that the appearance of the site remains appealing and consistent throughout. You may need additional styles if you are allowing end-user customization or if you have several Portal pages that require a different look. Unlike layouts, the connection between a style and the pages that use it is always maintained, so changes to the style will be immediately reflected in page's appearance.

Create and Edit Default Page Layouts

Page layouts define the look and feel of the user experience and how portlets will be organized on a page. Portal provides three simple layouts, with one, two, or three columns each. You may wish to create and save your own layouts if you need more columns or want to change the amount of space occupied by each column. Use the Navigator and move to the Pages tab. Click on the Page Layouts link to see the three default page layouts. You may use any of these layouts to create your page layouts, or you may create your own generic layouts that may be used by others to create pages. Log in as PATM for these exercises and let's see how this is done.

Exercise 3.7: Creating a Default Page Layout

1. From the Navigator Pages tab, click the Create link next to the Page Layouts link.

2. In the Display Name field, type `Two Column Stacked Layout`.

3. In the Description field, type `This Page Layout contains two columns. The first column is divided into two rows.`

4. In the Page Layout Usage area, click the Make Public check box and click Next.

5. Click the Add Column icon in the test page to create two columns side by side. If you make any mistakes, you can click the red X to back out your changes.

6. On the left-side region, click the Add Row icon to create a row within the column, as shown in Figure 3-24.

7. Click on the Edit Region icon on the right-side region to go to the Region Properties dialog box.

8. In the Width column, type `60%` to give this column 60 percent of the page width. You may express the width in pixels but it is better to use percentages to ensure that pages are rendered consistently between browser types and with various browser font or type settings.

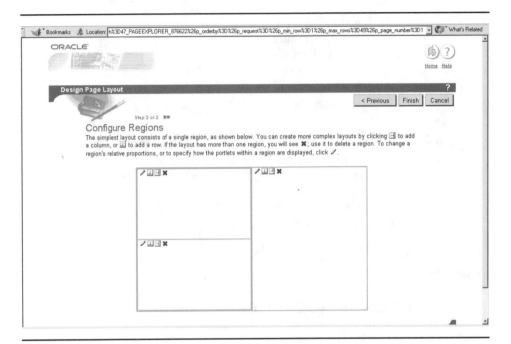

FIGURE 3-24. *Creating a new row in a region using the Default Page Layout Wizard*

9. Set the Display Portlets As field as Column (rather than the default Rows).

10. Set Space Between Portlets as 4 pixels.

11. Set Space Around Portlets as 5 pixels.

12. Click Apply and then Close.

13. Click Finish.

You should create default layouts at the beginning of the project and use one or more standard page layouts to keep a uniform look and feel throughout the site. In order to use a page layout, you select a default layout at the time you create a page. The layout is an initial setting, and no link between the page and the layout exists after the page is created. You use the default layout only as a starting point for developing any actual Portal page. Changing a default page layout after a page is deployed on the Portal site will not modify the actual page that was previously created with that default layout.

Try to develop a comprehensive choice of standard page layouts so that minimal customizing will be required to the default layouts when a page is initially created. You may delete a page layout or copy a page layout, rename it, and change its look and feel to avoid additional effort in creating a new default layout from scratch.

Creating and Editing Default Page Styles

Page styles support the look of the site and offer a method to standardize colors, fonts, and themes. Page styles support banners, titles, tabs, links, and other page characteristics.

Portal offers a facility to edit current page styles or create new ones. The colors that you may choose from are based on the universal hexadecimal color scheme that is the basis for color representation on the Internet. The colors available on the Style page of Oracle Portal are considered browser-safe across platforms. If you delete a page style that has been made public, all users of that page style will revert back to the default out-of-the-box Portal page style.

The page Caching option allows a page style to be cached in memory. Validation-based caching only checks for a new page style on a previously rendered page if a change was made to the page style since the last time it was accessed. Expires-based caching refreshes the page style on a defined time interval regardless of whether the style has changed. Use validation-based caching because it strikes the best balance between ensuring that your page style is current and the ultimate performance gained by retrieving cached styles from memory without checking to ensure it's the latest applied style.

You may create a page style from scratch by accessing the Build tab from the Portal home page and clicking on the Create Page Styles link. Alternatively, you may copy an existing page style from the Navigator Page Styles link and rename it so that you can have a head start in creating a custom page style. We will start by creating a new page style and apply this page style to the pages we will create for eXYZ Corporation.

Exercise 3.8: Creating a Page Style in Oracle Portal

1. Go to the Build tab of the Oracle Portal home page and click on Create Page Styles. (Alternately, access the Navigator's Pages tab, click on the Page Styles link, and click Create New... Page Styles)

2. In the Display Name field, type eXYZ Page Style.

3. In the Description field, type Page Style for eXYZ Corporation.

4. Under the Page Style Usage section, check Make Public to allow other users to view and utilize this page style, as shown in Figure 3-25.

5. In the Page Style Caching section, check Validation Based Caching and click Next.

6. The Page Style Element field shows that the page color is initially set to #FFFFFF, the hexadecimal representation of white, as shown in Figure 3-26.

7. In the Page Style Element field choose the colors and fonts listed in Table 3-3 for the page elements. You may press Apply at any time to see how your page would look.

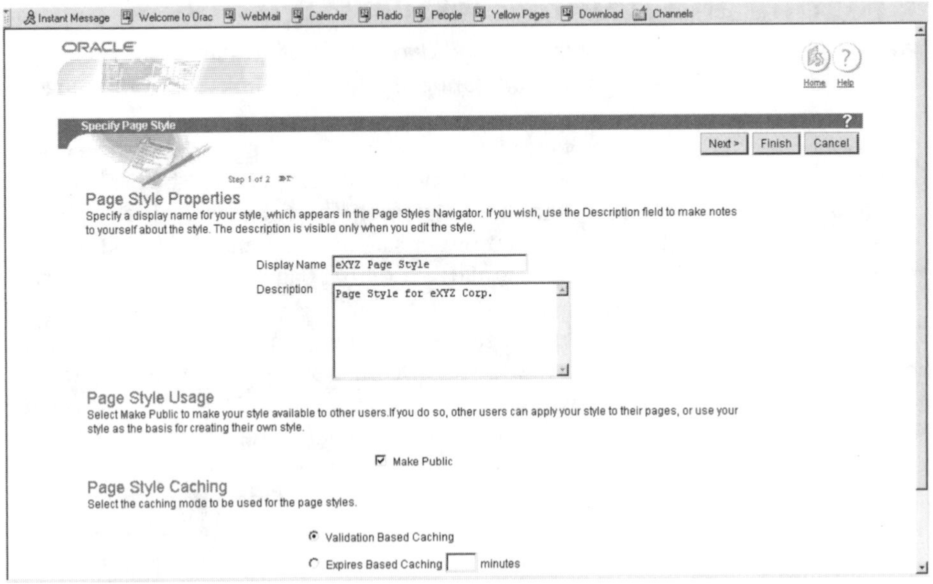

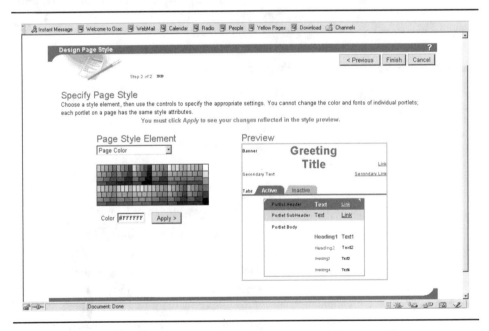

FIGURE 3-25. *Create page styles to standardize colors and fonts for all pages*

FIGURE 3-26. *Use the Design Page Style screen to apply page colors*

Page Style Element	HEX Color Value
Page Color	**#FFFFFF**
Banner Title	#000000
Banner Greeting	#000000
Banner Link	**#000099**
Banner Secondary Link	**#000099**
Banner Secondary Text	#000000
Active Tab Color	**#000099**
Active Tab Text	#FFFFFF
Inactive Tab Color	#D4D4D4
Inactive Tab Text	#330099
Portlet Header Color	#D4D4D4
Portlet Header Text	#000000
Portlet Header Link	**#000099**
Portlet Header Style	Normal
Portlet SubHeader Color	#FFFFFF
Portlet SubHeader Link	**#000099**
Portlet Heading1	#000000
Portlet Text1	#000000
Portlet Heading2	#000000
Portlet Text2	#000000
Portlet Heading3	#000000
Portlet Heading4	#000000

TABLE 3-3.   *The eXYZ Page Style Elements*

We created this page style as Public so that anyone building a page can apply this style to a Portal page. Later we will apply the page style and page layout we just created to our Portal pages to standardize the look and feel of the eXYZ portal.

Because this is a rapid prototype designed so management can see our concept, we will start by taking advantage of the built-in styles provided with Oracle Portal. In Chapter 4, we will show you how to design the portal to reflect your corporate image and how to define the functionality required by management. In Chapter 5, we will perform the administration functions for the Portal site and get the environment prepared for a team of developers to begin work on the portal. For now, we will just address the basic requirement, which is to demonstrate a customizable Portal page with specialized tabs for each department in the organization. It will have a Welcome tab displayed to all users, and the remaining tabs will be displayed for various corporate business units.

The Create Page Wizard

Start by creating a Portal page using the Portal Page wizard. As the lead developer, you will develop the system as PATM, so log in to Portal as PATM with a password of PATM. Starting from the Oracle Portal home page, make sure you are on the Build tab. Click on Create a New Page to enter the Create Page wizard.

The first step will ask you to specify the name and display name for the page, as well as an optional description of the page. The name is used internally to identify the page in code, and it must conform to Portal's rules for an identifier. These require that the name be 40 characters or less with no spaces or special characters except the underscore ("_"). You will want to come up with a naming standard that helps you identify the type of object being referenced with a recognizable identifier. The standard that we use specifies the suffix "_page" for pages. The display name shows up in the development interface any time a list of pages is displayed, and so should be descriptive. It allows mixed case and spaces, making it easy to define it with a meaningful title.

The next section of this page, under the heading Display Options, asks you to set two check boxes. We will look at each one separately. The first is Display Banner, and it allows you to choose whether to keep the banner across the top of the page. This choice is a matter of design—the banner takes up some extra screen space, but at the same time it provides a convenient place to put your corporate logo, a welcome message, and a few navigation links. It can also be used in combination with JavaScript to display banner advertising or flash important messages in real time. Our design requires the banner, so leave the check box checked.

The next option asks whether you would like to display subpages as links. If you're dealing with an extremely complicated set of pages, you may find it necessary to create additional pages, known as subpages, linked as children to this one. By leaving this box checked, you create an easy navigation path between the parent and child pages. The links display automatically on a line between the banner (if used) and the beginning of the page contents. We are using tab pages to manage the complexity of our site, because with tab pages we can control access and display for each tab by the user's privilege level. Subpages do not offer the same level of dynamic security, but if your users prefer the links to the tab pages and all users have the same security level, you may choose to use subpages. Either way, you can leave this box checked for our application—it won't affect our display since we are not using them, and it gives you the freedom to experiment if you like.

Finally, the Page Caching section asks you to choose the extent of caching you will use for this page. The default suggests that you will "Cache page definition only", and this option is sufficient for most applications. It caches the display page structure without caching the portlet contents. If the actual values contained in the portlets themselves won't change frequently, then you can use "Cache page definition and content", and you will have to set a time (in minutes) to allow the content to be cached. When this time expires, Portal will automatically refresh the content.

Use caution with this setting—a user could enter values into a form, and expect to see those values the next time they view a corresponding report. If the Report portlet is in the cache, they may not see the new values immediately and will assume the data isn't there. The last choice is "Don't cache", and while this is the only way to ensure the page is always up-to-date, it implies regeneration of the page every time it is used, and could have serious performance implications. Performing the following exercise, let's create a page.

Exercise 3.9: Create the eXYZ Home Page

1. In the Name field, enter `exyz_page`.

2. In the Display Name field, enter `eXYZ_Home_Page`.

3. In the Description field, enter `eXYZ tabbed Home Page`.

4. In the Display Options section, choose "Display page banner" and "Display sub-pages as links", as shown in Figure 3-27.

5. In the Page Caching section, choose "Cache page definition only".

6. Click Next to proceed to select the layout template and style. Here we'll set the initial layout for the page regions and choose a style for the colors and fonts. In the Layout Template section, choose `Two Column Layout`.

7. In the Style section, choose `Style for Design-Time Pages` and then click Next.

Exercise 3.10: Add Portlets

Here is where you will add portlets, subdivide the screen using tab pages and/or additional regions, and customize the banner at the top of the page. Because you are going to develop the site as you progress through this book, it will look a little sparse at first. Think of the initial cut as a framework that will help your customers visualize the eventual interface. You can show it in a demo, allowing the customers to comment on the style and arrangement of the screen. This interaction is intended to spark discussion of the placement and functionality of the portlets on the site and elicit additional requirements. We will use a few built-in portlets to begin, and add additional portlets as we specify and develop them. We will begin the process of setting up portlets by subdividing the home page into tabs by business unit.

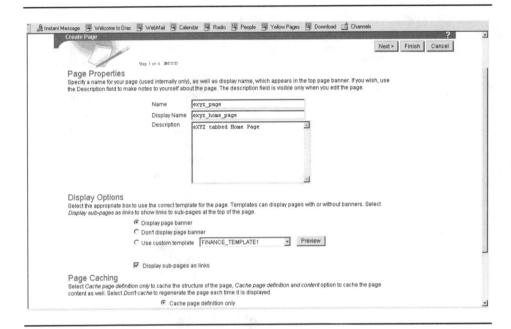

FIGURE 3-27. *The eXYZ Create Page dialog box*

Tab Pages   In the initial analysis phase for this project, the customer established that there are several distinct business groups, each having their own application needs. You will set up the framework so that each business unit has its own tab page on the portal. When you create all of the user accounts in Chapter 5, you will set up the security so that each group has access only to the tab pages appropriate to their job function. The tabs we'll include are as follows:

- The Welcome tab displays for everyone.

- The My eXYZ tab which users can customize and display their own portlets.

- The HR tab contains employee maintenance functions for the Human Resources staff.

- The Sales tab allows order entry and verification of available stock.

- The Management tab contains information to enable managers to analyze company performance.

To create the first tab, use the Add Tab icon on the right-side region, as shown in Figure 3-28. After you create the first tab, a set of icons will be displayed next to

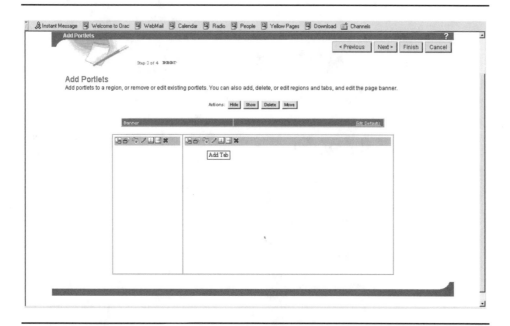

FIGURE 3-28. *Use the Add Tab icon to create tabs in a region*

the tab, as well as beneath it (in the original region). To create the remaining four tabs, use the Add Tab icon to the right of the new tab that you just created. If you use the one within the first tab region, you will get nested tabs, which is not what you want.

After creating all five tabs, edit the properties of each one. Use the Edit icon on each tab to set display names to Welcome, My eXYZ, HR, Sales, and Management. Be sure to click the Apply button before you click the Close button. We will modify the page access privileges in Chapter 5 to restrict access to certain groups using the Advanced tab options. We will not use images for our tabs. When you are finished, your screen will look as it does in Figure 3-29.

Customize the Banner   The banner will display across the top of the page. To set the banner, perform the following:

1. Click on the Edit Defaults link on the Banner region.

2. Set the Greeting to Portal Home Page.

3. In the Banner Logo Settings, change the Label to eXYZ Home. The Label appears as pop-up text when the mouse passes over the image.

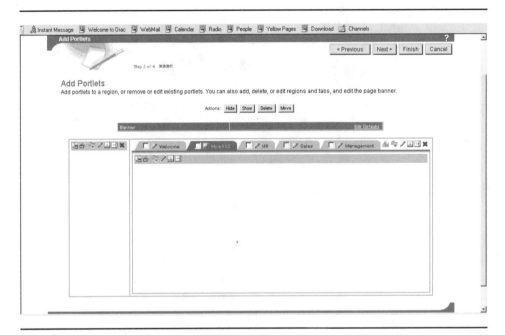

FIGURE 3-29. *The eXYZ home page with all tabs created*

4. Copy the `exyzlogo.jpeg` image to the `IAS_HOME/isuites/portal30/images` directory.

5. Use the Browse button next to the Logo field and find the `exyzlogo.jpeg` file. In the resulting File Upload pop-up window, make sure you change "Files of type" to `All` files (*.*) to make sure you can find the logo properly.

6. The URL will work as it is, because the PORTAL30.home link will always take the user to the home page defined for that user.

7. Scroll down to the bottom of the page, where you will find check boxes that allow you to display some of the default options provided with Oracle Portal. Because end users will not use the Navigator, uncheck the box that allows them to see this link. Leave the remaining check boxes checked, as these will provide default functionality that will come in handy later. Note that we can add links to other applications from this banner. The Edit Banner Portlet page should look like Figure 3-30.

8. Click Apply and then OK to continue.

Add Built-in Portlets   The initial portlets you will add are tools for all employees in the company, so you will put them in the left-side region. The first

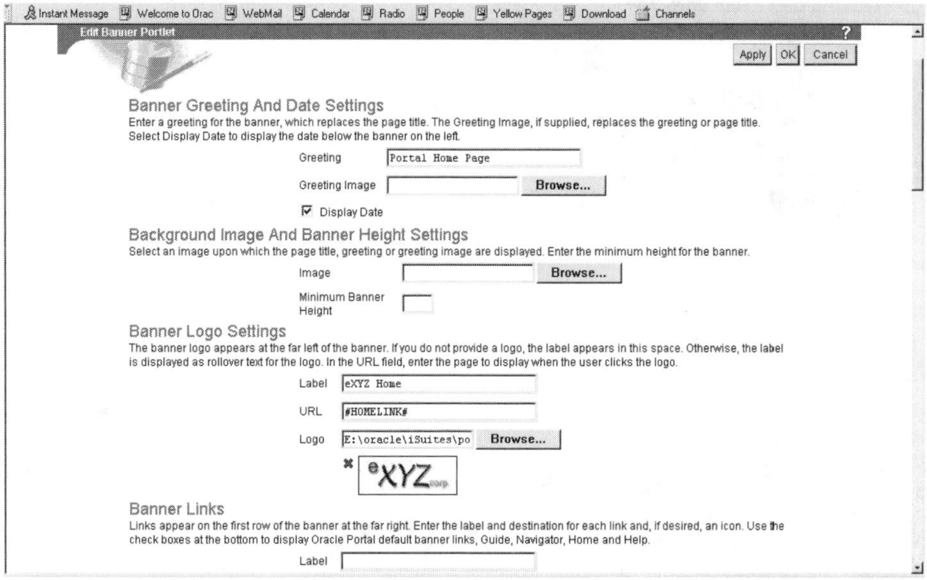

FIGURE 3-30.   *The Edit Banner Portlet dialog box controls the look of the Portal page banner*

portlet contains built-in functionality to look up "people," or Portal users. This will serve as a company directory.

1. Click on the Add Portlets icon, the leftmost icon, in the left-side region.

2. This will bring up a new window displaying the Portlet Repository and an interface to choose from the list of existing portlets you may want to use. Underneath the Seeded Providers link, click on the People APP link. Click on the People portlet under General to move it into the Selected Portlets window, as shown in Figure 3-31.

3. Click on the Portlet Repository link to return to the portlet providers page Then, still under the Seeded Providers section, click on the Oracle Portal link. Repeat the preceding step to add in the Favorites portlet to the list of select portlets.

4. Go back to the Seeded Providers section, choose the Login Server provider and move External Applications into the Selected Portlets list.

5. Click OK.

6. Highlight the My eXYZ tab, where you will add some default portlets. Click on the Add Portlets icon inside the My eXYZ tab.

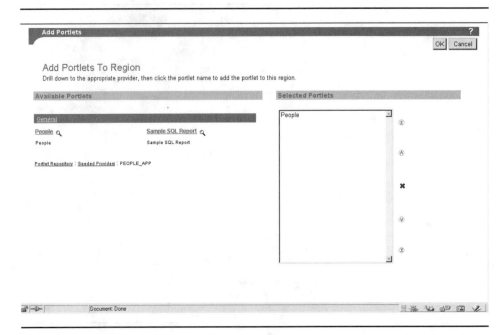

FIGURE 3-31. *The Add Portlets window displays available portlets you may render on a page*

7. Click on the Personal Content link and add the Saved Searches and User-Owned Folders portlets to this tab. You will customize this later when you integrate the unstructured content. Click OK.

8. By default, the portlets are displayed on top of one another in rows. To change this so they are side by side, click on the Edit Region icon for the tab page.

9. Change Display Portlets As to Columns and then click Apply and Close. The portlets will now show up as columns when you add them to this region.

10. To add more "slots" for portlets, you can subdivide the tab page into additional regions. Click on the HR tab and then find the Add Column icon beneath it.

11. Click once to create an additional column.

12. Click Next and note the Control Access page. We will fine-tune access in Chapter 5 after we have created all users and groups.

13. Click Finish. The screen should look like Figure 3-32.

FIGURE 3-32.   *The completed eXYZ Portal page*

Navigate around the resulting page to view the functionality you have created. You can navigate through all of the tabs on the page and use the portlets on the page. Earlier we discussed the Customize links that are available on each Portal page. Let's look at the eXYZ home page and personalize it using the Customize link. From the eXYZ home page, perform the following steps:

1. Click on the Build tab to ensure you are on the first tab of the home page.

2. Click on Customize Page link. You should be looking at an editable eXYZ home page, as shown in Figure 3-33.

3. Click on the blue tab. Arrange icon on the right side of all the tabs.

4. Highlight the My eXYZ tab and use the down arrow at the very bottom to demote this tab to the end. Click OK.

5. Click on the Edit icon (the pencil) on the new tab.

6. In the Edit Tab | New Tab dialog box, type My Tab in the Display Name field (as shown in Figure 3-34).

7. Click Apply and then Close.

8. Click Close on the Customize Page | eXYZ_home_page Edit screen.

9. You should see a new Portal home page with a new Tab with the My eXYZ tab moved to the far right and a new tab called My Tab showing last.

You may make changes in this manner to any page that has the Customize link on it. The Customize link will only enable you to customize your own view of the page. You are essentially making changes to your copy of a page that others also use. They can make their own changes to their pages without affecting the look of your page.

If you have Developer or higher privileges using the Edit Page link, then you can make changes for everyone. Be careful with the way you handle these privileges as an administrator. You don't want to have users knocking on your door wondering why your "Personal" page is showing up on everyone's desktop!

Manage Page Styles Throughout the Site

Anyone may change the page style for a personalized stylized view of the Portal site. An administrator can change the style of all pages in the site by setting a style

FIGURE 3-33. *The Customize link customizes your own pages without affecting others*

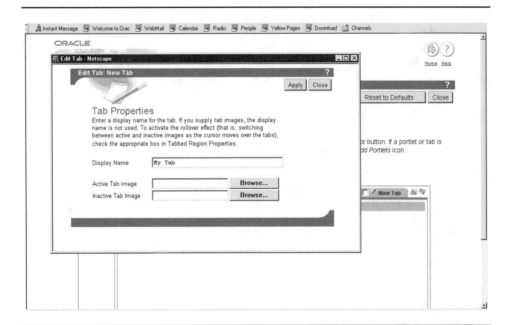

FIGURE 3-34.   *The Edit Tab dialog box lets you change the name and display of a tab*

as the default style for the site. A user who chooses their own personalized style for their view of the site using the Customize link from the home page can always override the default style set for a page. If the Portal administrator does not make a default choice for a page style, the initial system default for Portal page style will automatically prevail.

To set the default page style for the entire site, log in as the Portal administrator, use the Navigator, and choose the Pages tab. Click on the Page Styles link and promote any of the page styles that are listed to the default page style by clicking the Make Default link. You may also change the default page style from the Portal home page Administer tab using the Global Settings link under Services. From the Default Style window, you may choose the default style from the list of page styles available.

If you wish to choose your own page style from the list of page styles for your own page style view, use the Navigator Pages tab to find the page that you want to modify. Click Edit and choose the Style tab. Under the Page Style section, choose the page style you want to see on your page from the Available Styles window. The style you choose will apply only to the page you are editing and will only affect your own page style. Only by setting the default page style for the portal will uniform standards apply throughout. A user of the system who desires their own page style look and feel can override the standards at any time. Once again, personalization of the Web experience is a characteristic of portals and it is facilitated with the end-users' ability to change their own page style and override the default page style set by the administrator.

Now let's go ahead and apply the eXYZ page style we created to a specific page using the page we previously created for eXYZ Corporation.

Exercise 3.11: Applying a New Page Style to Portal Pages

1. Log in to the PATM account and, using the Navigator, highlight the Pages tab.

2. Click on the Top-Level Pages area and choose the Edit link next to the eXYZ home page.

3. Highlight and click on the Style tab.

4. From the list of available styles, choose eXYZ page style.

5. Click OK and then click on the eXYZ Home Page link to view the new page style.

6. Now go back and repeat your steps but choose <Use User's Default Style> from the list of available styles.

7. Click on the Pages link in the Path field to go back to the root Pages tab directory and click on the Page Styles link.

8. Choose the Make Default link next to the Style for Design-Time Pages to promote this page style to the default for PATM.

9. Go back to the root path, choose Top-Level Pages, and click on the eXYZ home page to see how the user default style for PATM has changed the appearance of the eXYZ page.

You will be adding to the XYZ page and editing it throughout this book. You can change the Portal page to the look that you want at any time. You will set up the security controls later—for now, it's time to give the boss a demo.

Conclusion

In this chapter, we have walked through the Portal user interface and met with management about our upcoming Portal project, and you have created your first Portal page. It is a functional demo that will get you started building the remaining application components. In the next chapter, you will define the requirements, understand design issues, and design the portal. In later chapters, you will set up the required security scheme, build content areas to handle unstructured data storage and retrieval, and create application components to interface with the database tables. The result of this process will be a fully functional intranet site that supports all of the organization's business needs.

CHAPTER
4

Designing the
Enterprise Portal

A t this point you should have a clear idea what Oracle Portal can do. Before we get into the mechanics of developing a working Portal site, it is important to understand what constitutes a successful enterprise portal. Portal projects that are successful require a substantial investment in preparation and design. The enterprise architecture must be defined, structured and unstructured corporate data assets uncovered, the look and feel of the site conceived, and navigation standards adopted. Most of all, the requirement for the Web portal itself must be developed and understood before any other effort is expended in putting the portal together. The requirement for the portal must be dictated and determined by the ultimate users of the portal.

This chapter will provide a user-centric methodology for developing a corporate enterprise information portal. The methodology begins by determining the makeup of the project team and the roles they will fulfill in developing the system. The next step is to define corporate goals, objectives, and requirements for the portal at a high level. How should the portal be set up—by line of business, by business process, by product type, or by other criteria? Is the goal to provide information, provide direct customer support, support internal applications in the form of a corporate dashboard, or facilitate some or all of these? The methodology then addresses how to refine requirements and identify and classify structured and unstructured data resources based on the stated goals of the system.

Once requirements are adequately defined, it's time to discuss the design of the system. The design characteristics include look and feel, graphics and branding, applications and content, organization of the Web site content, navigation methods, labeling, themes, and application design. Last, we will identify how to iteratively develop the portal application, seeking feedback at all stages of the project from the users of the system.

At all times during this process, it is imperative to get feedback from the customer— the prospective users of the system. The old adage that the customer is always right is especially important when developing enterprise portals. The visibility and openness of a Web portal ensures that if you don't listen to your customer, you will certainly hear about it later.

The Project Team

As a collaborative tool, Oracle Portal encourages groups of specialists to work together to create enterprise portal applications. Portal defines a set of default group roles that the members of the Portal team can assume in the process of developing the portal application. Additional group roles can be set up for the project team and for the users of the system (as we'll see in Chapter 5), but the primary development groups available for Portal development are:

- Portal Administrator
- Portal Developers
- Portal Publisher
- Portal DBA
- Authenticated Users

All members of the team who develop application components, create content, and work with the database, as well as users of the system, will be assigned to one of these roles. Let's see how these Portal roles might apply to people who are part of a Portal development team.

One of the most important individuals on the development project team is someone that will likely never develop an application or contribute any content: the *corporate sponsor*. Like any enterprise project, a Portal development effort must have the support of a strategic corporate sponsor, someone with vision and a corporate perspective who understands the needs of the organization and has some idea of the scope that the project must take on. The corporate sponsor will not be on the project team full time, but in many ways he or she will be the most important member of the team. The corporate sponsor will undoubtedly be called on to break stalemates in the approach to site development after hearing all sides of an argument. More than anything, the corporate sponsor must work with the development team to support and manage end-users' expectations.

The corporate sponsor should not be a consultant, although consultant support can offer a fresh perspective to any Portal project. Whoever serves in this capacity should be able to understand and think like an insider in all operations of the corporation and see the big picture. The corporate sponsor should also be able to think like someone new to the company and provide or endorse innovative ideas free of political bias. They should be able to get away with asking hard questions and be able to command the respect needed to get the answers and not cause political disruptions. After all, the information age has created individuals that depend on "their" information for job security. A sound enterprise portal ensures that job security is not tied to proprietary individual or line-of-business interests, but to the needs of the enterprise. A corporate sponsor must enforce this tenet at all costs.

Any barriers that have been erected within the organization to prevent strategic sharing of corporate knowledge must be broken down. It is up to the lead *Portal architect* (as shown in Figure 4-1), in conjunction with the corporate sponsor, to collaborate, communicate, facilitate, and ultimately dismantle these barriers in order to demonstrate the value added of the Portal to everyone in the organization. The Portal architect serves as the project manager of the Portal development effort, and it is up to this individual to identify the individuals that understand the business case

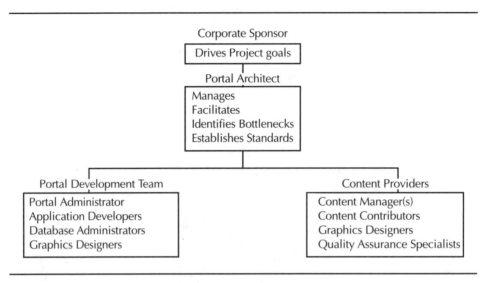

FIGURE 4-1. *The suggested Oracle Portal project team*

for the system within the organization. These business-savvy functional proponents of the system can end up as the most valuable allies on the project, regardless of whether they are predisposed to be knowledge hoarders or knowledge purveyors.

The Portal architect and their team will spend many hours working with line-of-business managers identifying Portal site goals, requirements, and design issues. The architect must be a skilled negotiator, understand corporate politics, understand budgets and aggressive deadlines, recognize when the "horse is dead," be able to facilitate group discussions, be able to understand current corporate business processes and recommend changes, and have direct access to corporate management. In addition to possessing management skills, the Portal architect should ideally have some technical ability so that they can understand and communicate with members of the technical team about aspects of database design, Web site design, Web security issues, and general information management concepts. Needless to say, one individual possessing all of these skills could be a tall order, but success is predicated on the Portal architect or the management team possessing a majority of these skills.

Oracle Portal is a database-driven tool and this makes the *database administrator* (DBA) a very important team member. Depending on a corporation's reliance on database management systems, it may or may not already rely on a DBA for the internal setup and administration of enterprise databases. Although there are similarities between database management systems, all databases are different and an Oracle Portal effort will require a DBA skilled in administering the Oracle DBMS. MS Access is *not* a database in the Oracle sense, and it is not wise to think that if you can figure out MS Access, Oracle will be an easy progression. At a minimum, the DBA will be responsible for setting up the database, database sizing, backup and recovery, performance tuning, and maintaining links to other database instances that Portal will connect with.

In a corporation with robust database-oriented applications, the DBA is an indispensable team member for many projects and he or she will be tapped to review SQL code for efficiency, ensure software releases are kept current, and identify application bottlenecks that are caused by poor database tuning, poorly written application code, or network bandwidth problems. These skills can be especially important in a Portal environment that employs extensive application coding using forms, reports, charts, and heavy document management searches. The Portal administrator will assign the DBA to the DBA group role within Oracle Portal.

A DBA may be supported by one or more *data analysts.* The data analyst will evaluate data throughout the enterprise and ensure that information rendered within the portal from that data is consistent and valid. The data analyst should have some knowledge of database design and data modeling in order to understand the interrelationships between systems and database tables. Additionally, the data analyst will work closely with business analysts throughout the enterprise that are the most knowledgeable about company legacy systems and data.

To develop forms, reports, calendars, graphs, or other applications using Oracle Portal, you will need to have at least one *application developer* on staff. In a small organization, the DBA and/or the Portal architect may perform these duties. Forms and reports design and PL/SQL code development involve vastly different skill sets from those possessed by a graphics or design artist. An application developer must be familiar with the principles of relational database theory and design, and should understand one or more application development techniques, including SQL, JavaScript, HTML, and Java. Application developers work with and for the Portal architect and develop application specifications in conjunction with end users. In a small organization, a developer will devise design specifications for application components, and in a larger organization an applications system analyst will develop specifications. The application developer will be assigned to the *Portal developers* group at a minimum, and possibly to the DBA group as well.

In a larger organization, a *graphic designer* will be employed to render the look and feel of the site, identify themes and concepts, provide graphical artwork, and develop the page styles, colors, and layouts for the site. Some of this work can be accomplished using Portal templates, color schemes, page styles, and layouts that are part of the out-of-the-box Portal administration framework that will be discussed in the next chapter. In order to create fresh graphical content, artwork, and other design styles, it is advisable to use a tool like Adobe Photoshop. Access a site such as www.zdnet.com to identify other commercially available tools that can enhance and create graphical content for your Portal site.

Graphics design is a highly specialized and artistic field; for this reason, the function of graphics design is often outsourced to a company that specializes in quality Internet artwork. If you typically outsource your graphics requirements to an outside firm, make sure you obtain all graphics, including logos and any branding colors or artwork, in JPEG, HTML, or GIF format for inclusion in your Portal site. Don't lock yourself into previously designed brochure artwork when designing your site, but if you consider your brochure graphics artwork to represent a corporate look and feel, then by all means include that work within the Portal site. Don't reinvent the wheel! The graphics designer will work closely with the content administrator. In a small shop this may be a combined role in conjunction with some outsourced graphics design work.

The *content administrator* will serve as the lead information architect of the enterprise portal. This job function is the key to the success of the informational enterprise portal whether many team members or a specific individual performs it. This person will be the lead information architect responsible for identifying the informational assets of the organization and working with line-of-business managers and employees to include those assets in the portal. Since new information is constantly being developed, the job of the content administrator never ends. The content administrator specifies and enforces standards for documents that will be included in the Portal site. The content administrator defines classification guidelines for documents within the Portal content areas and develops guidelines for searching, retrieving, and navigating to documents and information located within the site. They will also be responsible for identifying any security considerations that should restrict a document from being seen by a specific individual or group of individuals.

The content administrator will identify and work closely with *content contributors* throughout the enterprise to ensure that individuals are designated to add items to the Portal site. This is an important function because it ensures that members of the organization are empowered to add content to the enterprise portal. The content administrator should ensure that guidelines are published within the portal, which content administrators can use to determine what documents are important and should be included within the portal. Content administrators must also ensure that all content is checked into the system properly and in the proper format.

Finally, one or more individuals within the organization should be designated as *quality assurance (QA) specialists*. QA specialists should not be members of the development team, but should be familiar enough with the project to understand the stated goals and requirements for the Portal site and understand the design guidelines set forth for system navigation, search criteria, and document classification. For instance, a QA specialist can test keyword searches within the system as they are approved and test hits on documents and content using the Monitor tool to ensure accuracy for the intended searches. This method of testing should be used to minimize the number of erroneous hits that can take place when searching for a specific topic and can assure that the portal meets the requirements of the organization. If navigation or page styles are inconsistent, the QA specialist can report problems back to the project team for resolution. The QA specialist may work closely with data analysts to ensure data quality is consistent in the production system. The QA function is crucial to ensure a solid working Portal site and for the continued success of the Portal site.

Identifying Corporate Goals

In Chapter 3 we had an initial meeting with the management of the eXYZ Corporation where the requirements of the Portal site were initially stated. The eXYZ Corporation has many choices in determining the type of enterprise portal to build. Generally, portals come in three varieties or a combination of these three:

- **Internet** Portal to facilitate Internet-wide searches for information on specific or general topics. Examples include Yahoo.com, MSN.com, and Google.com.

- **Intranet** A private network that typically resides behind a firewall that is used by individuals within a corporation or other entity to share corporate information.

- **Extranet** A portion of a corporate intranet that is securely shared with suppliers, partners, vendors, and customers to facilitate sharing of information and improved business processes.

Let's look at an Internet portal first. Oracle Portal can power an Internet site that could convey a corporate brand and facilitate e-commerce applications and online purchases. It can also simply serve as the platform for an Internet Portal site that provides a sophisticated informational search engine for Web research and topical analysis. Oracle encourages partner corporations and third-party vendors to develop applications to seamlessly fit into the Oracle Portal architecture. Customer relationship management (CRM) applications, online e-commerce engines, and other Web-based applications will soon be standard components of Oracle Portal. The list of pre-approved and certified third-party applications and shareware that interface with Portal can be found on the Oracle Web site at www.oracle.com.

These third-party applications can give significant added value to your Internet portal development efforts. A corporate development approach to an Internet portal development effort is significantly different from the approach to an intranet or extranet portal. The mere fact that an Internet portal is a fully public site that could attract an unlimited number of concurrent users makes security and bandwidth considerations alone major design issues. In Chapter 1 we discussed the classic intranet application, a design that is particularly well suited to the Oracle Portal architecture. Intranets are designed to help employees collaborate to perform the business of the company, as shown in Figure 4-2.

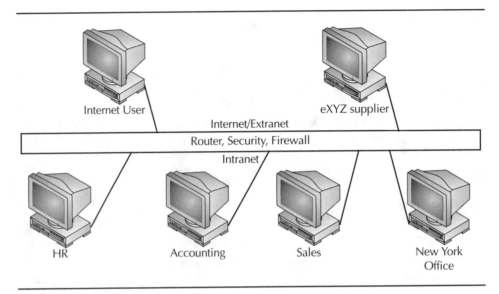

FIGURE 4-2.   *Corporate intranets can also support extranet and Internet viewing*

While the tendency for most companies is to build and design the portal according to line of business, many companies are beginning to subscribe to the idea of building corporate intranets to conform to specific business processes. For instance, if eXYZ Corporation is developing a new product, the Research and Development, Manufacturing, and Marketing departments should collaborate to ensure that the product is developed properly and has effective marketing collateral available by the time it goes to market. Developing such an integrated strategy is just what a corporate intranet should be designed to accommodate. Too often, intranets are developed along organizational lines and not cross functionally by business process; the end results of such efforts can be disappointing. Designing a cross-functional intranet can be more difficult and time-consuming, but the end result is typically a more effective enterprise intranet portal.

A corporate extranet combines the openness of the Internet with the business function of an intranet to securely share portions of a business's operations with suppliers, customers, and partners. For example, partners can access the extranet as they would a corporate intranet to view information about products and services, to view catalogues for most recent product pricing for resale opportunities, and to collaborate on other joint business opportunities. Extranets can speed up the business cycle by offering a secure way for all internal and external corporate interests to work together to promote common business goals. Security is a key consideration for extranets. With Oracle Portal's role-based security and single-source login functionality, it is particularly well suited for extranet applications.

In order to set the corporate goal for the Portal site, the functionality of the site should generally fall under one or more of the three classifications described previously. Goals and design requirements for these three types of sites fall into two general categories: consumer-oriented commercial sites and informational sites.

An Internet site can be a consumer-oriented site, geared to promote brand awareness and to sell goods and services directly or indirectly to the product consumer. A consumer site can be designed for fun, glitz, and flash in an effort to promote a product line or catch the user's eye. Navigation should get and keep the user in the site, promote products through trials or promotions, and acquire information about the users of the site in exchange for trial products or services. Alternatively, a consumer site can be understated, with a rich and elegant look that promotes a service or highlights the power and reliability of a services-based company. Either way, keeping content interesting for the consumer is paramount, and sales and marketing techniques to attract consumers are important.

Internet or intranet Portal sites are most frequently informational and quickly provide users with requested information. Such sites are suited to be database driven in order to utilize the power of sophisticated search engines and generate dynamic content. Data must be presented to the user in a way that does not lead to information overload, but provides a solid, crisp, and accurate response to the search for specific information of interest. In this regard, the promise of XML is significant to information-based sites because XML-tagged documents and text result in more finely tuned searches. There are generally fewer graphics in an informational Internet portal, and the site is built for quick response. Typically, user input is geared to provide parameter-driven searches for content (both structured from the database and for unstructured text and documents), rather than aiming to collect data from users to update a database. Links to other URLs outside of the Portal site are more prevalent in an intranet environment where support for job function and information is more important than attracting consumers.

While intranets typically are exclusively informational sites that provide reports and document search capability to internal users, extranets supply information to internal users, partner corporations, and suppliers, while often extending portions of the site to consumers. Design considerations for extranets can include the glitzy aspects of consumer and informational sites designed to attract consumers in conjunction with more mundane information-oriented pages designed for research. Portal's role-based characteristics allow both types of pages to be accessed from one Portal instance for each of these types of content consumers. Content area design is an important function and performed differently in each of these instances. The remainder of the book will focus on developing an enterprise information portal that allows corporate content consumers and extranet suppliers to understand the business practices of an organization and optimally serve the needs of the corporation.

Determining Project Scope

The scope of a Portal project can quickly escalate unless the objectives for the Portal site are well defined based on the goals outlined by management. Scope creep is unavoidable unless the following key criteria are embraced:

- Project goals are well identified in a basic mission statement.

- Specific requirements and objectives for the site are defined and refined by the end user in conjunction with the project team.

- All requirements, short and long term, are identified.

- User expectations are set by the project team for each project milestone and phase.

- User satisfaction with the end product is quantifiable.

The planning phase of a Web development project is often the most overlooked and least understood by an end user. Most users don't understand why a team of developers can't just develop a home page and connect it to the rest of the site. They look at the process as a creative endeavor and not the exercise in structure and architecture that it really is. A Web site is like a building: If it does not sit on a firm architectural foundation with a solid infrastructure, the site will quickly fall apart and be impossible to use. Users must understand the need for up-front planning; it is the goal of the Portal development team to educate them to this fact. Scope creep is nearly always the fault of the project team not communicating and managing the end users' understanding of the project and their expectations for the final deliverable. Scope creep rarely happens, even with the most demanding of end users, if they are clear on the fact that additional demands for the Portal site will mean time delays and additional costs. Midcourse corrections in a Web development effort are always costly and can be avoided if a project is scoped properly.

Mission Statement

Organizations often prepare mission statements to define succinctly what the goals of the corporation are and what the company stands for. Since the focus of an enterprise information portal is to improve corporate business processes and knowledge management throughout the enterprise, the company mission statement would seem like an appropriate place to begin to define the portal's goals, scope, and requirements. Many companies do not have a formal mission statement, and developing one often leads to greater clarity in the mission and purpose of the organization as a whole. Merely stating that the company sells something or is in a particular business area is not enough. The mission statement should define what you do, how you do it, and how you expect to accomplish it. It should be as goal-oriented as possible and that goal should be measurable, if possible. If you are a manufacturing or distribution organization like eXYZ Corporation, your mission statement might be the following:

> *The mission of eXYZ Corporation is to provide the highest level of customer satisfaction in our line of gift products by effectively utilizing e-commerce one-to-one sales methods and state-of-the-art rapid distribution processes, and measuring that satisfaction through customer relationship management (CRM) techniques.*

This mission statement says, first and foremost, that eXYZ is committed to customer satisfaction. Nothing else comes before that. Secondly, eXYZ's primary product offering is a line of gift products. The company is focused on selling one set of products and it is intent on ensuring that each client and prospective client recognizes that eXYZ is the best company out there at producing those products. That is the goal and that is what eXYZ is committed to. Lastly, eXYZ intends to use e-commerce, world-class distribution methods, and CRM processes to maintain quick turnaround, responsiveness, and client satisfaction. This mission statement also identifies how the success in accomplishing the stated goal will be measured—using CRM to measure customer satisfaction. This is a crucial component of the mission statement.

A nonprofit or trade association might have a mission statement that looks more like the following:

> *The mission of the National Association of Dog Lovers is to use our privately funded Web site to promote the education, understanding, knowledge, and love of all canine breeds to individuals worldwide.*

This mission statement identifies the goal of the organization as promoting the love of dogs worldwide. The site is privately funded and it is assumed that donations from users of the Web site and other sources make up a large part of the funding. Since the organization promotes dogs on a worldwide basis, multilingual documents and content should be maintained. The National Association of Dog Lovers is a knowledge-based organization that promotes its cause using its Internet Web site. This statement identifies the corporate goals and how we expect to accomplish them. Presumably the Web site will have a hit count or other measuring stick to identify the degree of success the company is having with the goal of promoting the love of canines.

Both of these mission statements offer a basis for beginning to understand organizational objectives and business goals. From this initial platform, we can delve deeper into the organizational structure and business processes of these corporations.

Business Objectives of the Portal

An enterprise portal should reflect business objectives that support the organization and its structure, not the other way around. Too often businesses build Web portals that resemble the organizational structure of the company with specific tabs and content for, say, HR and Accounting. Although this design supports the HR and Accounting divisions separately, it does not necessarily support collaboration between the HR and Accounting divisions quite as effectively. The design, structure, and content of the portal must support the portal's requirement to be open and collaborative while also enforcing role-based security and information access as appropriate.

Continuing to take a top-down approach, once you've defined the corporate goals with the mission statement, you should define specific corporate objectives for the Portal site from that mission statement, as shown in Figure 4-3. Keep in mind throughout this process that Portal development is iterative, meaning that it takes place in steps, and the job of building and maintaining the Portal never really ever ends. Web site development can also be a very political process that requires educating end users in order to break down the barriers to success.

Corporate Objectives Document

Overall Corporate objectives—management	Relative Importance
Share knowledge within the business	
Lower costs	
Improve operating efficiency	
Communicate more effectively	
Share understanding of corporate goals	
Promote an integrated team approach to the business	
Understand customers and their needs	
Sales objectives	
Understand customer buying habits	
Have ready access to sales collateral	
Have quick access to current product pricing	
Improve lead generation by integrating Sales Force Automation	
Understand competition and the market	
HR objectives	
Improve benefits delivery and understanding	
Provide access to 401K mutual fund latest pricing	
Improve timeliness and support of employee review process	
Improve access to company policies and procedures	
Provide on-line time sheet management	

FIGURE 4-3. *Defining corporate business objectives*

As an example, our project team recently took on a job to reorganize a company's Web site. The original objective of the job was to improve the navigation within the site and to facilitate future maintenance and enhancement efforts by developing a simpler site structure. It quickly became much more than that. In looking at the original structure of the site, we first noticed that all of the content was laid out by divisions within the organization and by office rather than by process. In our project scoping phase, we also noticed a great deal of commonality among the content and the Web directory hierarchies among the various offices in the organization. Every directory contained training, seminars, sales or merchandise, and newsletters. Each of these subdirectory names constituted key components of the business and what the organization was actually "selling."

In reviewing these content directory structures, we found extensive content and many icons maintained in more than one of the directories—a sure sign that corporate collaboration was not being achieved and too much work was being expended to maintain redundant information. When we suggested eliminating the redundant corporate hierarchy structure from the site, we ran into our first taste of corporate politics. Each office wanted to maintain their identity and keep the corporate structures that they were used to. Office managers worried about a loss of "control" if the structure of the site changed and things were maintained by business process rather than by line of business. This is the phase of the project where education, facilitation, and patience with the user must prevail.

It is very important to push for an open dialogue when discussing objectives. The more discussion and thought-provoking testiness you can facilitate in these discussions, the better. Start with an initial set of one-on-one interviews with the key proponents of the site. If you are a consultant or new to a company, first find the trusted "insider" who can tell you about the nuances of the individuals you will be interviewing. Some of the people you will be interviewing will have strong opinions about what the site should be. Some will have political ambitions for the site or hidden agendas. It is important to know all you can before the interviews start.

In the interview process, find out everything you can about the goals and aspirations that each individual has for the site. Use a questionnaire similar to the one shown in Figure 4-4 and tailor it to the company you will be working with. First, spend some time educating the interviewee about the general capabilities of a portal from the aspect of technology and functional possibilities. Be general at this point—don't skew the vision of what the portal could be and use the corporate mission statement and any stated goals of the project to illustrate what the project will be about. Ask what their short-term and long-term goals will be for the site for their branch and for the company or organization as a whole.

Some people will have more vision about the site than others. Take notes on everything that is said, including pie-in-the-sky ideas. Notions that no one has thought of seriously sometimes end up adding the most value. Stress that you are just trying to understand the need and individual goals for the project so that those goals can be prioritized and translated into requirements for the effort. Also stress that portals are iterative, and that if the objectives that they outline in the interview are not met

Portal Goals and Objectives	Relative Importance (Rank 1 low to 5 high)
Return on Investment	
Reduced development costs	
Ease of system use	
Business Integration	
Document Management	
Improved corporate knowledge flow	
Improved Customer Satisfaction	
Improve response time to customer needs	
On-line customer survey results	
Customer trend analysis	
Product White papers readily available	
Improved Sales Opportunities	
On-line competitive analysis	
Links to competitors sites	
Integration with R&D information	
Online collateral and current pricing	
IT Requirements	
Integration with existing systems	
Scalability	
Fast response times	
Software ease of use	
Workload reduction	
Questionnaire	
What are your line-of business requirements at eXYZ Corporation?	
How do you want this Portal to support your line-of-business mission requirements?	
Are your existing support applications web enabled?	
Are your existing application reports adequate for your needs?	
What are your short and long term goals for this system?	
Who are your customers inside and outside the company?	
How do you support your customers?	
How could you serve your customers better?	
Would you like to see document information online?	

FIGURE 4-4. *The corporate portal interview sheet*

initially, they may be addressed later in a subsequent phase based on a process of management decision and approval.

This interview does two things. First and foremost, it makes the line-of-business managers and interviewees part of the process. It is so important for the enterprise collaborative aspects of a portal to ensure that everyone will be a contributor to the portal when it is actually deployed. If a portal is developed and deployed in a vacuum, without collaboration, it is doomed to failure. Key individuals who are left out of the objectives and requirements gathering process have less incentive to see the project succeed than those that have a voice in its final look and feel.

Portals require the contribution and understanding of everyone in the organization to be successful, and the earlier you get individual and overall corporate buy-in to the objectives of the site, the better. Politics are quickly eliminated when open communication and dialogue prevail. Secondly, the initial interview process opens the floodgates for possibility and offers members of the organization some creativity in how they would like to see the organization use the portal to improve the business. Every idea can be noted in this initial interview, and all ideas will later be prioritized to define the scope and objectives of the project in phases.

After everyone is interviewed, the Portal team must find the commonality in the objectives mentioned and produce a single document that defines the project's short-term and long-term objectives. Prioritize all objectives and put any requests that aren't realistic on the back burner, but think through reasons for all priorities you assign and be ready to explain diplomatically why something wasn't considered a high priority. Attach a weight to the objectives in terms of degree of difficulty. Cost-benefit analysis should be applied to the objective and priorities to determine whether a particular objective is too costly to implement in the short term given project resources and deadlines. Work with management and the corporate sponsor to understand the relative importance of each objective. Try to assign a rough order of magnitude to the costs associated with accomplishing each objective so that this cost-benefit analysis can be presented as accurately as possible in the draft Statement of Objectives document.

It is a good idea to call a meeting after the draft objectives have been written to present this goal-oriented document to all line-of-business managers and to the corporate sponsor of the project to get final consensus. Try to present the document first to the corporate sponsor and work with them to anticipate where there will be political clashes of will or disagreements that will require more thought or maybe a change in the approach. This is a living document that will require changes, but it is important to identify any changes early on so as to minimize the impact to the project scope and associated timeline and costs. A meeting with all interview participants may be too much to handle because ideas may be too wide ranging. It is often difficult to make decisions by committee in this manner. Participants in this meeting should be very familiar with the interviews that have taken place and they must be in a position to voice opinions and make decisions. These meetings tend to be lively and frequently result in the identifying of some new and important objectives that didn't come out in previous discussion.

Afterwards, disseminate the results of the meeting, prioritize and weight the objectives once more, and offer a final objectives document for acceptance and sign-off by all managers and the corporate sponsor. This document will define the goals of the company and the short-term and long-term goals and objectives of the Portal site, as shown in Figure 4-5. The objectives should be presented to the client in phases that

---

Final eXYZ Portal Objectives Document
Project Scope
To develop an integrated automated system that supports the business processes and mission of eXYZ Corporation. The system will support the highest level of customer satisfaction in the companies' gift products by effectively utilizing sales and competitive data, integrated and proactive enterprise information sharing, and timely immediate reporting to promote one-to-one sales methods and state of the art rapid distribution processes.
Project Goals
Facilitate effective proactive reporting, information retrieval, and information analysis on demand by implementing a corporate Enterprise Information Portal (EIP) to promote improved corporate business processes in the core areas of sales, marketing, finance, Human Resources, and Distribution.
Project Objectives
  1. Integrate corporate data and unstructured information using corporate information standards
     · Identify common business processes between business units
     · Define a core metadata standard and naming convention for all corporate data elements
     · Identify and resolve all information and data conflicts
     · Improve data quality and manageability
     · Identify all unstructured assets within the organization that support the business
  2. Improve enterprise customer responsiveness and sales through supportive web-based applications
     · Create corporate content areas for best practices and procedures
     · Create corporate content area for white papers
     · Create internal discussion forum for customer service topics
     · Create forms, reports, and charts that improve customer responsiveness
     · Improve customer database with improved data validation techniques and standards
     · Create calendars for internal scheduling and communication
     · Identify customer needs and trends through automation
     · Deliver all information to our employees in a focused role-based manner

---

FIGURE 4-5.   *The objectives document is crucial to the definition of the Portal project scope*

coincide with the overall corporate budget for the project. Management does not always understand the complexity of a Portal development effort. The objectives document must clearly state the correlation between the scope of the project objectives and the general cost of the effort so there is no ambiguity. Management should see in the document the relative weight and complexity of individual key components of the effort. If these points are not clearly laid out and discussed or negotiated, the project team will begin the effort at a disadvantage and scope creep will be inevitable. Management must always understand the cost of adding new requirements to a project and they must be reminded that changes have an associated cost.

Going back to our earlier example, it was apparent early on in our interview process that our company client needed much more than a simple reorganization of their Web site. They wanted to offer online membership registration, credit card authorization and acceptance, a store front, streaming video for intranet training and meetings, a members-only Intranet, and listserv capability for communicating with their membership. Obviously, this was not all going to be accomplished within the original budget, which was supposed to pay for simply reorganizing the site. In fact, the architecture changes to accommodate streaming video and e-commerce alone required a substantially higher investment.

After extensive interviews with strategic line managers and employees, we conducted the group meeting, laid out alternatives, and suggested an approach that would improve the site navigation and structure and enhance the look and feel of the site. The suggested structure was open so that future enhancements could easily be accommodated. It was recommended that the site be moved to an outside hosting company that provided 24x7 support and superior bandwidth to support streaming video and e-commerce. Finally, the good news was that all of the development effort to reorganize the site to give it a new look and feel could be met within budget. Additional hardware and hosting services would cost more and would be required now, or later, to proceed with future goals. After the site infrastructure was improved and the look and feel was accepted, the organization could proceed to implement future goals in additional phases of the effort.

Management's understanding of what could be accomplished for the existing budget and their understanding of long-term costs for the various organizational objectives that had been identified resulted in a hard look at near- and long-term priorities. Corresponding changes in scope were made to accommodate the strategic short- and long-term objectives in a timely manner. Management was able to use the objectives road map to understand how to accomplish their corporate goals for the Portal site in a multiphased development approach. They also had a clear understanding of the budget and timeline for each phase.

NOTE
Budget and timeline are the keys to project scoping. If these can be understood in a relative sense by management, you have accomplished all the goals of the scoping phase of the project.

Refining Portal Requirements

Once the project scope is determined, it is time to identify the absolute requirements for the system. If goals and objectives answer the question of *what* needs to be accomplished, requirements define *how* the needs of the business will be met by the Portal project. In an intranet portal, requirements include

- Define who will use the site and what their roles and privileges should be.

- Define user tasks and business processes or reengineered processes.

- Perform an enterprise information assessment.

- Define unstructured documents and content standards.

- Identify required structured data and determine data quality.

- Organize information (according to categories and perspectives).

- Define the look, feel, and branding concepts for the site.

- Define site hardware, software, and security requirements.

Understanding the users of the system, what their job requirements are, what their information needs will be, and defining the best method of presenting that information are the goals of the Portal requirements definition phase, as shown in Figure 4-6.

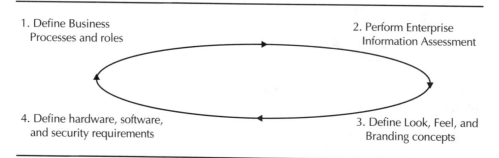

FIGURE 4-6. *Steps to complete in the Portal Requirements phase*

Identifying Portal Users and Roles in the Organization

The mission statement and goals of the company define what the business is about. Objectives analyses define the business objectives of the Portal site and what groups of users will benefit from them. Understanding who your users are and the business processes that they must use to meet operational requirements goes a long way toward defining your site architecture and Portal user interface. Will your portal be laid out along strictly business lines or by business process? The answer to these questions will define the page layout and role-based interface to your Portal site.

Oracle Portal uses roles and privileges to display content or hide it based on the group the user is assigned to and the privileges allocated to the group. In determining what users will need from the site and how content will be portrayed, it is helpful to develop a matrix of business units within the organization and map corporate business processes to each business unit. The business units of our hypothetical eXYZ Corporation include Corporate Management, Finance, Human Resources, Sales, Logistics, and Information Technology. Many of the business processes of the company cross over functional bounds and require common reporting or user interfaces. If there is information that everyone requires, or if certain business units will need to share particular applications, it is important to identify that in a matrix, as shown in Figure 4-7.

By identifying business units and the business process functions that each unit is responsible for, we can see how Portal pages could be developed along lines of business, with shared business processes or content available to foster collaboration among units that need them. It's important for the enterprise collaborative aspects of the portal to ensure that content and applications rendered on pages accurately represent the current business functions and requirements of each business unit. As we get further into the definition process, we will identify all individuals by the specific role they serve in the business and identify specific tasks within each business process that these individuals will be responsible for. Chapter 5 will show how to register these individuals in Oracle Portal and assign them to groups that will allow them to share common duties, responsibilities, applications, and content according to job function. It's important to identify users and groups early on in the requirements stage and set groups up so that appropriate security can be maintained from the outset.

Business Unit Areas: 1 – Management 2 – Finance and accts.	3 – Human Resources 4 – Marketing 5 Sales	6 – R&D 7 – Logistics 8 – Production			9 – Distribution 10 – IT 11 – Customer Service						
Business Processes		1	2	3	4	5	6	7	8	9	10	11
(a) BUSINESS ANALYSES												
(1) Budget		X	X	X	X	X	X	X	X	X	X	X
(2) Sales trends		X	X			X	X		X			X
(3) Cost, Cost/Benefit Analyses		X	X			X			X			
(4) Market analysis		X			X	X			X			
(5) Financial statements		X	X			X						X
(b) MARKET ANALYSIS												
(1) Competitive market data		X	X		X	X	X					X
(2) Product viability analysis		X			X	X	X					X
(c) INFRASTRUCTURE ASSESSMENTS												
(1) Physical Infrastructure Requirements		X	X					X	X	X		X
(2) Technology assessments		X	X				X	X	X	X	X	
(3) Fleet Management		X	X					X	X	X		
(4) Plant depreciation		X	X					X	X	X		
(5) Plant demographic analysis		X			X	X		X	X	X		X
(d) PRODUCT SALES												
(1) Product sales analysis		X	X			X	X		X			
(2) Sales projection analysis		X	X			X	X					X
(3) Client sales analysis		X	X			X			X	X		X
(4) Demographic sale analysis		X	X			X		X	X	X		X
(5) Sales profitability analysis		X	X			X	X					
(6) R&D for new products and sales projections		X	X			X	X					
(7) Inventory management		X				X		X	X	X		X
(g) CUSTOMER SUPPORT												
(1) Product Delivery		X		X		X		X		X		X
(2) Product documentation and customer training		X		X					X		X	X
(3) Product quality assurance and repair		X		X	X	X		X	X			X
(4) Customer Service support		X		X	X	X			X	X	X	X
(5) Product upgrades to maintain satisfaction		X			X	X	X		X		X	X
(h) EMPLOYEE SUPPORT												
(1) Employee training		X	X	X	X	X	X	X	X	X	X	X
(2) Employee benefits		X	X	X	X	X	X	X	X	X	X	X
(3) Employee salaries and reviews		X	X	X								
(4) Employee retention plans		X	X	X	X	X	X	X	X	X	X	X
(5) Project support		X	X	X	X	X	X	X	X	X	X	X

FIGURE 4-7. *The business unit – business process cross-reference matrix*

Defining Individual User Tasks and Business Processes

By understanding business tasks and the roles that individuals serve in performing these tasks, we can also identify what portlets will be required. As explained in Chapter 3, portlets are applications, functions, URLs, content, or any other function that will be displayed on a Portal page for consumers to view. We can see from the business process cross-reference matrix in Figure 4-7 that HR might need to have access to stock quotes on a daily basis in order to monitor the companies that eXYZ has invested in for the company 401K benefit plan. Sales might require online travel information to book flights and reservations for sales trips. Both Management and Sales need access to corporate and national news content, and IT needs to access database monitoring information. These tasks must be identified early on in the requirements stage and prioritized and cross-referenced by business unit according to need.

Each task will become one or more portlet providers designed to meet the business requirements of one or more business units. Database monitoring portlets to support the needs of the IT staff come ready-made within Oracle Portal. The HR department can develop a stock portlet application or specify links to various sites on the Web that provide sophisticated online access to stocks. The Sales staff can link to Expedia.com or another travel service to obtain travel information and online booking services.

By identifying shared tasks and proper user access to those tasks, we can begin to facilitate the process of delivering information to those who need it within the organization. At the same time, we can restrict access from those that should not have access to information. We can identify external applications such as the corporate Web-based accounting system or Expedia.com that can be tied into the portal seamlessly using Portal's single sign-on feature. Lastly, we can identify new applications or functions such as personal productivity pages, calendaring, and scheduling that can offer more streamlined and effective ways of doing business. Do not shy away from using the Portal development effort as a way to reengineer the business. An enterprise portal can be a very effective business process reengineering tool.

Also, don't be afraid to offer corporate users controlled access to content or sites that provide stock quotes, weather, and local traffic reports. These "quality of life" enhancements will be appreciated by end users and might reduce the amount of wasted web surfing that takes place outside of the portal environment that reduces worker productivity.

The Enterprise Information Assessment

By far the hardest task in developing an enterprise portal is the analysis and assessment of strategic corporate information assets, identifying where the information can be found, and understanding how it can be organized and presented. Standards must be set for all data and information that will be presented in the portal.

Data quality is an important consideration regardless of the database structures. Old information can be useful in one business unit but useless in another, depending on the need and the requirement within the organization. Information takes on a different flavor and relevance depending on who is looking at it.

For example, an old electronic copy of a client purchase order may be important to a sales analyst who is reviewing buying trends for a marketing survey. It is not useful at all to the Logistics department, which is responsible for fulfilling current outstanding orders. Web information consumers want timely and relevant information that is well presented—not contradictory—and that makes sense from their business perspective. The information that comes from the corporate portal must be correct and be the one source for information on a particular topic. Information that is contradictory, inconsistent, or considered incorrect by the consumer will lead to frustration with the Portal site.

Data quality must also be considered according to the type of information it conveys. Take the case of older customer information in the database or in documents. Is it relevant? Should it be made available to Portal information consumers? Or is a customer address so old that it is really irrelevant at this point. Some of the information available in various legacy application systems or written in different content documents is contradictory—the same customer may be listed under several slightly different names. Which one of them is correct? These and other decisions must be made in order to understand what information will be selected for display within the portal. You can choose to display everything to show historical context but a Portal project is really the opportunity to "clean your desk" and develop corporate standards for data and information quality and access.

Identifying and Defining Document Content

The first step in developing standards for information is to understand the users of the information. In a corporate intranet portal, the intended consumers are internal to the organization. In every organization there are individuals in each business unit that everyone just gravitates to for information. Whoever these people are, and however many of them there may be, you need to find them because they will be your content providers for unstructured and structured information during the initial setup and long-term maintenance of the portal. You should identify one of these individuals per business unit or by business process, depending upon how the Portal UI is designed. They will become portal content contributors at a minimum, or content administrators if they have the technical expertise. These individuals will be the key to the working portal, ensuring that content is available, current, and accessible.

Unstructured information standards may be difficult to formulate precisely because the documents can come in any form. Oracle Portal can handle unstructured information in many different formats including HTML text; URLs; files that include Word, Excel, and PowerPoint; and images in JPEG or GIF format. All of these unstructured file types can be checked into a folder in one or more content areas and categorized according to the document type (categories) and who would be interested in the document (perspectives). The ability to search and retrieve documents checked in to Portal is the most important aspect of the unstructured content of our Portal site. Searches can always be performed on the definitions, titles, and classifications that the content administrator or provider created when checking the document into the content area.

You may extend Portal's search characteristics by installing interMedia, Oracle's full-text search engine. Using interMedia, the portal can fully index unstructured documents and search text for keywords, phrases, themes and "gists." Oracle interMedia, formerly known as Oracle ConText, facilitates text mining of unstructured documents and other multimedia information such as image and sound that is stored in the database, stored in files, or stored as URLs. Text mining involves sophisticated algorithms including natural language computing to find keywords in documents and facilitate presentation of those documents to the end user via Portal. interMedia comes bundled with the Oracle 8i database, and once it is optionally installed, it is fully integrated into the Oracle Portal product. interMedia adds a tremendous value to the enterprise information portal where knowledge management requires the segmentation, indexing, summarization, and query of high volumes of unstructured textual information. interMedia provides a much greater search capability for all document types and should be used if full-text document searches are important.

Web content is always difficult to obtain. The initial interview process addresses the issue of where to find content. In the meetings our project team had with the company we discussed previously, everyone in the organization was initially interested in making documents available for consumption to end users. When a group meeting was held to finalize results, two individuals who had not previously made a contribution suddenly started to argue animatedly that document content should not be offered universally to outsiders. One expressed the opinion that much of the content he developed was for limited consumption only because he expressed views that could be considered controversial to many. He did not want the organization held at risk from a broader audience for opinions that he currently expressed to a select few by email. The second individual expressed concern that the documents that he researched and made available to clients were extremely subjective and could be misread by anyone that did not have the right kind of background and expertise. When it was pointed out that this individual had a document search engine only in his head, the reply was the same—no one should be researching these documents but the specialists that know them well or they would be misinterpreted.

Each of them had valid points that changed the approach to how documents would be viewed on the Web site. In the first case, a members-only section of the site was developed to hide controversial opinions from the public at large. Valuable commentary and viewpoints would be available to the organization's clientele on a members-only intranet rather than to only a select few by email. This new concept of open communication would be a valuable tool and a "new" client benefit that would attract additional sales for the company. In the second case, it was decided that an interMedia document management search engine would be helpful to research and make documents available on an internal intranet basis due to the interpretive nature of the documents. In this way, all documents could be more easily found by experts who needed them, without a tedious manual search for documents on the network or on paper. As an added benefit, if key members of the organization left or were ill, documents would already be classified and categorized to ensure that newer members of the organization could understand the documents' significance and could search and retrieve documents in the proper context. The proper attribution and classification of the documents themselves would replace the more subjective search criteria that had been employed to date.

Content Standards

In order to realize these kinds of gains, each division of an organization must begin to organize and collect unstructured content according to basic standards that should be set for everyone. Some of these standards may be subjective and others may be more concrete. Begin by developing a form after the initial interviews, like the one in Figure 4-8 that identifies broad categories of content type. These content areas can be broken down by section within the organization, identifying the relative priority of the content type for the section and a rough order of magnitude of number of documents. This gets everyone in the organization thinking about broad content category types that will likely result in defined Portal categories or separate content areas if the number and priority of the content type is high enough.

After the content type form is completed and the content areas for the portal are identified, designated content contributors should begin to collect unstructured content from within the organization. The best way to begin that process is once again by distributing a form such as the one in Figure 4-9 to each branch of the organization. Brief the users on the proper use of the form and have content administrators and contributors hand them out and collect them in a timely manner. The best way to start is to identify the documents that are most important to the organization and that are critical to daily operation. Remember, the process of gathering, classifying, and deploying content, and documents to the Web is a never-ending process, and it is not necessary to gather everything immediately. This can be a step-by-step process that leads to a solid content management system that everyone uses.

In fact, rather than collecting information on paper documents, you should take this opportunity to develop a prototype with Portal, and use this form to collect information electronically from everyone. In this way, you can demonstrate the collaborative manner in which Portal can be used. You can also control and monitor the process of identifying the types of documents destined for the portal.

For instance, at eXYZ Corporation, HR wants to include the employee manual, 401K plan, and other employee documents online rather than keeping up with them in paper form. This is an outstanding use of a portal and a no-brainer in terms of whether the documents should be stored and maintained electronically. They absolutely should! The Sales division wants to store the historical electronic MS Word copies of purchase order forms that were used to purchase and resell products. Management wants this despite the fact that all purchase orders are in the database by date and

The following form will be used to identify corporate content types by organization. Please take the time to fill it out by identifying (and attaching) examples of document types, files, spreadsheet types, raw text, Image types, and URL links that you use on a frequent basis or that are crucial to your business unit on a day to day basis. Please try to indicate in the description field the relative amount of space each category of content takes up on your hard drive or on the network server.

CONTENT PLANNING FORM			
Content Category	**Content Description**	**Organization**	**Contact and Phone**
Company Directory	Directory of phone numbers and business units	All	
Financials	Corporate sales and financials (Excel)	Sales and Management	
Sales Brochures	Sales and marketing collateral	Sales	
Product Pricing	Pricing brochures	Sales	
Employee Manuals	Employee manuals and benefits	HR	
Employee Reviews	Employee review dates (Excel)	HR	
Reseller links	URL links to corporate reseller	Sales/Management	
Corporate technical documents	IT, Sales, and Management docs (Word)	All	

FIGURE 4-8.   *The content category and classification form*

can be regenerated in electronic form from database tables using Portal reports at any time. This redundancy is not necessarily a good use of the portal.

At the outset of a project, decisions on what to include in the portal may be difficult to make because the users of the system can't see the results and can't visualize what the portal will look like. This is when a prototype of the system comes into play. The Sales division can make a better decision about what PO information to store after they see the HR employee manuals online alongside the electronic stock reports and structured reports or forms that display employee review dates. A formal demo of a working prototype can go a long way toward easing the decision-making process

---

Content Item Inventory Form
The following Form will be used to identify and collect all items of content that you consider useful in your day-to-day work within your business unit. Please identify _all_ content including Word documents, files, Excel spreadsheets, raw text, Images, and URL links. If others use the same files, please note that, if possible, but include everything that you consider useful.
All content must be turned into the designated Sales Content Administrator by Friday, August 17. If you have questions contact Steve Vandivier or Kelly Cox at <u>administrator@exyz.com</u>

Content Area Name: Sales Content

Description of Content Area: Content, web sites, and documents utilized by the Sales branch

Content Consumers (circle one): Internal External (including suppliers)

  Internal (Circle all that apply): Sales Marketing HR Management IT

  External (circle all that apply): Suppliers Partners Customers Other

Content Item file Format (circle one): HTML file   Word file   PowerPoint file
        Excel file   image/image map   PL/SQL   Text   URL   Java application
        Zip file   Portal Component

Content Classification (circle one): Sales Collateral Presentations   Pricing
        Sales data   Marketing   Customer Information   Products   Product families

Update Frequency (circle one): daily   weekly   monthly   yearly

Item Attributes:

Name:	Title:	**Description:**
Category:		**Perspective(s):**
Author:		**Expiration date:**

FIGURE 4-9.   _The content collection form_

of what does and doesn't go into the portal and how content and applications should be rendered. If after the demo the Sales division makes a decision to keep the same structured and unstructured data in the portal in a redundant way, they will have made that choice with a little better education about what a portal is all about.

Identify Structured Information and Determine Data Quality

Every organization that implements a Portal solution usually has internal or external application systems or database management systems that support corporate business processes. Smaller organizations might have a stand-alone accounting system or human resources application. Larger organizations rely on integrated enterprise resource planning (ERP) solutions that combine accounting, HR, management reporting, supply chain management, and CRM to support the business operations. Portal can tap into these applications and the databases behind them to provide a single source for structured information throughout the company. There are issues that the Portal development team must understand and plan for before portal access to these database structures is granted.

Before you can begin to uncover your database assets and understand the information stored therein, you must understand what kind of data you have accumulated. Many companies don't really know what lies behind their database management applications; they just know that they key information in and they get reports out. The problem with this approach is that it is impossible to understand how to collaborate between systems and within an organization without some kind of enterprise understanding of the overall corporate data information architecture.

The glue that holds the enterprise information architecture together is *metadata*. Metadata is typically defined as "data about data" and it has a very important function in an information management environment, where it describes logical and physical data formats, data security, provides uniform data descriptions, and offers data version control information. From a user's perspective, metadata provides a business view of the information available in enterprise legacy systems broken down along business lines by subject area, business items, and description using business terms that make sense and don't require in-depth knowledge of physical details of the underlying database and application system. A solid metadata management approach by the Portal project team is integral to the success of a portal development effort. Tools such as Oracle Designer are available for documenting and managing metadata.

It is important to develop a metadata repository that defines the technical data resident in the database in easy-to-understand business terms. When everyone understands how data is represented, it greatly enhances the usability of end-user reports and the understanding of information presented in them. A good first task for the database administrator or programmer is to reverse engineer or enter into the metadata repository all legacy tables, columns, and relationships for all databases in the organization, as well as business-oriented descriptions for these objects. It's important to show relationships between tables, as shown in the eXYZ data model in Figure 4-10, and make sure all table columns have well-defined meanings and consistent naming conventions. Pay particular attention to fields (in different tables) that have similar names but may contain data with different meanings.

For example, assume that an accounting system contains a Purchasing table with a field named ORDER and a CRM system contains a separate table with a field named CUSTOMER_ORDER. After inspecting the data and doing some research, it is discovered that, in fact, both the ORDER and CUSTOMER_ORDER fields refer to orders for the same products tracked separately in the accounting and CRM systems. However, the accounting system ORDER field has been kept up-to-date and represents all customer orders that have been placed and fulfilled. The CRM system contains all orders that are in the works but that have not been fulfilled. Furthermore, not everyone in the Sales department uses the CRM system for order fulfillment, so the CUSTOMER_ORDER information is found to be suspect. This type of information must be captured in the metadata repository or in a business process flow diagram. Understanding table interdependencies or correcting data conflicts between tables that are identified and documented ensures that information retrieved or updated in Portal will be consistent and appropriate.

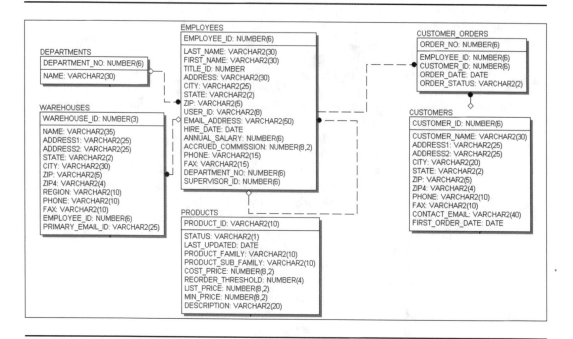

FIGURE 4-10. *Data model for eXYZ Corporation*

Using this *data-driven* approach to setting corporate standards for structured data, you should be able to understand all legacy data information assets and decide which should be populated in the Oracle database. Using the Portal database tools available (and described in Chapter 12), a data quality analyst (assigned the role of database administrator) should spend time drilling down into detail data. Reviewing the results of database queries can be an excellent method to discover data anomalies and problem areas. Non-Oracle and legacy database systems that are Web-based must also be checked for data quality. Such Web-based systems can be easily integrated into the Portal environment as external applications accessible via Portal's single sign-on feature. Strategic data from these non-Oracle systems can also be inserted into the Oracle database using extraction and load utilities or accessed directly using Oracle's Gateway products that tie directly into non-Oracle databases.

Data quality is a key issue and problem at many companies, and a source of frustration and lost productivity. Many companies do not even realize they have data quality problems until they start an enterprise portal project. Data problems can occur due to bad data entry, badly designed software applications, lost data from hardware failure, poor backup and recovery routines, and inconsistent updates due to lack of understanding of the database structure and poor data standards. For example, consider an application that has allowed users to freely enter data in a City field. For the city of Baltimore, the data contains such variations as "Balt", "Baltimo", "Ballmor", and even a few "Baltimores". A DBA or developer can write a SQL script that changes all the existing variations to "Baltimore". However, having clean data will be short-lived unless the application is fixed to prevent the entry of inconsistent data. The remedy can be as easy as applying a standard list of values (LOV) to the form that allows users to enter data into the city name. Database integration, quality, and consistency are the goals of a portal. A side benefit of developing a portal is that in the process of enforcing data consistency and integrity, developers can make changes in the legacy systems of the corporation to ensure they are more accurate and serve the organization better.

Designing the Enterprise Information Portal

Now that we have identified how to obtain and classify documents and identify and integrate data structures, it's time for the actual design of the portal, the last design task before we begin development. Up until now we have been laying out all the pieces to the puzzle, understanding all the facets of the job that will need to be included to create a successful Portal site. Now we will take all that we have learned from interviews and use it to rough out the components of the Portal site to make sure the site communicates the organization's message effectively.

When designing the Oracle portal, don't sacrifice intuitive organizational layout of your information for glitz and graphics. If your site looks sexy but information is hard to get to and it takes too long to download, you will have lost the battle and the war. Less is almost always more on a Web site, and organization of content is the key to the success of the site.

In designing the enterprise information portal, we will want to work through a logical process as we did in the requirements definition phase. Design steps will include

- Organize the portal for end users

- Group content according to business process

- Organize structured database information

- Organize information on Portal pages

- Define site navigation controls

- Brand the Portal site with a corporate look and feel

- Establish application design standards

- Plan the project

Some of these tasks can be conducted concurrently, but all should be completed before any development is started. Too often projects of the magnitude of a typical Portal project are begun with inadequate planning due to budget constraints or lack of management understanding. Invariably, these efforts end up becoming much more costly than projects that have a reasonable amount of design time factored into the project plan.

Organizing the Portal for End Users

The methodology for the requirements gathering phase stressed identifying structured and unstructured content and organizing it according to user need and business process functionality. In the design phase, it is important to develop a plan to logically present all of the identified information to the users that need it. In order to organize the site properly, it is critical to get to know each and every type of user of the system in more depth than was possible while working with these individuals earlier. By defining who the users of the system are and what their experience will be on the site, we can begin to lay out the Portal site structure in a way that our users will appreciate. Otherwise, we may end up creating a site biased by our own misconceptions and initial impressions.

The development team will be using information collected from the interviews conducted earlier with line-of-business employees and managers to define scenarios for the Portal experience in a storyboard format. Have the development team create the storyboard for each line of business based on the previous interview process, identifying all types of users and embellishing a picture of what each user's experience will be when they log on and begin using the portal.

For instance, at eXYZ we can create scenarios for Mr. John "All World" Sales and walk John through the process of logging onto the portal and performing the tasks and functions that comprise his typical workday. John may perform many of the following functions on the Web site:

- Research and analysis of competitors' products

- eXYZ product pricing and research

- Sales goals analysis by region and type of client

- Review product collateral materials from the Marketing department

- Query for personal year-to-date commissions earned

- Research relevant PowerPoint presentations for use in sales calls

- Search for Web content that is related to a specific product line

These and other scenarios can be embellished to define what is most important to John Sales and how he would like to see the information presented. Some of the information that John wants to see is content oriented. Some of the research that will be performed will come from the database management system. And some of the information that will be important to John may be found on external Internet sites such as competitors' commercial sites or in subscription sites belonging to third-party analysts like the Gartner Group.

Make sure that all types of users are identified and one or more storyboards are created for each of them. Discuss the completed scenarios with line-of-business managers and other prospective Portal users who will add to your descriptions or contradict your assessment as they see fit. These will be the users of the portal, so listen carefully and seek their input. Look for commonality in processes and requirements across business lines. This will help to establish how content will relate to business roles within the company. These storyboard sessions will have immense benefits for you:

- You will understand the type of content each type of user is interested in.

- You will understand what content is most important to your users, and you will know how to organize it on Portal pages within and across functional lines.

The next step in the Portal design phase is to take the content and structured database information that was identified earlier and link it to broad categories that will be used to organize the site. In order to understand the process of organizing content on a site more fully, let's review how Oracle Portal is organized.

Grouping Content According to Business Process

A site can contain multiple content areas. As we discussed in Chapter 3, Portal initially comes with three working content areas: Oracle Portal Online Help, Monitor, and the Portlet Repository. Each of these has a distinctive (and distinct) function. Online Help provides help documents for developers within Oracle Portal. The Portlet Repository provides definition and classification for all applications that will be developed within Oracle Portal. The Portlet Repository lists portal providers, application containers for objects that are segmented and classified, along with the portlets that have been checked into each of them, as shown in Figure 4-11. The Monitor content area is a series of items that allow users to analyze the efficiency and use of a developed portal.

Each of these content areas has a wide and varied, but well-defined, use. You should strive for the same structure for your site in terms of the content areas you will create. Minimize reliance on many content areas unless it makes logical sense. A Help content area can provide online context-sensitive and functional help for your entire enterprise Portal site and should be created. On the other hand, choosing to create Sales, Marketing, HR, and Accounting content areas does not make sense for

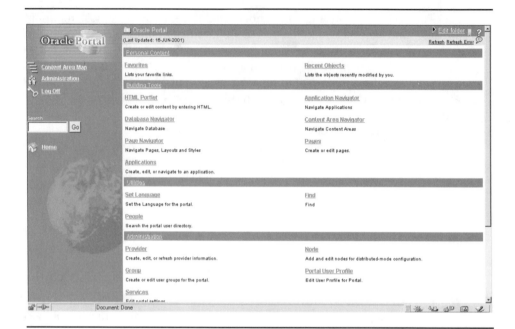

FIGURE 4-11. *Portlet Repository classified by portal provider*

an organization that wants to provide cross-functional capability across its various lines of business.

If a company is focused on one product line, it may make sense to create one content area that provides resources and content for everyone. Role-based security can be enforced throughout the content area, even down to the item level, to ensure that documents are only visible to those that need to see them and are not available for those that shouldn't view them.

Folders and subfolders can be created to classify documents and content within a content area. A content area for all of eXYZ Corporation can be subdivided into folders that have names such as Finance, Personnel, IT, Marketing, and Sales to identify the types of resources and content available. A company that has radically different business lines might build content areas shareable only within a specific division. For example, AOL and Time-Warner may not need to share content information due to their (currently) different business requirements. The folder structure can reflect the aspects and functionality of each division and the content area will be classified and categorized using the separate business terms and processes for each.

A content area can be broken down into folders that are named Products, News, Training, and Information Links if it is more appropriate to segment content by business function rather than line of business. For maintenance and content administration purposes, you should take into account not only who is going to view content but also who will contribute content. Name folders within content areas and assign control to those folders in such a way that the contributors have full control over their designated content at the folder level.

NOTE
It is a good idea to identify and name folders according to a business process, function, or specialty within the corporation that can have a specific individual designated as the primary content contributor tied to that process and folder. Folder-level security and content access is more easily maintained in this manner and multiple content contributors will not be working at cross-purposes within one folder to categorize and secure specific content. Just make sure content contributors know the value of their content and documents for other elements of the organization or the result will be a lack of collaboration between business units.

However you decide to create and name your content areas, remember that content areas are the logical and physical way to store primarily unstructured content within Oracle Portal and they should be created and named based on a broad business process. As you develop the organizational structure of your content areas, keep in mind who will use and create the content that is organized by business process, how it will be viewed, and who will view it so that content can be categorized accordingly.

Once content and information has been identified, it is important to organize the information within content areas and in applications. It is also important to display it logically on Portal pages so that users can make sense of it and retrieve it easily. Well thought out categories and perspectives can greatly enhance the ability to search for unstructured documents. The next design task is to devise the categories, perspectives, groups, folders, and portlet providers that will allow us to segment and categorize unstructured and structured information assets so that we can later render them on pages and display them logically for users.

Web content can be wide-ranging and varying. Company information can be as innocuous and wide open as a list of employee birthdays or as focused as documents that convey the strategy for selling specific products. Such information can be displayed from the database or conveyed in a static HTML document. The various formats in which information can be portrayed include URL links to other Web pages, image files, zip files, or database information. The ability to store this information and classify it succinctly dictates the use of a database management system to control the environment. In Oracle Portal, unstructured and structured content is all stored in the database. Unstructured content is kept in content areas that are made up of folders and categorized using categories and perspectives. All of these varied requirements use the Oracle database to coordinate, categorize, and facilitate user interaction with the portal.

Folders act as containers for items of information. Folders can be organized into parent/child hierarchies consisting of subfolders, until a child folder finally contains specific items of information. Folder naming conventions must be distinctive and unambiguous so that there will be no confusion as to what folder an item of information belongs to. Content contributors and content consumers are given write and read privileges, respectively, to a particular folder. Security privileges assigned at the folder level are inherited by subfolders and items within the folder hierarchy to control access for groups of users.

Categories allow classification of information using a single attribute definition. A category will answer the question: What is this? In a Human Resources category, you might want to create subcategories for HR Forms, HR Policies and Procedures, HR Guidelines, HR Employee Manuals, and HR Misc Information. Documents will be checked into the content area and assigned to one and only one category. The same categories can be used across multiple content areas to provide definition for content items that are checked into the Portal Repository. Items are linked to one category. Items in different subfolders or folders can be linked to the same category. Categories therefore can cross-reference items between branches in a company and facilitate collaboration according to business process. In fact, categories linked to the names of business processes can be a very powerful way to collaborate between business units.

Perspectives identify the types of individuals that may be interested in a specific item of information. Web sites are developed for a wide variety of users, most of whom will have different ways of looking at things. As you define perspectives, make sure you think in terms of your user base and establish a naming convention that is intuitive within the organization. Use business terminology familiar to everyone to define perspectives. You can use perspectives to define groups of users such as Sales, Logistics, HR, and Management. Or, you can define perspectives about a type of object, like what's new. Defining perspectives should be an iterative process, and you can expect to add new perspectives as the portal grows and changes.

Don't confuse perspectives with groups. Perspectives classify documents for the types of corporate users that may want to view them, using descriptive terms that might spark interest in a piece of information. Folders and items are controlled by the privileges that users and groups are given. Users or groups are given the ability to update folders or merely to view their contents. Or groups can be totally restricted from viewing an item or items within a folder. Groups allow role-based restrictions to be placed on content to control access privileges. Perspectives are tight classifications of terms for items stored in the database that encourage access to the type of information you may be looking for.

Categories and perspectives can be thought out in the process of collecting information from branches within the company. As individuals fill out the items that they want to check into the portal, they should consider a hierarchy of categories and perspectives for all items. The Portal team should meet after collecting the Content Item Inventory forms and content planning forms displayed in Figure 4-8 and evaluate and classify all types of information into logical groupings according to type of information and type of information consumer. Upon completion of the sorted forms, present them to management, and to a select user base (including content administrators), to validate the structure. Once completed, you are ready to create the content area structure and begin checking in unstructured content to the portal.

Organizing Structured Database information

Structured information is organized in a much different way than unstructured information. Earlier we discussed the need to reverse engineer the data and we saw the results of the data model in Figure 4-10. When organizing database information, it is important to know how to deliver that information to individuals by their functional role within the organization. Table information must be segmented using database roles so that only the data that is required or allowed is accessible to the end user.

An example is the Employees table at eXYZ Corporation. This table contains a great deal of useful information concerning all employees at the company, including their name, address, email address, and phone and fax numbers. Each record also contains the employee's salary information. All of this information is appropriate to expose on an HR Portal page for review, reporting, and update by a qualified eXYZ HR specialist. It is not appropriate to display employee contact and salary information in a report accessible to all employees on the Portal home page.

An analysis of the roles that individuals perform in the organization and the degree of information they should see is required before Portal applications can be developed. If it is not performed, too little or too much information will be delivered within applications and confusion (at best) or security breaches (at worst) will be the end result. Developers need to understand what data the end user needs in each application before the application development process begins. Role-based delivery of information to the end user according to their business need is a central tenant of a portal.

Don't rely strictly on database information that is available in Oracle. If data is resident on homegrown systems such as FoxPro, Access, or some other local-based system, consider migrating that data to Oracle or capturing it on a recurring basis into the Oracle database. Reengineered business processes, databases, and applications are common side benefits in Portal development efforts. Even a partially reengineered system that integrates into the enterprise portal information scheme can pay large dividends. Unless the systems are small, fully reengineering a system as part of a portal development effort may not make much business sense. If non-Oracle legacy systems are Web enabled, consider incorporating those systems into Portal using a link to the legacy application URL and add in support for the integration of the system within Portal by supplying single sign-on functionality. We will discuss how to do this in Chapter 11 and 12.

When reengineering a legacy system, define the data elements and table structures of the legacy application and design the new database structure in Oracle. When complete with the new design, map all elements of the old structure to the new Oracle-based structure and then mimic or develop functionally superior forms and reports that map to the new structures. Convert the data from the old table structures to the Oracle structures using the SQL*Loader utilities on a one-time or recurring basis. If the portal is a report-only mechanism in the new environment, you will need to continue to convert and transform data to the new structures on a recurring basis. By reengineering and modernizing legacy systems into the portal, you will develop a much more integrated approach to your enterprise reporting needs and users will be able to find and update information from one source.

Organizing Information on Portal Pages

Organizing and collecting information from within the business is only half the battle of developing a successful enterprise portal. Presenting that information in a meaningful way on the Portal site is the other.

There are many ways to organize information within Portal. In content areas, Portal maintains unstructured information in folders and organizes it using categories and perspectives. Application components such as forms or reports present data and information from structured database tables. Application components or content areas can be designated as portlets and they are then checked into a specific application portlet provider where they will be categorized according to function. The portal can have a portlet provider for all of eXYZ Corporation or one for each division of the company. As application forms, reports, or charts are developed, they are placed within the appropriate application and portlet provider repository by the developer and the application can be made available to all users or specific users or groups as a candidate for placement on a Portal page for user viewing, as shown in Figure 4-12.

Most organizations divide their enterprise Portal site into page categories by organization, as we did at the end of Chapter 3. It's fast, it's easy to organize along organizational lines, and it can be more intuitive to the end user to break pages into organizational categories using Portal tabs. But this has its drawbacks, as we discussed earlier. What if the company reorganizes the business drastically? Strict layout according to organization often sacrifices the ability to collaborate between lines of the business. The people in Sales may not know what the Marketing department is up to. The R&D department may be producing new products without making the Sales and Marketing departments aware of them so that they can position clients for these new products in advance.

Defining the site according to business process or product type is another option, but there can be many gray areas here, too. A business process might cross over many business lines, making it difficult to know who should be given access. A great deal more thought must go into a process-oriented Portal site, but the rewards can be great because this workflow format offers a way to reengineer business processes and to work in a defined process.

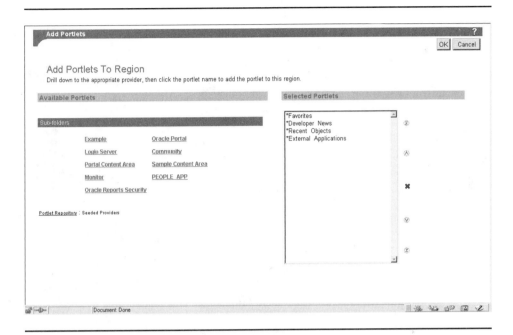

FIGURE 4-12. *Portlet applications are checked in and rendered on Portal pages*

Ensure that role-based security fits within this scheme. Users can get very frustrated when the role they have been assigned does not allow them to perform a designated function that is part of their job requirement. Ensure that forms and reports that are rendered on the Portal pages track with the roles that have been given out within the organization to users by line of business. If someone in HR is responsible for updating employee salaries, they—and only they—need to be able to access the forms and reports that allow them to update the database. Make sure that if a user's role should prevent them from working with salaries or any other HR function that the tab associated with HR is not made available to that user within Portal.

Consider using other simple methods to define portions of the site, including by geography, by topic, or by listing in chronological order. For instance, in our earlier discussion of our corporate Web site development effort, we used a chronological listing to promote an organization's seminars and lecture series by highlighting the most current lectures at the top of the page on a Seminars tab. The Seminars page could also be re-sorted by topic in chronological order so that seminars on a specific topic offered next week would display first and similar seminars offered next month would appear further down the page. This can easily be done from a sorted parameter-based report accessing a seminar table from the database or from a content area sorted by a content area category that contains a list of topics to choose from.

More complicated methods for organizing display on the site include using themes or metaphors for organization of the site. Abstract concepts can create interest in the site and provide a good visual. For example, a company that sells plants and shrubs online might use themes like a dogwood flower to identify the flowering trees and shrubs section of their site. Or, the home page of a furniture store could use pictures of the rooms of a house so that clicking on the dining room leads to pages devoted to dining room furniture. Similar conceptual imagery within a company's enterprise portal application should involve images familiar to everyone in the organization. Images must be recognizable and meaningful or theme-driven sites lose effectiveness quickly.

Most sites combine two methods to organize and link information schemes together: URL links and page hierarchies. As mentioned in Chapter 1, hyperlinks have been around since the early days of the Internet. The problem with hyperlinks is, first of all, they can be broken when a page is moved or dropped, and secondly, you can easily get lost in a site with too many hyperlinks. Hyperlinks work best when the user understands the site and has a good frame of reference for where the hyperlink is taking them.

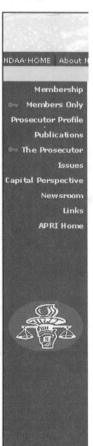

In order to ensure that this is true, it is important to have a navigation bar that stays current throughout the site, as shown in the illustration. With proper and consistent navigation control, the user can choose between using the browser Back button or clicking on a site location on the navigation bar to go directly to a defined area within the site. Keeping terminology focused and standardized on the navigation bar and throughout the Portal site is another key to promoting user confidence in the site and ensuring sound navigation and understandable site organization. Site maps also are an extremely useful method to promote navigation and user understanding of the entire site. Just make sure that the site map is kept up-to-date. Users will get frustrated quickly with a site map that doesn't reflect the current Portal site.

Most Web sites have a recognizable hierarchy that always begins with the home page. Hierarchies must be thought through and structured according to the category schemes discussed earlier. For instance, eXYZ Corporation's site might have a home page that is focused on the latest news within the company, common applications, and a feed of the latest stock price. Off of that page, we might have tabs for HR, Sales, Marketing, Accounting, Logistics, and a Personal tab that each represent the next layer down in the hierarchy. Each of these tabs provides a springboard for information necessary to the operation of each of these organizations, as shown in the hierarchy in Figure 4-13.

Hierarchies should never be too shallow and wide or too narrow and deep. Shallow hierarchies only go down a few levels, but they typically have many options at the second level of the hierarchy.

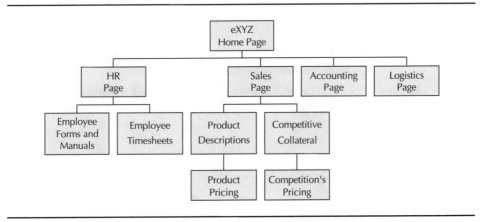

FIGURE 4-13. *A possible hierarchy of information for a company*

Presenting the user with too many initial choices indicates poor organizational layout of the site; the result will probably be a lost user suffering from a quandary of choices. Conversely, a structure with only a few options at the secondary level but many layers below will leave the user equally confused. An even distribution of choices at the second level of the hierarchy with no more than four or five layers of depth below any one tab is what any Web development team should strive to implement.

The best way to work through the hierarchy and concept issues for a Portal site is to sketch it out manually or electronically. For each page, identify the page title or theme, what kinds of users will be viewing the page, what applications will be required, and what general categories of content will be available. Lay out the site as you conceptualize it, and encourage different ideas and layout formats. Developing a logical presentation structure for the Portal site involves a great deal of thought and creativity. Once again, let the end users drive the process of determining site layout at the page level. First, determine what type of general organizational scheme you wish to use for the entire site. Choose a few options to present to your users before you actually develop the site. Consider dividing your development team into two groups, give everyone some ideas, and offer a reward for the most creative team that organizes the site in an innovative but effective manner. Chances are you will get some good feedback that will ultimately involve ideas generated by both teams.

After you have decided what kinds of application components and content go on each page and how to lay out the design hierarchy, start to think about how to lay the content out on the page. Oracle Portal allows each page to be broken out and sized in regions, as shown in Figure 4-14. Each region is a self-contained unit that houses content and/or portlet applications. Keep in mind that your users will be scanning

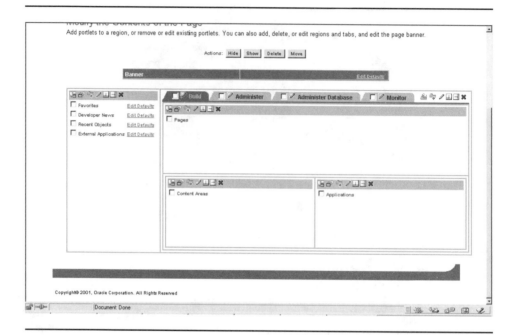

FIGURE 4-14. *Portal pages contain content and applications within regions on a page*

the page as they would a book, reading from left to right and top to bottom. So, catch them immediately with a graphic or picture or compelling application component in the upper left-hand corner. You have roughly five seconds or so from the time your page has been fully rendered on the browser to capture their interest or excitement or they will move on. First impressions go a long way toward a favorable overall impression of the site.

Another critical design feature is white space. Many Web developers attempt to crowd as much information as possible on a single page under the mistaken impression that there is only a small window of opportunity to say everything that needs to be said. A page that is cluttered with links, poor navigation control, and too much information crammed together has lost its audience already. Use white space artfully to separate and delineate text and graphics, and don't crowd too much information onto one page. Keep every page simple.

This is especially true on the home page. It should be designed to create an immediate impression. Offer current topics that are of interest to the majority of users and provide an immediate feeling of comfort to the user based on their job function. Leave them with confidence that their information needs will be met with a concise, clear, and direct path to topics of interest. Wherever possible, design pages to a percentage of available space, not fixed space—this will ensure all available space will be taken up properly regardless of browser type or PC resolution. Portal has this facility available when designing pages and placing portlets on pages. Make full use of this facility and don't get hung up on how many specific pixels should be taken up by an object. Let the Portal product do the work for you in this area.

When thinking about the appearance of your pages, remember also that each tab on a Portal page contains applications that will all be requested by Portal when the page is first requested. Too many tabs with full applications on each tabbed page will require substantial time to render upon startup. If your pages take longer than ten seconds to render, you have lost your audience. Shoot for five seconds per page. If a page takes too long to come up on the typical user connection, go back to the drawing board and break it up into separate pages. Look to move an application onto a separate page or work with page or application caching to render a page faster. We will discuss details of page rendering, caching features, and performance considerations throughout the book and specifically in Chapter 12.

Defining Site Navigation Controls

Oracle Portal offers various controls that provide consistent navigation throughout the Portal site. Shortcuts such as Home, Help, and Logout should be available throughout the site in the banner. Don't rely on the Web browser for navigating within your site. Users are familiar with the Back and Forward navigational features of any browser and the ability to bookmark pages, but they should not be forced to use them to navigate through the site. Provide a consistent mechanism to go directly to any desired area of the site and make sure it is visually pleasing, complements your design hierarchy, and provides concise, well-understood terminology.

You can create a navigation bar in the site content area that can be rendered on each page of the Portal site to provide a consistent navigation interface to any other area of the site. Use image icons on the navigation bar if they are recognizable, consistent, and render quickly. Use GIF images rather than JPEG, if possible, because GIFs render more quickly in Portal with its more limited color palette.

NOTE
Navigation controls should not take up more than 25 percent of your Web page. Remember, content is king and navigation controls are the servants. Whenever there is a question, allow more space for content on a page and reduce the percentage of space for navigation controls.

Text-based navigation controls may be preferable to images because of the fast and efficient rendering of pages inherent in text. Whichever way you decide to implement, make sure that the speed of the page rendering is acceptable if the

Portal site will be used extensively from a dial-up access line. Always design and develop so performance is adequate over your slowest connections. If you have a large page that extends beyond the initial user view of the page, consider navigation controls to either send the user immediately back to the top or provide navigation controls from the bottom of the page, as shown in Figure 4-15. The user should not have to scroll all the way back to the top of a page to navigate.

Navigation bars can be displayed on pages and within content areas, and are programmable to offer custom searches for information, a site map, logon and logoff, and key links and task bar functionality. The content area for Portal Help contains a representative navigation bar on the left side of the screen. It is displayed as a frame, an independent region rendered on a Portal page that acts as the driver for the other region(s) on the page. A frame adds consistency to the Portal users' navigation and control.

Frames do take up space, sometimes unnecessarily, and can confuse the user if they do not synchronize adequately with the other region of the page and with the task at hand. Keep frames task oriented and consistent throughout the site for a designated task. You may develop a frame-based navigation aid that is slightly different for each tab that aids with site navigation within the designated line of

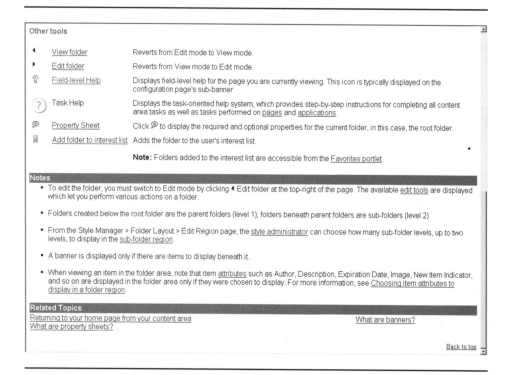

FIGURE 4-15. *Place navigation controls at the bottom of long pages*

business or business process tab. Or, you may develop one for all rendered pages in the site. Use consistent fonts, colors, and graphics throughout to promote consistency and an intuitive user interface. Independent Search fields, site maps, indexes, and alphabetical listings can be used to augment system navigation bars. Make sure that, as the site is changed, site maps and indexes are modified to ensure that all items are searchable and available from these alternate search mechanisms.

Banners also offer a consistent method to organize information on the Portal site and should be nominally the same on all pages and under all tabs (see illustration). Banners typically contain the logo of the company on the left, a title in the center, and primary and secondary links on the right hand side that facilitate navigation and shortcuts. The banner will always be at the top of the page and will provide support for universal navigation throughout the site, but also for branding within the confines of a tab or site. The banner can include personalization for the user, including a user welcome, date, and messages that apply to the user's job function. The banner plays a major role in the look and feel of the site, known as *site branding*.

Branding the Portal Site

Design artists will tell you that beautiful graphics, rich colors, and complex fonts make or break a site. Don't believe them. If you look at most Internet Portal sites that supply information to users, including Oracle's own Web sites, there is enough iconic imagery and graphics to keep things interesting but it is usually on the minimalist side. Web Portal sites are structured for optimum navigation, speed, and solid search mechanisms. Nothing else really matters. An intelligent use of fonts, simple color schemes that convey an image, and limited but effective graphics, icons, and pictures will go a long way to support a Portal site and an identifiable corporate image. Don't sacrifice the proper presentation of information or task-based support of your organization just to make it all look good. A great looking nonfunctional Web site is still a nonfunctional site. Make sure when you do use graphics that they are used consistently, render quickly, and enhance the end user's Web experience. The content area administrator or the portal administrator will assign the duty of creating colors, fonts, and page styles to the style administrator.

As the style administrator, you should ensure that when you are developing the color palette for the site that you use simple colors from a browser-friendly 216-color palette, not 256. Users with older PCs, PCs with less sophisticated graphics cards, or lower-resolution monitors are stuck with poor resolution and a weaker color palette and can't display the full 256-color scheme. This is a realistic concern, even today with the advances in high-resolution monitors and graphics cards. Again, you are developing for your weakest user and it is not really necessary to gear the site to a finer grain of color and resolution. Keep colors to variations of the primary colors of red, green, or blue. Use reds, white, and black to wake up your user or subtle darker blues, yellows, or greens to convey a rich color image. If your company has specific colors, fonts, or themes that are used in the corporate logo or business cards, play off of those and reflect the corporate scheme throughout the Web site on all pages and content areas.

NOTE
Oracle Portal uses a browser-friendly 216-color style palette.

Try to use blue text with underlines to identify links and change the text color to light blue or red for links that have been visited. Similarly, highlight tabs in the primary color scheme of the site and ensure all unused tabs are displayed in gray or a subtle lighter version of the same color. Offset the banner with an identifiable logo and a complementary color. Don't use too many colors or color gradations. Although graphics cards are getting more sophisticated and provide full color and enhanced resolution, it is still better to use an older PC with 800 × 600 resolution and 256 colors to test out the look and feel of the Portal color scheme as you develop it. Use both the MS Internet Explorer and Netscape in your tests to ensure all users will view content the same. We looked at the process of developing color schemes as the style administrator in Chapter 3.

Graphics that will be used as background images or logo icons should be checked into the content area as JPEG images that use all 256 colors in the palette. Logos and key graphical content should appear more like they do in elegant print graphics and not as a washed-out image. Otherwise, JPEG should be used sparingly—for pictures and for branding icons only, and not for smaller images. JPEG compresses images, and when uncompressed, images rarely look the same as they did when they were created. Use GIF for everything (other than brand images) that does not absolutely require sharp contrast and rich color, because they decompress and render quickly. Don't embed text in graphics because it takes longer to render and causes maintenance problems in mixed-language sites. An image should be recognizable without text. Images should be created and used with similar themes throughout and they should not be divergent. Mixing heavy images of power and influence with something that is fun and goofy within the same site is just not great design. The operative idea throughout the site is consistency.

Terminology is a key to the consistency, navigation, and corporate branding of the Portal site. Be consistent with keywords and have your users validate terminology for consistency and meaning. Screen all terms for political viability. Some terminology that you may find useful may have negative connotations in the corporation. Any politically incorrect terminology can be identified by your users.

Terminology will come into play in a major way when developing content areas. Categories and perspectives must offer clear definitions to the end user to enable intuitive document searches. Parent/child and other defined relationships will be implemented using specific terms. Terminology and relationships must be worked through and refined in an iterative manner over time. Assign terms and names to folders, categories, and perspectives and then test them out with a limited assortment of documents and other content until you have it right. In addition, the Oracle Intermedia advanced text search option utilizes a dictionary of terms that can be modified in the thesaurus component of the interMedia search engine.

Application Design Standards

Application components that interface with a database will most likely be part of your Portal site. Oracle Portal supports development of forms, reports, calendars, menus, charts, and other customized components. Portal components are generated from the database and utilize PL/SQL objects. Forms, reports, charts, and other applications can be reused or replicated from prior development efforts. Try to reuse code wherever possible. If you find a chart or form that looks good to you, mimic it or use the actual form and modify it to your specifications if possible. Keep the same colors, fonts, graphics, and background images for all developed applications to promote uniformity within the site.

When developing forms and reports, keep entry or query fields to an acceptable length that conforms to the length of the database table field. Try not to wrap fields or make them unwieldy. Make sure there is some blank space going down the page between fields and don't bunch fields together. Rather than placing fields all over the form, place the entry fields linearly going down the page in an alignment that looks much like the form in Figure 4-16. Place field name tags to the left of each field and right-justify them flush with the field they identify. Try to keep the form centered on the page and don't allow the form to go off the page to the right. Let it go beyond the bottom of the page only if necessary. Try to align the header for the form or report with the fields of the form to reinforce the left margins of the form and keep the lines of the form looking cleaner. Keep terms simple and use abbreviations when necessary— and only if they are easily understood and meaningful.

With reports, consider using an alternate row color for subtotals and totals, but only if it blends in with the corporate color scheme of the site and only if it looks attractive to your users. Once again, direct the report down the page and try not to allow reports to "overflow" off the page to the right. If multiple colors are important to your charts, choose them. Otherwise, choose one color that does not clash with the look and feel of your Web site.

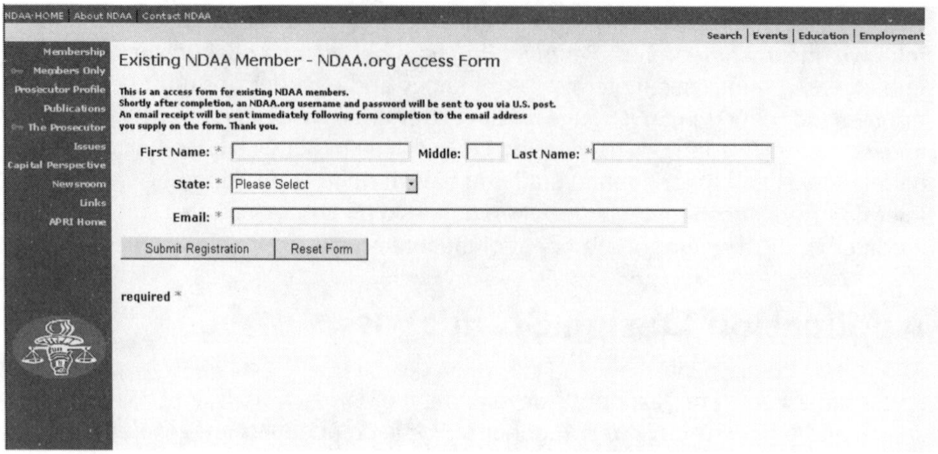

FIGURE 4-16. *Forms and reports should be clean looking and use simple field names*

Section 508 Internet Compliance

The Internet has opened up a whole new world of possibilities to everyone, especially the disabled. Special browser functions allow the blind to "see" Web pages through browser tags that read Web pages to them. Assistive technology is also available to help the physically handicapped and hearing impaired. Section 508 of the federal Rehabilitation Act now requires "equivalent" access to all of the federal government's electronic and information technology for persons with physical or cognitive impairments. The law covers all types of electronic and information technology in the federal government. It applies to all federal agencies and contractors when they develop, procure, maintain, or use Web-based technology. The scope of section 508 is limited to the federal sector but, unofficially, it is strongly adhered to at the state and local level and in the private sector. States receiving assistance under the Assistive Technology Act State Grant program are required to comply with section 508 laws.

The criteria for disabled access to Web-based technology and information are based on guidelines developed by the Web Accessibility Initiative of the World Wide Web Consortium. Many of these provisions ensure access for people with vision impairments who rely on various assistive products to access computer-based information. These technologies include screen readers, which translate what's on a computer screen into automated audible output, and refreshable Braille displays. Certain conventions, such as verbal tags or identification of graphics and format devices, like frames, are necessary so that these devices can "read" them for the user in a sensible way.

The standards do not prohibit the use of Web site graphics or animation. Instead, the standards aim to ensure that this information is also available in a disabled-accessible format. Generally, this means use of text labels or descriptors for graphics and certain format elements. HTML code already provides an "ALT Text" tag for graphics that can serve as a verbal descriptor for graphics. The law also addresses the usability of multimedia presentations, image maps, style sheets, scripting languages, applets and plug-ins, and electronic forms.

Accessible sites offer significant advantages to any user that goes beyond disabled access. For example, those with "text-only" options provide a faster downloading alternative and can facilitate transmission of Web-based data to cell phones and personal digital assistants. If you generally use the following methods to develop a Portal site, you will ensure that Section 508 disability compliance is followed:

- **Provide text equivalents**   Provide a text equivalent for any information presented with graphics, videos, or applets. Text will describe the content and/or function of the graphic.

- **Alternate navigation controls**   Develop screens to provide text links on pages where appropriate, in addition to image maps for site navigation.

- **Color**   Don't use color as a primary means of imparting information. If budget items hit a certain target threshold and they are displayed in red text, they should be grouped together under a text header that says: "Warning, budget exceeded!" in addition to the red highlight.

- **Links**   Label links clearly as links and describe the destination for the link.

- **JavaScript alternative**   Some browsers don't support JavaScript, or users may have it disabled. JavaScript alternatives should be offered for any critical functions on the site.

- **Frames**   Frames and pop-up windows should be avoided as they often introduce accessibility concerns.

- **Images**   All images should provide an ALT tag, as these are often used by the alternative browsers.

- **Testing**   Web pages should be run through a compliance software package such as "Web Bobby" to ensure that compliance is met for all Web pages (http://www.cast.org/bobby).

Project Planning

This section presents a method for iteratively developing an enterprise portal that involves the end user throughout the design and development process. One of the most important facets of user-centered design is setting the end user's expectations of the project, including setting up project milestones and deliverables and walking users through the steps of the development process. Without clear guidelines that set parameters on the effort, end users will begin to expect too much and the project team will lose focus.

In setting up a project plan, it is a good idea to develop a Gantt chart, such as the one shown in Figure 4-17, that identifies a timeline for the effort with specific milestones. Use tools such as Microsoft Project to identify project constraints, team resources, and project deliverables. In our chart, we identify preliminary meetings and the project scoping effort. Then we define requirements and sketch out initial design ideas for user acceptance and approval. As we move more into the design process, we develop user storyboards, identify structured and unstructured information assets, and develop organizational structures and labels for information.

Next, we identify branding criteria and sketch the outline of the Web site with rough internal mockups identifying the look and feel of the site, including navigation controls and banners. At the same time we are developing the design, we begin to perform the administration duties for the site as defined in Chapter 5. Once the user has accepted the completed design, the Portal team will begin developing forms, reports, charts, and calendars, assembling documents and unstructured content in content areas, and generally creating the infrastructure for the site. Finally, the team will assemble the site on pages throughout the effort as the content areas and application components are completed and checked into Portal application areas as portlets.

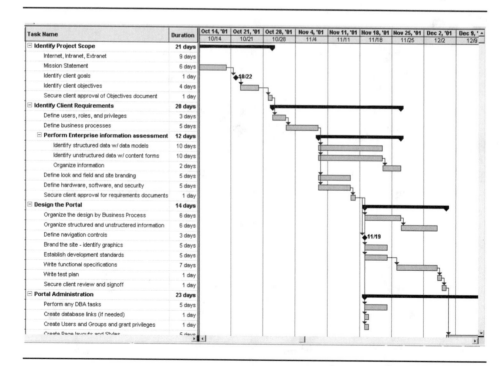

FIGURE 4-17. *A Gantt chart details the project plan and critical milestones*

Throughout the analysis and design effort, specific milestones are identified to solicit user feedback and suggestions. As suggestions are made and accepted, the portal is refined and enhanced to improve performance, functionality, and usability. The continuing effort to build and improve the portal serves to improve workflow throughout the organization. For this reason, it is important to consider building the portal in phases, keeping an enterprise perspective on the availability of information within the system for all areas of the business. As new processes are introduced to the enterprise, the portal should be open enough in its design to accommodate and embrace new ways of doing business. In this way, the enterprise portal facilitates process improvement and enhances the productivity of all who use it.

Conclusion

We have learned in this chapter the basic principles of portal design. It is imperative if you want to develop a polished end product that you follow the basics of this methodology to ensure a successful enterprise portal that will be embraced by your end users. In the next chapter we will discuss administering the Oracle Portal, setting up users and group roles, and laying the groundwork and infrastructure for your Oracle Portal project. If you are ready, let's put on the administrator hat and go to the next step!

PART

II

Developing the
eXYZ Application

CHAPTER
5

Portal
Administration

ow that we have defined requirements and designed the portal, we can create the Portal development infrastructure and setup routines, focusing on Portal and page security and application administration. The Portal administrator leads this effort, and can grant access to team members to perform the specific duties identified in Chapter 4. The ability to spread out the work in a project-focused way to Portal team members is a central tenet of Portal development.

Many administrative functions can be performed concurrently after the Portal administrator delegates authority to the other senior members of the team including the content area administrator, DBA, style administrator, and application developers. The Portal administrator will begin by setting up users and groups who can in turn delegate authority to others to support Portal development. Setting up this collaborative work environment will ensure that the project gets off to a fast start and supports rapid application development. Let's begin by setting up groups and the rest of our users.

Portal Security Administration

Initial Portal administration is required to set up users and to develop the basic architecture of the Enterprise Portal. In this section on Portal administration, we will discuss

- Creating and editing groups

- Bulk loading users and assigning them to groups

- Granting user access to Portal pages, applications, and content areas

Creating and Editing Groups

Upon installation, Portal provides five groups consisting of the following:

- PORTAL_ADMINISTRATORS

- AUTHENTICATED_USERS

- DBA

- PORTAL_DEVELOPERS

- PORTLET_PUBLISHERS

Each of these groups has different privileges that allow varying degrees of control and access within Oracle Portal. Each group identifies a different role that a Portal user will play in creating and maintaining the Enterprise Portal as shown in Figure 5-1. Groups allow the administrator to assign those privileges in bulk form, easing the process of user administration. Users can be assigned to multiple groups to provide support in multiple areas.

Portlet_Publishers
Page Privileges – None
  All Portlets – Publish
Content Area Privileges – None
Application Privileges – None
Administration Privileges – None

Portal Developers
Page Privileges – None
Content Area Privileges – None
Application Privileges – Create
  Shared Components – Manage
Administration Privileges – None

DBA
Page Privileges – Manage
Content Area Privileges – Manage
Application Privileges – Manage
Administration Privileges – Manage

Authenticated Users
Page Privileges
  All Pages – Create
  All Styles – Create
  All Layouts – Create
Content Area Privileges – None
Application Privileges – None
Administration Privileges – None

Portal Administrators
Page Privileges – Manage
Content Area Privileges – Manage
Application Privileges
  All Applications – Manage
  Shared Components – None
Administration Privileges
  All Users – Manage
  All Groups – Create
  All Schemas – None
  All Logs – Manage

FIGURE 5-1.   *Groups provide create and maintenance access control within
the portal*

Each group provides certain explicit privileges to create or manage Portal objects,
as shown in Figure 5-2. Any user assigned to the PORTAL_ADMINISTRATORS group
can perform any task within Portal except for creating database objects, managing
shared components, and editing or managing existing groups. The AUTHENTICATED_
USERS group comes with privileges to create pages, styles, and layouts, and to create
other groups. These privileges are assigned by default to everyone that becomes a
member of this group with the exception of PUBLIC users, whose only privilege is
to view pages. If group privileges are changed, the changes will automatically be
propagated to every member of the group. Anyone that logs into Oracle Portal
successfully is member of the AUTHENTICATED_USERS group by default.

The DBA group has the greatest level of privileges. This has been set up because
the Portal software is a database-driven product and requires some knowledge of the
Oracle database to control it. Anyone given DBA privileges will have full access to
everything in Portal and will have Manage rights to all privileges.

Don't confuse the PORTAL_ADMINISTRATORS or DBA group role with the
PORTAL30 user account. PORTAL30 is the user that was created in the Portal install.
The PORTAL30 user account is a member of all groups and thus has full privileges
and access to everything within the site, including database object manipulation.

To create application components, developers must have the PORTAL_ DEVELOPERS
privilege. The default PORTAL_DEVELOPERS group has some privileges to manage

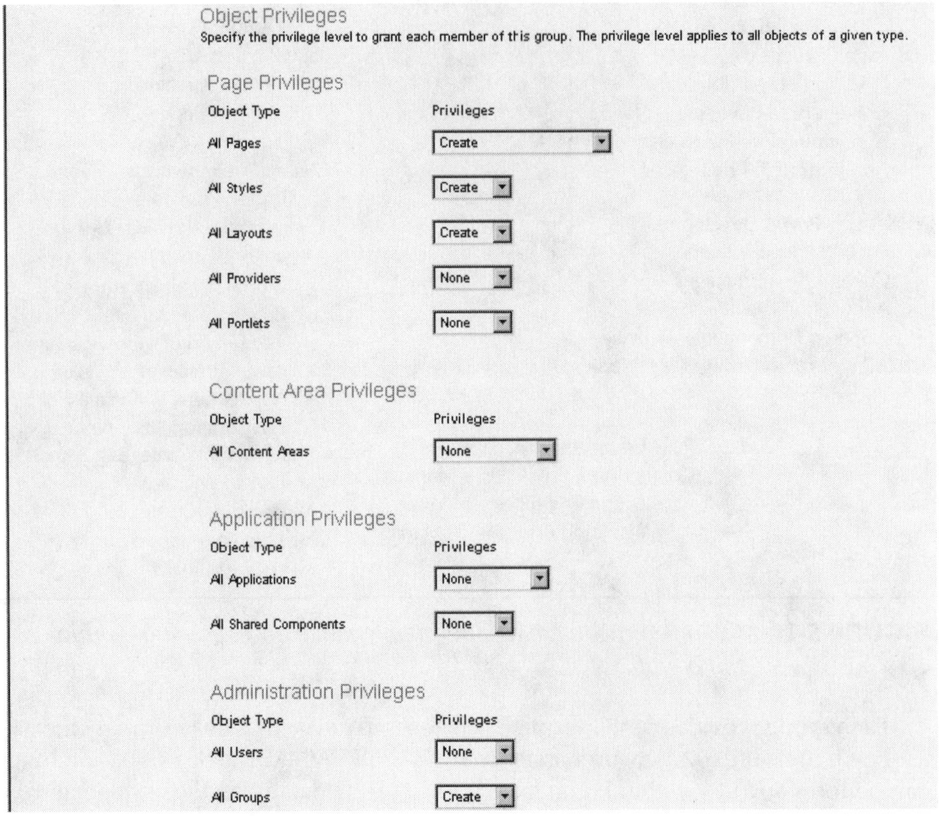

FIGURE 5-2. *Group accounts contain Portal privileges that can be assigned or revoked*

database objects that are necessary for developing Oracle Portal applications. This group also is assigned privileges to create applications and manage shared components so that developers can share reusable application components.

Members of the PORTLET_PUBLISHERS group have the ability to create or accept components from others such as folders, forms, reports, or charts and, upon their acceptance, designate the application or content as publishable as a valid portlet. This group and the DBA group alone have publishing capability for any portlet to a specified page or pages in the Portal.

Overview of Create Group

Each group you create should be assigned a distinctive name, as shown in Figure 5-3. The name should be a term that would apply to a group of people like SALES_USERS

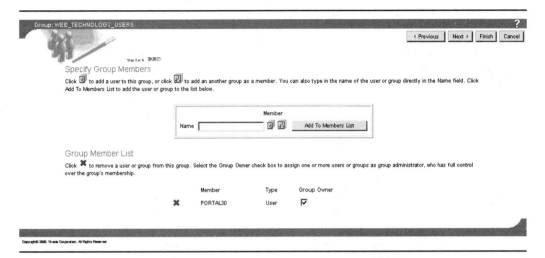

FIGURE 5-3. *Assign users to Group privileges using the Specify Group Members icon*

or MANAGEMENT_USERS. The Applies To radio button can be used to allow group privileges to all objects and object areas across Portal so that any privileges granted will be given for any content area or Portal application repository. Choosing the Applies To Content Area option restricts the group to the specified content area. The Description field is a short description of the type of user that will be a candidate for this group.

The Group Visibility area allows a group to be hidden from all members of the group with the exception of the group administrator. Hiding a group does not affect the group characteristics such as group membership privilege settings—it only prevents members of a group from knowing who the other members are. The Group Home Page specifies the group's default home page. For an HR_USERS group, this might be an HR Portals page or content area that members of HR are responsible for maintaining. This page is used as the default if the user chooses this group as their default, and the user does not override this preference and choose a different home page in their personal default page when specifying their account info.

The default style allows a default page style template to be applied to all pages that any member of this group can access. Again, individual preferences can override the group default.

NOTE
Individual preferences generally override group preferences unless the user is trying to gain more privileges than they are actually allowed within their group.

Users or other groups are assigned to the group that is being created in the Specify Group Members dialog box. Users are selected using the Browse Users LOV icon to the right of the Name field and assigned to the group. If a user does not appear in the LOV, you do not have privileges to assign that user to a group.

It is best to start by offering broad authority to a group for a specific function. Then, within that group, offer additional authority and privilege to specific individuals. For instance, you may want to set up an HR_USERS group that allows users to view pages and content for HR but not to create applications, check components in as portlets, or check in content to content areas. In this case, create HR_USERS with very few general group privileges that apply to everyone and grant selected individuals in the HR office the privileges to create and maintain content, pages, and perform other limited administration duties.

Groups can also be assigned to other groups by using the Browse Groups LOV next to the Browse Users LOV. You must have privileges to assign another group to your own group. You may delegate the ability to own a group and change its characteristics to another individual by clicking on the Group Owner check box next to the name of the user or group. In this way, if you don't have all of the authority you need to modify or add to a group, you can get it from someone else or delegate your own authority by clicking on this check box. An example would be to assign the MANAGEMENT_USERS group to the HR_USERS and SALES_USERS groups so that management can view anything that applies to either HR or SALES users.

Available Group Object Privileges

The Object Privileges page offers the opportunity to grant groups of users control over the objects within Oracle Portal. It is important, particularly with a large number of Portal users, to create as many groups with specific privileges as possible to eliminate excessive security and privilege administration. Group privileges cannot be selectively revoked at an individual level. Offer as many privileges as possible to the broadest cross section of the group you are creating privileges for and then allocate a few special privileges to a select few in that branch—individuals that understand the responsibility that these select privileges require. Different levels of privileges are available for each type of Portal object. Table 5-1 lists all privileges that can be granted to group users for pages, content area, applications, and administration, and their meanings.

Manage is the highest-level privilege and allows the user to create objects and assign privileges to other groups or users. Since the Manage privilege is so powerful, it may be best to not include it in group privileges, because it would be granted to every member of the group. Instead, offer Manage authority only to individual members of the group in the separate Edit User function. Alternatively, create a group with the appropriate Manage privilege and assign the group to only one or two people. For example, LEAD_DEVELOPER, SENIOR_DBA, or SALES_CONTENT_MANAGER

Page Privileges	**Privilege**	**Description**
All Pages	Manage	Change all private or public versions of a page.
	Edit Contents	Change all private or public versions of a page as follows: Add portlets to the existing regions on a page.
		Add, hide, or delete any portlets/tabs.
		Manage Style: Create or delete page styles and apply new styles to a page.
		Customization (Full): Change the user's private version of the page.
		Add, hide, or show portlets placed on a page by the page's creator.
	Customization (Add-Only)	Change the user's private version of the page only as follows: Add portlets to the existing regions on a page.
		Delete only those portlets placed there by the user.
		Cannot: Create, hide, or delete regions or hide portlets placed on the page by the page's creator.
	View	Look at any page in Oracle Portal.
	Create	Create a page.
All Styles	Manage	Create, edit, or delete any page style.
	View	View any page style.
	Publish	Make the page style public for others to use.
	Create	Create a page style.
All Layouts	Manage	Create, edit, or delete any aspect of any page layout.
	View	View any page layout.
	Publish	Make the page layout public for others to use.
	Create	Create a page layout.
All Providers	Manage	Display and refresh the portlet repository.

TABLE 5-1. *Group Object-Level Privileges*

Page Privileges	Privilege	Description
	Publish	Register portlet providers through the local provider via nodes.
All Portlets	Manage	Create and delete portlets.
	Publish	Publish any object as a portlet so it can be included on a page.
Content Area	**Privileges**	**Privilege Description**
All Content Areas	Manage	Perform any task the content area administrator can perform.
	Manage Styles	Create, delete, and edit any folder style.
	View	View any folder in the content area.
	Make Public	Make any content area object public.
	Create	Create any content area object. May not create content areas.
Application Privileges	**Privilege**	**Description**
All Applications	Manage	Create/delete components within an application, delete and export applications, assign privileges.
	Edit Contents	Edit or export components within an application. May not modify the application itself or its privileges.
	View Source	View package specifications/body for a component and run the component. Intended for users who may want to look at an application's source so they can call it from a component.
	Customize	Run and customize all applications.
	Run	Run all applications.
	Create	Create a new application. Application creators are automatically granted Manage privileges for their own applications.

TABLE 5-1. *Group Object-Level Privileges* (continued)

Administration Privileges	Privilege	Description
All Users	Manage	Edit any aspect of a user account.
	Create	Create users.
All Schemas	Manage	Create, edit, or delete database schemas.
	Modify Data	Modify data in existing schemas.
	Insert Data	Insert data into all or specific schema objects that your Portal group has privileges to.
	View Data	View schema data.
	Create	Create schemas.
All Groups	Manage	Create, edit, or delete groups.
	Create	Create groups.
All Logs	Manage	Edit or purge any logs; ability to grant this privilege to other users.
	Edit	Edit or purge any logs.
	View	View any logs.

TABLE 5-1.   *Group Object-Level Privileges* (continued)

groups could be created to provide Manage authority for application components, database objects, and specific business unit content, respectively. Manage is a broad privilege that should be controlled, and it cannot be revoked individually from users assigned to a group with manage authority. Group privileges are either granted to everyone or taken away from everyone.

Additional groups can be created to support Portal development and usage infrastructure. We will create users in bulk and assign them to groups later in this section. Before we do that, we will need to create some eXYZ-specific groups. The HR_USERS group will support the Human Resources branch and all HR user access to pages and HR applications. Log on with the Portal30 account and perform the following.

Exercise 5.1: Creating Groups from the Administer Tab

1. From the Administer tab, click on the Create New Groups link.

2. In the Name field, type HR_USERS.

3. In the Description field, type Used by the Human Resources staff to assign HR permissions.

4. Leave the Hide Group check box under Group Visibility unchecked.

5. To set the group home page, click on the LOV next to Default Home Page. On the list of Pages, expand the node for Top-Level Pages. Click Set as Default for Oracle Portal Navigator (NAVIGATOR), as shown in Figure 5-4.

6. Choose Navigator Page Style as the Default Style.

7. Click Next at the top of the page.

8. To specify group members, click the Browse Users icon next to the Member Name field to display a list of users. Choose your name from the list. Then Click Add to Members to add PATM to the HR_USERS group.

9. Click Next.

10. Under Page Privileges, choose View for All Pages, All Styles, and All Layouts. Leave None for All Providers and All Portlets.

11. Under Content Area Privileges, choose Create for All Content Areas.

12. Under Application Privileges, leave None for All Applications and All Shared Components.

13. Click Finish.

Repeat the steps in Exercise 5.1 to create MANAGEMENT_USERS and SALES_USERS.

Edit Group Function

For a more controlled Portal environment, it would be a good idea to revoke the Create Groups privilege from the AUTHENTICATED_USERS group. This would control the proliferation of groups within the Portal. You can do this with the Edit Group function if you are the owner of a group or have DBA group privileges to edit a particular group. If you do not own a group or have DBA authority, you will not

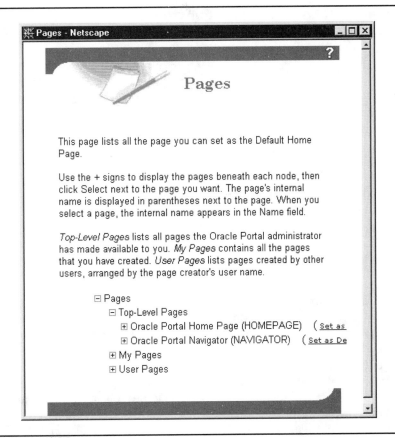

FIGURE 5-4. *The default home page can be changed for a group to the Navigator*

have the ability to edit a group and you will not see any groups under the Edit LOV list in the Administer tab.

NOTE
There is a fine line between opening up the Portal to control from many and various individuals and enforcing standards that everyone can conform to. The enforcement of standards is usually left to a few people, while a Portal is geared to contributions from many people throughout the organization. It is up to the Portal architect/manager to find the right balance between the two and assign group privileges accordingly.

Exercise 5.2: The Group Edit Function

1. Log in to Oracle Portal as PORTAL30.

2. Click on the Administer tab.

3. Click on the Window icon to the left of the Edit button. Choose AUTHENTICATED_USERS from the list of available groups. Then click Edit.

4. Click on the Privileges tab in the upper right-hand corner of the Edit Group screen.

5. Scroll down to Administration Privileges and change the Administration Privileges for All Groups from Create to None.

6. Click OK.

In this configuration, PORTAL_ADMINISTRATORS would be the only group that has the privilege to create new groups.

It may also be appropriate to assign the Create privilege to developers and portlet publishers to ensure that control of groups is in the hands of those individuals that will be controlling the applications and site content. Portal developers should also have View privileges for all schemas so they can understand the tables and objects available for them to use.

Using the steps above, select the PORTAL_DEVELOPERS group. From the Privileges tab, change the Administration Privileges for All Groups role to the Create role and for All Schemas change the privilege to View Data. Next, give the PORTLET_PUBLISHERS group the Create All Groups privilege. Lastly, edit the SALES_USERS and HR_USERS group and add the group MANAGEMENT_USERS as a member of each of these groups.

Delete Groups

Users may delete groups if they have privileges to do so. To delete an existing group, find the group using the Edit Group function. Click Edit after you have found the group name and press the Delete button in the upper right of the Edit Group Details screen. You will receive a warning saying that you are about to delete the group you have chosen. Clicking Yes will delete the group and all of its privileges, but will not delete any users associated with the group. Any privileges that users have from other groups or individually are undisturbed. It is a good idea to create groups first and ensure that all privileges and combinations of privileges correspond to some set of job responsibilities you might assign to an actual person working on a Portal project.

Automating the User and Group Load Process

Corporations with a large number of users may want to automate the process of setting up users and groups. Oracle Portal contains a set of documented utilities to automate this process. After all users are created and assigned to groups using these utilities, the administrator can use the Administer tab to assign Manage privileges to key users who oversee the administrative functions for their business unit. In this section we will discuss the automated methods Portal provides for setting up users and groups.

Let's start by looking at the Oracle database procedures used to create users in order to better understand the whole process. The first procedure, CREATE_USER, is within the package WWSSO_API_USER_ADMIN. In order to view this procedure, do the following:

1. Click on the Navigator icon and then the Database Objects tab.

2. In the Find field, type `WWSSO_API_USER_ADMIN` and click Go.

3. Click on the Show Properties link under Actions. Scroll down the page until you see the Public functions/procedures label in the package.

4. Click on the CREATE_USER procedure icon to view the parameters for this procedure, as shown in Figure 5-5.

The CREATE_USER package creates a user account in the PORTAL30_SSO. WWSEC_PERSON table with basic information supplied to the following fields:

- **Username**   The Portal username you wish to create (for example, PATM).

- **Password**   The password for the account.

- **Email**   The email account for the user under the SSO account (default is NULL).

- **Activation Time**   The date the account is activated in DD-MON-YYYY format (default is SYSDATE).

- **Termination Time**   The date the account should be terminated (default is NULL).

- **Lsadmin**   Login Server privilege level (default is False for end user).

Username and Password are the only fields required for the bulk user load procedure, because the PORTAL30_SSO.WWSEC_PERSON table is used exclusively for single sign-on authentication. The user's email address can be entered at a later time. This email address is not mandatory. The email address supplied will be used for all Portal-related administration functions, as they apply to the single sign-on account and password administration. The email address is also established seperately in the PORTAL30 schema and used in the PEOPLE application that we incorporated on our eXYZ Portal page in Chapter 3. The activation time defaults to the date when the script is run. Unless you intend to activate accounts at a later time, accept the default for this.

This script will return a 0 error code if successful. If there is an exception, the following errors will be recorded in the P_ERROR_CODE field used as an output parameter by the CREATE_USER procedure:

- -7 - DUP_USERNAME

- -8 - USER_NOT_FOUND

- -9 - PASSWORD_RULE_FAILED

- -10 - NOT_IN_VALID_AUTH_MODE

- -11 - INCORRECT_OLD_PASSWORD

- -12 - EXTERNAL_CHANGE_PASSWD_ERROR

- -1000 - UNKNOWN_ERROR

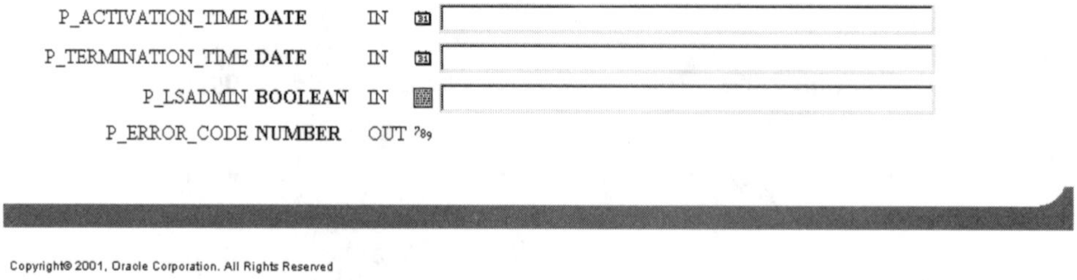

FIGURE 5-5. *The CREATE_USER procedure for loading users into the SSO account*

Click Close at the top of the page of the CREATE_USER procedure. Feel free to scroll down the page to view the package specification for the WWSSO_ API_ USER_ADMIN package. All of the procedures are well documented and include the purpose for each, warning messages and error procedures, and mandatory fields and defaults. When you are done, click on Return to Navigator at the top of the page.

The next step requires adding a Portal user profile to the PORTAL30.WWSEC_ PERSON table. This table contains the characteristics of the Portal user, including name, address, and email, and it equates to the function of the Portal User Profile link on the Portal home page Administer tab. It is slightly different, but is more or less a mirror image of the PORTAL30_SSO WWSEC_PERSON table. This table contains all of the information about the authenticated user. You will add the information by invoking the `WWSEC_API.ADD_PORTAL_USER` package procedure. Take a look at this package by typing `WWSEC_API` in the Find search window and clicking Go. Two packages named `WWSEC_API` are listed, one owned by PORTAL30, the other owned by PORTAL30_SSO. We are only interested in the PORTAL30 WWSEC_API package, so click on Show Properties for the PORTAL30. `WWSEC_API` and look at the procedures and functions available.

Scroll down to the Public Functions/Procedures and you will see a number of procedures as we noted in the WWSEC_API_USER_ADMIN package, but also a number of functions. We will be using the `ADD_PORTAL_USER` procedure, and the `ADD_USER_TO_LIST` procedure to create the single sign-on account for all eXYZ users. Click on the `ADD_PORTAL_USER` function icon and look at the fields that we can manipulate, and understand what this function will do.

Although you may include all of the input criteria for the user with the ADD_ PORTAL_USER function, it makes more sense for users to add their own personal information and for the bulk load routine to add only what is necessary to the table to allow the user to log into Portal and have appropriate group permissions. We will provide the following parameters as input to this function:

■   **Username**   The Portal30 username that matches the PORTAL30_ SSO username.

■   **DB_USER**   The user's login server default database privilege— PORTAL30_PUBLIC is the default for most users.

If the function completes successfully, it will return the user's ID number in the WWSEC_PERSON table in PORTAL30. This number is the same unique ID number as the one in PORTAL30_SSO.WWSEC_PERSON. The ID number returned by the function will be used in the PL/SQL group load to ensure that the same user will be added to the proper group for security purposes and also updated properly with whatever personal information is in our eXYZ EMPLOYEE table.

Lastly, the procedure to create a Portal user needs to add users to a group and assign them group user privileges. This is done by running the WWSEC_API.ADD_ USER_ TO_LIST procedure that assigns all users to a specific group. This can be done in the same PL/SQL routine that creates the PORTAL30 user account in the WWSEC_ PERSON table. You may view this package to see the information that will be entered by clicking on the Package icon. Scroll down the page and view the package specifications for all of these packages and procedures to get a better idea of what they all do.

NOTE
These APIs are documented and available for your use, but be careful how you use them. Mistakes can result in a corrupted single sign-on environment. Any work done with the APIs outside of the Portal structure is difficult for Oracle to support. Make sure you document what you do so you can retrace your steps if you need technical support, and check technet.oracle.com first for assistance.

Exercise 5.3: Using Automated Procedures to Create eXYZ Users and Groups

1. Log in with SQL*Plus to the Portal30 user account by typing in Connect field PORTAL30/PORTAL30@<Host String> (assuming your password for PORTAL30 is PORTAL30). Type the following exactly or invoke the script CREATE_PORTAL_USERS.SQL that was included in the Portal iAS Portal Handbook download file:

```
--create_portal_users.sql
--Connect as PORTAL30 to run
set serveroutput on

DECLARE

--declare a variable to hold the generated username
  new_username VARCHAR2(40);
--declare error number field
  v_err        NUMBER;
--declare variables to store user_id and group_id
  uid          NUMBER;
  gid          NUMBER;
```

```
/*
Declare a cursor based on the employees table,
to copy the information into the portal tables.
Select for update allows us to record
the portal user name in the employees table.
*/

CURSOR  c_employees IS
  SELECT *
  FROM   corp_site.employees
  FOR UPDATE;
BEGIN

 FOR r_employee IN c_employees LOOP

--Set up the user name
   new_username :=
r_employee.first_name||SUBSTR(r_employee.last_name,1,1);

/*
 Call the SSO create_user, supplying the generated user name
 for both username and password. Users will be responsible
 to change their password when they log in for the first time.
*/

    portal30_sso.wwsso_api_user_admin.create_user
    ( p_username => new_username,
      p_password => new_username,
      p_error_code => v_err;
    IF v_err <> 0 THEN
      dbms_output.put_line ('Error '||v_err||' occured for user '||
                            new_username||'.');
      --do not proceed if error
    ELSE
/*
 Store the portal user id in the employees table to provide
 a link between the two
*/
      UPDATE corp_site.employees
      SET    user_id = new_username
      WHERE  current of c_employees;
/*
 Call ADD_PORTAL_USER, supplying information
```

```
from the employees table. Copying the employee_id
to the portal user information table is redundant,
because the portal username is stored in the employees
table, but it represents another way to tie the
two tables.
*/
      uid := portal30.wwsec_api.add_portal_user
             ( p_user_name => new_username,
               p_db_user => 'PORTAL30_PUBLIC',
               p_empno => r_employee.employee_id,
               p_display_personal_info => 'Y',
               p_last_name => r_employee.last_name,
               p_first_name => r_employee.first_name,
               p_email => r_employee.email_address,
               p_work_phone => r_employee.phone,
               p_fax => r_employee.fax,
               p_home_addr1 => r_employee.address,
               p_home_city => r_employee.city,
               p_home_state => r_employee.state,
               p_home_zip => r_employee.zip,
               p_hiredate => r_employee.hire_date);
/*
Check to see what department the employee belongs to,
and assign that user to the group accordingly.
According to our data model, we want the following groups
based on the following departments.
```

Dpt No	Dept Name	Group Name
1	Human Resources	HR_USERS
2	Sales	SALES_USERS
3	Information Technology	PORTAL_DEVELOPERS
4	Logistics	MANAGEMENT_USERS
5	Management and Operations	MANAGEMENT_USERS

```
The add_user_to_list expects a group ID, so we will user the group_id
function to get the numeric group ID from the name.
If the user does not have a department number assigned,
they will just get the default group AUTHENTICATED_USERS,
and a new group is not added.
    */
        SELECT DECODE(r_employee.department_no,
                      1, portal30.wwsec_api.group_id('HR_USERS'),
                      2, portal30.wwsec_api.group_id('SALES_USERS'),
                      3,
```

```
          portal30.wwsec_api.group_id('PORTAL_DEVELOPERS'),
                         4,
          portal30.wwsec_api.group_id('MANAGEMENT_USERS'),
                         5,
          portal30.wwsec_api.group_id('MANAGEMENT_USERS'),

          portal30.wwsec_api.group_id('AUTHENTICATED_USERS'))
                INTO gid
                FROM dual;

                portal30.wwsec_api.add_user_to_list
                  (p_person_id => uid,
                   p_to_group_id => gid,
                   p_is_owner => 0);

          END IF;
          END LOOP;
        COMMIT;
    END;
    /
```

You may now log into Portal using the account for anyone in the eXYZ EMPLOYEE table. Try logging in as NICKC with a password of NICKC. You will immediately see that the Build tab is all that appears on the Portal home page. If you check the Account Info link, you will note that you have name information on the Main tab and address information on the Contact Info tab. If you check the Preferences tab, you will note that there is no default group chosen. Click on the Browse Groups icon to the right of the Default Group field and choose PORTAL_DEVELOPERS from the list of choices. Click OK and go back to the Portal home page. Note that if you choose the Navigator link and the Database Objects tab, you have access to open and query all database objects from the NICKC account.

Now that we have created all of our users and assigned them to groups, let's look at how we can offer security access to pages for all of our eXYZ users based on the groups that they have been assigned to. The PORTAL30 user will remain our ultimate PORTAL_ADMINISTRATOR and PATM will serve as the DBA.

Portal Page Security

It is important to provide security for the Portal site and standards for Portal page design. It is not absolutely imperative to even build a Portal page if your entire site will be content oriented and you do not intend to build applications. Role-based access to the pages in Portal and the content and application components that are displayed on them is fundamental to the Portal development process. We have assigned all of the users at eXYZ to the groups that coincide with the roles they serve in eXYZ, including SALES_USERS, HR_USERS, MANAGEMENT_USERS, PORTAL_DEVELOPERS, DBA, and PORTAL_ADMINISTRATORS. Now we will grant access to the page we created for the eXYZ Portal to our users utilizing the group privileges assigned to them in the bulk user load process in the last section.

Page Security Privileges

Granting user or group page access involves specifying the type of access that a user can have to a page or tab. This function is performed in the Grant Access section of the Access tab of the Edit Page dialog box. Previously granted access privileges can be changed at any time. Table 5-2 identifies the page privileges that are available for granting to a user or group.

You can always accept the Display Page To Public Users default that allows the page to be displayed as a nonauthenticated page to anyone accessing the Portal site with or without a user ID and password. Setting a page display for public use and ensuring that all tabs have Inherit Access Settings From The Page checked will display the page on the Internet without any authentication security. Since the page is visible to the public, all content and applications must also have public privileges or they will not be viewable on the page. All page content and application components must also have public access grants. Be very careful about how you disseminate component and content on publicly accessible pages.

Privilege	Access Granted
View Only	Allows grantee to view the page, set it as their default, and copy the page to a private page (if they have privilege to do that).
Customization (Add Only)	Allows grantee to add new portlets to existing regions. These portlets are specific customizations for this user and will not appear for any other users. Grantees can remove the portlets they have added, but they cannot remove portlets placed there at design time. Users with only this privilege may not create, delete, or modify regions, nor hide or delete any portlets placed on the page by the page's creator.
Customization (Full)	Allows grantee full customization on their private version of the page. Their customizations will not appear for any other users. This includes the ability to hide or show portlets placed there by the page's creator.

TABLE 5-2. *Page Privileges*

Privilege	Access Granted
Manage Style	Allows grantee to select a new style for the private or public version of the page.
Edit Content	Allows grantee to change the private or public version of the page as follows: Add other portlets to existing regions on the page. Add or delete any portlets/tabs. Hide or show portlets/tabs. Users with this privilege may not create or delete regions, even for their private version of the page.
Manage	Allows grantee to change the private or public version of the page in any way, which includes Edit the properties of the page (title, name, description) Add or delete portlets/tabs Hide or show portlets/tabs Add or delete regions Choose a different style Specify access privileges for the page Note: Creators automatically have full control over any pages that they create. In addition, DBAs, portal administrators, and those with the Manage privilege for all pages have full control over all pages.

TABLE 5-2. *Page Privileges* (continued)

If the page or tab requires authentication, you will uncheck the Display Page To Public Users and identify the user or group in the Grantee field. If you do not know the exact name of the group or user that you would like to grant access to, you can use the user or group Browse icons to display the groups or users available. By choosing a user or group, selecting the security privilege to apply to the user, and clicking on the Add button, a user or group will receive privileges to view, work with, or manage all or part of a Portal page.

Let's log onto the PATM account and have PATM assign access to the eXYZ Portal pages.

Exercise 5.4: Assigning Access Privileges to the eXYZ Page and Tabs

1. Using the Navigator, choose the Pages tab and click on the My Pages link. Click the Edit action next to the eXYZ home page.

2. Choose the Access tab and uncheck the Display Page To Public Users.

3. In the Grantee field, click the Browse Groups icon and choose AUTHENTICATED_USERS as shown in Figure 5-6. In the Privileges field, choose Customization (Add-only) and click Add. The AUTHENTICATED_ USERS (GROUP) will appear with the list of users and groups in the Change Access section.

4. Click Apply and then click on the Portlets tab.

5. Check the check box on the Welcome tab and click the Edit (pencil) icon to create tab privileges for the tab.

6. Click on the Advanced Options tab and ensure that the check box for Inherit Access Settings From The Page is checked. Leave the Display Tab To Public Users box checked. This setting is overridden by the Page privilege that provides authorization to access anything on the page only to AUTHENTICATED_ USERS (and the page's creator).

7. Check the My eXYZ tab, click on the Edit icon, and check the Specify Access Settings radio button.

8. In the Grantee field, choose the Browse Groups icon and choose AUTHENTICATED _USERS. Give Manage authority to AUTHENTICATED _USERS for this page. Click Apply and Close.

9. For the HR tab, give the Edit Contents privilege to the HR_USERS group and the View privilege to MANAGEMENT_USERS group.

10. For the Sales tab, give the Edit Contents privilege to the SALES_USERS group and the View privilege to the MANAGEMENT_USERS group.

11. For the Management tab, give the MANAGEMENT_USERS group Customization (Full) privileges. Click Add, Apply, and Close.

12. Click Close to exit from the Edit Page dialog box.

13. Lastly, let's make our page available in another category that makes it more readily available for others to work with by clicking the Make Top-Level action link. You will now see the eXYZ home page under My Links and under the Top-Level Pages.

Click on the Home link to go back to the Portal home directory and let's move on to look at Portal's extensive application development environment.

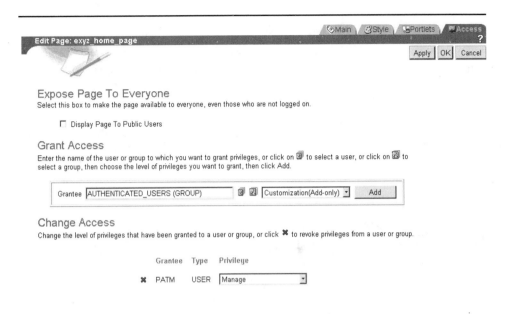

FIGURE 5-6. *The Edit Page Access tab creates page access privileges for users or groups*

Application Administration

The next few chapters will be devoted to developing content areas and application components. Before you begin developing Portal applications and content, you should set up application standards, the development environment, reusable components, LOVs, and scripts that will support the development standards your team will follow to support a common look and feel within the Portal. In this section we will discuss the following:

- Applications overview

- Setting up the application development environment

- Creating and managing application components

- Reusable component objects

- Managing shared application components, including colors, fonts, images, JavaScripts, and user interface templates

- Managing application security

Applications Overview

Oracle Portal offers a sophisticated environment for developing Web-based applications that interface with the database. Portal applications are made up of one or more forms, reports, charts, calendars, hierarchies, menus, URLs, links, LOVs, frame drivers, XML components, and dynamic pages. Each of these application types is known as a component. A wizard-based development approach will walk you through the process of creating each of the components and integrating them into an application. We will explore all of the components and their interrelationships in depth throughout the book.

It is important to note just what an application component consists of. As mentioned in Chapter 3, components are really Oracle packages and procedures that are stored in the database. Components are processed by the Oracle 9iAS application server and rendered in an HTML and/or JavaScript user interface within Portal. A record of the component you develop is stored in the database to identify the component by name, to support version control, status, Portal user ownership, and granted privileges. This information about the component is stored in the WWV_MODULE$ table, as shown in Figure 5-7. Let's see how the application component development process works.

ID	VERSION	TYPE ID	NAME	OWNER	REQUIRED ROLE	STATUS	CREATED ID ON	CREATED BY	STATUS	L(O(
1211501563	7	16	CATEGORY_FORM	TASK_APP	(null)		(null) 16-JUN-01	PORTAL30	PRODUCTION	(n:
1027225244	3	12	DETAIL_RPT	WWV_SYSTEM	(null)		(null) 16-JUN-01	PORTAL30	PRODUCTION	(n:_
1140063967	8	16	DEVELOPER_FORM	TASK_APP	(null)		(null) 16-JUN-01	PORTAL30	PRODUCTION	(n:
1041586961	1	6	DYN_SEARCH	PEOPLE_APP	(null)		(null) 16-JUN-01	PORTAL30	ARCHIVE	(n:
1041586961	2	6	DYN_SEARCH	PEOPLE_APP	(null)		0 09-JUL-01	PORTAL30	ARCHIVE	(n:
1041586961	3	6	DYN_SEARCH	PEOPLE_APP	(null)		0 09-JUL-01	PORTAL30	ARCHIVE	(n:
1041586961	4	6	DYN_SEARCH	PEOPLE_APP	(null)		0 09-JUL-01	PORTAL30	PRODUCTION	(n:
1136634245	1	31	EUL4_BATCH_QUERIES	PBC_ADMIN	(null)		0 05-JUL-01	PORTAL30	EDIT	05 01
1134463535	1	31	EUL4_BATCH_REPORTS	PBC_ADMIN	(null)		0 05-JUL-01	PORTAL30	EDIT	05 01
1184702996	1	80	EXAMPLE_APP	PORTAL30_DEMO	(null)		(null) 16-JUN-01	PORTAL30	(null)	(n:
1120627757	1	15	EXAMPLE_CAL	EXAMPLE_APP	(null)		(null) 16-JUN-01	PORTAL30	ARCHIVE	(n:
1120627757	2	15	EXAMPLE_CAL	EXAMPLE_APP	(null)		0 08-JUL-01	PORTAL30	ARCHIVE	(n:
1120627757	3	15	EXAMPLE_CAL	EXAMPLE_APP	(null)		0 08-JUL-01	PORTAL30	ARCHIVE	(n:
1120627757	4	15	EXAMPLE_CAL	EXAMPLE_APP	(null)		0 08-JUL-01	PORTAL30	ARCHIVE	(n:
1120627757	5	15	EXAMPLE_CAL	EXAMPLE_APP	(null)		0 08-JUL-01	PORTAL30	ARCHIVE	(n:
1120627757	6	15	EXAMPLE_CAL	EXAMPLE_APP	(null)		0 08-JUL-01	PORTAL30	ARCHIVE	(n:
1120627757	7	15	EXAMPLE_CAL	EXAMPLE_APP	(null)		0 08-JUL-01	PORTAL30	PRODUCTION	(n:
1024	1	22	EXAMPLE_DEPTNO	EXAMPLE_APP	(null)		(null) 16-JUN-01	PORTAL30	PRODUCTION	(n:
1002285333	4	6	EXAMPLE_DYNAMIC_PAGE	EXAMPLE_APP	(null)		(null) 16-JUN-01	PORTAL30	PRODUCTION	(n:

FIGURE 5-7.   *Information about developed components is stored in the WWV_MODULE$ table*

Setting Up the Application Development Environment

The first step in developing application components is to create the application that will contain the components. This can be done in the Build tab under the Create a New Application link. Alternatively, you may access and create applications from the Navigator by clicking on the Applications tab, then clicking on the Create New Application link on the upper left. Users can and should build multiple application containers to differentiate applications from one another. The application name should reflect the system name, business unit, or business process covered by the application.

To develop Oracle Portal applications, a developer must be able to access and manipulate database schema objects. The application itself, including all its components, is stored in a single schema. A developer who is granted the privilege to create a component in an application is by default granted privileges to build components in the application's schema. When an application is granted access to database objects such as tables, views, and procedures, the users and developers of the application schema are by default granted access, as shown in Figure 5-8.

We will create three applications for eXYZ Corporation: APP_SALES, APP_HR, and APP_PTS. Log in as user PORTAL30 and create an application in the following way.

Exercise 5.5: Create a New Application

1. Click the Create a New Application link from the Build tab or access the Create New … Application link from the Applications tab of the Navigator.

2. In the Application Name field, type `APP_SALES` and in the Display Name field type `Sales Application` as shown in Figure 5-9.

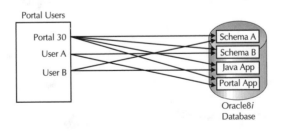

FIGURE 5-8. *Access privileges to schema objects are granted through Portal to users*

3. As the Schema, choose CORP_SITE. (If this is not available, you must grant permissions from PORTAL30 to this schema).

4. Click OK and then click on the Access tab on the next screen.

5. Check the Expose as Provider check box to allow this application to serve as a portlet provider and to display components as portlets in the Portlet Repository in the APP_SALES portlet provider.

6. In the Grant Access section, use the Browse Groups icon to choose the PORTAL_DEVELOPERS group, granting all members of this group access to this application.

7. Choose Edit from the drop-down list of privileges. Edit permissions allow application developers to create, edit, and delete components in the application.

8. Click the Apply button.

9. Click on the Browse Users icon and choose PATM.

10. Grant PATM Manage privileges, as shown in Figure 5-10, to allow full privileges within the APP_SALES application. With Manage privileges, PATM will be able to grant privileges to other users or to drop the application.

11. Click OK.

Anyone in the PORTAL_DEVELOPERS group will be able to access and edit the APP_SALES application area. All applications developed and placed in this container will support the Sales division of eXYZ. Additionally, all components within the

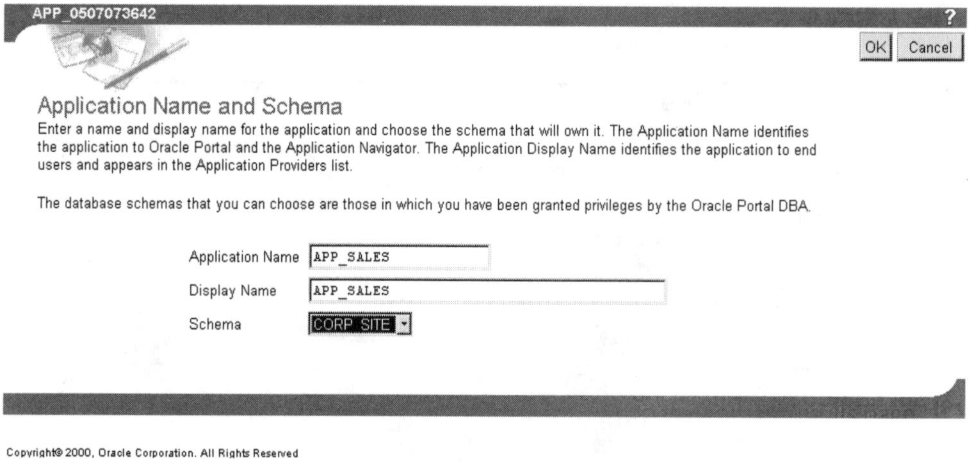

FIGURE 5-9. *Creating a new application entitled APP_SALES*

Provider Access

Check the Expose as Provider option to make this application available as a portlet provider.

☑ Expose as Provider

Grant Access

Enter the name of the user or group to which you want to grant privileges, or click on 🔳 to select a user, or click on 🔳 to select a group, then choose the level of privileges you want to grant, then click Add.

Grantee [   ] 🔳 🔳 [Execute ▾] [Add]

Change Access

Change the level of privileges that have been granted to a user or group, or click ✖ to revoke privileges from a user or group.

	Grantee	Type	Privilege
✖	PATM	USER	[Manage ▾]
✖	PORTAL30	USER	[Manage ▾]
✖	WEB_TECHNOLOGY_USERS	GROUP	[Edit ▾]

FIGURE 5-10. *User PATM has full management authority within APP_SALES*

APP_SALES application will use a single schema, CORP_SITE, to store the components created within the application. We will be able to create categories in the Portlet Provider Repository that will relate components to business processes so that any components that are developed with cross-business line functionality can be displayed accurately.

Now, create two more applications, APP_HR and APP_PTS, that will be application containers for all HR and project tracking system components. Make these applications portlet providers using the Expose as Provider check box. If you want to restrict access to the application's components, you can leave this check box blank. There is really no good reason to not expose an application as a portlet provider unless you are in the early stages of a project and you want to limit end-user access to portlet components that may be incomplete or not fully tested.

Using and Managing Components

Now that we have created an application repository, let's look at an existing application and understand what the development environment within the application will look like. Log in with the Portal30 master account and start by looking at the EXAMPLE_APP, accessible from the Applications tab in the Navigator window. You will notice first of all that the EXAMPLE_APP has a number of actions that can be applied to the application. You can work on all of the components within EXAMPLE_APP either by clicking on the link of the name or by clicking on the Open Action item. If you click on the Edit link, you can change the name of the application. By clicking Delete, you can delete the application and all of its components. Clicking on the Manage link allows you to edit, delete, or export the application.

An *export* allows you to save a copy of the contents of the application to a binary file. This file can later be imported back into Portal on another instance of the database. Exports are a way to capture the contents of the database or a portion of the database at a point in time. It is a good idea to create exports on a recurring basis much as you would save the contents of your PC or network server onto a backup medium. If you lose the application or it is accidentally deleted, you can import (restore) it at any time using the most recent export file.

Lastly, you may grant access to an entire application using the Grant Access link. This allows individuals or a team of Portal developers to access an application and the components it contains. Developers can explore the development techniques of other developers and reuse code by copying components and changing them for the end users' requirements. The Grant Access link also allows you to make an application a portlet provider. Exposing an application as a portlet provider allows the application to be viewed in the Portlet Repository content area if one or more components that make up an application are also published portlets.

You can access this tab by clicking on the Grant Access link for any component in the Applications tab of the Navigator, or by clicking on the Manage link and then the Access tab. You can grant access to specific groups or individual users by entering the user or group name in the Grantee field. If you do not know the name of the group or user to which you want to grant access, use the user or group Browse icons to show a list of existing groups or users. When you select one, it will be returned into the Grantee field and you can click the Add button to provide the grant.

Click on the EXAMPLE_APP name link or the Open link next to it to look at the components for this sample application. Click on the down arrow for the Type column and sort the application component types in descending order to show Reports on top. If you scroll through the page, you will see that these are all of the applications that you have been given access to within Portal. You will notice a number of Actions links next to each component as shown in Figure 5-11. These include:

- **Manage**   Brings up the Develop tab of the Component Manager.
- **Run**   Executes the component code in a separate full browser window.
- **Edit**   Places the component in edit mode to enable code and display changes.
- **Delete**   Deletes component versions or the entire component.
- **Grant Access**   Brings up the Access tab of the component where access and portlet provider privileges are granted.

Click on the EXAMPLE_SQL_REPORT to take a look at the component development environment beginning with the Develop tab.

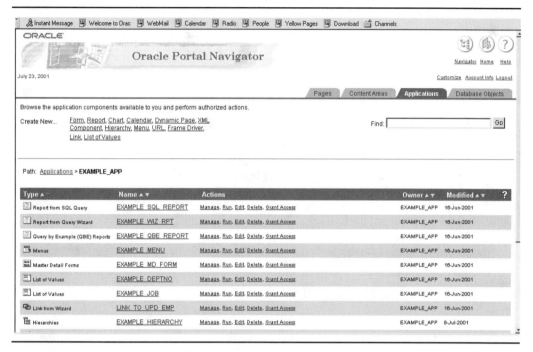

FIGURE 5-11. *The Component Management Actions links*

Develop Tab

The Develop tab of the Component Manager displays information about an existing application component. After you have created a new application component, you will be placed on the Develop tab page where you can test the component and edit it, if necessary. As we can see in Figure 5-12, the report name, the application name, the last date the component was changed, and the run link that will be the actual URL link of the component within Portal are displayed, as well as links to display the PL/SQL source code (Package Body and Package Spec) and the Show link that details the call interface for the component.

The Develop tab includes options to edit a component, test it as a full screen application or portlet, and customize the report with additional sort criteria, parameters, breaks, layouts, and titles. You can quickly add the component to your list of favorites, view the component attributes from the About tab, or delete versions of the component.

Component Version Control   Whenever you save changes to a component, Portal produces a new component version. The most recent version of a component is always the PRODUCTION version of the component and is the one that is executed when you run it. All other versions are ARCHIVE versions. Only the production version has a corresponding package that can be run. If there is an archived version of the component, you may edit it and save it, and create another valid package for

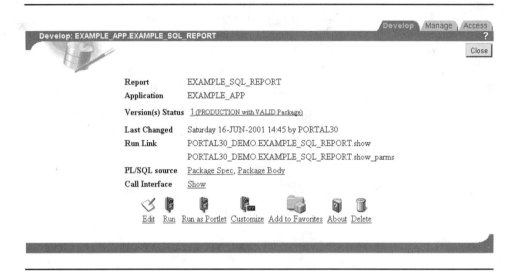

FIGURE 5-12. *The Component Manager user interface*

the component. If you delete the production version of the component, the component itself will be deleted along with all previous versions.

All versions of the component are stored in a Portal configuration management repository that includes the WWV_MODULES$ and WWV_MODULE_DETAILS$ tables and other supporting tables. Click on the About link at the bottom of the Manage Component page to see information about the most recent version of the component.

Edit Component   Click on the Edit link for the EXAMPLE_SQL_REPORT and note that there are a number of tab pages, as shown in Figure 5-13. Each of these tab pages corresponds to a portion of the wizard-based process that was used to create the component. If you place your cursor on each of the tabs to display bubble help, you will see that the tabs are, in order: SQL Query, Column Formatting, Formatting Conditions, Display Options, Customization Form Display Options, Report and Customization Form Text, and Additional PL/SQL Code. Click on each tab to get a feel for the type of dialog you will encounter as you modify a component. Don't worry about understanding all of this at this point—you will get a much better feel for the process of editing components as you progress through the book.

Run and Run as Portlet   You can test any application component using the Run and Run as Portlet links. Both links execute the production package that is listed in the Version Status line and documented in the PL/SQL source Package Spec and

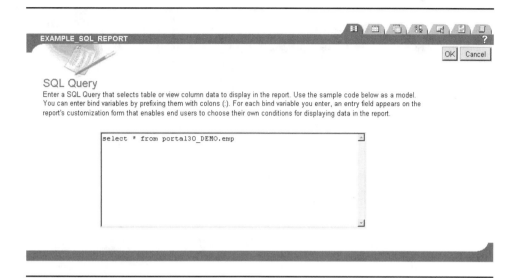

FIGURE 5-13. *The EXAMPLE_SQL_REPORT Edit tabs*

Package Body description. The full page or portlet display options are based on the choices made in the Display Options tab of the Component Edit window for all nonforms-related components. You can control the look and feel of these components within a portlet or on a full page report using the Display Options tab. Find the Display Options tab on the EXAMPLE_SQL_REPORT in Edit mode and note the section for Full Page Options and Portlet Options, as shown in Figure 5-14.

Click on the Run link for the EXAMPLE_SQL_REPORT to execute the report in a full separate browser window. The package in the database is invoked, all links and input parameters are passed to the package, and HTML code is generated to display the report. You may use the browser print facility to print the report. Click on the link for SMITH, or on any other name on the report, to view the form that is linked to the report that has all the information for SMITH listed. Links are powerful application features that allow users to "drill down," to find data anomalies and trends in reports and update the database, if needed.

What you are viewing is a working application. On the form, change the salary for Smith from 800 to 850 and click on the Update button, and notice that the record has been updated. Click the Reset button to clear the fields. In the Name field of the form, type ALLEN in all capital letters and click on Query; the information for ALLEN is now on the screen. Type 250 in the Commission field and update the record. Now use the browser Back button to return to the report and then use Refresh to reload the page to see the changed values. Make sure your users understand that a refresh or reload is needed to reflect updated data in the database. The reload issues a call

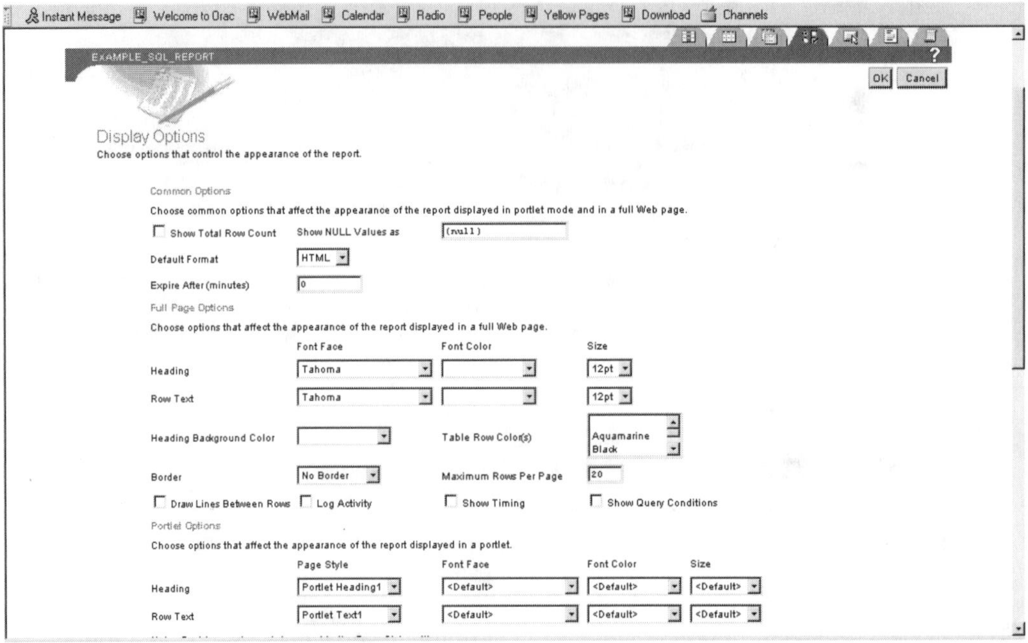

FIGURE 5-14. *The Display Options tab controls the display of a component on a page*

to the database to rerun the report package and retrieve the current information from the database. Lastly, click on the body of the report with your right mouse button and select View Source to see the code that generated the report. You will see HTML that was generated to render the report on the screen.

Close the report window and go back to the Manage Components page. Click the Run as Portlet link and note the report is more compact and lacks the customization form template that wraps around the output on the full-page report. The linked form appears on the Portlet view of the report as well. The portlet report will display within a region on a page and will need to be more compact when it is rendered. You can use these two ways to run a component to test them and view them for accuracy and for look and feel.

The Customization Form   Customization forms work in conjunction with reports and other application components to allow users to enter runtime parameters and specify other options for the component. The only component type that does not use a customization form is a form because everything, including queries if they are allowed, is performed from the form interface. If a report appears on the page with a Customize link, the customization form is available for the user to customize the output format. If you remember, Customize Applications is a group and user object privilege. Users with only Run privileges will not be able to customize their reports or charts.

The customization form allows users to submit query criteria that were defined in the development process. Reports and other components allow both user-defined and system parameters. In the customization form, the user will enter values for parameters to narrow search criteria. You specify which parameters are to be displayed, and you can format those parameters with custom prompts and LOVs to help users choose the value to submit. To use a customization form, users must have the Customize privilege for the application or component as we explained in the group and user application security section. If the report is displayed in a portlet, the Customize link will take the user to the portlet-oriented view of the same form.

Users can change the default title for the report, set query parameters using drop-down lists and radio groups, and change the sort order for the data. Additional options for setting break columns and changing the style and output format of the report are also available. Bring up the EXAMPLE_SQL_REPORT Develop tab, click on the Customize link, and perform the following:

1. Change the Display Name to read eXYZ Management Report.

2. In the Row Order Options area, change the first Order by field to Job, Descending and in the second Order by field, change the order to Ename Ascending.

3. In the Break Options, choose Job as the First Break Column, as shown in Figure 5-15.

4. Click the Run Report button to see how the report changes.

Manage Tab

The Manage tab of the Component Manager page provides facilities to monitor and manage a component. Go to the Manage tab for the EXAMPLE_SQL_ REPORT. On the top of the page there is a Show SQL Query Info link. This link displays the SQL that was generated by Portal for any report component such as reports, charts, and calendars; it does not work with forms.

Click on Show SQL Query Info. You will be placed back in the Develop tab where you can click the Run link. At the top of the report, the SQL queries that were used to generate the report are displayed. Close the report and go back to the Manage tab: the first link now says Hide SQL Query Info. When you are ready to place a report component on a page, ensure that the Show SQL Query Info link is visible on the production version of the component.

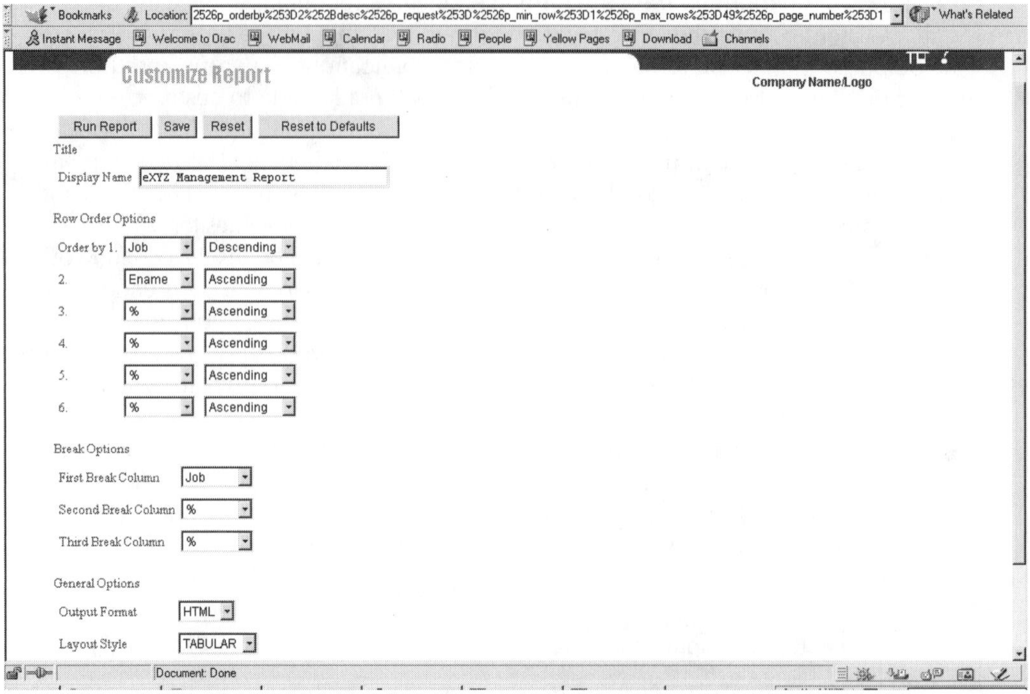

FIGURE 5-15. *Customization form for eXYZ management*

A component is locked when you are working on it, so that others cannot access and manipulate your code at the same time that you are trying to change it. This is a fundamental configuration management control that is provided by Portal. Inadvertent locks can occur if you finish editing the component any way other than clicking OK, Finish, or Cancel. If you exit a session without performing one of these three functions or log out in the middle of an edit session, a lock will remain on the component and you will need to unlock it. The Show Locks on this Component link lets you identify and clear existing locks on a component so that you or another developer can access it again. This is an important link, because people often make this mistake.

Export/Import of Components   We briefly discussed the export process with the application, but it is important to deal with it in a little more depth. Every component or application can be exported at any time. Since version control is enforced within Portal, it is possible to go back to a prior release of a component by editing older versions and clicking OK to make that version the most current—and thus the production version of the component. If you accidentally delete a component or version and you have a recent export file of it, you can use the export file to import it back to the database and recover the code.

Exports can be used to copy an application or component from one Portal installation to another as long as they are both the same version of Oracle Portal. If you have two Portal nodes with similar requirements, you can export an application or component from the local node and import it into the remote node and have the same code resident on both machines. While there are other ways within Portal to get the same results, this is the only way to physically take a copy of the database object from one machine and place it on another. Remember that this is just a copy of the object at a specific point in time. To export the EXAMPLE_SQL_REPORT, follow these steps:

1. Click on the Export link on the Manage tab.

2. Click on the "here" in "Click here to download the export script file".

3. Type `Example_SQL_Rpt` as the name for the export file in the Save As dialog box and click the Save button, as shown in Figure 5-16.

4. Click Close.

The exported component will be in the directory designated in the Save As dialog box.

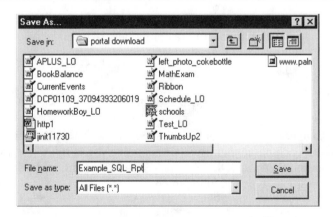

FIGURE 5-16. *Type the export file name in the Save As dialog box*

The import process is a little trickier. To import the component, it is easiest to invoke SQL*Plus, preferably from the command line. You may test the import process by first renaming the EXAMPLE_SQL_REPORT as EXAMPLE_SQL_ REPORT_TST and then importing the original EXAMPLE_SQL_REPORT back into the EXAMPLE_APP application by performing the following:

1. On Windows NT, go to the command prompt and change your directory to the Oracle database home directory.

2. Type `sqlplus PORTAL30/PORTAL3@<export name>.sql` (In our case, the file name is example_sql_rpt.sql).

3. At the command line for Parameter 1 = Import Mode, CHECK or CREATE prompt, type 2.

4. At the Parameter 2 = portal schema prompt, type the following: `portal30` (or schema owner with SYS privilege).

5. At the Parameter 3 = login user name prompt, type `portal30` (or the login user).

6. At the Parameter 4 = login user password prompt, type `portal30` (or the password).

7. At the Parameter 5 = application schema prompt, type `portal_demo` (or the schema where the application or component will be created).

8. At the Parameter 6 = application name prompt, type `example_app` (or the application name for the component or application).

9. At the Parameter 7 = log file prompt, type `imprpt.log` as shown in Figure 5-17.

10. Hit RETURN and the import will execute.

If the package is already resident in the schema, the import will fail. An alternative to responding to each parameter prompt interactively is to run the script as one command from the DOS or UNIX command line. If you choose to do that, based on the above example, type the following:

```
Sqlplus portal30/portal30@or8i @example_sql_rpt.sql CREATE portal30
portal30 portal30 portal_demo example_app imprpt.log
```

This will create the report package in the PORTAL_DEMO application schema with the same characteristics and version that were in the export file that you created earlier.

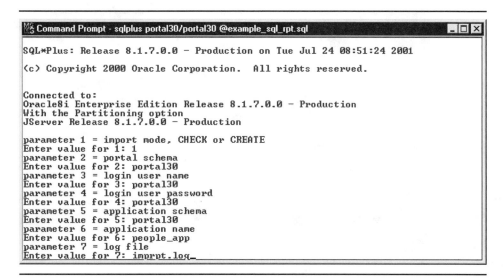

```
Command Prompt - sqlplus portal30/portal30 @example_sql_rpt.sql                    _ □ ✕

SQL*Plus: Release 8.1.7.0.0 - Production on Tue Jul 24 08:51:24 2001

(c) Copyright 2000 Oracle Corporation.  All rights reserved.


Connected to:
Oracle8i Enterprise Edition Release 8.1.7.0.0 - Production
With the Partitioning option
JServer Release 8.1.7.0.0 - Production

parameter 1 = import mode, CHECK or CREATE
Enter value for 1: 1
parameter 2 = portal schema
Enter value for 2: portal30
parameter 3 = login user name
Enter value for 3: portal30
parameter 4 = login user password
Enter value for 4: portal30
parameter 5 = application schema
Enter value for 5: portal30
parameter 6 = application name
Enter value for 6: people_app
parameter 7 = log file
Enter value for 7: imprpt.log_
```

FIGURE 5-17.   *The Oracle Portal component import using SQL*Plus*

Other Manage Features   The Manage tab's copy function allows a copy of a
component to be placed in another application. This is a useful feature if you wish to
share components with developers building other applications. To copy a component,
perform the following:

   1. Click Copy.

   2. Identify the application you wish to copy the component into. For this
   exercise, choose the PEOPLE_APP.

   3. In the New Component Name field, type SAMPLE_SQL_RPT.

   4. In the New Component Display Name field, type Sample SQL Report,
   as shown in Figure 5-18.

   5. Click OK and navigate to the PEOPLE_APP to find the SAMPLE_SQL_RPT.

Similarly, you may rename a component within your own application using
the Rename link. You can replace the New Component Name, the New Component
Display Name, or both. The new name will appear in the list of component packages
under your application.

EXAMPLE_APP.EXAMPLE_SQL_REPORT

OK Cancel

Create A Copy Of This Component
Create a new component based on this one. The new copy can be created in this application or another application that you
can access.

Current Owner	EXAMPLE_APP
Current Component Name	EXAMPLE_SQL_REPORT
Current Component Display Name	Report from SQL Query
New Owner	PEOPLE_APP
New Component Name	SAMPLE_SQL_RPT
New Component Display Name	Sample SQL Report

FIGURE 5-18. *The Portal component copy page*

The Generate command will compile the PL/SQL package for your component
and store it in the database. It is not necessary to use the Generate command unless
the package you created is invalid, or if you have migrated from one version of Portal
to another and some of your portal package components are listed as invalid. In
this case, modify the package if necessary and use the Generate link to create a
valid package.

Lastly, the Monitor link displays a chart of the component that identifies all users that
have requested the component, and the frequency of those requests by user. A frequently
accessed component on a site might be a good candidate for analysis to determine if the
component could be cached in memory to improve response time. A component that
is used infrequently can be moved to a different portion of the site that is more accessible,
it can be granted additional privileges to more users and groups that are applicable,
or it can be removed from the site due to a lack of interest. These decisions can be
made based on the information provided from the Monitor report.

Access Tab

You may grant access to an application component from the Access tab of the
Manage Components page for that component. By default, all components in an
application will inherit the privileges that have been defined for the application. You
may overwrite the application security for the EXAMPLE_SQL_REPORT by opening
it up in the Applications tab of the Oracle Portal Navigator.

Grant Security Privileges with the Grant Access Link

I. Click on the Grant Access link next to the EXAMPLE_SQL_REPORT.

2. Check the Publish to Portal check box, uncheck the Inherit Privileges from Application check box, and click the Apply button.

3. The page will be refreshed and a Grant Access and Change Access region will appear on the page.

4. Notice that numerous individual and group users already have access to this page from the inherited privileges of the application. You may change any of these privileges by editing or deleting the existing group and individual users or by adding new users or groups. Click OK to exit from this window.

The Access page dialog box is the same for components as it is for the application it resides in, but privileges apply only to the component. In the previous exercise, only users with PORTLET_PUBLISHERS permissions will see the Publish to Portal check box that we checked. If you are not an owner or manager of a component or application, you will also not be able to see the Grant Access dialog box. If you need these privileges as part of your role in building the Portal and don't have them, have the Portal administrator grant you PORTLET_PUBLISHERS permissions. At an individual user level, the administrator may grant you Manage or Create permission to an application or component.

To grant access to a specific application component for nonauthenticated users, grant PUBLIC (USER) authority to the component. You may do this for the EXAMPLE_SQL_REPORT by performing the following:

I. Open the Oracle Portal Navigator, and click on the Applications tab.

2. Choose the EXAMPLE_APP and pick the EXAMPLE_SQL_REPORT from the list of components.

3. Click on the Grant Access link for the EXAMPLE_SQL_REPORT.

4. Choose PUBLIC (USERS) in the Grantee field and press the Add button.

5. Leave the Privilege as Execute so that nonauthenticated users will not be able to modify anything in the application or on the page. Click OK.

You can follow the same example to modify permissions for an entire application. Always leave any public user privileges as Execute so that security is enforced and nonauthenticated users cannot make changes that will affect other users adversely.

Reusable Objects

An advantage of Oracle Portal is that it is based on packages and procedures that can be shared among developers. The Chapter 4 design review discussed the importance of code reuse and, particularly, setting standards in advance of development. In this section we will discuss some of the object components that should be developed in advance of any applications for a Portal site. Additionally, we will discuss the Shared Components link and the features that are available in the Shared Components library that are available for all developers. Shared components constitute an application library that contains reusable objects that can be incorporated in any application component.

Links

Links are the easiest way to call one component from another and dynamically pass parameters based on the current row. There are other ways to link components and pass parameters, including the call interface we saw previously from the component Develop tab, but links are reusable objects that are easily called by components. They simplify management—if you rename the component, it only changes in one place if all other components use a link. You can create several links to the same component that pass different parameters, to simplify the process of calling components.

Go back to the EXAMPLE_APP. Find the LINK_TO_UPD_EMP link component and click on its Edit action. You will see that the link target type is an Oracle Portal component and its name is EXAMPLE_APP.EXAMPLE_FORM. Click on the second tab, Enter Link Target Inputs, to see the link parameters that will be passed to the form from the calling component. These links correspond to all of the fields available on the EXAMPLE_FORM and the fields within the form that accept parameters. If the form did not accept parameters, you would not be able to link to it. You can also pass a specific parameter such as DEPT = 'SALES' as a condition to limit the result set of the query to only the Sales department.

Exit from the link and let's look at how a link is invoked. Using the Navigator, edit the EXAMPLE_QBE_REPORT. Edit the report and click on the second tab, the Column Formatting tab, as shown in Figure 5-19. Notice that the Link column on the EMP.ENAME field refers to the link we just looked at, LINK_TO_UPD_EMP. Click on the Cancel button at the top of the page and at the Develop tab click on the Run icon. Click on the link in the ENAME field for SMITH; and the link will pass the name parameter from the report to the form that comes up. Information about SMITH now appears in the form based on the ENAME parameter passed from the report.

Links can also be used with URL's to pass parameters to external Web-based applications. For example, Portal could use links to invoke Oracle Discoverer and execute its Web-based workbooks. Use the Link component, check the HTML link, and type the URL link to the external Web source. The following link would invoke Discoverer 4i: http://<servername>:7777/discwb4/html/english/ms_ie/start_ie.htm.

EXAMPLE_OBE_REPORT

OK Cancel

Column Formatting

Choose how to display the results of your QBE report. If size is not specified, the Width Type can be ignored.

Column	Column Heading	Sum	Type	Align	Display as	Format Mask	LOV	Link	Edit Link	Width Type	Size
EMP.EMPNO	Empno	☐	⁷⁸⁹	Right	Text			%	✎	Pixel	
EMP.ENAME	Ename	☐	A	Left	Text			LINK_TO_UPD_EMP	✎	Pixel	
EMP.JOB	Job	☐	A	Left	Text			%	✎	Pixel	
EMP.MGR	Mgr	☐	⁷⁸⁹	Right	Text			%	✎	Pixel	
EMP.HIREDATE	Hiredate	☐	📅	Left	Text			%	✎	Pixel	
EMP.SAL	Sal	☐	⁷⁸⁹	Right	Text			%	✎	Pixel	
EMP.COMM	Comm	☐	⁷⁸⁹	Right	Text			%	✎	Pixel	
EMP.DEPTNO	Deptno	☐	⁷⁸⁹	Right	Text			%	✎	Pixel	

FIGURE 5-19. *The Column Formatting tab identifies the link between components*

Additional parameters can be added to the end of this link to provide input parameters or conditions. External Oracle applications are automatically invoked without requiring a separate sign-on authentication.

Lists of Values (LOV)

One of the easiest ways to ensure consistent data entry is to give end users a list of valid values from which to choose. Lists of Values (LOVs) are a separate Portal application component that provide data entry support for forms or validated parameter input for reports.

In Oracle Portal, you can create a List of Values (LOV) component based on a query from a lookup table or a hard-coded list. Lists of Values belong to the application in which they are used, and are not shared among applications. Once created, an LOV can be displayed in any of the following formats.

Combo Box   This is the common drop-down list, shown at the end of this section. If the list allows nulls and no default is specified, the list will appear blank at first. Clicking on the down arrow will reveal the available choices. Most browsers also allow users to choose a value from the list by typing the first letter of the desired choice until the choice appears. For example, a list of 50 states is long enough to make scrolling cumbersome. A user living in Virginia could click on the list item and type a V and the first state (Vermont) beginning with V would appear as the selected option in the list. Typing V a second time would move down in the list to the next state, Virginia. A combo box allows only one choice to be selected.

Pop-Up   A pop-up is a prebuilt component that displays the list in a separate window. A small clickable list icon appears to the right of a field with an associated pop-up. When the user clicks the icon, a separate window appears to display the items in the list. At the top of the window is a "Find" box that supports wildcard searches. When the user clicks the link in the display value list, the return value is automatically passed back to the form and the pop-up window closes. The pop-up list can only be used to select a single item, but is especially useful for long lists.

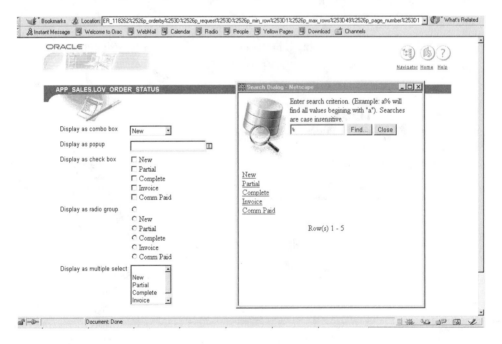

Check Box   With check boxes, all choices are displayed as a text list, with a check box to the left of each value displayed. The user can check any number (or none) of the items. The list of return values is passed as an array (in the form of a PL/SQL table) to the form, which must be designed to handle multiple values for the field. Some components are naturally suited for this structure, while others require a little manipulation to get it to work.

Radio Group   A radio group is a list of items shown with radio buttons to the left of each display value. When a value is selected, the corresponding radio button is filled in, and the return value is passed to the parameter. An advantage of Portal radio groups is that they can be generated dynamically, a difficult task in most client/server development environments. Radio groups limit the selection to one value.

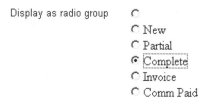

Multiple Select   The multiple select LOV shows the list of display values as a box containing many values, with a scroll bar on the right side of the box that allows the user to view all of the values. The height of the box determines the number of items visible at any one time, and is set when using the multiple select list in a form. The multiple select list allows the user to select more than one value by holding down the CTRL key while clicking on each of the desired values. A value of NULL is selected by clicking the blank item. As with check boxes, the form or report in which the multiple select list is used must be able to handle multivalued input for the field associated with the list.

Exercise 5.6: The Order Status LOV

eXYZ's ordering system allows users to check the status of an order. There are five possible entries for the Status field, and we will create a hard-coded list to support these entries. Veteran programmers may object to coding this as a static list rather than a dynamic list based on a lookup table. By creating the list in Portal, we retain many of the advantages of a lookup table. First, we can reuse the list in any application component, so we are not copying hard-coded list values from one code fragment to another. Second, this list is actually dynamic, because it is stored in Portal database tables. The list can be edited at any time, and the components will use the current values as soon as they are saved. If we wanted to be certain of our data integrity, we could add a check constraint to the table. Whether you choose a static or dynamic list will depend on your application needs, but we will work with both types in this chapter. So let's get started.

1. To create this LOV, go to the Navigator tab for Applications and click on the APP_SALES application.

2. Click on List of Values at the top of the screen by the label "Create New ...".

3. Choose Static List of Values. You will be taken to a screen that lets you specify all the details of the LOV.

4. Name your LOV LOV_ORDER_STATUS, set the Default Format to "Combo box", and leave the Show Null Value field set to Yes.

NOTE
Even if you don't want to allow nulls in a field, you may want to include NULL values in the LOV, so that when users perform a query, they can leave the field blank. The item can still be set to mandatory when creating the form. Another option is to set the Show Null Value field to "%", which causes the "%" sign to display when the list value is NULL. Some users may find this more intuitive in query mode, because the "%" sign is a standard wildcard character in Oracle.

5. Type the values as in the table here so that your edit screen looks like Figure 5-20.

Display Value	Return Value	Display Order
New	N	1
Partial	P	2
Complete	C	3
Invoice	I	4
Comm Paid	CP	5

6. Click Apply, then OK. On the main screen, click Run to see how the LOV works in a variety of formats. Close the Run window when you are done.

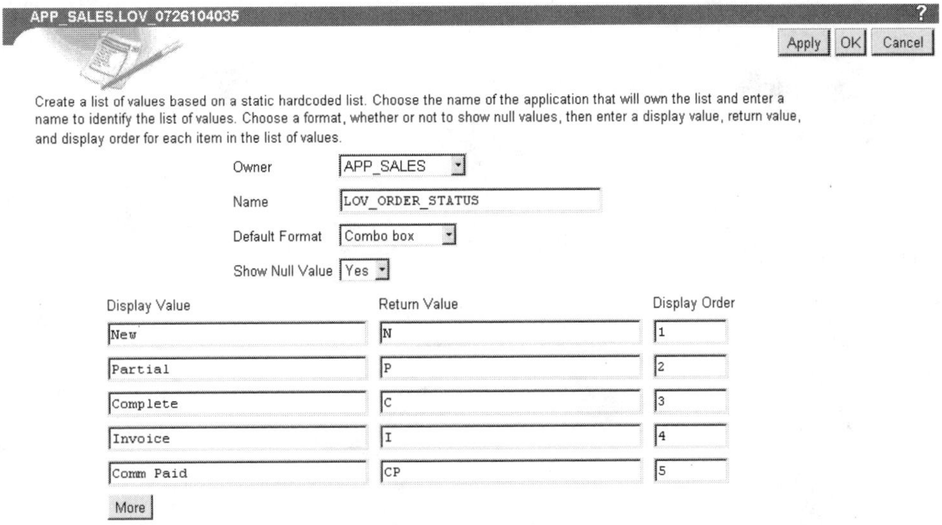

FIGURE 5-20. *The main Navigator page for the Sales application*

Exercise 5.7: Customer List

An LOV of customers should be dynamic, because customer data is typically volatile and changes frequently. The Customer LOV will be based on a database table. To create a dynamic list, you will specify a valid SQL query with exactly two columns in the SELECT list. The first column is always the value displayed in the list, and the second column is the value returned when a list element is selected. Set the default display format to a pop-up list, because any other type of list will be unwieldy for displaying all of eXYZ's customers.

1. Return to the main Navigator screen for APP_SALES, and create a new List of Values.

2. This time choose Dynamic List of Values.

3. Name the list `LOV_CUSTOMERS`, set the default format to "Pop up", and set Show Null Value to No.

4. Type the query as below. Use the concatenation operator (||) to display both the customer name and the city where the customer is located.

```
SELECT customer_name||'--'||city, customer_id FROM customers
```

5. Click OK and then click Run to test the Customer LOV.

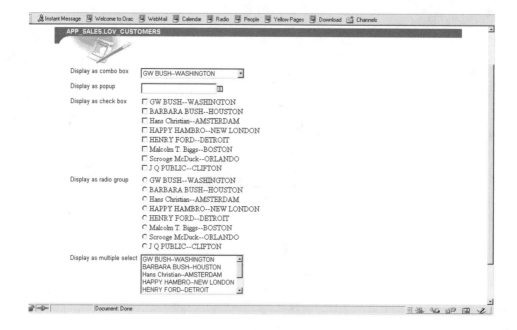

Managing Shared Application Components

You may add to or edit a library of shared components that include color palettes, fonts, images, code, and application templates. The application development team will use these components to enhance the look and feel of applications that will display as portlets on Portal pages. All of these application colors, fonts, images and code are available for use when developing applications within Portal. Colors can be used to enhance the background of an application or for colorized text within an application. Most standard fonts are included in the Portal install, but you may add additional specialty fonts. Custom JavaScripts, corporate images, and custom application templates may be added to support standards among the development team.

Exercise 5.8: Add Colors to the Application Template Color Scheme

1. Log in as the Portal administrator and use the Navigator to go to the Applications tab.

2. Under Applications, click on the Shared Components link.

3. Click on the Colors link or click Open under Actions next to the Colors link.

4. Under Create New, click on the Colors link.

5. Under Color Value, type #1E90FF.

6. In the Color Name field, type dodgerblue.

7. Click Preview to view the color in a separate window.

8. Click Create and then click Close.

Dodgerblue will now be available for application development with forms, reports, charts, and other application components, as shown in Figure 5-21. Dodgerblue will not be available for the page styles color palette by adding this color to the applications components. This is an application-only color scheme. When you choose standard colors to add to the color palette, ensure that they are browser safe. On the Internet, you may search for the URL www.htmlref.com /reference/appe/safepallette.htm to see a list of colors that are browser safe for all standard browser types.

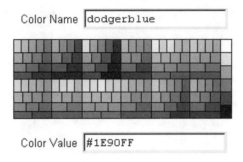

FIGURE 5-21. *Shared components color allows the addition for new application colors*

Exercise 5.9: Add Fonts to the Application Template

You may add in additional fonts that are made available to developers when developing applications. Any standard font can be added into the list of fonts available to the application development team. Add a new font by performing the following:

1. Log in as the Portal administrator and use the Navigator to go to the Applications tab.

2. Under Applications, click on the Shared Components link.

3. Click on the Fonts link or click Open under Actions next to the Colors link.

4. Type `Sans Serif` in the Font Name field.

5. Type `sans-serif` in the Font Name field.

6. Click Create and then click Close.

   You can now see that Sans Serif is added to the list of fonts that are available to developers. Click on the View link and you can see what the font will look like. Note also that you can edit the name of the font, delete the font, export it to another Portal instance, or make a copy of the font and give it a new name that will be more familiar to users. An example of a copy would be copying the Helvetica font and naming the new font "eXYZ standard font" so that all developers will use this font as their standard for all eXYZ applications.

Exercise 5.10: Adding Images to the Shared Components Images Directory

You may add additional images that will be used as iconic imagery or Portal image links within your Portal applications. A large number of installed images are available in the shared components Images directory. You may want to add additional images for use by the development team in creating page background and customization form templates. The image types should be JPEG, GIF, or PNG. The Portal image definition process includes a definition of the image to include the size of an image from Icon 16 x 16 to Icon 32 x 32 or more descriptive terms such as "arrow" or "Logo". To add the eXYZ logo image to the list of shared component images, first copy the image from <drive>:/portalhandbook/content/exyzlogo.jpeg to the Portal virtual images file location at <drive>:/IAS_HOME/portal30/images. Your images will not be visible within Portal unless they reside in the Apache virtual directory. Next, perform the following:

1. Log in as the Portal administrator and use the Navigator to go to the Applications tab.

2. Under Applications, click on the Shared Components link.

3 Click on the Images link or click Open under Actions next to the Images link.

4. Type eXYZ logo in the Image Name field.

5. Type <drive>:/oracle/isuites/portal30/images/ exyzlogo.jpeg in the Image Filename field.

6. Choose a logo from the Image Type LOV choices.

7. Click OK and click Close.

8. Find the eXYZlogo logo image and double check to ensure that it appears properly.

JavaScripts

LOVs are used to validate a value entered against an element of a list. If the validation you need is not list-based, but value-based, you will need to use JavaScript to validate the input. JavaScript is a scripting language that augments HTML code and provides field validation, editing and control, and event-driven Web support. JavaScript is embedded in the HTML code that is generated from Portal. JavaScript is a much faster means to edit transaction-based forms because all code resides in memory on the end user's browser when a form or application is rendered on a page. Avoiding a form field validation check against the database means faster response times and better user interaction with the Portal applications, while still ensuring data entry integrity. JavaScript is best used in field- and form-level validations, for warnings, and for unique proactive procedures that cannot be accomplished using static HTML. The shared-component JavaScripts are meant to provide user edit checks for specific field- or form-level data entry validation when the user updates or inserts a new record.

Portal allows you to store JavaScripts for reuse in many application components. JavaScripts should be developed in a fairly generic manner, so they can be created and stored in the shared components application. When you use a JavaScript, you have the option to enforce the validation at the field or form level. When using field-level validation, users will not be able to navigate out of the field until the JavaScript validation is satisfied. Form-level validation, on the other hand, allows users to navigate out of the field, but will not accept the form until all of the individual field conditions are satisfied. JavaScript is an object-oriented language. As such, JavaScript may not be easy for someone used to procedural languages like PL/SQL to learn. Often the best technique for creating JavaScripts is to copy an existing one and modify it to suit your needs. After doing a few of these, you will become more comfortable with the language. If you need more information on JavaScript code, refer to Appendix A for a list of sources.

Exercise 5.11: Validating Input with JavaScript

In the HR application, we need to be able to pay a draw on commission for a salesperson. To ask for a draw of zero would not make any sense. Since we don't want to have to write our first JavaScript from scratch, let's see if any code already in Portal can be used: Navigate to the shared components application. Notice that it is owned by the Portal schema, by default PORTAL30—not CORP_SITE. Some shared components are created automatically when Oracle Portal is installed. These are available for use in any application. Navigate to the JavaScripts page and take a look at the available components. There is no entry that would validate that a number is greater than zero. There is, however, one that validates whether a number is in the range of 0–100; we can copy this script and base our new code on that. Navigate to the shared components application, JavaScripts, find the inRang0_100 script, and click on Copy.

1. On the Copy JavaScript page, specify `GreaterThan0` as the New JavaScript Name and click the Next button.

2. Change the JavaScript body so it looks like the following:

```
{
  if ( (theElement.value <= 0  ||
isNaN(Math.abs(theElement.value)) )
                                && theElement.value != "" )
  {
    alert( " Value must be a number greater than 0." );
    theElement.focus();
```

```
   theElement.select();
   return false;
 }
 return true;
}
```

NOTE

isNaN is a JavaScript built-in that checks to see if the value is "Not a Number". An empty value is not a number, so this function alone would enforce data entry in the field where it is used. To allow for nulls, we added the test for not equal to "", the JavaScript equivalent of a NULL.

3. Click Finish.

4. Find the JavaScript GreaterThan0 in the list and click on the Run link.

5. In the Text field, try a few different numeric values that would and would not meet the condition. What happens if you enter a non-numeric value or a negative number?

User Interface Templates

To promote application consistency and appearance, Oracle Portal provides user interface templates that give applications a uniform appearance on a Portal page. There are actually three ways to create a UI template. The easiest is to copy an existing template that is close to the look, feel, and characteristics that you want for your application template. Simply copy the template and replace the images and text with your own and rename the template. A second method is to create a structured UI template that walks through a series of dialog steps and generates the HTML UI wrapper that will surround your application components. The last method is to create an unstructured UI template that allows you to write your own HTML code for the UI wrapper. This last method requires more detailed knowledge of HTML code, but also offers a greater degree of control over how the UI template will look on the screen. Let's try copying an existing template and modifying it first.

Exercise 5.12: Creating a User Interface Template

1. From the Navigator, open Shared Components in the Applications tab.

2. Under User Interface Templates, find FINANCE_TEMPLATE1 and click on Copy.

3. In the Template Name field give the new template a name of EXYZ_ TEMPLATE. Then click OK.

4. On the User Interface Templates page, find EXYZ_TEMPLATE and click Edit.

5. The Template Definition will display HTML with some substitution parameters in the form of #parameter#. Your goal is to leave the HTML mostly as it is, substituting the logo and company name for eXYZ Corporation.

6. The first parameter that you should notice is #IMAGE_PREFIX#. This constant refers to the directory where Oracle Portal images are stored—by default, it is $IAS_HOME\portal30\images. Ensure that you copied the eXYZ corporate logo (exyzlogo.jpg) into this directory in the previous exercise. Change the text so that the image named news01.jpg in the Template Definition is now exyzlogo.jpg.

7. Right after the name of the image file, you will see a "width=" attribute—set this width to 114. You will need to figure out and test these settings whenever you substitute a custom image into a template.

8. Now scroll down to the bottom of the HTML and find the words "Company Name/logo" surrounded by Bold tags. Change this to read eXYZ Corporation. Remove the reference to the bottom logo by deleting the tag just above that reads:

```
<img src=#IMAGE_PREFIX#news_01b.jpg width=300 height=24 border=0>
```

9. Delete only this tag, not the table tags that surround it.

10. Click Apply and Click Preview to view your new template as shown in Figure 5-22.

11. Click OK and exit.

Note the substitution parameters, in the format #PARAMETER#. These will be substituted at runtime, so do not modify them directly, but do feel free to rearrange them. You may also create a template from the beginning by performing the following:

1. At the top of the screen, click on Create New . . . User Interface Templates and then choose Structured UI Template.

2. Give the Template a Name of EXYZ2_TEMPLATE.

3. Leave the Background Color at white.

4. Click on the list next to the Background Image and choose "wsd.gif".

5. In the Template Title Properties, set the Title Font Size to 12, the Title Font Color to Blue, Midnight, and the Title Font Face to "Arial Rounded MT Bold".

6. In the Template Header Properties window, set the Heading Background color to Quartz, and type in `exyzlogo.jpg` for the Application Image. In the Home Image field, type `homew.gif`. In the Home Image URL, type the URL for the Portal home page using the HTTP:// prefix. (ex. `HTTP://Exyz:7777/pls/portal30`). In the Help Image field, type `helpw.gif`.

7. Click Preview to view the template and OK to save and exit.

The unstructured UI template works the same way as what we demonstrated when we worked with the copy and replace function. Simply invoke the unstructured UI template from the Create New... User Interface Templates, give the template a name, and modify the HTML to create a new template. The copy function is much easier to work with to get started than beginning with an unstructured UI template.

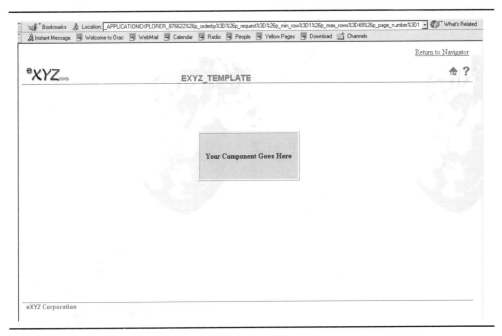

FIGURE 5-22   *The eXYZ application standard template*

Conclusion

We have performed many of the duties required in the administration of the Portal development environment before we begin developing the Portal Web site. It is very important to make sure that all users have correct access privileges before beginning development of the site. Common tables, triggers, procedures, and views should all be created and made available to developers so that they have all of the access that is needed to create and check in applications that utilize these objects. Even more important is to ensure that all developers work to the same standards as they develop the site using user interface templates, corporate style sheets, page styles, and page layouts. We will see in the next chapter how to apply these concepts to the development of content areas.

CHAPTER
6

Content Areas

ll companies have information resources that are not part of any formal data structure. There are policies and procedural documents, graphics, white papers, forms to fill out, and even software. Educational institutions have academic papers, research results, and protocols. Public service organizations may have press releases, announcements, and reference information. These resources, or *content*, are not usually formally catalogued or centrally stored, but scattered among various departments and storage formats. In fact, it was this very issue of distributed location and format that first led Tim Berners-Lee to conceptualize the notion of a "world-wide web." While the underlying Hypertext Transfer Protocol supports complete information transparency—defined as the ability to locate and access any document anywhere—the implementation has suffered from a few practical issues.

First, document formats are not necessarily uniform. Few organizations are ready to give up their proprietary word processing software, with all of its built-in customization and standardization features, in favor of the relatively immature HTML editors on the market. We continue to produce documents in our format of choice and ask Web administrators and browser vendors to find ways to make these documents accessible to end users. Second is the issue of security. Some documents should not be globally accessible, but only available to privileged users within the company, while others need to be available to the public. The ability to post a document to a public or internal Web site must be limited to those who can faithfully represent the organization's intent. To date, the security issue has been largely addressed by making the Web administrator the single point of contact for approving and posting site content, effectively creating a frustrating bottleneck.

Finally, while we may be able to access any document anywhere, the sheer proliferation of Web content has made searching for content something of a challenge. A simple entry in an Internet search engine for the keyword "Java" brings up thousands of sites containing information on programming languages, an Indonesian island, coffee, or a city in New York. The same search retrieves completely unrelated sites that use the word "Java" in their URL or in HTML source, but will not typically find Microsoft Word or Adobe Acrobat documents about Java. In searches limited to a single Web site, the search is often performed by examining file after file for the relevant keywords. When the site grows to hundreds or even thousands of files, search performance tends to degrade quickly.

Portal content areas offer a sharable, easy-to-maintain solution to these issues. With a simple create process, an administrator can build a structured repository that accepts, stores, organizes, and displays content in any browser-readable format. Content security is fully integrated with the Portal SSO security scheme, and permits a variety of privilege levels that determine who is allowed to view, submit, and approve content. The built-in search engine supplements simple keyword searches with information that identifies the expected audience and interest area of each document. Content areas can take full advantage of Oracle interMedia's document indexing capability to improve search performance and enable content-based, thematic searches.

When creating content, users can set an expiration date to automatically remove a document when its timeliness has passed, reducing the effort involved with keeping links up-to-date. Built-in auditing, versioning, and item checkout all facilitate change management and document history tracking. "Content" can be anything from files, links, and text to PL/SQL and Java programs, and it is all organized and secured in the same way regardless of content type. The framework is extensible, allowing you to create your own attributes and types to further customize the existing content types.

In this chapter, we'll start with a hypothetical example to illustrate basic content area concepts. We will then look at one of the content areas supplied with Oracle Portal to examine some techniques for content presentation. Finally, we'll apply this knowledge to build a content area for the eXYZ Corporation. Following these steps should help you gain both a theoretical and a practical familiarity with content areas that you can put to use in your own organization.

Fruits, Nuts, and Flakes: A Hypothetical Growers' Collective Site

This "nutty" example evolved from the notion that *categories* should be as distinct as "apples and oranges." Recently, we learned that a company named Agrifusion builds sites using Oracle Portal for growers' collectives to communicate agricultural and product information (see Appendix A for the URL). This bit of information proves the utility of Oracle Portal for such an application, but the discussion in this chapter is in no way related to the work being done by our colleagues at Agrifusion. Since fruits and vegetables are such a ubiquitous part of everyday life, the subject area just makes a good candidate for a generic discussion of Web content publishing.

Let's introduce the players in this hypothetical site (www.fruitsnutsflakes.org). This is an information portal, intended to be accessed by the general public, farmers, distributors, grocery operators, and representatives of the U.S. Department of Agriculture (USDA). The site allows for communication and sharing of information among the parties who are interested in fruits, nuts, and flakes. Most of the information on the site is not subject to security controls, but we take it as a given that some of the documents will be of interest only to a subset of the user population. Our task is to organize the site, using the content area framework, to be of maximum utility to each individual.

Content Submission and Folders

The first question we will ask is "How do we control the posting of information to the site?" We want the site to be a collaborative effort, but we do not want rogue users to post inflammatory documents about a particular kind of pest control method, for example, or to post something that impersonates an officially sanctioned document. Content area *folders* are the primary means to control content submission and approval privileges. They organize the site much like a directory structure, and each folder can be published as a portlet on a Portal page. If we have already created Portal groups to represent each of our constituencies, the next step is to create folders and determine the appropriate privileges for each folder. The available privileges, which can be granted to groups or individual users, are described below, from lowest to highest level:

View Content   Allows the named user or group to see and download individual items in the folder. Note that folders can be made public, which means that no login is required to view the folder content. View permission is not necessary for public folders, but it is used for nonpublic folders to ensure that only certain users can see the content. The View privilege is automatically granted with all of the other privileges. Users with only this privilege cannot submit any content and will not even see links suggesting that content may be edited.

Create with Approval   Allows the named user or group to add content to the folder, but these items are not published until a user with the Manage Items privilege approves them. A user must log in to create content. Items created by someone with this privilege are displayed in an area delimited by an "Items awaiting approval" banner and are visible only to the creator and to folder owners or managers. After approval, anyone with the correct privileges can view the item, but only a manager or owner can edit or delete the item.

Edit Style   Creates a folder style administrator, with permission to change only the colors and fonts used in the folder. This privilege is rarely used in sites seeking consistency, but is useful for sites that want to allow content folders to appear unique, perhaps to set each folder apart from the others. A separate privilege, Manage Style, can be granted on the content area (or all content areas) to allow an individual to change styles in any folder.

Manage Items   Creates a folder administrator. Users granted this privilege can approve content submissions and create content, but cannot alter security settings or folder properties. Manage Items also allows the grantee to delete and change existing items, and to manage versions.

Own Folder   Automatically given to the folder's creator, this is the highest privilege level. Folder owners can do everything described in the other privileges, and they have the additional ability to grant privileges to other users, and to edit the properties of the folder. There can be multiple owners of a folder, and ownership can be revoked just as the other privileges can. The content area administrator can prevent the folder owner from changing the folder's style.

NOTE
Any member of the Portal DBA group has full access to all folders, including create, delete, and ownership privileges.

A sample of the kinds of folders and privileges that we might create for such a site is depicted in Table 6-1. The table shows both primary folders and sub-folders, represented beneath their parent folder by indenting the sub-folder name. The *root folder*, which contains the entire content area, is not shown, as it is implicitly created when creating the content area. The root folder is public by default, but individual folders are not. We assume that the grower's collective, as the creator of the content area, owns all folders.

We've simplified matters a bit by only showing those groups that might have folder permissions, but it is more likely in a site like this that the management-level privileges would be assigned to specific users within each group. For example, USDA employees might all be granted the ability to create items with approval in

Folder	Public?	Group	Privilege Level
Official Announcements	Yes	USDA	Manage Items
Grant Applications	No	USDA	Manage Items
		Farmers	View Content
Growing Methods	Yes	USDA	Create with Approval
		Farmers	Create with Approval
Consumer Information	Yes	USDA	Create with Approval
		Grocers	Create with Approval
		Distributors	Create with Approval

TABLE 6-1.   *Sample Folder and Security Structure for www.fruitsnutsflakes.org*

the Official Announcements folder, but only one or two senior administrators would be given the ability to approve the submissions.

We created this content area with the above folders, accepting all of the defaults for style and item settings, so we could show how the concepts are implemented in the content area framework. Figure 6-1 shows the public view of the content area home page, and Figure 6-2 shows how it would look to a privileged user. Notice that in Figure 6-1, the nonpublic Grant Applications folder is not visible.

The folders we show here are all *container* folders; that is, they organize the content submission, approval, and security organization and hierarchy. Other types of folders, as you'll see later in this chapter, can be used to provide secure links on the home page or within another folder page to other types of content. For example, this site may require an auction application in addition to the user content. A PL/SQL or URL folder could serve this purpose well, by linking to an application written in PL/SQL (including Portal components) or Java. The benefit of using a folder to link to the application is that security is implemented in the same way as for container folders. The link will not display to users who are not allowed to participate in auctions, and the folder can be exposed as a portlet on a Portal page.

Personal Folders

If you want each of your users to have their own folder to store and share content, you can enable personal folders for all users, or you can create personal folders for individual users in the Portal User Profile portlet. All Portal users would then have a private content area for storing content that is unrelated to the main site. These folders are not displayed with regular folders, but can be published as portlets so

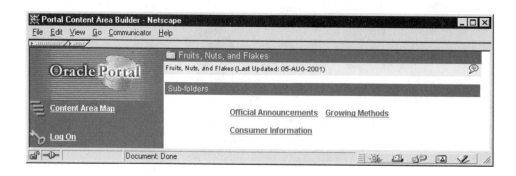

FIGURE 6-1. *Public view of www.fruitsnutsflakes.org*

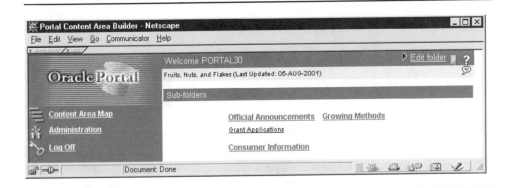

FIGURE 6-2. *Privileged view of www.fruitsnutsflakes.org*

users can easily work with their documents from a Portal page. In an intranet site, personal folders can be used like a "briefcase" to allow employees to access their work from any location.

A Portal administrator must enable personal folders using the Services portlet on the Portal Home Page Administer tab. In the Global Settings dialog, check the box labeled Create Personal Folders for New Users. All users created after this step will automatically get their own personal folder.

Categorization

While folders are primarily used to classify items according to privilege levels, *categories* evoke a broader classification scheme. Every item and folder can be assigned a category that describes a primary feature common to all members of the category. Categories span the entire content area, allowing a cross-typing or further refinement of content. They will subset the information in any given folder, to break up the folder's content into understandable divisions.

Categories represent "what" each document is about, and they work best when they are mutually exclusive. Because our site represents a variety of fruit and nut growers, users could potentially find hundreds of documents in each folder, of which only a few apply to their topic of interest. For example, most users will be interested in only one type of fruit during any given search, but the documents are created in folders that pertain more to ownership and less to the subject of the document. Because categories apply across all folders, a user can view information about "apples" in all folders or in a specific folder. The most obvious way to categorize this site is by type of fruit, nut, or flake. Categories can have sub-categories, allowing a hierarchical structure within the category framework. The following list shows the categories and sub-categories we have chosen for this site:

Fruits	**Nuts**	**Flakes**
Apples	Almonds	Bran
Oranges	Walnuts	Wheat
Pears	Macadamias	Barley
Kiwis		Corn

As items are created and assigned a category, the view of the content area begins to change. Each category is represented by a banner across the screen, delineating the items in each category. If an item is not assigned a category, it belongs to the General category, provided as part of the installation process. We added these categories to our hypothetical content area, and created a few items in each folder to show how the items will be displayed and organized by content area. Figure 6-3 shows the root folder with a few items added. The New icon is automatically displayed for a configurable time period.

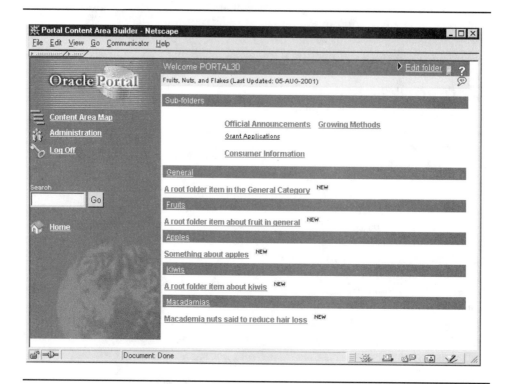

FIGURE 6-3. *The content area home page (root folder) with items added*

The interesting part begins when users start clicking on the category banners. It is the most natural thing (we assume) for a user who is interested in fruit, when presented with a link labeled "Fruits", to click on that link for more information. This switching back and forth is very useful for browsing: a user finds a folder of interest, and sees category banners. After seeing a category that may more closely represent the required content, the user can then click on the category name to view more items of that genre. Clicking on the Fruits link takes the user to a page populated by all of the items in the Fruits category, now subdivided by folder banners, as shown in Figure 6-4. Notice too that all of the sub-categories are clearly visible at the top, to allow for further investigation. The security settings continue to apply, and users will not see any folder banners for which they do not have at least View permission on the underlying folder.

Of course, it is often difficult to identify truly mutually exclusive categories. What if one of our farmers had identified a cultivation technique that works well for both apples and pears? The parent category, Fruit, could serve as a broader category, or we could create additional categories to represent common exceptions to the category structure. In this case, we could create an interim level of sub-categories to represent the general family of fruit that includes both apples and pears (using the scientific genus perhaps). The idea is to get the best division of content that also

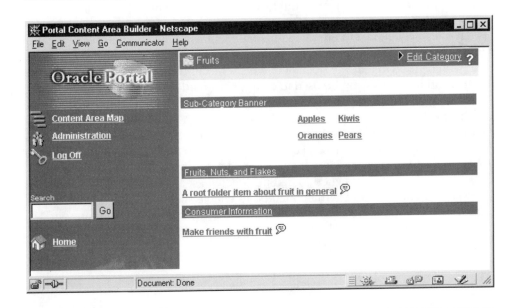

FIGURE 6-4. *The Fruits category page*

happens to correspond with the users' interest areas. Perspectives, discussed next, can serve to further classify content, and when all else fails, keywords can be used with each item to refine search criteria.

Perspective

Perspectives represent "who" might be interested in a particular item. In our example, a USDA agent might post an announcement that pertains to farmers, grocers, and the collective, or one that pertains only to farmers and the collective. Perspectives often mirror the groups set up for the user community, but not necessarily. They can serve to further refine the interest areas within each group, or to extend users' search capabilities. They have no security implications—documents assigned to a perspective are still subject to the security restrictions of the folder in which they are created. They are helpful on searches, however, as users can ask to view only documents in a particular perspective.

For example, within the group we have labeled "the public" for security reasons, there might be consumers, health care practitioners, and students interested in agriculture for research reasons. An item about nutrition might be interesting to all of these groups, but a medical alert describing diagnosis and treatment protocols for a food-borne illness would only be interesting to health professionals. Documents pertaining to pest control techniques might be of interest only to farmers and agriculture students, but anyone could view these documents if they wanted to.

Every item can have multiple perspectives, and another common use of perspectives is to indicate additional information about a document. Because perspectives can be configured to display an icon adjacent to every item containing that perspective, they can be used to indicate document type, for example, Microsoft Word or Adobe PDF. In addition, they can be used to create a standardized set of keywords, using often-queried or other subject-matter-specific words that help to indicate the nature of the document. For our site, some possible perspectives include organic farming, fertilizer, food storage tips, nutrition information, recipes, and distribution channels.

If used, the perspective icon(s) create a visual cue to the contents of the document. When a user clicks on the icon, they will see a page, much like the category page, that displays all items assigned to that perspective, separated by folder banners. Perspectives provide an alternate method to enable such browsing. Figure 6-5 shows the Consumer Information folder with perspectives added to represent student, health, organic, and buyer perspectives.

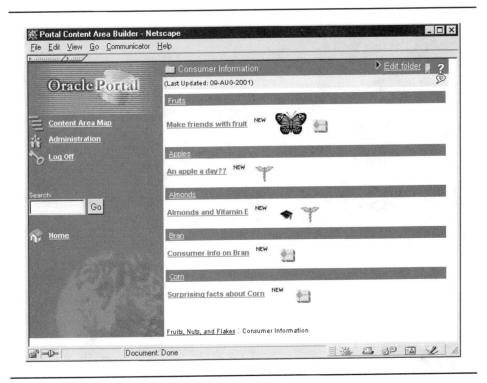

FIGURE 6-5.   *A content area folder showing perspective icons*

Figure 6-6 shows how the display changes when the user clicks on the health perspective.

Of course, perspectives do not have to have icons. The primary reason to use a perspective without an icon is to support perspective-based searches through the content area search facility. As you will see when you build a content area, you will also have the option of adding perspectives to the navigation bar, to make them more apparent to the end user.

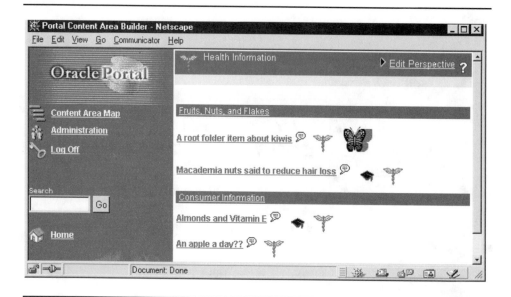

FIGURE 6-6. *The view from the Health perspective*

Screen Regions

A final way to differentiate items in a content area is to create them in a designated screen region, in order to highlight the importance or relevance of a particular item or set of items. Using a screen region is not a categorization technique, and an item's region does not affect searches in any way. Screen regions are used simply to position the content on the screen.

The default location for items is the Regular Items region, and all of our example content so far was created in this region. The list below describes the way each region is displayed by Portal when using the default style. We will show in a later section that the layout, location, and format properties of regions are configurable.

- **Quickpicks** Display at the top of the folder page, centered in two columns.

- **Announcements** Display below the Quickpicks, also centered but in a single column.

- **Sub-folders** Display below announcements, if any exist.

- **News Items** Display next and are left-justified, each on its own line.

- **Regular Items** Display in the main folder area separated by category banners.

NOTE
There is no way to create items in the Sub-folders region, as its purpose is to display the available sub-folders.

Figure 6-7 shows how our site would look after adding content to each of these regions. With the exception of increasing the number of columns in the Quickpicks region to four, so that all of the fruit icons would display on a single line, we left all of the default display settings for the regions. Notice that the News and Sub-folders

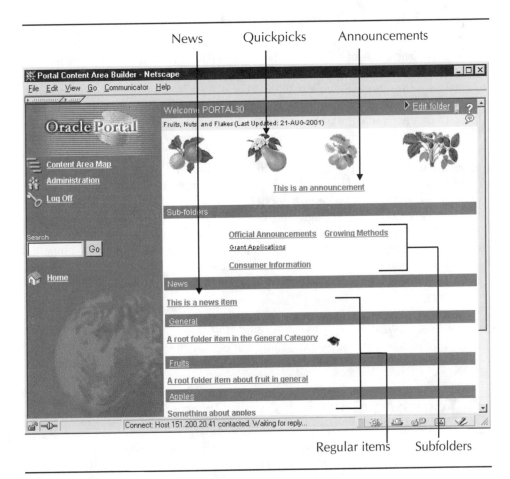

FIGURE 6-7. *Content regions help delineate content by importance*

regions have banners, but the other regions do not. The placement of the Quickpicks and Announcements regions at the top of the screen indicates their importance, making the banner unnecessary. If you prefer to have a banner for each region, you will be able add them when you configure the regions.

NOTE
Graphic icons courtesy of The Garden Link
(http://www.thegardenlink.com).

Using a Content Area

Now that we have introduced content areas from a theoretical point of view, we can show the practical side of how a content area is used. You will use this information as you build your content area and train your users.

In this section, we will work with the Oracle Portal Online Help system, because it is a complete content area with plenty of content available to illustrate our examples. It is part of any Oracle Portal install, and will be available if you completed the installation steps in Chapter 2. For this part of the chapter, you should be logged in as PORTAL30, so that you can see the full range of administrative functions available. If you are working in a production site and don't have access to the PORTAL30 schema, ask your site administrator to temporarily grant Administer privilege on the content area to PATM or your user account.

To access this built-in content area, go to the Content Areas tab of the Navigator. There you will see a list of content areas. Click on the Oracle Portal Online Help link (the name of the content area) and Portal will display the content area interface in the current browser window, as in Figure 6-8.

NOTE
You can also get to the content area by clicking on the large Help icon displayed in the upper right-hand corner of any Portal page. Doing this will display the help system in a separate browser window.

A Tour of a Content Area Page

Overall, this site is quite similar to our fruits, nuts, and flakes example. It has a navigation bar on the left and the content display area on the right. The appearance has been customized by adding graphics, custom links, and other elements, but otherwise this is a typical content area page. We will examine each element of the page to become familiar with some of the possibilities of a Portal content area.

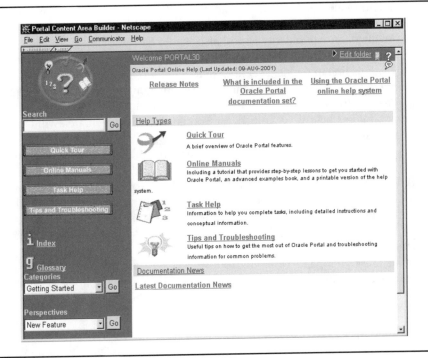

FIGURE 6-8. *The Oracle Portal Online Help system is a content area*

The designers of this site have substituted a custom image for the main content area logo, displayed at the top of the navigation bar. Below the image is the built-in search element, available on any navigation bar. There are four folder links, represented by the images below the search box (Quick Tour and so forth). The Index and Glossary elements are links to static HTML files installed in a directory mapped to /help on the Apache server. The available categories and perspectives have been exposed in combo boxes (drop-down lists) to help users jump directly to a category or perspective of interest. If you scroll down a little, you will see two more links: one to the Content Area Map and a second that reads "Send us your comments". The Content Area Map is a navigation bar element, provided by Portal, that constructs a hierarchical tree view of the content area folders. The "comments" link is another link to a static file in the /help virtual path.

The content display area shows a personalized banner across the top of the page, if you are logged in. (If you are not logged in, the banner displays the name of the folder and a folder icon, as you saw in Figure 6-1.) The personalized banner welcomes you by username, or by your full name if you have entered it in the

Account Information dialog (which is accessible from the content area Administration link or the Account Info link on a Portal page). If you have any privileges (other than View privilege) on the folder, you will also see an Edit Folder link. The Edit Folder link is the starting point for editing and managing all content in the content area—we will revisit this link in the next section. Below the top banner is a sub-banner with the name of the content area and the last date any content was changed. The rest of the page contains the regions we described earlier, with three Quickpicks at the top and regular items below. Of course, the contents of this screen area will change as you navigate the site.

The root folder for this content area shows two categories: Help Types and Documentation News. There are actually four sub-folders in the root folder, but the designers have chosen to hide them for aesthetic reasons. Instead, they created items (folder link items, to be specific) that would serve the same purpose. By choosing to display the sub-folder links as items, the designers replaced the formulaic and possibly meaningless "Sub-folders" banner with a more representative category banner. As you can see in Figure 6-8, the folder link items—Quick Tour, Online Manuals, Task Help, and Tips and Troubleshooting—are displayed with descriptive text and jazzy icons. This technique improves the appearance of the page and emphasizes the Help Types category as the focus of the page.

Exercise 6.1: Navigate the Online Help system

This exercise will give you the opportunity to become familiar with content area navigation and folder structure. You will also gain a comfort level with the help system, which should prove beneficial for future development work. If you haven't already done so, log in as PORTAL30 and navigate to the Oracle Portal Online Help content area as described earlier.

1. Click on the Task Help link. This page shows the usual display of folders and sub-folders, offering an organized, text-based list of tasks you might wish to accomplish in Portal. It displays two levels of sub-folders—the top level is indicated by the larger font and blue color, and the sub-folders of that level are in a smaller black font. Navigating to any folder will display its sub-folders and items, and clicking on any of these allows users to drill down further into the content area.

2. Now click on The Basics, to drill down one more level. In this folder view (shown in Figure 6-9), there are four sub-folders at the top, and the items belonging directly to The Basics folder are separated by category banners (Getting Started and Concepts). Notice the row of links at the bottom of the page. This list, shown in each folder below the root folder, provides a reference to your location in the folder structure. Clicking any of the links allows you to navigate up to any folder above the current one.

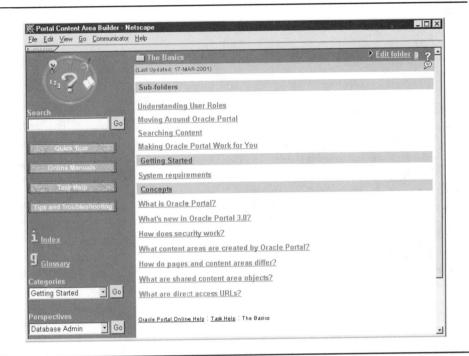

FIGURE 6-9.   *The Basics folder contains both sub-folders and items organized by category*

3. Click on a few of the items in this folder to see how the items are displayed. You will see that they are configured to open a new browser window for each item. To return to the content area, close the new window or navigate back to the window using ALT-TAB.

4. Click on the Oracle Portal Online Help link at the bottom of the page to return to the top level.

Searching and Navigation

If clicking on folder links were the only way to get to content, a Portal content area would not be very different from any other Web site. Content would tend to get lost deep in the folder hierarchy, and users would become frustrated with the number of actions they had to take to get to what they need. Fortunately, the content area provides the means to get to content from many angles, and you can incorporate any or all of these means into your content area, without a lot of programming or administrative effort. The content area automatically enables rich text, category, and perspective-based searching and navigation for your users. You do not have to build any search engines or document locator tools. You can optionally store searches, or you can allow users to create and save their own search mechanisms without having to build a single utility. We will examine each of these techniques from the user's point of view.

Categories and Perspectives

As we saw earlier, the Oracle Portal Online Help system incorporates drop-down lists on the navigation bar for both categories and perspectives. To go directly to a category or perspective page, users need only to select the category or perspective from the list and click the appropriate Go button. This technique exposes the category and perspective concepts at the first view of the page. We will show later how to substitute your own terminology for the list labels, in case the supplied terms don't make sense to your users.

The categories are designed with respect to the types of tasks you will perform in Portal. Not all documents are about tasks, so three additional categories were created to handle these other topics. The Getting Started category provides a category for introductory topics, Concepts suits documents that are not task-oriented, and a final category offers Examples. Category membership is reasonably clear and distinct. If a technical writer creates a document about how to do something in a page, that does not contain examples and is not conceptual or appropriate for first-time users, it goes in the Page Tasks category.

Notice, too, that the first category we saw, Help Types, is not displayed in the drop-down list. The content areas designers obviously felt that this category did not describe a topic area, so they chose not to display it in the drop-down. Its main purpose is to provide the banner on the main page that replaced the Sub-folders banner.

The perspectives mostly represent roles within the Portal user community, in keeping with the conventional definition. Some documents may apply to several user roles, and the notion of perspectives allows this, as a document may appear in many perspectives. One perspective, New Feature, is used to highlight items that may have been added since the last release, regardless of any other category or perspective membership. Adding this perspective allows a New icon to remain attached to the items permanently, or at least until the next release.

Content Area Map

A simple way to navigate the entire content area or view its structure is to use the Content Area Map, shown in Figure 6-10. This map will display all content areas containing public folders or folders on which you have permission. Folders and sub-folders will be displayed regardless of whether they were hidden in their parent folders. The Content Area Map is also the only way to access personal folders from the content area interface.

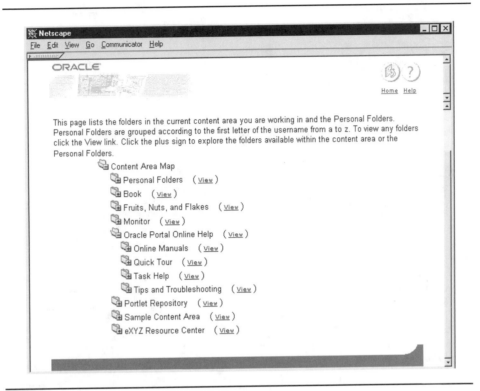

FIGURE 6-10.   *The Content Area Map page*

TIP
*Another way to access personal folders is to allow
users to publish them as portlets and add them to their
home page, using the customize link.*

Basic Search

The basic Search element appears on any navigation bar created by Portal (by default).
It is limited to text-based searching of item and folder titles, descriptions, and keywords.
If interMedia is enabled, the engine will also search the contents of each item,
regardless of document type. A basic search will find category and perspective titles
containing the search text, to provide the user with some alternate places to browse.
When a search completes, links to the items, folders, categories, and perspectives
that matched the search terms are displayed in an attractive tabbed browser window,
as in Figure 6-11.

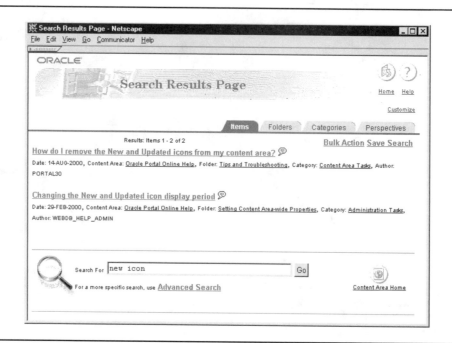

FIGURE 6-11. *The Search Results page displays after a search on "new icon"*

At the top of the page are links that offer two very convenient functions—Bulk Action and Save Search—described in the next few paragraphs. At the bottom of the page, you can execute a new search, go to the Advanced Search page, or return to the content area's home page. Advanced searches are the subject of the next section.

The Bulk Action link allows you to apply a mass change to the items returned by the search. This feature is invaluable when you realize that you need an additional category, folder, or perspective after the content area has been in use for some time. You can create the new classification, then use the search to find items that need to be moved or updated with the new category or perspective. Click on Bulk Action to display the page shown in Figure 6-12. To use this page, select all the items by checking the box next to Display Name or select individual items, then choose an action. You can delete the items, move or copy them to another folder, or click Attributes to change their category or perspective settings.

The Save Search link lets users store their search criteria for future execution, so that they can get current results of their favorite searches at any time. After clicking Save Search, the user gives the search a name and returns to the Search Results page. To reference saved searches later, the Saved Searches portlet must be available on the user's home page. Like many of the built-in portlets, Saved Searches is sensitive to the login name, and only displays the searches saved by the currently connected user.

FIGURE 6-12.   *The Bulk Actions page lets you make changes to many items at once*

Advanced Search

As users become more comfortable with the content area interface and develop an understanding of categories, perspectives, and folders, they will tend to find the Advanced Search utility increasingly useful. In addition, as the content area becomes more successful and thus more heavily populated, the sheer volume of content will make more precise search options necessary. Users can get to the Advanced Search utility from the Search Results page (see Figure 6-13), or you can add it to the navigation bar so they can get there directly.

As you can see in Figure 6-13, the Advanced Search page allows you to search by keyword, content area, folder, language, category, perspective, or any combination of those. If you want the sub-folders to be searched, check the Include Sub-folders check box. You can elect to return only items of a particular type, only folders, or all matches regardless of object type. You can also search on built-in or custom item attributes, using a `Contains`, `Greater Than`, `Less Than`, or `Equals to` operator. The built-in attributes include such descriptors as the item's author or creator, creation or expiration date, description, image name, and keywords. When you search on attributes or keywords, you have the choice to require a match on all specified conditions or to return documents matching at least one condition (Any). Provided on the page is a Search Tips link, which offers help on searching, and a link back to the Basic Search, in case the Advanced Search is no longer necessary.

You can save advanced searches in the same way that you saved a simple search, and display links to your saved searches on the Portal home page. If you want the saved search to be available to all users, you must create it as a search folder, described in a later section. You can also customize the navigation bar so that it will display links to your search folders.

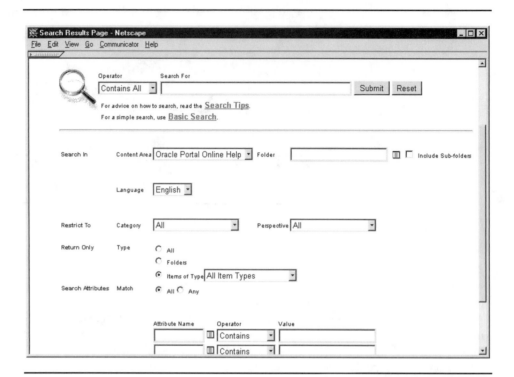

FIGURE 6-13. *The Advanced Search page allows for highly customizable searches*

Exercise 6.2: Getting Around in a Content Area

In this exercise, you will put the search and navigation techniques covered in this section to use. We will continue to use the Oracle Portal Online Help system, so you can get a feel for all of the navigation options. The steps are intended to show each navigation technique—you don't have to follow them directly, and feel free to browse the content at will, and view any items of interest.

1. Using the Categories drop-down list on the bottom left of the screen (on the navigation bar), choose the Administration Tasks category and click Go. The banner at the top of the screen now represents the category title rather than a folder title, and all of the items listed belong to that category.

2. Click the Next 20 Items link at the bottom of the page to browse the Administration Tasks category.

3. Click the Monitoring Oracle Portal banner (which should be in the second set of 20 items) to view the contents of that folder. Click the Concepts banner to view the Concepts category.

4. Now select the Authorized User perspective from the Perspectives drop-down list. Browse this content using the Next 20 Items link.

5. Look for the Building and Customizing Pages banner on the second page. Click the New icon next to the item named "Adding your personal folder to a page". You are now in the New Feature perspective page.

6. Click the Content Area Map link on the navigation bar. Expand the Personal Folders node by clicking on the small gray "+" button by the folder icon. Expand the "p" node to see the personal folders for PORTAL30 and PORTAL30_ADMIN.

7. Navigate to PORTAL30's personal folder by clicking the View link. We will see how to add items using the Edit Folder link in the next section.

8. Try a basic search. Type content in the Search field and view the results of your search. Review the search results for Items, Folders, Categories and Perspectives by clicking on the corresponding tab. Notice that your search has returned results from all content areas. This happens because you initiated your search from the navigation bar on your personal folder, which is not associated with any content area.

9. Find a link on the page to the Oracle Portal Online Help content area (there are several) and click it to go back to the help system home page. Reenter your search on content and click Go. The search results are now limited to the Oracle Portal Online Help content area.

10. Click the Advanced Search link at the bottom of the page. Search for content again, but this time limit your search to the Concepts category and the Content Contributor perspective.

11. On the Search Results Page, click Save Search and give the search a name of Content Area Concepts.

12. To see how the saved search works, return to the Portal Home Page by clicking the Home link. Find the eXYZ Home Page in the Navigator or Portal Home Page and view the page. Notice that the Saved Searches portlet on the My eXYZ tab now has your saved search in it, as you can see in Figure 6-14. Click the link to return to the Search Results page.

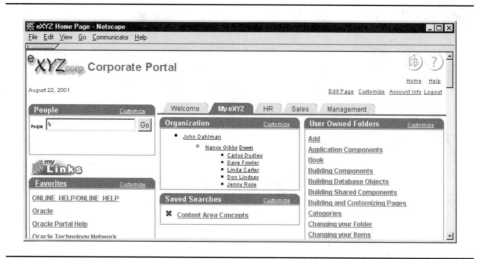

FIGURE 6-14. *The Saved Searches portlet links to searches that you have created*

The eXYZ Home Page's My eXYZ tab will resemble Figure 6-14 when this exercise is complete. The User Owned Folders portlet should make a little more sense at this point, as it lists all of the content area folders created by the current user. Since PORTAL30 owns most of the folders in the content area, its list of folders is quite long.

Edit Mode

Most of the screens you have seen so far in this chapter have a link in the upper right-hand corner labeled Edit Folder (Edit Category or Edit Perspective on the category and perspective pages). Clicking this link puts the page in edit mode, which allows you to add, edit, or delete content, and change the properties of the folder, navigation bar, or content area. Figure 6-15 shows the Edit Folder view of the Oracle Portal Online Help system for the PORTAL30 user. Other users may see fewer options in edit mode, as the page will only display icons and links for actions you have privileges to perform.

The view changes significantly and now displays *dashboards* above the page banner and navigation bar. The dashboard provides links to general actions at the folder or navigation bar level. The Edit Folder link has changed to View Folder, which returns you to the view mode for the page.

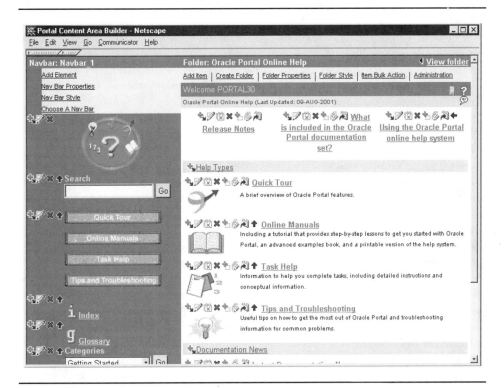

FIGURE 6-15.   *The Oracle Portal Online Help system in edit mode*

Navigation Bar Dashboard

The navigation bar dashboard allows you to modify the navigation bar from within the content area interface. Clicking Add Element brings up the Navigation Bar Element wizard, which will allow you to add an element to the bottom of the navigation bar. (To add an element to another location on the navigation bar, use the Add Element icon at the place where the new element will go.) The Nav Bar Properties link takes you directly to the full properties page for the navigation bar, where you can set general properties, change the style, or add new elements. Nav Bar Style lets you modify only the style, and Choose a Nav Bar lets you substitute a completely different navigation bar for the current page. All of these choices are available in the Portal Navigator container for navigation bars, and we will illustrate the process of building and customizing navigation bars in a later section.

Folder Display Area

On the folder side, the dashboard lets you add items, create sub-folders, modify the properties or just the style of the current folder, perform bulk actions on the contents of the folder, and navigate to the Administration page. Adding an item using the Add Item link in the dashboard adds the item "generically"—that is, you have full control over the screen region and category. This is a little different from the Add Item icon, which will create the item in the region or category where the icon was clicked. The folder utilities in the dashboard link to the same property pages you would see if you created or edited the folders in the Navigator, which you will do when you create your content area in the next section. The Item Bulk Action link takes you to a screen like the bulk action screen you saw in the Search Results page, but now the action applies to the items in the current folder.

Administration Page   The Administration page, shown in Figure 6-16, links to all of the Navigator utilities for managing styles, categories, perspectives, and so on. It is divided into sections named Content Area Managers, Content Managers, and Personal Information. The sections displayed depend on the current user's privileges— for example, end users will only see the Personal Information section, which allows them to update their information and change their password. Within each section are links to either the Navigator pane or the property page for each of the content area objects. This page is provided as a convenience, so content area administrators can easily navigate to the tools they need without having to leave the content area interface. If you are only using the content area interface, and not portal-style pages, you will need this link to let users set and reset their passwords.

Editing Items

All of the items now display icons that allow items to be edited, expired, deleted, moved, copied and added. Table 6-2 explains each of these icons.

Versions   When enabled, the Portal versioning system stores multiple copies of a versioned item. If an item has more than one version, the Versions icon will appear, allowing users to browse the properties of each version and to reset the item to a prior version. The versions browser for a Fruits, Nuts, and Flakes item is shown in Figure 6-17. To examine the changes between versions, click the Property Sheet icon. You will be able to see who created the new version, and all of the properties of each version. Be careful not to edit the properties here, though, as you will only

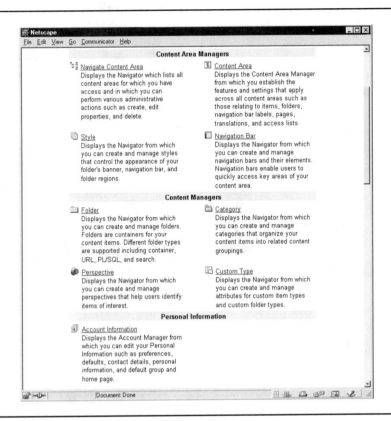

FIGURE 6-16. *The Administration page lets you link to all of the possible content area utilities*

create a new version of the item. As in the content display area, clicking the item's name here displays the item.

We won't offer an exercise just yet for adding or modifying content, because we don't want to alter the online help system. In the next few sections, you will create a content area for eXYZ Corporation, create and modify folders, and then work with a variety of content types.

Icon	Name	Description
	Add item (or element)	Adds an item or navigation bar element. Items added using the icon automatically adopt the properties of the screen region where the icon was displayed.
	Edit	Modify the properties of the item or element.
	Expire	Cause the item to expire immediately.
	Delete	Remove the item from the content area or the element from the navigation bar.
	Add a subitem	Add a subitem, to create a hierarchical structure of related items.
	Copy	Copy an item to another folder, optionally specifying a new category.
	Move to another folder	Move an item to another folder.
	Move Up	Move the item or element within a screen region to change the display order.

The following icons are only displayed when the corresponding features have been enabled.

Icon	Name	Description
	Check-out	Check out an item to prevent others from changing it while you are working on it.
	Versions	Brings up the list of versions, which allows you to revert to an earlier version or delete old versions.
	Undelete	Restore a deleted item—only available if you have set up the content area to retain deleted items.

TABLE 6-2.   *The Edit Folder icons*

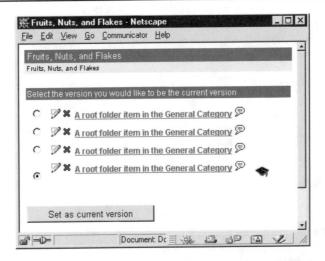

FIGURE 6-17.   *The versions browser lets you choose the current version and delete old versions*

Creating Content Areas

With a conceptual foundation in place, we can now look at the mechanics of creating a Portal content area. eXYZ Corporation will use this content area to make internal documents, forms, and other modes of communication available to the appropriate personnel. It will use the built-in search and classification facilities we've discussed, and will be flexible enough to allow the company to gradually move away from the paper-based systems in place now to a more Web-oriented system for internal communication.

There isn't much to say about creating a content area—it is simply a matter of giving it a name. However, a content area has many properties that customize how users will interact with it, and it will contain the folders, categories, and perspectives discussed in the introductory section. We'll begin by creating the content area for eXYZ Corporation, then we will review its properties in detail. You should be logged in as PATM for this and the remaining exercises.

Exercise 6.3: Create the eXYZ Content Area

1. In the Portal Navigator, go to the Content Areas tab and click the Create New ... Content Area link at the top of the page.

2. Name the content area EXYZ_RESOURCES and give it a Display Name of eXYZ Resource Center.

3. Click the Create button.

4. That's it! You have created a content area. You are now presented with the option to create another content area, or to "Click on eXYZ Resource Center to edit the content area". Clicking on this link will display a set of tabs you will use to customize the content area. We will discuss these in the next section, but for now, you probably would like to see what you created.

5. Close the content area wizard page and return to the Navigator. You should see the new content area in the list. Click its name, and you will see the empty content area, ready for customization.

Content Area Properties

Had you clicked the content area name just after creating it, you would have seen the content area properties page. You can get to this page from the Navigator by clicking Edit Properties next to the content area name, or from the Administration page for this content area by clicking the Content Area link. The Edit Content Area tab pages allow you to manipulate properties that control the high-level settings of the content area and provide a place to set defaults for many of the folder properties. The high-level settings are mostly administrative—they control such things as storage, caching, versioning, terminology, and granting administrative access to others. The following sections describe the properties in detail.

Main

The Main tab contains the basic information that you entered when creating the content area, and some general content area settings. In addition, it allows you to specify the email address of the content area administrator. This email address is displayed on all pages as a `mailto` link, and allows users to easily contact the administrator. It can be overridden at the folder level, making it very easy to distribute the "webmaster" responsibility to the people closest to the content.

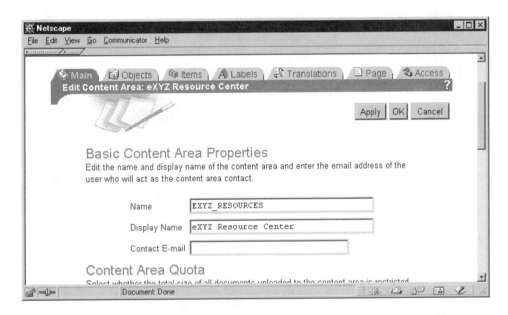

Content Area Quota   The Content Area Quota section allows you to set the maximum size of the content stored within the content area. The option of setting a quota is not available to PATM. Because this option affects database storage, it is only accessible to a user with DBA privilege, or a user with Manage privilege on all content areas. The default quota is unlimited, and this is fine for our purposes, but if you need to limit the space used by a content area, you will need to log in as a DBA. You will then have a choice between keeping the quota unlimited or setting a quota (in megabytes). The illustration on the following page shows how the Content Area Quota section would look to a DBA.

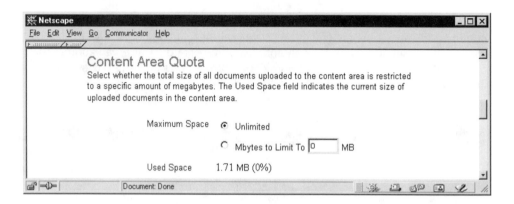

Folder Properties   The Folder Properties section is where you will specify whether individual folder owners can control the style of the folder. Allowing folder owners to control the style creates a risk to the content area's consistency. It is only useful when the folders are relatively independent of one another and you would like each folder to appear personalized or unique to the folder's subject area.

This section also allows you to control how folders are cached. If you would like to use caching for any of the folders within the content area, you must enable it here. Caching can be disabled for individual folders containing rapidly changing content. Portal content area caching is both expiration- and validation-based. By default, caching is enabled and the cache is retained for 24 hours, which means that the cached version will expire at least every 24 hours. Folders that have not changed will always be served from this cache, but the cache is automatically invalidated when content is added, changed, or removed. Enabling folder caching for a folder that is constantly changing creates additional overhead, because each change requires writing the revised folder page to the cache. For most folders, the benefit of caching outweighs the potential performance penalty, because there is no risk to currency.

Content Area Logo   Finally, you will specify the content area logo. The content area logo is optionally displayed in the navigation bar. It should be an image that represents the entire site, as its position lends itself to "branding."

Objects

The Objects tab is used to restrict the types of objects that users can see or create in the content area. You may limit the displayed perspectives or categories to a subset of the available perspectives or categories. This is particularly useful if there are perspectives or categories in the Shared Objects content area that are not appropriate to the current content area. (As you saw in Chapter 3, the Shared Objects content area allows you to create global objects accessible to all content areas.) You may also limit the kinds of items and folders that the content area will accept. For example, if you do not want anyone creating PL/SQL folders, you will remove that from the Visible Folder Types list.

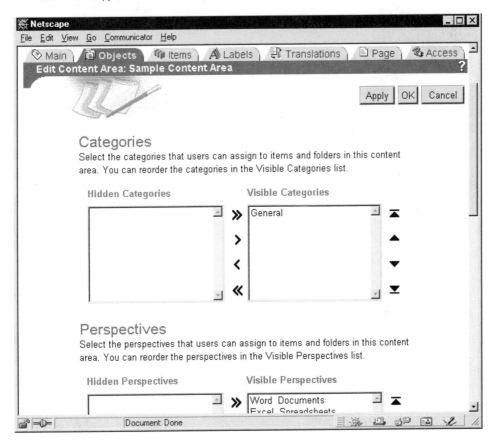

Items

The Items tab provides options for handling item versions, deleting items, and handling new or expired content. It is both a configuration tool and a maintenance utility, and you will periodically revisit this tab to remove outdated content.

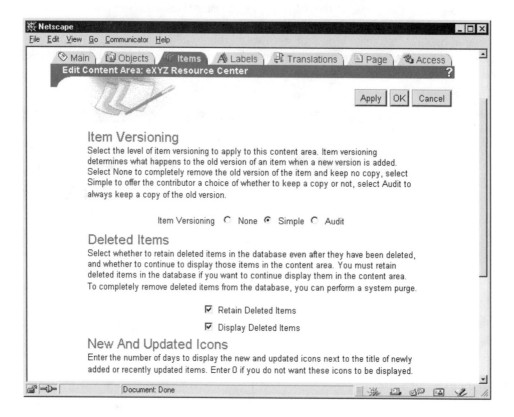

Item Versioning   Sometimes you may need to track changes to a document over time, keeping information about who made changes, when the changes were made, and what each version of the item contained. You may have strict requirements, needing to track "who, what, and when" for all documents, or you may just need to store prior versions of a few documents for historical purposes. Portal versioning simply stores a new copy of an item each time any property is changed, rather than tracking the actual changes.

Portal provides three levels of item versioning: None, Simple, and Audit. None implies there will be no versioning, and will not allow users to create multiple versions of any item. This is, of course, the fastest and the easiest method to manage, because there is no need to track prior versions or identify the current version when retrieving content from the database. Simple versioning makes the version process optional. When editing an item, the user has the choice to just replace the item with the changed version or to create a new version of the item. This option is likely to be the most useful for many organizations, since it allows users to keep history for the more important documents without wasting storage for trivial changes. The key to successfully using simple versioning is educating users about which items and changes require version history and which do not. Audit versioning keeps a history of all changes to all items, so that when a user edits an item, a new version is always created. Some additional site management may be required if you use versioning, as prior versions of documents remain until they are manually removed. As long as the prior versions exist, you can revert to those versions if necessary.

The level of versioning set for the content area can be increased for individual folders and sub-folders, but never decreased. For example, if versioning is set to None at the content area level, owners of sub-folders can upgrade the versioning to Simple or Audit. A sub-folder can never have less auditing than its parent folder, so if the content area uses simple versioning, auditing cannot be removed at the sub-folder level. Setting the versioning at the content area has essentially the same effect as setting it in the root folder's properties.

Deleted Items   To make it easier to recover from accidental deletes, you may wish to keep deleted items around until an administrator performs a system purge, as explained shortly. If so, you will check the Retain Deleted Items check box in this section. If you do retain deleted items, you need to decide whether they should be displayed to end users. Deleted items will always be visible to the folder owner or anyone with Manage privilege on the folder, but they display with the word "Deleted" shown in red. Additionally, the Undelete icon (shown in Table 6-2) appears, allowing users with appropriate privileges to recover the item. If you want logged-in users to see the deleted items as well, check the Display Deleted Items check box. Deleted items only display in the edit view of the folder, so this setting applies only to logged-in users, and never to public users.

CAUTION
Whether you elect to retain deleted items or not, deleting a folder permanently deletes all of the folder's content, with no possibility for "undelete."

New and Updated Icons   Portal automatically displays a New icon to highlight recently added items. Set the number of days that this icon will display, or to disable this feature altogether, set the Icon Display Period to 0. An Updated icon is also available, subject to the same time limitation, but it is not displayed by default. To show the Updated icon, you will need to edit the region's properties in the style editor. A later section on content area styles offers more detail on this subject.

System Purge   System purge (found at the bottom of the Items tab) is a maintenance feature that you should plan to use from time to time to prevent the content area from using excessive storage space in the database. With a single click, you can remove all of the deleted and/or expired items in the content area. If you have elected not to retain deleted items, a purge will only affect items that have expired. The expiration date is set when creating items, and helps to keep the system free of outdated content, such as announcements for events that have already occurred. Users can also manually expire items at any time. Expired items can be purged here en masse or manually deleted one at a time in the folder's edit view.

Labels

As we discussed in Chapter 4, the value of terminology cannot be underestimated— it may make the difference between user acceptance and rejection of the site. On the Labels tab, you can supply your own terms for some of the standard features of a content area. If your users prefer "Connect/Disconnect" to "Log On/Log Off", "Webmaster:" to "Contact:", or other familiar terms for standard features, substitute that text here. Most of the custom labels apply to navigation bar elements. When you design the navigation bar in a later step, you will choose whether to use an element; here you will only set the text and/or icon to display when the element is used. Several elements allow an icon, and you can either remove the icon entirely or replace it with one that is consistent with your site design.

The two labels that do not apply to navigation bar elements are the Sub- Category Banner and the Sub-Perspective Banner. These display only on the category or perspective page view, if sub-categories or sub-perspectives exist (as in Figure 6-4). If you have chosen another term for categories or perspectives, you would want to ensure that the sub-banner is consistent. For example, if you are referring to categories as "Focus Areas", your sub-category banner might read "Sub-Focus Areas" or "Focus Area Specifics."

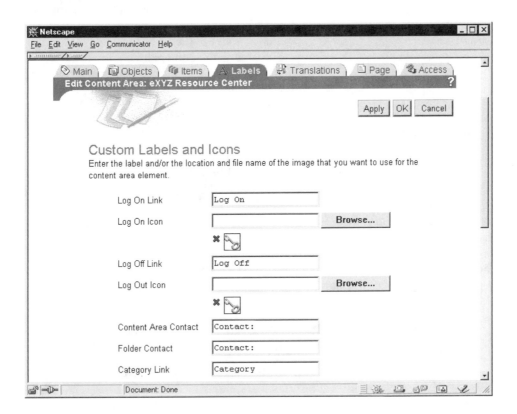

Translations

The Translations tab allows you to build the content area in more than one language. This powerful feature means that each item can have multiple versions, one for each supported language. When users access the content area, Portal checks the browser's language setting and displays the items in the correct language, if enabled. New items are tagged with the language given by the creator's browser setting. You may add translated names for categories, perspectives, folder names, and labels in each supported language. To enable translations, you must install the message files, using the `langinst.cmd` script (`langinst.csh` for UNIX users) found in the `<IAS_HOME/portal30/admin/plsql>` directory, for each language that you will use in the content area. Then use this tab to make the language(s) available to the content area. While you are in the process of creating the translated content, you may wish to restrict access to the translation; use the Edit Translation section to mark a translation as online or only accessible to the content area administrator(s).

To remove a translation, use this tab. Deleting any language version of a category, perspective, folder, or item will remove *all* translations of the object, removing it entirely from the content area.

Page

When you create a content area, a page is automatically created to display the content in the default arrangement (navigation bar on the left and the content display area on the right). This page is essentially the same as the Portal pages you saw in Chapter 3, but is not managed under the Pages tab in the Navigator. You can edit this page only from within the content area properties editor, but you have the same abilities to add portlets and rearrange regions as you do in any Portal page. You could, for example, move the navigation bar to the top or right side of the page, and add custom portlets to the content area. To create a new content area page, enter a Name and Display Name, and click Create. The new page is automatically laid out with the navigation bar and content regions.

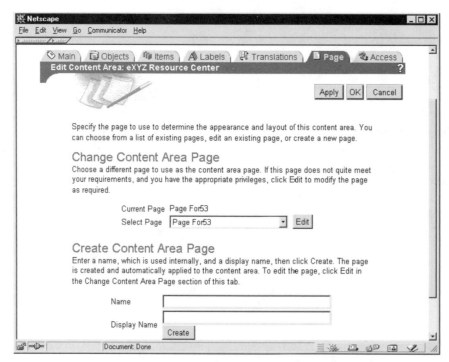

Access

The Access tab for the content area allows you to create content area administrators. Do not use this tab for content security, only to create a backup administrator. Administrators have full privileges on the content area, and can change all properties, and access and manage all content. Manage Style allows the grantee to change and apply styles to folders, and Make Public allows the user to modify any style or navigation bar so that it is visible to other users and other content areas.

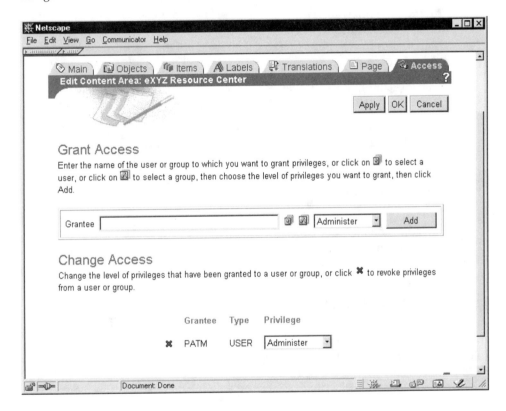

Exercise 6.4: Customize Content Area Properties

Navigate to the properties page for the eXYZ Resource Center to begin this exercise. You may find it helpful to edit the properties from within the Navigator, and keep a separate window open to show the content area home page, so you can easily reload the page to see the effects of your changes.

1. In the Basic Content Area Properties section of the Main tab, enter patm@exyz.com for the Contact E-mail field.

2. In the Folder Properties section, uncheck the box labeled Enable Folder Owners to Control Style. This content area should have a consistent user interface.

3. Replace the Content Area Logo with the logo provided on the distribution (`exyzlogo.jpg`) and click Apply at the top of the page.

4. Skip the Objects tab, so that all categories, perspectives, and item types will be available.

5. On the Items tab, set the Versioning to Simple and leave the remaining defaults.

6. On the Labels tab, change the label for Content Area Contact to `Please direct technical inquiries to:`, for Folder Contact to `Questions about the contents of this page? Contact:`, and for Content Area Map to `Resource Center Map`. Remove all of the icons by clicking the red X by each one.

7. Skip the Translations tab unless you have more than one language installed. If you do, create a translation for all the languages you will use on the site.

8. We will create a style administrator for our content area, so that changes to the look and feel can be accomplished without the need for developers. Click the Access tab and select `GAYLED` from the Browse Users list associated with the Grantee field. Choose `Manage Style` from the drop-down list of privileges and click Add.

9. We won't modify any of the remaining properties, so click OK and return to the content area home page. It should look like the image in Figure 6-18. The style and navigation bar aren't how we would have them in the finished site, but we will improve those in a later exercise.

Folder Properties

All content areas are automatically created with a root folder, the container folder that will hold the rest of the content area. The properties you can set for the root folder are the same as for other container folders, but the root folder has the distinction of being the "home page" for the content area. Any folders subsequently created in the content area will automatically inherit its properties. These properties

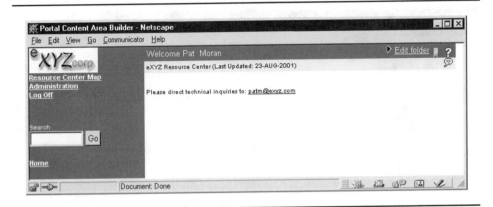

FIGURE 6-18. *The customized eXYZ content area*

can be overridden for lower-level folders, and their sub-folders will inherit the
revised properties. To modify the root folder properties, click on Edit Root Folder
next to the content area's name in the top level of the Navigator Content Areas tab,
or click Folder Properties in the edit view of the main content area page.

In this section, we will discuss each of the tabs in the Folder Properties page.
These properties apply to all folders, but our site contains only the root folder at this
point. Refer back to this section as necessary when you create lower-level folders in
your content area.

Required

The Folder Properties section of the Required tab simply reflects the basic properties
set when the folder was created. The root folder was created automatically—its name,
display name, and description default to the names derived from the content area,
and the Category field always defaults to the General category. You may change the
name or display name, but this shouldn't be necessary if you chose appropriate
names for the content area.

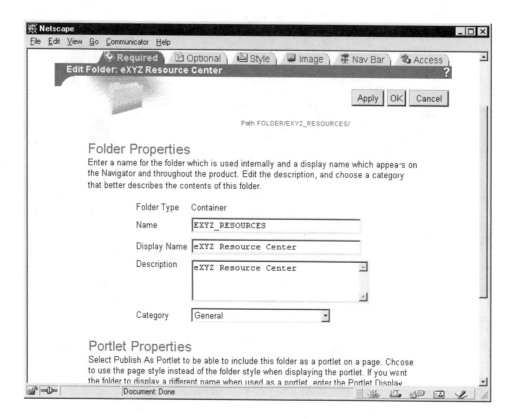

Use the Portlet Properties section to make the folder available as a portlet to any Portal page. You can make any folder available as a portlet; publishing the root folder makes the entire content area accessible in the Portal page. Depending on the context, you may wish to only make individual sub-folders available as portlets. When users navigate into sub-folders, the portlet interface is preserved, but they can also navigate to the content area home page by clicking on the portlet title. If you do publish the folder as a portlet, you can optionally allow the page style to override the content area style, so user pages appear consistent. Use the Portlet Display Name field to specify a different title to use when displaying the folder in a Portal page.

Optional

The Optional tab allows you to control the item versioning level, override the contact email, and enable or disable caching for an individual folder. As we discussed in the section on content area properties, each of these is initiated at the content area level, but can be changed on a folder-by-folder basis.

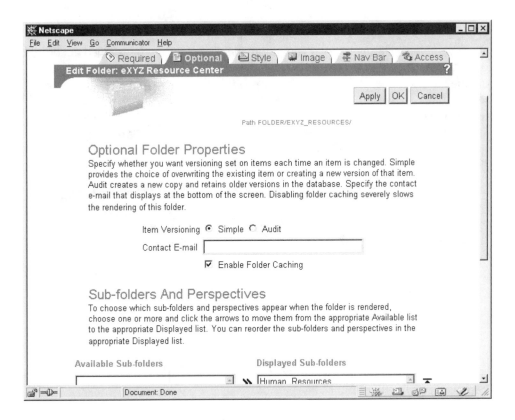

Further down on the same tab, the Sub-Folders And Perspectives section shows a pair of select lists that allow you to hide sub-folders from the main folder display. All folders are initially displayed when created—to hide a folder after creating it, edit the properties for the parent folder and move it from the Displayed Sub-folders list to the Available Sub-folders list. Hiding folders eliminates the sub-folders banner and sub-folder list at the top of the folder page, as you saw in the Oracle Portal Online Help content area. You can also use the Displayed Sub-folders list to change the display order of sub-folders—just move the folders up and down within the list.

While the Available Perspectives and Displayed Perspectives lists are in the same section, they have a slightly different meaning. Folders can have perspectives, just as items can. Moving a perspective into the Displayed Perspectives list assigns that perspective to the folder. Folders do not display perspective icons as items do, but the folder will be retrieved in perspective-based searches. Our content area has no sub-folders or perspectives yet.

Style

When you create a content area, you automatically get two styles, named according to the content area name. (The folder style has the same name as the content area, and the navigation bar style is the content area name with "Navbar Style" appended.) On the folder's Style tab, you will be selecting and/or editing the style to apply to the content display area—we will look at the navigation bar style in a later section. As with page styles, editing the style will affect all folders that use that style. Any new folders you create inherit the style of the root folder, but you can override this inheritance and each folder can have a different style, if desired.

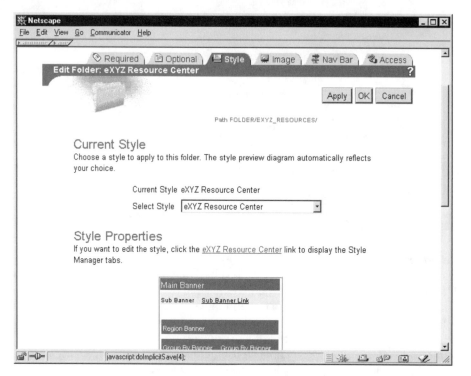

The Current Style section of the Style tab shows the currently selected style and allows the option to select another style. When you choose a style, the preview shown in the Style Properties section will change to reflect the properties of the new style. To edit a style, click the style name link in the Style Properties section, and Portal will display the content area style editor. See the section on content area styles for more information on the style editor.

Image

You may specify up to three images, to be used in different contexts, for each folder. The title and rollover images are only used when a folder link is placed on a navigation bar. As the name implies, the rollover image is shown when the user's mouse "rolls over" the title image. Portal supplies the JavaScript to make this happen. The banner image is displayed at the top of the page, just below the banner, when the user is viewing a folder page. The banner image does not appear in the portlet view.

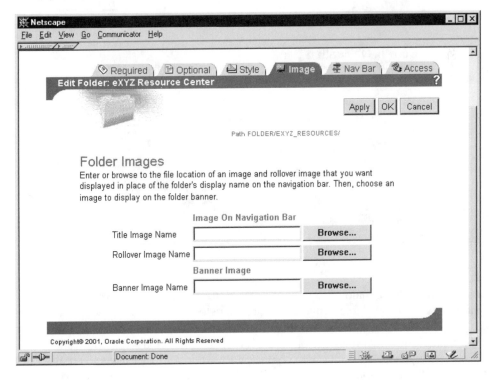

Nav Bar

As with styles, Portal creates a default navigation bar when you create the content area, and allows you to choose a different navigation bar, edit the default navigation bar, or create a new navigation bar from the Nav Bar tab. You can also create or edit navigation bars from the Navigator, and we will devote an entire section to navigation bar design. Each folder can have its own navigation bar. At first glance, this might seem a good way to disorient users, but the ability to switch navigation bars for individual folders allows you to supply folder-specific text, links, and graphics on each folder page.

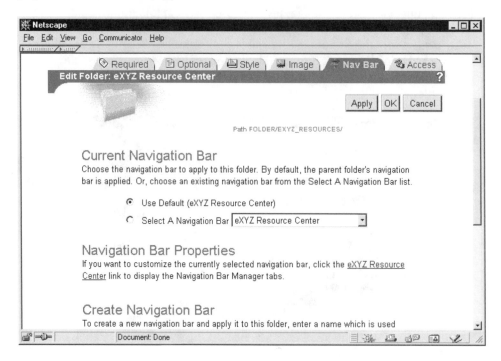

Access

As we have seen, a major design consideration for folders is security. Some folders must be publicly available, while others are restricted to a particular user population. You may have "power users" who can create content in some areas, subject to the approval of the folder manager or a designated content manager. If you wanted to create a truly dynamic public interchange, you would allow all users to create content without an approval cycle. Finally, you may wish to allow certain individuals the ability to change the appearance of the folder without modifying the content. By default, all of these security controls apply at the folder level, and all items within a folder inherit the folder's security scheme. Each folder has its own access list, which can be cascaded to sub-folders as needed.

If you are not concerned about security, or do not wish to force your users to log in simply to view content, you can make a folder public. This means that all items in the folder can be viewed by anyone with access to the site, even users without a Portal account. Creating or modifying content in any folder always requires a valid logon, regardless of whether the folder is public. Folders that have not been made public can only be viewed by valid, logged-in users with at least View privilege for the folder.

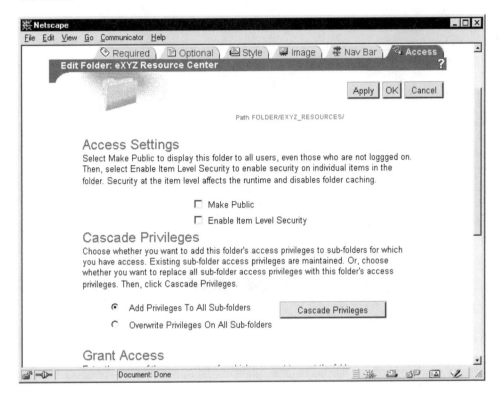

To override folder-level security and create access lists on an item-by-item basis, check the box labeled Enable Item Level Security.

NOTE

Avoid using item-level security if possible. Item-level security requires a check against a security table for each item displayed in the folder, which could cause the folder to render slowly. It will also disable the folder content cache, because each user's view of the folder may differ. In addition, maintaining access lists for individual items could become dreadfully complicated.

Cascade Privileges   When you change privilege settings for a folder, you have the option to cascade the new settings to lower-level folders. This option is provided for convenience so that you may easily add groups or alter privileges after folders have been created. There are two methods to cascade privileges to sub-folders: Add and Overwrite. Add copies any new privileges to sub-folders without disturbing any existing access lists, while Overwrite removes the existing access lists and replaces them with the settings for the current folder. You must use the overwrite method to cascade any operation that revokes privileges from groups or individuals.

Grant Access   The Grant Access section works the same as the Access tab for a page or application, but the available privileges differ. You will select a user or group from the list in the Grant Access section, then check the check boxes to assign privileges. Be sure to click Apply after each change. The list of users comes from the main list of users for the Portal site, so content area users must first be Portal users. The available security levels were described in detail in the "Content Submission and Folders" section at the beginning of this chapter.

This completes our tour of the available folder properties. Next, we'll begin creating folders in the eXYZ Resource Center content area.

Exercise 6.4: Root Folder Properties

Most of the default root folder properties will work well for our site. We only need to ensure that the security settings are correct. For now, we don't want the content area to be viewed by anyone other than employees with a valid user ID, so we will make the root folder nonpublic. We can always change this later if we decide to produce some extranet or Internet content. Start this exercise from the root folder properties page, which you can reach from the Navigator by clicking Edit Root Folder by the content area name, or by clicking Folder Properties from the content area dashboard.

1. On the Access tab, uncheck the box labeled Make Public and click Apply.

2. In the Grant Access section, select AUTHENTICATED_USERS from the Browse Groups list and click Add to Access List. By default, this group will be given View Content privilege on the root folder. This is fine for our purposes—we will grant additional privileges to other groups on lower-level folders.

3. Click OK to close the root folder properties page.

Creating Folders

Portal offers four kinds of folders in which to display your content. The most-used folder type in any content area is likely to be a container folder, as we have seen in the previous examples. The earlier discussions of items, versions, and privileges apply mostly to container folders. This is the only kind of folder that can contain items and sub-folders, and that can accept content submissions from end users. The other types—URL, Search, and PL/SQL folders—are used primarily to mimic folder behavior while showing custom content. This section gives a brief overview of the creation process for each type of folder. In the exercise to follow, we will create several folders for eXYZ Corporation.

There are a couple of different ways to create folders. In the Navigator Content Areas tab, click on the Contents link for the content area you want to use. On the contents page, you will see a list of object types. To create a new folder, just click Create on the line for Folders, or click the Folders link to go down into the folders page and create the folder from there.

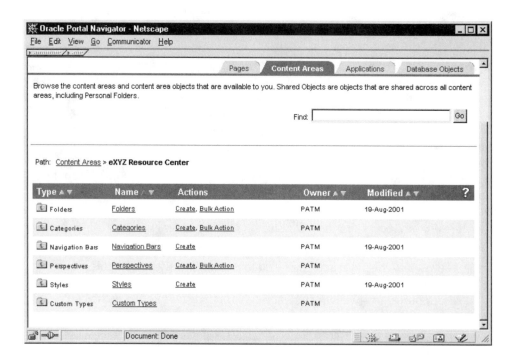

If you prefer to work in the content area interface, navigate to the content area (click its name on the Navigator Content Areas tab). Click the Edit Folder link, then Create Folder. Both techniques will put you into the Create New Folder wizard, which first asks which type of folder you want to create—Container, URL, PL/SQL, or Search. Depending on the folder type you select, the remaining wizard steps will ask for different information. The sections below outline the properties for each type of folder. You will probably find the Navigator interface faster and easier to use, but if you are already working in the content area, you do not have to leave to create new folders.

Container   Creating a container folder is as simple as giving it a name and a display name to be used when the user sees it in the content area. You can optionally specify a category for the folder, which is used only in searches. Folders assigned to a category or perspective will not display (as items do) when users navigate to the category or perspective page. All of the properties discussed in the previous section on the root folder are available for container folders. When you click Finish, you can use the folder properties editor, as you did with the root folder, to set up the folder's details.

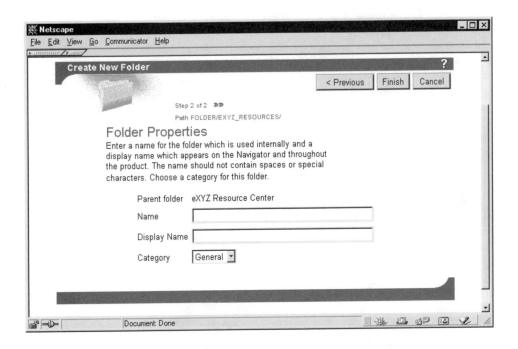

A container folder, by definition, can have sub-folders. To create sub-folders in the content area interface, navigate to the folder where you want to create the sub-folder and click Create Folder. In the Navigator, you will have to go to the folders page (Content Areas tab | Contents | Folders) and click Create next to the folder where the new folder is to go.

URL A URL folder links to any valid URL. Use a URL folder to display another Web site or to link to an application written in another programming environment (such as Java or ASP) within your content area. You can choose to have the new URL replace the contents of the screen or to preserve the navigation bar, displaying the URL as though it was a part of the content area. Specify the full URL, including the HTTP service identifier (follow the default text `http://` in the URL field). Without the service identifier, the URL is interpreted relative to `http://<yourhost>/ pls/portal30/`, a path that would only be correct for Portal component URLs and custom PL/SQL routines.

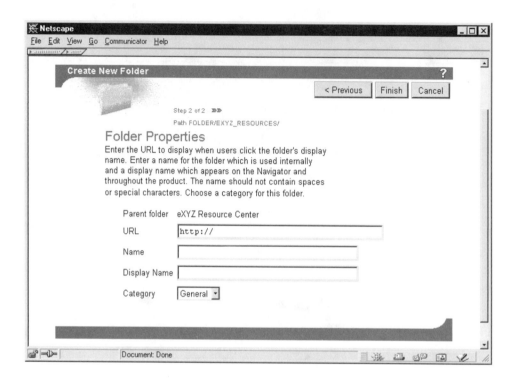

Search The search folder lets you create a "canned" search for your users. When you create a search folder, you can either reference a previously created saved search or enter new search criteria in a third wizard step.

The search criteria entry form is similar to the advanced search page you saw earlier in Figure 6-13, and allows you to specify keywords, content area, folder, language, category, perspective, types of items to return, and attribute values. Search folders are great for marketing purposes—an example might be a toy vendor who creates a search folder that identifies all toys with the perspective of "2-year old" in the "Educational Toys" category. Putting a link to this and similar search folders on the navigation bar or in an image map would ensure that shoppers found what they were looking for, and the search results would always be current. In an intranet site, search folders can be used to cull content on a particular topic that crosses folder and category and/or perspective borders. Users do not need to understand categories, perspectives, or advanced search techniques in order to use a search folder, because the search has been set up for them.

PL/SQL A PL/SQL folder allows free-form entry of PL/SQL code or a reference to a custom package or procedure that uses the PL/SQL Web Toolkit. Use a PL/SQL folder when you want the results of PL/SQL routine to appear as though they were content area items, accessible only to users granted permission on the folder. You will not be able to add or manage individual items to a PL/SQL folder, but must generate all of the content dynamically. A PL/SQL folder is useful for displaying highly customized content or content that is already stored in a database table. It can also help you integrate legacy code into the content area, so you can take advantage of the content area's structure and administrative benefits.

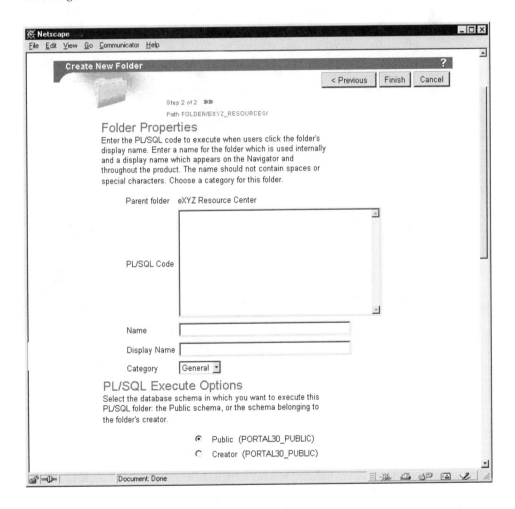

To create a PL/SQL folder, you must specify some PL/SQL code to execute when users click the folder name. Usually this PL/SQL is a call to a database stored procedure, but you can enter the entire text of the PL/SQL routine directly into the wizard page. You will not need to enclose the code block in a BEGIN-END pair, unless you are declaring local variables, but you will need to end all statements with semicolons, according to standard PL/SQL syntax rules. You will set the Name, Display Name, and Category as you did for other folders.

For PL/SQL folders, you will need to specify the database schema in which to execute the code. As you recall from Chapter 5, all Portal users are mapped to a database schema to determine their runtime permission for database references. The default database schema for Portal users (PORTAL30_PUBLIC) is created during the installation, but users can be mapped to different database schemas to allow for variation in database security levels. The PL/SQL code must be executable by one of three possible database schemas. The PORTAL30_PUBLIC schema is the default, but the Portal user who creates the folder can specify that the code will always run under his or her associated schema, which might be something other than PORTAL30_PUBLIC. Finally, if the folder creator or editor is a member of the Portal DBA group, any schema can be used for the PL/SQL execution privilege. The latter option permits direct access to the schema that owns the tables, packages, or procedures referenced in the PL/SQL folder code, without compromising security on that schema at runtime.

Exercise 6.5: Adding Folders

1. Create the following container folders in the root folder, leaving the Category at its default value of General:

Name	Display Name
FLDR_HR	Human Resources
FLDR_SALES	Sales and Product Information
FLDR_CONTRACTS	Contracts

2. Create a Search sub-folder under the Human Resources folder. If you are working in the Navigator, click the Folders link and then click Create in the Actions column for Human Resources. If you are in the content area, click on the folder name and then click Create Folder while in edit mode. Name this folder FLDR_TAX and give it a Display Name of Tax Information. This folder will pull together all of the tax-related documents from the site to simplify the employees' access to tax forms. Click the Next button to view the Search Criteria page.

3. In the Search For field, enter tax irs. Limit the search to the Human Resources folder by clicking the list icon to the right of the Folder field in the Search In section. In the popup window, click on Return Object next to

the folder named Human Resources. Check the box labeled Include
Sub-folders in case any are added later. Leave the remaining items at their
defaults and click Finish.

4. Next, you will create a simple PL/SQL folder that lets PATM check the
number of items awaiting approval by folder name, to keep track of potential
backlogs. The PL/SQL code that this item will invoke is provided in the
procedure `item_count`. It has been created in the CORP_SITE schema,
but if you want to review the code, you can find it in `item_count.sql`
on the distribution directory for this chapter. From the root folder, create a
PL/SQL folder. Set the PL/SQL Code to `corp_site.item_count;` (don't
forget the semicolon). Set the Name to `FLDR_WORKLOAD`, and the Display
Name to `Show Workload`. Leave the PL/SQL Execute Options set to Public
(PORTAL30_PUBLIC), as we have granted EXECUTE permission on this
procedure to PORTAL30_PUBLIC. Click Finish and test the folder link.
There should be no items awaiting approval at this point, so the screen will
look like that shown in Figure 6-19.

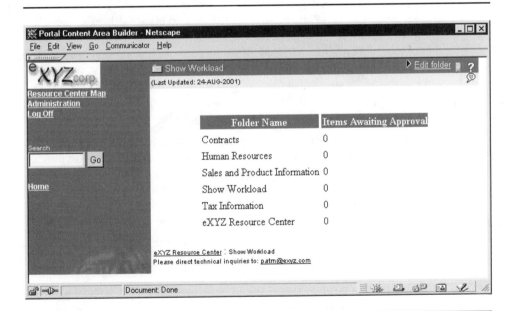

FIGURE 6-19. *The Show Workload PL/SQL folder*

NOTE
We could have easily created this report as a Portal component, making use of style standards for the site. We chose to implement it as a PL/SQL folder to demonstrate how you might integrate existing Web PL/SQL code with the content area.

5. Now that the folders are created, we need to set up the security scheme and individual folder properties. To simplify the process, we will first copy the privileges from the root folder to the lower-level folders. Return to the properties page for the root folder (by clicking the Edit Root Folder link on the top-level Content Areas tab or Edit Folder from the top level of the content area) and click on the Access tab. Click Cascade Privileges to copy the AUTHENTICATED_USERS View Content privilege to the sub-folders. Click OK to exit this page.

6. Navigate to the properties page for the Human Resources folder. Click the Access tab and add the HR_USERS group to the access list. Give this group the Manage Items privilege and click Apply. Give the AUTHENTICATED_ USERS group Create With Approval privilege and click Apply. On the Optional tab, specify `carlos_dudley@exyz.com` for the Contact E-mail. Remove the Tax Information folder from the list of Displayed Sub-folders. (We will use a navigation bar icon to link to this folder.) Finally, we will publish the folder as a portlet, so we can add it to the HR tab to give users a quick view of the forms and policies for the company. On the Required tab, check the box labeled Publish As Portlet. Click OK to save your changes.

7. Edit the Contracts folder and remove the AUTHENTICATED_USERS group from the access list by clicking the red X next to the group name on the Access tab. This folder will only be available to a subset of users. Add the MANAGEMENT_USERS and SALES_USERS groups to the access list, as well as users JOHND and NANCYG (eXYZ's president and COO). Give JOHND and NANCYG Manage Items privilege, and give the MANAGEMENT_ USERS and SALES_USERS groups Create With Approval and click Apply. On the Optional tab, specify `nancy_gibbs@exyz.com` for the Contact E-mail field. Specify Audit versioning, and click OK.

8. For the Sales and Product Information folder, give the SALES_USERS Manage Items privilege. Set the Contact E-mail to `dave_fowler@exyz.com`.

9. For the Show Workload folder, remove the AUTHENTICATED_USERS group. Only PATM will be able to view this folder for now. On the Required tab, publish this folder as a portlet so PATM has the option of adding it to the home page.

10. Finally, we will add some images to the Tax Information sub-folder. Because we've hidden this folder in the content area, you will have to use the Navigator to get to it. In the folders page for eXYZ Resource Center (Contents | Folders), click the Sub-Folders link for Human Resources, then click Edit next to the Tax Information folder name. On the Image tab, set the Title Image Name to `tax1.gif`, found in the distribution directory for this chapter. Set the Rollover Image Name to `tax2.gif`. Click OK.

11. Refresh your content area page if you kept a separate window open, or return to the top level of the Content Areas tab in the Navigator and click on the content area name to view the results of your changes. The only visible change was the addition of sub-folders, as shown in Figure 6-20. You may wish to try logging in and out a few times using different user IDs, so you can experiment with the available privileges in each folder.

12. Now you can add your first custom content to the eXYZ Home Page you created in Chapter 3. Go to the Pages tab in the Navigator, and click the My Pages (or Top-Level Pages) link. Click Edit on the line for eXYZ Home Page. Click the HR tab, then the Add Portlets icon. The eXYZ Resource Center should now show up in the Other Providers section. Click this link and click the Human Resources link to add the folder as a portlet on the HR tab. Click OK, then view your page. It won't look like much, because we haven't added any content, but should appear as it does in Figure 6-21. Notice that the folder contact has overridden the contact area contact information. Click the Customize link on the portlet header to see the kinds of things you can change about how the folder is displayed in portlet view.

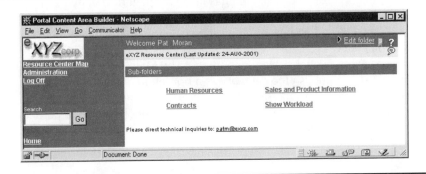

FIGURE 6-20. *eXYZ Resource Center after adding new folders*

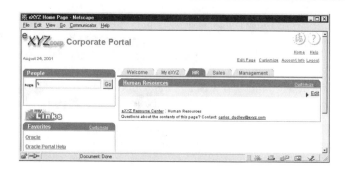

FIGURE 6-21. *The eXYZ Home Page with the Human Resources folder added*

The folders are now set up and ready to go. Let your users know they can test the content area. We can now move on to creating categories and perspectives.

Categories

The hardest part about creating categories is the design—figuring out what categories you need to completely describe the contents of your site, yet still keep the categories well differentiated so the choice of category is obvious for any item. Creating the categories is nothing more than clicking on the Create link on the Categories line in the eXYZ Resource Center contents page. You can get there from the Navigator Content Areas tab, or from the content area Administration page. Give each category a name and a display name, and click Create. Portal makes it easy to rapidly add categories by producing a blank Create Category page after you create each new category. Each content area has its own categories, but you can create global categories in the Shared Objects content area. Create sub-categories by clicking on the Create link next to an existing category in the Categories page.

After you create a category, you have the option to edit it. In the category properties page are two tabs: Main and Image. The Main tab lets you edit the basic information, and to publish the category as a portlet, just as you could with folders. A category portlet displays the same information as a category page, as you saw in Figure 6-4, but in portlet mode. You have the same options for other portlets—that is, you can specify the portlet header (Portlet Display Name) and whether to use the page style.

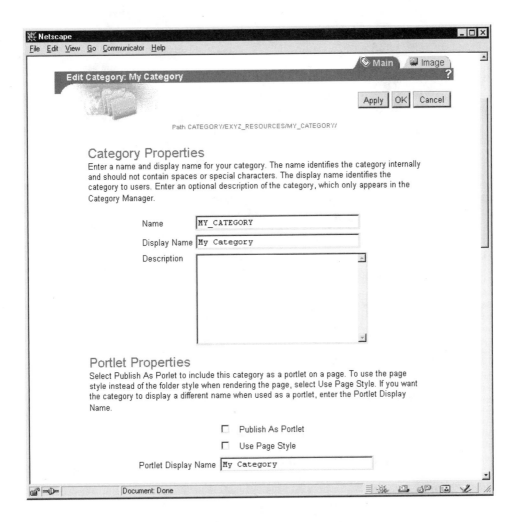

On the Image tab, you can add images to enhance the display. As with folders, you can specify a title image and a rollover image for use in the navigation bar, and a page header (Banner) image. Additionally, you can specify a small icon to be used in the banner displayed at the top of the category page (Icon Name).

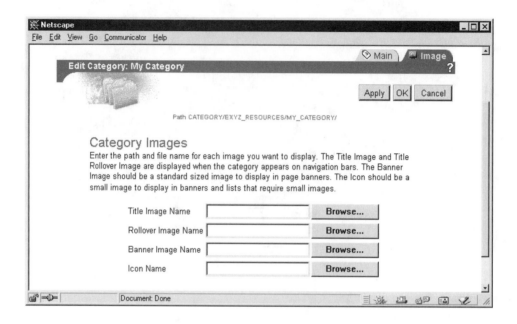

Exercise 6.4: Creating Categories

1. In the Navigator Content Areas tab, go to the contents page for the eXYZ Resource Center.

2. Create the following categories for the eXYZ Resource Center. We won't specify images for our categories, because we won't use them in the navigation bar and we would like to keep the look and feel as simple as possible.

Name	Display Name
CTG_REFERENCE	Reference Information
CTG_FORMS	Forms
CTG_POLICY	Policies and Procedures
CTG_LINKS	Useful Links
CTG_GRAPHICS	Images and Corporate Templates

3. Close the Create Category page when you are finished. We won't be able to see the categories until we have created some items.

Perspectives

Perspectives are created much like categories. Starting from the contents page in the Navigator, simply click the Create action on the Perspectives line. As with folders and categories, you can specify images to be used in the navigation bar, the perspective page header, and the perspective page banner. You can also publish a perspective page to the portal, displaying the always-current results of a perspective search. One thing that distinguishes perspectives from the other objects is that the icon specified for a perspective will display with every item in that perspective. This option can be turned off on the Main tab of the perspective properties page, using the Display Icon With Items check box. If turned off, the perspective's icon would not be displayed with the items, but would be displayed in the page banner.

TIP
16 x 16 pixel icons work well for perspectives.

Exercise 6.5: Specifying Perspectives

1. In the Navigator Content Areas tab, go to the perspectives page (under Contents) for the eXYZ Resource Center.

2. Create the following perspectives, removing the check mark for the box labeled Display Icon With Items:

Name	Display Name
PS_ALL	All Employees
PS_MANAGER	Managers
PS_ENGR	Engineering
PS_LEGAL	Legal

3. Navigate to the Shared Objects content area and create the following perspectives. After creating each perspective, edit the properties to set the corresponding icon name.

Name	Display Name	Icon
PS_WORD	Word Documents	wordicon.gif
PS_EXCEL	Excel Spreadsheets	excel.gif

```
PS_COMPONENT    Portal Components    comp.gif

PS_ADOBE        Acrobat Documents    pdficon.gif
```

4. As with categories, we won't see the effects of these changes until we add content, which we will do next.

Adding Content

When it gets right down to it, the items make up the real content (the "stuff") of the site. Items can only be created in the content area edit mode, not in the Navigator. As you saw in an earlier section, the properties of a created item depend to some extent on where you click the Add Item icon. Items can be submitted by one person, approved by another, edited, removed, versioned, checked out, and set to expire on a given date.

Portal supports many different types of items to support any possible addition to the content area—programmatic or static. When you create an item, Portal will not validate its existence or make any assumptions about file type or structure. The validation is left to the download action—for example, an empty file item will result in a "Document contains no data" error from the browser. Portal will generate the appropriate MIME header to represent the file type to the browser when the item is downloaded. It is up to the user to ensure that the browser is properly configured to view that type of document.

NOTE
A MIME (Multipurpose Internet Mail Extension) header identifies the type of content being delivered. The browser configuration determines, based on the MIME type, whether the document should be displayed in the browser window or sent to a helper application or plug-in. Portal bases its generated MIME header on the file extension, so be sure to save all files with the usual extension for the program used to access them. For example, use .pdf for PDF files, so that Portal will generate the correct MIME header to instruct the browser that it needs to run Acrobat Reader to display the file.

Common Properties for Items

The Add Item wizard begins by asking for the item type, so it can correctly set up the following wizard steps. The available types are File, Text, URL, Folder Link,

PL/SQL, Application Component, Image, Java Application, and Zip File, described in detail in the following pages.

After selecting the item type, you will go to the second page of the wizard and select the folder region in which the item will appear, as illustrated previously. The remainder of this page lets you set general properties. When you return later to edit the item's properties, this page is shown as the Required tab. All items, regardless of type, have a display name (which serves the link to show the item's content), a category, and a description, to be displayed under the item's link. For most items, the Display Name field is optional. If omitted, the file name or URL associated with the item will display as the link text, or, if specified, the item's image can supply the link. The Publish Date defaults to the current date, but it can be edited to delay publication of the item. You can set any item to expire within a number of days from publication or on a set date. The default is that the item never expires. Expired items will remain visible to owners and managers until they are deleted or until an administrator performs a purge of expired items.

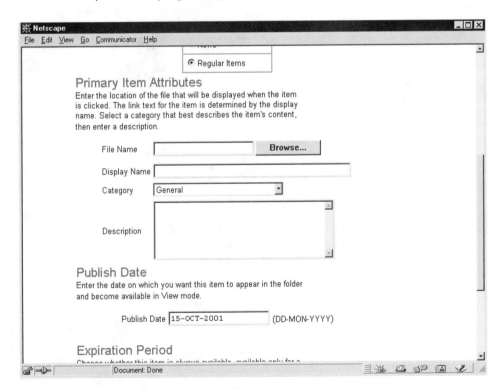

The last page of the Add Item wizard corresponds to the Optional tab that you will see when you subsequently edit the item. Here you will assign perspectives, optionally choose an image to display next to the item, add search keywords, and set a few more details, depending on the item type. The specified image can be displayed in any position relative to the item's name link. Enter free-form search keywords separated by spaces, and enclose search phrases in double quotes. If you design your perspectives well, you may be able to minimize the use of unstructured keywords. The advantage of perspectives over keywords is that users have a predefined list from which to choose, both when creating items and when searching. The item's author automatically defaults to the name of the currently logged-in user, but you can set this field to anything you like. An internal attribute, Creator, records who put the item into the content area, so the Author field can record the actual author of the document. Enabling item check-out allows users to lock items while they are working with them, in order to prevent destructive updates. Item check-out is independent of the versioning settings for the content area or folder, and is always available. Finally, you can hide items so they are only visible to those who have Manage or Own privilege on the folder—a useful setting for communication among the content managers.

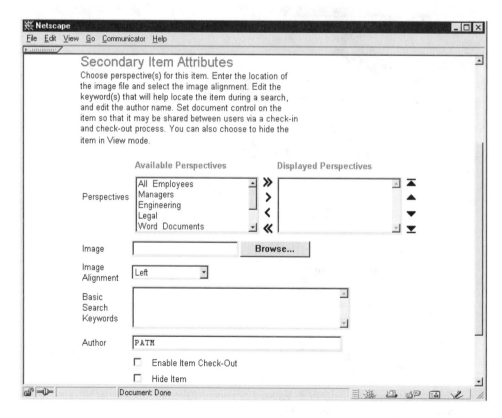

Each of the item types has specific properties and behavior. The wizard differs minimally for each item type, to handle the required fields and optional display characteristics appropriate to each one. We have not illustrated each minor difference, but will discuss the important fields in the text.

File Items

When a user creates a file item, the file is actually uploaded into the database and stored as a BLOB (binary large object) in the WWDOC_DOCUMENT$ table. DBAs should note that this will result in extra storage requirements for the document tablespace. Specify the file by typing a full path name or click the Browse button to find the file using an operating system dialog box. If the display name is omitted for a file item, the file's name will be used in the link, unless the file is an HTML file. In this case, Portal will search the file for `<TITLE></TITLE>` HTML tags, and will set the link text to whatever it finds between those tags.

When users click on the name of a file item, the file will be downloaded to the desktop. (Unlike many of the other item types, you do not have a choice to display a file item within the content area window.) Downloading the file will launch either a helper application (MS Word, for example) to work with the file in a separate application or a browser plug-in such as Adobe Acrobat, which will display the file directly in the browser window. When a browser plug-in automatically replaces the content area window with the file view, users must click the Back button to return to the content area. If the browser does not recognize the file type, users will be prompted to save the file locally.

TIP
Use a zip file item, described at the end of this section, to load large numbers of files in a single operation.

Text Items

Text items are simply free-form text that the creator types into the Add Item wizard. The text is displayed when the user clicks the name of the item, and as with other items, the text in the Description field shows on the main folder page with the item. You may use HTML tags to format the text, but any complex HTML is probably better created as a file item.

The main advantage of using a text item over an HTML file is that it allows you to choose where the content will display. You can display text items in the content display area (preserving the navigation bar), in the full browser window (losing the navigation bar), or in a completely new browser window. You can also display the item directly in the folder display area, which shows any description text followed by the actual item text. The Display Options section is at the bottom of the third page of the wizard, or the Optional tab in later edits.

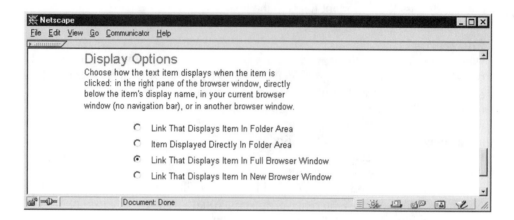

URL Items

URL items allow you to link to any valid URL. The URL could point to a page from another site, a CGI program or another application that produces a page, or a page on the local site. URL items can incorporate content from other sites into your content area, or simply offer useful links to the user community. As with URL folders, you must specify the full path to the resource.

The decision of whether to use a URL folder vs. a URL item depends on where you want the item displayed and how you want to control the security of the item. You can have many URL items categorized in a list, but this is not possible with URL folders. You have the same choices in the Display Options section for URL items that you did for text items—the only difference for this item type is that you now specify a URL rather than a file name or text.

Folder Link Items

As we saw in the Oracle Portal Online Help content area, folder links can be used to make the display of sub-folders more attractive than the default display. You may link to any existing folder or sub-folder from anywhere in the content area by choosing it from the list associated with the Path field. This list is similar to the Content Area Map, and lets you select the folder using a Return Object link. The Path field will now contain a display-only folder name, and the actual path is stored with the folder link item. Creating a folder link item allows you to override the actual folder structure, and add additional attributes such as a different display name, an image, an expiration date, a category, or perspectives to the folder display. If the link is in the same folder as the original folder, you can hide the original folder by editing the properties of its parent.

PL/SQL Items

PL/SQL items, like PL/SQL folders, let you run custom PL/SQL code, typically from a stored procedure. A PL/SQL item must use the PL/SQL Web Toolkit to return any information to the user. You must also consider execution privileges when setting up a PL/SQL item, as you did with the PL/SQL folder. As before, the PL/SQL Execute Options section allows the choice between using the public schema or the creator's schema, with the added option to name a schema if the creator is a Portal DBA. As with most of the other item types, you have the choice of where to display the results of the procedure.

PL/SQL items are one of the ways you might integrate existing PL/SQL Web Toolkit code into your Portal site, if you want it to be searchable and identifiable as content. The same considerations we discussed between URL folders and URL items apply when deciding between a PL/SQL item and a PL/SQL folder. If you want many links to PL/SQL procedures to appear as items in a folder, or if you want a PL/SQL link to appear in a folder along with other item types, use PL/SQL items. If you want the results of a single PL/SQL procedure to appear as folder contents, use a PL/SQL folder. Keep in mind, too, that it is preferable to set security at the folder level, so if the security varies for your PL/SQL items, you may be better off with PL/SQL folders.

Application Component Items

If you want to create your entire site as a content area, or wish to have application components organized and displayed with other content, use an application component item to provide access to previously developed Portal forms and reports. You can link to any application component that has been published to the portal, following the same rules for adding portlets to a page. The component can be displayed as though it was a part of the content area, providing visual consistency with the remaining content. In the Display Options section, you can opt to display the customization form first rather than the component itself, so users can add any custom parameters before running the component.

Image Items

An image item can be static or active. A static image (without an image map) is used to enhance the appearance of the folder display page, or to actually serve images as content. Image items would allow you to produce a searchable gallery of images and/or photographs, complete with keywords, perspectives, and categories, which are especially useful for searching in this type of site. This kind of gallery could be produced using image items or file items. The difference between the two approaches is that the actual images will display in the content area when using image items, as opposed to a list of links to the image files.

An active image also supplies an image map, which is a navigation device that assigns distinct URLs to different parts of the image, so that clicking parts of the image directs users to different resources. The image map itself is an HTML-encoded overlay that divides the image into geometric regions, each with an associated URL. The links can be any valid destination, including links to other parts of the content area or Portal site. Probably the best example of an image map is an actual geographic map, where a user can click on a city or state to identify information specific to that area. Using an image map is not limited to actual maps; you can specify "hot" areas of any interesting graphic to aid in site navigation. These would allow you to create a secondary, but graphically appealing, navigation tool for the content area. To add the image map, specify its name and then type the HTML for the named map area directly into the Imagemap field.

NOTE
Your favorite HTML reference will contain the syntax to specify image maps.

Java Application Items

You can integrate existing JavaServer Pages (JSPs) into a content area using the Java Application item. Java Application items will always replace the current content area page, and can use the full feature set of the Java language in combination with Oracle Portal content features. To integrate a JSP application, deploy your JSPs as a Java archive (JAR) file in any directory. In the Add Item wizard, specify the JAR file name and the name of the initial page to display, in addition to the usual item attributes. Portal will upload the JAR file into the WWDOC_DOCUMENT$ table and generate the path to call it through the Apache JServ engine. Your content area is now Java-enabled without any configuration changes to the Apache server. In addition, end users do not have to do anything special to their browser to use JSPs, because JSPs, like servlets and PL/SQL Web Toolkit routines, deliver results in HTML (and possibly JavaScript).

Zip File Items

A zip file item can be used to post a zip file for download and searching, but how is that different from any other file item? The difference is that Oracle Portal recognizes a zip file upon creation, and will create a link for each zip file that simply says "Unzip". This little link is the key to bulk-loading file items, a long-desired feature for content areas. The process will create items for each of the files contained in the zip file, as well as sub-folders for directories represented in the zip file (use the "Save full path info" check box when creating the zip file). The unzip process is subject to the same security controls as regular item creation, and any properties (such as categories and perspectives) set on the original zip file item will be applied to all files in the extract. This feature is invaluable when first setting up a site or migrating to a Portal content area, as it eliminates the tedious process of creating items one at a time.

NOTE
The zip file item does not appear to support UNIX `tar` *or other compression methods in this release.*

To upload a set of files or to transfer files from an existing file server to a Portal content area, zip them using PKZIP or WinZip, then create a zip file item in the content area with the resulting file. Set any item properties that you want to cascade to the unzipped items, and close the item wizard to return to the folder where you created the zip file item. Click the Unzip link to display the Bulk Load page. Choose the target parent folder (you must have appropriate permission) and uncheck the box labeled Run Unzip in Background—leaving it checked seems to prevent the unzip from working. Choose the item type from among File, Image, and Zip File (for nested zip files). If you have created any custom types based on those three item types, these will also be in the list.

Finally, choose the File Posting mode. You can overwrite existing files, create new versions (if the folder is set up with at least simple versioning), or rename the files as they are extracted. The rename feature appends the current date to the file name, and ensures a distinct internal name for the new items. Click the Unzip button when you have set up the process to your satisfaction. After the unzip completes, close the Bulk Load page and browse the new content. When you are satisfied that all files have been correctly unzipped, you may delete the original zip file item, or leave it available to end users.

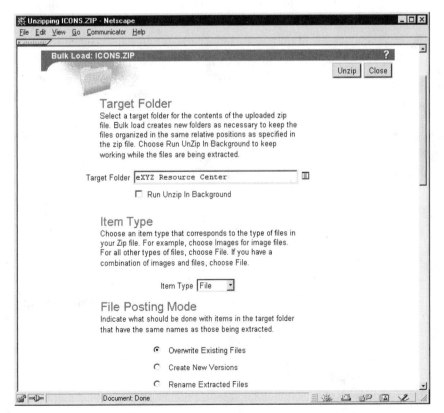

Exercise 6.6: Adding Items

In this exercise, we will add items to our content area. Use the items provided in the distribution directory for these exercises, and feel free to experiment with additional items from your own resources. Begin the exercise in the content area home page.

1. Go to the Human Resources folder and click Edit Folder. Click Add Item, choose `File` for the Item Type, and then click Next to continue.

2. Leave the Folder Region setting at Regular Items.

3. Under Primary Item Attributes, use the Browse button to locate the `handbook.doc` file in the distribution directory. Give the item a Display Name of `eXYZ Employee Handbook`. The Category is Policies and Procedures. You may leave the Description blank or enter a few words to describe the employee handbook. Leave the Publish Date and Expiration Period at their defaults and click Next.

4. Under Secondary Item Attributes, move the perspectives for Word Documents and All Employees to the Displayed Perspectives list. Check the box to Enable Item Check-Out so that the handbook will be unavailable during changes and click Finish.

5. Now add the employee review form. Click Add Item, and add another File item—this one is named `reviewform.pdf`. Set the Display Name to `Employee Review Form` and the Category to `Forms`. Give it the Managers and Acrobat Documents perspectives, and click Finish.

6. There are several other human resource forms, named `*form.doc` in the distribution directory for this chapter. Create items for any or all of them, if you like.

7. Now let's create a few URL items. Click Add Item, and select URL for the Item Type.

8. In the URL field, enter `http://ftp.fedworld.gov/pub/irs-pdf/fw4_01.pdf`. Type `W-4 Form` for the Display Name. For the Category, select Forms, type `Download official W-4 Form` in the Description, then click Next.

9. Give the item Perspectives of Acrobat Documents and All Employees. Add `IRS` and `tax` as Basic Search Keywords. Leave the remaining defaults and click Finish.

10. Repeat steps 5–7 for the 1040 form. This time the link is `http://ftp.fedworld.gov/pub/irs-pdf/f1040.pdf` and the Display Name is `Federal Form 1040`.

11. Create one more URL Item, this time for a direct link to the IRS Web site. The URL is `http://www.irs.gov` and the Display Name is `IRS Web Site`. Set the Category to Useful Links and give it a description (optional). Use the same perspectives and keywords as the other two IRS links, but this time set the Display Options to `Link That Displays Item In New Browser Window`.

12. Click Finish. Switch back to view mode by clicking View Folder. Examine your new content, test the links, and try a perspective search by clicking on one of the perspective icons. The page should look as it does in Figure 6-22. You also may want to return to the eXYZ home page to see the new content on the HR tab.

13. Now you will create an announcement in the Sales and Product Information folder. This will be a text item so that the involved parties can add comments to the item as new developments arise. Go back to editing the folder, click on Add Item, choose Text, and click Next.

14. Set the Folder Region to Announcement, and in the Text field, enter the following:

```
At the end of December, we will be upgrading our order
fulfillment system to Oracle 9i, and installing the new 9i
Application Server. The following schedule is approximate and
likely to change:
    <br>Dec 29—Upgrade test server
    <br>Dec 30—Port Production Data to test
    <br>Week of Dec 31—Run full usability tests on new server
    <br>Jan 5—Install 9iAS on new web server machine
    <br>Jan 6—Upgrade Production server
    <P>
    Please send any comments to <A
    HREF="mailto:patm@exyz.com">Pat Moran</A>, and post any
    issues you have with the schedule here.
    </P>
```

15. Set the Display Name to `Upgrade Schedule Released` and leave the Category at General. In the Description field, enter `Please view and add comments or changes if necessary. Add initials to any changes.` Set the Publish Date to a date in the next week. Set Expires On to next January 31st. Click Next.

16. Add the `Engineering` perspective to the Displayed Perspectives list. Change the Display Options to `Link That Displays Item In Folder Area`.

17. Click Finish and test the item. Notice that it does not show up in the normal view of the folder, because it has not been published. It does show up in edit mode, and it will appear in normal view starting on the publish date.

18. The last item is a zip file item that will let us load previously created specifications for eXYZ's products. Navigate to the Sales and Product Information Folder and add an item, setting the type to `Zip File`, and then click Next.

19. Locate the `products.zip` file from the distribution directory using the Browse button. Leave the Display Name blank, and choose `Reference Information` for the Category.

20. Click Next to specify a perspective of `Acrobat Documents`, and click Finish.

21. When you return to the folder page, you will see an Unzip link next to the zip file name. Click it to unzip the file. In the Bulk Load page, uncheck the box that says Run Unzip in the Background and click Unzip. Close the Bulk Load page after the unzip process completes. Notice that all of the files preserved the settings for the Category and Perspective fields. You may edit these on an item-by-item basis, and add perspectives if you wish. Delete the original zip file using the red X in edit mode.

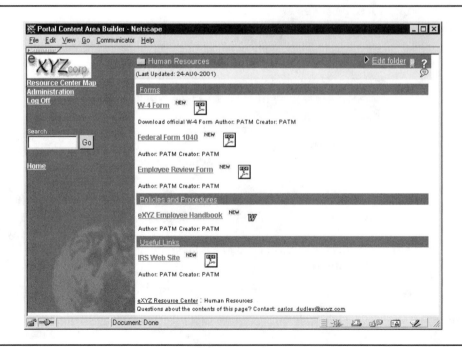

FIGURE 6-22. *The Human Resources folder with new content*

Congratulations! You now have content in your content area. These examples are intended to be typical of the kinds of content you will use in your own intranet application, and to give you a feel for the uses of each item type. If you wish to extend your items and folders to track custom information, you can create custom items and folders with user-defined attributes, as you'll see at the end of this chapter. In later chapters, as we create components, we will integrate these as content area items as well.

Content Area Styles

Content area styles differ from page styles in several respects. First, content areas have two different styles—one is applied to the navigation bar and the other is applied to the content display area. It is acceptable to use the same style for both the navigation bar and the content display area, if your goal is to hide the distinction between the two sections. However, most sites will want to use different colors, and perhaps fonts, to distinguish the navigation bar from the content display area. Second, a content area style has an additional feature to alter the layout of page regions: the Quickpicks, Announcements, Sub-folders, News, and Regular Items we discussed earlier in this chapter. Finally, and hopefully most obvious, content area elements are not the same as portal page elements. You will set fonts and colors for the background, banners, and items of the content area rather than the text and headings as you did for portlets.

To work with content area styles, choose either the Folder Style or Nav Bar Style link from the dashboards in the content area. Alternatively, you can go the Styles section of the Navigator (Content Areas | eXYZ Resource Center | Contents | Styles). You can link to the style editor for the current folder style from the folder properties Styles tab, or you could create a new style in the Navigator and edit the folder to assign the style later.

Properties

Setting style properties uses the same technique you used with page styles in Chapter 5. Choose the element, then specify the appropriate color and/or font settings. For example, select the Main Banner (text) or the Main Banner Color as the element to customize, then specify the properties (color and/or font) to assign to that element. When you press Apply, your changes will be reflected in the Preview panes on the right of the screen. But here's the confusing part: both the Preview: Folder and Preview: Navigation Bar will change, even though the style you're working on will apply to either a navigation bar or a content display area (folder), but not usually both. Additionally, the element names can sometimes serve a dual purpose. For example, if you are editing a navigation bar style, the Item Content/Navigation Bar Text element refers to static text displayed on the navigation bar, but if you are editing a content area style, the same element will set the text style for the item content. To make sense of it, you can just ignore the preview and elements that don't pertain to the style you're editing.

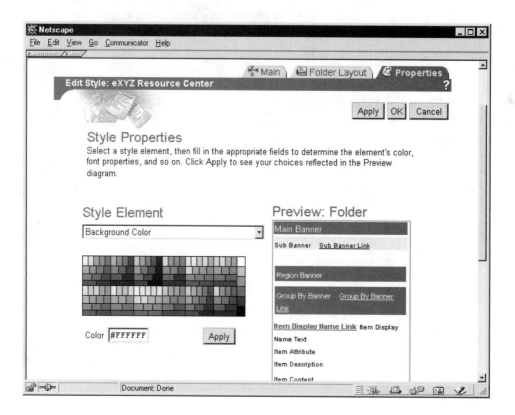

Folder Layout

The Folder Layout tab, applicable only to content area styles, offers five choices of arrangement for the folder's regions. The region layouts are predetermined—for the most part, you won't be able to choose which region will be displayed in each page area. You will be able to choose the layout that works best for you, and then modify how items display within each region.

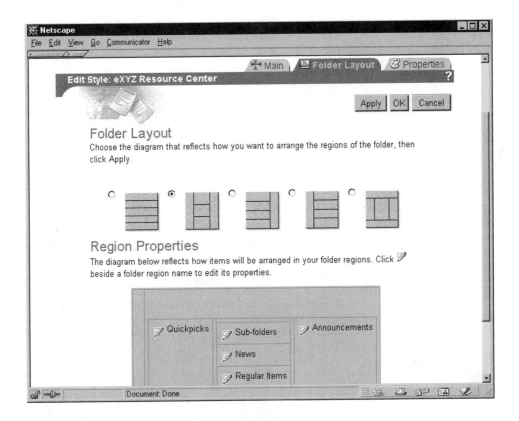

Region Properties

To modify the display of items within each region, click on the Edit icon (pencil and pad) for the region. All regions have an optional banner to set off items within the region—if you display the banner, you can change its text using the Display Name field. If you select the radio button to say that this region will display sub-folders, you will be able to switch the region with the Sub-folders region. This is the only way we could find to move regions around within a preset layout. The Region Content Properties section allows you to specify which of the items' attributes will be displayed. Several of the attributes are display elements that enhance the appearance of the region, but most are properties stored with the items, as shown in Table 6-3.

Attribute	Description
<Carriage Return>	Inserts a carriage return between items. Only affects items displayed in columns.
<Space>	Inserts a space between items. Only affects items displayed in rows.
<Blank Line>	Inserts a blank line between items, for additional whitespace. Only affects items displayed in columns.
Application Type	Only applies to Java Application items—displays the type of application (for example, JSP), so users know what the link will do.
Associated Functions	Enables the display, next to the item name, of the results of functions associated with custom types.
Author	Displays what was entered in the Author field when item was created.
Create Date	Item's creation date.
Creator	Displays the Portal user ID of the user who created the item.
Description	The text description that users can enter when creating items.
Display Name	Enforces that the item's display name is used when displaying the item.
Display Name or Image	Uses the image to show the item if it exists; otherwise, uses display name.
Document Size	Shows the size of the item.
Expire Date	Item expiration date.
Gist	Add a document summary generated by interMedia.
Help URL	Only applies to Portlet Repository content area—displays a "?" icon with a link to help for the item.
Image	Always show the image associated with the item.

TABLE 6-3. *Available Item Attributes*

Attribute	Description
Image URL	Displays a link to the image.
In Place Item Display	Enables item content to be displayed within the folder page view—without it, "display in place" has no effect.
Initial Page Name	Displays the name of the starting JSP within the JAR file for a Java application item.
Jar File	Displays the name of the Java archive file for a Java application item.
Keywords	Shows all keywords associated with the item.
New Item Indicator	Displays the New icon according to the rules set in the content area.
Perspectives	Shows all perspectives associated with the item.
Portlet Id	Shows the internal ID of a portlet—applies only to the custom item type for portlets in the Portlet Repository content area.
Provider Id	Shows the internal ID of a portlet provider—only in Portlet Repository.
Provider Name	Shows the portlet provider name—only in Portlet Repository.
Property Sheet	Displays an icon that, when clicked, shows a pop-up property sheet.
Themes	Displays themes generated by interMedia.
Translations	Displays all available translations for the item.
Updated Item Indicator	Displays the Updated icon, according to the rules for the content area.
Versions	Displays a link to view all versions of an item.
View as HTML	Ensures that HTML tags entered within a text item or description field are interpreted as HTML and not literally.

TABLE 6-3.   *Available Item Attributes* (continued)

As you can see, just about any descriptive information about items can be displayed in the folder page view. This list will grow as you add custom attributes, so you can choose whether to display their values. Use these display features to provide users with the information they need about your content.

Below the attributes lists is a group of properties that allow you to change essentially all of the default characteristics of the region's display. You can replace the category banners with banners to subdivide the region by `Author`, `Date`, or `Item Type`, or you can do away with "Group By" banners altogether. You can change the sort order (using the Sort By and Sort Order fields) to sort alphabetically or by document size, in ascending or descending order.

NOTE

The usual sort order is determined by the placement of items in the folder. A sequence field in the WWV_THINGS table stores the creation order, which is modified based on the rearranging of items on the page.

The Item Icon Height and Width fields force all icons in the region to the same size—but be careful with this setting, because not all icons will shrink gracefully. It's better to design your icons to the right size when you create them. Next, you can specify whether the items will be aligned left, center, or right (Item Alignment), and you can force them to display in multiple columns (or rows), to create a newspaper-style layout. Use the Number of Columns or Number of Rows setting to control this arrangement—a blank value is interpreted as unlimited. Finally, you can change the background color of each region to set it off from the others.

Main Tab

The Main tab lets you change the style and make the style public. A public style is available to all users with rights to modify their folder style, and so can be very useful if you want to predefine a few color schemes or view orientations.

To sum up, the combination of all these settings makes the content area an extremely flexible content display device, but the proliferation of choices may seem overwhelming. We highly recommend taking a "baby steps" approach when modifying content area styles. Make a few small changes at a time, and thoroughly test the results of each change before proceeding to the next one. Make sure you keep your users involved throughout the process.

Exercise 6.7: Modify Content Area Styles

We will only make a few simple changes to improve the appearance of the navigation bar, and change some colors.

1. Navigate to the root folder and click Edit Folder. Click Nav Bar Style to enter the editor for the navigation bar style, then click the eXYZ Resource Center Navbar Style link to go to the style editor.

2. Make the following changes by first selecting the element from the Style Element list. Be sure to click Apply after each change.

Element	New Value
Background Image	Remove the image by clicking the red X
Navigation Bar Search Field Width	15
Navigation Bar Width (Pixels)	160
Item Content/Navigation Bar Text	Set Font Size to 9pt
Item Display Name/Navigation Bar Label	Set Font Size to 9pt

3. Click OK (twice) and reload your content area page in view mode to see the navigation bar changes.

4. Now switch to edit mode and select Folder Style from the folder dashboard. Click the eXYZ Resource Center link under the Style Properties section to navigate to the style editor.

5. On the Folder Layout tab, click the Edit icon for the Announcements region. Choose the palest yellow (#FFFFCC) for the Background Color field. Move Expire Date to the Displayed Attributes list. Click Apply, then Close, and return to the content area.

6. Navigate to the Sales and Product Information folder and view the changes. (You will have to preview the change in edit mode, because the announcement is not yet published. If you like, edit the item properties and change the Publish Date to today's date, so you can see the item in view mode.)

Navigation Bar

Now that we have discussed all of the possible item types, classification schemes, display strategies, and search techniques, we can show you how to customize your navigation bar to provide users with easy access to the advanced features you have developed.

Creating a good navigation bar is critical to successful implementation of a content area. The navigation bar is not displayed when viewing content published to the Portal page, but can be published independently to the portal, to be used as an entry point to the content area. It is, however, the main method of getting around in the content area interface. Navigation bar elements can be links to specific categories, perspectives, or folders, or can be independent lists of all categories, perspectives, or folders. If you create folder links on the navigation bar, they will only display to users with the correct privileges on the folder. A Search element is provided, as is a link to the Advanced Search page. Custom text, links, and images can be added to enhance the overall appearance or functionality of the navigation bar.

A default navigation bar is provided with every new content area. You will modify this navigation bar to suit your needs, or create new ones to attach to lower-level folders. Each folder within a content area can have a different navigation bar, so you can customize the functionality available at each level. The navigation bar is usually displayed at the left of the screen, but because the content area page is implemented as a Portal page, you can place it anywhere you like by editing the content area properties.

To modify a navigation bar, you can use the Nav Bar Properties link in the navigation bar dashboard. To specify a different navigation bar for any folder, you can use the folder properties page or the Choose A Nav Bar link in the folder page. You can create new navigation bars and edit existing ones from within the Navigator, using the Contents link for the appropriate content area. Finally, you can add elements that help the user find content directly from the edit view of any folder, using the Add Element icon or link. There are several types of navigation bar elements, and anytime you create an element, a new region is created within the navigation bar. The regions are simply used to group related types, because each element type has distinct properties. This explains why you may see several sets of edit mode icons in a navigation bar.

The Add Element wizard first asks for the type of element you wish to add, then displays a property screen where you can customize the element. The choices differ depending on the element type, as explained in the sections that follow.

Basic Elements

Basic elements require no custom settings, and simply require that you move the element from the Available list to the Selected list in the wizard. Basic elements that can be incorporated into a navigation bar are explained in Table 6-4.

Element	Description
Content Area Logo	The main graphic for the content area.
Content Area Name	The name of the content area—not usually necessary because the name is displayed at the top of the content display area.
Log On/Log Off link	Links to the login page or logs the user off, depending on whether the user is currently logged in or not.
Category List	A drop-down list of all currently defined categories.
Perspective List	A drop-down list of all currently defined perspectives.
Administration Link	A link to the content area administration page, which displays utilities subject to the user's privileges. This is the simplest way to provide a link for users to change their passwords in a content area-only application.
Basic Search	Displays a text entry box for simple keyword search.
Advanced Search	A link that takes the user directly to the advanced search page.
Content Area Map	A link that displays the folder structure of the content area.
--BLANK LINE--	Creates some space in the navigation bar for visual balance.
Content area contact	A `mailto` link to the specified site contact's email.
Portal Home	A link to the Portal home page for the current user.

TABLE 6-4.   *Basic Navigation Bar Elements*

Categories, Folders, and Perspectives Elements

The basic elements include drop-down lists for both categories and perspectives, but these simple lists do not allow you to be selective about which categories and perspectives to show, and they offer no choice of display format. If you want to display a subset of categories or perspectives, or want to display them as links or images, you must create a category or perspective element. This technique applies to folders as well, and it is the only way to show folders in the navigation bar.

All three element types work the same. You can optionally specify a label to set off the section of links or to serve as a prompt for the drop-down list. Then choose the categories, perspectives, or folders you would like to display. Sub-folders, sub-categories, and sub-perspectives are indicated by preceding dots (" . "), one for each level below the parent. Finally, set the Display Mode. The Default setting will display the title image associated with the object if it exists; otherwise, a text link will display. The Drop-down List choice displays a list, and the Link(s) choice displays all elements as text links.

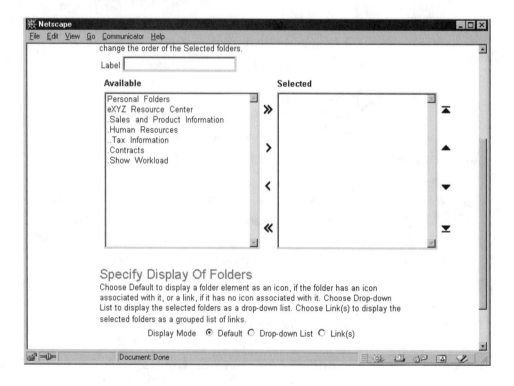

Image Element

The image element allows you to add images to the navigation bar, in addition to (or instead of) the content area logo and navigation bar background image. You can specify an image map as you can for image items, to create a navigation element.

Text Element

A text element lets you add helpful text to the navigation bar. It can be any text, and you can add as many text elements as you like.

URL Element

A URL element lets you add any link to the navigation bar—it is the only way to provide a link to an external resource from the navigation bar. URL elements can display text or images within the link. The image, like the object images, can support both a default and a rollover image.

Exercise 6.8: Improving the Navigation Bar

You may recall that the Oracle Portal Online Help system made use of direct folder links, a couple of custom URLs to the Index and Glossary, and lists for categories and perspectives. In this exercise, we will add similar functionality to the navigation bar for the eXYZ Resource Center.

1. Bring up the properties of the navigation bar for the eXYZ Resource Center, using either the Navigator or the Nav Bar Properties dashboard link.

2. Click on the Elements tab, and then click on the Edit icon to edit the navigation bar elements.

3. Remove the Administration Link by selecting it and clicking the left arrow to move it back to the Available list.

4. Move the Content Area Map to the bottom of the page, just above the Portal Home link.

5. Add an Advanced Search link by selecting it from the Available list and clicking the right arrow. Move it so it displays below the Basic Search box.

6. Offer your users a choice of perspectives by adding the Perspective List. Display this list just above Basic Search. Add a second BLANK LINE below the Perspective List, and a third at the end of the list. At this point, your screen should look like the following illustration. Click OK to save your changes.

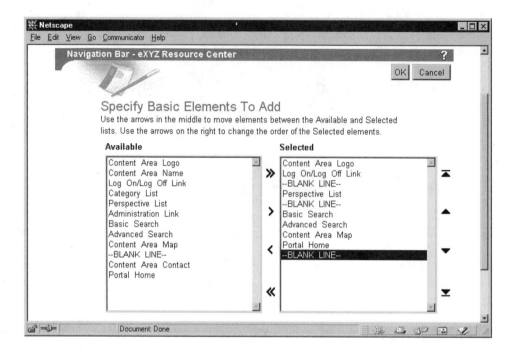

7. Now you will add an element to let users jump to the search folder we created for tax information. Click on the "Add an element after this element" icon and choose Folders for the Element Type, then click Next.

8. Move the Tax Information folder into the Selected list and click Finish.

9. Click Close and then return to the folder to see how your new navigation bar works. Test the elements, and modify it as you wish.

You have now completed the final step in building a content area by adding the custom navigation bar. The content area has its own style and graphics, and allows users to quickly find corporate resources using a variety of methods. While there are a lot of new terms and techniques to master, working with content areas quickly becomes an intuitive and dynamic process.

Extending the Content Area

We've shown a considerable number of customization techniques, but Portal content area customization can go far beyond altering the layout, terminology, and structure of the content area. Portal allows you to create your own attributes to attach to custom item and file types, and then pass those attributes to custom PL/SQL routines or any code that you can call using HTTP. You can also considerably extend the accuracy and utility of your searches by enabling interMedia.

Custom Types

You may find as you build your content area that you wish to track additional information about a particular class of item. Keywords and perspectives are useful to a degree, but when you need to standardize the information, supply custom fields, or enforce data entry, you will want to add named attributes. Custom item attributes can be validated against a list of values, made mandatory, and searched in the Advanced Search page. You can also add code to a custom item and choose how to execute that code.

For example, if your content contained technical papers presented at user conferences, you might want to track the name and year of the conference where the paper was presented, and the name and other information about the presenter(s). For each conference paper, you could add a custom code link that would display the presenter's biographical information. In this section, we will create custom attributes, add them to custom item types, and add code to these types.

Attributes

To build a custom item, you must first create and set properties for its attributes. From the Navigator Content Areas tab, you can click the Contents link, then the Custom Types link to begin creating attributes. After you have created the attributes, you can then create the custom item type, specifying your attributes. Creating an attribute is as simple as giving it a name and display name, then choosing its datatype from among the following types: Boolean, Date, File, Number, PL/SQL, Text, URL, or Application Component. The datatype is used to validate user input.

After creating an attribute, you can further refine its properties. Use the Edit Attribute page to add an LOV to assist with and validate user input, or to enable translations for the attribute. Enabling translations ensures that the attribute will display with all language versions of the item.

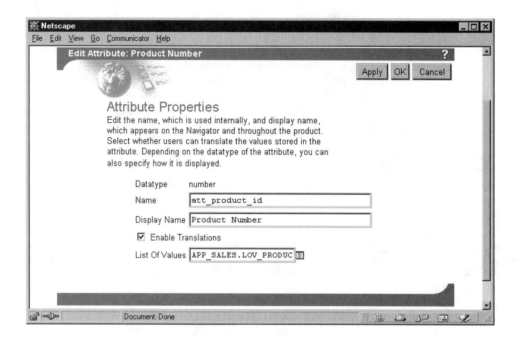

Item Types

Create an item type in the same page where you created the attribute. The item type can be based on any of a number of default item types within Portal, or it can be completely custom and not based on any type. In the latter case, you would have to add custom code for the item to function. You can base custom types on any of these default types: File, Folder Link, Image, Java Application, PL/SQL, Text, URL, or Application Component.

Once you have created the type, you will edit its properties to add attributes and custom code. You can optionally add a description and an icon to represent the item type on the Main tab.

On the Attributes tab, you will specify the attributes to associate with the type by moving them into the Selected Attributes list. Click Apply, and you will have the opportunity to specify a default value and set the attribute as Primary. Primary means that the attribute is an identifier of the item, and is the way to make an attribute mandatory.

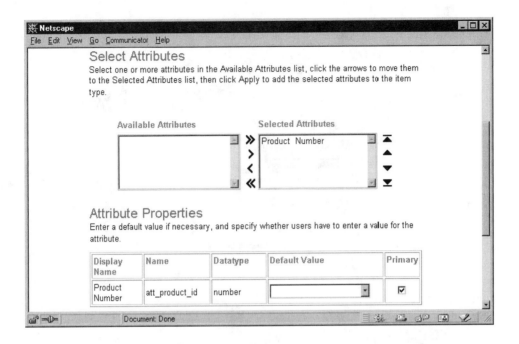

Finally, you can add any number of custom code links to the type. The Procedures tab allows you to specify procedure calls, either to HTTP resources or to PL/SQL programs. HTTP resources can be any program that can accept a CGI query string, and PL/SQL programs can refer to custom code, or to components developed in Portal. Each procedure call will display as a link with its own distinct link text or icon, unless you elect to display the procedure results with the item. The latter option is useful to display price, quantity, or other related details that you may need to retrieve from the database or an external data source. Because different programs may use different parameters names for the same information, you can specify the name of each attribute (using the "Pass As" field) as expected by the called procedure. When users create items based on the custom type, they will set values for the custom attributes. These values will be appended as arguments to the URL or PL/SQL procedure call, creating unique links for each item instance.

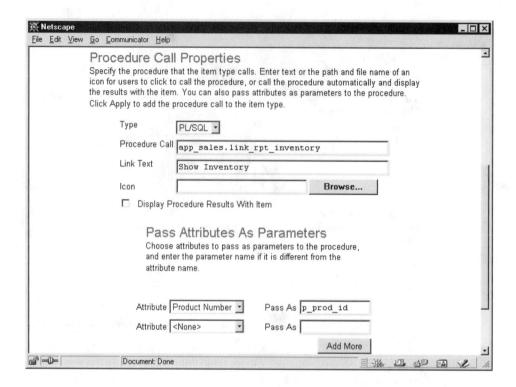

Folder Types

With custom folder types, you can use the same customization techniques on a folder type as you could on an item type. All of the properties and steps are the same, but now the type can be used to create folders with additional attributes and functionality. All four folder types can serve as the basis for a custom folder type, and the usual properties of the base folder type will still be available to users creating or editing folders in your custom type.

Exercise 6.9: Custom Types

In this exercise, we will devise an alternate item type for the product specification papers, so we can link the specification to the product ID.

   1. Go to the Navigator Content Areas tab and click on the Contents link for eXYZ Resource Center. Click on Custom Types, and then click Create on the Attributes line.

2. Give the Attribute a Name of `att_product_id` and a Display Name of `Product`. Set the Datatype to `Number`, and click Create.

3. Click on the Attribute name to edit it. In the LOV field, use the list icon to choose `APP_SALES.LOV_PRODUCTS`.

4. Now create an item type, specifying `it_prod_spec` for the Name and `Product Specification` for the Display Name. Set the Base Item Type to File.

5. Edit the item type, and on the Attributes tab, add Product to the Selected Attributes list. Click Apply, then OK.

6. To create items in this custom type, we will use the file item as we did in Exercise 6.6. Delete all of the product specifications in the Sales and Product Information folder, then repeat the steps to upload and unzip the file, but this time choose Product Specification for the Item Type in the Bulk Load page.

7. Edit the properties of one or two products, to see that the Product field now exists. Select the corresponding product name from the LOV and click OK.

To use `att_product_id` in links to procedures, it must be populated for each of the items, or the procedure code must be able to handle a `NULL` value for the product ID. In the exercise, you set a few of the product IDs manually, but when you have a large number of content area items, you will need a method to set the attributes using a SQL statement or PL/SQL procedure. You can add attribute values using an `INSERT` statement against WWV_THINGATTRIBUTES, but the data in this table is made up of ID references to several other tables in the Portal repository. A little reverse engineering on the repository will easily yield the correct data relationships. Look on the Oracle Press Web site for a companion volume to this book that explains the Portal repository.

interMedia

Oracle interMedia facilitates text mining of unstructured documents and other multimedia information, such as image and sound, that is stored in the content area. Text mining involves sophisticated algorithms including linguistic processing to find keywords, related words, meaning, and themes in documents. interMedia can search any document in the content area, such as word processing documents, PowerPoint presentations, Internet URLs, images, audio, and PDF files. It is not limited to use within a content area, as it can mine information from files stored on disk or even through URLs, but we will narrow the discussion to its use within a content area.

To use interMedia, you must install it in the database using the Oracle Universal Installer. It is installed by default when you use the "Typical Configuration" option, but there are some post-installation steps to ensure that it is correctly configured. These steps are beyond the scope of this book—see your installation documentation for more details on installing and configuring interMedia.

interMedia works by creating a special kind of index for all documents to be included within its realm. Oracle Portal automatically creates these indexes on the columns that contain the content area items, but the quality of these indexes depends on the configuration that you do prior to creating them. The configuration settings, also outside the scope of this book, include ways to define terms that are important to your industry, terms to ignore, languages you will enable, and even document sections (depending on document type) of particular importance. In addition, you can create or import a thesaurus that defines relationships among terms within your industry, in accordance with a set of rules for thesaurus definition.

The need for thesauri may not be immediately obvious, but consider this example: the word "film" is synonymous with "movie" if you are in the motion picture industry, and you would most likely want a search on "film" to return documents containing "movie". However, if you were in the plastics business, the film you work with is not at all synonymous with movies, and it would be a considerable waste of your time to have to sort through the unrelated content.

In addition, interMedia can identify the *theme* of a document by using natural language algorithms based on frequently occurring nouns and verbs to try to "understand" the document. A *gist* uses those nouns and verbs to provide, as the name implies, the gist of what the document is all about, and is remarkably accurate (given a good configuration). Themes and gists can be displayed along with the items in the content area.

Once you have interMedia installed and configured to your satisfaction, you must enable it for the Portal installation. When you enable interMedia, you do so for all content areas within the Portal installation. To begin, log in using an account with Administrator privileges and navigate to the Portal home page Administer tab. In the Services portlet, click Search Settings, and scroll down to the bottom of the page. You can enable interMedia text searches independently of the themes and gists features, and you can optionally choose a different color or text style for interMedia to use to highlight found keywords. Select your settings, then click Create Index. This will take a while, particularly if you have a lot of content, as interMedia is examining each document for elements to index. The creation and maintenance of indexes is best saved for times when the database transaction volume is low.

Once you have an index created, the button will change to Drop Index. You will periodically rebuild the index by dropping and re-creating it, so that the index remains current with any new or updated content.

With the index, a search that returned only a few documents before may return many more, because the search is now able to see inside each document, rather than just checking keywords, titles, and descriptions. In addition, the Search Results page will offer more details about the expected relevance of each returned document.

Conclusion

In this chapter, we introduced and described all of the basic content area components. We walked you through the process of building content area folders, adding items, and customizing searches, navigation, and style. We enabled interMedia text searches to help users find content, and created custom types to further extend the site. In the next few chapters, we will move on to building interactive forms to solicit data from the end user, and creating application components.

CHAPTER
7

Developing
Enterprise Forms

V irtually any type of application needs to request information from end users. Whether that information is to be stored in a database table for later use, or used in the processing and discarded, a Web application needs some mechanism to request and process user input. For example, you may need to collect demographic information about your clients, obtain order details, or allow users to submit expense information to create reimbursement requests. If you have been working with Oracle for some time, you probably have preexisting PL/SQL packages or procedures that you would like your users to access from the Web site. When working with content areas, you may decide to provide users with custom tools for content submission. The uses of online forms are unlimited, and Oracle Portal provides some convenient techniques to automatically create online forms.

Using wizards, you can produce simple forms with a customized user interface quickly and easily. You can then add data validation options to ensure that corporate business rules are enforced by the form. More complex requirements or business rules can be addressed with customized processing before or after the form is executed. In this chapter, you will create several forms, so that you can see first hand how form components work within an application.

Types of Forms

Three different form options are available in the Oracle Portal development environment. They are *forms based on tables or views; master-detail forms;* and *forms based on procedures.* The first two are wizard-based, and support query, UPDATE, INSERT, and DELETE. Forms based on procedures will do anything the associated PL/SQL procedure does—they simply serve as an interface to request parameters for the procedure. All three types have similar options for customization and data validation, and all three can be passed default values when called from another component. The choice of which type of form to use depends simply on your requirements, as you'll see in this section.

TIP

There is actually a fourth kind of "form," which is useful when you need a single component that supports reporting, search, data entry, and data modification on the same table. This is a query-by- example, or QBE report. The QBE report offers less flexibility in terms of the programming options, but supports a much richer set of display choices. In the QBE report, for example, the query results are displayed in full as a table, while the form components can only display one record at a time. You may wish to review the QBE report section in Chapter 8 before you commit to designing a form and a separate report based on the same table. Another option for custom coding your form is the dynamic page component, which we will cover in Chapter 10.

Form Based on Table or View

The form based on a table or view is the simplest way to provide an interface to a single table. If you need to provide access to multiple tables, or to only a subset of rows in a table, you can still use this form—you will just base it on a view that you have already created in the database. When you create the form, you will select the table or view of interest, then choose whether and how to display each column. You will control the operations allowed in the form by showing or hiding buttons that are preprogrammed to query, INSERT, UPDATE, or DELETE records. You can extend this type of form by adding list-based validation, derived fields, and custom buttons.

You will create two of these simple forms. The first allows managers to document the employee review process in an online form instead of using the older paper-based method. You will see how to prevent DELETES and INSERTS in this form, pictured in Figure 7-1. The second, pictured in Figure 7-2, allows users to create events for display in the corporate calendar.

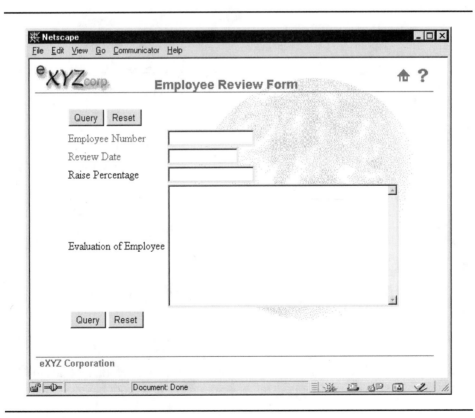

FIGURE 7-1. *The employee review form allows managers to document reviews without a paper process*

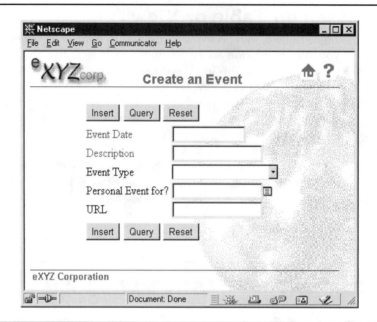

FIGURE 7-2. *The events form allows users to create both personal and company-wide events*

Master-Detail Form

When you need to display data from two tables that are (or could be) related by a foreign key, the simplest approach is to use a master-detail form. This type of form is designed with the commonsense notion that the relationship is best represented by displaying a single record from the parent table at the top of the screen and multiple related records from the child table below. Records from both the parent and child tables can be edited and queried, and all of the formatting and validation controls available with the form based on table or view are available in this form as well.

You will create a master-detail form that allows the sales crew to create orders in the system, as shown in Figure 7-3. This sort of an order entry system is intended to be used on an intranet or extranet site, because it assumes that users know and understand the product line. If you need to build a shopping interface, a content area combined with a form to accept the user's purchase information is probably more appropriate. The design techniques would be a little different, too, because you would want to provide more detailed help screens and more bulletproof data entry devices.

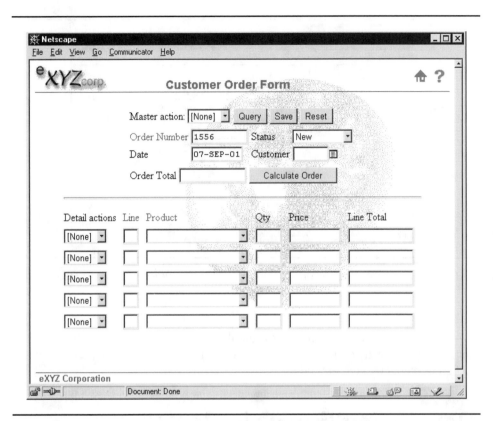

FIGURE 7-3. *Sales personnel will use this master-detail form to create customer orders*

Form Based on Procedure

When the complexity of your business logic exceeds the basic capabilities of a form based on one or more tables, you may be able to code the logic as a stored procedure. You can then use a form based on procedure to solicit the required parameters from the user. The form based on procedure is simply an interface to existing code, and so can be used to integrate legacy PL/SQL into the portal as a portlet, or to quickly produce an interface to a complex routine. The advantage of using a form to retrieve data for a procedure is that you can attach lists of values to support parameter validation, and customize the display to match the look and feel of the other site components. You can also manage the security directly through the Portal interface, a significant administrative benefit. There is a little added maintenance, because you will have to manage the PL/SQL procedure separately from the component.

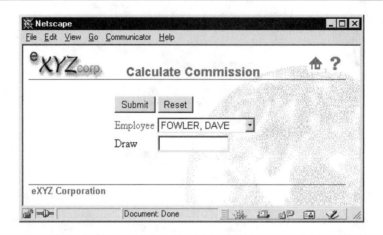

FIGURE 7-4. *Forms based on procedures are a convenient way to access existing code through a portlet interface*

eXYZ Corporation has a process to calculate and pay commissions due to sales staff, which is already coded in a PL/SQL procedure. Later in this chapter, you will build the interface to the procedure, shown in Figure 7-4.

Developing Forms in Portal

The environment in which you will be working is consistent across all types of forms. Creating any component, as you have already seen, involves clicking on a link at the top of the Navigator page for the application. When you create a new form, you first specify the type of form: form based on a table or view, master-detail form, or form based on a procedure. The wizard steps are essentially the same in all forms, except the master-detail form, which has an extra step to set up the Detail block. We will begin by walking through the process for creating a form based on table or view in detail, and then illustrate the differences in the wizards for the other form types. If you are a hands-on learner, feel free to create a form in Portal as you read through this section. If you accept all the defaults as you click through the wizard, you will produce a simple form for the SCOTT.EMP table. In this way, you will be able to see first hand the settings and dialogs available in the wizard, rather than trying to interpret the settings from the illustrations, which cannot always show all of the possible options. Following each section will be an exercise in which you can build a sample form.

Form Based on Table or View—Step by Step

Once you have chosen to create a form based on table or view, you will specify the form name and application, as shown in the illustration. The Name is used internally and in the Navigator to uniquely identify the form. The Display Name is used as the title for the displayed form, in the Portlet Repository for the link to access the component, and as the default portlet title. The Application can be changed in this step, too, in case you accidentally clicked the create link in the wrong application.

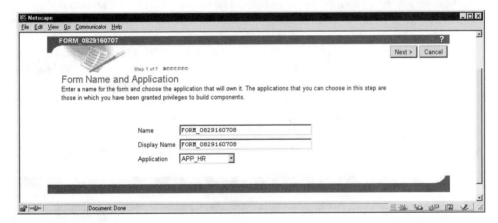

Table or View

The next step is to specify the table or view that you will use in the form. This kind of form can be based on only a single table or view, as shown below. Clicking on the list icon brings up a list of tables and views accessible to the application owner. See the "Modifiable Views" box (on page 9) for information on working with views in forms.

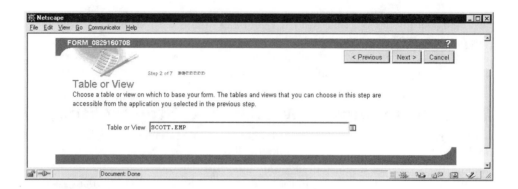

Form Layout

The next step is the choice of layout options. The default is a tabular layout, which orients the fields within a series of nested HTML tables. Custom layout allows you to modify the default HTML for the form, but is not necessary in most cases, and can be difficult to work with. However, if it's flexibility and style you're after, the custom layout is the way to go. When you choose a custom layout, you will have an additional step in the wizard to edit the HTML. A few of the settings for formatting items will not appear in the Formatting and Validation Options page (discussed next), because the assumption is that you will modify those settings by editing the HTML. The wizard simply exposes the exact same HTML as would be generated for the tabular layout. We won't use a custom layout for forms, but will illustrate this technique for a report in Chapter 8.

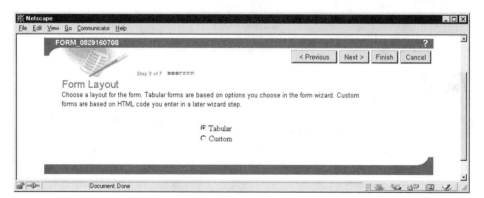

Modifiable Views

If you want to allow INSERT, UPDATE, and DELETE in a form based on a view, you will need to ensure that the view is modifiable. An updatable view must contain no aggregate functions (that is, AVG, SUM, MIN, MAX, COUNT), no implicit joins through object references, and no set operators (UNION, MINUS, INTERSECT). If the view contains a join, only key-preserved tables can be updated. A key-preserved table is one whose primary key would match the primary key of the view, if the view could have a primary key. Deletes are allowed if there is only one key-preserved table in the view, and inserts are allowed as long as each INSERT statement references a single key-preserved table.

For example, consider a view that joins employee data to department data, so that the name of the department for which the employee works can be displayed along with each employee record. The primary table of the view (EMPLOYEES) is key-preserved, since one row in the view corresponds to exactly one row in the EMPLOYEES table. The lookup table in the view (DEPARTMENTS) is not key-preserved, since multiple rows in the view could map to a single DEPARTMENTS row.

In Figure 7-5, we show a simple form with the table borders exposed so that you can see how each part of the form is rendered in the nested tables. Notice that the template creates a table, with one row each for the template header section, the component, and the template footer section. Within the component, the top buttons are rendered in a single-row table, each button occupying a table data cell. A second table is opened for the middle section, which contains the data fields. Each field (by default) displays within a single table row, with a data cell for the label and another to contain the input field. The bottom button items are contained within another table, with the same format as the top section, except there is a placeholder for Previous and Next buttons. These are only visible when the form contains multiple rows as a result of a query.

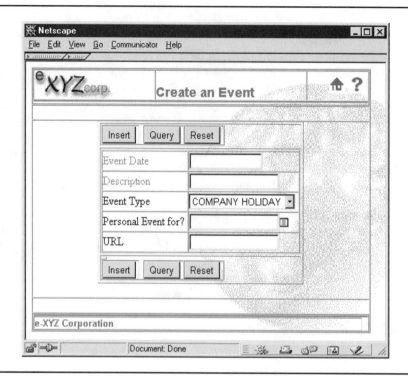

FIGURE 7-5.   *The HTML of this form has been edited to illustrate the nested HTML tables*

Formatting and Validation Options

Next is the detailed Formatting and Validation Options page, by far the most complex of the form wizard pages. Here you will specify complex validation, customize the display, or add your own JavaScript event handlers, if you need to alter the default behavior of individual fields in any way. As you can see in Figure 7-6, the Formatting and Validation Options page contains four frames. The top frame lets you navigate to the next page, and the bottom frame simply completes the graphic element as seen on all wizard pages. The real work is done in the two middle frames (left and right), as you'll see in the pages to follow.

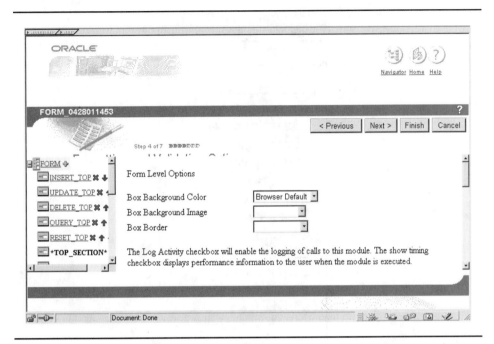

FIGURE 7-6.   *The Formatting and Validation Options screen*

Form Navigator   In the left frame is a hierarchy of items contained in the form, organized by form section. The sections govern the display location of the item in the set of nested tables that make up the form, as you saw in Figure 7-5. The top and bottom sections are usually used for buttons and other control items, and the middle section is where the form data fields go. Where you place an item on a form has no effect on the execution of the form, but does help with organizing the user's view of the interface.

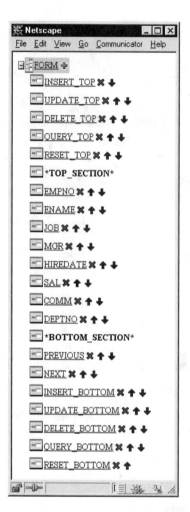

The wizard automatically generates a set of default buttons and one form field for each column in the table or view. To create a custom item in the form, click on the green + sign at the FORM node, give the item a name, then move it to the appropriate location. Use the blue arrows to move items up and down in the form, changing the display order. The red X deletes an item from the form, making its value inaccessible to any custom code in the form. You can create an item to replace one that was accidentally deleted by naming it the same as the corresponding database column. Use a distinct name to add a new item to the form, either to enhance the display or to hold hidden or calculated values.

TIP

When working in the Formatting and Validation Options screen, you may find it helpful to reduce the font size in the browser. In Netscape, click in the hierarchy frame and type CTRL-[*until you can see the up arrows for all fields. In Internet Explorer, try the following menu choice: View | Text Size | Smallest.*

Clicking on the name of any of these items, including the form itself, displays the corresponding property sheet in the right frame. Each property sheet differs, based on the selected item type, as you'll see in the descriptions to follow.

Form Properties   The top of the hierarchy is the FORM item, and it is there that you will change basic properties of the form. Form level options are summarized in Table 7-1.

```
┌─────────────────────────────────────────────────────────────────────────┐
│ ※ Netscape                                                     _ □ ✕     │
│ File  Edit  View  Go  Communicator  Help                                 │
│ ┌─────────────────────────────────────────────────────────────────────┐ │
│ │ Form Level Options                                                    │ │
│ │                                                                       │ │
│ │  Box Background Color          [Browser Default ▾]                    │ │
│ │  Box Background Image          [              ▾]                      │ │
│ │  Box Border                    [No Border    ▾]                       │ │
│ │                                                                       │ │
│ │  The Log Activity checkbox will enable the logging of calls to this   │ │
│ │  module. The show timing checkbox displays performance information    │ │
│ │  to the user when the module is executed.                             │ │
│ │                                                                       │ │
│ │                          ☐ Log Activity                               │ │
│ │                          ☐ Show Timing                                │ │
│ │                                                                       │ │
│ │  Order by     [%        ▾]   [Ascending ▾]                            │ │
│ │  Then by      [%        ▾]   [Ascending ▾]                            │ │
│ │  Then by      [%        ▾]   [Ascending ▾]                            │ │
│ │  Then by      [%        ▾]   [Ascending ▾]                            │ │
│ │  Then by      [%        ▾]   [Ascending ▾]                            │ │
│ │  Then by      [%        ▾]   [Ascending ▾]                            │ │
│ │                                                                       │ │
│ │  On successful submission of a form, execute this PL/SQL block or     │ │
│ │  PL/SQL procedure:                                                    │ │
│ │  Hint:                                                                 │ │
│ │  You can redirect your browser to a PL/SQL procedure, for example a   │ │
│ │  procedure that creates a Web page, using either of these methods:    │ │
│ │                                                                       │ │
│ │    1. call('<url>', '<parameter name for back url>');                 │ │
│ │       Redirects the browser to the procedure and passes a parameter   │ │
│ │       containing the URL back to the form.                            │ │
│ │    2. go('<url>');                                                    │ │
│ │       Redirects the browser to the procedure but does not pass a URL  │ │
│ │       to return to the form.                                          │ │
│ │  ┌──────────────────────────────────────────────────────────────┐    │ │
│ │  │                                                              │    │ │
│ │  └──────────────────────────────────────────────────────────────┘    │ │
│ └─────────────────────────────────────────────────────────────────────┘ │
│ ⚐ =□=      Document: Done                  ☰ ⬚ ⬚ ⬚ ⬚ ✐                │
└─────────────────────────────────────────────────────────────────────────┘
```

Property	Purpose
Box Background Color	Change the color for the generated HTML table that contains the form items and labels.
Box Background Image	Set an image to be used as the background for the table.
Box Border	Specify thick, thin, or no border for the table.
Log Activity	Create a log entry for each use of the form. (See Chapter 12 for more details on logging component activity.)
Show Timing	Create an entry at the bottom of the page to report the time it took to display, query, or process a change to the form's data.
Order by	Change the sort order of the rows displayed as the result of a query. Allows specification of up to six columns from the source table, each in descending or ascending order. Default is to sort on Oracle `ROWID`.
On successful submission	Allows you to redirect the user to another page or form upon a successful `INSERT`, `UPDATE`, or `DELETE`. Overrides the default redirection, which resets the form and gives the user a message describing the successful operation. Use the `call` or `go` procedure to create a succession of forms in a complex data entry situation. The `call` syntax allows you to create "back" links in each successive form, and requires that the target procedure accept a parameter (named here) to hold the current form's URL.

TABLE 7-1. *Form-Level Properties for the Formatting and Validation Options Page*

Form Items   There are 15 types of items available for placement or customization on a form. Several of these are merely to enhance the display, and these have few or no properties, while the others correspond to HTML input types. The Blank item type simply creates some white space on the form, and the Horizontal Rule creates a line within the table—these have no additional properties. To add a static image to a form, use the Image item type and upload the image to be stored in the database with the form definition. Label Only allows you to add custom text or hyperlinks anywhere within the form. The remaining types allow data entry or create buttons to handle user actions, and are described in Table 7-2 and the "Buttons" section that follows. Below is an illustration of the properties page for a TextBox item, which contains most of the properties discussed.

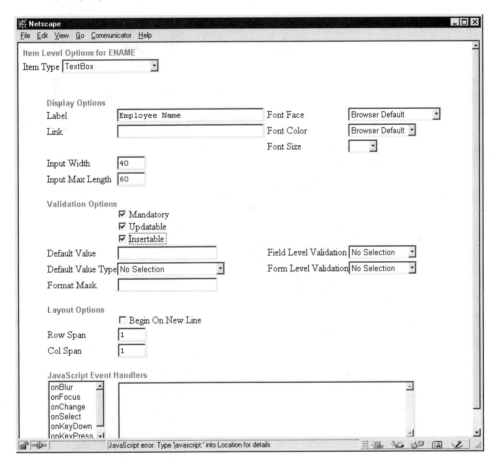

Property	Purpose	Applies to
Item Type	Choose any of the standard HTML input types in which to display your data.	All items
Image Location	Use to upload an image for an image item.	Image

Display Options

Label	The label displayed with the field. Can be blank.	Button, CheckBox, Combobox, File Upload, Label Only, Password, Popup, Radio Group, TextArea, TextBox
Link	Specify a URL to turn the label into an active link.	All items with a label, except Buttons—in that case, the label is the button text
Font Options	Set Font Color, Font Face, and Font Size for the label. Required fields default to Red, others to Browser Default.	All items with a label, except Buttons—button text uses browser default
Input Width	Sets the size of the data entry field. Ignored for combo boxes and radio groups, which are always wide enough to display all text.	Combobox, File Upload, Password, Popup, Radio Group, TextArea, TextBox
Input Height	Sets the height of the data entry field. Ignored for radio groups and pop-ups. Causes a combo box to show the specified number of items, but does not create a multiple-select list.	Combobox, Popup, Radio Group, TextArea
Input Max Length	The maximum number of characters that can be entered in the field, regardless of input width.	Password, TextBox

Validation Options

Mandatory	Enforces data entry. Does not apply to list items—use the list or a JavaScript Event Handler to restrict NULL values.	File Upload, Password, TextArea, TextBox

TABLE 7-2. *Item Properties*

Property	Purpose	Applies to
Updatable	Allows the value to be used in a database UPDATE statement—if unchecked, the field will display as plain text on queries, rather than as modifiable data within a text box.	Combobox, File Upload, Hidden, Password, Popup, Radio Group, TextArea, TextBox
Insertable	Allows INSERT—unchecked means the field will not be used in the database INSERT statement.	Combobox, File Upload, Hidden, Password, Popup, Radio Group, TextArea, TextBox
List Of Values	Choose an LOV to supply the values for the field from among those in the current application.	Combobox, Popup, Radio Group
Default Value	Specify a constant or expression to use as a default value for the field. For list items, the value should correspond to one of the return values in the list, and will cause that value to appear selected on first entering the form. Provides the INSERT value for a hidden field. A shortcut for evaluating database expressions is to prefix the expression with a pound sign (#), which does not require you to set the Default Value Type field (next).	Combobox, Hidden, Popup, Radio Group, TextArea, TextBox
Default Value Type	If using an expression, set this to help Portal figure out how to evaluate the expression. Use SQL, database function calls, and JavaScript expressions, by datatype.	Same as Default Value field
Format Mask	Alter the display format of dates and numbers. Applies only to queried records, but the user must know to remove any format characters (such as currency symbols) when updating a numeric value. Work around this with a JavaScript select() statement in an onFocus event handler to automatically select the existing value so the user's typing will replace the field contents (see "JavaScript" section for more information).	Hidden, TextArea, TextBox

TABLE 7-2. *Item Properties* (continued)

Property	Purpose	Applies to
Field & Form Level Validation	Choose a predefined or custom Javascript (from the Shared Components application) to validate the entry. Field-level validation does not allow the user to leave the field until the value is correct. Form-level validation checks the value when users submit the form.	File Upload, Password, TextArea, TextBox

Layout Options (not available when using Custom Layout)

Property	Purpose	Applies to
Begin On New Line	Causes the item to display on the next line. Remove the checkmark to display fields side by side.	Button, CheckBox, Combobox, File Upload, Image, Label Only, Password, Popup, Radio Group, TextArea, TextBox
Row Span	Sets the number of rows the field will occupy in the generated table. Increase to allocate additional vertical room to the item.	CheckBox, Combobox, File Upload, Image, Label Only, Password, Popup, Radio Group, TextArea, TextBox
Col Span	Sets the number of columns the field will occupy in the generated table. Increase to allocate additional horizontal room to the item.	CheckBox, Combobox, File Upload, Image, Label Only, Password, Popup, Radio Group, TextArea, TextBox
JavaScript Event Handlers	Allows you to add custom JavaScript events to each item. See the "JavaScript" section later in this chapter for more detail. Different field types have different associated JavaScript events from which to choose.	Button, CheckBox, Combobox, File Upload, Password, Popup, Radio Group, TextArea, TextBox
PL/SQL Event Handlers	Use to specify custom actions (for buttons only) using PL/SQL. See "Buttons" section for more information.	Button

TABLE 7-2.   *Item Properties* (continued)

Buttons   The default buttons provided by the wizard perform queries, execute UPDATE, INSERT, and DELETE operations, reset the form, and navigate to the previous and next records in a query result set. You can change the label for any of these buttons to make your form more intuitive to your users, and you can remove buttons for functions you do not wish to allow.

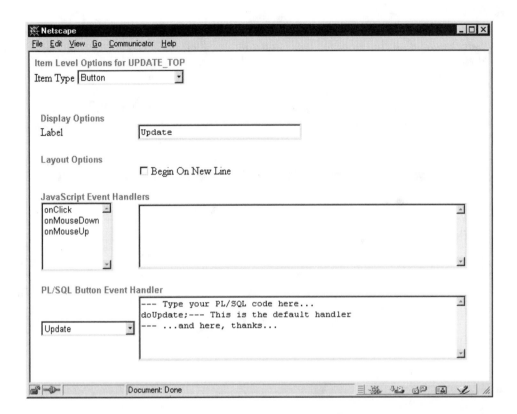

The default buttons each have a corresponding *default handler*. The default handler is a PL/SQL procedure generated within the form's package that performs the operation. You can override or add to the default processing of these buttons using JavaScript or PL/SQL.

To create a custom button, create the item and then set the Item Type to Button. Choose Custom from the PL/SQL Button Event Handler list and type your PL/SQL or specify JavaScript event handler code for the onClick, onMouseDown, or onMouseUp events. The default handlers will not be available to you directly if you are using a custom button. Regardless of whether you specify JavaScript or PL/SQL event handlers, clicking any button causes a form submission operation, because Portal assumes all actions require database communication. You can easily work around this limitation by adding JavaScript comment tags at the end of your custom code to prevent the built-in submit code from executing. Exercise 7.10 offers a practical example of how this would work.

Form Text

After you have set up all your fields, you can customize the text and graphics on the page surrounding the form. The first item allows you to choose a template in which to display the form. Next, you have an opportunity to change the Display

Name you entered in the first wizard step. This will be used as the window title or portlet header, and is included here so it can be edited later. (The first wizard step does not appear when reentering the wizard.) The remaining fields allow you to create helpful supporting text. Anything you enter in the Header Text field is displayed above the form, and the Footer Text is displayed below. Help Text is only accessible if the template contains a Help icon or link. When users click Help, the help text replaces the page and they must use the browser Back button to return to the form. These text fields each accept up to 30,000 bytes of text, HTML, or JavaScript.

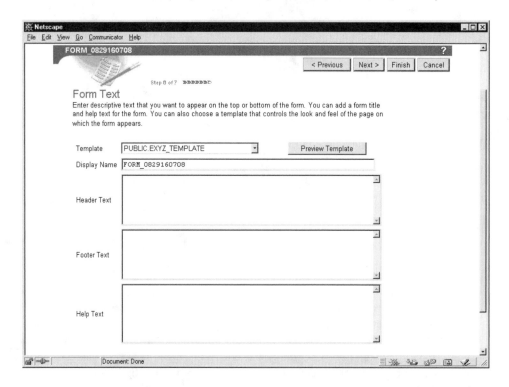

Additional PL/SQL Code

The Additional PL/SQL Code page allows you to add custom PL/SQL code at several points in the form execution process. These points, and some examples of the kinds of things you would do at each point, are shown in Table 7-3. The fields accept any PL/SQL, separated by semicolons. BEGIN-END pairs are not necessary unless you are declaring local variables. You may wish to call an existing procedure, update a related table, or display database values using the PL/SQL Web Toolkit. There is a significant advantage to using PL/SQL code rather than HTML, as you did on the Form Text page. With PL/SQL, you can easily access the database and use logic to determine what to display and how it should be formatted.

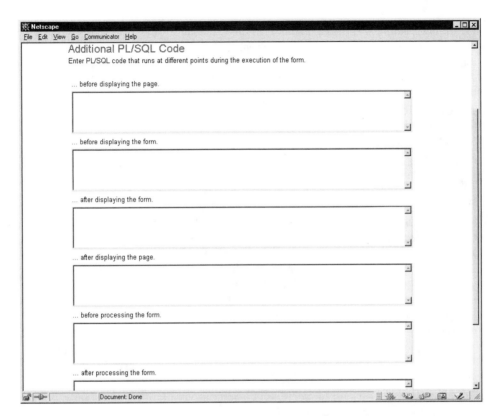

Something as simple as a welcome message can be personalized to welcome users by name, for example. Another option would be to provide users the ability to suppress the display of additional text in forms, and use PL/SQL to check the users'

Processing Step	Typical Usage
Before displaying the page	Set up any headers, JavaScript functions, or hidden values
Before displaying the form	Change form values, set defaults, display personalized messages
After displaying the form	Supply footer text or add custom links and images
After displaying the page	Add page footer text, links, images
Before processing the form	Test and alter values submitted by the user
After processing the form	Perform post-processing steps based on form results

TABLE 7-3.   *Sample Applications of Additional PL/SQL Code Fields*

preferences before displaying the text. In the last section of this chapter, we will explain the processing model and give you some insight into how you can access the runtime values in the form.

This is the last step of the wizard. When you click Finish, you will return to the Manage Component page. In the exercises to follow, we will guide you through the process of creating a form based on a table to support eXYZ's requirements. Portal forms are quick and easy to develop, so let's get started. In this section, you will build two of the forms pictured at the beginning of this chapter, and integrate them with the site using several different techniques. The data model and design are based on the requirements identified in Chapter 4.

Exercise 7.1: Employee Review Form

Before beginning this exercise, verify that you have the database and Portal set up correctly. If you skipped any of the exercises in Chapters 2-6, you may need to run a few scripts to prepare your Portal installation for the remaining exercises, to ensure that the necessary applications and pages are ready to go. Instructions for running the scripts are found in a `readme.doc` file in each of the chapter directories, and in the main `Table Data` directory. The `Table Data` directory contains the scripts to generate the database tables and procedures that we will use in the exercises. You will do all of the development exercises as the PATM user, the lead developer.

We'll begin with a simple form to record the results of employee performance reviews. This online form will replace the paper-based form now stored in the content area. We won't integrate it with the portal page or worry too much about validation, because it will be accessed through the content area and later from a calendar component. A trigger on the EMPLOYEES table creates the first review entry with the date set to six months after the hire date, and each subsequent review creates the next annual review. We'll implement this latter requirement, as well as the salary increase, in post-processing code. The review is initially created with no data in the comments or recommended salary increase fields, and the job of the reviewer is to fill in those details. Let's get started!

1. In the Navigator Applications tab, click on the APP_HR application and then click the word Form under the "Create New ..." listing.

2. Choose Form based on table or view.

3. Name the form FORM_REVIEW and give it a Display Name of Employee Review Form.

4. Click the Next button and you will be asked to enter the Table or View on which to base the form. Click the list icon and choose CORP_SITE.EMPLOYEE_REVIEWS.

5. On the next screen, choose a Tabular layout.

6. We won't allow any INSERTS or DELETES from this form, so click on the red "X" by the INSERT_TOP, DELETE_TOP, INSERT_BOTTOM, and DELETE_BOTTOM items, found in the form navigator.

7. Click on the word FORM at the top of the list. In the middle of its properties frame, you will see an Order By section. Change this so that the records are ordered by REVIEW_DATE, in Descending order.

8. Click on EMPLOYEE_ID and change the Label to Employee Number.

9. Click on REVIEW_DATE and change the Label to Review Date.

10. Click on RECOMMEND_INCREASE and change the Label to Raise Percentage. Set the Field Level Validation to the built-in Javascript inRange0-100. (You might consider creating a stored Javascript routine to limit the salary increase to a more realistic number—after your review, of course.) Remove the Form Level Validation by changing it to No Selection.

11. Click on REVIEW_COMMENTS and change the Label to Evaluation of Employee. Change the Item Type to TextArea, and set the Input Width to 40 and the Input Height to 10.

12. Click Next to see the Form Text page. Set the template to PUBLIC.EXYZ.TEMPLATE.

13. That's it! Click Finish; then click Run to test your form. Try a query to see the existing data, and give someone an evaluation. (You may find that we are a little behind on our review process.) The form displays both completed and pending evaluations, which allows us to use it in the context of both performing a review and viewing the results of a review. Using links, we can specify whether to show completed (defined as having non-NULL raise percentage and comments), pending, or specific reviews for an individual.

We will revisit this form and add the code to give the raise and schedule the next review in the last section of this chapter. For now, we need to ensure that the paper form will no longer be used. We will return to the content area and replace the review form item with a link to this form.

Exercise 7.2: Integrate a Form with the Content Area

1. Before leaving the Manage Component page, click on the Access tab and check the box labeled Publish to Portal. Click Apply and then Close.

2. Bring up the eXYZ Resource Center home page. (Use the Navigator Content Areas tab, a bookmark if you created one, or the eXYZ home page HR tab.)

3. Click on the Human Resources folder, then click Edit Folder.

4. Create a new item in the Forms category of type `Application Component` and click Next.

5. In the Primary Item Attributes section, set the Application Component field to `Human Resources Application: Employee Review Form`. Set the Display Name to `Employee Review Form` and click Next. Click Finish.

6. Choose `Portal Components` as the Displayed Perspective, and set the Display Options to `Link That Displays Item In Folder Area`. Click Finish.

7. Remove the PDF version of the employee review form.

8. Test your new form in the Content area.

Exercise 7.3: Event Form

The eXYZ home page will display a calendar of events, based on the CORP_CALENDAR table, and users will need a form to create new events. Events can contain a URL that provides more information about the event, but this is optional. An event with a user ID specified is intended as a personal event, which will only display on the calendar for that user. This way, the employees can use the calendar to track their own schedule as well as company events.

1. In the Human Resources Application, create an LOV named `LOV_EVENT_TYPES` with a default format of `Combo` box. Set Show Null Value to `Yes`, and use the following query:

```
SELECT event_type_desc, event_type_id
FROM CORP_SITE.event_types
```

2. Create a second LOV entitled `LOV_USERNAMES` with a default format of `Pop up`. Use the following query:

```
SELECT last_name||', '||first_name, user_id
FROM CORP_SITE.employees
```

3. Create a new form based on table or view named `FORM_EVENTS`, and give it a Display Name of `Create an Event`.

4. In the Table or View page, choose `CORP_SITE.CORP_CALENDAR` from the pop-up list.

5. Leave the Form Layout at Tabular and click Next.

6. At the `FORM` level, set the default Order By to `ACTION_DATE`, `Ascending`.

7. Change the Label for `ACTION_DATE` to `Event Date`. Set the Field Level Validation to `isDate`.

8. Change the Label for `EVENT_DESCRIPTION` to `Normal Font Description`.

9. For the `EVENT_TYPE` field, change the Label to `Event Type`. Set the Item Type to `Combobox` and specify `LOV_EVENT_TYPES` as the List Of Values.

10. For the `RESPONSIBLE_PARTY` field, change the Label to `Personal Event for?` and set the Item Type to `Popup`. Choose `LOV_USERNAMES` from the list.

11. For the URL field, change the Label to `URL`.

12. On the Form Text page, set the Template to `PUBLIC.EXYZ_TEMPLATE`.

13. Click Finish and test your form. Create a few events if you wish.

This form is only of limited interest by itself, but we will use it to demonstrate how to link to a form from another component. It won't be displayed directly on the eXYZ Home Page, but will be called from the calendar component, which we will build in Chapter 9.

Master-Detail Form—Step by Step

The Master-detail form wizard begins in the same way as the wizard for the form based on table or view, but in this case you are asked to specify two tables. The first is the master table, which is the parent table in a parent-child relationship. It will be displayed one record at a time at the top of the generated form. The second is the detail table, and you may choose any number of records to display for this table. For the remaining wizard steps, we will discuss only where they differ from the wizard for the form based on table or view.

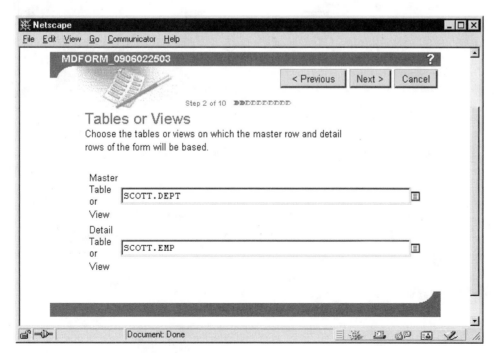

Join Conditions

Next, you will specify the join condition or conditions that relate master and detail records. If a database foreign key exists between the two tables, this join condition would be pre-populated with the columns from each table that are referenced in the key. In the case of a multi-part key, each part of the join condition is represented by one row on this page. You can use this form even in the absence of a database foreign key, as would be the case if you were basing the form on views rather than tables. Just specify the columns that would relate a single row in the master table or view to zero, one or many rows in the detail table or view, based on an equality condition.

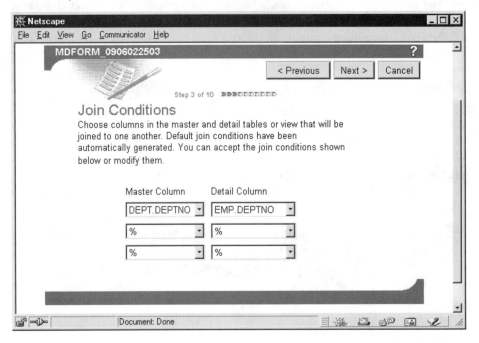

Formatting and Validation Options

Because this form has two sections, there are two of these pages—one for the master section, and the other for the details. They will still display on a single page in the generated form, but they each have their own set of navigation buttons and top and bottom sections. There are a few properties on each of these pages that are unique to master-detail forms, as we'll see.

> **NOTE**
> *You may see references to blocks when working with master-detail forms. This legacy term refers to the individual sections, and is used in identifying the field names in the generated form. There is a master block and a detail block on each master-detail form, but only a "default block" for other form types.*

On the form-level properties page for the master row, you will see a checkbox with a label of "Cascade Delete Detail Rows on Master Delete". If checked, this means that when users delete a master row, the corresponding detail rows are deleted along with it. Without it, the master delete will result in an error when detail rows exist. Whether to use this feature is a question of application design. Some master- detail relationships, such as orders to line items, naturally lend themselves to cascade delete. Others, such as departments to employees, are better represented without cascade delete, to protect the data from inadvertent removal. Database foreign keys offer similar delete cascade functionality, and if your database key specifies cascade delete, do not use this feature in the form. Doing so would cause two conflicting delete attempts, and would result in an error.

In a master-detail form, the actions are presented to the user in the form of a list, accompanied by a Save button. The form items that represent the lists are MASTER_ACTION for the master row and DETAIL_ACTION for the detail row, and for both the Item Type is Action List, a type we have not discussed. Instead of separate buttons for Update, Insert, and Delete, there will be a single Save button, which is automatically created as a part of the Action List. Users decide which action they will perform by selecting the action from the list, and then click Save to execute the action. Queries are only supported on the master record.

The remaining pages are the same for all form types. For the master-detail form, any custom text or PL/SQL is displayed before or after the entire form, and there are no options to interject text or processing between the sections. In the exercise that follows, you will create a master-detail form that is considerably more complex than the forms we developed in the last section.

Exercise 7.4: Placing Customer Orders

The customer order form will be a master-detail form based on the CUSTOMER_ ORDERS and ORDER_LINE_ITEMS tables. You will create a new LOV to support lookups to the PRODUCTS table, and use the LOV you created in Chapter 5 to look up customers. Continue to work under the PATM login name in this section, but use the APP_SALES application to hold this component.

1. Create an LOV named LOV_PRODUCTS in APP_SALES, using the following query and leaving the remaining fields to their defaults:

```
SELECT INITCAP(description), product_id
FROM   products
ORDER BY INITCAP(description)
```

2. Test your LOV, then close the Manage Component page and create a new master-detail form.

3. Set the form Name to MDFORM_ORDERS and the Display Name to Customer Order Form.

4. Set the Master Table or View to `CORP_SITE.CUSTOMER_ORDERS`, and the Detail Table or View to `CORP_SITE.ORDER_LINE_ITEMS`.

5. On the next page, you will see that the join condition to link the tables on the ORDER_NO column has been automatically created, based on the database foreign key constraint.

6. Skip the next page, as we will use the default Tabular layout.

7. In the Formatting and Validation Options for Master Row page, start by moving some of the fields around. Click on the up arrow to move `MASTER_ACTION` to the very top of the form, above the buttons in the top section. Move the `ORDER_STATUS` field until it is just below `ORDER_NO`. Move the `ORDER_DATE` field to just below `ORDER_STATUS`. Move `EMPLOYEE_ID` to the bottom of the middle section.

8. Click on `ORDER_NO` and set the Label to `Order Number`, the Input Width to `10` and Input Max Length to `6`, and uncheck Updatable. We will generate this field from a sequence, but the order number must be visible so that the sales rep can provide it to the customer when the order is complete. Set the Default Value to `#seq_order_no.NEXTVAL`.

NOTE
The pound (#) sign is an indicator to the Portal engine that a function is to follow, and does not require that you set the Default Value Type. Use it as shorthand with simple functions like `SYSDATE` *or mathematical operations.*

9. After the `ORDER_NO` field is populated with the sequence value, the user could possibly change it before they save the record, because it is no different from any other form field. HTML does not have a read-only input attribute, but we can prevent changes to the field with a little JavaScript trick. At the bottom of the details screen for `ORDER_NO`, in the section labeled "JavaScript Event Handlers", click on `onFocus` to create the handler for that event. Enter the following code:

```
if (this.value != '') blur();
```

This will have the effect of navigating the user out of the field every time they enter it! The purpose of the `if` statement is to allow the user to enter data in the field during a query, when all fields are `NULL`. When the field is populated with an order number, the user will not be able to enter the field at all.

10. Next, click on ORDER_STATUS and change the Item Type to Combobox, then select LOV_ORDER_STATUS for the List Of Values. Set the Label to Status and the Input Width to 9. Set the Default Value to N (for a New Order) and the Default Value Type to Constant. Under Layout Options, uncheck the box labeled Begin On New Line.

11. For ORDER_DATE, change the Label to Date. Make it Mandatory and nonupdatable and set the Default Value to #SYSDATE. Change the Font Color to Red to indicate that this is a required field. Set the Input Width and Max Length to 9. Leave the Format Mask as it is, and apply the isDate Javascript for Field Level Validation.

12. Click on CUSTOMER_ID and set the Item Type to Popup. Set the List Of Values to LOV_CUSTOMERS. Change the Label to Customer and the Input Width to 6. Clear the Begin On New Line checkbox.

13. Click on EMPLOYEE_ID and change the Item Type to Hidden. Uncheck Updatable. In the Default Value field, type the following statement:

```
SELECT employee_id FROM employees
WHERE user_id = PORTAL30.WWCTX_API.GET_USER
```

and choose SQL query returns number from the drop-down list for Default Value Type.

14. Click Next, and you will see a similar screen to set up the Detail Rows. Change the Order By to ORDER_LINE_NUMBER.

15. Remove the UNIT_MARGIN and COMMISSION_EARNED fields.

16. Click on ORDER_NO and change its type to Hidden so that the order number does not display with the detail records. Uncheck Updatable and move the field down so it is the last field in the middle section.

NOTE
In the 3.0.9 release, Portal creates an HTML table data element for all fields, including hidden fields. If you leave this hidden value in its default location, the table headings will be improperly aligned with the data entry fields, because there is no column heading for the hidden field. Another workaround is to use a custom layout.

17. Click on ORDER_LINE_NUMBER and change the Label to Line. Change the Input Width and Input Max Length to 2, and uncheck Updatable.

18. For the PRODUCT_ID field, choose Combobox as the Item Type and select LOV_PRODUCTS from the list. Change the Label to Product.

19. For QTY_SOLD, change the Label to Qty and reduce the Input Width and Input Max Length to 4. Set the Field Level Validation to isInteger. (The Form Level Validation is automatically set to isNumber, because QTY_SOLD is a numeric column, but we want to improve on that. We will ensure that no one orders fractional quantities, and we want to catch any data entry error before they leave the field, so users won't have to go back and correct multiple rows. You can remove the Form Level Validation to save on processing.) Set the Format Mask property to 999.

TIP

A format model of '999' fills empty leading digits with spaces to the length of the model, and then pads the resulting string with another leading space. The number 52 would therefore translate to the string '^^52' (where the caret represents a space). Use this to your advantage by setting the length of the field to at least one character greater than the length of the format mask. By doing so, you enforce right-justification in your numeric fields and the numbers don't "roll off" the edge of the field. Format masks only apply on query retrieval. To format numbers as they are entered, you would apply a JavaScript onChange event.

20. Change the Label for UNIT_PRICE_SOLD to Price, and set the Input Width and Input Max Length to 9. Set the Field Level Validation to isNumber. Give the field a Format Mask of 9,999.00.

21. Click on TOTAL_PRICE_SOLD and change the Label to Line Total. Set the Input Width and Input Max Length to 12. Specify a Format Mask of $999,999.00.

22. Click Next and select PUBLIC.EXYZ_TEMPLATE for the Template field.

23. Click the Finish button to get a preliminary test of the form.

At this point, you have a working form. Try it out, entering a few orders and order items. Try to change the order number, and attempt to enter an invalid date for the order date so you can see how the validation works. Check all of the lists to ensure they are working as expected. Notice that you have to select the actions from the list and then save to get your orders created. Try a query of existing orders as well.

TIP

To query, press the Query button twice—once to put the form into query mode, where you can optionally enter query criteria, and again to execute the query.

The form is missing a couple of key features. The line item numbers are blank, but they should be populated automatically. The line total (extended price) field should be a calculated value, and it should never be changed by the salesperson. And what about the price of each product? We could populate this field automatically with a SQL statement, but the sales force wants some flexibility with the price to allow negotiating room. The PRODUCTS table stores two prices—the list price and the minimum price—for each product. What we need is to ensure that the negotiated price falls within this range. All of the features described here can only be implemented with the aid of JavaScript, and the functions are not simple. The last section of this chapter will introduce the advanced JavaScript and PL/SQL code that allows you to accomplish all of these things. For now, we will integrate the form with the eXYZ portal page.

Exercise 7.5: Integrate the Order Form with the Portal

1. Click on the Access tab in the Manage Component screen for MDFORM_ ORDERS, or the Grant Access link in the Navigator. Check the box labeled Publish to Portal, click Apply, and then close the Manage Component screen.

2. In the Navigator, go to the Pages tab and click on My Pages, then Edit for the eXYZ Home Page or navigate to the page itself and click the Edit Page link.

3. On the Sales tab, click the Add Portlet icon and select the Sales Application from the Other Providers section.

4. Click the name to add the Customer Order Form portlet to the region. Click OK, then Close and test your new page. (If you are working in the Navigator, click the page name to display it.) Your page should look like the one shown in Figure 7-7.

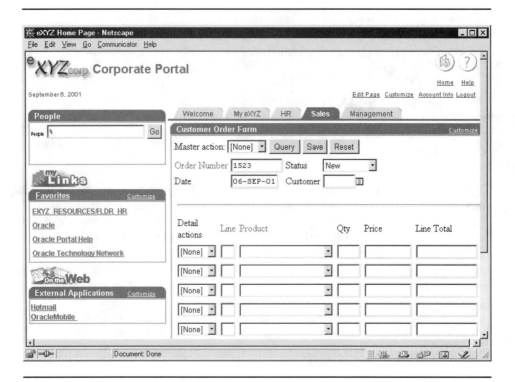

FIGURE 7-7. *The eXYZ home page now shows the customer order form*

Form Based on Procedure

The wizard process for the form based on procedure is no different from the wizards we have already discussed. What is different, however, is that you will now base the form on an existing stored procedure. The arguments to the procedure now function in the same way as the table columns did in the other two form types—they provide the form items for you to customize. There are no built-in buttons for INSERT, UPDATE, or DELETE, but only Save and Reset buttons. The Save button passes the parameters to the procedure and executes it. You can customize the input fields in the same way as you could for tables, creating a clean and simple interface to a stored procedure. If you use the redirection utilities in the "on successful submission" option provided on the form-level properties page, your users will not see any results from the procedure, but the procedure will execute. You can customize this form with additional text and PL/SQL code as you could with the other forms.

Exercise 7.6: Calculate Commission and Draw

This form will be in APP_HR, and will simply provide an interface to an existing procedure. We have provided this procedure for you—it should have been installed when you created the CORP_SITE schema. The procedure name is `calc_commission`, and it accepts an employee ID and an optional amount, if the employee wishes to draw on earned commission. It updates the employee's accrued commission, marks the commissions as paid, then feeds back some information to the user about the results. We'll create an LOV to list only the names of the sales personnel and pass the employee ID parameter in the background.

1. Navigate to the APP_HR application and create a new dynamic list of values.

2. Name the LOV `LOV_SALESCREW`, set Show Null Value to `No`, and enter the following query:

   ```
   SELECT last_name||', '||first_name, employee_id
   FROM CORP_SITE.salescrew_view
   ```

3. Click OK, then test the LOV. Close the Manage Component page to return to the Navigator.

4. Create a new form based on procedure, in the same application.

5. Name the form `FORM_COMMISSION`, and give it a Display Name of `Calculate Commission`.

6. On the next page, choose `CORP_SITE.CALC_COMMISSION` for the procedure name.

7. Leave the Form Layout page to the default Tabular layout.

8. On the Formatting and Validation page, enter the following PL/SQL in the "on successful submission" text area in the `FORM` properties page:

   ```
   htp.anchor('javascript:history.go(-1)','Return to Portal');
   ```

9. Click on `P_EMPLOYEE_ID` and change the Item Type to `Combobox`. Choose `LOV_SALESCREW` as the List Of Values. Change the Label to `Employee`.

10. In the field settings for `P_DRAW`, make sure that the field is not mandatory—this procedure can be used to calculate commission without requesting a draw. Change the Label to `Draw`, and set the Field Level Validation to `isNumber`. Set the Input Width and Input Max Length to `12`.

11. Click Next and set the Template to `PUBLIC.EXYZ_TEMPLATE`.

12. That's it! Click Finish, then Run and test your form.

The output from the procedure is simple HTML generated with the PL/SQL Web Toolkit, a Back icon and link appended by Portal, and then our return link. We did not use the `call` or `go` routines because we wanted users to see the feedback from our procedure before returning to the portal page. The easiest way to generate a return link is through the JavaScript `history` command, but you may specify a particular page in the anchor instead. This link gets the user back to the Portal interface, in contrast with the generated Back icon and link, which takes them back to the form in full-page mode. Users would be able to get back to the home page either way, because the full-page form's template contains a Home link. In most cases, users will find it preferable to return directly to the portal interface.

Exercise 7.7: Integrate the Commission Form with the Portal

1. Click on the Access tab in the Manage Component screen, or the Grant Access link in the Navigator. Check the box labeled Publish to Portal, click Apply, and then close the Manage Component screen.

2. Bring up the editor for the eXYZ Home Page.

3. On the HR tab, click the Add Portlet icon and select the Human Resources Application from the Other Providers section.

4. Click on Calculate Commission to add the portlet to the region. Click OK, then Close, and test your new page.

Advanced Programming Techniques

The forms you've created so far in this chapter are functional but lack one or two essential features. To really make the best use of Portal technology, you'll need some knowledge of advanced PL/SQL and JavaScript. The PL/SQL is used primarily in obtaining additional information from the database or from the Portal session objects, represented as PL/SQL variables. JavaScript comes in when you need a screen component to "do something" within the browser display. HTML, including that generated from the Portal engine, has no capability to respond to on-screen events, except to request another server resource in response to a form submission. If you want something to happen without forcing the user to leave the on-screen form, you have no choice but to pick up a little JavaScript. As mentioned previously, this is not a simple undertaking. In this section, we will introduce you to JavaScript and provide a few examples that you may extend for your own requirements. We will also expose the underlying PL/SQL session framework so that you may access Portal variables and data elements in your code.

Working with JavaScript

It's time to face facts. Your career as a Web development professional can only go so far without knowing the ins and outs of JavaScript. You may have seen bits and pieces of JavaScript code when viewing the source of other Web pages, but it was so cryptic and hard to read that you opted to leave that part of coding to someone else. If you are already comfortable with JavaScript, feel free to skip ahead to the exercises, because you will understand the code, and all you need is an understanding of how to integrate it into Portal components. The rest of you should probably peruse this brief introduction. It is, of necessity, brief, because this is a book about Oracle Portal—not JavaScript. It is also not written from the perspective of an expert, but someone, like you, who needed to pick up enough of the language to meet user requirements. It is not intended to be a definitive reference on the language. There are many good references to JavaScript, both online and in print form, and these are listed in the bibliography for this chapter. Please use these to fully develop your knowledge of the language.

First, the name "JavaScript" is something of a misnomer. It is a scripting language, but it also has most of the features of a full-fledged programming language. You can define variables and subroutines, and create conditional and iterative control structures. JavaScript has a server-side component that can be used to generate entire applications, and with Netscape's proprietary LiveWire Database Service it can retrieve and modify data. Second, JavaScript has just about nothing to do with Java! A bit of the syntax and some of the conventions and object models are similar to Java, but JavaScript is an independent language in its own right.

NOTE
The Apache Project is working with an experimental open source module called XANG that enables database application development using JavaScript and XML, but it is still in the early phases of its life cycle.

Integrating JavaScript

The first issue we need to address is, "Where and how does JavaScript operate?" JavaScript works in the browser, and wise readers may already be asking the question, "But oh, aren't browsers different, and configurable?" Yes, gentle reader, they are, and this is one of the risks of using JavaScript. Microsoft and Netscape each have their own implementation, as do other browsers. Fortunately, there is a basic standard, as there is with HTML, that most browsers will accept. There are also different versions of JavaScript, and older browsers will, of course, only recognize older versions. Finally, users have the option to turn off JavaScript, and some do—often based on overprotective recommendations from corporate security officers. Fortunately for you, your users are already pre-qualified as JavaScript- enabled, because they couldn't even get to the main Portal page without JavaScript.

The convention is to hide JavaScript in comments so that older browsers will ignore the code and the page will still display properly. So whenever you create a JavaScript function or code fragment, it will be enclosed first in a SCRIPT tag, optionally indicating the compliance version, then in comments, as below:

```
<SCRIPT LANGUAGE="JavaScript1.1">
<!-- Comment out script for old browsers
  …some javascript here …
//-->
</SCRIPT>
```

A SCRIPT tag can go just about anywhere in a page, and there are scoping rules that determine what code is accessible at any point in the document.

Scripts can be stand-alone lines of JavaScript code, or they can be incorporated into functions. The advantage of using a function, as you already know, is that the code can be reused in multiple places. The scoping rules are mostly a matter of order of appearance in the HTML page. Functions must be defined before they are invoked, and any object referenced by the function must appear in the page before the function call. Functions can be called from other functions, from simple scripts, and from event handlers, which we will discuss shortly. They can accept parameters, and can return values as well. This is a sample template for a JavaScript function (it would be enclosed in the SCRIPT and comment tags shown earlier):

```
function myFunction (arg1, arg2)
  {
    … some javascript commands …
    return some_value;
  }
```

The return command is optional. Without it, the JavaScript behaves as a procedure, but there is no separate construct for a procedure in JavaScript.

One final introductory comment: JavaScript *is* case-sensitive, so be aware of case when you are referencing form fields, functions, and commands. JavaScript can be difficult to debug, and this is one of the first things you should check. If your errors seem to indicate that something hasn't been defined, when you know it has been, chances are it's a case or scoping issue.

The JavaScript Object Model

To understand how JavaScript handles form items, we must first understand a little of the Document Object Model (DOM). JavaScript treats each page as a document made up of other components, like forms, images, frames, and tables. Each of these components is in turn made up of other components. We will concentrate on form components, or elements, because they contain the form data that we would like to modify at runtime. Figure 7-8 shows the DOM in a tree structure. Notice that the

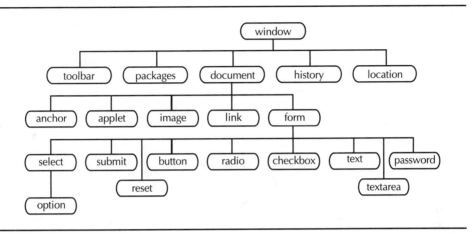

FIGURE 7-8. *The JavaScript DOM*

top of the tree is a window, which can contain pages and other elements, like navigation history.

There are methods and properties associated with every object in the tree. For example, a document object has properties that specify default font, link and background colors, as well as its URL. You can test the values of these properties, as well as set them. Document methods include open(), close(), and write(). The open() and close() methods refer to the output stream of the document, as distinct from the open() and close() methods of a window, which would physically open or close the browser window. Any string passed to the write() method is written in the indicated document, and will appear in the page when it is rendered. An example of this usage to render a simple page in JavaScript follows:

```
document.open();
document.write("Hello World");
document.close();
```

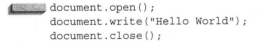

TIP
There are several acceptable ways to terminate JavaScript statements: a semicolon, a new line, or a change in scope (for example, the end of an event handler). To avoid confusion, make it a practice to end each JavaScript statement with a semicolon.

The preceding syntax will work because there is only one document available to the JavaScript at any given time. The text will be written to the document in which the JavaScript is executing. In some cases, particularly in the case of forms, you will need to specify the index of the object. When thinking about indexes, it is helpful to think of the document as an array of arrays. The document contains an array of forms, and each form contains an array of elements. Some of the elements (lists in particular) contain an array of values.

All JavaScript indexes start at 0 and increment in the order of specification in the HTML. So, if you have a single form with two inputs (including hidden fields), the first input could be referenced as `document.forms[0].elements[0]` and the second as `document.forms[0].elements[1]`. The `document` portion is optional, because as we have mentioned, there is only one document. Objects can also be referenced by their names as defined in the HTML tag that created the object, but not all HTML tags require a `Name` attribute. This could create a little havoc, but the issue is solved by combining approaches. So if your form does not have a name, but you want to use field name references, you can specify `forms[0].myField` to reference a named field within the first form. If you name your forms, you can use only the name references—that is, `myForm.myField`. There is (at least) one more way to reference JavaScript objects. The `this` keyword is used to refer to the current object, and its equivalent for the current window is `self`.

NOTE
Portal-generated HTML forms do use the Name attribute, but the name changes with each new version of the form, so it cannot be used in code. This technique is intended to prevent users from continuing to use an old version of a form (because of browser caching) after a change to the form's definition.

Note that JavaScript uses dot notation in a few different contexts. In the first example of `document.write`, the dot signified a reference to one of the object's methods. In the second example, the dot signified a traversal of the DOM hierarchy down to the element. Yet another example would be to reference a property of an object, as in `myForm.myField.value.`, which traverses the hierarchy to obtain the value of `myField`. These three meanings (and one or two others) can coexist peacefully because of the way JavaScript is interpreted.

A special case of the form element contains yet another level of sub-items. The HTML `SELECT` list, which is available as a combo box or a multiple selection field, has a sub-element array that allows you to reference the choices in the list. The array contains the value and text associated with each option in the list, in the order they appear in the HTML document. There are a few properties and methods specific to this kind of element.

Table 7-4 lists a few of the properties we will work with in this book.

Property	Applies to	Purpose
name	Forms, elements	Returns the name of the object.
value	Elements	Returns the data in the element.
form	Elements	Returns the identifier for the form that contains the element.
options[n]	Selection lists	An array depicting all of the available choices in the list—access the entire array or the *n*th value.
selected Index	Selection lists	Returns the ordinal number in the list of the currently selected item.

TABLE 7-4. *Commonly Used JavaScript Properties*

Variables and Datatyping

JavaScript is a loosely typed language, but does support explicit variable declaration and typing. Because of this, variable declaration is simple and not subject to intense scrutiny by the browser. You can declare variables anywhere, with or without the var keyword, and with or without a datatype. Be warned, however, that the looser your code, the greater the likelihood of unanticipated runtime errors. The more explicit you are, the better your success rate. For example, the following lines of JavaScript all do essentially the same thing, but may be interpreted differently in subsequent usage:

```
myVar ;    myVar = "text1" ;
var myVar ;    myVar = "text1" ;
var myVar = "text1" ;
myVar = "text1" ;
var myVar = String ("text1") ;
myVar = 1 ; myVar = "text" + myVar ;
```

You must use the keyword var to declare variables within a function, but it is otherwise optional. The String method enforces the interpretation of the variable as a string; without it, numeric text could be interpreted as a number and any text could be interpreted by the eval () top-level function (see next section) as a command. Notice that the datatype of a variable can change on the fly, if assigned a different value (inadvertently or intentionally).

Variables declared outside of any function or event handler are global, and accessible to subsequent functions and event handlers. Scoping is simple—any variable or function that has been declared earlier in the document is available to other code. Again, this presents a bit of an issue. If you inadvertently reference a variable before the intended declaration or initialization, you will create a new undefined variable.

JavaScript is rich in the flexibility it offers to declare variables, arrays, and even user-defined objects. We won't get to the level of user-defined objects in this book, so please refer to the bibliography for more information about those. We will use a few arrays, and if you're going to use JavaScript at all, you should have a basic familiarity with array processing. A simple declaration for a loosely typed array of ten elements looks like this:

```
myArray = new Array (10);
```

To access the values in an array, use the index value. The following statement sets the value of the sixth element (because JavaScript arrays are zero-based) to "myText":

```
myArray[5] = "myText";
```

You can use a loop to process an entire array, as you'll see in the section on conditional control.

Operators, Methods, and Top-Level Functions

JavaScript objects can be modified with standard operators, property settings, methods, and top-level (built-in) functions. You can test their values using conditional Boolean operators. Table 7-5 summarizes the most often-used operators. Parentheses can be added for clarity, and the usual precedence and override of precedence rules apply.

Operator	Meaning	Example
=	Assignment	a = b ;
*, /, +, -	Mathematical operations	a = b + c / d * e ;
==	Equality condition	if (a == b)
>, <, <=, >=	Greater/less than conditions	if (a > b)
!=	Inequality	if (a != b)
&&	Logical AND	if (a >= b && b < c)
||	Logical OR	if (a >= b || b < c)

TABLE 7-5. *JavaScript Operators*

We will use a few methods, listed in Table 7-6, in our code as well. Methods apply only to the objects for which they are valid, and inappropriate method calls will result in JavaScript errors.

We have already seen one top-level function, `isNaN`, in Chapter 5, where we tested to see if a variable was not a number. The other top-level function that we will work with is the `eval()` function, and a powerful function it is. `eval()` takes any string variable and interprets it as if it were code, rather as a simple string. It allows you to dynamically build executable statements and execute them within the code. The following is a simple example of `eval()`:

```
myString = "4 + 5" ;
myResult = eval( myString ) ;
```

The variable `myResult` is now a numeric equal to 9. The `eval()` function has implications far beyond simple math, such as using variables in place of field names to create generic code that can be called from anywhere. When generating master-detail forms, Portal appends a number to each field name in the detail block, making it necessary for us to dynamically interpret the field name at runtime. We will see how this works in the line item totals calculation in Exercise 7.9.

Method	Applies to	Meaning
open (URL, name, properties)	Windows	Opens a new browser window with an optional name and properties, and populate it with URL.
split (string, "delimiter")	Strings	Converts a delimited string into an array with each piece of the string in a separate element, using the delimiter to mark the split points.
replace (RegExp, "new str")	Strings	Alters the contents of a string using regular expressions to match patterns.
focus()	Elements	Navigates to the element.
blur()	Elements	Leaves the element.
select()	Elements	Selects the data in the element, making it easy for the user to replace the text.

TABLE 7-6. *JavaScript Methods*

Conditional Control

JavaScript has all of the `if`, `switch`, and loop statements you would expect to see in a professional programming language. The syntax for these statements is similar to the Java equivalents, so here Java programmers will feel right at home. We will only look at the `if` and `for` statements in this book. The `if` statement has the following form:

```
if ( conditions )
   {
     … statements …
   } else {
   … other statements …
   }
```

The conditions can be any Boolean variable or operation as described in the section on operators. You may use logical AND (`&&`) and OR (`||`), with or without internal parentheses, to combine multiple conditions. The curly braces around the statements are optional if there is only one statement and no `else` clause, but we recommend that you use them always for clarity. And of course the `else` clause is optional.

A `for` loop example is next. In our application, we will need to loop through an array to determine the correct price for an item. Another common use of a `for` loop construct is to search for a specific field name and set or return its value. The example below would be part of a function that accepts the form object and the designated field name as parameters (that is, `theForm`, `theField`), and returns the value of the requested field. It is specifically oriented to the Portal field naming conventions, described in the Note that follows.

> **NOTE**
> *The JavaScript in this example works with the naming convention used by Portal when creating the detail record lines. Each element's field name takes the form of FORM.BLOCK.ITEM.NUMBER (for example, MDFORM_ORDERS.DETAIL_ BLOCK.ORDER_LINE_NUMBER.02), where NUMBER is the line number on the screen. Only multiple-record blocks, like those in the detail section of a master-detail form, will have a line number greater than 01. The forms and blocks in this case are Portal concepts, not JavaScript, and the naming applies to each field within the document object model. The dot notation is in addition to the DOM dot notation. They help the code generators enforce a manageable and consistent naming scheme, but can cause problems within JavaScript because of the additional "dots".*

```
for (var i = 0; i < theForm.length; i++)
  {
    slicedName = theForm.elements[i].name.split(".");
    tmp = slicedName[2];
    if (!tmp)
      { continue; }
    objName = tmp;
    if (objName == theField)
      {
        return theForm.elements[i].value;
      }
  }
```

The first line of the statement is where we set up the loop. We initialize a variable i to act as an iterator starting at 0, and then we specify the exit condition, determined by the number of elements in the form (theForm.length). The last component increments i by one for each iteration of the loop. Note that the increment happens after the exit condition is evaluated, so we exit when the iterator is one shy of the form's length. This last iteration will be over the last element of the form. The code breaks each field name found into its component parts, and tests the third part (slicedName[2]), which represents the true field name, stripped of the form name, block name, and line number. If the field name did not follow this convention, it is not a database field or button, so we skip it using the continue statement. If the current field in the loop matches the provided field name, we get its value and exit the function. We could add line number checking to this code by testing slicedName[3].

This is one method to work around the naming conventions used by Portal-generated code, but it is suspect in terms of its performance. Who wants to evaluate every field on the screen to obtain a single value? It is an alternative to the more focused technique mentioned earlier and illustrated in Exercise 7.9. Basically, you have the choice to either loop through all the fields on the form to find the one whose value you need, or use the split() and eval() functions to parse and precisely identify the field name.

Event Handlers

Many of the objects in the DOM have event handlers associated with them. You may be familiar with one that is commonly used in rogue Web sites to prevent you from leaving without viewing their incessant advertisements. This is the window's onUnload event, and it "fires" when you try to close the window. These shameless souls spawn a new window from the JavaScript event handler every time you close one, so that you are trapped in an endless loop. (Quick mouse action can usually beat this game—if you close the window fast enough, the browser won't have time to process the event handler.) Events are associated with JavaScript objects. They are defined not in JavaScript, but in the HTML tag that creates the object. The code looks like simple attribute code, and is ignored by any browser that does not recognize the attribute. A sample of a call to a previously defined function in an event handler is shown here:

```
<INPUT TYPE="text" VALUE="" NAME="myField" onBlur="myFunction()">
```

The `onBlur` event fires when the user navigates out of the field. Those who are familiar with Oracle Forms programming (or any event-based environment) will recognize event handlers as similar to triggers, although the set of available event handlers is substantially smaller than the set of available Forms triggers.

Event handlers are really two parts. The first part is an attribute (`onBlur` in the example) that specifies when to fire, or what event causes the response. The second part, specified as an attribute value, is the response. In the response portion, which is enclosed in double quotes, you can call a function as we did in the example or just enter JavaScript commands, separated by semicolons. We will provide examples of both in the exercises.

The subset of events that we will work with in this book is described in Table 7-7. There are many more events available to JavaScript programmers, but we have found that these are used most often in Portal components, and we will limit the examples to them.

Hopefully this brief explanation of the JavaScript framework and processing model has given you enough of an overview to understand what you are doing in the following exercises. You have actually already written a simple event handler. Remember the way we prevented users from changing the Order Number field? You entered `blur();` in the JavaScript Event Handler field for the `onFocus` event in the form wizard. This single-statement event handler forced the focus to leave the field every time the user attempted to navigate to it.

In the exercises, we will begin with a simple event handler to calculate the line number in the Customer Orders form, and move on to a more complex function that calculates and updates the line item totals. The final exercise shows you how to integrate database values with JavaScript.

Event	Fires When ...
onBlur	The user leaves the object
onFocus	The user enters the object
onChange	The user enters or changes a value in the object
onClick	The user clicks a button or image

TABLE 7-7. *JavaScript Events*

Exercise 7.8: Calculate a Line Number

1. Edit the MDFORM_ORDERS form you created earlier.

2. Click on the Formatting and Validation Options for Detail Row tab.

3. Click on ORDER_LINE_NUMBER.

4. Scroll down to the JavaScript Event Handlers section, then click on the onFocus event and enter the following code:

```
var itemname = this.name;
var pieces = itemname.split('.');
this.value = pieces[3];
blur();
```

5. Run and test your form. Do the line numbers work? What happens when you save an order and then query it?

NOTE
Notice that we are using the blur() *method to prevent the user from changing the value as we did with the ORDER_NO item. This is but one of many ways to set a line number. If the user never clicks on the Line Number field, this value will not be populated. You might want to copy the same code into an* onFocus *event for another field, such as PRODUCT_ID, to ensure that it is always set properly. As we'll see in the next exercise, setting one field's value from another is not a trivial task, due in part to the naming convention described earlier. After going through the next exercise, you can go back and apply the same logic to this event handler.*

Exercise 7.9: Setting Field Values

In this exercise, you will use a JavaScript function to calculate the line item total. It will fire any time the user changes either the product quantity or unit price. Because we want to call this from two different places, we will code it as a function. You have several options as to where to put JavaScript functions, but the simplest place to put them in the wizard is the Header Text section of the Form Text tab. You can put any HTML or JavaScript commands there, as you can put any PL/SQL on the Additional PL/SQL Code tab (which we will use in the next section).

1. Return to the editor for the Customer Orders form.

2. Click on the Form Text tab. In the Header Text field, enter the following JavaScript:

```
ex0709.js
<script language="JavaScript1.1">
  <!--
    function setTotal(form,fieldName)
      {
        var pieces = fieldName.split(".");
        var totalfield = new String( pieces[0] + "." + pieces[1] +   "."   +
                              "TOTAL_PRICE_SOLD" + "." +  pieces[3] );
        var pricefield = new String( pieces[0] + "." + pieces[1] +   "."   +
                              "UNIT_PRICE_SOLD" + "." +  pieces[3] );
        var qtyfield = new String( pieces[0] + "." + pieces[1] +   "."   +
                              "QTY_SOLD" + "." +  pieces[3] );
        var price = form.elements[eval(pricefield)].value;
        var qty = form.elements[eval(qtyfield)].value;
        if (price != "" && qty != "")
          {
            var total = price*qty;
            form.elements[eval(totalfield)].value = total ;
          }
      }
  //-->
</script>
```

3. Navigate to the Formatting and Validation Options for Detail Row tab. Click on the QTY_SOLD field and create an onChange event handler with the following code:

```
setTotal( this.form, this.name );
```

4. Repeat Step 3 for the UNIT_PRICE_SOLD field.

5. To prevent users from changing the calculated total, add an onFocus event handler to the TOTAL_PRICE_SOLD field. Use the blur(); method as before.

6. Run and test your form. Does it work as expected?

Exercise 7.10: Order Total

With respect to the total order value, our database is normalized. This means that we do not store the calculated sum of the line item totals with the order record. Typically, though, the customer will want to know the total amount when they place the order. We will use a custom JavaScript button to calculate the order total, which we will then display in a non-database item.

1. Edit MDFORM_ORDERS once again. This time you will be working in the Formatting and Validation Options for Master Row tab, displayed by default as soon as you re-enter the wizard.

2. Create two new items, and set their properties as follows:

Item Name	Item Type	Begin on New Line	Label
ORDER_TOTAL	TextBox	Yes	Order Total
CALC_ORDER_TOTAL	Button	No	Calculate Order

3. For the ORDER_TOTAL, set Input Width and Max Length to 12. Notice that the Insertable checkbox is off by default—this is how Portal prevents the form from trying to insert the ORDER_TOTAL into a nonexistent database field. Create an onFocus Event Handler, specifying only the blur(); method to prevent changes.

4. For the CALC_ORDER_TOTAL button, add the following code in the onClick event:

```
calc_order_total (this.form); //
```

TIP
Use the comment symbol (| |) to prevent the default button handler, do_event, from running. do_event causes a form submit, and is used with the other button types to refresh the form for a query or reset operation. We do not want to submit the form when calculating the total value, but simply update the displayed field.

5. On the Form Text page, add the following function to the existing <SCRIPT> tag in the Header Text field, either above or below the setTotal function (note that you will have to change the form name in the second-to-last line if your form is named anything other than MDFORM_ORDERS):

```
ex0710.js
function calc_order_total (form)
{
  var order_total = new Number(0);
  for (var i = 0; i < form.length; i++)
    {
      slicedName = form.elements[i].name.split(".");
      tmp = slicedName[2];
      if (!tmp)
        continue;
      objName = tmp;
      if (objName == "TOTAL_PRICE_SOLD")
        {
          order_total = order_total +
```

```
                                    Number(form.elements[i].value.replace(/\$/,""));
                                    //use the replace() method to strip the "$" formatting
                }
            }
        var ordertotalfield =
            new String("MDFORM_ORDERS.MASTER_BLOCK.ORDER_TOTAL.01" );
        form.elements[eval(ordertotalfield)].value = order_total ;
    }
```

6. Click OK to test this functionality.

The button works regardless of whether there are detail line items specified. To allow the order total feature to work when records are queried, create a function that sums the records at the database, then reference the function in the Default Value field for ORDER_TOTAL.

Exercise 7.11: Lookups to Other Tables

Except in the case of LOVs, Portal doesn't offer an easy way to retrieve values from related tables and use them in form fields. If the requirement is to validate some data entry against data stored in a separate table, an LOV doesn't really fit the bill. You could use a dynamic page or even a report (because the SQL is more flexible) to incorporate this kind of lookup, but then you lose some of the benefits of forms. Oracle may add a "lookup" feature to the product in future releases, but for now we have developed a wonderful JavaScript workaround. It's very complex, and it uses PL/SQL to generate the JavaScript from the data in the database.

eXYZ Corporation allows its sales force to quote prices within a range, from the minimum price to the list price. The PRODUCTS table stores both prices. We would like to inform the salesperson of the range in some way, and protect against invalid data entry outside of the range. The users have agreed that the best way to represent this requirement is to automatically populate the UNIT_PRICE_SOLD field with the list price of the product being ordered, and allow the salesperson to change it. If the change causes the price to go below the minimum, we'll alert the salesperson and prevent the change until the price is valid.

The reason this requirement is difficult is that Apache does not handle database calls from JavaScript. Some servers do (and there are plans to add this kind of module to Apache), so if you frequently need to do database callbacks, you may consider the possibility of setting up a separate server to handle them. The point is that we can't call a JavaScript routine, passing a product_id parameter, and expect it to go to the database to get the maximum and minimum price values for that product. What we will do instead is use PL/SQL to generate JavaScript commands in the page. The commands will set up some arrays that contain the product ID, and minimum and maximum prices for the product. This technique is similar to the idea of using a PL/SQL table held in memory. Then we will use a JavaScript function to set the default price when the user enters the field and check it if the user changes it. We have to generate all of the JavaScript from PL/SQL because of JavaScript scoping rules. The arrays have to be declared and populated first in the page, so the function can reference them. The function has to be declared before the form is drawn on the page. The page text boxes that we used before only allow header text and footer text. If we put the function in the header, it would be above the arrays because the PL/SQL-generated code is always generated after the header section. The way to get PL/SQL to generate JavaScript is just to use the `HTP.p` or `HTP.print` commands and pass your JavaScript as an argument.

So here it is. The PL/SQL was complex enough that we created it as a procedure. We can only do this because we do not reference any session variables (explained in the next section) in the code. Because a separate PL/SQL procedure runs in a different context, you may not always have access to everything you can access from a Portal component. Be sure to grant `EXECUTE` permission to the PORTAL30_PUBLIC schema any time you reference code belonging to any other schema. (We have done this for you in the scripts that build the CORP_SITE schema.)

1. Open the MDFORM_ORDERS for editing.

2. On the Additional PL/SQL code tab, enter the following code in the "… before displaying the page" text area:

```
corp_site.gen_pricelookup;
```

3. On the Formatting and Validation Options for Detail Row tab, click on the `UNIT_PRICE_SOLD` item. Create an `onFocus` event with this code:

```
this.value = get_price (this.form, this.name, 'LIST');
setTotal( this.form, this.name );
```

NOTE
You must reset the total in the event handler, because JavaScript does not cascade its events. In other words, if the value changes because of an `onFocus` *event, the* `onChange` *event does not fire.*

4. Add the following code to the onChange event for `UNIT_PRICE_SOLD`, before the existing `setTotal` command:

```
var min_price = get_price (this.form, this.name, 'MIN');
if ( this.value < min_price )
   {
   alert ('Minimum price for this item is ' + min_price );
   this.focus();
   }
```

5. Run and test your form.

The text of the `gen_pricelookup` procedure is included below. The comments highlight some of the more important techniques we are illustrating.

```
gen_pricelookup.org
CREATE OR REPLACE PROCEDURE gen_pricelookup IS
/* use a cursor to get all the prices */
  CURSOR c_prices IS
   SELECT product_id, min_price, list_price
   FROM   CORP_SITE.products;
   v_count NUMBER;

BEGIN

  SELECT COUNT(*)
  INTO   v_count
  FROM CORP_SITE.products;
/* begin your Javascript, substituting values from the
   cursor as necessary */
  HTP.p('<script language="JavaScript1.1">');
  HTP.p('<!-- ');
/* initialize the arrays */
  HTP.p(' var product_id_arr = new Array('||v_count||'); ');
  HTP.p(' var min_price_arr = new Array('||v_count||'); ');
  HTP.p(' var list_price_arr = new Array('||v_count||'); ');
/* populate the arrays */
  FOR r IN c_prices LOOP
    HTP.p ('product_id_arr['||to_char(c_prices%ROWCOUNT - 1) ||'] = '
                                     ||r.product_id||';');
    HTP.p('min_price_arr['||to_char(c_prices%ROWCOUNT - 1)||'] = '
                                     ||r.min_price||';' );
    HTP.p('list_price_arr['||to_char(c_prices%ROWCOUNT - 1)||'] = '
                                     ||r.list_price||';' );
  END LOOP;
/* use this variable to determine the size of the array */
    HTP.p ('var num_products = '||v_count);

/* create the function--accept a parameter that tells
   you whether to return the minimum or list price
   for maximum flexibility  */
    HTP.p ('function get_price (form, field, min_or_list)
      {
       var pieces = field.split(".");
       var productIDfield = new String( pieces[0] + "." +
                                 pieces[1] + "." +
                                 "PRODUCT_ID" + "." +
                                 pieces[3] );
/* first find out which item they chose from the product_id list */
       var IDinlist = form.elements[eval(productIDfield)].selectedIndex;
```

```
/* then get the value of that item */
       var productID =
           form.elements[eval(productIDfield)].options[IDinlist].value;

/* loop through the array until you find the right product ID */
       for (var i=0 ; i < num_products ; i++)
          {
            if (product_id_arr[i] == productID)
              {
/* return the correct price */
               if (min_or_list == "MIN")
                  { return min_price_arr[i]; }
               else
                  { return list_price_arr[i]; }
              }
           }
        }' );
/* close out the JavaScript */
  HTP.p ('//-->');
  HTP.p ('</SCRIPT>');

END gen_pricelookup;
```

To be thorough, you would probably want to add an onChange event to the PRODUCT_ID field that covers you if the user went back to choose a different product. How would you code this? (Hint: Use the setTotal function as a model.) Where could the code go, keeping in mind JavaScript scoping rules? Would this be a good solution if your PRODUCTS table contained thousands of rows? What are some alternate solutions? Using a trigger on the table would work in any circumstance, provided that the trigger could communicate the appropriate error message back to the user. A network of linked forms would also be an option, so the user can click on a link that navigates to the price lookup form. We will illustrate links as we develop the other components.

The PL/SQL Session Model

When you need to do anything with the current field values on the form, such as using them to update another table or to decide whether to allow an action, you will need to use PL/SQL code blocks. To access the underlying data, you must first understand the session model used by the Portal code generators.

What happens, in brief, is that every time a record is retrieved from the database, it is stored in the session object. When the form is cleared with the Reset button, the session object is also cleared. The session object is always called P_SESSION, and it is defined as an object of type WWA_API_MODULE_SESSION. It contains the values of all the items on the form, as well as the ROWID of the current row and some status, state, and current position information. It also contains, when performing a query, the WHERE clause created by the query form submission process, the number of records to fetch at one time, and the ORDER BY clause as specified at form creation time. These are all modifiable when you access the session object in PL/SQL code.

The session object methods we'll be most concerned with are those that allow retrieval and assignment of session variables, especially those that represent the data on the form. There are three methods to get values, depending on the datatype of the source item, and one method to set values. The get methods are functions that return the datatype indicated by the name, and the set method is a procedure. They are called as follows:

```
my_number  := P_SESSION.get_value_as_number ( p_block_name => 'block name'
                                             , p_attribute_name => 'attribute' );
my_varchar := P_SESSION.get_value_as_varchar2 ( p_block_name => 'block name'
                                             , p_attribute_name => 'attribute' );
my_date    := P_SESSION.get_value_as_date ( p_block_name => 'block name'
                                          , p_attribute_name => 'attribute' );
P_SESSION.set_value ( p_block_name => 'block name'
                    , p_attribute_name => 'attribute'
                    , p_value => new_value_to_set );
```

The block name is always 'DEFAULT' for forms based on tables, views or stored procedures, and either 'MASTER_BLOCK' or 'DETAIL_BLOCK' for master-detail forms. 'attribute' refers to the form item name, prefixed by A_. Therefore, if you were looking for the current value of EMPNO, you would substitute 'A_EMPNO' for the attribute name. For master-detail forms, there is another parameter, p_index, to identify the row number as displayed on the screen. You cannot actively change on-screen data with PL/SQL, but you can get the data as it is retrieved from the database and change the values before the screen is rendered. You can also reset data before it gets to the database, and prevent operations based on the retrieved data. Let's delve into this topic with an exercise.

Exercise 7.12: Post-Processing in Forms

In the first form you developed, the requirement stated that after updating an employee review, the employee should get the raise as specified on the form, and a new review should be created for the next year. We will accomplish this using the PL/SQL session object and post-processing code.

    I. Find FORM_REVIEW in the Navigator under the HR_APP application.

2. Click Edit and you will be on the main Formatting and Validation Options tab at the FORM level. Scroll down to the text area that allows you to enter code "On successful submission of a form". Enter the following PL/SQL code:

```
ex0711.sql
DECLARE
  v_empid NUMBER := p_session.get_value_as_number
                      ( p_block_name => 'DEFAULT'
                      , p_attribute_name => 'A_EMPLOYEE_ID' );
  v_raise_pct NUMBER := p_session.get_value_as_number
                      ( p_block_name => 'DEFAULT'
                      , p_attribute_name =>
                      'A_RECOMMEND_INCREASE' );
  v_review_date DATE := p_session.get_value_as_date
                      ( p_block_name => 'DEFAULT'
                      , p_attribute_name => 'A_REVIEW_DATE' );
BEGIN
  UPDATE employees
  SET annual_salary = annual_salary * ( 1 + v_raise_pct/100)
  WHERE  employee_id = v_empid;
  INSERT INTO employee_reviews (employee_id, review_date)
  VALUES (v_empid, add_months(v_review_date, 12));
END;
```

3. Click OK and test your form. You might want to query the EMPLOYEE_ REVIEWS and EMPLOYEES tables before and after entering a review to verify that the code succeeded.

In a production system, you would probably want to code the above updates as a procedure and pass the session variables as parameters.

Conclusion

In this chapter, you created simple forms, customized their appearance, and modified the code to get them to do exactly what the users needed. We introduced you to the world of JavaScript, and showed how to use JavaScript and LOVs to ensure consistent data entry. We provided an overview of the PL/SQL session object that you can now use and extend to your own requirements. In the next chapter, you will see how to create and customize Portal reports.

CHAPTER
8

Developing
Enterprise Reports

very organization needs reports in some form. The traditional business report is typically a static paper document that captures data at a point in time. We never think of a report as an active document, but as a simple snapshot of some part of a company's operations. Wouldn't it be nice if reports could do more? Rather than just inform users that inventory levels are low, why not highlight the low inventory and provide a link to the purchasing application?

In Oracle Portal, a report is more than a list of data. Of course, you can produce simple reports in Portal, but even these have the advantage of showing up-to-the-minute data. For many applications, last month's printed summary is out-of-date as soon as it is distributed. Portal reports are always online and always current, and users can download the results into a spreadsheet or text file for ad hoc analysis. By adding links to other components and resources, developers can turn a report into an active part of the business process, rather than a simple mechanism to reflect results.

NOTE
If you need high-quality printed output, use Oracle Developer to produce your standard business reports and integrate these with the Portal. The advantage of using Developer Reports is that they can be generated as Adobe PDF documents, which are printer friendly and highly customizable. Technet offers more information about Developer Reports integration, in the Reports section (technet.oracle. com/products/reports). Look for the white paper entitled "Security Tips in Oracle9iAS Reports Services 6i with Oracle9iAS Portal Release 3.0".

In this chapter, we will examine the features, benefits, and drawbacks of each Portal report type. Each report you build will be tied in to the business processes of eXYZ Corporation, and integrated with the Portal interface as portlets or as linked application components.

Types of Reports

Oracle Portal offers several ways to produce reports: the *Query by Example (QBE) Report,* the *Report From Query Wizard*, and the *Report From SQL Query*. The QBE Report provides users with the ability to update, insert, and delete records and builds in significant options for customizing the report output. Its drawback is that it supports only a single table or view. If you don't need the data modification features, you can use the Report From Query Wizard or the Report From SQL Query. The Report From Query Wizard walks you through a series of dialogs to build the query. It is very easy to use, but can only support the most straightforward of queries. The Report From SQL Query asks you to supply the SQL that will produce the report's data. If you need to use any complex SQL, or embed HTML with your data, you can use the Report From SQL Query.

All reports offer similar options for column display formats and end-user customization. For example, in any report, you may set format masks, change font characteristics, hide values, display HTML retrieved from a database column, or specify a link on a column that takes the user to another URL. You may change the format of individual rows or values based on the data. Finally, all reports support customizable sort and break groups, with summaries at the report or break level. Deciding what type of report to use depends on the structure of the data you will be reporting and the expected sophistication of the end users, as you will see here.

QBE Report

The Query By Example (QBE) Report is a form, report, and query engine rolled into one. It only supports a single table or view, but it has the advantage of being a "one size fits all" solution. You control whether users can update, insert, and delete records, and whether they can view or modify individual columns. A modifiable join view can serve as the basis for a QBE Report, allowing you to provide information from more than one table and still use the features of the QBE Report. The QBE Report does not have all the power and features of Portal Forms. If you need significant customization of the data entry controls, such as validation, custom JavaScript, default values, or post-processing code, or if you simply do not need the accompanying Web-based reporting capability, use a Form component instead. If the fields to be displayed on the report differ from the data entry fields, either in format or in security level, then you will need both a Form and a Report.

The output of a typical QBE Report is shown in Figure 8-1. If enabled, users can click the Update link and navigate to a prepopulated form that allows update of the available fields. The Delete link, also optional, deletes the record associated with each displayed row. Users will be prompted to confirm the delete before it proceeds.

The QBE Update screen, shown in Figure 8-2, is a part of the component and requires no additional effort on your part to produce. All of the fields displayed on the QBE Report are updatable.

For some users, the QBE Report may seem complex. A single screen, known as the *customization form*, is used both for inserts and for user customization of queries. It supports both value-based and freeform WHERE clause conditions, and allows changes to the column alignment, format masks, and case sensitivity of the query. It has a few options that you, as a developer, cannot remove, and others that you can control.

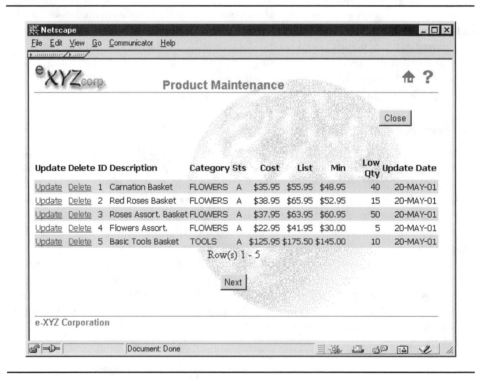

FIGURE 8-1. *The QBE Report allows managers to maintain the product list*

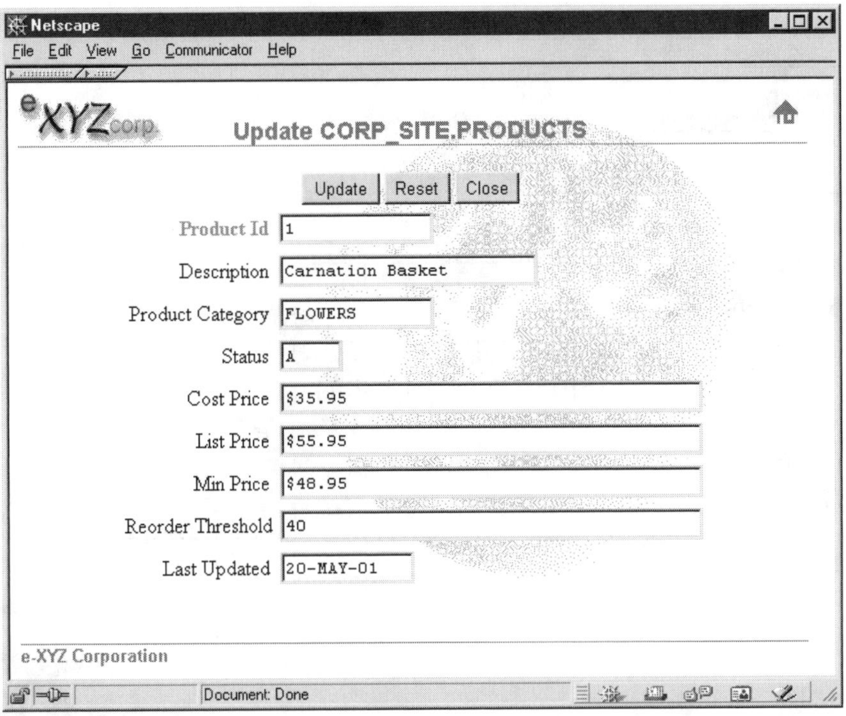

FIGURE 8-2. *The QBE Update screen is used to update product information*

A QBE customization form like the one you will build in this chapter is shown in Figure 8-3. Notice the Insert and Query buttons at the top, and the available options for changing the report's format or query criteria. Not shown are similar options for changing the sort order, break columns, output format, columns to sum, and general query settings. The target audience for a QBE Report customization form is the "power user," or someone who understands the nature of database operations—it is not intended for casual users with simple reporting requirements. Users have more options in the QBE Report for customizing their view of the data than in any other report, and for the correct audience, this report provides a range of options and flexibility.

Report From Query Wizard

When you need a quick report to output the results of a simple join query or you do not want the complexity and power of the QBE Report interface, the Report From

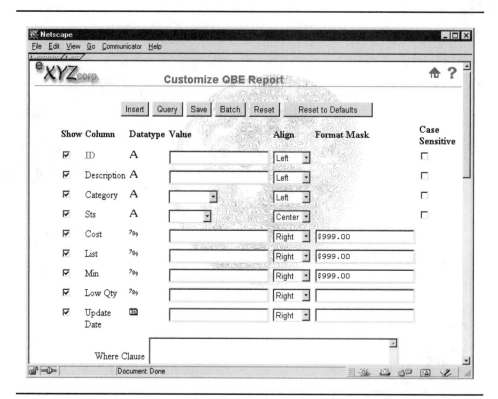

FIGURE 8-3. *The QBE Customization Form for the Product Maintenance report allows managers to create new products and execute customized queries*

Query Wizard is the solution. With only a few clicks, you can produce a nicely formatted report with an optional customization form for user-specified parameters. Conditional formatting, summations, links, and other generic report features are available. The main drawback of the Report From Query Wizard is that it supports only simple queries—those that do not use outer joins, subqueries, the HAVING clause, or functions in the column list or WHERE clause. A sample view of this kind of report is shown in Figure 8-4.

Report From SQL Query

The Report From SQL Query is the most flexible of Portal's report offerings, as it is limited only by your ability to write creative SQL. It is the only report that allows a query with outer joins, subqueries, the HAVING clause, and functions in the WHERE

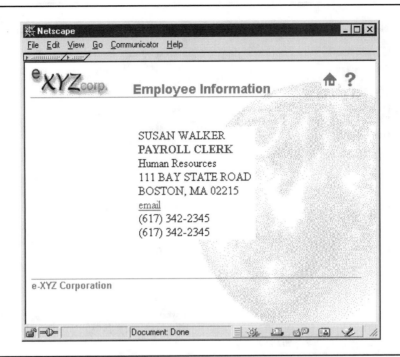

FIGURE 8-4. *The Employee Business Card was produced with a Report From Query Wizard and a custom layout*

and SELECT clauses. Of course, these complex conditions could be coded into a view and you could use any report on the view, but creating a view for every report could quickly become cumbersome.

Programmers familiar with SQL, PL/SQL, and Web programming may find the Report From SQL Query more to their liking than the wizard-driven approach. The SQL is explicit and can be customized to do precisely what you want it to do. The query you write can return static data, active links, JavaScript, or any other HTML markup—even <FORM> and <INPUT> tags. Of course, every <FORM> tag you generate requires a corresponding action program, so you may find yourself writing lots of custom PL/SQL to support these extended reports.

A Report From SQL Query would be a good candidate for the "View Cart" page in a shopping cart application, because each row (depending on how you code it) requires a separate HTML form to handle changes to individual items.

To produce a "report" like this, you would concatenate the appropriate HTML to the data retrieved from the shopping cart table, and then write the code to respond to the buttons separately. The main drawback is that the query would be extremely

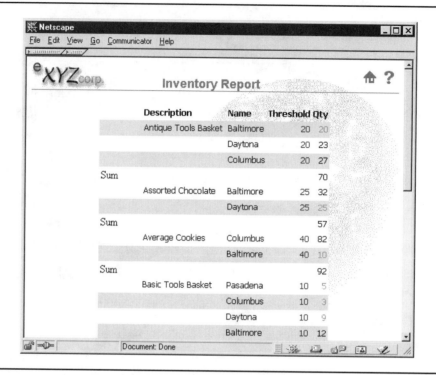

FIGURE 8-5. *The Inventory Report is based on a Report From SQL Query*

difficult to read and maintain. The case studies presented in Chapters 13 and 14 will illustrate the concept of using the Report From SQL Query as an application driver.

To showcase the Report From SQL Query, we base our example on a report that requires several flexible parameters and a calculated field. Shown in Figure 8-5, the Inventory Report also demonstrates the use of conditional formatting and PL/SQL to change the report appearance.

Developing Portal Reports

The process for developing reports is similar to that for forms, and in this section we will walk through the wizards to give you an idea of all the options available to you in Portal reports. To create a report, go to the Navigator Applications tab, click on the name of the application that will own the report, then click the Report link in the "Create New ..." list at the top of the page. The choices of report type are displayed in a screen like the one next.

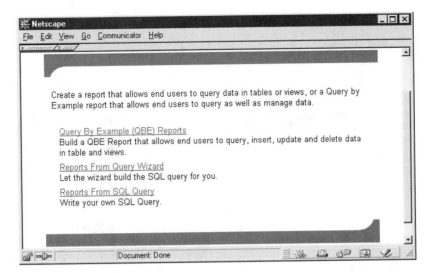

The wizards are similar for all of the report types, but the meaning of each field differs a little for the QBE Report. We will walk through the QBE Report wizard first, then explain the differences in the wizards for the Report From Query wizard and the Report From SQL Query. At the end of each section, you will have the opportunity to build the type of report discussed.

QBE Report: Step by Step

In the first step of the wizard, you are to specify the Name of the report and the Display Name, as you did with forms. This step is the same for all components.

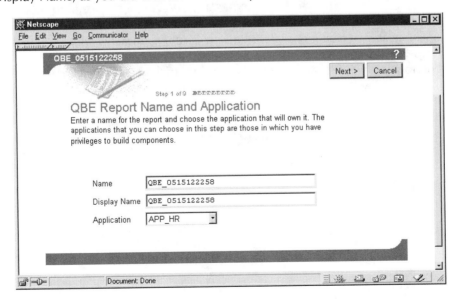

Choose the Table or View

A QBE Report is based on a single table or view. Use a view if you need to combine information from several tables. Use the pop-up list to select the table or view, or type the name of the table or view into the field. The table or view must be accessible to the component schema.

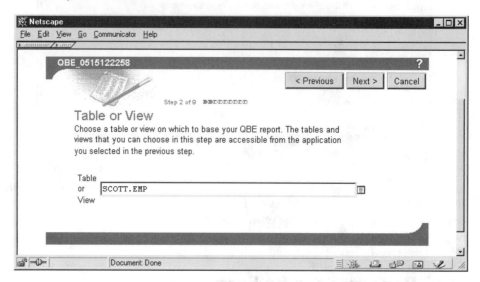

Choose Table or View Columns

Next, choose the columns you'd like to work with in the report. If you need the value of a column for comparison, for INSERT or UPDATE, or for passing to another component, but do not want to display it in the QBE Report view, include it here. You will be able to hide it in a later step. Any column you select will be available for INSERT and UPDATE, if you enable those functions. There is no way in a QBE Report to selectively allow operations on a subset of the columns. If, for example, you want to allow INSERT on all columns but limit UPDATE to one or two columns, you will need to use a Form.

To include a column in the report, highlight the column in the Columns list on the left, and then click on the right arrow to move it into the Selected Columns list. To move all of the columns in one step, click the double right arrow. The order of the columns in the Selected Columns list dictates the display order in the eventual report. Set up the desired display order by moving the columns up and down in the Selected Columns list. The up and down arrows move a highlighted column up or down one time, and the arrows with a bar above or below move the column to the top or bottom of the list.

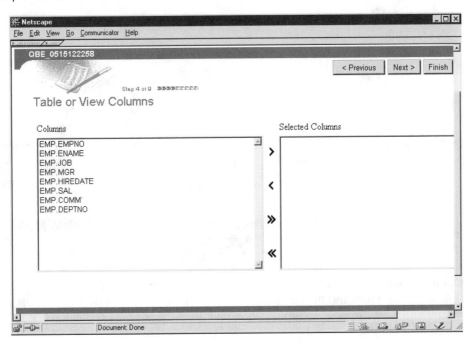

Column Formatting

The Column Formatting page allows you to define each column's functional characteristics and any custom links and display features. Each column selected in the previous step is displayed in its own row on this page, and the settings appear as columns going across the screen. The only display characteristics that you will set on this page are the alignment for the columns and, if desired, the column width. Font size, face, and colors are set later in the Display Options page, or for column, row, or data-specific formatting, in the Formatting Conditions page.

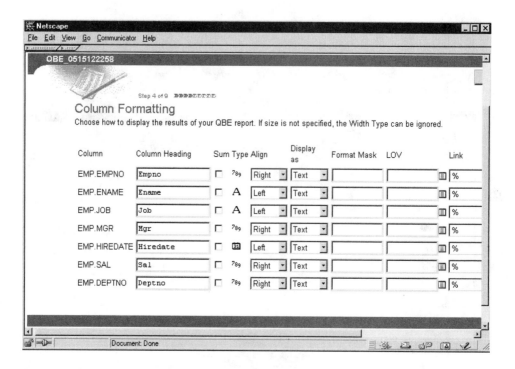

Column Heading   The Column Heading serves as the field label in the Customization Form and the column heading in the tabular view of the data. Use meaningful words to describe your data, rather than the defaults generated from the column names.

Sum   Checking the Sum check box causes the report to display a sum of that column for each break group, or for the entire report when there are no break groups. (See the discussion of break groups in the "Break Options" section that follows.) The Sum check box only acts on numeric fields.

Type   The Type column is provided for reference so you can easily see the field's datatype.

Align   Align allows you to justify the data to right, left, or center. Numeric fields default to right justification and text defaults to left justification. You may find that changing the default justification greatly improves the appearance of your report.

Display As   Display As allows for different uses for the data. The default value, Text, simply displays the information as selected from the table or view, and applies any formatting you specify. If you want to include custom HTML in your report, you will have to change this value to HTML. (Otherwise the complete source of the HTML tags are faithfully displayed and formatted in the generated report!) You might use this setting if you have stored HTML in a table, or if your view definition has concatenated HTML in the SELECT statement. This technique lets you generate custom image, anchor, or other tags using names or parameters stored in the database. The browser can then evaluate the tags as HTML, creating nonstandard report features in your output. You will want to remove any formatting defined on these columns in the wizard, as any custom formatting may affect the generated HTML. Finally, the Hidden option hides columns whose value you need for INSERT, UPDATE, or conditional formatting, but that you do not wish to display in the report view.

Format Mask　The Format Mask option allows you to display dates and numbers in a custom format, and uses all of the standard format strings that you would normally use with SQL. For example, the default date format is 'DD-MON-RR'. If you wanted to display a four-digit year, you could change the Format Mask to 'DD-MON-YYYY'. For a complete explanation of format masks, refer to the Oracle Server documentation, specifically the Oracle SQL Reference.

LOV　LOV allows you to specify a previously defined LOV for the field. For QBE Reports, the LOV will display on the Customization Form to help the user with queries and inserts.

Link　The Link option turns the column into an active link instead of plain text. Choose any previously defined Link from the list and click the Edit Link icon to map static or column vales to the link's parameters. You can make any column an active link regardless of which columns will be used to supply parameter values. Each row will show the link, and the report will pass values from the current row (as configured) to the destination component.

Width Type and Size　Finally, you can modify the size of each column in the generated report. The cell width in HTML tables is controlled by the browser, and sometimes you may find that the text wraps in unusual places or that the column headings appear too close together on the screen. Shortening column headings may solve some of the format issues, but if you want to force a table cell to a particular width, set its size here. The Width Type and Size options work together to allow you to set the column's width in pixels, number of characters, or as a percent of the screen. A percentage would give the most consistent results for different screen sizes, but an absolute number in pixels or characters would guarantee that certain text does not wrap.

Formatting Conditions

The Formatting Conditions page lets you change the default format of the data based on Boolean conditions. To set up a conditional format, first choose the column whose data you will test. If you want the format to apply regardless of the data, choose <NO CONDITION> from the list. Next, if you choose a column, set the Condition operator to be used to test the data. You can test using equality, inequality, greater than or less than, NULL or NOT NULL, LIKE and IN. In the Value field, type the test condition, or the value that will trigger the conditional formatting. You may use static text or numbers, a wildcard (%) for the LIKE operator, and a colon (:) to separate multiple values in a list for the IN operator. If you are testing for NULL or NOT NULL, do not enter anything in the Value field. Next, you will choose the column to which the format will be applied. Choose <ROW> to set the format for the entire row, and a column name otherwise. If you want two or more columns formatted in this way, but not the entire row, create the same condition for each column that needs the format.

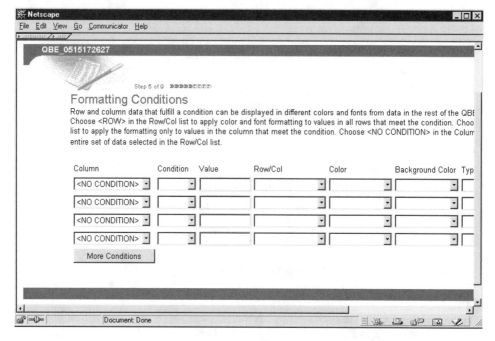

After setting up the condition, choose which formats to apply. You only have to set the formats that you wish to change. For example, to preserve the default font face but make it a different color, leave the Type Face setting blank and set only the Color field. The Color field lets you change the font color, and the Background Color field allows you to specify a different color for the table cell. Choose a font face if desired, and check any of the boxes that represent bold, italics, underline, or blinking text.

The sequence field (Seq) dictates the order in which the conditions are to be evaluated. Use the Seq field when multiple format conditions could conflict. For example, to set a two-level format condition, such as one that displays the text in blue when the price exceeds $100 and in red when the price exceeds $1000, you would need to make sure that the more restrictive condition (i.e., price > 1000) is evaluated last.

The <NO CONDITION> setting implies that the special format should always be used, and so can be used to change the display characteristics of a column or the entire report. The Formatting Conditions page allows the use of bold, italic, underline, or blinking fonts, which are not available on the Display Options page. If you want to use one of these for your entire report, you can specify them as formatting conditions using the <NO CONDITION> and <ROW> options. Between the Display Options and Formatting Conditions settings, there exists a somewhat confusing array of format possibilities. Table 8-1 outlines the combinations based on what you might want to accomplish.

If you want to:	Use:	Set Column to	Set Row/Col to
Change font face, color, or size for the entire report	Display Options page	N/A	N/A
Specify bold, italic, underline, or blinking for the entire report	Formatting Conditions page	<NO CONDITION>	<ROW>
Override formatting for all values in a single column	Formatting Conditions page	<NO CONDITION>	Choose column to format
Apply dynamic formatting for a single column based on conditions	Formatting Conditions page	Column to test— also set Condition and Value	Choose column to format
Change the format of entire row based on conditions	Formatting Conditions page	Column to test— also set Condition and Value	<ROW>

TABLE 8-1.   *Options for Controlling Static and Dynamic Format*

Display Options

The Display Options page allows you to set up the default behavior of the report in terms of sort order, break groups, font settings, summaries, and more. It is divided into five sections: Common Options, Full Page Options, Portlet Options, Break Options, and Row Order Options.

Common Options

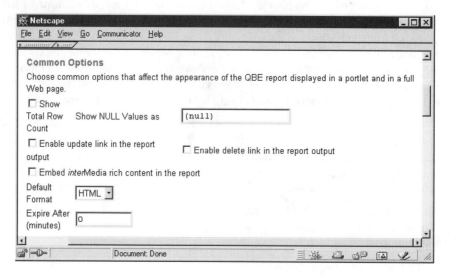

The Common Options settings apply whether the report is displayed in full page mode or as a portlet—hence the name. The settings are defined in Table 8-2.

Setting	Description
Show Total Row Count	Adds a footer to identify the record numbers displayed on the page (e.g., "Rows 11 - 20").
Show Null Values as	Allows you to specify text to substitute for NULLs in the report output.
Enable update link in the report output	Permits updates to the data from this component.
Enable delete link in the report output	Permits deletes from this component.

TABLE 8-2. *Common Options Settings*

Setting	Description
Embed interMedia rich content in the report	Allows you to include graphics and sound.
Default Format	Choose from HTML, Excel, or ASCII text. Excel setting permits download of the data in spreadsheet form.
Expire After (minutes)	Specify how long the data is valid—increase this value to enable caching of report output.

TABLE 8-2. *Common Options Settings* (continued)

Full Page Options   The Full Page Options dictate how the report will look when viewed in full page mode. The column headings are generated with the HTML table header <TH> tag, so most browsers will add bold to the font settings you choose here. You may specify a different font face, color, or size for your column headings using the drop-down lists by the Heading entry. The Row Text entry sets the default format for the data, which will be overridden by any conditional formatting set on the Conditional Formatting page.

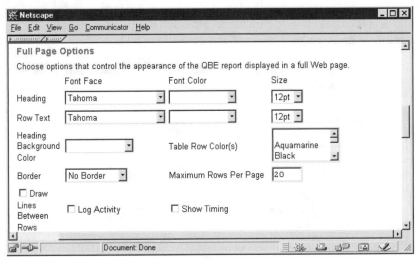

You may set the Heading Background Color field independently from the Table Row Color(s) field. The latter field is a multiple select list, and you may choose as many colors as you like from the list. The list is generated from the Colors defined in the Shared Components application. The colors will be used in alternating fashion, and if well chosen, can really jazz up your report output. If you set no colors for the table rows, you will get alternating dark gray and white background for the rows, and a transparent background for the headings. Alternating colors tend to help the users track the data as they read across the row.

There are two other ways to delineate the rows. You can use the standard HTML Border setting, which is set to No Border by default and offers the choice of a Thin (1 pixel) or Thick (2 pixel) border. Your other choice is to use the Draw Lines Between Rows check box to separate the data with horizontal lines, but not vertical column divisions. These are drawn as HTML horizontal rules (the <HR> tag), but within table cells, so they look like broken lines in the finished report. Both are helpful for improving the report's legibility, but definitely should not be used together.

Maximum Rows Per Page sets the number of rows to display on each page. It will not restrict the total number of rows retrieved. The Log Activity and Show Timing check boxes provide the same functionality as they did for the forms you developed in Chapter 7.

Portlet Display Options   For portlets, you can set font face, size, and color explicitly, but the preferred method is to use preexisting Portal *style elements*. When you created styles in Chapter 5, you set font characteristics for several levels of text and headings. These text and heading levels, as well as background colors, banner settings, and portlet headers, are all style elements that are used any time a Portal page is rendered. For maximum flexibility, use the style elements to format your report in a portlet. This way the report can be used seamlessly with any page style, even one that has been customized by the end user. You may choose from any of the four levels of both text and headings provided in the list. Typically, the higher the number (e.g., `Portlet Text4`), the smaller the text.

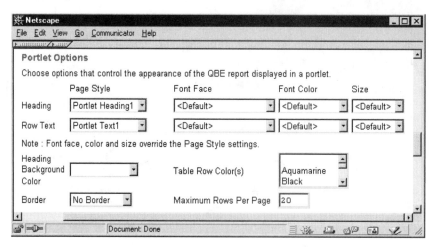

The background and row colors, borders, and rows per page all work the same in the portlet as they did for Full Page Options. You may wish to reduce the number of rows displayed so the component will fit nicely in the portal page, or use a more sedate color scheme to reduce the possibility of conflicts with the page style.

Break Options   Break groups create subdivisions of the rows by value. They must work in concert with the row ordering to be meaningful. A break group suppresses repeated values in a column and displays summaries (if specified) at each change of value. This concept is illustrated below—notice that the break groups would not work very well on unsorted data.

No Break Groups			Order by Deptno, Break on Deptno		
20	SMITH	800.00	10	CLARK	2450.00
30	ALLEN	1600.00		KING	5000.00
30	WARD	1250.00		MILLER	1300.00
20	JONES	2975.00	sum		8750.00
30	MARTIN	1250.00	20	SMITH	800.00
30	BLAKE	2850.00		ADAMS	1100.00
10	CLARK	2450.00		FORD	3000.00
20	SCOTT	3000.00		SCOTT	3000.00
10	KING	5000.00		JONES	2975.00
30	TURNER	1500.00	sum		10875.00
20	ADAMS	1100.00	30	ALLEN	1600.00
30	JAMES	950.00		BLAKE	2850.00
20	FORD	3000.00		MARTIN	1250.00
10	MILLER	1300.00		JAMES	950.00
				TURNER	1500.00
				WARD	1250.00
			sum		9400.00
			sum (report)		29025.00

The only Break Style option in the current release is Left Break. This means that the column(s) you choose to break on will be displayed first in the generated report, in order of First Break Column, Second Break Column, and Third Break Column, from left to right. These columns will also be sorted in the same order to ensure that the break groups have appropriate meaning. Any Order By setting that you specify (see next section) will be applied after the sort for the break groups.

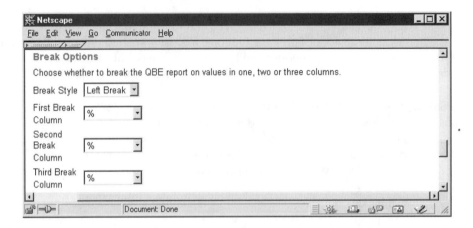

Row Order Options   The Order By choices will set the ORDER BY clause for the query that retrieves the report data. They are numbered to reflect successive sort levels. To specify a sort order, choose the column(s) by column name for each sort level, and specify Ascending or Descending. You may allow the user to change the sort, as we'll see in the next section.

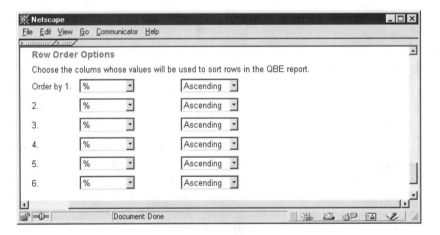

Customization Form Display Options
If you allow access to the customization form at all, you will want to evaluate what the user is allowed to change. Novice users may not understand break groups, query conditions, or even output format, so be sure you understand your user base or train them on the available options as you decide what to offer in terms of customization.

The customization form give the users significant power to format, alter, and display their own queries within the context of the table defined for the QBE Report. If you want to use these features without allowing access to the customization form, you can specify some of these options in links and any of them in programmatic calls to the component. In other words, you can use another component or your own custom page to serve in the place of the customization form.

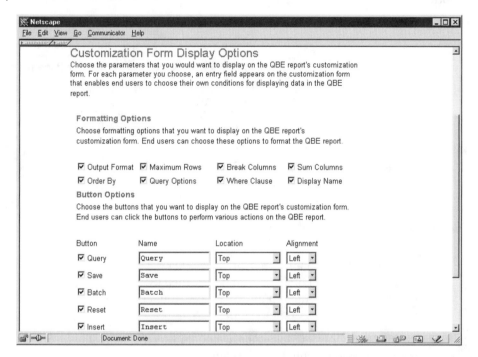

Formatting Options   With the exception of the Query Options and Where Clause check boxes, the choices available in the Formatting Options section let you expose some of the customization features of the wizard to your end users. We have discussed these features at length, so instead of explaining them again here, we refer you (in Table 8-3) to the wizard feature that corresponds to each check box. The Where Clause check box does not have a direct mapping-it enables user to enter freeform WHERE clause criteria. The Query Options check box enables a variety of useful options, described in the next section.

Query Options   The Query Options setting displays a multiple select list with several options from which users can choose to alter the format of the report. Some of these have corresponding settings in the report wizard, but not all. There is no way to display a subset of these options on the customization form—it's an all-or-nothing feature. The options are described as follows:

- **Show SQL**   Displays the SQL statement used to generate the report.
- **Display Results in Table with Borders**   Same as setting the Border to Thin Border on the Display Options page.

Customization Form Option	Maps To
Output Format	Display Options page, Default Format field
Order By	Display Options page, Row Order Options section
Maximum Rows	Display Options page, Maximum Rows Per Page field
Break Columns	Display Options page, Break Options section
Sum Columns	Column Formatting page, Sum check box—allows user to select from a list of all numeric columns to add summaries
Display Name	Report Name and Application page (first step)—allows user to change report heading or portlet title

TABLE 8-3. *Customizing the Customization Form*

- **Show Total Row Count**   The only way other than custom PL/SQL to display a true count of all rows to be returned by the query—this is (surprisingly) different from the Total Row Count on the Display Options page (see Table 8-2, Common Options Settings).

- **Count Rows Only**   Displays a row count instead of the data—very useful if you allow ad hoc query against large tables.

- **Show Paging Buttons**   Paging buttons appear any time there are more rows than the Maximum Rows Per Page setting, so this option has no effect.

- **Show HR Between Rows**   Maps to the Display Options page, Draw Lines Between Rows check box.

- **Replace ASCII New Lines with HTML Breaks**   Replaces any line feeds in the datat with line break (<BR>) tags—otherwise, they are ignored in the report output.

Button Options   If you allow a customization form and you want the users to be able to view records, you will need a Query button. The Reset button is also essential so users can set the customization form back to its defaults and enter a new query. The Save button allows users to save the customization options they've entered, so that the report always displays with their settings. They can modify the settings for a single run of the report, or save different settings later to change their default view. If this is more of a management-directed report, you may not wish to allow saves, but they are entirely appropriate for reporting utilities designed for ad hoc query.

Finally, the Insert button allows the users to create records from within the QBE Report. For the insert to succeed, you must include all required fields in the QBE Report, or set their values with database default values or triggers.

If the QBE Report is based on a multi-table view, the only fields that will be insertable are those from key-preserved tables. Values from non-key-preserved (lookup) tables will be disabled on the customize form, and therefore the user will not be able to directly query those fields either. They may enter conditions using the Where Clause field if you included it in the Formatting Options section above. Removing the Insert button enables these lookup fields for query.

Wizard Wrap-Up

The final two pages of the wizard are the same two pages you saw for forms, with a slight twist. The Text page and the Additional PL/SQL Code page both have two columns now, one that supports enhancement of the displayed results and another for enhancing the customization form. You may add different text or preprocessing and postprocessing code to either the report or the customization form, or both, and create different Help Text entries for each.

Of course, these pages are optional, and we will demonstrate some handy uses for them in the exercises to follow. The Finish button takes you out of the wizard at any time, so you can return to the Manage Component page to test your report in full page or portlet mode, or test the customize form.

Exercise 8.1: Maintain Products

eXYZ's product managers need a way to view the product list, add new products, edit product descriptions, status, or pricing, and delete products that the company no longer offers. Given these requirements, and because all of the required information is in a single table—with no need for default values, hidden fields, lookups, or complex validation—this is a good candidate for a QBE Report.

1. In the Navigator Applications tab, click on the APP_SALES application.

2. Click Report at the top of the screen to Create a New report.

3. Select Query By Example (QBE) Reports.

4. Name the report QBE_PRODUCTS and give it a Display Name of Product Maintenance.

5. On the Table or View selection page, use the list icon to select CORP_SITE.PRODUCTS and click Next.

6. Select all the columns by clicking the double right arrow. Using the up and down arrows, order them according to the column names in Table 8-4 (ignore the column headings for now).

7. Click Next to go to the Column Formatting page. Change the Column Headings to match the headings in Table 8-4. Add a Format Mask of $999.00 to the three PRICE fields. Set the alignment for LAST_UPDATED to right-aligned, and for STATUS to centered.

8. This report won't use any Formatting Conditions, so click Next until you get to the Display Options page.

9. On the Display Options page, check the box under Common Options to Show Total Row Count and enable both the update and delete links in the report output. In the Full Page Options section, change the Font Size to 10pt for both the heading and row text. In the Portlet Options, set Maximum Rows Per Page to 10.

10. Skip the Customization Form Display Options page for now so that you can test the default options in your initial run of the report.

11. On the QBE Report and Customization Form Text page, change the display name for the QBE Customization Form to Insert and Query Products, and choose the EXYZ_TEMPLATE in the Template field. Click Finish to build and test the report.

Column Name	Column Heading
PRODUCTS.PRODUCT_ID	ID
PRODUCTS.DESCRIPTION	Description
PRODUCTS.PRODUCT_CATEGORY	Category
PRODUCTS.STATUS	Sts
PRODUCTS.COST_PRICE	Cost
PRODUCTS.LIST_PRICE	List
PRODUCTS.MIN_PRICE	Min
PRODUCTS.REORDER_THRESHOLD	Low Qty
PRODUCTS.LAST_UPDATED	Update Date

TABLE 8-4. *Columns and Headings for the Product Maintenance Report*

Exercise 8.2: Using the QBE Report

1. To test your report, click the Run or Run as Portlet link in the Manage Component page. Try to update a record or two, and see how the update page works. Return to the list of records to see your changes. The Update Date changes due to a trigger on the table.

2. Next, click the Customize link to test queries and inserts. Try inserting a new record—enter the values for each field in the row, using A for the Status and any value for the Category, and then press Insert. Repeat one or two more times, experimenting with different values. Is there any validation when you enter these fields? What happens if you specify the same ID twice?

3. Now query for specific records, either by entering the query value(s) in the corresponding fields on the customization form or by writing a custom Where Clause, or both. Try displaying only a subset of the columns using the check boxes.

4. Test the Delete link on records that you have inserted.

Exercise 8.3: Validation in a QBE Report

The only field-level validation option available for a QBE Report is to attach an LOV. In this exercise, you will create two LOVs, then attach them to the report to ensure consistent data entry for the STATUS and CATEGORY columns.

1. Close the Manage Component page for the report so you can return to the Navigator.

2. Create a new dynamic list of values.

3. Name the LOV LOV_PRODUCT_CATEGORY, using the following query:

```
SELECT DISTINCT INITCAP(product_category), product_category
FROM    corp_site.products
```

4. Leave the remaining defaults and click OK.

5. Click Close and create a Static LOV named LOV_PRODUCT_STATUS with the following values:

Display Value	Return Value	Display Order
Avail.	A	1
Discont.	D	2
New	N	3

6. Click OK, then return to the Navigator page. Click on the Edit link by QBE_PRODUCTS to add these LOVs to the report.

7. On the Column Formatting tab, click the LOV list icon for PRODUCT_CATEGORY and select LOV_PRODUCT_CATEGORY. Repeat to select LOV_PRODUCT_STATUS for the STATUS column.

8. Click OK and test the new LOVs. Be sure to try a query, an insert, and an update to see how the LOV works in all situations.

In this section, you have seen how to build and use a QBE Report, and have seen the types of applications where it is most appropriate. We have elected not to put the product maintenance report directly on the eXYZ home page, because it is more useful and more flexible in full page mode. In portlet mode, the Customize link allows users to restrict query options, but it does not allow insert. eXYZ's product managers need the insert functionality, so in Chapter 10 you will build a menu component that will offer several options for working with the products. The menu component will be deployed as a portlet to serve as a gateway for all product management-related functions. If you would like your users to have the option of adding the product report as a portlet to their customizable pages, click on the Access tab of the Manage Component page and check the Publish to Portal box. This way, any users who would like to see the product list can see it at a glance on their home page.

Reports from Query Wizard: Step by Step

Most of the steps in the Report From Query Wizard are similar or identical to those in the QBE Reports Wizard. In this section, we will focus on the differences between the wizards rather than take you through the entire wizard again. Because the first step (specifying the report name and display name) is always the same, we can start with step 2.

Tables and Views

The first thing you should notice about this wizard step is that tables and views are mentioned in the plural, and the interface to select them is a little different. The

Report From Query wizard can handle any number of tables or views, provided you supply join conditions to link them together. Because of this, you need to click the Add button after selecting each table or view to include it in the report. To remove a table after adding it, click the red X that appears to the left of the table or view name in the Selected Tables/View list. When you are finished choosing all of the tables and views you will use, click the Next button.

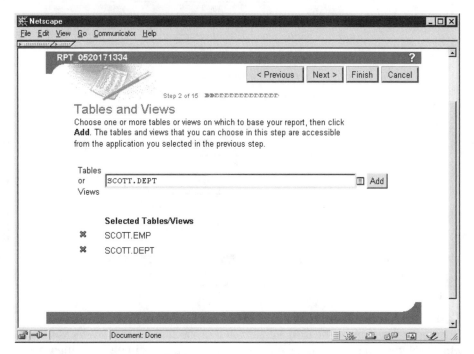

Join Conditions

The Join Conditions page is where you will link the tables and views you selected for the report. If the tables are related by foreign key constraints in the database, Portal will pick up those relationships and display them as defaults here. If they are not related by foreign keys, or if you are joining views, use the combo boxes to select the corresponding columns from each side to complete the join. Be sure to specify all of the columns involved in a multiple-column join condition, or the report will display a Cartesian product, which maps every row to every other row.

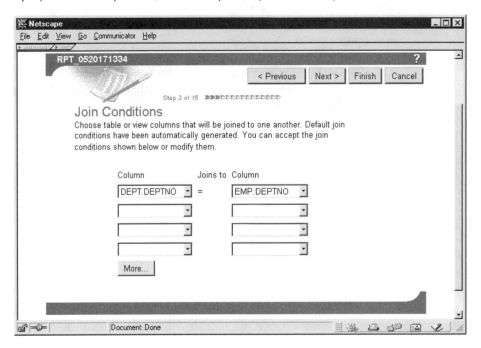

Table or View Columns

This step is the same as the QBE Wizard step of the same name, where you specify which columns to use in the generated report. If you are joining more than one table, you may choose not to display the join columns. The join will still function properly. As with the QBE Report, you can hide columns in a later step, if you need the value but don't want it displayed.

Column Conditions

Each column condition that you enter on the Column Conditions page will generate an additional WHERE clause expression to limit the data returned by the query. To create a column condition, select the Column Name from the list, choose a Condition, and type a Value. The Conditions that you can choose are shown in the illustration.

You can only use static values for the Value entry. If you need to use functions or parameters in your conditions, use the Report From SQL Query. The LIKE operator works as it does in SQL. It supports the percent sign (%) for multiple-character wildcard substitution and the underscore (_) for single-character substitution. For NULL and NOT NULL comparisons, do not enter a Value. The list for the IN and NOT IN operators is delimited by colons (:) and is not surrounded by parentheses.

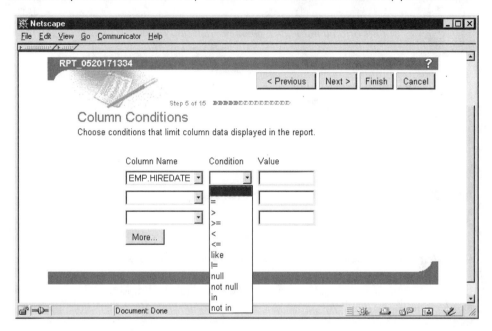

Report Layout

As with the forms you developed in Chapter 7, the remaining reports allow you to choose the layout style. (The QBE Report did not allow you to change the layout, because much of its interface depends on the tabular structure.) The Tabular layout is used most often with reports, and it presents the data as a table with rows and columns that map to database rows and columns, much like you would see when selecting data in SQL*Plus. In Portal, the table is represented in HTML, with table header tags for each of the column labels, a table row for each row of the data, and a table data cell for each column. The Form layout is also an HTML table with one table row for each row of data, but all fields are shown together in a single cell in the HTML table. Labels are displayed next to each field, and line breaks inside the table cell separate the fields. The Custom layout generates the HTML for a Tabular layout, and adds an extra step in the wizard where you can edit the HTML for custom formatting.

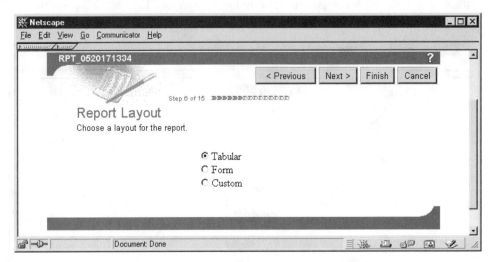

Column Formatting and Formatting Conditions

These steps correspond to the equivalent steps in the QBE Report wizard. The Column Formatting page allows you to customize labels, alignment, and format masks, and to add links to the displayed columns. The only difference from the QBE Report is that the option to specify an LOV for a column does not exist, because this report is not a data entry form. If you need an LOV for a query parameter, you will add it in the Customization Form Display Options page.

The Formatting Conditions step allows you to set up formatting based on conditions that occur in the data, exactly as you did in the QBE Report.

Display Options

The Display Options page is similar to that for the QBE Report, with a few minor exceptions. First, there is no way to enable Update and Delete links in the Report From Query wizard, because they are just not supported. Second, the Full Page Options section includes an additional check box to Show Query Conditions. If selected, this option will echo the parameter settings back to the user in the displayed report; it is quite useful for testing and for providing the user with additional information. The remaining settings in this page are the same for all reports.

WARNING
If your report uses more than one table (in version 3.0.9), you must specify at least one Order by field in the Row Order Options section. If you do not, the default is to use ORDER BY ROWID, *which cannot work against a multiple table query (i.e., the* ROWID *of which table?).*

HTML Code

You will only see the HTML Code page if you choose a Custom layout for the report. It displays the HTML and field and label placeholders that will be used to generate the report. You may modify this HTML to display the data in the exact format you require. Keep in mind that the output will still be contained within an HTML table with one table row for each row retrieved by the report, and there is no way to override the outer table.

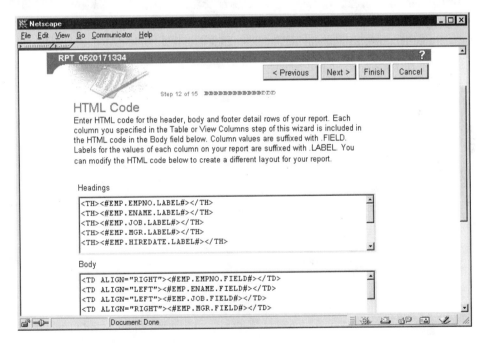

Customization Form Display Options

The Customization Form Display Options page allows you to set up the exact parameters you need, provided each one corresponds to a column in the report.

This is quite unlike the QBE Report, where all of the columns shown in the report were automatically allowed as query parameters, and you were unable to override that setting. Choose a column from the Column Name list to make it a parameter on the customization form, and create as many parameters as you like, clicking on the More Parameters button if you need more than three. Check the Value Required box if a parameter must be supplied to run the report, and optionally specify a prompt, an LOV, and the display format for the LOV. If you do not specify a prompt, the column's name will be used by default—it will not be blank.

At runtime, the Report From Query wizard customization form displays a text entry field or LOV, with the prompt, for each parameter you choose. In addition, it displays a combo box with the same comparison operators that were available in the Column Conditions page, so that users can query using the less than, not equal, LIKE, and IN operators, to name a few. You may want to explain these operators and their usage in the Help Text field.

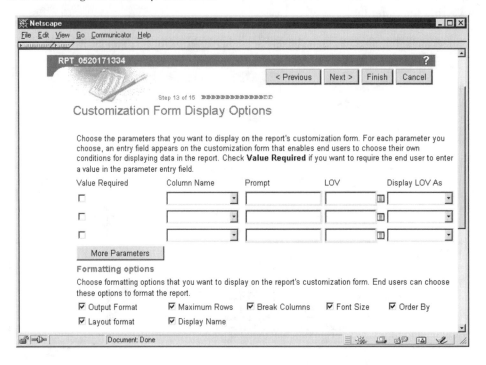

The Formatting Options section allows a little less flexibility than it did in the QBE Report. In the Report From SQL Query, you can allow users to change the Layout Format to Tabular or Form layout. Users cannot alter the summary columns you have set up, but you can let them change the font size of the generated report. Finally, the freeform Where Clause field and the general Query Options list are not available in the Report From SQL Query.

In the Button Options section, the Query button is replaced by a Run button, which essentially does the same thing. Of course there is no Insert button option, because this report does not accept inserts.

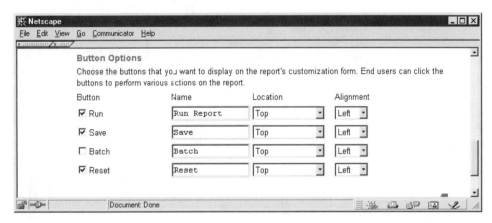

The final two steps are the same in all components. They allow you to customize both the text displayed with the report and the default processing with PL/SQL.

Now we can try our hand at building a Report From Query wizard.

Exercise 8.4: Employee Details

You will use the Report From Query wizard to build a simple report that shows a "virtual business card" for an employee. A legacy application creates the actual personnel records, and a trigger on the EMPLOYEES table creates a Portal user for every new employee, using code similar to the user creation script you saw in Chapter 5. We would like to be able to get employee details from within the Portal, without relying on the self-service account information, because we have no guarantee that users will enter their "Contact Info" there.

The report itself is simple, so we will make it more interesting by creating a custom layout. We'll call this report later from another component, using it to show details of the employee record.

1. Create a New Report From Query Wizard in the HR Application.

2. Name the report RPT_EMP_DETAILS, and give it a display name of Employee Information.

3. On the Tables and Views page, select the following tables for the report:

    ■ CORP_SITE.EMPLOYEES

    ■ CORP_SITE.DEPARTMENTS

    ■ CORP_SITE.TITLES

Click the Add button after selecting each table. Your screen should look like the one below after all the tables have been added. If so, continue to the next page of the wizard.

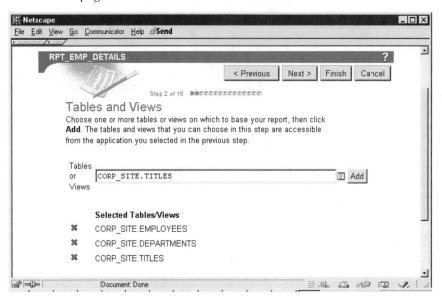

4. Specify the join conditions to relate EMPLOYEES to DEPARTMENTS based on DEPARTMENT_NO and to relate EMPLOYEES to TITLES based on TITLE_ID. The correct join settings are illustrated below.

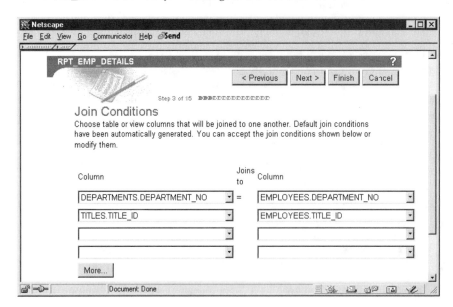

5. Click Next and select the following columns to use in the report, ensuring that they are displayed in the order below (either select them in the specified order or use the up and down arrows to the right of the column list to rearrange them):

- `EMPLOYEES.EMPLOYEE_ID`
- `EMPLOYEES.FIRST_NAME`
- `EMPLOYEES.LAST_NAME`
- `TITLES.TITLE_DESC`
- `DEPARTMENTS.NAME`
- `EMPLOYEES.ADDRESS`
- `EMPLOYEES.CITY`
- `EMPLOYEES.STATE`
- `EMPLOYEES.ZIP`
- `EMPLOYEES.EMAIL_ADDRESS`
- `EMPLOYEES.PHONE`
- `EMPLOYEES.FAX`

6. Skip the Column Conditions page.

7. Specify a Custom layout for the report.

8. On the Column Formatting page, set the EMPLOYEE_ID column to Display as `Hidden`. Remove all of the Column Headings and click Next.

9. On the Formatting Conditions page, create a format condition to display the employee's title in blue. Set the Column field to `<NO CONDITION>`, the Row/Col field to `TITLE.TITLE_DESC`, and the Color field to `Blue, Midnight`. Use the check box at the far right (under the "A" displayed in bold) to display it in bold font.

Create another condition, so that if the employee is the president of the company (TITLE.TITLE_DESC = PRESIDENT), the report will override the first condition and display the title in Red. See the illustration to verify these settings are correct.

```
Netscape                                                        _ □ ×
File  Edit  View  Go  Communicator  Help  ✍Send

Formatting Conditions
Row and column data that fulfill a condition can be displayed in different colors and fonts from data in the rest of the report.
Choose <ROW> in the Row/Col list to apply color and font formatting to values in all rows that meet the condition. Choose a column
to values in the column that meet the condition. Choose <NO CONDITION> in the Column list to apply the formatting to the entire se

Column                    Condition  Value    Row/Col                    Color              Back
┌──────────────────┐      ┌─┐  ┌─┐   ┌──────────────────┐  ┌─┐ ┌──────────────┐
│<NO CONDITION>    │ ▾    │ │▾ │ │    │TITLES.TITLE_DESC │ ▾  │Blue, Midnight│▾  │
└──────────────────┘      └─┘  └─┘   └──────────────────┘  └─┘ └──────────────┘
┌──────────────────┐      ┌─┐  ┌────────┐  ┌──────────────────┐  ┌─┐ ┌──────────────┐
│TITLES.TITLE_DESC │ ▾    │=│▾ │PRESIDENT│  │TITLES.TITLE_DESC │ ▾  │Red           │▾  │
└──────────────────┘      └─┘  └────────┘  └──────────────────┘  └─┘ └──────────────┘
┌──────────────────┐      ┌─┐  ┌─┐   ┌──────────────────┐  ┌─┐ ┌──────────────┐
│<NO CONDITION>    │ ▾    │ │▾ │ │    │                  │ ▾  │              │▾  │
└──────────────────┘      └─┘  └─┘   └──────────────────┘  └─┘ └──────────────┘
┌──────────────────┐      ┌─┐  ┌─┐   ┌──────────────────┐  ┌─┐ ┌──────────────┐
│<NO CONDITION>    │ ▾    │ │▾ │ │    │                  │ ▾  │              │▾  │
└──────────────────┘      └─┘  └─┘   └──────────────────┘  └─┘ └──────────────┘
┌──────┐
│More...│
└──────┘

☞ Document: Done
```

10. On the Display Options page, remove the (null) text from the Show NULL Values as field. In the Full Page Options section, remove all formatting from the Row Text fields, including Font Face and Size. This will cause the text to be displayed in the browser's default font. As you will see, we will use a mailto link in the custom HTML. The text formatting would prevent this technique from working, because it would nest FONT tags within the mailto address. Under Row Order Options, choose EMPLOYEES.LAST_NAME as the first Order by condition.

TIP
If you would like to combine a significant amount of HTML with database data, you will find it easier to write the query yourself in a Report From SQL Query.

11. In the HTML Code page, remove all the text from the Headings field. Technically, we don't have to do this because we removed the labels earlier, but we're just getting rid of unnecessary HTML. Edit the HTML in the Body field or paste it in from the accompanying file to make it look like a form-style report and include the `mailto` link, as shown here:

```
File: ex0804.txt
<#EMPLOYEES.EMPLOYEE_ID.FIELD#>
<TD ALIGN="LEFT" BGCOLOR="WHITE">
<#EMPLOYEES.FIRST_NAME.FIELD#>  <#EMPLOYEES.LAST_NAME.FIELD#> <BR>
<#TITLES.TITLE_DESC.FIELD#> <BR>
<#DEPARTMENTS.NAME.FIELD#> <BR>
<#EMPLOYEES.ADDRESS.FIELD#> <BR>
<#EMPLOYEES.CITY.FIELD#>, <#EMPLOYEES.STATE.FIELD#>
<#EMPLOYEES.ZIP.FIELD#> <BR>
<A HREF="mailto:<#EMPLOYEES.EMAIL_ADDRESS.FIELD#>">email</A> <BR>
<#EMPLOYEES.PHONE.FIELD#> <BR>
<#EMPLOYEES.FAX.FIELD#> <BR>
</TD>
```

12. On the Customization Form Display Options page, specify the employee ID as a required parameter—check the Value Required box and select EMPLOYEES.EMPLOYEE_ID as the column name. You won't need an LOV or a prompt, because we will call this report from another component. Remove all of the formatting options by removing the checkmarks from the boxes, and do not display the Save button.

13. Choose the `EXYZ_TEMPLATE` on the Report and Customization Form Text page.

14. Click Finish and test your report. You must use the Customize link to view the report output. Some sample values for a valid Employee_Id include: `1111`, `5556`, `4000`, and `9835`. Be sure to test the company president (employee `5556`) to see that the special formatting on the title worked. Try to send an email to the employee whose card you are viewing.

That's it! This was a simple report, and we will see in Chapter 9 how it can be used in conjunction with an organization chart to allow lookup by the corporate hierarchy.

Report from SQL Query: Step by Step

The Report From SQL Query differs from the Report From Query wizard in only a few ways, all based on the concept that you write the query to produce the report's output. For example, joins and WHERE clause conditions come from the query, so the wizard does not display those steps. All of the columns selected in the query are available to the report and they can be hidden as with the other reports.

If you want parameters in a Report From SQL Query, you will have to include them as bind variables in the query—you will not have the option to create new parameters in the Display Options screen. You will also have to do some extra work in the query to allow for range criteria or the `IN` or `LIKE` operator, because the customization form does not display the conditional operators as it does in the other reports. For example, to allow a query to support a greater than or less than condition, you would have to create two parameters—a `value` for the user to enter, and a `flag` (preferably supported by an LOV) to indicate the type of query. A fragment of the WHERE clause to support such a report is below.

```
WHERE col = :value AND :flag = 'eq'
OR    col > :value AND :flag = 'gt'
OR    col < :value AND :flag = 'lt'
```

You could extend this model to support a wide range of query criteria, but be sure to specify default values for parameters that would cause the query to fail if they are `NULL`. The following modification to the query compensates for the possibility of `NULL`s in the parameters by returning all rows if the `value` is `NULL`, and assumes an equality condition if the `flag` is `NULL`.

```
WHERE (col = :value AND (:flag = 'eq' OR :flag IS NULL)
OR     col > :value AND :flag = 'gt'
OR     col < :value AND :flag = 'lt')
OR     :value IS NULL)
```

Everything else about this report is the same as the Report From Query wizard, so we don't have to walk through the wizard in detail. Instead, let's start immediately with an exercise.

Exercise 8.5: Inventory Report

At eXYZ Corporation, the Inventory Report needs to be implemented as a Report From SQL Query, because it will use a calculated value to highlight records when the inventory level is below the predetermined threshold. The warehouse staff and salespeople must be able to check current stock levels, which are held in the INVENTORIES table. This table maps warehouses to product numbers, and the rows store the quantity available of each product at each location.

The Inventory Report will accept three parameters: `product`, `warehouse`, and a parameter that will let users display only those products that are below threshold. All parameters are optional, and you will use LOVs for the product and warehouse selection. When the user selects a `product`, the report will list quantities of that product at each warehouse. When the user selects a `warehouse`, the report will list quantities of all products at that warehouse. If both are selected, the report will display one line, and if none are selected, the report will display all quantities at all warehouses. Low stock levels will be flagged with a font color change, and users will have the option to download the report data into Excel.

This example illustrates how you would get a single component to perform a variety of functions. The same requirement could be met with three (simpler) reports, but because of the component's ability to use custom parameters and complex SQL, we can reduce the number of components in the application and still meet the users' needs.

1. Create a new Report From SQL Query in the Sales Application.

2. Name the Report RPT_INVENTORY, and give it a display name of Inventory Report.

3. On the SQL Query page, enter the following query:

```
File ex0805.sql
SELECT p.description, w.name, p.reorder_threshold
       ,i.qty_available
       ,(i.qty_available - p.reorder_threshold) low_ind
FROM   products p, warehouses w, inventories i
WHERE  p.product_id = i.product_id
AND    w.warehouse_id = i.warehouse_id
AND    p.status = 'A'
AND    TO_CHAR(w.warehouse_id) LIKE :warehouse
AND    p.product_id LIKE :product
AND    SIGN(i.qty_available - p.reorder_threshold) <= :low_qty
```

Let's explain this query: The LIKE operators for the product and warehouse criteria allow the option of specifying an individual product or warehouse or displaying all of them. When you use LOVs in parameters, as you will in this report, the NULL value always returns a percent (%) sign. This way, if the user enters no parameters, the query will use the % sign to retrieve data on all products and warehouses. Because the Warehouse_Id column is defined as numeric, you must use the TO_CHAR function to convert it for this comparison.

Using the SIGN function in the WHERE clause is a clever workaround to enable flexible queries without requiring two parameters. SIGN returns 1 if its argument evaluates to a positive number, 0 if its argument evaluates to zero, and -1 if its argument evaluates to a negative number. Subtracting the threshold from the quantity available yields a negative number if the quantity is below the threshold. We will use this indicator value as a parameter to allow users to report only below-threshold items.

4. On the Layout Options page, leave the default Tabular layout for the report.

5. On the Column Formatting page, change the column heading for REORDER_THRESHOLD to Threshold, and for QTY_AVAILABLE to Qty.

Click the check box for Sum on the QTY_AVAILABLE column to generate totals for the report. Change the Display as field for LOW_IND to Hidden and click Next.

6. In the Formatting Conditions page, create a condition on the LOW_IND column so that the value displays in blinking text when the quantity falls below or is equal to the threshold value. Choose LOW_IND for the Column, <= for the Condition, and type 0 into the Value field. In the Row/Col dropdown, select QTY_AVAILABLE and check the box under the word Blink.

7. In the Full Page Options section of the Display Options page, reduce the font size for both headings and row text to 10pt. In the Break Options section, set the first break column to DESCRIPTION. Also, set the order by to DESCRIPTION in the Row Order Options section.

NOTE
In the QBE Report, the break column automatically changes the sort order, but it does not appear to do so in the Report From SQL Query. Since we will allow the user to change the break column, we will have to build in some code to ensure that the sort changes accordingly.

8. Next, in the Customization Form Display Options page, set the product parameter to use LOV_PRODUCTS that you created in Chapter 7, and set Display LOV As to Combo box. Set the Default Value for both the product and the warehouse parameters to %. Set the default value for LOW_QTY to 1. Leave the remaining settings to their defaults.

9. On the Report and Customization Form Text page, choose EXYZ_TEMPLATE in the Template combo box.

10. Click Finish to test the report.

Exercise 8.6: Testing the Inventory Report

1. Click Run to view the entire report in full screen mode, then return to the Manage Component page and click Run As Portlet to see how it will look as a portlet. In both cases, the rows should display neatly divided by

product, with a sum for each product and a sum for the page. Look for the blinking text that serves as a warning that quantity is low, and use the Next and Previous buttons to navigate the data.

2. Return to the Manage Component page and click the Customize link. In the Customization Form, try selecting a single product, and view the report to display the warehouses that have it in stock.

3. Now try displaying all the products for a single warehouse. Return to the customization form (use the browser Back button) and set the `warehouse` parameter to 3. Set the `product` parameter to %. Does the report look right? Go back to the customization form and change the first order by column and the first break column to Name, so the output will be sorted and grouped by warehouse name. Rerun the report to see if these changes improve the report output. It should look much better with the revised break and order settings.

4. Finally, try displaying all products that have low inventory levels. Go back to the Customization Form and click on the Reset to Defaults button. Set the `low_qty` parameter to 0 to display all products that are at or below their reorder threshold, and view the results. Try setting the parameter to -1 to see only products that are below the threshold.

Exercise 8.7: Enhancing the Inventory Report

This report needs a few enhancements. First, we should probably add an LOV for the `warehouse` parameter, so users do not have to guess at the Warehouse ID. Second, we need to try to second-guess the users' intentions, and set the sort and break orders accordingly. We don't want to rely on the ability of the users to figure out the appropriate sort order and break settings when they view the report, so we will do it for them. We will also add an LOV for the `low_qty` parameter so users don't have to know the details of this construct. Finally, we will clean up the display a little.

1. Close the Manage Component page and go back to the Navigator so you can create an LOV for the WAREHOUSES table. Create a new dynamic list of values.

2. Name the LOV LOV_WAREHOUSES, and set the default format to Combo box. Leave the Show Null Values list set to Yes. Use the following query:

```
SELECT name, warehouse_id
FROM   corp_site.warehouses
```

3. Click OK, then Close the Manage Component page.

4. Create a static LOV named LOV_THRESHOLD. Set Show Null Value to No, and leave the default format as Check box. Enter the following values and click OK:

Display Value	Return Value	Display Order
Show All	1	1
Restock List Only	0	2

5. Back at the Navigator page, click the Edit link for RPT_INVENTORY.

6. Click on the Customization Form Display Options tab, and add LOV_WAREHOUSES to the parameter for the warehouse. Display this as a Combo box. Add LOV_THRESHOLD to the parameter for the quantity indicator, displayed as a Radio group, and set the low_qty Prompt to . This HTML shorthand for a nonbreaking space will display a space where the label should go, effectively removing it.

7. Add some text to help the user understand the customization form. Click on the Report and Customization Form Text tab, and in the Header Text field for the Customization Form, enter something like the following:

```
Welcome to the Inventory system. To get a list of products at any one warehouse,
choose the warehouse from the list. To check availability of a product at all
warehouses, choose the product from the list. Use the Restocking List Only option
to get a list of items in need of ordering. Click Run Report when you are ready to
see the results. For more assistance, click the question mark.
```

In the Help Text field for the Customization Form, enter:

```
This is a Customization Form. You may change the name of the displayed report,
change Query Options, and change the report's format. <UL><LI>To leave the
defaults, just click Run Report. <LI>To save your customizations, click Save.
<LI>To download a report into Excel, choose Excel from the Output Format list.
<LI>Set the Maximum Rows/Page to a high number if you do not want page breaks.
</UL>
```

TIP
The text areas can contain any HTML tags, and you may wish to improve on the format of your help system. In the case of the help text, we're using the unordered list (<UL>) and list item (<LI>) tags to list these options in a bulleted list, making the options easier to read.

8. Changing the order by and break columns when the report is run is a little more complex. Enter the following code on the Additional PL/SQL Code tab, in the "… before displaying the page" field for the report:

```
IF get_value ('warehouse') <> '%' THEN
  FOR i IN 1 .. l_arg_names.COUNT LOOP
    IF l_arg_names(i) = '_orderby_col_1' THEN
      l_arg_values(i) := 'NAME';
    END IF;
    IF l_arg_names(i) = '_break_column_1' THEN
      l_arg_values(i) := '2';
    END IF;
  END LOOP;
END IF;
```

Here's how to understand this code. First, we have to find a way to see if the user is selecting a particular warehouse. We'll do this by examining the array of arguments passed to the show procedure in the report package from the customization form. All arguments in Portal make use of two arrays: one contains the argument names, and the other contains the argument values. They are related by a common index value, so if the fourth entry in the name array was "warehouse", then the fourth entry in the value array should contain the passed Warehouse ID. Portal provides a get_value function in each generated package to simplify access to the two arrays. If the user did not select a warehouse, get_value would return the default of %.

Overriding the values passed by the Customization Form requires a different technique. Because there is no equivalent set_value function in reports, we will have to resort to the method of looping through the name array until we find the name of the parameter we need to set. Once found, the value array's corresponding entry is set with the correct value. In this release, order by parameters use the column's name, but the break parameters use the column's number. This number refers to the column order when you created the query in step 2 of the wizard, and will remain the same even if the break order changes the order of the columns in the report display.

9. Now click on the Formatting Conditions tab. Change the Font Color to red for the condition you created earlier, to make it a little more visible. If you do not like the blinking text, you may remove the checkmark that makes the text blink.

10. Add another condition, this time with <NO CONDITION> to change the REORDER_THRESHOLD to display in Blue, Dark. This will distinguish the value a little more from the actual inventory data.

11. Run and test your report again. Use the customization form to choose a warehouse. Does the display work as expected this time?

NOTE
Because the PL/SQL Code and the default values automatically set the sort order and break columns, you could remove these options from the report's Customization Form.

Exercise 8.8: Publish the Inventory Report to the Portal

The version of the Inventory Report that we want on the Portal home page is the one that shows which products have dangerously low stock levels. Let's see how we can create a portlet with some default customizations.

1. Once you are satisfied with the functionality of the report, click on the Access tab of the Manage Component screen and publish the report to the Portal.

2. Edit the eXYZ home page, using either the Navigator Pages tab or the Edit Page link on the page itself.

3. Click on the Management tab. Divide the region into two columns by clicking on the Add Column icon.

4. Now click on the Add Portlets icon for the right-side region. Click on the Other Providers: Sales Application link and then on Inventory Report. Verify that the portlet was added to the Selected Portlets list and click OK.

5. While still in the Edit Page view, click on Edit Defaults for the Inventory Report portlet. Change the display name (Title) to Restocking List and the radio group to Restock List Only. Set the first break column and order by column to Name, and click OK.

6. Click Close, and run and test your page. Does this portlet meet the requirements? Users will be able to modify the portlet settings using the Customize link, provided you have given them that privilege. Do not offer the privilege if you do not want them to change the defaults.

Linking Reports to Reports

Portal supports linking between pairs of components for almost all of the component types. The first link that we will look at is a link between two reports, which could be used to create a "drill-down" into further levels of detail. In later chapters, we will show you how to build links from other components to the reports we created in this chapter.

To use a Portal link, you must first create the link to the component you want to call in the Navigator. After you have created and tested the link, you can reference it in any other component, specifying parameters from the component to be passed to the link. We'll demonstrate this technique by linking the Product Maintenance QBE Report to the Inventory Report.

Exercise 8.9: Linking Reports

When the product managers at eXYZ are looking at the product list, they may need additional information about the inventory levels of each product. We will make this very easy for them by creating a link on the product name to take them to the inventory report, passing the product ID as a parameter.

1. In the Navigator page for APP_SALES, create a new link.

2. Name the link `LINK_RPT_INVENTORY` and click Next.

3. In the "Target Component or URL" field list, select the `RPT_INVENTORY` report.

4. Click Next to see the list of available parameters. We will only pass the `product` parameter to this report, but all parameters are available in case we need them for other references to this link.

5. Click Finish, then Close to return to the Navigator.

6. Edit the QBE_PRODUCTS report and navigate to the Column Formatting tab.

7. On the line for PRODUCTS.DESCRIPTION, choose `LINK_RPT_INVENTORY` from the Link combo box. Click the Edit Link icon to specify link parameters. In the pop-up window, select PRODUCT_ID from the Column Name list for the `product` parameter. When you return to the wizard, click OK and test the report with the new link. Does it pass the value as expected?

By linking the two reports, you represent the normal flow of business processes explicitly in the application, making the application work hard for the users. As we continue to build the site in Portal, we will expand on this concept even further.

Conclusion

In this chapter, we have created three powerful reports using Portal components and shown how to create links between them. These reports go beyond the typical hard copy reports found in most companies and fully support business processes from the Portal. In later chapters, we will enhance the reports by integrating them with other Portal components.

CHAPTER
9

Graphical Display
Features

he preceding chapters of this book have dealt mostly with text-oriented display and data entry techniques. Though these are a major and important component of most business applications, they do not lend themselves to a quick, summarized view of the data. Even with conditional formatting to highlight exceptional data, text listings take more time for users to process and understand. Typically, text-based components can only show top-down relationships among data elements, and they often do not represent the data as it would normally appear to users. For example, a list of dates and associated events has much less impact than a calendar page that shows an event on the date it occurs. In this chapter, we will investigate the use of the more graphically oriented components of Oracle Portal, specifically charts, calendars, and hierarchies. We will build a sample of each component and show how to integrate the component with the Portal and with other application components.

Developing Charts

When users need a quick way to view and compare data values against each other, a chart is often the best solution. When the data is displayed as a chart rather than as a list of numbers, users can easily see the largest, smallest, and average values, as well as the range of differences between them. In this release, Portal offers a simple bar chart, with the option of showing the bars vertically or horizontally. Future releases will include Java-driven charts, which will offer more choices of chart display formats.

The first chart that we will develop is shown in Figure 9-1. It shows the sales figures summarized by product category, and it will link to a second chart that shows the sales by individual product (see Figure 9-2). This chart, in turn, will link

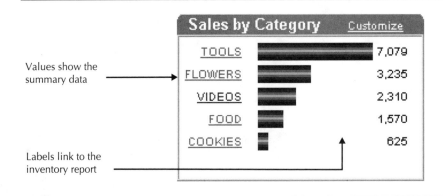

FIGURE 9-1. *The eXYZ Home Page with the Sales by Product Category chart added*

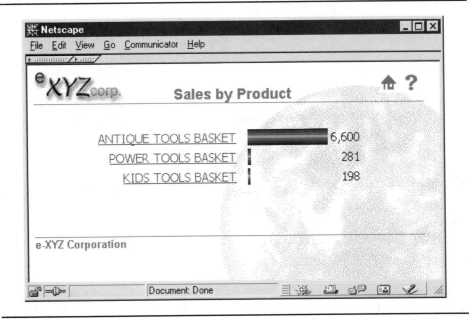

FIGURE 9-2. *Sales by Product*

to the inventory report you developed in Chapter 8, so that users can check stock levels for the best-selling products.

The procedures for developing charts and reports are quite similar. You can choose between using a wizard to generate the query for you or specifying the exact query for more complex data requirements. Charts can be used with templates, and as with all Portal components, you can specify custom text and PL/SQL at essential points in the processing. You can allow users to set some or all of the customization options, or provide a default chart with no user modification allowed. The decisions unique to building charts will be what data will go into the chart, and then how to summarize the information shown.

To create a chart, click on the Chart link from the "Create New ..." section at the top of the Applications tab in the Navigator. You can use the query wizard to generate the SQL to produce the chart for you, or write the statement yourself. Of course, the query wizard is simpler, but it only allows a query against a single table. If the data to be charted is in a separate table from the column that provides the labels, you will have to use the Chart From SQL Query. For example, you may want to chart the average salary by department. The data you wish to chart is in the EMPLOYEES table, but the department name is in the DEPARTMENTS table. If you could get away with only showing the department number, you could use the Chart From Query Wizard. Even if all the data was in the same table, but you wanted to display two columns concatenated together (as in the employee's first and last name), you would have to write the query yourself. You will find that for most requirements, you will choose the Chart From SQL Query.

In the explanations that follow, we will show how to build a chart with the query wizard or using your own SQL statement. The process is the same, except that when you use the Chart From SQL Query, the three steps for the query wizard are replaced with a single step where you specify the query.

Chart from Query Wizard: Step by Step

As with most components, the first step is always to specify a name and display name, and choose the application in which to create the component. The application name always defaults to the name of the application whose page you were viewing when you started the process.

Table or View

Next, you'll choose the table or view on which to base your query. As usual, you may type the table or view name or select it from the list that accompanies the Tables/Views field.

Table or View Columns

The Table or View Columns page asks you to enter four items. The Label field specifies a database column to use for the bar labels. These labels describe "what" you are charting. A column that contains descriptive text about the rows involved in the chart is a good choice, if available. If the column specified in the Label field is nonunique, you can summarize the values for each distinct label by setting the Group Function field (more on groups to follow). The optional Link field makes the label active, to invoke an existing Link component. Use the Edit Link icon (the pencil) to specify parameters that will be passed via the link to the called component. You might use a link to navigate to a form so users can update information about the row, or to drill down into another, more detailed chart or report for the row.

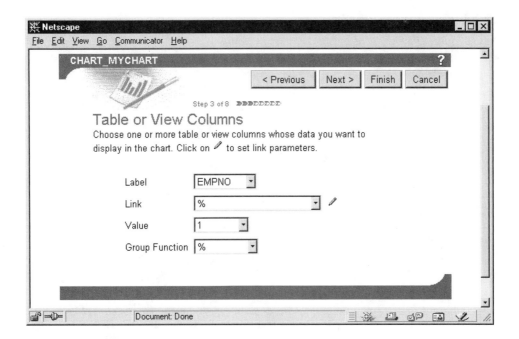

The Value entry specifies the database column to show or summarize in the chart. These values will determine "how big" each bar should be. Since only numeric values can be charted, the drop-down list shows only the numeric columns. To summarize the values, select a function from the Group Function list—this will change the query, adding a GROUP BY clause. The available group functions are SUM, COUNT, AVG, MAX, MIN, STDDEV, and VARIANCE.

Group structures only make sense if the column selected for the label represents a higher level of abstraction than a single row. In essence, you can either chart individual row values, or create a summary chart that includes a grouping function. For example, a chart based on the EMPLOYEES table, showing salary by employee, would not include a group function since there is only one row in the table for each employee. However, if the chart were to show salary by department, you would group the salaries using one of the supplied group functions. The Value field list includes a 1 expressly for the purpose of the COUNT function, so you can chart the number of rows in each group without having to access the underlying data.

TIP
*Counting a static value often results in better
performance compared with counting actual
column values, but do not use the 1 when you
are concerned with counting column values. For
example, if you are only interested in counting
commissioned employees, use the* COUNT *function
with the Accrued_ Commission column as the Value;
this will not count employees whose commission
is* NULL.

Column Conditions

The last query wizard step allows you to add WHERE clause conditions to restrict
the rows displayed. Choose the Column Name and Condition, then add your own
criteria against which to test the values. You may enter any valid condition to limit
the rows in the chart. If you need to filter out rows that contain NULL in any column
other than the one you are charting, create a NOT NULL condition here. In the Display
Options screen, you will have the option to include or exclude NULL values in the
chart (Value) column. To restrict rows using the IN clause, choose IN from the list
of conditions and separate the values with a colon (:). You may use functions in
your conditions if you prefix them with the pound sign (#).

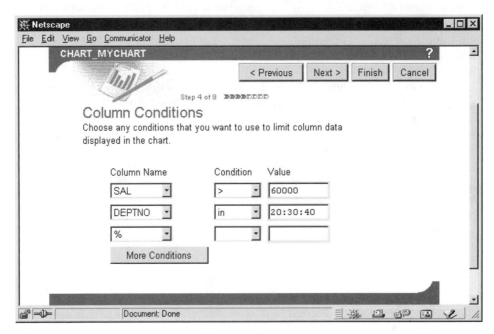

Display Options

Use the Display Options page to set up the ordering of the bars in the chart, the handling of NULL values, and the display formats for both full page and portlet views of the chart.

Common Options   The Common Options section lets you set up the ordering and specify how to handle NULLs. Set the Order By field to sort by ascending or descending ORDER BY VALUE if you want to make it easier for users to see the relative ranking of values. This would produce a chart with bars increasing or decreasing according to their size. For ease of reference to a particular item, use ORDER BY LABEL or ORDER BY LABEL DESC.

Check the Include Null Values check box to allow display of NULL values, and if you do include NULLs, enter a value in the Treat Null Values as field to indicate how they should be represented on the chart. The default of 0 is usually a good choice, but this depends on your requirements.

Full Page Options   In the Full Page Options section, the Type Face, Font Color, and Font Size fields all refer to the font in which to display the labels. The Chart Type can be either Horizontal or Vertical bars—choose the orientation that looks best with your data, or that fits best on your Portal page.

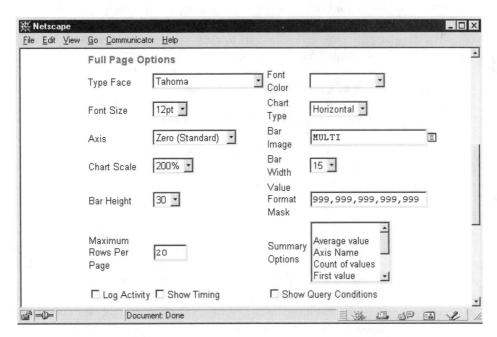

The Axis setting can really affect the way your chart looks. You can choose the standard zero-based axis, which charts all values from zero, or you can create a comparative chart against the average, minimum, maximum, first, or last values. A comparative chart based on the average would show the axis in the middle and all the data as a delta from the average. Values that are below average would show as bars below or to the left of the axis, and those that are above average show how much above or to the right of the average line they are. Similar comparisons can be built using a basis of the highest or lowest value in the chart, or the first or last value displayed.

The Bar Image list allows you to choose the color in which the bars are displayed, but you may specify any GIF or JPEG file. The color choices in the provided list are simply 1 × 1-pixel images of each color, which will be stretched to represent the data. The MULTI or Multiple Colors choice creates the chart in a variety of bright colors. If you really want to jazz up your chart, specify your own bar image. The key is to create an image that looks good when stretched, vertically or horizontally, to various lengths. To supply your own images, copy them into the Portal images directory, usually `$ORACLE_HOME/portal30/images`, and type the file name in the Bar Image field.

For horizontal charts, set the Bar Height field (specified in pixels) to make each bar wider or narrower along the value axis, and for vertical charts, use the Bar Width field to control the bar's width. When reducing bar dimension for vertical charts, keep in mind that Portal still needs room to display the label text under the corresponding bar; this may cause the bars to appear widely spaced. Reduce the font size accordingly to mitigate this effect.

The Chart Scale field determines the baseline size for the largest chart value—when set to `200%` (the `%` is a bit misleading), the largest bar on the chart will stretch to 200 pixels. The length of all other bars will be calculated as a percentage of that bar. For any chart whose axis is set to something other than `Zero`, `Maximum Value` or `Minimum Value`, the chart scale will determine the total chart width. The width is then split below and above the axis according to the data values. These concepts are illustrated in Figure 9-3, showing the same data values (2, 2, 3, 3, and 5—average is 3) charted several different ways. Notice that the scale always determines the length of the bars, but horizontal and vertical charts each have their own setting for the width. Setting the axis to `Average Value` shows the difference from the average, rather than the actual data values.

The Value Format Mask setting is used to format the numeric values corresponding to each bar, and can be set to any valid SQL format string. (See the *Oracle8i SQL Reference* for a full list.) Beware of the Maximum Rows Per Page setting, because each page is formatted separately according to the rules above. The scale is reset for each page, as is the axis, meaning that an average value axis would be recalculated based on the values displayed on each page. This implies that each page will use a different scale, and that the first bar on each page always appears at the maximum

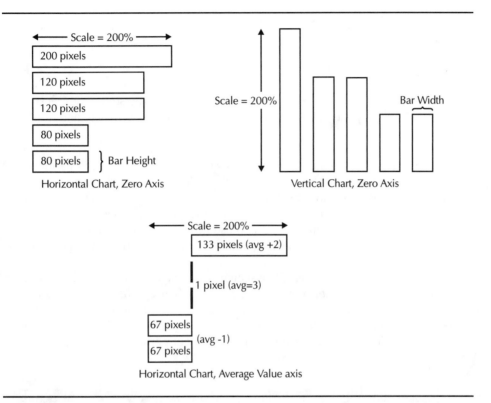

FIGURE 9-3. *Three methods of charting the same data result in very different charts*

width. As a result, it would be impossible to compare data spread across multiple pages simply by eyeballing the relative sizes of the bars. Consequently, you may want to set the Maximum Rows Per Page field high enough to ensure that all of your data values fit on a single page.

You can create a summary for the entire chart, displaying any or all of the following Summary Options:

- `Average Value`
- `Axis Name (echoes the Axis setting)`
- `Count of values`
- `First value`
- `Last value`

■ `Minimum value`

■ `Maximum value`

■ `Sum of values`

These, too, are calculated at the page level, so to get true summaries, ensure that all rows display on one page, or use custom PL/SQL to calculate and display the summaries.

Portlet Options   The most consistent way to set the font characteristics for portlet display is to associate the text with a predefined Portal style object, using the Page Style field. The default is to set the text to a `Portlet Text3` object, which is one of the smaller Portal text styles. Depending on the styles you have created and the data you are displaying, you may want to use `Portlet Text2` or even `Text1`. You will have to experiment by adding a few test charts as portlets to your pages, to see how they look.

The benefit of using the Page Style setting is that the chart's style will be consistent with the design of the other portlets on the pages where it is used. If you want the text to display in a particular way regardless of the Portal page settings, you may override it by specifying values for the Type Face, Font Size, and Font Color fields. If you use a style that could possibly clash with other portlets on a page, you run the risk of making the page unattractive.

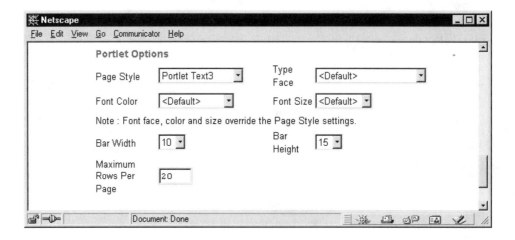

For most portlets, setting Bar Height (or Width for vertical charts) to `10` is sufficient and compresses the chart well. The Chart Scale setting, although in the Full Page Options section, affects the portlet in the same way it affects the full page display. The portlet can have a different setting for Maximum Rows Per Page, to minimize the space required, but the same warnings about multiple-page charts apply.

Customization Form Display Options

The Customization Form Display Options page controls what users will see on the customization form. You can always prevent customization altogether using privileges, and in that case, you would skip this screen. If you allow any customization, you'll want to evaluate what the user should be able to change, and set up the options here.

You may add as many parameters as you need, in the same way as you did with reports. On the customization form, users will be able to choose the condition on which to base the parameter, much as you did in the Column Conditions page. These conditions will be added to the WHERE clause used to generate the chart data. You may optionally specify an LOV to help with these choices.

Using the appropriate checkboxes, you can control whether end users can change the Display Name for the chart, the Chart Type, Axis, Summary values, Maximum Rows Per Page, and whether to Include NULLs in the generated report.

Finally, you can specify which buttons appear and customize the labels. The users only need the Run and Reset buttons to operate the Customization Form. Giving them the Save button would allow them to alter the default view of the chart. Although the chart will be changed only for that user's personal view of the data, this may be a dangerous privilege to give novice users. They may forget that they changed the settings and call you when the data seems to have disappeared!

Chart and Customization Form Text

The Chart and Customization Form Text page should look familiar as well. It allows you to specify the template and text to display above and below the chart. You may also specify help text, which displays only if the user clicks the "?" icon in the upper right-hand corner. As with reports, there are separate fields for text on the chart display area and for the customization form.

Additional PL/SQL Code

Another familiar sight, the Additional PL/SQL Code page, lets you run PL/SQL at several points in both the chart and customization form display processes. For charts, you might use additional code to check or reset parameter values or to populate temporary tables and clean them out after the chart is run.

A particularly handy use of the Additional PL/SQL Code page is to calculate and display (using HTP.print or equivalent) true summaries for multiple-page charts. In the PL/SQL, you would reference the sum (or average, maximum, minimum, etc.) from all the database values and display it instead of the default summaries provided with the components. If you allowed the user to customize the chart in this case, you would need to access the argument arrays (as we did in the Inventory Report in Chapter 8) to ensure accurate summaries.

The exercises reflect our assertion that most charts will be based on a custom query, so we will not demonstrate using the query wizard. Instead, we will explain the differences in the wizard when creating a Chart From SQL Query, and then create and link two of these charts.

Chart From SQL Query—What's New

The main difference in the Chart From SQL Query is that you will write the query to retrieve the chart data, rather than use the three query wizard steps to specify the table columns and WHERE clause. As you'll see, there are some subtle differences in the other wizard steps that imply a slightly different development technique for this kind of chart.

SQL Query

The SQL Query page allows you to specify the query that provides the data for the chart. This query always returns three columns. The first column supplies the link for the label text–you may specify any combination of static text and database values that evaluates to a valid URL. If you do not need a link for the label column, specify NULL in the first column. The second column provides the labels for the bars, and the third column supplies the values to be charted.

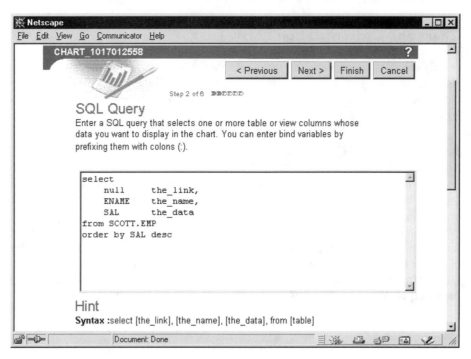

The remainder of the query is up to you, and you can use any valid FROM, WHERE, GROUP BY, ORDER BY, and HAVING clause conditions. You can join multiple tables, use a UNION operator to combine result sets, and perform any kind of function on the data before it is rendered into a chart. If you want to specify a sort order for the data, you must add an ORDER BY clause to the query, as the Display Options page does not have a Row Order Options section.

To accept parameters, you must include them in your query as bind variables, prefixed by a colon (:). As with the Report From SQL Query, users will not be able to choose a condition on the the customization form, as they can with the charts and reports based on the query wizard. Build your SQL statement to handle as much flexibility as they will need. Here is yet another example of a flexible WHERE clause condition. It supports queries on a range of values, with optional boundary conditions on both the upper and lower bound.

```
WHERE annual_salary BETWEEN NVL(:lower_bound, 0)
            AND GREATEST(NVL(:upper_bound,0), annual_salary)
```

Links

To access links created in Portal, use the WWV_USER_UTILITIES.get_url function. It accepts as arguments the name of the link component and up to 30 parameters in name-value pairs. So, to link to another chart that accepts p_employee_id as a parameter, the statement would look something like this:

```
SELECT WWV_USER_UTILITIES.get_url('LINK_EMP_CHART'
                                ,'p_employee_id', employee_id)
      , last_name
      , annual_salary
FROM    employees
ORDER BY annual_salary DESC
```

To pass a parameter with an explicit condition (subject to the component's design), specify the condition in a separate name- value pair. Each parameter has an associated background parameter to specify the condition, in the form _<param_name>_cond. You can use this technique to call a form in "query mode"—that is, the parameter is understood to be a query parameter, and the form attempts to retrieve data that matches. The returned data is then available for editing as specified in the form. The following statement will create a link that brings up the form view of the employee record:

```
SELECT WWV_USER_UTILITIES.get_url('LINK_EMP_FORM'
                                ,'p_employee_id', employee_id
                                ,'_p_employee_id_cond', '=' )
      , last_name
      , annual_salary
```

```
FROM    employees
ORDER BY annual_salary DESC
```

Display Options

A spiffy technique you can use with the Chart From SQL Query is to create a custom axis using the UNION ALL operator. The following SQL statement is an example of such a query. The first row returned (via the first SELECT command) established the baseline. You must set the Axis to First Value and use UNION ALL to prevent a sort from rearranging the rows in the result set. (The baseline row must be the first row returned by the query.) You will have to ensure that all rows fit on a single page, as the baseline will be reset for each page.

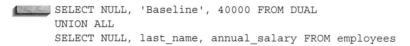

```
SELECT NULL, 'Baseline', 40000 FROM DUAL
UNION ALL
SELECT NULL, last_name, annual_salary FROM employees
```

Exercise 9.1: Product Sales by Category

This typical chart uses an SQL query to show summary values from one table (ORDER_LINE_ITEMS) using labels from another (PRODUCTS). It will display the product categories, charting the dollar value of sales within each category. Most users will want a drill-down into the category to see which products are the sales leaders within each category. The next few exercises will address that requirement.

1. Create a new Chart From SQL Query in the APP_SALES application.

2. Name the chart CHART_SALES_BY_CAT and give it a Display Name of Sales by Category.

3. Enter the following query in the SQL Query screen:

```
SELECT
    NULL                    the_link,
    p.product_category      the_name,
    sum(li.total_price_sold) the_data
FROM  corp_site.order_line_items li, corp_site.products p
WHERE li.product_id = p.product_id
GROUP BY NULL, p.product_category
ORDER BY the_data DESC
```

4. On the Display Options page, set the Chart Scale to 100% and the Bar Image to blueline.gif. In the Portlet Display Options section, set the Page Style to Portlet Text2.

5. On the Customization Form Display Options page, remove the checkmark from the Save button, but leave the remaining options.

6. Choose EXYZ_TEMPLATE on the Chart and Customization Form Text page.

7. Click Finish and test your chart in both portlet and full screen modes.

8. On the Manage Component page, click the Access tab. Check the box labeled Publish to Portal.

That's it! A simple chart is easily produced when you can directly write the SQL.

Exercise 9.2: Integrate a Chart into the Portal

You can integrate this chart directly into the Portal, as it requires no parameters. It will go on the Management tab so executives can get a top-level view of product performance.

1. Go to the Pages tab in the Navigator. Find the eXYZ Home Page and click the Edit link.

2. Click on the Management tab. You will use the empty region on the left. Click the Add Portlets icon within that region.

3. In the Add Portlets window, under Portlet Repository: Other Providers: Sales Application, click on Sales by Category to add it to the Selected Portlets window.

4. Click OK and then Close and click on the page name to test the new portlet.

Exercise 9.3: Sales by Product

Because eXYZ has 20 or more products, a chart that shows sales of all products might not fit very nicely into our Portal. The solution to this is to display high levels of detail on the Portal page, and then draw users into a more detailed view for each category. The category chart from the previous exercise is the entry point—clicking on any category name will direct users to a new chart, displayed in full screen mode, that shows the sales for individual products. You will create the chart here, and in the next section, you will build the components necessary to complete the link between the two charts.

1. Create a new Chart From SQL Query in the Sales Application.

2. Name the chart CHART_SALES_BY_PRODUCT and give it a Display Name of Sales by Product.

3. Enter the following query in the SQL Query text area:

```
SELECT
    NULL                    the_link,
    p.description           the_name,
    sum(li.total_price_sold) the_data
```

```
FROM  CORP_SITE.products p, CORP_SITE.order_line_items li
WHERE p.product_id = li.product_id
AND   (p.product_category = :category OR :category IS NULL)
GROUP BY NULL, p.description
ORDER BY the_data DESC
```

4. Adjust the display options as you did for the SALES_BY_CATEGORY chart. Under Full Page Options, set the Chart Scale to 100% and specify blueline .gif for the Bar Image. Under Portlet Options, set the Page Style to Portlet Text2.

5. On the Customization Form Display Options page, the category parameter is already created for you. Since end users will never run this chart from the customization form, we do not need an LOV. The parameter will be passed in the background. Under Button Options, remove the checkmark from the Save button.

6. Specify the EXYZ_TEMPLATE on the Chart and Customization Form Text page.

7. Click Finish and test the chart by clicking the Customize link. Supply a valid category from the list below to test the report. (The query is case-sensitive, so be sure to enter the category name in uppercase.)

   ■ COOKIES

   ■ FLOWERS

   ■ FOOD

   ■ TOOLS

   ■ VIDEOS

   ■ CHOCOLATE

We have created several charts that display high-level information about corporate sales, and integrated one of them into the Portal. To make the Portal page more effective, we'll need to create links between the charts.

Linking Charts and Reports

In this section, we will see how to link charts to each other, and how to link charts to reports. We introduced links in Chapter 8, but to use a link in a chart, we need to reference the link using the API. We will create some links now to implement the drill-down for sales information.

Exercise 9.4: Link to Detail Chart

1. In the Sales Application, click on the Link item in the "Create New ..." list.

2. Name the link `LINK_SALES_BY_PRODUCT`.

3. On the Link Target Type and Name page, click on the list icon for the Target Component or URL field and select the `APP_SALES.CHART_SALES_BY_PRODUCT` component.

4. On the Link Target Inputs page, you can see that the component accepts one user parameter, `category`, and several system parameters. Make a note of the user parameter name, because you will need to reference it within the SQL query in the component that will call this link. Click the Finish button.

That's all there is to creating the link. Next, you will modify the Sales by Category chart to use the link. To do this, we need to use an API utility to reference the named link and pass in the `category` parameter.

5. Close the Manage Component screen for the link and click Edit for the CHART_SALES_BY_CAT chart.

6. Replace both occurrences of `NULL` in the query with the following (the second occurrence is in the `GROUP BY` clause):

```
PORTAL30.WWV_USER_UTILITIES.get_url
('APP_SALES.LINK_SALES_BY_PRODUCT',
                    'category', p.product_category)
```

7. Click OK, and test the revised chart. The link should take you to the next chart. Test the behavior in the Portal page as well. Notice that the Portal interface goes away when you get into the detail chart. This is expected, as the Portal page is intended to be a starting point; when users require more detail, you should use the entire browser window.

NOTE
To keep the styles consistent, use the same template for the page as you use for your components. The ability to apply a template to a page is a new feature in version 3.0.9.

4. Because we have not integrated the Sales by Product chart into the Portal page, users have no way to customize their view of the chart. They may want to see all products in the full page mode. To give them this ability without giving them access to the customization form, edit SALES_BY_ PRODUCT and add the following on the Additional PL/SQL Code page to the "…before displaying the footer" text area for the Chart column:

```
HTP.anchor(PORTAL30.WWV_USER_UTILITIES.get_url
          ('APP_SALES.LINK_SALES_BY_PRODUCT')
       ,'View all products');
```

Continuing this technique, you can develop a full-scale executive information system. For our purposes, the next screen that needs to be displayed is the Inventory Report you developed in Chapter 8. eXYZ employees want to be able to verify inventory levels for the most popular products. We can now reuse the link from Chapter 8 to the Inventory Report, and let this chart navigate to it as well.

Exercise 9.5: Link to a Report

1. Edit CHART_SALES_BY_PRODUCT.

2. Replace both occurrences of NULL in the query with the following:

```
PORTAL30.WWV_USER_UTILITIES.get_url
('APP_SALES.LINK_RPT_INVENTORY','product', p.product_id)
```

3. Click OK and then Close the Manage Component page.

4. To test this link, start from the eXYZ home page, and go to the Management tab. The Sales by Category chart should be displayed. Click on a category name to view the Sales by Product chart, then click on a product name to view the inventory levels for that product.

These links allow managers to navigate between charts without having to know individual product IDs or how to work a customization form. Starting from the Portal interface allows an intuitive process of connecting components.

Calendars

How many of us are slaves to the all-important calendar? We have wall calendars, pocket calendars, personal digital assistants, desktop software, and Web calendars. Wouldn't it be nice to have all your calendar entries in one place, accessible from anywhere? Many public portal sites offer calendars for personal use, but these wouldn't allow a business to create calendar entries for its employees, for privacy reasons. They also lack a programmatic interface to support automatic calendar entries based on application requirements.

Portal calendar components are based on database queries, so they support any kind of customization and programmatic technique that is possible in a relational database. You could even make such a calendar available on an Extranet Portal so that clients or suppliers could set up meetings with employees. We will build a calendar for eXYZ Corporation, complete with a data entry component that allows users to create new calendar entries. The calendar will look like the one shown in Figure 9-4.

Portal calendars display one or more months at a time, showing the events or reminders in the appropriate date cells. Calendars can be used to remind staff of due dates, company holidays, payroll deadlines, and other important milestones. They can also be used to schedule conference rooms or other resources. In this discussion, we will use the generic term "event" to describe the entries in the calendar cells.

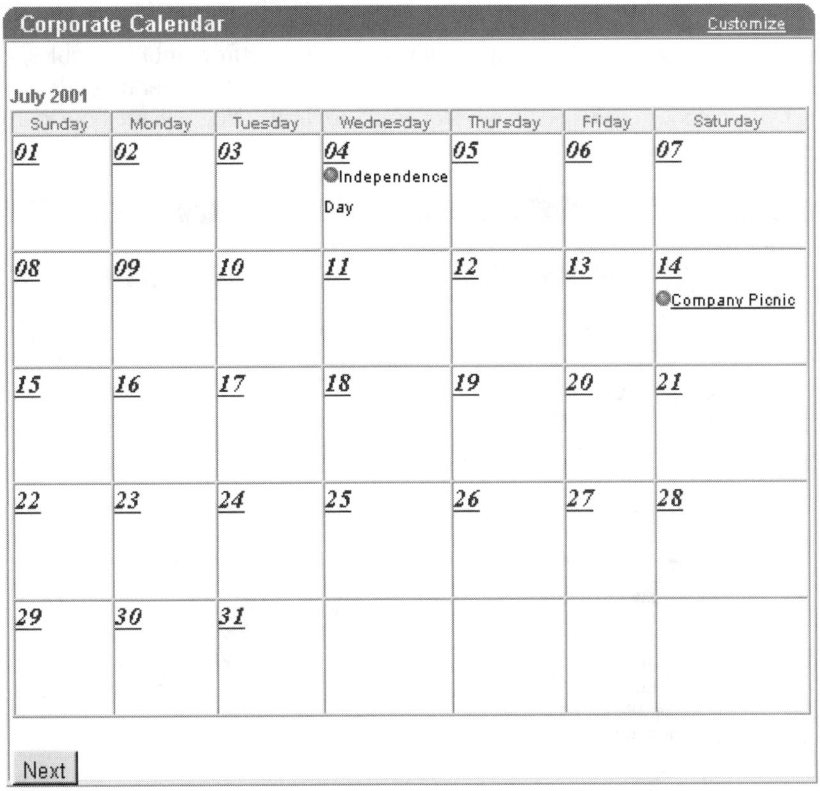

FIGURE 9-4. *The eXYZ Corporate Calendar*

The foundation of a calendar is a query that returns the event dates and the text that is to be displayed with each date. The query only needs to select the dates on which events exist, and you may choose whether to display or hide months with no events. The simplest calendar only lists events, and provides no links to related information. By adding a URL column to the query, you can make each event an active link. You may also add a link for the date so that when users click on the day of the month, they are taken to another component that lets them create or edit events.

Developing Calendars

There is only one type of calendar, and the wizard is a mere six steps. We'll start with the SQL Query page.

SQL Query

The most important step in creating calendars is writing the SQL query. It can be as complex as necessary, as long as it returns the appropriate values in the right number of columns. You may use a UNION operator to collate events from multiple tables, and you may also use parameters to limit the events displayed. A parameter might be useful to allow users to choose only certain types of events to display. You will see how to implement this feature in the exercise at the end of this section.

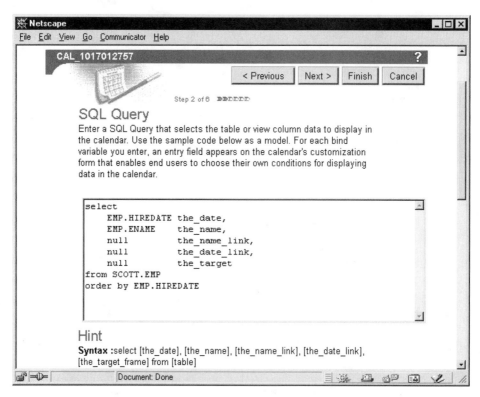

The columns of the query are described in Table 9-1, listed in the order they must appear in the query. To skip an optional column, specify NULL in the column list. As with charts, the FROM, WHERE, and GROUP BY clauses are limited only by your requirements. The ORDER BY clause is not so flexible, as we will see.

The default behavior for calendars is to start with the earliest month containing dates returned by the query, and to display only months in which there are events. Portal includes settings to modify that behavior, but you can also use the query to dynamically alter the dates displayed. For a forward-looking calendar, such as one that would display upcoming events, you would want to ensure that the query only returned rows where the date is greater than or equal to the current date. The WHERE clause condition would use the SYSDATE built-in function to restrict the rows appropriately, as follows:

```
WHERE event_date >= SYSDATE
```

To show all events in the current month and forward, try:

```
WHERE event_date >= TRUNC(SYSDATE, 'MM')
```

Column	Required?	Description
the_date	Y	The event's date—must be returned as a DATE datatype.
the_name	Y	Brief text that describes the event.
the_name_link	N	A URL or component link that provides more details about the event—turns the_name into a link.
the_date_link	N	A URL or component link selected from the database or generated using concatenation or WWV_USER_UTILITIES.get_url. The day number will link to this URL.
the_target	N	A window name in which to display the output of the above link(s)—use only if you want the URL to display in a different browser window.

TABLE 9-1. *Calendar query columns*

NOTE
*TRUNC(SYSDATE, 'MM') returns the first day of the
current month.*

The ORDER BY clause must sort the dates in ascending order. Any other sort order
will cause the calendar to work improperly. It will either fail to display events, or will
not allow "Previous" navigation to earlier months. Be sure to include the ORDER BY
on the date column in your query.

Display Options

Second only to the query in terms of importance in designing a calendar, the Display
Options screen allows you to modify the default behavior of the calendar to make it
more suitable to your requirements. It is divided into three sections: Common Options,
Full Page Options, and Portlet Options.

Common Options   The first decision is whether to display weekends. Corporate
calendars may be better served with only Monday through Friday displayed, but
leaving off Saturday and Sunday will cause any events on those days to be hidden.
A company picnic or special work session that falls on a weekend will be overlooked.
The next decision is whether to show months with no events. To build a fully functional
calendar application, you will most likely want to show all months. Users tend to
get a little surprised when the calendar skips over months, and if you want to allow
users to create events, they need to be able to view each month.

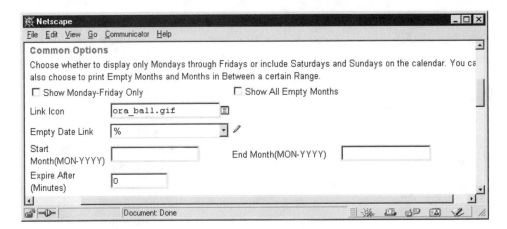

The link icon will display next to every event. It serves to draw attention to the
events in a busy calendar. To leave it off, just delete the reference to ora_ball.gif.

The list associated with the Link Icon field retrieves all 32 × 32-pixel icons defined as images in the Shared Components application. You may use one from the list or type your own icon name into the field. To use a custom icon, copy it into the images directory for Portal, as we explained in the section on charts, or use any of the thousands of images supplied there. If you want your icon to show on the list, you must create it as a 32 × 32-pixel image in the Shared Components application. This size is a bit large for portlet display, so the approach of typing the icon name is preferred.

Alternatively, you can supply the link icon dynamically, as part of the SQL statement. Delete the icon name on the Display Options page and append an image tag to the event text in your query, using the DECODE statement to determine the appropriate image name based on event type or some other criteria. A sample SELECT clause to accomplish such a feature is shown below, but you may choose to move the code that generates the image tag to a separate PL/SQL function, or to store the image names in a database table for lookup in the query.

```
SELECT events.date                                    the_date,
       '<IMG SRC="/images/'||DECODE (events.type, 'PARTY', 'balloon.gif'
                                   , 'CORP',  'minilogo.gif'
                                   , 'oraball.gif')  --else
                    ||'">'||events.description     the_name
```

The Empty Date Link field allows you to specify a date link for cells with no events. (the_date_link specified in the query is only active on dates where there are events.) This link could be the same as the link specified in the query, or a different link, perhaps to a form that lets users create new events.

Next, you can specify the start and end months for the chart. Use these to ensure that certain date ranges are always displayed—otherwise, the calendar will always start with the first date returned by the query and end with the last date. These values cannot be based on variables (at the time of this writing), so you may have to modify the calendar periodically to ensure the range stays consistent with the objectives (e.g., a year in advance). Fortunately, modifications to components in the production application are easy to implement and will not affect the end users, except perhaps briefly while the component is being recompiled. As mentioned earlier, you can also use the query to restrict the displayed dates.

Finally, you can set the content to expire after a number of minutes. As with charts, leaving this at the default of 0 causes the query to be re-executed each time the page containing the calendar is loaded. If your calendar does not change very frequently, set the Expire After field much higher.

Full Page Options   Each part of the calendar can be formatted independently of the others. The first few fields allow you to set the font face, color, and size for the Month text at the top of the screen, the Day number, and the Cell text describing the event. In full page mode, the day font settings will be the same for both the day-of-the-week headings and the numbers in each cell. You can set the background color of the main calendar area (using the Table Background Color field) and set a separate color as the background for the day-of-the-week headings (Heading Background Color). If you want your background image to show through, make the calendar transparent by selecting the blank item in this list.

To make the calendar smaller on the page, reduce the Page Width setting. The calendar will be sized as a percentage of the browser screen, so this is only a relative size setting; when users reduce the size of their browser window, the calendar will shrink along with the window. Generally speaking, this is desirable behavior, but it implies that you should test your calendar with a variety of window sizes. If you are displaying a large amount of text, the calendar may be difficult to view in smaller windows, or page regions.

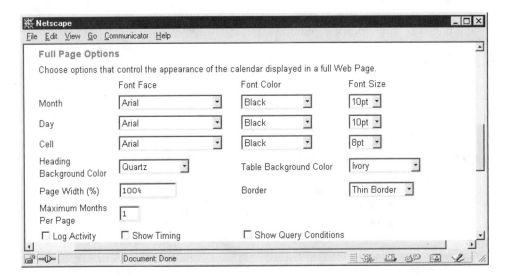

You can set a maximum months per page, which would permit you to display a quarterly or annual calendar. The Border options are thin, thick, and none. A calendar with no border at all might be a little difficult to read, but for some applications may appear more elegant. The remaining full page options are the standard log activity, timing, and query conditions display features.

Portlet Options   The options for setting the portlet formats are the same as for full page, with a few minor distinctions. The font settings allow you to choose a predefined style object or to override the page style with hard-coded font face, color, and style. The initial size of the calendar is set to 50% of page width so the calendar is smaller for portlet display.

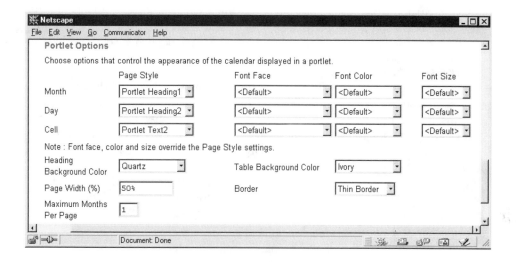

Customization Form Display Options

As with the other components, the Customization Form Display Options page allows you to specify the options available when users click the Customize link on the portlet header, or when you allow users to access the customization form. Formatting options specific to calendar components map to the settings on the Display Options page, and the familiar button options and parameter specifications are available for customization.

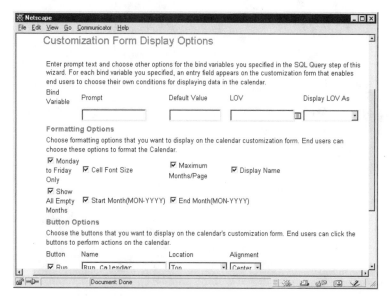

The remaining two wizard pages are the same as in every other component—the Text and Additional PL/SQL Code pages. Use these to add custom text and to perform pre-processing and post-processing on the data, as we have done in the other components.

Exercise 9.6: Company Calendar

The calendar you will build is extremely flexible. By default, it will display the current and subsequent months, but users will be able to modify it to display prior months. It will display all events except those that are assigned to a single individual. In that case, only the individual will see those events. This will give users the ability to create personal events to be shown only in their view of the calendar. eXYZ's CORP_CALENDAR table has an Event_Type column, which will allow users to display only certain types of events. By default, all events will be displayed. If the user entered a URL when the event was created, the event name will link to that URL. The days will link to the Events form that you created in Chapter 7.

1. Since this is primarily an employee-related calendar, we'll put the calendar and the link in the Human Resources Application. Start by creating a new link named LINK_EVENT_FORM.

2. Set the Target Component to APP_HR.FORM_EVENTS. Click Finish and then Close to exit the Manage Component page.

3. Create a new static LOV named LOV_Y_N to handle a Yes/No parameter. Set the Default Format to Radio group and do not display Null Values. The values for the LOV should be as follows:

Display Value	Return Value	Display Order
Yes	Y	1
No	N	2

4. Continuing in the Human Resources Application, create a new calendar.

5. Name the calendar CAL_CORPORATE and give it a Display Name of Corporate Calendar.

6. Enter the following query:

```
SELECT
    action_date                         the_date,
    event_description                   the_name,
    URL                                 the_name_link,
    PORTAL30.WWV_USER_UTILITIES.get_url
            ('APP_HR.LINK_EVENT_FORM',
            'action_date', action_date,
            '_action_date_cond', '=') the_date_link,
    null                                the_target
FROM CORP_SITE.corp_calendar
```

```
WHERE ((action_date >= TRUNC(SYSDATE,'MM')
                   AND :first_date IS NULL)
       OR
       (action_date >= :first_date AND :first_date IS NOT NULL))
AND    (responsible_party IS NULL
        OR responsible_party = PORTAL30.WWCTX_API.get_user)
AND    (event_type IN (:event_type)
        OR :show_all = 'Y' )
ORDER BY the_date
```

NOTE

The (`action_date >= SYSDATE AND :first_date IS NULL`) line in the query will restrict the rows returned to current and future events, but only if the `first_date` parameter is unspecified. Otherwise, the (`action_date >= :first_date AND :first_date IS NOT NULL`) line will apply, restricting the rows to those on or after the requested date.

    7. On the Display Options page, check the box labeled Show All Empty Months. Select LINK_EVENT_FORM for the Empty Date Link. Click the icon to edit the link parameters. For the `action_date` parameter, choose TODAY in the Column Name list. Do not specify the Condition. In the Portlet Options section, set the Page Width (%) field to 100%.

TIP

Use the Condition operator only when you want to perform a query to retrieve matching records. Without it, the form assumes the parameter is intended to supply a default value for the field. In this case, we are supplying the current date from the calendar as the default date for a new event.

    8. On the Customization Form Display Options page, specify an LOV for `event_type`, by typing its name (APP_HR.LOV_EVENT_TYPES) in the LOV field. Display the LOV as a Check box. Set the Default Value for :`show_all` to Y, change the Prompt to Show All Event Types, and set the LOV to APP_HR. LOV_Y_N.

NOTE

In version 3.0.9, a minor bug prevents the list attached to the LOV field from working properly. Typing the LOV name works around this issue, which is fixed in the next release.

9. Under Formatting Options, uncheck the Start Month checkbox, because the query and `first_date` parameter will provide this functionality. We will allow users to specify an End Month if they wish.

10. Set the Template to `EXYZ_TEMPLATE` on the Calendar and Customization Form Text page. Enter the following in the Header Text field for the Customization Form:

```
To display all events, choose "Yes" for Show All Event Types. If
you would like to see only certain event types, choose "No" and
check the boxes for the types of events you would like to view.
```

11. Click Finish and test your calendar. Run the customization form and test a few different values for First Date. Try showing only a subset of event types. If there are no events for the current month, create a few so you'll have some data to test.

12. Before closing the Manage Component screen, click on the Access tab and choose Publish to Portal.

This calendar displays all the dates listed in the CORP_CALENDAR table, making it very easy for users to view corporate events. After seeing the calendar, the supervisors requested that it also display employee reviews on their schedule. We could meet this requirement by adding the review dates to the CORP_CALENDAR table, but to do so would create the potential for problems associated with duplicate data. Instead, we'll use a `UNION` to select from both tables and link to the employee review form from the calendar entry.

NOTE
In practice, a view that performs the UNION may be simpler to work with.

Exercise 9.7: Extending the Calendar

1. First create a link to the employee review form. Name the link `LINK_FORM_REVIEW` and choose `APP_HR.FORM_REVIEW` in the Target Component or URL field.

2. Edit the calendar and add the following SQL above the `ORDER BY` clause, but after the entire `WHERE` clause:

```
UNION
SELECT r.review_date, 'Review for '||e.last_name,
       PORTAL30.WWV_USER_UTILITIES.get_url
```

```
                    ('APP_HR.LINK_FORM_REVIEW',
                     'employee_id', r.employee_id,
                     '_employee_id_cond', '=',
                     'review_date', r.review_date,
                     '_review_date_cond', '=')   ,
             PORTAL30.WWV_USER_UTILITIES.get_url
                    ('APP_HR.LINK_EVENT_FORM'
                     'action_date', r.review_date))   ,
             NULL
    FROM    employee_reviews r, employees e, employees s
    WHERE   r.employee_id = e.employee_id
    AND     e.supervisor_id = s.employee_id
    AND     r.recommend_increase IS NULL
    AND     s.user_id = PORTAL30.WWCTX_API.get_user
    AND     (3 IN (:event_type) OR :show_all = 'Y')
    AND     ((r.review_date >= TRUNC(SYSDATE,'MM')
                          AND :first_date IS NULL)
         OR
        (r.review_date >= :first_date AND :first_date IS NOT NULL))
```

NOTE
We offer another complex query to get the reviews for each supervisor, merged by a UNION with the first. We select from the EMPLOYEES table twice, once to get the employee name, and a second time to get the supervisor's user id so we show only reviews for that supervisor. Completed reviews will not be shown, because we only show those reviews with NULL in the Recommend_Increase column. We must use similar WHERE clause conditions to restrict the dates to current and future dates, and to show only the requested event types (event type 3 is a review). The name link takes us to the review form, and the date link takes us to a blank event form with the current date (where the review is shown) as a default.

3. Click OK and test the calendar. PATM is not a supervisor, so try logging in as LINDAC, DONL, or JENNYR to see scheduled reviews.

Next we'll put the calendar into a prominent position on the company home page so that users will always be kept up-to-date on corporate events.

Exercise 9.8: Integrate the Calendar with the Portal

1. In the Pages tab of the Navigator, find the eXYZ Home Page. Click Edit.

2. Divide the Welcome tab into two regions, of 70% and 30% respectively. (Click the Add Column icon to create an additional region, then edit the properties of both regions.)

3. Click on the Add Portlets icon for the left-hand region.

4. Click on Other Providers in the Portlet Repository window and choose Human Resources Application.

5. Click on Corporate Calendar to add it to the Selected Portlets list and click OK.

6. Click Close to return to the Navigator.

7. Click on the page name to test your new portlet.

Terrific! Now the corporate Web Portal has a highly useful calendar on the Welcome tab. Users can communicate events to others, and view upcoming events at a glance. When we built forms to create new users and perform reviews, we inserted records into the EMPLOYEE_REVIEWS table to schedule these events for the supervisors. Now if you log in as any user with a title of supervisor, you will be able to see the reviews that they are scheduled to perform.

Hierarchies

We are all familiar with the standard organization chart published by almost every company to show the top-down management relationships. This "org chart" is usually created by an administrative person using software expressly designed for that purpose, or manually using a drawing package. Wouldn't it be nice to automatically generate an organization chart directly from the database? There are many advantages to this. First, the relationships would always be current, so the administrative staff would not need to constantly update a separate document. Second, if we could display it as an active component, it would come alive. Users could navigate up and down the tree, showing the level of detail that they choose. Then they could link to a form that allows them to update the data on the fly.

Organization charts are not the only hierarchical relationships used in business models. A bill of materials or assembly instructions is hierarchical as well. These are often known as "gizinto" charts, because they show that one part "goes into" another, and serve to document the component makeup of a finished product. Project plans can also be thought of as hierarchical, since a task is often composed of multiple subtasks and each of those could have subtasks as well.

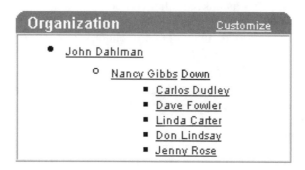

FIGURE 9-5.   *The top-level hierarchy of eXYZ Corporation*

When you need to illustrate a hierarchical relationship and allow users to navigate up and down the tree, the best choice is a *hierarchy*, shown in Figure 9-5. It shows the organization chart from the top down and links the name to the employee details report from Chapter 8. When users click the Down link next to an employee name, the hierarchy traverses the tree and displays the next level, with that employee as the new parent. That employee's subordinates are now displayed as the tree branches, with an optional reference to show that employee's manager. At lower levels of the tree, users will see an Up link, to help them return to the top levels of the hierarchy. This drill-down and drill-up behavior is directly supported by the hierarchy component.

Building Hierarchies: Step by Step

To use the hierarchy component, the data design must support a hierarchical listing. The table involved must have a recursive relationship, one in which the foreign key column points to the primary key of the same table. In the organization chart, each employee has a manager. The manager's employee ID is stored (as Supervisor_Id) with the row for the employee, and can be used in a self-join to get information about the manager. An example of a self-join on this recursive relationship was shown in Exercise 9.7.

Veteran Oracle developers may be familiar with the CONNECT BY clause, specific to Oracle's implementation of SQL. It produces a hierarchy, or tree structure, of information when used to access a table with just such a recursive relationship. It is notoriously difficult to conceptualize and write, but its advantage is that it can display this kind of data in a top-down fashion. You can use the CONNECT BY clause to start from the highest level in the hierarchy and display each successive level and sublevel, or to display individual branches of the hierarchy. Fortunately, Portal provides the hierarchy component to generate this SQL for you.

The hierarchy also supports links to other components, to allow users to view more information about each item in the tree. Create a hierarchy by clicking on its link on the Applications tab, just like any other component.

Table or View

Of course, this table must have the recursive relationship discussed earlier. The hierarchy component only supports a single table or view, but in this case, even the view must be based on a single table. This is not a limitation of Portal but of Oracle itself—the CONNECT BY clause cannot be used on a join, even if the join is "hidden" within a view.

Table or View Column

This is the crucial step in creating a hierarchy. The field settings here will dictate the structure of the SQL statement that Portal generates. The Primary Key Column field refers to a unique or primary key column in the table (such as Employee_ID) that is used in the lookup to find the related information (such as the supervisor's name). The Parent Key Column field is the column that supplies the value for this lookup (such as Supervisor_ID). The component does not support multiple-column keys.

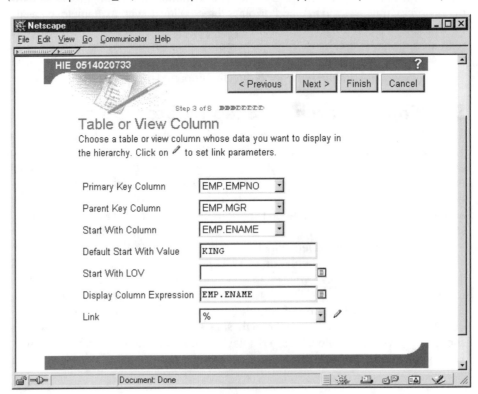

The Start With Column field dictates where to start in the hierarchy. Though it can be any column in the table, you should choose a column that the users will typically query to set up their hierarchies. For a bill of materials, you could choose the product name, and for employees, you could choose the person's name or maybe a title to ensure that the hierarchy begins with the company president. The Start With Column field is used with the Default Start With Value field to produce the condition that finds the first (parent) row in the hierarchy. If the Start With Column entry is not unique, the user will see multiple top-level nodes when displaying the hierarchy, because the component will create a separate tree for each distinct Start With Value. You may optionally provide an LOV to make it easier for users to choose the starting value.

TIP
A typical design technique when working with hierarchies is to set the top-level relationship column equal to NULL. This implies that the person has no manager or that the part is a top-level part. Unfortunately, the hierarchy component does not support NULL in the Default Start With Value field, and you'll have to work around this in the data. You could use a separate field to indicate the top-level item, or choose a unique column as the Start With Column. In this example, we can use the person's title, since we know the highest-ranking person in the corporation in the president.

The Display Column Expression dictates what text will be displayed at each node in the hierarchy, and unlike many of the other Portal wizard fields, supports concatenation and complex functions. Configure a link in the Link field to make this expression active, allowing users to navigate to a related Portal component or URL.

Column Conditions

The conditions that you enter on the Column Conditions page will be used to generate WHERE clause conditions for the hierarchy. The biggest caveat about WHERE clause conditions in a hierarchy component is that you may inadvertently remove entire branches of the tree. For example, if you added a condition on the Salary field that caused a supervisor to not be displayed, all of that supervisor's employees would also disappear, regardless of their salaries. The WHERE clause essentially stops the tree anytime a row fails the condition. Be extremely careful when using column conditions, and make sure you test rigorously if you do.

Display Options

The Display Options page has quite a few settings that are unique to the hierarchy component. In the Common Options section, you will control how the hierarchy will display, and in the Drill Up/Down Options section, you will specify the details of the navigation. The Full Page and Portlet Options sections are similar to those we've seen in other components.

Common Options   In the Common Options section, you will first decide the maximum number of child levels to show (1 or 2), then you will choose whether to show the parent level as a reference point to the current level. This Parent Level option is actually a "grandparent" to the displayed tree branch, as you can see in Figure 9-6. All told, you could show anywhere from two to four levels at one time (including the grandparent). These relationships are best illustrated with a schematic diagram. In Figure 9-6, we define all the levels of the tree and indicate which are optional using these settings. You may limit the number of children displayed at each child level using the Max Children option, perhaps to save on screen space. If this setting is smaller than the number of children, there will be no way for the user to view the remaining children.

Next, you will decide how to display the hierarchy. In the Hierarchy Type field, you have the choice of stacked HTML Tables or a "Break Down." Both are excellent ways to represent the information, but the Break Down style tends to take up less

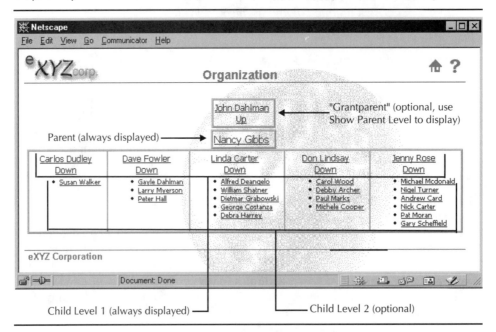

FIGURE 9-6.   *The HTML Table view of the eXYZ organization hierarchy illustrates the four display levels*

screen space and is more appropriate for portlet display. In full page mode, the Break Down style centers the list entries and the bullets don't line up as nicely.

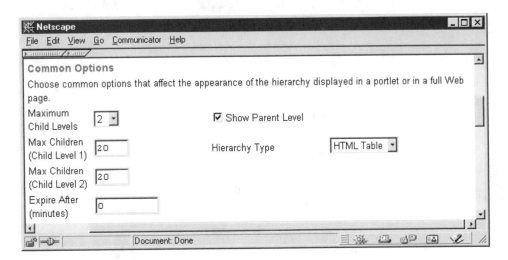

The reason for this distinction is that most templates, including the one we've developed in this book, insert the #BODY# section, or the actual component, into a <TD> tag with alignment set to center. This works well for most components, but if you prefer to see your hierarchy Break Down view aligned left, create a second template with all of the same settings except change the <TD> tag surrounding the #BODY# to align left. Alternately, you could add the following code to the "…after displaying the header" PL/SQL entry on the Additional PL/SQL Code page. This code closes the centered <TD> tag and opens a new one with left alignment.

```
htp.print('</TD>');
htp.print('</TR>');
htp.print('<TR>');
htp.print('<TD ALIGN=LEFT VALIGN=TOP>');
```

Drill Up/Down Options   You can use text, an image, or an iconic button (using the Value Type field) for the Drill Up and Drill Down links that allow the user to navigate the tree. The Drill Up and Drill Down options are specified independently of each other. If you use text or a button, you may specify your own custom text— just type the text into the Value field in place of the default text. The list attached to the Value field is for images only. It includes all of the images of type Icon (any size) from the Shared Components application. If you would like to use custom images (say, up and down arrows), create them as icons in the Shared Components application.

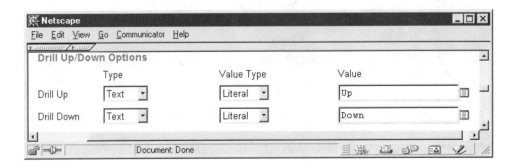

TIP
*There are some very nice up and down arrows in
the Portal images directory.* `arrowu.gif` *and*
`arrowd.gif` *are large and yellow;*
`ed-movdn.gif` *and* ed-movup.gif *are the small
blue arrows you saw in the form wizard. If you
would like to use them, upload the files into the
Shared Components application.*

Finally, you can use a column value to provide the navigation text. This is a fine
way to sneak a little extra information into the hierarchy. Just select Column in the
Value Type field and type the column name in the Value field. The data from the
column will display with each hierarchy entry, highlighted as active text to let the
user navigate up and down. A good candidate column to provide this text might be
the employee's title if stored in the source table.

Full Page Options   Each node in the tree can be formatted with a different font
face, color, and size. The Child font options apply to Child Level 1 and the "grandparent"
level shown for reference, and the GrandChild option applies to Child Level 2. You
are allowed two Background Color settings: the Parent Background Color for the
parent; and the Child Background Color for everything else, including the grandparent
reference. The colors do not apply when the hierarchy is displayed in a Break Down
style—this is just a text-based list, and it displays over the page background.

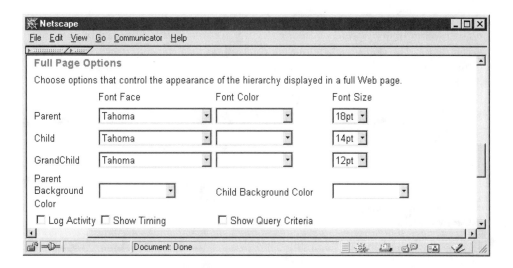

Portlet Options   As with Full Page Options, you will set the fonts independently for each level, but as usual with portlets, you may reference page style objects. The background colors can also be set independently, but you'll have to be careful not to clash with page styles. There is no page style object that you can access to specify the background of hierarchy components, so you'll want to be conservative with these colors.

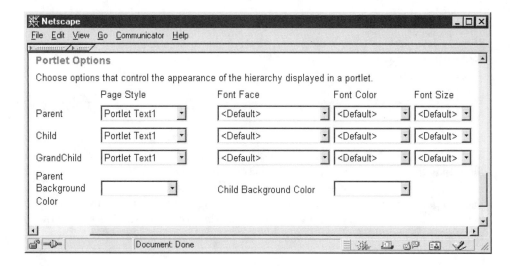

Customization Form Display Options

As with other query wizard components, any column in the table can be used as a parameter. The query will be modified based on user input to the customization form. All options on this page should be familiar from creating report, calendar, and chart parameters.

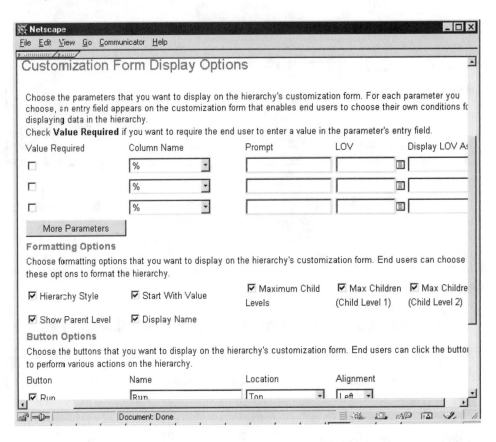

The Form Text and Additional PL/SQL Code pages offer the same flexibility as they do with other components. Use the Form Text page to set the template and add information text to the screen or Help page, and use the Additional PL/SQL Code page to perform pre-processing and post-processing actions. The discussion of these pages in earlier chapters should give you some ideas of their usefulness. For now, let's build a hierarchy.

Exercise 9.9: Organization Chart

Before we get started on the organization chart, we will need a link to display detail records for the employees and an LOV for the customization form.

1. Create a Link in the HR application named `LINK_RPT_EMP_DETAILS`.

2. For the Link Target, choose the Oracle Portal Component `APP_HR.RPT_EMP_DETAILS` from the list. Click Finish and then Close.

3. Create a dynamic LOV named `LOV_TITLES` with a Default Format of `Combo box`, using the following query:

```
SELECT title_desc, title_id
FROM   titles
```

4. Create a Hierarchy in APP_HR named `HIE_ORG_CHART` with a Display Name of `Organization`.

5. For the Table or View field, choose `CORP_SITE.EMPLOYEES`.

6. On the Table or View Column page, the Primary Key Column is `EMPLOYEES.EMPLOYEE_ID`, and the Parent Key Column is `EMPLOYEES.SUPERVISOR_ID`. Set Start With Column to `EMPLOYEES.TITLE_ID` and Default Start With Value to `5` (for PRESIDENT). Choose `APP_HR.LOV_TITLES` for the Start With LOV. For the Display Column Expression, enter `INITCAP(EMPLOYEES.FIRST_NAME|` `|' '||EMPLOYEES.LAST_NAME)`. In the Link field, choose `LINK_RPT_EMP_DETAILS`. Click the pencil icon to edit the link, and set the `employee_id` parameter to equal the value contained in the `EMPLOYEES.EMPLOYEE_ID` column. Click OK, then continue with the wizard.

7. Skip the Column Conditions page.

8. In the Common Options section of the Display Options page, change the Hierarchy Type to `Break Down`. Leave the Drill Up/Drill Down options at their defaults, so that the literal text "Up" and "Down" provides navigation links through the tree. In the Full Page Options section, change the Font Size fields as follows:

Parent	12pt
Child	10pt
GrandChild	8pt

In the Portlet Options section, reduce the Page Style to `Portlet Text2` for all levels of the hierarchy.

9. Remove all the checkmarks from the Formatting Options section of the Customization Form Display Options page, except for those labeled Start With Value and Display Name. This allows users to change the portlet heading and the default view of the tree. We'll allow users to save their customizations, if they wish, so that their default view shows their own branch of the organization.

10. Specify the `EXYZ_TEMPLATE` on the Hierarchy and Customization Form Text page.

11. Click Finish and test your hierarchy in both portlet and full page modes. Ensure that the link works as expected; try drilling up and down, and click on an individual's name to see their virtual business card.

Exercise 9.10: Integrate the Hierarchy with the Portal

1. Before closing the Manage Component screen for the hierarchy you just created, click on the Access tab and publish it to the Portal.

2. Edit the eXYZ Home Page.

3. On the My eXYZ tab, click the Add Portlet button in the left-hand region.

4. Click on Organization in the Other Providers: Human Resources Application section. Move the Organization portlet above Saved Searches and click OK.

5. Click Close and then test your revised Portal page. Click on the Up and Down links to see how the display changes. Click Customize, change the Start With LOV field to `COO`, and change the Display Name if you like. Test this setting and a few others and notice that at the lower levels (i.e., `PROGRAMMERS`), you will see multiple trees. This is due to our Start With Value setting, and you must plan for this when designing your hierarchy or disallow modification of the Start With Value. Save the customization settings for the view that you prefer.

Conclusion

In this chapter, we have presented some alternative methods of displaying output, namely charts, calendars, and hierarchies. These graphic-oriented components are extremely useful for showing a quick summary of your data. They tend to fit nicely within Portal pages, and allow users to comprehend the data at a glance.

CHAPTER
10

Integration
Components

t this point, you have learned how to create the building blocks of any business Web application. You have created forms for data entry, and active reports, charts, and hierarchies to display and format database records. You have linked these together, and created a content area to provide structure to otherwise unstructured information.

But what about the miscellaneous requirements, those little details that glue an application together or provide special services? Many requirements don't map neatly to a predefined shape or format. Others do, but require a custom call interface that just isn't possible using the stock components we have seen so far. What about incorporating other HTML resources or applications that have already been deployed? How do you meet XML-based requirements in a Portal design? Are you resigned to finding other tools in which to develop code to meet those requirements? To some extent, you may be. (That was not the answer you were expecting, was it?) While Portal supports many development techniques, there may be times when you have to develop code, whether it is HTML, PL/SQL, Java, or XML, outside the Portal environment. The components we will discuss in this chapter help you to integrate or link to this external code in a Portal site, and provide some very flexible options for those requirements that don't fit the models we have discussed.

As you have already seen, building components to meet complex requirements sometimes requires creating PL/SQL validation or formatting routines outside of the Portal interface. You may need to customize more than the validation and formatting, though. You may have some conditional logic or complex HTML that is not easy to reference in a report or form, or you may want to show different customization options to different users. If your organization has been working on an intranet site for a while, you may have some components already developed that you would like to be able to reference in the portal without rewriting them. You may need to produce a more menu-oriented interface, so that one part of the screen populates data in another part of the screen. Or, you may have so many components that you can't fit them all in the portal—what then?

The components we will discuss in this chapter (dynamic pages, frame drivers, menus, XML components, and URL components) are related only by the simple fact that they seem to address these "other" needs. Each provides one possible way to solve a problem, and patient work with any of the other Portal components, with some extra coding, could potentially achieve the same objective. The choice of how to meet a particular user requirement will often depend simply on your personal style (or standards set by your organization). Would you rather write code from scratch, or do you enjoy the challenge of customizing the generated code that handles all the basics of data manipulation? Who will maintain the code—someone who enjoys writing and debugging PL/SQL or someone who is more comfortable working in a graphical environment? If you are more of a "coder" than a "clicker", the components in this chapter are more likely to suit your style. You may create code anywhere you like, and use these components to "plug in" to the portal.

Keep in mind that there is one level beyond these catchall components, as well. Highly complex requirements, or highly complex programmers, will be more suited to the Portal Development Kit (PDK), where the code is all written in good old 3GL style, and integrated using a published framework. The PDK is the subject of the next chapter.

Dynamic Pages

The dynamic page is a flexible component that allows you to combine any HTML, SQL, and PL/SQL, and display the result in the portal. There are two potential situations where this flexibility is beneficial. One is when you need to display lots of HTML markup, graphics, or even animation, but also a few items of live data. This kind of page is best designed in an HTML editing tool suited for the page requirements. The database information can then be added after the fact, using a dynamic page.

NOTE
This division of labor is a central concept in JavaServer Pages (JSP) and PL/SQL Pages (PSP). The idea is to get the page design right, then add any custom logic in a separate step. The HTML can be maintained separately from the code in this way, but with dynamic pages, you will have to edit the component, paste in the new HTML, and regenerate any time the HTML changes.

Another handy application of a dynamic page is when you have highly customized logic that does not readily map to the provided components. Some examples might include a visit counter, a "message of the day" portlet, or a fully customized internal application. These are the requirements that you never read about in books like these, because they are so hard to predict, but that come across your desk every day. In Chapter 7 we saw one way to incorporate completely customized logic. The Form Based on Stored Procedure first displays a parameter entry form and only displays the results of your custom code after users click the Run button. When you don't need to request input from users, but instead want to display a PL/SQL-generated page as a portlet, a dynamic page is probably your best bet. The dynamic page that we will build in this chapter, a simple message-of-the-day portlet, is displayed in Figure 10-1.

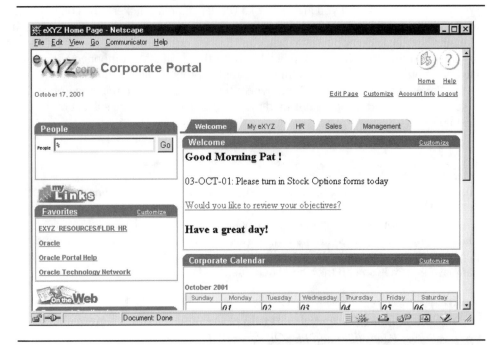

FIGURE 10-1. *The eXYZ Home Page will display a simple dynamic page portlet to greet the user upon logging in*

Building a dynamic page involves writing HTML, then adding SQL or PL/SQL to retrieve data or perform conditional logic. All SQL and PL/SQL code is embedded within special <ORACLE> tags to signal Portal to execute the statements before sending the page to the browser. The following is an example of simple dynamic page code:

```
<HTML>
<BODY>
<H3> The EMP table contents: </H3>
<ORACLE>select * from scott.emp</ORACLE>
</BODY>
</HTML>
```

Only one SQL statement may be contained within each set of <ORACLE> tags, and there is no semicolon to terminate the line. Figure 10-2 shows how this page would look in a browser window. There is no way to alter the default format for the data retrieved by the embedded SQL, but you may specify any formatting for the page content above and below the generated result set.

For more control over formatting, you would embed PL/SQL, using the PL/SQL Web Toolkit routines to produce the output. PL/SQL statements within the <ORACLE>

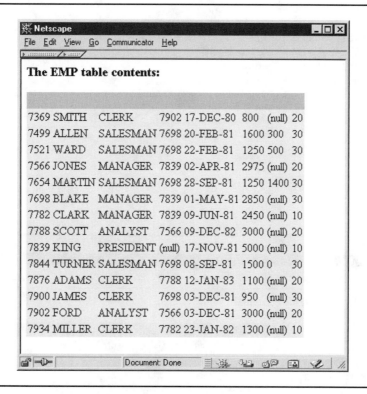

FIGURE 10-2. *SQL statements in dynamic pages are automatically formatted*

tags require semicolons to terminate each line, as well as BEGIN and END statements, regardless of the number of lines of PL/SQL. Below is the code to produce a different rendering of the same data, as pictured in Figure 10-3.

```
<HTML>
<BODY>
<H3> The EMP table contents: </H3>
<TABLE BORDER>
<TR bgcolor="BLUE">
  <TH>EMPNO</TH><TH>NAME</TH><TH>JOB</TH><TH>MGR</TH>
  <TH>HIREDATE</TH><TH>SALARY</TH><TH>COMM</TH><TH>DEPT</TH>
</TR>
<ORACLE>
BEGIN
 FOR x IN (SELECT * FROM SCOTT.emp) LOOP
  HTP.tablerowopen(cattributes=>'bgcolor="LIGHTBLUE"');
```

```
       HTP.tabledata(x.empno);
       HTP.tabledata(x.ename);
       HTP.tabledata(x.job);
       HTP.tabledata(NVL(TO_CHAR(x.mgr),'(null)'));
       HTP.tabledata(x.hiredate);
       HTP.tabledata(x.sal);
       HTP.tabledata(NVL(TO_CHAR(x.comm),'(null)'));
       HTP.tabledata(x.deptno);
     HTP.tablerowclose;
   END LOOP;
 END;
 </ORACLE>
 </TABLE>
 </BODY>
 </HTML>
```

EMPNO	NAME	JOB	MGR	HIREDATE	SALARY	COMM	DEPT
7369	SMITH	CLERK	7902	17-DEC-80	800	(null)	20
7499	ALLEN	SALESMAN	7698	20-FEB-81	1600	300	30
7521	WARD	SALESMAN	7698	22-FEB-81	1250	500	30
7566	JONES	MANAGER	7839	02-APR-81	2975	(null)	20
7654	MARTIN	SALESMAN	7698	28-SEP-81	1250	1400	30
7698	BLAKE	MANAGER	7839	01-MAY-81	2850	(null)	30
7782	CLARK	MANAGER	7839	09-JUN-81	2450	(null)	10
7788	SCOTT	ANALYST	7566	09-DEC-82	3000	(null)	20
7839	KING	PRESIDENT	(null)	17-NOV-81	5000	(null)	10
7844	TURNER	SALESMAN	7698	08-SEP-81	1500	0	30
7876	ADAMS	CLERK	7788	12-JAN-83	1100	(null)	20
7900	JAMES	CLERK	7698	03-DEC-81	950	(null)	30
7902	FORD	ANALYST	7566	03-DEC-81	3000	(null)	20
7934	MILLER	CLERK	7782	23-JAN-82	1300	(null)	10

FIGURE 10-3. *The EMP data with minimal PL/SQL Web Toolkit and custom HTML formatting*

The PL/SQL may quickly get too complicated to manage in the simple editing area provided with the dynamic page component. If this is the case, you can create a database stored procedure and simply invoke the procedure here. A good PL/SQL Integrated Development Environment (IDE) will be invaluable for writing and testing this code. We have listed a few of these in Appendix A.

Developing Dynamic Pages: Step by Step

Before you get started with the dynamic page wizard, you will usually build and test your HTML or PL/SQL in a language-appropriate editor. Once you are satisfied with the design and/or logic, go ahead and create the component.

Dynamic Page Content

If you developed your HTML in an HTML editor, the first thing you will do is paste it into the HTML Code text area. Otherwise, you can type HTML directly into this text area, or edit the default HTML. The next step is to add the <ORACLE> tags and embedded PL/SQL or SQL statements. If your data requirements are simple and you want to use the default formatting, enter a single SQL statement within each set of tags. Otherwise, type the anonymous PL/SQL block that will make calls to existing packages, procedures, or functions.

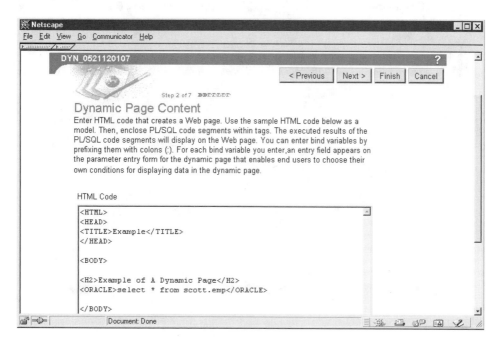

You may use bind variables within the <ORACLE> tags, indicated by a leading colon (:). Dynamic pages can have a customization form, just like most other components, which allows users to enter or choose values that affect the displayed results.

The page can contain custom images, media, JavaScript, or any other Web construct, with a couple of caveats. First, links to images and other external resources must be absolute references or formed with respect to the Portal page path and be accessible to the Apache server. The simplest technique for including images would be to place them in the Portal images directory, referencing a path of /images/. Second, a dynamic page that will be used in a portlet must be designed with the portal page in mind. Excessive graphics and interactive media would cause the page to display very slowly, and some HTML tags could cause the page to display incorrectly. For example, specifying frame sets would cause the portal interface to disappear, replaced entirely by the frame. Images and HTML tables specified with absolute rather than relative sizing would tend to push other portlets off the page if they were too large.

PL/SQL Code Segments
On the PL/SQL Code Segments page, the wizard displays the PL/SQL or SQL code from the <ORACLE> tags on the Dynamic Page Content page. This allows you to double-check the code you entered. There will be one text area for each set of <ORACLE> tags. You may edit the code here, and your changes will be saved to the component. This page is most useful in later edits, because you won't have to hunt through the HTML to find the PL/SQL to edit.

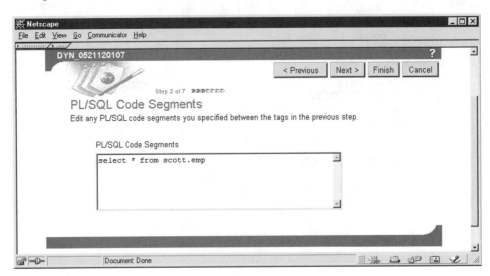

Full Page Display Options

The only options on the Full Page Display Options page are the Log Activity and Expire After settings. This is because all formatting and display features must be produced by the page code, rather than by Portal settings.

Customization Form Display Options

If you used bind variables in the page code, you may set the prompt, associate an LOV, and choose the LOV display style. The only formatting option that users can change is the display name of the page or portlet. The button options are the standard Run, Save, Batch, and Reset.

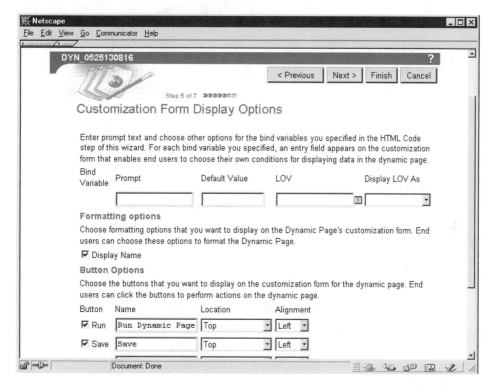

Wrap-Up

The dynamic page itself cannot use a template, and it does not support custom header and footer text, or additional PL/SQL. All formatting must be specified using custom HTML, as supplied on the Dynamic Page Content page. However, the customization form is displayed like any other. You may specify a template, additional supporting text, and additional PL/SQL code before and after the customization form header and footer.

Exercise 10.1: The Welcome Portlet

eXYZ has expressed a need for a way to welcome employees when they first access the home page. Each employee will be greeted by name, and any messages added by managers or the system administrator will be displayed. A customization form option will allow employees to restrict the number of messages displayed. If an employee is on the sales staff, the portlet will display the employee's year-to-date sales total and quota for the year, along with a message indicating their progress toward the goal. Otherwise, it will display a link to the employee's last review, to remind the employee of the objectives set there.

1. Since this is mostly a Human Resources function, navigate to HR_APP and create a new dynamic page.

2. Name the component DYN_WELCOME and give it a Display Name of Welcome.

3. In the HTML Code text area, replace the default HTML with the following:

```
File ex (001.htm)
<HTML>
<BODY>
<H3>Good Morning
<ORACLE>
BEGIN
 HTP.print (get_name('FIRST', PORTAL30.WWCTX_API.get_user));
END;
</ORACLE>
!
</H3>
<ORACLE>
BEGIN
 IF :num_msgs IS NOT NULL THEN
  motd_portlet_proc(PORTAL30.WWCTX_API.get_user, :num_msgs);
 ELSE
  motd_portlet_proc(PORTAL30.WWCTX_API.get_user);
 END IF;
END;
</ORACLE>
<H3> Have a great day! </H3>
</BODY>
</HTML>
```

NOTE

The `motd_portlet_proc` *procedure and the* `get_name` *function are provided with the CORP_SITE schema. Review the code to see how each piece works.* `motd_portlet_proc` *references LINK_FORM_REVIEW, created in Exercise 9.7—without it, the component will not function properly. If you did not build the link, build it now or run the script named* `ex0907link.sql` *in the directory for Chapter 9, substituting your Portal schema name when prompted.*

4. Click on the Next button to review the PL/SQL Code Segments, then click Next again until you come to the Customization Form Display Options page.

5. Set the Prompt for the bind variable to `Number of Messages to Display`, and set its Default to `1`.

6. Click Finish.

7. Test the component using the Run and Run as Portlet links. We have inserted a few messages into the MOTDS table, but feel free to add your own.

8. Try logging in as a member of the `SALES_USERS` group (try `GAYLED` or `DAVEF`) to see how the portlet displays the sales information.

Exercise 10.2: Publish the Welcome Portlet

1. Click on the Access tab, and check the box labeled Publish to Portal and click Apply.

2. Close the Manage Component page and find the eXYZ Home Page.

3. Edit the page and add this portlet to the Welcome tab, above the calendar. Close the Customize Page window to test the portlet integration.

Dynamic pages are in some ways the best of all worlds, and in other ways the worst of all worlds. You have complete freedom over the HTML and the PL/SQL or SQL used to generate the component's output. You can easily integrate graphics or multimedia content, and display the output in portlet or full screen mode. Dynamic pages support a customization form, so you don't have to develop separate pages to solicit input data. They are a simple and quick way to get data onto your site. On the minus side, there is no debugging environment, and all code is modified by hand. You must manually accommodate any changes to database structure, and you will probably have to use additional tools to generate and test your HTML and PL/SQL code.

Frame Drivers

A *frame driver* is a frame set where one frame, known as the *driving frame*, populates the other, *target frame*. This is a common way to build a menu interface in many Web applications, but the advantage of the frame driver component is that the menu content is generated dynamically, based on the results of a SELECT statement. All that is required of this statement is that it produce labels for each of the choices in the driving frame, and the corresponding URLs to populate the target frame based on the user's selection. It could access a table that stores labels and links created specifically for a dynamic menu system. Even better, it can build links on the fly, using query results to provide the parameters for a Portal component or another URL. If you are running into problems displaying LONG, RAW, CLOB, or BLOB fields in Portal forms or reports, you can use a frame driver to display or allow edits to the field in the target frame.

NOTE
In version 3.0.9, Portal forms offer limited support for BLOBs only, and reports can display only LONG and RAW datatypes.

Because a frame driver accepts parameters, you can limit the entries displayed in the driving frame using WHERE clause conditions. As with dynamic pages, frame drivers are an excellent way to provide an interface to existing Web applications.

Frame driver components will not display as portlets, because they rely on the <FRAMESET> tag to display the two frames. <FRAMESET> is a top-level tag, used in place of the entire <BODY> section of an HTML page. When a <FRAMESET> tag appears within the body section of another HTML page, such as the Portal home page, all body section HTML is ignored and the frames display instead. So, rather than include the frame driver component as a portlet, create a link to it from anywhere in the portal application. You may use one of the banner links, another component, or a menu, as you will see in the next section.

Figure 10-4 shows the frame driver we will build in this section. A list of vendor links comprises the menu on the left side of the page. Clicking on one of these links

FIGURE 10-4. *The Vendors frame driver displays links to our vendors' Web sites*

displays the vendor's home page in the target frame on the right. Both the vendor names and home page URLs are extracted from the VENDORS table in the CORP_SITE schema. The frame driver accepts a parameter that limits the list of vendors to suppliers of a particular product, so that when we are running low on something, we can shop around to find the best price. We will link this component to the Inventory Report produced in Chapter 8, to make reordering products very convenient.

Developing Frame Drivers: Step by Step

Building a frame driver requires some preliminary design. What data will you use to populate each frame? Are you planning to call a component, link to an external URL, or simply display stored text? Whichever technique you use, you will have to ensure that you can use a query to build the links. This may involve modifying existing table structures or adding new tables to meet your requirements, or just figuring out and testing the call interface to the target resource.

SQL Query

The SQL query for a frame driver requires two columns. The data from the first column provides the labels in the driving frame list. You may format this column using any SQL or PL/SQL Web Toolkit function or concatenate multiple values together to produce a meaningful label. The second column must evaluate to a text string, but it will be interpreted in one of three ways, depending on the Target Link Type setting, as follows.

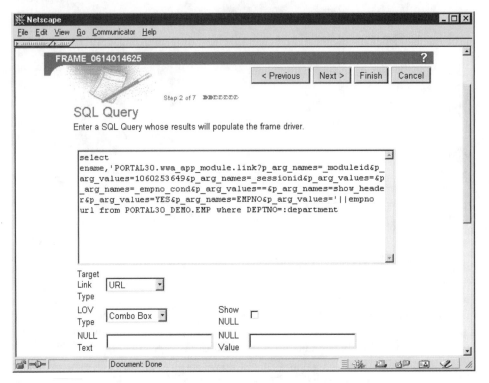

HTML/TEXT Links If you choose HTML/TEXT for the Target Link Type, the text string will be treated as a literal and displayed directly in the target frame. You must set LOV Type to Combo Box or Radio Group to display text data in this way. Any embedded HTML tags will be interpreted by the browser to format the data, so you could produce a page "on the spot" by simply formatting the returned data. For example, to simply display the contents of a CLOB column containing HTML, use a query similar to this:

```
SELECT id, DBMS_LOB.substr(clob_col,2000)
FROM   table_with_clob_data
```

This technique has quite a few limitations, but it works in simple cases. To provide the capability to edit this data, you would have to create PL/SQL procedures to display an edit form and to process the changes, and use a PL/SQL link type. To display BLOB, LONG, or RAW data, large CLOBs, or CLOBs containing complex HTML, you will have to create a procedure to read, interpret, and display the data, then reference it here. The actual code will depend on the datatype, and with BLOB and RAW data, on the content of the column.

URL Links   The URL link type will interpret the string as a call to another Web resource, which could be a simple site address or concatenated text that calls a Web-based routine with a query string generated from the data. You may specify any valid URL, keeping in mind the current path within the context of the Portal DAD. To link to a resource outside of the portal, you must use the absolute URL, beginning with `http://`, but you may use relative addressing for Portal resources. For example, every component has a call interface so that it can be referenced in a URL, in the form

`http://server/pls/portal_schema/application_schema.component_name.show`

To populate the target frame with this component, you need only to specify *APPLICATION_SCHEMA.COMPONENT_NAME*.show as the URL, because the current path will always be `http://server/pls/portal_schema/`. The same method would apply to the show_parms procedure, which displays the customization form for the component instead. To reference a predefined Portal link component, use the built-in function WWV_USER_UTILITIES.get_url, which constructs a URL based on the supplied parameters. In fact, you could display any PL/SQL Web page using a URL link type, provided you grant execute permission on the page code to PORTAL30_PUBLIC. You may use a custom PL/SQL function to build the URL, which would tend to improve the readability of the frame driver code. When using a PL/SQL function, do not enclose it in quotes, so that the SQL query engine will execute the function and return the URL string to Portal to be rendered via the browser.

PL/SQL Links   The third link type, PL/SQL, allows one or more PL/SQL commands in the string. The PL/SQL will be executed at the time the link is chosen in the frame driver—the string must be enclosed in single quotes to prevent the SQL query engine from trying to evaluate it. Any PL/SQL that the application schema can execute is valid, including Web Toolkit routines that are otherwise not directly accessible from a URL. You can leverage this feature to add custom headers or footers to existing PL/SQL Web pages, or to display the results of more than one PL/SQL Web page in the same frame. The PL/SQL link type would even support a sequential process in which, for example, you create a record in the database for each visit to a particular link, display your own custom header, then display the requested page. You would code each step as a database procedure, and specify them all (each terminated by a semicolon) in the target link. Whenever a user accesses the driving frame and selects this link, the procedures will execute, and the results will display in the target frame.

NOTE
At least one of your procedures must return results to the browser via the PL/SQL Web Toolkit, or users will see the following error message: "No data returned from stored procedure. The PL/SQL gateway invoked a stored procedure as part of processing the URL but the procedure returned no data."

LOV Type   You may display the values in the driving frame as a Combo Box, Radio Group, or List. The List option displays all the values as hypertext links. The Radio Group option displays the values as radio button choices, and the Combo Box option displays a drop-down list of the values. Both the Combo Box and Radio Group options require that users click once to choose the value and again to click the Submit button. Consequently, users may prefer the List option, because they have only to click once on the name link to display the corresponding Web page.

NULL Value and Text   If you want one item in the driving frame that does something different, you may use the NULL value as a special case. For example, you may have a frame driver that shows an update screen in the target frame for each record listed in the driving frame. The NULL choice could be used to display a summary screen for all records, or a data entry screen to create a new record. To use this feature, check the box labeled Show NULL, and specify the string that will populate the target frame for the NULL entry. The string must be of the same type used in the query. You may also specify NULL Text, which will display as a label (such as "Summary") with the other values in the driving frame, to give the user a better indication of what the option will do. Radio Groups and Combo Boxes will display the NULL choice regardless of whether there was a NULL in the data. Be sure to specify NULL Text for the Radio Group or you will have a rather unattractive blank radio button. If you are using a List to display your values, there must be a NULL in the data and NULL Text or you will not see the NULL choice. To generate a NULL row when the data has no NULLs, add the following code fragment to the beginning of your query:

```
SELECT NULL, NULL FROM DUAL
UNION ALL
```

Customization Form Display Options

You may configure the customization form in the same way that you have for the other components; it will only be useful if you plan to accept parameters before displaying the frame driver. Users can change only the display name of the frame driver, which is shown in the driving frame.

Initial Target Frame Content

Rather than let users see a blank target frame when they first load the frame driver, you may want to specify some "default" text, HTML, URL, or PL/SQL call. Otherwise, the target frame will not be populated until they choose an option from the list. The link types work the same as they do on the SQL Query page, and can be different from the link type used in the query. Use this feature to welcome your users, display help, or to provide some generic content as an initial entry page.

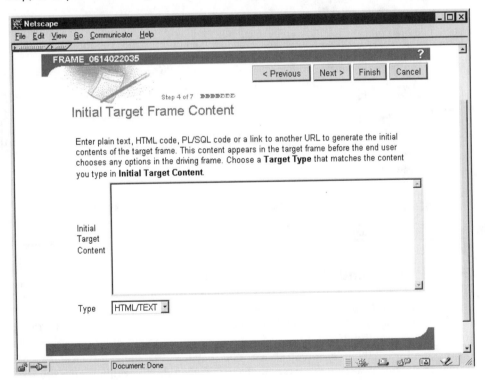

Display Options

The Display Options tab helps you customize the frame set's appearance. You can choose to Divide Frames By COLS (vertically) or ROWS (horizontally), and set the percentage of the screen that the driving frame and target frame should each occupy. These percentages should add up to 100 percent. The Border attribute dictates the width of the line between the frames; set it to 0 to remove the line. You may customize the list button name and its position (using Button Location) relative to the LOV (Left, Right, Above, Below). The button will only appear in conjunction with a combo box or radio-type list. The parameter button is a convenient feature that, when clicked, takes users to the customization form for the frame driver. Enable it using the Show Parameter Button check box, and set its label in the Parm Button Name field.

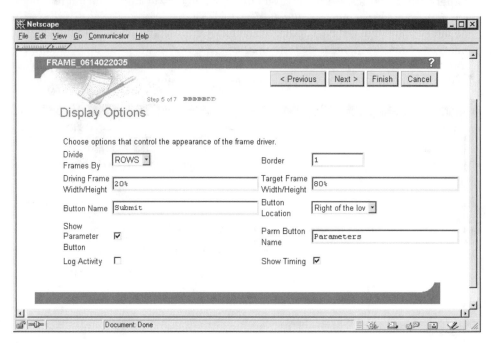

Frame Driver and Customization Form Text
Because the target frame will always be populated programmatically, you can only specify a template and additional page text for the driving frame and customization form. A single template choice applies to both the customization form and the driving frame. Keep in mind that, for the driving frame, the template will be displayed in only a fraction of the total screen space. You may find that the graphics and HTML tables that worked well in the template for full screen display don't work very well in a small space. The implication is that you may need to design a separate template,

or even create a "blank" template without graphics and with little markup, for the frame driver component.

Additional PL/SQL Code

You can add PL/SQL code to run before and after the driving frame or customization form, but not the target frame. Any additional code for the target frame would have to be specified as part of the link, as described earlier.

Exercise 10.3: Vendor Directory

The product managers have asked for a component that gives them a list of vendor Web pages for the items they sell, to simplify the order process for restocking the warehouses. To really turbo-charge this kind of utility, you would want to link directly to the order page or supply your customer ID for each vendor, but in this simplified example we only show the top-level home page and pass no parameters. It would be easy enough to change this by simply updating the URL column in the VENDORS table. The vendor directory component will accept an optional parameter of product_id, so that a manager can display a list of vendors for a particular product. If product_id is not specified, all vendors are displayed.

1. Create a new frame driver in the Sales Application.

2. Name the component FRAME_VENDORS, and set the Display Name to Vendor Directory.

3. Enter the following SQL statement on the SQL Query page:

```
SELECT DISTINCT v.name, 'http://'||v.url
FROM   CORP_SITE.vendors v, CORP_SITE.product_vendors pv
WHERE  v.id = pv.vendor_id
AND    (pv.product_id = :product_id OR :product_id IS NULL)
```

   Leave the Target Link Type set to URL, and change the LOV Type to List. There won't be any NULL values to contend with, so click Next to continue.

4. We will call this component using a link, so there is no need to set the LOV or Prompt for the product_id parameter; click Next on the Customization Form Display Options page.

5. The Initial Target Frame Content will be a blank screen—skip this step.

6. On the Display Options page, change the Divide Frames By setting to COLS and uncheck the Show Parameter Button and Show Timing boxes. Set the

Driving Frame Width/Height Ratio to 30 and the Target Frame Width/Height Ratio to 70.

7. Choose EXYZ_TEMPLATE on the Frame Driver and Customization Form Text page.

8. Click Finish, then Run to test your component. Try clicking on a few of the links to display the vendor Web pages.

The frame driver is a very convenient way to make a number of Web sites or Portal components available in a single page. Because it can't be displayed as a portlet, we will investigate some other options to link it into our portal. First, we'll look at using links to display it, taking advantage of the parameter to show only vendors for a particular product. In a later section, we'll use a menu to link to all vendors.

Exercise 10.4: Linking to the Frame Driver
We need a link for this frame driver, so we can call it from the Inventory Report. This way, when product managers see that they are running low on quantity for a particular product, they can go directly to the page that helps them order the product.

1. Return to the main Navigator page for APP_SALES and create a new link.

2. Name the link LINK_FRAME_VENDOR and click Next.

3. In the Target Component or URL field, choose or type APP_SALES.FRAME_VENDORS.

4. Click Finish and then Close.

5. On the Navigator page, click the Edit link for RPT_INVENTORY.

6. Add p.product_id to the SELECT list in the query, as below (leave the rest of the query as it was):

```
SELECT p.description, w.name, p.reorder_threshold
     ,i.qty_available
     ,(i.qty_available - p.reorder_threshold) low_ind
     ,p.product_id
```

7. Navigate to the Column Formatting page and change Display As for PRODUCT_ID to Hidden. For the DESCRIPTION field, choose

`LINK_FRAME_VENDOR` in the Link column. Click on the Edit Link icon and set the Column Name to `PRODUCT_ID` on the line for the `product_id` parameter. Click OK.

8. In the wizard, click OK again and then run the report to test the link. You may also wish to reload the eXYZ Home Page and click on the Management tab to see that the portlet version of the same report also displays the links.

In this section, you developed a frame driver to enhance the usefulness of the Inventory Report, and to provide a quick reference for the purchasing staff. There are many possibilities for the frame driver as a way to easily show a list of options and link the user to a related application. While it cannot be displayed in a Portal page, its big selling point is that it allows you to use values in one part of a page to affect the display in another part of a page.

Menus

Menus are another way to provide application navigation, and to link in code from other applications. Menus are made up of *items*, or hypertext links that call other components, customization forms, or URLs. Menus can have submenus to further organize the structure of the available choices, and they offer a Find option that lets users search the menu contents. Each menu item and submenu can have explanatory text to help users identify what each item does. You could create an entire application with only menu-driven navigation (anyone out there remember SQL*Menu?) by calling the menus in full screen mode, and forgo the portal page/portlet interface altogether. As we'll see in this section, you can also use a menu within a portlet to list several options in a small space in the page, and to explicitly call the customization forms that are not directly available as portlets. The menu you will add to the eXYZ Home Page is displayed in Figure 10-5.

Developing Menus

You will want to plan your menu structure before you begin working with the wizard. Do you want several top-level elements, or will you need a hierarchy to organize related links? Is the security of each menu item the same, or do you want to restrict access to some items by user privileges? Each menu item can have its own icon, so you may want to think about what images you'll use for these. Because the menu can be changed at any time, you don't have to decide every issue at this point,

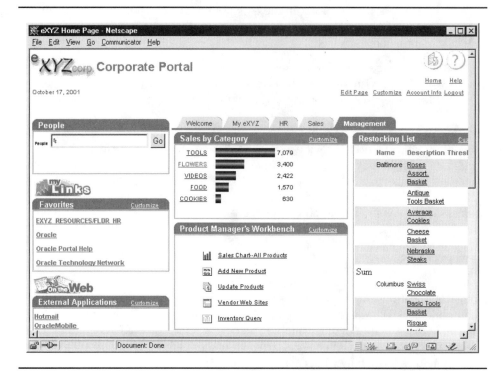

FIGURE 10-5. *The Product Manager's Workbench shows links to several components in a small space*

but you should have an idea of some of the basic requirements and the eventual complexity of the menu. Once you have an overall plan, use the wizard to create a new menu.

Menu Items and Submenus

Like the Form Formatting and Validation Options page, the Menu Items and Submenus page is made up of a left-side tree of elements and a right-side frame for setting properties. It's a little difficult to see everything at once, so as we discuss each item, we will isolate its frame in a separate illustration. The page you will use looks like the following illustration; subsequent illustrations are created only for clarifying the discussion.

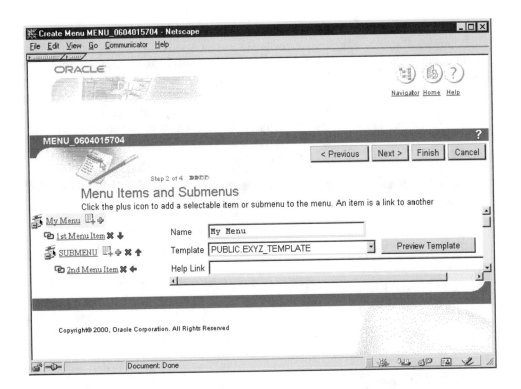

Working with Menu Items and Submenus   To create a submenu, click on the Add Submenu icon where you want the submenu to go. Each submenu can have additional submenus, creating a hierarchical structure. Menu items and submenus can be mixed at any level. To create an item, click on the Add Menu Item icon where you want the item displayed. To rearrange items and submenus vertically, click on the blue up and down arrows within the tree. Delete nodes using the red "X" and use the right and left arrows to move items into or out of submenus.

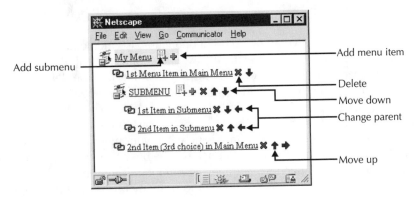

Menu Properties The top-level element is the main menu node, and its submenus and items will show on the initial display of the menu (by default). The main menu is a container for submenus and items, and never displays as a menu option. You may format the page that will display the contents of the menu by choosing a template, and adding text above and below the menu choices. Much like the Page Text page in many of the other components, the main menu property frame contains a Welcome Text field (similar to the Header Text field in other components) and a Footer Text field. Help works a little differently in menus, as you will have to supply a URL for the Help Text field rather than typing it in directly.

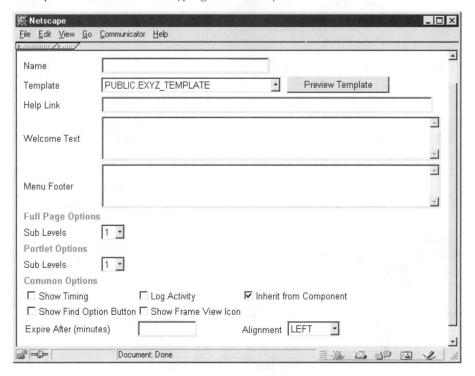

Display options for the overall menu component are also included on the Menu Properties frame. The only option specifically available for either Full Page or Portlet mode is the number of menu Sub Levels to display at one time. The default is 1, which means that only the direct children of the main menu will be visible on the menu entry page. The choice of the number of sub levels to display is a balance between reducing the complexity of the menu entry page and making the menu easy to use. This is a particularly important issue when your menu has many levels. A menu with many sublevels displayed at once will be busy and will require much screen real estate. A menu with fewer sub levels will look neater on the screen, but users may find it frustrating to have to delve into so many layers, and to have to frequently navigate up and down the tree. Set the Sub Levels according to how you assess your user requirements, keeping in mind that you may reduce the number of Sub Levels displayed in the portlet.

The Common Options section has a few settings that apply only to menus. The first, Inherit From Component, refers to the security settings of the menu. If everyone who will use this menu should be able to see all menu items, leave this box checked. The individual component security will still be enforced, even if users can see the menu choice. If a user does not have permission for the underlying component, clicking the link will display an error message rather than the component. A somewhat friendlier approach would be to uncheck the Inherit From Component box; you can then set the security individually using the multiple select list that will display for each menu item. Remember that the Security setting only affects whether or not the user will see the menu item, and is independent of the actual component security. This technique has the drawback of not being automatically tied to the Portal security scheme. Every newly created user or group will have to be added manually to the menu security, and the menu will have to be edited each time permissions change.

The Show Find Option Button check box displays a small search window at the bottom of the menu where users can type in text and press the associated button, labeled Find Menu Options, to search for menu items. This feature is quite useful in large, complex menus. The Show Frame View Icon check box displays an icon that lets users switch to a frame-based view of the menu as a navigable tree. The menu you will develop in Exercise 10-5 is shown as a frame view in Figure 10-6. The frame view shows the menu link in a target frame, much like the frame driver.

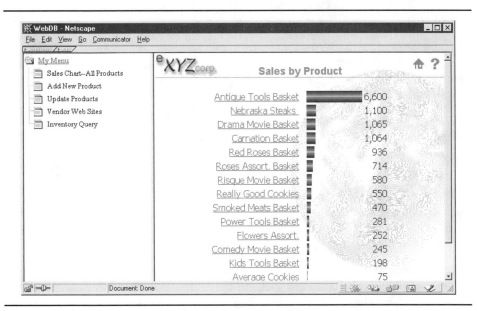

FIGURE 10-6. *The frame view of the menu shows all the menu choices in a hierarchical list, with results displayed in a separate frame*

Finally, you can choose how the menu items will be aligned in the normal view (LEFT, CENTER, or RIGHT).

Submenu Properties   Submenu properties are similar to the top-level menu properties, because when the user clicks on a submenu, the submenu replaces the display with its contents, and it becomes the parent menu. However, for submenus, you may specify font characteristics and Bullet icon, because the submenu name is displayed as a menu choice in higher-level menus, just like a regular menu item. The font details can be set independently for portlet and full page modes, and can be set differently for each submenu. While it may be unattractive to have a multitude of fonts and colors on a single menu, you can use this feature to draw attention to important or new submenus. The Description field allows you to enter descriptive text to be displayed below the menu link. This text can help users decide if the menu is the one they want.

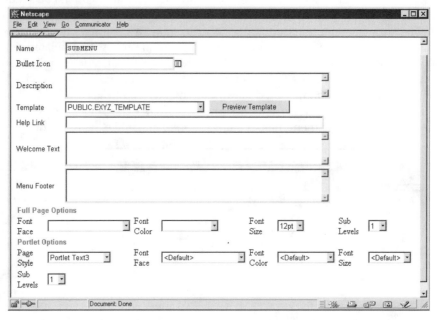

The Sub Levels setting applies only when this submenu's contents are displayed. The parent of this submenu has its own setting for Sub Levels, which is disregarded when the user enters the submenu. This allows you to display two sublevels on the main menu (for example), and more (or fewer) on the lower-level menu pages.

Menu Items   The only thing different about items is that instead of having sublevels, items have Links. The Link field specifies the URL or component associated with the menu item. The word "link" is used in the generic sense here, in that you may specify a direct link to a component or component customization form, a Portal link component, or any URL.

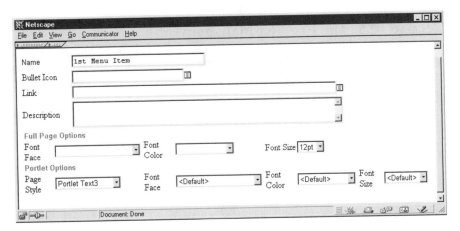

The same font characteristics, Bullet Icon, and Description fields are available for both submenus and menu items. The source of the Bullet icon list is, as before, images in the Shared Components application. You may wish to set the font or icon one way for items, and a different way to indicate a submenu.

Customization Form Display Options

On the customization form, you can allow users the option of turning off the Description field text, to simplify the display. Do not allow this option if you expect the menus to change frequently, because you will want your users to see current descriptions at all times. You can also let users override the number of Sub Levels to display and allow them to decide whether they want the Find Menu Option feature.

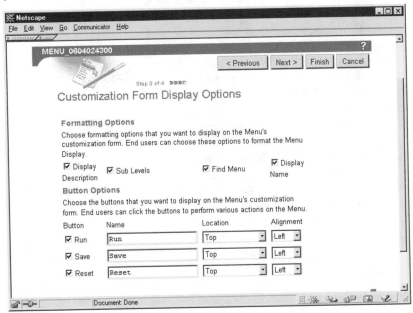

Exercise 10.5: The Product Management menu

We have developed quite a few components for the product managers to use, and are running out of screen real estate in which to display them. To save space, we'll create a menu of product-related options so the product managers can easily see the available tools.

1. Create a new Menu in the Sales Application.

2. Name the menu `MENU_PROD_MGMT`, and give it a Display Name of `Product Manager's Workbench`.

3. Add five menu items by clicking the green + sign. Set the properties as follows, and change the Page Style under Portlet Options to `Portlet Text2` for each one:

Name	Bullet Icon	Link
Sales Chart—All Products	chart.gif	CHART_SALES_BY_PRODUCT(SHOW)
Add New Product	form.gif	QBE_PRODUCTS(SHOW PARAMETERS)
Update Products	dyn.gif	QBE_PRODUCTS(SHOW)
Vendor Web Sites	frame.gif	FRAME_VENDORS(SHOW)
Inventory Query	report.gif	RPT_INVENTORY(SHOW PARAMETERS)

NOTE
The table above shows the Link name as it is displayed in the pop-up LOV associated with the Link field. The LOV returns the actual URL used to invoke the component. If you want to type the Link without using the LOV, the Link names are as follows (and are not case-sensitive):
CORP_SITE.CHART_SALES_BY_PRODUCT.show
CORP_SITE.QBE_PRODUCTS.show_parms
CORP_SITE.QBE_PRODUCTS.show
CORP_SITE.FRAME_VENDORS.show
CORP_SITE.RPT_INVENTORY.show_parms

4. Click Finish when you have added the menu items. (We will leave all of the defaults for Customization Form Display Options.) Click Run As Portlet to view the menu and test your links.

5. On the Manage Component page, click on the Access tab and publish the menu to the portal. Click Apply and then Close to return to the Navigator.

6. Find the eXYZ Home Page, and click the Edit or Edit Page link.

7. On the Management tab, click the Add Portlets icon in the left-hand region to add the menu portlet. In the Portlet Repository, it will be displayed in the Sales Application, under Other Providers. Click the Product Manager's Workbench to add it below the Sales by Category chart.

8. Click OK, then Close, to view your new page.

That's it! Now the product managers have easy access to several of the components we've built to help them manage the product line. Note that we used several components in different ways on this tab page, sometimes specifying parameters, sometimes linking to the component itself, and sometimes linking to the customization form. This is one of the real flexibilities of Portal, enabling you to use a single component for multiple purposes.

XML Component

Everybody is talking about XML these days, and Oracle is one of the leaders in the field. XML's advantage as a standard mechanism for exchanging data between heterogeneous environments and applications is growing rapidly, and users are demanding ways to incorporate XML into day-to-day business processes. Companies all over the world are working to produce standardized templates to generate content for a variety of devices, and provide all kinds of business-to-business data communication mechanisms.

There are several ways to work with XML within Oracle, and the XML component is only one of them. The XSQL Servlet, provided with the 9i Application Server, accepts and processes requests to perform database operations specified in special-purpose XML files. It uses its own markup language to manipulate data, execute procedures, and return results in XML format. It can also convert XML into SQL `INSERT`, `UPDATE`, and `DELETE` statements to support direct load of XML into the database, all from a browser interface. To access similar features directly from a PL/SQL program, use the lower-level packages `DBMS_XMLQUERY` and `DBMS_XMLSAVE`. Of course, the PL/SQL Web Toolkit can generate XML using `HTP.print` commands to produce the tags. A frame driver, dynamic page, report from SQL Query, or form based on stored procedure could be used to display XML results of any PL/SQL operation. To use the XSQL Servlet with Portal, you would have to configure it, then reference the full URL of the XSQL Servlet file in a URL component or as a link from any other component. This commentary mostly applies to outgoing XML that you generate from your data. If you have incoming XML that you would like to display as HTML or translate to another format, the XML component is a good choice.

A Very Brief XML Primer

XML stands for eXtensible Markup Language. To run the risk of trivializing it, XML itself is little more than a set of rules about how to label data using markup. The markup is specified in tags, as it is in HTML. However, HTML tags specify how an item is to be displayed, while XML tags specify the semantics of the item—for example, the fact that "01/04/2001" represents the purchase date for a purchase order. XML is quite flexible and can be used to represent data structures equivalent to almost any relational database structures. Its real power derives from the fact that these data structures can be standardized and implemented as a "grammar" representing a consistent way to describe data. Examples of such grammars include markup languages to support mathematical notation, voice response systems, and cell-phone display, as well as industry-specific data transfer. For example, Visa and the Open Financial Exchange (OFX) are working hard to establish XML specifications for such standard business processes as purchasing, invoicing, bank transfers, and stock purchases.

XML works in conjunction with these other resources using the concept of *namespace*, referenced using HTTP syntax. To reference constructs stored in other documents, a namespace is associated with an abbreviation, in the form `xmlns:abbr="URL"`. This allows developers to relate XML documents to other standards and reference those standards using the shorthand provided by the abbreviation.

The XML language itself has essentially no other commands or keywords, so data can be marked up in any way the developer sees fit. Typically, the tags will conform to an existing specification, or the developer will create a custom specification to indicate the purpose and structure of the XML document. This custom specification will either be in the form of a *schema* or a *Document Type Definition* (DTD) as described in the "Validating XML" section to follow. Unlike HTML, XML markup is very strict—tags are case-sensitive; all tags must be terminated with a corresponding closing tag or a closing symbol; and there must be a single root tag enclosing the entire document.

The following is a sample of XML that could represent a purchase order. It is simplified for presentation purposes, and not representative of the above-referenced specifications. It references a business-specific schema to specify the grammar of common objects and ensure the validity of the XML as an "international purchase order." In order to achieve compliance with the standard for XML schemas, it maps the standard for an XML schema instance to the abbreviation *xsi*. Notice that the address can take several forms; addresses in different countries have different characteristics, and the XML schema can support different type definitions within the same element. This particular purchase order consists of only one item, but multiple items may be specified.

NOTE

If you expect to use XML in your business applications, please consult www.w3.org, www.visa.com, or www.ofx.org for more information about emerging standards.

```xml
<?xml version="1.0"?>
<ipo:purchaseOrder
xmlns:xsi="http://www.w3.org/2000/10/XMLSchema-instance"
xmlns:ipo="http://www.example.com/IPO" orderDate="1999-12-01"
xsi:schemaLocation="http://www.example.com/IPO ipo.xsd">
  <shipTo export-code="1" xsi:type="ipo:UK-Address">
    <name>Helen Zoe</name>
    <street>47 Eden Street</street>
    <city>Cambridge</city>
    <postcode>126</postcode>
  </shipTo>
  <billTo xsi:type="ipo:US-Address">
    <name>Robert Smith</name>
    <street>8 Oak Avenue</street>
    <city>Old Town</city>
    <state>AK</state>
    <zip>95819</zip>
  </billTo>
  <Items>
    <item partNum="833-AA">
      <productName>Lapis necklace</productName>
      <quantity>1</quantity>
      <price>99.95</price>
      <ipo:comment>Want this for the holidays!</ipo:comment>
      <shipDate>1999-12-05</shipDate>
    </item>
  </Items>
</ipo:purchaseOrder>
```

NOTE

Just as there are specialized editors for working with and displaying HTML, there are specialized editors for working with XML. XML Spy (www.xmlspy.com) is one such editor. Certain XML examples are taken from XML Spy—reproduced here with permission from Altova.

Validating XML

In order to use an XML document to support a business process, you usually need to perform some level of validation on the XML. There are essentially two levels to XML validation. The first answers the question, "Is this an XML document?" To be considered XML, the document must be *well-formed*, which implies that all tags and quotes are closed, that there is a single root tag, and that no tags overlap each other. These are basic requirements of all XML documents, but they offer no insight into the document's ability to meet its defined purpose. For example, an XML document that represents a purchase order would probably need to have some line items in order to be considered a valid purchase order. Without the line items, the document may indeed be XML, but it does not meet the requirements for further processing.

A *valid* XML document is one that meets its stated purpose, as defined by a DTD or XML schema. These are alternate ways to represent XML data structures. The XML schema is the newer standard, only approved in May 2001. It is much more powerful and flexible than the DTD, and is highly recommended. Portal only supports DTD at this writing, because it was the only approved standard available when the product was originally released.

Below you will find a sample schema used to validate the purchase order XML document shown earlier. The schema is specified entirely in XML, and it includes several different types of elements. Attribute datatypes and valid values are specified explicitly, and we are declaring and reusing datatypes. Because of the complexity of our address types, and because we can reuse the address types in other schemas, they are specified in a separate file (`address.xsd`) and included here by reference. If you examine the schema in detail, you can see some of the design and integrity constraints built into the XML, such as the number of occurrences allowed for the repeating element items, and other "constraints" on the data.

```
<?xml version="1.0" encoding="UTF-8"?>
<schema targetNamespace="http://www.example.com/IPO"
xmlns:ipo="http://www.example.com/IPO"
xmlns="http://www.w3.org/2000/10/XMLSchema">
  <annotation>
    <documentation>
    International Purchase order schema
    </documentation>
  </annotation>
  <!-- include address constructs -->
  <include schemaLocation="address.xsd"/>
  <element name="purchaseOrder" type="ipo:PurchaseOrderType"/>
  <element name="comment" type="string"/>
  <complexType name="PurchaseOrderType">
    <sequence>
      <element name="shipTo" type="ipo:Address"/>
```

```
      <element name="billTo" type="ipo:Address"/>
      <element ref="ipo:comment" minOccurs="0"/>
      <element name="Items" type="ipo:Items"/>
    </sequence>
    <attribute name="orderDate" type="date"/>
  </complexType>
  <complexType name="Items">
    <sequence>
      <element name="item" minOccurs="1" maxOccurs="unbounded">
        <complexType>
          <sequence>
            <element name="productName" type="string"/>
            <element name="quantity">
              <simpleType>
                <restriction base="positiveInteger">
                  <maxExclusive value="100"/>
                </restriction>
              </simpleType>
            </element>
            <element name="price" type="decimal"/>
            <element ref="ipo:comment" minOccurs="0"/>
            <element name="shipDate" type="date" minOccurs="0"/>
          </sequence>
          <attribute name="partNum" type="ipo:Sku"/>
        </complexType>
      </element>
    </sequence>
  </complexType>
  <simpleType name="Sku">
    <restriction base="string">
      <pattern value="\d{3}-[A-Z]{2}"/>
    </restriction>
  </simpleType>
</schema>
```

The following is an equivalent structure, but specified as a DTD. Notice that the DTD uses a completely different syntax, and that there are no options to specify pattern matching or other data restrictions. There is no support for including additional files, and we can't specify different address types. The only datatype is #PCDATA, which stands for "parsed character data," or in other words, a string. Character data (CDATA) is not parsed, and is useful when you need to include special HTML characters, such as & and <>, in the text.

```
<?xml version="1.0" encoding="UTF-8"?>
<!--DTD generated by XML Spy v3.5 NT (http://www.xmlspy.com)-->
<!ELEMENT comment (#PCDATA)>
```

```
<!ELEMENT purchaseOrder (shipTo, billTo, comment?, Items)>
<!ATTLIST purchaseOrder orderDate CDATA #IMPLIED>
<!ELEMENT shipTo (name, street, city)>
<!ELEMENT billTo (name, street, city)>
<!ELEMENT Items (item+)>
<!ELEMENT name (#PCDATA)>
<!ELEMENT street (#PCDATA)>
<!ELEMENT city (#PCDATA)>
<!ELEMENT name (#PCDATA)>
<!ELEMENT street (#PCDATA)>
<!ELEMENT city (#PCDATA)>
<!ELEMENT item (productName, quantity, price, comment?, shipDate?)+>
<!ATTLIST item partNum CDATA #IMPLIED>
<!ELEMENT productName (#PCDATA)>
<!ELEMENT quantity (#PCDATA)>
<!ELEMENT price (#PCDATA)>
<!ELEMENT shipDate (#PCDATA)>
```

Displaying XML

XML is not a display language. Because XML has no formatting tags, the browser has no instructions about how to represent the data. Microsoft Internet Explorer can recognize an XML document, and includes some proprietary code to display the XML data and tags in a color-coded tree structure. This feature is handy when testing XML output from other programs, as it allows collapsing and expanding branches of the tree, but it is not suitable for general-purpose Web display. If you want to display XML data with attractive or functional formatting, you will need to use a related language, extensible Stylesheet Language (XSL).

XSL resembles a programming language more than a markup language—it uses conditional and looping constructs to evaluate each tag and substitute other tags or data as appropriate. An XSL document typically contains HTML tags to create the page structure and format, and XSL commands that extract or process the data contained in the XML document. In some cases, you may need to simply convert XML from one format to another—an XSL style sheet can contain any tags, including XML tags, to generate a document in a different markup language.

Once you have both XML and XSL documents prepared, you will need a process to run the conversion. This process is called an XSL Transformation (XSLT). The XSLT can run at the server and deliver the transformed document to the end user, or the browser can contain an XSLT either as a built-in function or as a plug-in. The standards are still evolving in this area, so you can expect to see the techniques change. For our purposes, the Oracle Portal XML component contains an XSLT so that the user will view the transformed document rather than the raw XML. The exercise includes an example of an XSL style sheet. See www.w3c.org for the full specification.

Developing XML Components

The XML component in the current Portal release validates the supplied XML, translates it with a built-in XSLT, and processes embedded SQL and PL/SQL commands. The wizard allows you to specify

- The XML to process, which can contain <ORACLE> tags

- An XSL style sheet for displaying the XML

- A DTD to validate the XML

An added benefit is that you can allow users to substitute URLs for each of the above documents. You might want to create an XML component for each type of XML document the organization will use. In the component, you would define a fixed style sheet and DTD, allowing users to specify only the URL of the XML page as a parameter. The component could then display any XML resource that complies with the DTD, in an easy to read format. If you allow the style sheet as a parameter, sophisticated users can supply their own style sheets, or you could programmatically build URLs to call the component with different style sheets, depending on the context.

The XML component also offers the ability to embed <ORACLE> tags in the XML code, so you can integrate database data with the transformed XML output. Within the <ORACLE> tags, you can use PL/SQL to generate additional XML tags for the data, as follows:

```
<emplist>
<ORACLE>
DECLARE
  CURSOR emp_cur IS
    SELECT * FROM scott.emp;
BEGIN
  FOR e IN emp_cur LOOP
    HTP.print ('<emp id="'||e.empno||'">');
    HTP.print ('<rownum>'||emp_cur%ROWCOUNT||'</rownum>');
    HTP.print ('<ename>'||e.ename||'</ename>');
    HTP.print ('<job>'||e.job||'</job>');
    ...
    HTP.print ('</emp>');
  END LOOP;
END;
</ORACLE>
</emplist>
```

If you wanted to produce XML for someone else to download—to send an invoice, for example—you would generate the XML and apply a simple style sheet that simply transforms the XML back into XML rather than HTML.

TIP
The style sheet is required, so to preserve XML in the component's output, simply use XML tags instead of HTML in the style sheet.

You can also insert a single SQL statement between the <ORACLE> tags, as you could in the dynamic page, and the formatting works the same way. The generated document (before applying the style sheet) will preserve the <ORACLE> tags and insert the preformatted HTML table containing the results of the query within those tags. Using the XSL style sheet, you can strip out the <ORACLE> tags and transform the table to any format you prefer. The XML component you will build in this section uses all of these features, and is shown in Figure 10-7.

The XML component wizard has nine steps, summarized in the following table:

Step	Name	Description
1	XML Component Name	Specify Name, Display Name, and Application.
2	XML Code	Enter a URL to an XML document or the actual XML. Embed <ORACLE> tags and use bind variables, if desired.
3	PL/SQL Code Segments	Echoes the contents of each set of <ORACLE> tags.
4	XSL Code	Enter a URL to an XSL document or the actual XSL to be applied to the XML code specified in Step 2. (Required)
5	DTD Code	Enter a URL to a DTD or the actual DTD code to validate the XML specified in Step 2. (Optional)
6	Full Page Display Options	The only options are Log Activity and Expire After.
7	Customization Form Display Options	Set up any bind variables, and decide whether to allow the user to choose any URL for the XML, XSL, and DTD.
8	Customization Form Text	Template, Title, and Header/Footer/Help Text apply only to the customization form—the XSL must produce all HTML for the results page.
9	Additional PL/SQL Code	Before and after code also applies only to the customization form.

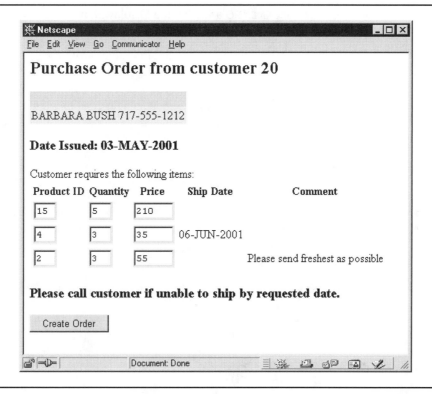

FIGURE 10-7. *An XML component can be used to convert an incoming purchase order to an approval form.*

Exercise 10.6: Accept XML Purchase Orders

This stylized example assumes that we have somehow allowed our customers to upload XML purchase orders to our site, and that they have agreed to a standard format that includes a SELECT statement enclosed in <ORACLE> tags. With the exception of the SELECT statement, the example is not too far-fetched. So long as you and your business partners can agree to a standard represented by either a DTD or an XML schema, you can use an XML component to read and process documents generated by any external (or even internal) system. We will use some advanced style sheet techniques to accept the data and format it as an HTML form. The resulting form's action procedure will insert the order details into the CUSTOMER_ORDERS and ORDER_LINE_ITEMS tables, and call our order form component so a salesperson can validate and save the order.

    1. Create a new XML component in APP_SALES.

2. Name the component XML_PO and give it a Display Name of Process Purchase Orders.

3. In the XML Code window, type or paste the following XML:

```
File ex 1006.xml
<?xml version="1.0" encoding="UTF-8"?>
<purchaseOrder orderDate="03-MAY-2001">
  <customerID>20</customerID>
    <oracle>
      select customer_name, phone
      from   corp_site.customers
      where  customer_id = 20
    </oracle>
  <Items>
    <item productID="15">
      <quantity>2</quantity>
      <price>210</price>
    </item>
    <item productID="4">
      <quantity>3</quantity>
      <price>35</price>
      <shipDate>06-JUN-2001</shipDate>
    </item>
    <item productID="2">
      <quantity>3</quantity>
      <price>55</price>
      <itemcomment>Please send freshest as possible</itemcomment>
    </item>
  </Items>
</purchaseOrder>
```

4. Click the Next button and verify that the SELECT statement appears in the PL/SQL Code Segments text area.

5. On the next page, enter the following XSL code:

```
File ex 1006.xsl
<?xml version="1.0" encoding="UTF-8"?>
<xsl:stylesheet version="1.0" xmlns:xsl="http://www.w3.org/1999/XSL/Transform" >
<xsl:template match="purchaseOrder">
<html>
<body>
<form action="CORP_SITE.process_order" target="_new">
<h2> Purchase Order from customer
    <xsl:value-of select="customerID"/>
</h2>
<input type="hidden" name="p_custid">
    <xsl:attribute name="value">
```

```
            <xsl:value-of select="customerID"/>
        </xsl:attribute>
</input>
<xsl:value-of select="oracle"/>
<h3> Date Issued: <xsl:value-of select="@orderDate"/> </h3>
Customer requires the following items:
<table>
  <th>Product ID</th> <th>Quantity</th> <th>Price</th> <th>Ship Date</th>
  <th>Comment</th>
<xsl:for-each select="Items/item">
  <tr>
    <td> <input type="text" name="p_prodid" size="3">
          <xsl:attribute name="value"> <xsl:value-of select="@productID"/>
          </xsl:attribute>
        </input>
    </td>
    <td> <input type="text" name="p_qty" size="3">
          <xsl:attribute name="value"> <xsl:value-of select="quantity"/>
          </xsl:attribute>
        </input>
    </td>
    <td> <input type="text" name="p_price" size="6">
          <xsl:attribute name="value"> <xsl:value-of select="price"/>
          </xsl:attribute>
        </input>
    </td>
    <td> <xsl:value-of select="shipDate"/> <br/> </td>
    <td> <xsl:value-of select="itemcomment"/> <br/> </td>
  </tr>
</xsl:for-each>
</table>
<h3> Please call customer if unable to ship by requested date. </h3>
<input type="submit" value="Create Order" />
</form>
</body>
</html>
</xsl:template>
</xsl:stylesheet>
```

NOTE
The XSL displays the XML data in a form, so that the values can be passed to the procedure. Notice how the XSL retrieves the values, and how these values are nested within a special case of the <INPUT> tag. The <INPUT> tag has to be constructed in this way to pass the values from the XML as attributes, setting the default value for each field. You could use similar techniques to produce a link or image tag from the associated XML.

6. Skip the DTD Code and Full Page Display Options pages, and on the Customization Form Display Options page, remove the checkmarks under Formatting Options for XSL URL and DTD URL.

7. Click Finish and then Run to test your component.

NOTE
The process_order procedure relies on the order form, which should be named MDFORM_ORDERS. If you named your form something else, you must edit the SELECT INTO statement that retrieves the module_id in process_order to use your name.

If you like, review the contents of the process_order procedure to see how the values are accepted and how to redirect to the order form component. (You may view this code using your favorite PL/SQL IDE, the Portal Navigator, or by simply examining the process_order.sql file in the distribution directory.) The procedure is relatively simple, and to some extent bypasses a few of our business rules. In a production application, you would probably need a trigger on the ORDER_LINE_ITEMS table to check for valid pricing, and an exception handler to deal with invalid prices or items.

The ideal way to use a component such as this one is to allow users to specify the URL so that they can retrieve and validate XML documents posted by their customers, and process the orders as they are posted. Even better would be to set it up programmatically, so that the URL is passed as a parameter. This way, you could set up a report of pending purchase orders with an embedded link to the XML component. When the user clicks the link, the purchase order is processed in the background and the user has only to confirm the resulting order. The only problem with this approach is that in the current release, the <ORACLE> tags are not supported when using the URL field. They only work if the XML is pasted into the component.

To test this feature, you can remove the <ORACLE> tags from our XML above, editing the other details if you wish, and save the XML as a file in a directory accessible to Apache. Run the component with the Customize link and specify the URL to your new XML file. We won't take you through all the details of this kind of system, because you would have to be able to set up a mechanism (such as a database table) to hold the URLs to the pending purchase orders, and a storage location for the test files. It would be a complex setup, but hopefully these examples will get you started on such a system if you expect to have this kind of requirement.

URL Component

The URL component is nothing more than a way to get a URL incorporated into your system. The wizard simply asks for a URL and creates the component. Users may customize the component to display a different URL, if given permission. As with the XML component, any custom text or PL/SQL applies only to the customization form.

The possibilities for using this component are as varied as the number of URLs on the Web, and we could not possibly do justice to the variety of needs addressed by it in this book. URL components can be published as portlets, but be careful with this feature. If the targeted Web resource is slow, large, or contains conflicting code, it could halt or ruin your portal page.

Conclusion

In this chapter, we have looked at some of the more programming-oriented components. These help when your requirements are not particularly suited for forms, reports, or graphical display, and they offer a measure of flexibility when building in advanced functionality. They represent the highest level of customization possible in the Portal environment, without resorting to developing your own portlets from scratch. This will be the subject of our next chapter, the Portal Development Kit.

CHAPTER
11

The Portal
Development Kit

ou have now seen just about everything you can do in the Portal development environment. You have built forms, reports, charts, menus, hierarchies, dynamic pages, and all the other component types. The stock components meet most of the requirements you would come across in a typical application environment, but you have also seen that each type of component has a limitation or two that might preclude its use in your application. You might want more control over the interface, you may need to access existing applications, or you might have some complex requirement to combine a variety of Web resources into a portlet. You may just be more comfortable writing 3GL code. In any case, the Portal Development Kit (PDK) provides a framework to fit completely customized applications into the portal.

At the core of the PDK is a set of rules about how custom portlet code must interact with Portal. The two main "flavors" of the PDK are PDK-PL/SQL, implemented entirely in PL/SQL, and PDK-Java, which uses Java for its call interface. They have similar capabilities, and both can access either Web resources or database services. Both can call Java programs, because Java programs can be called from PL/SQL if they are loaded into the database. Portal accesses PDK-PL/SQL applications by executing PL/SQL stored packages, and it accesses PDK-Java applications using HTTP calls to the application's main Java servlet. Because of the different invocation methods, PDK-PL/SQL applications are known as *database providers*, and PDK-Java applications are known as *Web providers*. There are two other minor pieces in the PDK tool kit. URL Services allow the PDK-Java to display portal content written in other languages, such as Active Server Pages (ASP) or Perl, also using HTTP. Integrating Technologies is a collection of supporting tools for administration and development within the PDK.

The PDK is not just a simple call interface with supporting tools but, more accurately, it's a constantly evolving shared code suite. The entire regimen is documented at the home site for Portal developers: portalstudio.oracle.com. The site is essential to developing custom portlets, as evidenced by its Portal home page "Community" link (in 3.0.9). It offers documentation of the application programming interface (API) in both languages, definitions of terms, and downloads for many types of sample portlets. The PDK community represents the evolution in software development made possible by the Internet. Rather than just offering a development environment with fixed functionality and annual updates, Oracle provides a framework and a set of resources with which to extend the product. Because the technology is constantly evolving, new PDK "versions" are released monthly.

The Portal Studio web site also provides mechanisms for sharing ideas, problems, and code. You can publish custom portlets here to be shared with others, download freeware portlets, and get information about Portal partners—companies who produce and license portlets designed to work with Portal. Some examples of downloadable code include portlets that you can configure to link your Portal to such external applications as Microsoft Exchange and Lotus Notes.

Portal Internals

If you've decided to try your hand at custom portlet writing, you'll need some background on how the Portal works before you start coding. So far in this book, we've been able to almost ignore the processes that build the pages and request portlets, because Portal takes care of all those tasks when you use built-in components. In this section, we'll walk through the background processes to assemble portlets and display them on pages, in an effort to prepare you to work within this framework.

Apache Listener and the PL/SQL Module

To begin, let's review the process, illustrated in Figure 11-1, by which PL/SQL Web pages are executed and delivered to the browser with Oracle 9i Application Server. First, the browser makes a request using a URL like the following:

```
http://myserver/pls/DAD/some_page
```

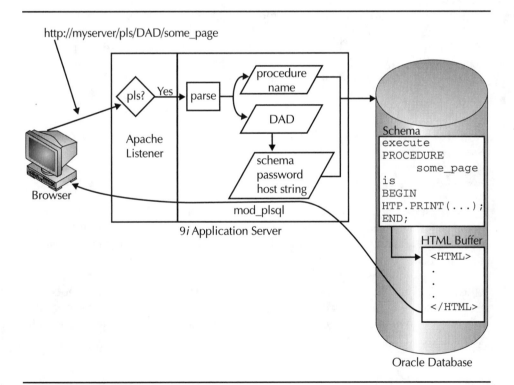

FIGURE 11-1. *PL/SQL page delivery with 9i AS*

The request is then routed over the Internet or corporate network to `myserver`, where the application server is running. The Apache listener, an HTTP server, handles all requests that come in over the requested port (in this case, the default port of 80 was requested). Apache then parses the rest of the request to decide how it should be handled. Because the request contains the string `pls`, Apache recognizes this as a PL/SQL request and passes execution responsibility to the PL/SQL module (mod_plsql). (The actual string to signal the request is configurable, but we will assume the default configuration for this discussion.)

mod_plsql then looks at the remainder of the string. The first component is the database access descriptor (`DAD`), which gives information about how mod_plsql is to connect to the database to execute the request. The DAD is also configurable, and you can have several DADs in any 9i AS installation. For the Single Sign-On (SSO) authentication method used by Portal, the DAD contains the username, password, and connect string of the Portal repository schema. The Portal page process initiates with this database connection, and accepts responsibility for end-user authentication.

Once a database connection is established, mod_plsql attempts to execute the PL/SQL procedure given by the last part of the URL—in this case, `some_page`. If no procedure is specified in the last part of the URL, mod_plsql looks for a default procedure name, also configurable, and runs that. The procedure executes and sends its results (generated using the PL/SQL Web Toolkit) to an HTML buffer. When the procedure completes, the contents of the HTML buffer are delivered back to the browser via mod_plsql and Apache, and the page is displayed on the browser screen.

Portal Page Processing

Now let's see what Portal adds to the mix. The default URL to display the Portal home page looks like this:

```
http://myserver/pls/portal30
```

The last part of the URL is `portal30`, which is the DAD associated with the Portal repository schema. The URL does not need to specify a procedure to execute, because the Portal DAD has been configured to call the procedure named `home` by default. As shown in Figure 11-2, the `home` procedure is actually a redirection to a Java servlet known as the Parallel Page Engine (PPE). (You may have noticed that the URL changes as the Portal home page loads.) Before redirecting, the `home` procedure first identifies the user's default home page as specified in Portal. If the user has not logged in, a login request is issued to identify the user. Then it calls the PPE with the correct page ID for the user.

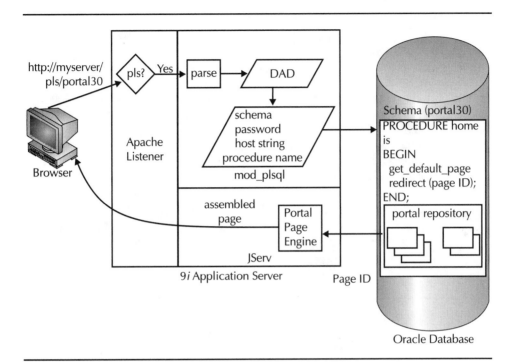

FIGURE 11-2. *PORTAL30.home (shown as pseudocode) redirects to the PPE*

NOTE
You may explicitly call a page using the PPE as well, in order to allow public access without a login. Simply refer to one of the following URLs, substituting your page ID for nn. To find out your page ID, click the page link in the Navigator and examine the URL when the page displays. Page IDs containing commas indicate a tab ID on the page.

```
http://myserver/pls/portal30/!PORTAL30.wwpob_page_util.redirect?_pageid=nn&_mode=3
http://myserver/servlet/page?_pageid=nn&_dad=portal30&_schema=PORTAL30&_mode=3
```

The PPE is the core of the Portal technology—it is responsible for requesting portlet content, building pages, and validating Single Sign-On security. When the PPE receives a request for a Portal page, the first thing it does is access the Portal repository to obtain the page definition. The page definition (metadata) comes in two parts. The first part defines the *portlet instance*, or its usage on the page. It identifies the source and unique ID of the portlet, as well as the path where user-defined preferences might be stored for this instantiation of the portlet. The second part of the metadata is the page description, used to construct the skeleton of the page that will display the portlets. It contains generated HTML and JavaScript to render the page banner, and HTML tables containing "placeholders" to be filled with the portlet content as it is received.

The processes that request the portlets work in parallel to retrieve the portlets, hence the name Parallel Page Engine. When requesting the actual content, a *portlet runtime record* is sent to the provider to communicate details of the current environment to the provider. The page is held in a data structure in memory until all of the portlets are either retrieved or timed out. If any of the portlets on the page require authentication from the SSO server, the PPE sends the SSO Login page first. After authentication is complete, the assembled page goes to the browser. This process is illustrated in Figure 11-3.

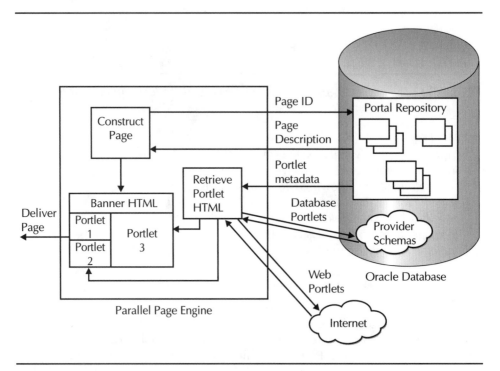

FIGURE 11-3. *The PPE assembles a page for display*

Configuring Custom Portlets

When you are ready to deploy your own portlets, you must register them with Portal so that the PPE can identify them, and so users can add them to their pages. The registration details differ depending on the implementation (database vs. Web), but the concepts are the same in both cases. The database implementation uses PDK-PL/SQL; the Web implementation uses PDK-Java. Both require that a *provider*, essentially a software-based list of portlets and implementation details, has been registered with Portal. A provider's job is to send the portlet metadata and content when a portlet is requested as in Figure 11-3, and to make a secure list of portlets available for adding to pages.

To add a portlet to a page, it must be listed in the Portlet Repository, the content area that is displayed when you access the Add Portlets window (shown in Figure 11-4 for reference). The Portlet Repository is organized by provider, and each provider offers a *portlet list* subject to the privileges of the current user. When you created content areas and applications, they were automatically

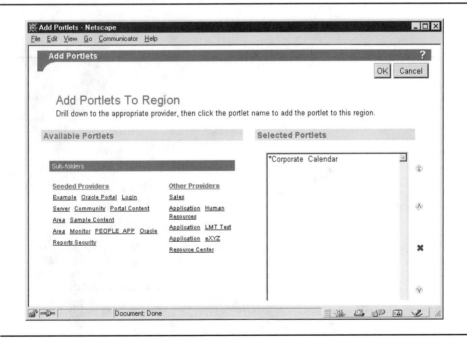

FIGURE 11-4. *The Add Portlets window contains portlets organized by registered provider*

registered as providers if you checked the Expose as Provider or Publish to Portal check box. For custom applications, you will need to create and register the provider, which is coded as a PL/SQL package in PDK-PL/SQL and as an XML file in PDK-Java. This package is like a control center—it knows about all of the portlets and their implementation details.

When users choose a portlet to be displayed on a page, Portal requires descriptive information about the portlet, such as its ID, name and display name, and whether it supports a preview mode, "Edit Defaults" customization, or end-user customization. All of this information is delivered by the provider in the form of a *portlet record*. Portal records the provider ID, portlet ID, page information, and customization information each time a portlet is assigned to a page.

Since users can copy Portal pages after adding portlets, you may need to specify what should happen to your portlet during a page copy operation—for example, should the defaults be copied or reset to their original values?

All of these functions are implemented in the portlet provider, which usually routes the requests to separate packages or URLs that implement the portlets. The portlet packages contain the actual code to show and work with the portlet, and any portlet-specific security or preference information. Portlets can be displayed in one of several modes, described in Table 11-1.

Mode	Purpose
mode_show	Shows the portlet
mode_show_details	Optional full-page mode; accessed by clicking the portlet title
mode_show_about	Produces an About page for the portlet; link is on portlet header
mode_show_edit	Displays the customization form; access from Customize link on the portlet header
mode_show_help	Displays a Help screen accessible from a link on the portlet header
mode_show_edit_defaults	Sets default preferences in page edit mode
mode_show_preview	Shows a preview in the Add Portlets utility or Portlet Repository

TABLE 11-1. *Potential Portlet Display Modes*

Given this framework, the generic process for developing custom portlets will involve the following steps. All steps must be completed to deploy custom portlets and you may modify the portlet code at any time.

- Write the portlet code, in PL/SQL stored procedure(s) or Java, or determine the URL or database path to existing code. If you are writing new code, you may wish to use the APIs described in this chapter to format the portlet according to page style settings.

- Create a provider—a PL/SQL package for database providers or an XML file for Web providers—to act as a communication channel between Portal and the portlet code.

- Register the provider with Portal.

- Add the portlet(s) to Portal pages.

Database Services (PDK-PL/SQL)

When you use PL/SQL to produce custom portlets, you will typically create a package for each portlet and a single provider package to handle the portlet requests. This separation of code is not entirely necessary, but is useful for code maintenance. The Portal Studio Web site offers several sample PL/SQL portlet and provider packages, but you are not bound to their implementation. As long as your code returns the expected datatypes (as we will enumerate) and produces portlet content, it will work within the framework. We will provide some alternate samples for you to evaluate and implement—and feel free to improve upon our techniques!

PL/SQL Provider API

Before we begin to look at the code for portlets and providers, we must describe the API that you will reference as you build your custom portlet application. The API defines the required datatypes and provides utilities for handling security, errors, portlet rendering, and end-user customization. The API is owned by the Portal schema, but you will most likely develop your portlet and provider packages using a separate schema. To make the necessary API packages available to a development schema, you must run the `provsyns.sql` script found in `$IAS_ HOME/portal30/admin/plsql/wwc`. (It may change with each version of Portal.) Log in to SQL*Plus as the Portal schema owner and type the following, substituting your development schema for `PROVIDER_SCHEMA` (and the appropriate `$IAS_HOME` path):

```
@C:\oracle\isuites\portal30\admin\plsql\wwc\provsyns.sql <PROVIDER_SCHEMA>
```

Provider API Types

The main API package for providers is `WWPRO_API_PROVIDER`, which defines types, constants, and exceptions that the provider will use to communicate with the PPE. Each type of request for portlet information has a corresponding record type. These are described below.

PORTLET_RECORD The `PORTLET_RECORD` is requested during the Add Portlet process, when editing the page to which it is added, and when displaying the Portlet Repository.

```
TYPE portlet_record IS RECORD
(
    id                      INTEGER,         --unique ID within provider
    provider_id             INTEGER,         --provider ID, supplied by PPE
    name                    VARCHAR2(30),    --unique name, no special characters
    title                   VARCHAR2(200),   --for portlet and page headers
    description             VARCHAR2(200),   --full text description
    image_url               VARCHAR2(1024),
    thumbnail_image_url     VARCHAR2(1024),
    help_url                VARCHAR2(1024),  --URL to use for Help Link
    timeout                 INTEGER,         --# of seconds before timing out request
    timeout_msg             VARCHAR2(200),   --override to default timeout message
    implementation_style    INTEGER,         --Web or Database
    implementation_owner    VARCHAR2(2000),  --schema owner of portlet package
    implementation_name     VARCHAR2(2000),  --portlet package name
    content_type            INTEGER,         --XML or HTML
    api_version             INTEGER,         --for version compatibility; always 1 now
    has_show_edit           BOOLEAN,         --show an Edit link in portlet header?
    has_show_edit_defaults  BOOLEAN,         --show Edit Defaults link in Page editor?
    has_show_preview        BOOLEAN,         --does the portlet have a preview mode?
                                             --if false, show portlet as preview
    language                VARCHAR2(30),    --NLS language of portlet content
    preference_store_path   VARCHAR2(2000),  --location of preferences for export
    created_on              DATE,
    created_by              VARCHAR2(30),
    last_updated_on         DATE,
    last_updated_by         VARCHAR2(30)
);
```

PORTLET_TABLE The `PORTLET_TABLE` is used when listing all of the provider's portlets in the Add Portlets window and the Portlet Repository. It consists of a PL/SQL table of `PORTLET_RECORD`.

```
TYPE portlet_table IS TABLE OF portlet_record
        INDEX BY BINARY_INTEGER;
```

PORTLET_PARAMETER_RECORD When a portlet needs to accept parameters, it must describe them in the following record format. The datatypes can be one of the following system-defined constants: STRING, NUMBER, INTEGER, CURRENCY and

DATE. The usage_type can be used internally by the portlet code as an additional descriptor for the parameter.

```
TYPE portlet_parameter_record IS RECORD
(
  name          VARCHAR2(30),    --parameter name
  datatype      VARCHAR2(30) DEFAULT STRING_TYPE,
  usage_type    VARCHAR2(30) DEFAULT PORTLET_PARM_PARAMETER,
  description   VARCHAR2(200),   --text description of parameter
  language      VARCHAR2(30)     --NLS language of parameter
);
```

PORTLET_PARAMETER_TABLE   Since there could be more than one parameter, the parameter list is passed as a PL/SQL table.

```
TYPE portlet_parameter_table IS TABLE OF portlet_parameter_record
          INDEX BY BINARY_INTEGER;
```

PORTLET_RUNTIME_RECORD   When a page containing the portlet is displayed, the PPE creates a PORTLET_RUNTIME_RECORD and passes it (via the provider) to the show method for the portlet. The purpose of this record is to inform the portlet of the details of how and where it is being called, and to allow the portlet to set up any caching information. The exec_mode identifies what sort of content the user wants to see—that is, the customization form, the portlet itself, a full-page view of the content, the Edit Details window, or Help, About, or Preview mode. It is numeric, but you can use the keywords shown in Table 11-1 to identify the requested mode, as they are defined as named constants in WWPRO_API_PROVIDER.

```
TYPE portlet_runtime_record IS RECORD
(
  portlet_id          NUMBER,           --unique ID of portlet
  provider_id         NUMBER,           --provider's internal ID
  node_id             NUMBER,           --provider's node ID
  reference_path      VARCHAR2(100),    --path where preferences are stored
  language            VARCHAR2(30),     --NLS language of browser
  exec_mode           NUMBER,           --mode of request
  back_page_url       VARCHAR2(4096),   --use to generate "Back" links
  page_url            VARCHAR2(4096),   --URL of page displaying the portlet
  page_type           VARCHAR2(200),    --type of page
  has_title_region    BOOLEAN,          --show the portlet header
  has_border          BOOLEAN,          --show the border
  caching_key         VARCHAR2(55),     --key for validation-based caching
  caching_level       VARCHAR2(30),     --SYSTEM or USER-level caching
  caching_period      NUMBER            --time for expiration-based caching
);
```

PORTLET_INSTANCE_RECORD   The portlet instance record is the metadata used when constructing the page. When a user adds a portlet to a page, Portal stores the relationship in a table, WWPOB_PORTLET_INSTANCE$, which is a child of the main page information table (WWPOB_PAGE$). When the PPE constructs the page, it accesses these tables to determine which portlets to load.

```
TYPE portlet_instance_record IS RECORD
(
    provider_id             NUMBER
    portlet_id              NUMBER
    reference_path          VARCHAR2(100)
    page_type               VARCHAR2(200)
);
```

COPY_PORTLET_RECORD   This record type is used when a user wants to copy a page. The main issue when copying pages is how to handle any user-defined customizations. Each portlet instance can have its own preference path, so users can set preferences differently for each page on which the portlet is displayed. If you allow customization, you will set the new preference path and add any customization in the copy_portlet procedure.

```
TYPE copy_portlet_record IS RECORD
(
    provider_id             NUMBER,         --internal Provider ID
    portlet_id              NUMBER,         --unique portlet ID
    srcReferencePath        VARCHAR2(100),  --original preference path
    dstReferencePath        VARCHAR2(100)   --new preference path
);
```

COOKIE_RECORD   This is a record structure containing the details for a cookie. You may retrieve and set cookie values within the portlet.

```
TYPE cookie_record IS RECORD
(
    cookie_name         VARCHAR2(4096),
    cookie_content      VARCHAR2(4096),
    cookie_domain       VARCHAR2(200),
    cookie_path         VARCHAR2(200),
    cookie_expires      DATE,
    cookie_update       BOOLEAN,
    provider_id         INTEGER,
);
```

COOKIE_TABLE This is a PL/SQL table containing a list of cookies.

```
TYPE cookie_table IS TABLE OF cookie_record INDEX BY BINARY_INTEGER;
```

Required Provider Functions
The functions defined by the API allow the provider to send information to the PPE about itself and about each portlet. Every provider implementation must contain these functions, and they should be able to respond to requests for all portlets serviced by the provider. Usually the provider package simply routes the request to the appropriate portlet package, but it can contain the actual code to respond to the request. Each function is described below, and in the sections to follow, we will show examples of their usage. The bulleted lists describe the expected parameters for each function, and the return datatype and possible exceptions follow. All parameters are IN parameters unless otherwise noted.

get_api_version Provided for compatibility with future versions—for now, it always returns the below-named constant that evaluates to 1.

- p_provider_id (INTEGER) Used to identify the provider—not necessary unless you are combining multiple providers in a single package (not recommended).

   Returns: API_VERSION_1

get_portlet Retrieves the portlet record for the portlet repository and the Add Portlet utility.

- p_provider_id (INTEGER) Used to identify the provider.
- p_portlet_id (INTEGER) Unique ID of portlet for which information is requested.
- p_language (VARCHAR2) Language of browser making the request.

   Returns: PORTLET_RECORD
   Exceptions: PORTLET_NOT_FOUND_EXCEPTION if the requested portlet ID is not available from this provider.

get_portlet_list Retrieves a list, using get_portlet, of all available portlets from this provider. p_security_level is a Boolean value that indicates whether or not each portlet in the list should first be subjected to a security check. When it is false, all portlets are to be displayed. This is used to save processing overhead when the logged-in user is a portal administrator or when the request is internal. When users add portlets to their pages, `p_security_level` will be true, so they will only see the portlets that they have permission to access.

- `p_provider_id` (INTEGER)
- `p_start_row` (INTEGER)
- `p_rowcount` (INTEGER)
- `p_language` (VARCHAR2)
- `p_security_level` (BOOLEAN)
- `p_type` (INTEGER)   The type of list required; always `LIST_PORTLET` (a constant) for custom providers.

Returns: `PORTLET_TABLE`

is_portlet_runnable   Allows you to specify whether a portlet can run. You may use any of the security APIs to identify the currently logged-on user and check for group membership and privilege levels. If the user is allowed to view the portlet, you may alternatively return `true`—`false`.

- `p_portlet_instance` (PORTLET_INSTANCE_RECORD)

Returns: Boolean
Exceptions: `PORTLET_NOT_FOUND_EXCEPTION`

describe_portlet_parameters   Any time the PPE needs to verify parameters, it will make a call to this procedure.

- `p_provider_id` (INTEGER)
- `p_portlet_id` (INTEGER)
- `p_language` (VARCHAR2)

Returns: `PORTLET_PARAMETER_TABLE`

Required Provider Procedures
Of the API procedures, the one that does the majority of the work is `show_portlet`. It handles the display for all show modes, and is really "the portlet." The remaining

procedures are more like event handlers—they allow you to add custom processing or respond to events in the portlet and provider life cycle.

show_portlet   This procedure displays the content. It can contain PL/SQL Web Toolkit procedures, API rendering calls, calls to other URLs, and even calls to Java classes in the database. Portal offers a set of utilities that you can use to create your portlet and customization form in the current page style. The procedure must respond to each of the display modes that it claims to support in the portlet record returned by get_portlet or it will produce an error. The runtime record specifies user preferences, such as whether to show the portlet's border or banner and communicates the customization preference path to the portlet code. It also contains context information about where the portlet is being displayed and the browser language.

- p_portlet_record (PORTLET_RUNTIME_RECORD IN OUT)

register_provider   This is an event handler used to set up default paths and any other preferences when the provider is registered. Provide a NULL statement if there is no initialization for the provider.

- p_provider_id (INTEGER)

deregister_provider   The opposite of register_provider, this event handler allows you to clean up any settings you created upon registering the provider. Use it when sharing your provider with other Portal installations, or just code a NULL statement if there was no initialization for the provider.

- p_provider_id (INTEGER)

do_login   Allows you to read and write cookies before the portlet is displayed. When you register the provider, you can specify whether login processing should occur every time the portlet is displayed, or only the first time in each session. Read cookies using the input table p_browser_cookies, and set them using the output table p_provider_cookies. You cannot issue any other HTML output from the do_login procedure.

- p_provider_id (INTEGER)
- p_browser_cookies (COOKIE_TABLE)
- p_provider_cookies (COOKIE_TABLE OUT)

register_portlet   Similar to the `register_provider` routine, this event handler allows you to set up the preference path and any other initialization features when the portlet is added to a page.

- `p_portlet_instance (PORTLET_INSTANCE_RECORD)`

deregister_portlet   Similar to the `deregister_provider` routine, this event handler allows you to clean up customization when the portlet is removed from a page.

- `p_portlet_instance (PORTLET_INSTANCE_RECORD)`

copy_portlet   In this procedure, you will perform the steps necessary to support the new instance of a portlet when a user copies a page. You must create a new preference path with the appropriate default settings for the new portlet instance.

- `p_copy_portlet_info (COPY_PORTLET_RECORD)`

The Portlet Package(s)

The portlet code renders the actual portlet content and communicates with the portlet provider. In this code, usually developed as a package, you will have procedures and functions that answer the requests from the portlet provider, constructing the necessary record types or output to send to the page. You may call existing applications or write your display code within the package itself. The beauty of the Portal API is that you have all of Portal's user interface (UI) routines available to render your portlet using the page styles defined by the end user. With a little effort, your portlet can be indistinguishable from the built-in components.

NOTE
Portal includes many API packages, each with a specific purpose. To clarify, when we refer to the PDK-PL/SQL or provider API, we are referring to the types, functions, and procedures defined in WWPRO_API_PROVIDER and described in the previous section. Other components of the Portal API include user interface (UI) tools, security tools, and content area tools.

The portlet package will contain custom logic to determine the contents of the portlet. This logic comes from your requirements, and we can only provide sample content here. The remaining procedures and functions are dictated by the PDK-PL/SQL call interface; you must be able to respond to each of the calls issued by the PPE via the provider package. You will have to return the PORTLET_ RECORD when requested, and display the portlet's content in each of the modes you have decided to support. The names of the procedures, functions, and parameters do not have to match the PDK-PL/SQL API exactly, because the provider routes the request. When you write the provider package, you will specify the exact API names and add your custom calls to each of the portlet packages. All portlets should support a portlet display mode, and you have the option to display a customization form, a full-page mode, Help, About, and an Edit Defaults feature. You may use the Portal UI API packages, described in Table 11-2, to assist with these display modes.

NOTE
In the examples to follow, we do not qualify the API routines with the name of the Portal schema owner. The provsyns.sql *script only builds synonyms for* WWUI_API_PORTLET *and* WWUI_ API_PORTLET_DIALOG. *If you use any of the others, you will need to prefix their names with your portal schema name (for example,* PORTAL30.WWUI_API_UTIL) *or create additional synonyms for them.*

Package Name	Purpose
WWUI_API_PORTLET	Main package for rendering portlets; open and close the portlet, draw text in correct style
WWUI_API_PORTLET_DIALOG	Renders customization form objects; use is optional—could draw and format text directly with WWUI_API_UTIL
WWUI_API_UTIL	Contains functions to render the styles for customization forms
WWUI_API_STATUS	Produces a page to display error or status messages
WWUI_API_PROGRESS	A utility to display "Step n of m" object; used internally
WWUI_API_BODY	Displays a page body; usually for internal use, but may be helpful for full-page display
WWUI_API_TABSET	Displays tab pages; mostly for internal use

TABLE 11-2. *Portal UI API Packages*

We will concentrate in this section on the routine that produces the guts of the portlet. Recall that the `show` routine is responsible not just for drawing the portlet, but for displaying the customization form and other supporting pages. The full text of a portlet package, showing the entire PDK-PL/SQL—required implementation, will follow the discussion of the major `show` concepts.

Rendering the Portlet

Your job in the `show` routine is to display the custom content within the Portal framework. You must support any end-user preferences and decide which links to show in the portlet header. Because users can customize page regions and elect not to display portlet headers and/or borders, you will need to check these settings in the `PORTLET_RUNTIME_RECORD`, and then comply with the user preferences. You will also need to call `get_portlet` to obtain the portlet title and other pertinent details. If the user has requested it, you will display a header with the appropriate links for your portlet. You will then add your content in any way you see fit. If the portlet is to be displayed with borders, you must open and close the border. All of these steps are supported with the API packages listed in Table 11-2.

Portlet Header   To see if the portlet is to be displayed with a header, check the value of the `PORTLET_RUNTIME_RECORD.has_title_region` setting. If it is true, you will need to display the portlet header using `WWUI_API_PORTLET.draw_portlet_header`. This procedure has the following specification:

```
WWUI_API_PORTLET.draw_portlet_header
    (
        p_provider_id     --provider ID, obtain from portlet_runtime_record
       ,p_portlet_id      --portlet ID, obtain from portlet_runtime_record
       ,p_title           --obtained from get_portlet
       ,p_has_details     --set to true if you have a full-page mode
       ,p_has_edit        --set to true if you have a customization form
       ,p_has_help        --set to true if you have a help page
       ,p_has_about       --set to true if you have an about page
       ,p_referencepath   --obtain from portlet_runtime_record
       ,p_back_url        --obtain from portlet_runtime_record
    );
```

Portlet Content   Before you write any HTML within the portlet, you must open it for write. The procedure to open the portlet accepts a single Boolean parameter to indicate whether to draw borders around the portlet. You may pass the value of `show_border` from the portlet runtime record, as follows:

```
WWUI_API_PORTLET.open_portlet (P_PORTLET_RUNTIME.has_border);
```

The remaining code of the portlet is up to you. The API functions to format text using the page styles are described in the next section. You must close the portlet after you produce your custom content, using the `close_portlet` procedure:

```
WWUI_API_PORTLET.close_portlet;
```

NOTE
The code found in many of the PDK samples seems to indicate that the `close_portlet` routine is only required for a portlet with borders, but `close_portlet` is necessary to close the table data cell containing the portlet. Without it, the page displays as a blank page in Netscape and could have problems in Internet Explorer.

Formatting Text

The `WWUI_API_PORTLET` package allows you to format your text in the user's page style. It contains functions that return the user's style settings for both regular portlet text and portlet headings. You will use these in combination with the PL/SQL Web Toolkit to produce the portlet text. The code fragments below indicate how these would be used to display headings and text within the portlet. Each function accepts two arguments: the string to be formatted and the style level to apply. The styles are implemented using Cascading Style Sheets (CSS), and each function simply appends the appropriate CSS tags to the text string. As a shortcut, you could view the HTML source of any page that uses the styles you need, then manually replicate the style tags in your print routines.

```
-- attach the Portlet Heading3 style to the string,
-- then display the string on the page within a table header:
v_header := WWUI_API_PORTLET.portlet_heading( 'News', 3 );
HTP.p('<TH>'||v_header||'</TH>');
-- the above code could also be accomplished in a single step:
HTP.tableHeader ( WWUI_API_PORTLET.portlet_heading ( 'News', 3 ) );
-- create the string, then attach the Portlet Text3 style
-- to the string and display in a table cell:
v_text := 'The first News item of the day';
HTP.tableData ( WWUI_API_PORTLET.portlet_text ( v_text, 3 ) );
```

The remaining functions in `WWUI_API_PORTLET` allow you retrieve formatting information for the portlet header text and background color, and the portlet body background color, as listed below. Use these in the same way as the preceding examples. There are functions to help with subheader formatting, but no utility to create one, as with `draw_portlet_header`. The subheader would be created manually, using the style obtained from `portlet_subheadertext` nested within a table data cell.

- `portlet_headertext`

- `portlet_subheadertext`

- `portlet_headerlink`

- `portlet_subheaderlink`

- `portlet_subheader_color`

- `portlet_header_color`

- `portlet_body_color`

- `draw_xml_header` (for use with portlets displaying XML)

Enabling End-User Customization

You can allow users to change the portlet's display features, such as the title, or to provide runtime parameters that will affect the portlet's content. To enable any of these modifications, you will have to do the following:

- Create a preference path when users add the portlet to a page (in the `register_portlet` procedure). The preference path links the instance of portlet to the saved preferences.

- Register the names of the preferences that you will allow for customization (also in the `register_portlet` procedure).

- Add data entry fields on the `MODE_SHOW_EDIT` page (the customization form) for the parameters that will be modifiable.

- Create a procedure that will accept the values from the customization form, save them to the preference path, and return the user to the main page.

- Modify your code to use the new parameters.

The packages involved in creating, setting, and identifying user preferences are `WWPRE_API_NAME` and `WWPRE_API_VALUE`, explained in the next few sections.

NOTE
When enabling end-user customization, you will have to explicitly grant EXECUTE permission on the portlet package to the schema you are using for Portal users (usually PORTAL30_PUBLIC). This ensures that Portal can execute the "save preferences" procedure, which is not registered as part of the provider package.

Preference Path   The preference path is made up of a constant name that you determine, concatenated to the reference path to the particular instance of the portlet on a page. Every preference path has three levels at which it can store values, listed below in the order in which they are tested at runtime:

- User level

- Group level

- System level (used to set system-wide defaults)

A sample of how you would create a preference path when users register a new instance of a portlet follows. While you can name the constant portion any way you like, our example follows a convention, naming the provider and portlet as the last two entries in the period-delimited list. The reference path is provided by the PPE in the portlet instance record that is always passed to the `register` procedure.

```
WWPRE_API_NAME.create_path ( p_path =>
                            'oracle.portal.custom_provider.crosstab_portlet'
                            ||p_portlet_instance.reference_path );
```

You will need to delete the path when the user removes the portlet from the page. The following code, called from the `deregister_portlet` procedure, removes the path and all custom settings:

```
WWPRE_API_NAME.delete_path ( p_path =>
                            'oracle.portal.custom_provider.crosstab_portlet'
                            ||p_portlet_instance.reference_path );
```

Naming the Preferences   Each preference must be created before it can be set or retrieved—in a sense, similar to declaring variables. This is done in the `register` procedure by creating a name to associate with each value you will allow the user to save. A preference name requires a path, a name, and a datatype, which can be NUMBER, DATE, STRING, INTEGER, CURRENCY, or any custom type defined and handled in the WWTYP_API_DYNAMIC_TYPE type definition (see the type specification for full details). The following example creates a name for a title preference using the STRING datatype and indicating that the descriptive information is to be stored in the current user's browser language. If you were working with multiple languages, you would provide appropriate translations for the description parameter.

```
WWPRE_API_NAME.create_name ( p_path =>
                            'oracle.portal.custom_provider.crosstab_portlet'
                             ||p_portlet_instance.reference_path,
                            p_name => 'PORTLET_TITLE',
                            p_description => 'Allows user to customize title',
                            p_type_name => 'STRING',
                            p_language => WWCTX_API.get_nls_language) ;
```

Setting and Retrieving Preference Values   To set a value for a preference, you will use one of the procedures listed in Table 11-3, depending on the datatype you have chosen for the preference. If the preference's datatype does not match the type implied by the procedure name, a VALUE_ERROR is raised. (In other words, you can't use set_value_as_number to set a value for a VARCHAR2 preference.) If the preference does not exist, a GENERAL_PREFERENCE_EXCEPTION is raised.

The code below illustrates how any of these would be called. The only difference among the specifications is that the expected datatype of p_value will be the same as the datatype indicated by the procedure name. p_level_type can be any of the following defined constants: WWPRE_API_VALUE.USER_LEVEL_TYPE, WWPRE_API_VALUE.GROUP_LEVEL_TYPE, or WWPRE_API_VALUE.SYSTEM_LEVEL_TYPE. p_level_name will be the user or group name for which to set the preference. If setting a system-level preference, supply NULL for p_level_name.

```
WWPRE_API_VALUE.set_value_as_varchar2
(
  p_path  =>                              --predefined preference path
       'oracle.portal.custom_provider.crosstab_portlet'
       ||p_portlet_instance.reference_path,
  p_name  => 'PORTLET_TITLE',             --predefined preference name
  p_level_type => WWPRE_API_VALUE.USER_LEVEL_TYPE,
  p_level_name => WWCTX_API.get_user,
  p_value  => p_title                     --this is the value to set
);
```

NOTE
*There is one additional parameter, p_commit,
that we have omitted because it is now deprecated.
It has a default value and should not be used.*

You will notice in Table 11-3 that each procedure and function has an equivalent "`by_id`" procedure that allows you to supply the numeric user or group ID instead of the name when setting or retrieving preferences.

The `set_value_as_string` procedure is used to set any preferences defined with custom datatypes—it converts the supplied string value to a custom datatype, based on built-in functions or customizations you have made in `WWTYP_API_DYNAMIC_TYPE`. In addition to the parameters specified for the other procedures, `set_value_as_string` accepts an NLS language parameter that custom types can use to retrieve the preference in the appropriate language.

The retrieval functions have similar definitions to the equivalent set procedures, but are defined as functions to return the preference as the appropriate datatype. An addition level type, `INHERIT_LEVEL_TYPE`, is added for retrieval, to make use of the preference hierarchy. `INHERIT_LEVEL_TYPE` is the default, and it checks the user level first, then the group, and finally the system level, to find a value for the preference. If no value is found, either at a named level or through the inheritance technique, the functions return `NULL`. A `VALUE_ERROR` is raised if the datatype of the preference does not match the function call.

```
l_title := WWPRE_API_VALUE.get_value_as_varchar2
    (
        p_path => 'oracle.portal.custom_provider.crosstab_portlet'
                ||p_portlet_instance.reference_path,
        p_name  => 'PORTLET_TITLE',
        p_level_type => WWPRE_API_VALUE.USER_LEVEL_TYPE,
        p_level_name => WWCTX_API.get_user
    );
```

Set Procedure	Get Function
set_value_as_varchar2	get_value_as_varchar2
set_value_as_number	get_value_as_number
set_value_as_date	get_value_as_date
set_value_as_string	get_value_as_string
set_value_as_varchar2_by_id	get_value_as_varchar2_by_id
set_value_as_number_by_id	get_value_as_number_by_id
set_value_as_date_by_id	get_value_as_date_by_id
set_value_as_string_by_id	get_value_as_string_by_id

TABLE 11-3.   *Procedures and Functions Used to Set and Get Preferences*

Finally, you may clear values using either the `delete_value` or `delete_value_by_id` procedures, as follows:

```
WWPRE_API_VALUE.delete_value
(
  p_path  =>
        'oracle.portal.custom_provider.crosstab_portlet'
        ||p_portlet_instance.reference_path,
  p_name  => 'PORTLET_TITLE',
  p_level_type => WWPRE_API_VALUE.USER_LEVEL_TYPE,
  p_level_name => WWCTX_API.get_user
);
```

Rendering the Customization Form

If you want the customization form to look like the others that you've seen, you can draw the headers and footers in the same way as they are drawn in the components. The package `WWUI_API_UTIL` contains procedures and functions used to draw dialog (customization form) pages for the Portal components. Several of these are described below, and Figure 11-5 provides a reference for each customization form style.

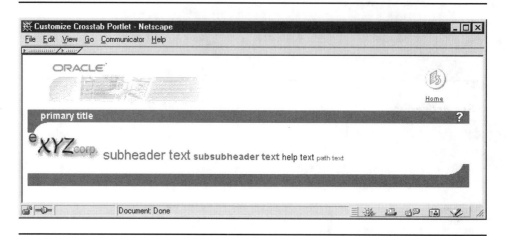

FIGURE 11-5. *A schematic customization form illustrates each style*

draw_title   draw_title draws the graphic object across the top of the customization form, using CSS styles and images found in the $IAS_HOME/portal30/images directory. It accepts the following parameters:

- p_title is the title bar text ("primary title" in Figure 11-5).

- p_sec_title should be a secondary title, but did not display in our test.

- p_help_url is a link to a help page. If provided, a question mark icon will appear in the title bar with a link to the specified page— otherwise, the question mark will not appear.

- p_language allows you to indicate the language in which to display the title text and help alternate text (displays as a pop-up when the mouse passes over the Help icon).

NOTE
The color and shape of the title bar are set using CSS styles, and do not appear to support any user customization. The only way (as far as we know) to modify the color and shape of the title bar is to produce the graphics yourself. The title bar is actually a borderless HTML table with a dark blue background, using style sheet classes unique to customization forms. The first row contains text and links, and the second row contains a curved shape image that overlays the table cell to produce the rounded edge. You can manually create a similar table with your own background color. For the graphic objects, use provided images to produce the curved shapes at the corners. In the $IAS_HOME/portal30/images directory, you will find images for each RGB color combination, with appended codes to indicate the type of curve: sl for top left, sr for top right, bl for bottom left, br for bottom right, and more.

draw_image   The image in the upper right-hand corner (eXYZ logo in Figure 11-5) is drawn using this utility, as is the above-mentioned curve (oddly enough). The default image used by the customization forms is `compedit.gif`. Supply this or another image name, with the correct URL path, in the procedure call.

```
wwui_api_util.draw_image('/images/xyzlogo.jpg');
```

Customization Form Text Formats   There are two ways to format the various text levels (subheaders, help text, and path text) shown in Figure 11-5. To print formatted text, either call the appropriate draw routine or use a "get style" function from `WWUI_API_UTIL` to format the text style in combination with another Web Toolkit procedure. The only exception is the "subsubheader", which does not have a draw routine. See the following examples:

```
--using the draw routines
WWUI_API_UTIL.draw_subheader ( 'subheader text' );
WWUI_API_UTIL.draw_helptext ( 'help text' );
WWUI_API_UTIL.draw_path_text ( 'path text' );
-- using the styles with other tags
HTP.p ( WWUI_API_UTIL.get_path_style ( 'path text' ) );
HTP.tabledata ( WWUI_API_UTIL.get_subsubheader_style( 'subsubheader text' ) );
```

draw_footer   draw_footer accepts no arguments. It draws the graphic object at the bottom of the page to close out the customization form.

```
wwui_api_util.draw_footer;
```

Data Entry Fields   You will have to create your own buttons and fields on the form, and supply the "action" procedure to modify the preferences based on the user's data entry. Oracle recommends that you use the same button names as you see on the built-in component customization forms—namely, Reset to Defaults, Apply, OK, and Cancel. All buttons should be submit-type buttons with the same name. You will need to supply button values for each of these actions, so that you can determine what to do in the procedure that handles the actions for the customization form.

For example, if the user clicks Reset to Defaults, you would restore the preferences to the system-level default (or nullify them if none existed), and return to the customization form. If the user clicks Apply, you will save the preferences and return to the form as well. OK would indicate that the user is finished and wants to return to the page, and Cancel simply returns the user to the page without changing preferences. This complex set of actions implies that the action handler must accept not only the button value and preference values, but also parameters for the customization form URL and the page URL.

In the example code provided, we will accept several preferences to modify the display of the portlet, and allow administrators to set defaults for other users. Refer to this code for examples of how to display the customization form, save the preferences, and return the user to the correct page.

The Crosstab Portlet

Now that you have sufficient background in the tools and techniques used to create custom portlets, we can review the code for a portlet package. The portlet we will produce displays a crosstab (matrix) report, something not otherwise available in Portal. Assume that the procedure exists and produces its own output—perhaps it was written in an earlier Web development effort. Figure 11-6 shows the current implementation of this report as a PL/SQL Web procedure, which you can test in your installation using the URL:

```
http://<yourserver>/pls/<portalDAD>/corp_site.crosstab
```

To fully "portalize" it, the code would have to be modified to use the portlet text styles, but we have simplified the example in this sense. If you wanted to allow it to run in both the old application and the Portal installation using the page styles, it could accept a parameter indicating the display environment, using the Portal styles only if called from Portal. The commented code is shown over the next few pages and contained in the files `crosstab_portlet.pks` and `crosstab_portlet.pkb`. The `crosstab` procedure was built when you installed the CORP_SITE schema. In the exercise to follow, you will build this package, but you will not be able to display the portlet yet. You will have to create the provider package before you can make it available to the portal.

	CHOCOLATE	COOKIES	FLOWERS	FOOD	TOOLS	VIDEOS
GW BUSH						$760.00
BARBARA BUSH			$1,055.85			$686.00
Hans Christian		$185.00		$275.00	$99.00	
HAPPY HAMBRO			$227.80			
HENRY FORD		$5.00	$5.00	$52.20	$979.95	
Malcolm T. Biggs						
Scrooge McDuck					$600.00	
J Q PUBLIC			$80.00			

FIGURE 11-6. *A crosstab report developed using the PL/SQL Web Toolkit*

NOTE
This code, with the accompanying `crosstab`
*procedure, illustrates a portlet with some complex
customization. The code is not as elegant as it
could be, and will take a while to run, but it does
offer some very powerful features. Feel free to
improve on our technique, or simplify as your
requirements dictate.*

```
--crosstab_portlet.pks
CREATE OR REPLACE PACKAGE crosstab_portlet IS

    FUNCTION get_portlet_info
      (p_provider_id IN INTEGER
      ,p_language IN VARCHAR2)
    RETURN wwpro_api_provider.portlet_record;

    FUNCTION is_runnable
      (p_provider_id IN INTEGER
      ,p_reference_path IN VARCHAR2)
    RETURN boolean;

    PROCEDURE register
      (p_portlet_instance IN wwpro_api_provider.portlet_instance_record);

    PROCEDURE deregister
      (p_portlet_instance IN WWPRO_API_PROVIDER.portlet_instance_record);

    PROCEDURE show
      (p_portlet_runtime IN WWPRO_API_PROVIDER.portlet_runtime_record);

    PROCEDURE copy
      (p_copy_portlet_info IN WWPRO_API_PROVIDER.copy_portlet_record);

    FUNCTION describe_parameters
      (p_provider_id IN INTEGER
      ,p_language IN VARCHAR2)
    RETURN WWPRO_API_PROVIDER.portlet_parameter_table;

    PROCEDURE show_edit
      (p_back_url        IN VARCHAR2
      ,p_page_url        IN VARCHAR2
      ,p_language        IN VARCHAR2
      ,p_reference_path  IN VARCHAR2
      ,p_portlet_runtime  IN WWPRO_API_PROVIDER.portlet_runtime_record
      ,p_edit_type IN VARCHAR2);
```

```
    PROCEDURE save_edit
      (p_action IN VARCHAR2 DEFAULT NULL
      ,p_reference_path IN VARCHAR2 DEFAULT NULL
      ,p_back_url IN VARCHAR2 DEFAULT NULL
      ,p_page_url IN VARCHAR2 DEFAULT NULL
      ,p_title IN VARCHAR2 DEFAULT NULL
      ,p_category IN PORTAL30.WWTYP_TYPE.v50_array
                      DEFAULT PORTAL30.WWTYP_TYPE.empty_v50_array
      ,p_edit_type IN VARCHAR2);

END crosstab_portlet;

--crosstab_portlet.pkb
CREATE OR REPLACE PACKAGE BODY crosstab_portlet IS

  FUNCTION get_portlet_info
    (p_provider_id IN INTEGER
    ,p_language IN VARCHAR2)
  RETURN WWPRO_API_PROVIDER.portlet_record
  IS
    r_portlet        WWPRO_API_PROVIDER.portlet_record;
  BEGIN
    r_portlet.id := 1;
    r_portlet.provider_id := p_provider_id;
    r_portlet.title := 'Crosstab Portlet';
    r_portlet.name := 'crosstab_portlet';
    r_portlet.description :=
      'This portlet displays a customizable crosstab report';
    r_portlet.timeout := NULL;
    r_portlet.timeout_msg := NULL;
    r_portlet.language := 'us';
    r_portlet.has_show_edit          := TRUE;
    r_portlet.has_show_edit_defaults := TRUE;
    r_portlet.has_show_preview := FALSE;
    r_portlet.content_type := wwpro_api_provider.CONTENT_TYPE_HTML;
    r_portlet.preference_store_path := null;
    r_portlet.created_on := sysdate;
    r_portlet.created_by := wwctx_api.get_user;
    r_portlet.last_updated_on := sysdate;
    r_portlet.last_updated_by := wwctx_api.get_user;

    RETURN r_portlet;

  END get_portlet_info;
```

```
    FUNCTION is_runnable
      (p_provider_id IN INTEGER
      ,p_reference_path IN VARCHAR2 )
    RETURN BOOLEAN
    IS
    BEGIN
/*
This security mechanism just checks if the current user is logged
on--we assume all internal users can view the portlet.
You may wish to restrict access by identifying the user or group first.
*/
      IF (WWCTX_API.is_logged_on) THEN
        RETURN TRUE;
      ELSE
        RETURN FALSE;
      END IF;

    END is_runnable;

    PROCEDURE register
      (p_portlet_instance IN WWPRO_API_PROVIDER.portlet_instance_record)
    IS
    BEGIN
    --Create a path name for the portlet instance
      WWPRE_API_NAME.create_path( p_path =>
                            'oracle.portal.custom_provider.crosstab_portlet'
                            ||p_portlet_instance.reference_path );
--Here is where we set up end-user customization

--Create preference names for the title and data to display
      WWPRE_API_NAME.create_name( p_path =>
                            'oracle.portal.custom_provider.crosstab_portlet'
                            ||p_portlet_instance.reference_path,
                            p_name => 'PORTLET_TITLE',
                            p_description => 'Allows user to customize title',
                            p_type_name => 'STRING',
                            p_language => WWCTX_API.get_nls_language);

      WWPRE_API_NAME.create_name( p_path =>
                            'oracle.portal.custom_provider.crosstab_portlet'
                            ||p_portlet_instance.reference_path,
                            p_name => 'CATEGORIES',
                            p_description => 'Allows user to choose categories',
                            p_type_name => 'STRING',
                            p_language => WWCTX_API.get_nls_language);


    --Set system-wide defaults
      WWPRE_API_VALUE.set_value_as_varchar2
                    ( p_path =>
                        'oracle.portal.custom_provider.crosstab_portlet'
                        ||p_portlet_instance.reference_path,
                      p_name => 'PORTLET_TITLE',
                      p_level_type => WWPRE_API_VALUE.SYSTEM_LEVEL_TYPE,
                      p_level_name => NULL,
                      p_value => 'Crosstab Portlet' );
```

```
    WWPRE_API_VALUE.set_value_as_varchar2
                ( p_path =>
                    'oracle.portal.custom_provider.crosstab_portlet'
                    ||p_portlet_instance.reference_path,
                  p_name => 'CATEGORIES',
                  p_level_type => WWPRE_API_VALUE.SYSTEM_LEVEL_TYPE,
                  p_level_name => NULL,
                  p_value => NULL );

  END register;

  PROCEDURE deregister
    (p_portlet_instance IN WWPRO_API_PROVIDER.portlet_instance_record)
  IS
  BEGIN
  --need to remove the path when the portlet is deleted from the page
    WWPRE_API_NAME.delete_path( p_path =>
                        'oracle.portal.custom_provider.crosstab_portlet'
                        ||p_portlet_instance.reference_path );

  END deregister;

  PROCEDURE show
    (p_portlet_runtime      WWPRO_API_PROVIDER.portlet_runtime_record)
  IS
    r_portlet        WWPRO_API_PROVIDER.portlet_record;
    v_category_list VARCHAR2(1000);
  BEGIN
/*
Ensure the user can view this portlet before displaying
*/
    IF (NOT is_runnable(
              p_provider_id      => p_portlet_runtime.provider_id
             ,p_reference_path   => p_portlet_runtime.reference_path)
        ) THEN
      RAISE WWPRO_API_PROVIDER.PORTLET_SECURITY_EXCEPTION;
    END IF;
/*
Retrieve the portlet information in preparation for show.
*/
    r_portlet := get_portlet_info(
                          p_provider_id   => p_portlet_runtime.provider_id
                         ,p_language      => p_portlet_runtime.language
                            );

    IF (p_portlet_runtime.exec_mode = WWPRO_API_PROVIDER.MODE_SHOW) THEN
      /* show the portlet */
      IF (p_portlet_runtime.has_title_region) THEN

/*
Override the default portlet title with the value provided
by end-user or system-level customization.
*/
          r_portlet.title := WWPRE_API_VALUE.get_value_as_varchar2
                        ( p_path =>
                            'oracle.portal.custom_provider.crosstab_portlet'
                            ||p_portlet_runtime.reference_path,
                          p_name => 'PORTLET_TITLE',
                          p_level_type => WWPRE_API_VALUE.INHERIT_LEVEL_TYPE,
                          p_level_name => NULL );
```

```
     /*
     Draw the portlet header and specify what links are available
     from that header (i.e. details, customize, help, and about).
     The has_title property is set at the page region level.
     */
            WWUI_API_PORTLET.draw_portlet_header
              (
               p_provider_id          => p_portlet_runtime.provider_id
              ,p_portlet_id           => p_portlet_runtime.portlet_id
              ,p_title                => r_portlet.title
              ,p_has_details          => TRUE
              ,p_has_edit             => r_portlet.has_show_edit
              ,p_has_help             => TRUE
              ,p_has_about            => TRUE
              ,p_referencepath        => p_portlet_runtime.reference_path
              ,p_back_url             => p_portlet_runtime.page_url
              );

         END IF;
     /*
     Open the portlet, with or without borders.
     The has_border property is set at the page region level.
     */
         WWUI_API_PORTLET.open_portlet(p_portlet_runtime.has_border);
     /*
     Get the list of categories the user would like to see.
     Note that we can do the same for customers if necessary,
     by adding a similar path and checkboxes for the customer list.
     */
         v_category_list := WWPRE_API_VALUE.get_value_as_varchar2
                              ( p_path =>
                                  'oracle.portal.custom_provider.crosstab_portlet'
                                  ||p_portlet_runtime.reference_path,
                                p_name  => 'CATEGORIES',
                                p_level_type => WWPRE_API_VALUE.INHERIT_LEVEL_TYPE,
                                p_level_name => NULL );
     /*
     Display the content of the portlet.
     The crosstab procedure produces the desired output, but should
     be modified to use the WWUI_API_PORTLET.portlet_text API.
     */
         crosstab(null,v_category_list,null);
     /*
     Close out the portlet.
     */
         WWUI_API_PORTLET.close_portlet;

       ELSIF (p_portlet_runtime.exec_mode = WWPRO_API_PROVIDER.MODE_SHOW_ABOUT)
       THEN
     /*
     Display the about page for the portlet.
     */
         htp.p('This portlet was developed for the 9iAS Portal Handbook,');
         htp.p(' to demonstrate the PDK.');
```

```
        ELSIF (p_portlet_runtime.exec_mode = WWPRO_API_PROVIDER.MODE_SHOW_EDIT) THEN
/*
Display the edit page for the portlet. Use this to accept parameters.
*/
        show_edit ( p_back_url        => p_portlet_runtime.back_page_url
                  ,p_page_url         => p_portlet_runtime.page_url
                  ,p_language         => p_portlet_runtime.language
                  ,p_reference_path   => p_portlet_runtime.reference_path
                  ,p_portlet_runtime  => p_portlet_runtime
                  ,p_edit_type        => 'USER'
                  );
      ELSIF (p_portlet_runtime.exec_mode = WWPRO_API_PROVIDER.MODE_SHOW_HELP) THEN
/*
Display the help page for the portlet. (demonstration only)
*/
        htp.p('This is a placeholder for any help you may wish to add');

      ELSIF (p_portlet_runtime.exec_mode =
                    WWPRO_API_PROVIDER.MODE_SHOW_EDIT_DEFAULTS) THEN
/*
Display the edit defaults page for the portlet.
*/
        show_edit ( p_back_url        => p_portlet_runtime.back_page_url
                  ,p_page_url         => p_portlet_runtime.page_url
                  ,p_language         => p_portlet_runtime.language
                  ,p_reference_path   => p_portlet_runtime.reference_path
                  ,p_portlet_runtime  => p_portlet_runtime
                  ,p_edit_type        => 'SYSTEM'
                  );

      ELSIF (p_portlet_runtime.exec_mode = WWPRO_API_PROVIDER.MODE_SHOW_DETAILS)
      THEN
/*
Display the page full view for the portlet. We are just repeating the
crosstab procedure here, but without customization to display all records.
*/
        crosstab;

      ELSIF (p_portlet_runtime.exec_mode = WWPRO_API_PROVIDER.MODE_PREVIEW) THEN
/*
Display the preview page for the portlet. We are not supplying a
preview page, but we include the option as a placeholder.
*/
        null;
      END IF;

   END show;

   PROCEDURE copy
     (p_copy_portlet_info IN WWPRO_API_PROVIDER.copy_portlet_record)
   IS
   BEGIN
      NULL;
   END copy;
```

```
FUNCTION describe_parameters
 (p_provider_id IN INTEGER
 ,p_language IN VARCHAR2)
RETURN WWPRO_API_PROVIDER.portlet_parameter_table
IS
   t_params     WWPRO_API_PROVIDER.portlet_parameter_table;
BEGIN
/*
Currently we don't accept any parameters, so we return an empty record.
*/
   RETURN t_params;
END describe_parameters;

PROCEDURE show_edit
  (p_back_url         IN VARCHAR2
  ,p_page_url         IN VARCHAR2
  ,p_language         IN VARCHAR2
  ,p_reference_path   IN VARCHAR2
  ,p_portlet_runtime  IN WWPRO_API_PROVIDER.portlet_runtime_record
  ,p_edit_type        IN VARCHAR2)
IS
--This procedure is used to display the customization form.
--It accepts an edit_type to indicate if this was called from
--the Customize link or from the Edit Defaults (admin) link.
   v_title   VARCHAR2(100);
BEGIN
 --get the current default title
 v_title := WWPRE_API_VALUE.get_value_as_varchar2
                        ( p_path =>
                            'oracle.portal.custom_provider.crosstab_portlet'
                            ||p_portlet_runtime.reference_path,
                          p_name => 'PORTLET_TITLE',
                          p_level_type => WWPRE_API_VALUE.INHERIT_LEVEL_TYPE,
                          p_level_name => NULL );

   PORTAL30.WWUI_API_UTIL.draw_title ('Customize the Crosstab Report');
     -- no help URL shown in title bar for simplicity

   PORTAL30.WWUI_API_UTIL.draw_image('/images/xyzlogo.jpg');

   HTP.formopen('corp_site.crosstab_portlet.save_edit', 'GET');
     -- the button bar
   HTP.tableopen(calign => 'CENTER',cattributes => 'WIDTH=80%');
   HTP.tablerowopen;
   HTP.tableData
     (
        htf.formsubmit ('p_action', 'Reset to Defaults')  ||' '||
        htf.formsubmit ('p_action', 'Apply')  ||' '||
        htf.formsubmit ('p_action', 'OK') ||' '||
        htf.formsubmit ('p_action', 'Cancel'), cattributes=>'ALIGN=right '
     );
   HTP.tablerowclose;
```

```
   HTP.tablerowopen;
   HTP.p('<TD>');
   PORTAL30.WWUI_API_UTIL.draw_helptext
      ('Use the dialogs below to customize your view of the crosstab. ');
   HTP.p('</TD>');
   HTP.tablerowclose;
   HTP.tablerowopen;
   HTP.p('<TD>');
   HTP.p ('Title: ');
   HTP.formtext ('p_title', cvalue => v_title);
   HTP.p('</TD>');
   HTP.tablerowclose;
   HTP.tablerowopen;
   HTP.p('<TD>');
   --generate a list of product categories
   HTP.print('Choose the categories you would like to see');
   HTP.br;
   FOR r IN (SELECT DISTINCT product_category FROM products) LOOP
     HTP.formcheckbox('p_category',r.product_category);
     HTP.p(r.product_category);
     HTP.br;
   END LOOP;
   HTP.p('</TD>');
   HTP.tablerowclose;
   --Create the hidden fields for the path and reference information
   HTP.formHidden('p_back_url', p_back_url);
   HTP.formHidden('p_page_url', p_page_url);
   HTP.formHidden('p_reference_path', p_reference_path);
   HTP.formHidden('p_edit_type', p_edit_type);
   HTP.formclose;
   HTP.tableclose;

   PORTAL30.WWUI_API_UTIL.draw_footer;

END show_edit;

PROCEDURE save_edit
  (p_action IN VARCHAR2 DEFAULT NULL
  ,p_reference_path IN VARCHAR2 DEFAULT NULL
  ,p_back_url IN VARCHAR2 DEFAULT NULL
  ,p_page_url IN VARCHAR2 DEFAULT NULL
  ,p_title IN VARCHAR2 DEFAULT NULL
  ,p_category IN PORTAL30.WWTYP_TYPE.v50_array
             DEFAULT PORTAL30.WWTYP_TYPE.empty_v50_array
  ,p_edit_type IN VARCHAR2)
--this procedure saves any changes to preferences
IS
  v_preference_path VARCHAR2(255) :=
      'oracle.portal.custom_provider.crosstab_portlet'|| p_reference_path;
  v_edit_type      VARCHAR2(4);
  v_level_name     VARCHAR2(60);
  v_category_list  VARCHAR2(1000);

BEGIN
--decide what sort of edits to save
  IF p_edit_type = 'USER' THEN
    v_edit_type := WWPRE_API_VALUE.USER_LEVEL_TYPE;
    v_level_name := WWCTX_API.get_user;
```

```
    ELSE
      v_edit_type := WWPRE_API_VALUE.SYSTEM_LEVEL_TYPE;
      v_level_name := NULL;
    END IF;

    IF p_action = 'Cancel' THEN
      owa_util.redirect_url(p_back_url);
    ELSIF p_action = 'OK' OR p_action = 'Apply' THEN
      WWPRE_API_VALUE.set_value_as_varchar2
        ( p_path  => v_preference_path,
          p_name  => 'PORTLET_TITLE',
          p_level_type => v_edit_type,
          p_level_name => v_level_name,
          p_value  => p_title
        );
  --Process the selections from the category list

      FOR i IN 1..p_category.COUNT LOOP
        v_category_list := v_category_list||''''||p_category(i)||'''',';
      END LOOP;
      v_category_list := rtrim(v_category_list,',');

      WWPRE_API_VALUE.set_value_as_varchar2
        ( p_path  => v_preference_path,
          p_name  => 'CATEGORIES',
          p_level_type => v_edit_type,
          p_level_name => v_level_name,
          p_value  => v_category_list
        );
      IF p_action = 'OK' THEN
        owa_util.redirect_url(p_back_url);
      ELSE
        owa_util.redirect_url(p_page_url);
      END IF;
    ELSIF p_action = 'Reset to Defaults' THEN
      WWPRE_API_VALUE.delete_value
        ( p_path  => v_preference_path,
            p_name  => 'PORTLET_TITLE',
            p_level_type => WWPRE_API_VALUE.USER_LEVEL_TYPE,
            p_level_name => WWCTX_API.get_user
        );
      WWPRE_API_VALUE.delete_value
        ( p_path  => v_preference_path,
            p_name  => 'CATEGORIES',
            p_level_type => WWPRE_API_VALUE.USER_LEVEL_TYPE,
            p_level_name => WWCTX_API.get_user
        );
      owa_util.redirect_url(p_back_url);

    END IF;
  END;

END crosstab_portlet;
```

Exercise 11.1: Create a Portlet Package

The portlet you will build creates the crosstab report as a portlet, something not otherwise available in Portal. We will assume that eXYZ Corporation had already built this functionality as a PL/SQL Web page, and now we simply wish to integrate it into the portal. The advantage of this approach is that the customization options are essentially unlimited. Users can choose which row and column values they wish to display, and we can add an option for administrators to change the source query and dimensions for the report. The crosstab procedure is built to handle dynamic queries and column display choices, but provides a default option to show customers against product categories. Each cell displays the amount customers spent on each category of product, to help the sales staff determine where their marketing efforts should be focused.

1. Review the source of the crosstab procedure using your favorite PL/SQL IDE. The procedure was created during the installation process for this book's schema, and its source can be found in the file crosstab.sql. It accepts three parameters: a common and limited list of columns as display in the matrix, another list for the rows, and a string that represents a query, which will produce the values to display in each intersection cell.

NOTE
For this procedure to work properly, considerable care and validation must be performed to ensure that the three parameters work together and produce sensible output. We have set working defaults for all three parameters, but you may modify and test these using your own data.

2. Display the crosstab report using the following URL:

   ```
   http://<yourserver>/pls/<portalDAD>/corp_site.crosstab
   ```

3. Log in to SQL*Plus as the Portal schema owner (for example, PORTAL30) and run the provsyns script appropriate for your installation, substituting the correct path to the 9i AS Oracle Home, as follows:

   ```
   @$IAS_HOME\portal30\admin\plsql\wwc\provsyns.sql CORP_SITE
   ```

4. Build the portlet package by first running crosstab_portlet.pks and then crosstab_portlet.pkb while logged in as CORP_SITE.

5. At the SQL prompt, type the following:

```
GRANT EXECUTE ON crosstab_portlet TO portal30_public;
```

6. That's it! The package is ready, but the provider is not, so you cannot view your portlet just yet.

Now that you have seen the complexity of the PDK-PL/SQL code, you may be wondering why you would go to so much trouble to write custom portlets, particularly in PL/SQL. Why not use a dynamic page, a form based on stored procedure, or a URL component? None of these allows true modification of the customization form, and none offers detailed control over each field. For example, you may have a customization form field that only certain users should be allowed to modify, or you may wish to have a simple and an "advanced mode" customization form. Alternatively, you may wish to allow the administrator to set certain defaults that are not supported by the built-in components. As you saw in the crosstab portlet, complete, flexible customization strategies are supported by PDK-PL/SQL.

Implementing a Portlet Provider

The next step in implementing custom portlets is to create and register a portlet *provider*. The provider is like a control center that manages all of the requests for portlet content and information and handles all the communication with the PPE. The PPE does not know anything about the individual portlet packages, except what it can learn from the provider. When you register a database provider, you must supply a PL/SQL package name as its definition. This package must meet the API specifications to supply the list of portlets available for page display, return metadata about each portlet, call the packages that show the portlets, and handle portlet security. As you've seen, portlets are usually coded in separate packages; the provider simply routes any calls to the appropriate function or procedure in the portlet package.

The following pages show the contents of the provider package we will use at eXYZ Corporation. It contains a single portlet, the crosstab portlet. To add more portlets, you would define constants to represent each one, and modify the procedures and functions to call the appropriate portlet package.

```
--custom_provider.pks
CREATE OR REPLACE PACKAGE custom_provider IS
/*
    To use this package as a template for your provider, add your
    portlets to the first section. It is simply a directory of the
    available portlets from this provider--we have only one.
    The constants are useful for later code references.
*/
    crosstab_portlet_id    CONSTANT INTEGER := 1;
```

```
FUNCTION get_api_version ( p_provider_id IN INTEGER )  RETURN INTEGER;

PROCEDURE register_provider ( p_provider_id IN INTEGER );

PROCEDURE deregister_provider ( p_provider_id IN INTEGER );

PROCEDURE do_login
(
    p_provider_id IN INTEGER
   ,p_browser_cookies IN WWPRO_API_PROVIDER.cookie_table
   ,p_provider_cookies OUT WWPRO_API_PROVIDER.cookie_table
);

FUNCTION get_portlet
(
    p_provider_id IN INTEGER
   ,p_portlet_id IN INTEGER
   ,p_language IN VARCHAR2
)
RETURN WWPRO_API_PROVIDER.portlet_record;

FUNCTION get_portlet_list
(
    p_provider_id IN INTEGER
   ,p_start_row IN INTEGER
   ,p_rowcount IN INTEGER
   ,p_language IN VARCHAR2
   ,p_security_level IN BOOLEAN
   ,p_type IN INTEGER
)
RETURN WWPRO_API_PROVIDER.portlet_table;

FUNCTION is_portlet_runnable
( p_portlet_instance IN WWPRO_API_PROVIDER.portlet_instance_record  )
RETURN BOOLEAN;

PROCEDURE register_portlet
( p_portlet_instance IN WWPRO_API_PROVIDER.portlet_instance_record );

PROCEDURE deregister_portlet
( p_portlet_instance IN WWPRO_API_PROVIDER.portlet_instance_record );

PROCEDURE show_portlet
( p_portlet_record IN OUT WWPRO_API_PROVIDER.portlet_runtime_record );

PROCEDURE copy_portlet
( p_copy_portlet_info IN WWPRO_API_PROVIDER.copy_portlet_record );

FUNCTION describe_portlet_parameters
(
    p_provider_id IN INTEGER
   ,p_portlet_id IN INTEGER
```

```
        ,p_language IN VARCHAR2
    )
    RETURN WWPRO_API_PROVIDER.portlet_parameter_table;

end custom_provider;


--custom_provider.pkb
CREATE OR REPLACE PACKAGE BODY custom_provider IS

  FUNCTION get_api_version  ( p_provider_id IN INTEGER ) RETURN INTEGER
   /* No change to this will be necessary in this release. */
   IS
   BEGIN
     RETURN WWPRO_API_PROVIDER.API_VERSION_1;
   END get_api_version;

  PROCEDURE register_provider  ( p_provider_id IN INTEGER )
   IS
   BEGIN
     NULL;
   END register_provider;

  PROCEDURE deregister_provider  ( p_provider_id IN INTEGER )
   IS
   BEGIN
     NULL;
   END deregister_provider;

  PROCEDURE do_login
   /* Change do_login only if you will use cookies */
   (
       p_provider_id IN INTEGER
      ,p_browser_cookies IN WWPRO_API_PROVIDER.cookie_table
      ,p_provider_cookies OUT WWPRO_API_PROVIDER.cookie_table
   )
   IS
   BEGIN
     NULL;
   END do_login;

FUNCTION get_portlet
/*

Here is where you will add calls to your own portlets, usually defined in
separate packages.
*/
(
        p_provider_id IN INTEGER
       ,p_portlet_id IN INTEGER
       ,p_language IN VARCHAR2
    )
```

```
RETURN WWPRO_API_PROVIDER.portlet_record
IS
BEGIN
  IF (p_portlet_id = crosstab_portlet_id) THEN
    RETURN CROSSTAB_PORTLET.get_portlet_info(
               p_provider_id  => p_provider_id
              ,p_language      => p_language
              );

  ELSE
        RAISE WWPRO_API_PROVIDER.PORTLET_NOT_FOUND_EXCEPTION;
  END IF;

END get_portlet;

FUNCTION get_portlet_list
  (
     p_provider_id IN INTEGER
    ,p_start_row IN INTEGER
    ,p_rowcount IN INTEGER
    ,p_language IN VARCHAR2
    ,p_security_level IN BOOLEAN
    ,p_type IN INTEGER
  )
RETURN WWPRO_API_PROVIDER.portlet_table
IS
  t_portlet_list  WWPRO_API_PROVIDER.portlet_table;
  i               NUMBER;
BEGIN
  i := 0;
  IF (p_security_level = false ) THEN
    i := i + 1;
    t_portlet_list(i) := get_portlet(p_provider_id  => p_provider_id
                                    ,p_portlet_id   => crosstab_portlet_id
                                    ,p_language     => p_language);
  ELSE
    IF ( CROSSTAB_PORTLET.is_runnable(p_provider_id    =>  p_provider_id
                                     ,p_reference_path =>  null) )  THEN
      i := i + 1;
      t_portlet_list(i) := get_portlet(p_provider_id  => p_provider_id
                                      ,p_portlet_id   => crosstab_portlet_id
                                      ,p_language     => p_language);

    END IF;
  END IF;

  RETURN t_portlet_list;

END get_portlet_list;

FUNCTION is_portlet_runnable
```

```
            (p_portlet_instance IN WWPRO_API_PROVIDER.portlet_instance_record)
RETURN BOOLEAN
IS
BEGIN
   IF (P_PORTLET_INSTANCE.portlet_id = crosstab_portlet_id) THEN
      RETURN CROSSTAB_PORTLET.is_runnable(
                  p_provider_id    =>  P_PORTLET_INSTANCE.provider_id
                 ,p_reference_path =>  P_PORTLET_INSTANCE.reference_path
                 );
   ELSE
      RAISE WWPRO_API_PROVIDER.PORTLET_NOT_FOUND_EXCEPTION;
   END IF;
END is_portlet_runnable;

PROCEDURE register_portlet
   (p_portlet_instance IN WWPRO_API_PROVIDER.portlet_instance_record)
IS
BEGIN
   IF (P_PORTLET_INSTANCE.portlet_id = crosstab_portlet_id) THEN
      CROSSTAB_PORTLET.register(p_portlet_instance);
   ELSE
      RAISE WWPRO_API_PROVIDER.PORTLET_NOT_FOUND_EXCEPTION;
   END IF;

END register_portlet;

PROCEDURE deregister_portlet
   ( p_portlet_instance in WWPRO_API_PROVIDER.portlet_instance_record)
IS
BEGIN
   IF (P_PORTLET_INSTANCE.portlet_id = crosstab_portlet_id) THEN
      CROSSTAB_PORTLET.deregister(p_portlet_instance);
   ELSE
      RAISE WWPRO_API_PROVIDER.PORTLET_NOT_FOUND_EXCEPTION;
   END IF;

END deregister_portlet;

PROCEDURE show_portlet
   ( p_portlet_record IN OUT WWPRO_API_PROVIDER.portlet_runtime_record)
IS
BEGIN
   IF (P_PORTLET_RECORD.portlet_id = crosstab_portlet_id) THEN
      CROSSTAB_PORTLET.show(p_portlet_record);
   ELSE
      RAISE WWPRO_API_PROVIDER.PORTLET_NOT_FOUND_EXCEPTION;
   END IF;

END show_portlet;

PROCEDURE copy_portlet
```

```
  ( p_copy_portlet_info IN WWPRO_API_PROVIDER.copy_portlet_record )
IS
BEGIN
  IF (P_COPY_PORTLET_INFO.portlet_id = crosstab_portlet_id) THEN
    CROSSTAB_PORTLET.copy(p_copy_portlet_info);
  ELSE
    RAISE WWPRO_API_PROVIDER.PORTLET_NOT_FOUND_EXCEPTION;
  END IF;

END copy_portlet;

FUNCTION describe_portlet_parameters
  (
      p_provider_id IN INTEGER
     ,p_portlet_id IN INTEGER
     ,p_language IN VARCHAR2
  )
RETURN WWPRO_API_PROVIDER.portlet_parameter_table
IS
BEGIN
  IF (p_portlet_id = crosstab_portlet_id) THEN
    RETURN CROSSTAB_PORTLET.describe_parameters(
               p_provider_id      =>  p_provider_id
              ,p_language         =>  p_language
              );
  ELSE
    RAISE WWPRO_API_PROVIDER.PORTLET_NOT_FOUND_EXCEPTION;
  END IF;

END describe_portlet_parameters;

END custom_provider;
```

Exercise 11.2: Create the Provider

You are now ready to register your provider with Portal using the
CUSTOM_PROVIDER package.

   1. Build the CUSTOM_PROVIDER package in the CORP_SITE schema by
   running custom_provider.pks and then custom_provider.pkb
   from your choice of IDE.

   2. Log in to Portal as the Portal administrator (PORTAL30). On the Portal
   home page, click the Administer tab. Choose Add a Portlet Provider from
   the Provider portlet.

   3. Give the provider a Name of EXYZ_CUSTOM, and set the Display Name to
   eXYZ Custom Portlets. Leave the Implementation Style set to Database.

4. Leave the defaults in the User/Session Information section.

5. In the Database Providers section, set the Owning Schema to CORP_SITE and the Package Name to CUSTOM_PROVIDER. Click OK.

6. Back in the Navigator, click on View Portlet Repository. If your provider (eXYZ Custom Portlets) is not displayed in the Other Providers section, click on the Refresh link in the upper right-hand corner.

TIP

Click Refresh Error if the provider is still not displayed after a refresh. Usually the errors indicate that the provider and portlet packages did not compile successfully. Resolve any compilation errors and return to this page to refresh the repository.

7. Click on the eXYZ Custom Portlets link to view the contents of the repository. Click on the portlet name to see the preview mode.

8. Now you are ready to integrate this portlet with the eXYZ Home Page. Navigate to this page and click on the My eXYZ tab.

9. Click the Edit page and then the Add Portlets icon for the left-side region of the My eXYZ tab. From the Other Providers section, choose the eXYZ Custom Portlets provider and then add the crosstab portlet to the region.

10. Click Close and test your new portlet. Try all the links, including the portlet header, to see how each of the show modes works. Your screen should look something like that in Figure 11-7.

In sum, PDK-PL/SQL can be used to produce a completely customized Portal application. It requires a little extra work to use it, but experienced PL/SQL programmers will adapt rapidly to these methods. We have only introduced PDK-PL/SQL, and have not addressed some of its more advanced features. These include setting and maintaining session storage objects, controlling the caching and refresh frequency of individual portlets, logging, error handling, and NLS language features. Please visit the Portal Studio web site for more information on these topics.

Keep in mind that PDK-PL/SQL may be affected by new Portal versions, as the APIs tend to change over time. Be sure that you fully research the effects of any upgrades before you begin, and keep backup copies of your code for future modifications.

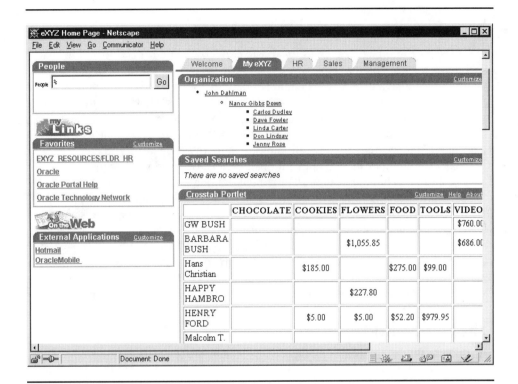

FIGURE 11-7. *The eXYZ home page with the crosstab portlet added*

As we went to press, Oracle released a provider generator utility that, given an XML file similar to the one used for PDK-Java (described in the next section), produces the PL/SQL for the provider package. Access the generator using the following URL:

```
http://psprovider.oracle.com/generator.html
```

This is but one way to simplify your provider implementation. You could also create a repository with your own portlet registration process, and write the provider so it accesses the repository for each portlet. In addition, Oracle Designer is capable of generating portlet and provider packages from application modules, beginning in version 6i R4. It generates the provider and portlet package wrappers, as we did manually, around the existing generated PL/SQL Web pages. See the bibliography for more information on Designer Web page generation.

Web Services (PDK-Java)

The PDK-Java interface uses the same basic concepts as PDK-PL/SQL, but instead of specifying the call interface in PL/SQL, it is now specified in Java. In organizations with significant Java expertise, this framework unleashes the full power of Java within the Portal application. Because PDK-Java can call and display essentially any Web resource, it is a good choice for integrating external content or media. Legacy applications can be integrated with ease as long as they are accessible over at least one of the many communication modes supported by Java. You can use the PDK- Java utilities in Java applications, servlets, or JavaServer Pages, so you are not even limited in your deployment options.

PDK-Java is thoroughly documented on the Portal Studio web site using the JavaDoc standard, and in `$IAS_HOME\portal30\jpdk\jpdk.zip`, installed with the 3.0.9 release of Portal. This zip file also contains a complete sample application with several types of portlets available for testing or as a basis for your PDK-Java application. We could do little justice to it here by comparison, so we will simply compare notes and summarize the important features of PDK-Java. In the next section, you will create a Web provider from a third-party vendor implemented in PDK-Java.

JServ Configuration

If you're planning to use PDK-Java, you need to have some familiarity with the Apache JServ servlet engine. Because the provider is implemented as a servlet, it must be accessed through JServ. JServ uses the term *zone* to refer to the path and location of servlets. The default root zone is physically located at `$IAS_HOME\Apache\JServ\servlets`, and is mapped to the `/servlets` virtual path in Apache. Configuration is accomplished by modifying `zone.properties` found in this directory, and `jserv.properties` in the `$IAS_HOME\Apache\JServ\conf` directory. You can use this zone for your provider servlet, or create a separate zone and virtual path for the provider.

Providers

Communication outside of the Portal environment (over HTTP) requires some translation between requests generated by Portal and responses by Java servlets and other URLs. All communication funnels through a program known as the Provider Adapter. The servlet `oracle.portal.provider.v1.http.HttpProvider` is the adapter provided with PDK-Java, and it must be used when you wish to use PDK-Java services. You can either develop your own provider by subclassing `HttpProvider` or use a configuration technique to reference the default Provider. The former method would only apply if you need to create some advanced features not available in the default provider.

Subclass Technique

To subclass `HttpProvider` and write your own provider servlet, you will simply reference it and supply your own provider name in an override to the `getProviderClass` method, as follows:

```
public class HelloProvider extends
oracle.portal.provider.v1.http.HttpProvider {
// supply your name
    static final String providerClassName =
"mysample.provider.HelloWorldProvider";
//this overrides with your name
    public Class getProviderClass() throws ServletException {
      try {
            return Class.forName(providerClassName);
        }
      catch (ClassNotFoundException e)
        {
          throw new ServletException(
                  "Unable to find Provider class " + providerClassName);
        }
    }
}
```

You may have reasons to override several of the other default methods in the `HttpProvider` class. If so, you will use this technique and override any part of the class to provide your own provider functionality. This is an advanced technique, requiring a thorough understanding of Java programming and the interfaces required by Portal.

Configuration Technique

To implement a provider by configuration, you need only to specify an XML file (`provider.xml`) that lists information about the available providers and their portlets and configure JServ to locate your customizations. The configuration method is similar in nature to the `get_portlet` and `get_portlet_list` APIs discussed earlier, but PDK-Java contains a `DefaultProvider` with methods to register, call, and list the portlets based on the contents of `provider.xml`. The default behavior of the `getProviderClass` method (without the above override) is to check the contents of this XML file to determine what the provider has to offer. In order for `getProviderClass` to find your implementation, you must relate a customized name to the `HttpProvider` class in `zone.properties` and then set some initial parameters.

First, create a short name or alias for the class. The following line in `zone.properties` would create the name "hello" for the provider:

```
servlet.hello.code=oracle.portal.provider.v1.http.HttpProvider
```

The next step is to set up the initial parameters using `initArgs`. There are only two: one specifies the location of the code and, more important, the `provider.xml` file; and the other specifies a session timeout parameter. An `initArgs` parameter like the following would indicate that the `provider.xml` file can be found in the `\provider\hello` subdirectory of the Apache root directory, and that a timeout will occur after 3 minutes (specified in milliseconds):

```
servlet.hello.initArgs=provider_root=\provider\hello,sessiontimeout=180000
```

Once this configuration is complete, you will create the `provider.xml` file in the specified directory. Its format is documented at Portal Studio and in `jpdk.zip` (see `xml_tag_reference.txt`), but the following sample provider containing a single JSP portlet is provided for reference. Notice how all of the information that was contained in the `portlet_record` in PDK-PL/SQL is now specified using XML tags.

```xml
<provider class="oracle.portal.provider.v1.http.DefaultProvider">

    <portlet class="oracle.portal.provider.v1.http.DefaultPortlet">
        <id>1</id>
        <name>HelloWorldJsp</name>
        <title>Hello World JSP</title>
        <description>
            This portlet is a "hello world" sample implemented by JSP.
        </description>
        <timeout>30</timeout>
        <timeoutMessage>Hello World JSP timed out</timeoutMessage>
        <showEdit>false</showEdit>
        <showEditDefault>false</showEditDefault>
        <showPreview>false</showPreview>
        <showDetails>false</showDetails>
        <hasHelp>true</hasHelp>
        <hasAbout>true</hasAbout>
        <acceptContentType>text/html</acceptContentType>
        <renderer class="oracle.portal.provider.v1.RenderManager">
            <appPath>/servlets/helloworld</appPath>
            <appRoot>d:\ias\Apache\JServ\servlets\helloworld</appRoot>
            <renderContainer>true</renderContainer>
            <contentType>text/html</contentType>
            <charSet>UTF-8</charSet>
            <showPage>hello.jsp</showPage>
            <helpPage>hellohelp.html</helpPage>
            <aboutPage>helloabout.html</aboutPage>
        </renderer>
    </portlet>

</provider>
```

With this information complete (and the 9i Application Server restarted), you can register your provider in Portal. The registration process is similar to registering a provider, but for the Web provider, you will specify the URL of the provider servlet or the alias ("hello") you registered in `zone.properties`.

Writing the Portlets

Unless you have a complex display or call interface, you will usually not have to write any Java code to perform the actual rendering of the portlets. As you can see in the `provider.xml` file above, the portlet element contains a reference to a default `PortletRenderer` class, supplying the path of the application code. For each portlet show mode, a file name indicates the resource to display. The `PortletRenderer` class does all the work to locate the resource, optionally draw the borders and title, and put the output of the resource into the portlet. The resource can be any file in any language on any server (provided the full path has been specified), as long as the output of the resource is HTTP-compliant. This opens up the enormous possibility of using PDK-Java to integrate and share diverse Web resources. Most portlets will be implemented in Java, to take advantage of the PDK-Java "runtime" utilities, a set of default handlers including the `PortletRenderer` discussed here.

Additional runtime utilities include the `PortletPersonalizationManager`, which supports end-user customization of portlets. Reference this class in your Java portlet code to store and retrieve user settings for each portlet. The `PortletSecurityManager` assists with identifying users and groups and determining appropriate privileges for each. Note that none of these additional classes are required to write custom Java portlets; they are merely helper applications to save you from having to write significant amounts of code. Additionally, if you want to use parts of the classes but don't like the way particular methods are implemented, you can subclass and override less desirable methods.

Finally, PDK-Java provides utilities similar to the `WWUI_API_UTIL` and other packages in a Java class named `HttpPortletRendererUtil`. This class contains methods to draw the title bar, write text and HTML, and specify how to cache the portlets' content, among others.

Using PDK-Java, you can reference any Web resource, or write your custom portlets as JSPs or any other Java implementation. We have only summarized PDK-Java here, but you can access the Portal Studio Web site as well as the `jpdk.zip` file for more detailed information.

Portlet Leasing and Purchase Options

When you need customized portlets, particularly those that provide general interest content, but simply do not have the time or expertise to develop them in-house, you might consider obtaining them from a third party. Because the Portal framework is an open API, it creates a marketplace in which vendors can create canned portlets that simply plug in to your installation. You can even outsource custom development, one portlet at a time. The connectivity aspect of the Internet protocol means that the portlets can reside anywhere and retrieve content from anywhere. Information about vendors in this business can be found on the Portal Catalog tab of the Portal Studio Web site.

Generally, one of two models is used in a portlet licensing transaction. The portlet will either be hosted by the vendor and accessed using a Web provider, or it will be downloaded, configured, and installed locally. The latter method is less convenient and subject to many possible points of failure and version conflicts, but it does allow more control over the displayed content. If the source is available, you can modify the portlets to suit your own needs, but you will then be responsible for its maintenance. The vendor-hosted model is more suitable for general-purpose content, such as news, weather, and stock quotes, or for access to large industry-specific information repositories. A sample of portlets offered by YellowBrix, an Oracle Portal Partner, is shown in Figure 11-8. Depending on the actual implementation, you may be able to customize even a vendor-hosted provider.

Exercise 11.3: Incorporate Third-Party Portlets

To illustrate the simplicity of the vendor-hosted model, we obtained a trial release of portlets available from YellowBrix. To complete this exercise, you will need to register for the 30-day trial offered on their Web site at

http://www.yellowbrix.com/pages/www/corporate/portlet_register.nsp

Using the YellowBrix Portlets application is optional; you may obtain any third-party portlet provider demo. Just be sure to follow the vendor's instructions for Portal integration.

1. Log in to Portal as the Portal administrator. On the home page, click on the Administer tab.

2. Ensure that your proxy settings are configured properly for Web Services, as described in the section of that name on the Global setting page. In order for Portal to make any Web calls, it needs to know how to get through the proxy server

3. Click Add a Portlet Provider. Set the Provider Name to YellowBrix, and the Display Name to YellowBrix Portlets. Increase the Timeout to 100 seconds.

4. Choose an Implementation Style of Web and scroll down to the section on Web providers. Set the URL to http://portal.yellowbrix.com/

`portlet/yellowbrix` and enter the Provider Key given in your trial license instructions.

5. Click OK, then view (and refresh if necessary) the Portlet Repository.

6. Now return to the eXYZ home page, where we will add one of the YellowBrix portlets.

7. Click on the Edit page and then click the Add Portlets icon for the left-hand region that displays for all tab pages.

8. Choose the My News portlet (or any of your choosing) and add it just below the Favorites portlet so it will be easily seen.

9. Click Close to view the page with the new portlet. Click the Customize link and choose a news topic to display. Try using the More News Headlines link to see another interface. Notice how the story details feed into the portlet on the right.

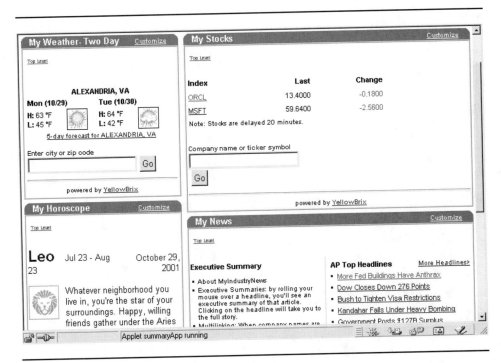

FIGURE 11-8. *YellowBrix offers portlets such as these on a subscription basis*

Vendor-supplied portlets can be an important addition to a Portal site. The example shown here is implemented as a Web Services provider using PDK-Java, and requires only minimal installation and no maintenance.

Conclusion

This chapter concludes the development section of this book. We have illustrated many development techniques to build, integrate, and display Portal applications. The big finish is a completely open-ended interface in which you can develop your own portlet code, either in Java or in PL/SQL. Whether you write the code yourself or license it from others, the possibilities are most certainly endless.

CHAPTER
12

Deploying, Tuning, and Maintaining the Portal

fully developed and approved Portal application is not necessarily ready for prime-time deployment until there is absolute certainty that the system is secure and scalable for the expected number of users. Security considerations must be well understood and security software and procedures in place before the system can go live. The database, the hardware, and the application server must be tuned and ready to accept the expected number of users. The Portal application itself must be evaluated to ensure that it is scalable and fine-tuned before users begin fully exploring its capabilities.

Lastly, a plan must be in place and procedures developed for maintaining the working portal and to ensure that fresh appropriate content keeps corporate interest and focus on the portal alive. The portal can be an exciting hub of enterprise computing or it can become an expensive toy that is greeted with excitement the first day and discontent due to poor security, slow response times, and stale content the next.

This chapter will identify the best methods for deploying a portal across the enterprise as an intranet, Internet, or extranet application and detail the best practices for tuning and maintaining the application. We will focus on the following:

- Oracle 9iAS Apache web server administration

- Methods for tuning and scaling Portal

- Portal security

- Database administration

- Monitoring the portal

Oracle 9i Application Server: Apache

The Oracle 9iAS Apache server is a very complicated piece of software that requires an in-depth understanding in order to configure, maintain, and tune it. In this section we will delve into an overview of the Oracle 9i Application Server powered by Apache, but we will limit our discussion to configuration of Apache within Portal, and an overview of the important configuration files and tuning concepts needed to ensure a dependable Portal site. We will discuss the following in this section:

- Apache server administration

- Apache startup and shutdown

- HTTPD configuration file

Apache Web Server Administration

The Apache Web server carries the bulk of the HTTP server market share, serving more than 60 percent of the world's Web sites. Apache is an open source code Web server, meaning that it is extensible and can be tailored to user needs. You will perform the bulk of the configuration and administration of the Apache server by editing the `httpd.conf` configuration file. Integrated Oracle extensions to the Apache server, such as Reports, Forms, XML, and PLSQL, are recognized and configured from the `oracle_apache.conf` file. Your primary job as the Apache administrator will be to ensure that the Apache server stays up, is secure, and has adequate performance.

With the 9iAS Portal tight integration with the database and the Apache server, it is extremely important to ensure that all Oracle database patches stay current. You may download Oracle database patches and apply them to your database from the Oracle Technology Network or Metalink Web sites at Oracle. Full documentation for the Oracle 9iAS server can be found by directing your browser to the machine your Apache server is installed on, identifying the machine and port number (`ex.` `http://<yourserver>:7777/`). This will bring up generic Apache documentation that covers a wide range of topics and issues related to Apache administration and programming.

Apache Startup and Shutdown

There are a number of ways to start and stop the Apache server. The easiest method in Windows NT is to start the server from the Control Panel under NT services. When the Apache server is installed, the OracleisuitesHTTPServer Service will install in the Services window as an Automatic startup function. To check whether it is up and running, you may proceed to Start | Settings | Control Panel | Services and browse down until you see the HTTPServer Services offering. You may see two of them if you did not deinstall the HTTP server that comes preinstalled with the database and you are hosting your Portal site all on one machine.

If this is the case, the HTTP server associated with the Oracle database home should be left as a manual service or deinstalled and the HTTP server associated with the Portal home should be left as an automatic service. An automatic service will begin as soon as a machine is started or rebooted. Ensure that there are no users on your system, highlight the HTTP server service, and click the Stop button to the right. You will be prompted as to whether or not you want to continue, click Yes and after a moment or two, the Apache server will stop and the Status field will be blank. While keeping the service highlighted, click Start and the Apache Server Status area will show Started when the server is up and running.

Another method to start and stop the Apache server is from the Programs menu. This method for startup and shutdown is the preferred method of the two as it tends to be more stable and offers better cleanup of processes. To stop the server using this method, click Start | Programs | Oracle – ISuites | Oracle HTTP Server | Stop HTTP Server Powered by Apache. To restart it, follow the same path and click Start HTTP Server Powered by Apache. It is important to wait a few minutes after you have stopped the Apache server before you restart it again to allow the server to stop gracefully and write to log files. The Apache server will take a while to stop when it is under an active workload. Trying to restart a server immediately, before it has shut down, will kill user connections from the last Apache session that is finishing up, which could result in loss of data in an application—or, at best, user angst.

Apache HTTPD Configuration file

There is no program to edit parameters or tune Apache. Almost every parameter that an Apache Administrator will need to work with Apache is found in the `httpd.conf` configuration file. The `httpd.conf` file is broken down into three sections:

- Global environment directives that set Apache's environment

- Main server directives that fine tune the global directives

- Virtual host setups, including SSL

Apache uses *container directives*, syntax arguments used to identify conditions and directives for handling specific conditions. Container directives are enclosed in less than/greater than brackets (<>). A sample syntax is as follows:

```
<Directory />
    Options FollowSymLinks
    AllowOverride None
</Directory>
```

The configuration file operates in a hierarchy where arguments at the beginning that generally apply to the Apache configuration can be overridden by specific arguments later on in the file. Section 1 includes log filenames, timeout limits, maximum concurrent user limits, and other global limits that affect performance and server function. The server hostname, port, root directory information, server administrator email address, and other higher-level information are available in the global environment directives in section 2. Fine-grain control such as Secure Socket Layer security and virtual hosts is identified and configured in the third section of the configuration file.

Entire books have been written about Apache server administration and some recommended ones are listed in Appendix A. We delve into configuration of virtual hosts and SSL in the next section of the book on Portal security. For the purposes of this book, we will highlight a few areas of the configuration file of interest.

The Alias command allows documents to be stored anywhere in the local file system in a directory other than the root directory. A URL specifying an icon in the `Oracle/Isuites/Apache/Apache/icons` directory will find it in the correct file system directory based on the alias that is defined in the current configuration file identified in the following code:

```
<IfModule mod_alias.c>
    Alias /icons/ "E:\ORACLE\iSuites\Apache/Apache/icons/"
    <Directory "E:\ORACLE\iSuites\Apache\Apache/icons">
        Options Indexes MultiViews
        AllowOverride None
        Order allow,deny
        Allow from all
    </Directory>
</IfModule>
```

If you wish to add additional aliases for images, you can add it into the preceding code. Include a Directory container directive such as the one above with it to define the location of the image directory and to identify the search criteria for finding the image.

Two other directives to pay attention to are `KeepAliveTimeout` and `MaxClients`. Every client that logs into Portal is taking up system resources. If they are taking up those resources needlessly, the `KeepAliveTimeout` directory prevents sessions from continuing to use resources after a period of inactivity. `MaxClients` should be used with care to restrict the number of HTTP server users. `MaxClients` refers to the concurrent http connections handled by the http server, and is not the same as the number of concurrent users. When a user issues a request for a page, it may result in multiple http connections to construct the page, with a separate http connection initiated to request each portlet and image on the page. If this number is consistently being reached, consider splitting up your configuration and distributing your load to multiple Web servers.

Tuning and Scaling Oracle Portal

The advantage of a portal is that it centrally delivers information to the end user from multiple applications and components. This corporate dashboard approach to enterprise computing is a blessing for end users that desire centralized corporate information delivered specifically to the desktop in a role-based manner. It is a little more daunting to the information technology professionals that must deliver that information in an efficient high-performance manner. It is particularly difficult when you must consider that a number of factors influence performance, including number of concurrent users, hardware performance and CPU speed, memory, network bandwidth, placement of the server on the network in relation to the majority of users, database considerations (including indexing and tuning), application efficiency, caching, and other factors.

In this section we will factor these varying considerations into our discussion of how to tune and scale a Portal site for maximum throughput for your users. We will concentrate on application, page, and content area tuning, and load-balancing systems. Let's get started with the basics of application tuning.

Application Tuning

At the beginning of the book and in the last chapter we discussed the architecture of Oracle Portal and discussed the Apache server, `mod_plsql`, Jserv, the Parallel Page Engine (PPE), and the database, and how they work together to support the development and generation of Portal pages for the user through a desktop browser. Let's look closer at how these important pieces of Portal work together and how they can be utilized to maximum efficiency.

Web applications normally work well and can scale upward for larger implementations in a multitier architecture, as shown in Figure 12-1. In this example, corporate end users request Portal pages and the content and applications rendered on them by making an HTTP request of the Apache Internet application server. When a page is requested, a number of activities are set into motion in order to deliver the

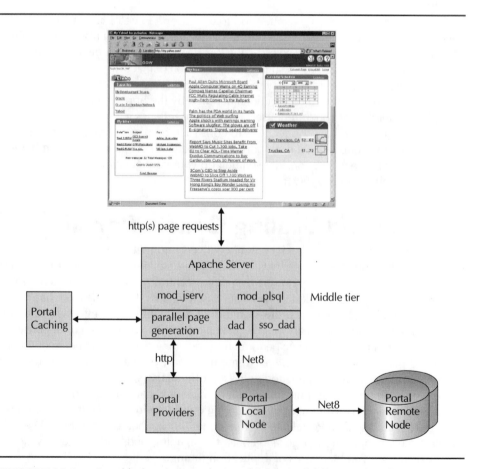

FIGURE 12-1. *Load balancing results in a highly scalable Portal architecture*

fully rendered page back to the end user's browser. The HTTP server directs all requests for database information to the `mod_plsql` engine that provides a direct connection to the Oracle database. `mod_plsql` identifies any local or remote Portal components or content that will be rendered on the page being requested. Any Java servlets that are needed to render the page are requested from the database at the same time and routed through `Jserv`.

The Java-based Parallel Page Engine makes calls to the `mod_plsql` routines to retrieves all of the data about the page, including page styles and layouts, internal and external Web content, and all portlets, and assembles all of the information to be delivered to the end user on the page. The PPE accesses and utilizes the caching definitions for all portlets, components, content areas, pages, and page styles to identify whether to assemble the page from memory using the Portal cache mechanism or to retrieve the page data and content directly from the database and assemble all or part of the page from scratch.

Lastly, the page is rendered back to the user's browser via Apache as a fully functional Portal page. As new requests are made within a session, this same process is invoked to render component applications on the screen, view content and documents, perform searches, or follow links to other Web sites. Knowledge of this architecture and the processes involved will allow you to make good decisions when it comes to identifying bottlenecks in the system and how to improve performance. Let's explore some general tuning considerations for Portal applications.

The first checkpoint for tuning is the database itself. Make sure that plenty of memory has been allocated to the `SHARED_POOL_SIZE`, `LARGE_POOL_SIZE`, and `JAVA_POOL_SIZE`. A minimum for all three should be 50MB for a medium-sized Portal application. Raise the limit to 75MB or more if you have memory to spare. Ensure that plenty of space has been allocated in the Portal tablespace for Portal growth. In general, follow best practices for configuring a large-volume production database that must accommodate frequent reads by many users and rely heavily on server-based code. These practices include, but are certainly not limited to, caching frequently used database tables and designing the physical database to optimize retrieval via different index or table types.

It is important to inspect the application components, content, and pages that you have developed, for potential bottlenecks. The first bottleneck that should be avoided is excessive graphics or rendering of images. Use images to augment text, but do it sparingly and only to improve the look of a page. Use the JPEG format for logos, images, and online photos, as it compresses more efficiently than other formats. Animated images should be avoided if possible. The overhead required to view them is not worth the extra viewing pleasure they might provide. Lastly, creating pages with subtabs within tabs is very inefficient—avoid this scenario at all costs.

Application components should be analyzed to ensure that they are executing efficiently. Standard procedure for ensuring a component is running at peak efficiency includes identifying all table indexes are utilized to maximum extent for all reports including charts, calendars, and hierarchies. Application tuning relies heavily on, but is not limited to, ensuring that the SQL commands used by the application are optimized to use indexed access, complying with the principles outlined in Oracle's online documentation as well as in books such as *Oracle PL/SQL Tips and Techniques* by Joseph Trezzo (Oracle Press, 1999) or *Oracle PL/SQL Best Practices* by Steven Feuerstein (O'Reilly & Associates, 2000), and others cited in Appendix A. Keep applications simple and small to ensure that they execute and render quickly on a page. Complex Portal pages with lots of applications on a page will be slow to render. Lastly, use the caching mechanisms within Portal as much as possible for everything.

Portal Caching

Caching applications, pages, and content offer by far the greatest tuning opportunities within Oracle Portal. Assembling a Portal page with full content and applications directly from the database is a very intensive operation that utilizes a great deal of CPU, network, and memory resources. Portal institutes a caching mechanism in the middle tier of the application using the PPE to determine whether caching is turned on or off for a specific page, piece of content, application component, or utility.

Caching is typically performed either in validation-based or time-based mode using the owa_cache package that is part of the PL/SQL Web Toolkit that you installed with Portal. When validation-based caching occurs, a page request signals the middle-tier applications to contact the database repository to identify the type of caching mechanism employed, to obtain information about the object or objects to be rendered within the user's browser, and to check page privileges for the requestor.

With validation-based caching, mod_plspl executes the procedure requested, and passes in the cache key information to the procedure via owa_cache. The portal, or portlet, procedure then determines whether the cache key is still valid based on any content or security changes that may have transpired since the cache key, and associated cached content, was generated. If the cache key is good, then the procedure simply returns, without spending the additional time and resource to generate new content, and indicates to mod_plsql that the cached content should be served up. If the cache key is no longer valid, then the new content is generated and the cache key is updated, indicating to mod_plsql that the cached copy should be replaced and the newly generated content returned to the requestor. All caching can be overridden by clicking on the Refresh link on the Portal home page. This action will refresh all page elements and objects from the database.

Time-based caching works in a similar way in that all pages are checked against the database metadata for the validity of the page timestamp and for security before the page is rendered. The PPE makes a call to the database to check the validity of the timestamp for the page metadata. As a next step, a security check is also made to see if the user should be able to see the page. These checks can be done very quickly— much quicker than regenerating the page each time. Next a check is made to ensure the page metadata is still valid. If the page definition has been modified or customized, a page has expired, or a programming change has occurred that changes the look of the page, the page metadata will be regenerated with a new timestamp and a refresh will occur to retrieve the full page from the database. However, if nothing has changed on the page it is rendered from cache until the expiration time refresh date has been reached, and then the page or object will again be refreshed from the database.

The Portal administrator can adjust the Portal cache settings by setting parameters at `http://myserver/pls/portal30/admin_/cache.htm` or by using the Cache Configuration Settings page, accessible from the Portal home page | Administer tab | Listener Gateway Settings link as shown in Figure 12-2. Always ensure that Enable PL/SQL Caching is set to `Yes`. The Cache directory specifies where the temporary versions of the cached pages will be written.

Only the Maximum Cacheable File Size (in bytes) setting is a hard limit for the amount of disk space allocated for caching objects. Set the log files on to capture caching information and always adjust the cacheable file size limit upward if the log reports show that caching hits the maximum limit on a recurring basis. Any request for a page that is made after the cache maximum file size is exceeded will result in automatic calls to the database to refresh the page, and degradation in performance.

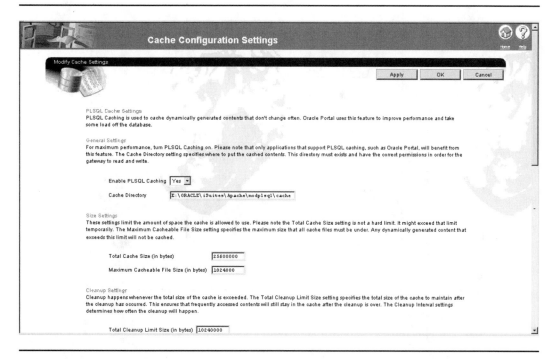

FIGURE 12-2. *Portal cache settings are adjusted in the Cache Configuration Settings screen*

Load Balancing

A frequently used method for scaling a Web-based application is load balancing. As the name implies, load balancing offers the ability to distribute the load of an application off onto multiple servers, thus minimizing the impact one server will have as the bottleneck in a production environment. Generally, because they perform most of the work processing applications, the middle tier (consisting of the Apache Jserv and the PPE) will be split out and distributed across multiple servers to achieve the greatest improvement in performance. Hosting the login server on a separate Oracle instance can result in some performance gains for an enterprise Portal application. Lesser performance gains can also be achieved by hosting the Apache listeners on separate servers and distributing the listener load for login requests, file handling, and file services.

Lastly, multiple nodes of Portal can be set up in the database on multiple servers to balance the content load on the database tier, as shown in Figure 12-3. Setting up multiple tiers in the Portal architecture, including the HTTP server, the middle-tier Jserv

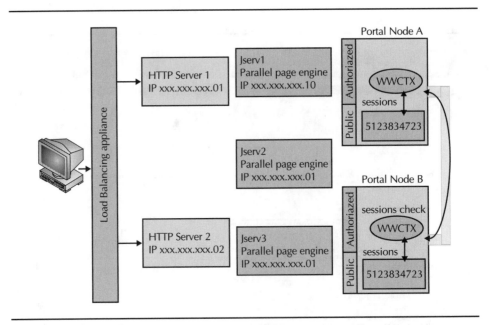

FIGURE 12-3. *Scaling a Web application up in a multitier architecture*

and PPE, and lastly the database engine of Portal, can serve to quickly improve the scalability of the Portal architecture and performance. Let's look at each of these options in some depth.

First, to achieve a simple three-tier architecture where the browser machine, middle-tier application server, and database server represent the three separate tiers of the architecture, simply ensure that the database server is on a separate machine when you perform the Portal install. Do this by keying in a connect string at installation time that identifies an Oracle database that is resident on another machine. Type the IP address or machine name:port name:sid. You will be prompted later on to configure the TNSNAMES.ORA file to ensure that the Portal middle tier can connect to the database.

To move a Portal application that is already developed in a multi-tier architecture to this configuration, it is probably easiest to install a new middle tier and point it to the existing database server that is sized to handle a production workload. Alternatively, you may wish to keep the existing server and install a more powerful database server. In this case you may export the applications and content from the single-tier database, install the new three-tier architecture, and then import the developed application and content into the new database. There are other ways to reconfigure an existing single-tier Portal application into a three-tier architecture, but this is the cleanest and safest.

Creating Remote Portal Nodes

You can further utilize and extend the three-tier architecture by distributing the database load of your enterprise Portal by employing additional Portal *nodes*. A Portal node is a single instance of Oracle Portal installed either on the local primary database or on a remote Portal instance. When you have successfully logged into Portal, you are logging into the local node of Portal. By recognizing and incorporating remote Portal nodes in Portal, you can distribute the content, application, and page load across database servers on the back end and realize performance gains on an overtaxed Portal host machine.

You may enter a remote note for another Portal instance using the Add a Remote Node link in the Node section of the Administer page. In order to add a remote node, you need to coordinate administration information between both Portal machines. You will need to know some information in the TNSNAMES file from the remote Oracle database, the remote node name for the Portal and the Administrator userid and password, the host address and port number for the Portal configuration, and the DAD settings for the remote Portal node.

Creating a Remote Node

To create a remote node, you will need to specify the following:

1. Enter the name of the remote node that you are linking to. If you are unsure what the name is, have the remote node administrator use the Edit the Local Node link from the Administer tab to see the local node name on the Portal instance you desire to connect to. Type the exact name of the remote node in the Remote Node Name field.

2. In the Oracle Portal Database User field, type the name of the remote node schema owner. The Portal user account should be the account that owns the Portal schema on the remote node, in our case PORTAL30.

3. In the Oracle Portal Database Password field, type the password for the Portal30 user.

4. In the Database Link Name field, type a name for the database link. By default, the Database Link Name will be the same as the remote node name if nothing is typed in this field.

5. In the Remote Database Information fields, you will key in information for connecting to the remote database. You can either specify a TNS Names entry, or alternatively, type the IP address in the Host Address field and key in the host service name and the host port number (usually 1521).

6. In the Host Listener Settings dialog box, you will specify the Remote Portal DAD name as defined in the listener settings for the remote instance, the remote listener URL used to connect to the portal (for example, www.exyz.com:7777/pls), and the remote listener port (7777), as shown in Figure 12-4.

Once the node is created, click on the Refresh Remote Provider Information from the Administer tab to recognize the remote node information in your local node. You may modify the local node name by using the Edit the Local Node link on the Node portion of the Administer tab. There should be no real reason to do this unless you want to have a standardized naming convention for Portal nodes across the organization. You may change the node to any name using a combination of letters, numbers, or underscores—not to exceed 200 characters.

When load balancing across nodes, consider distributing and balancing logical portions of your Portal among the various Portal nodes. For instance, if the sales division has an active Portal page or tab that has a tremendous load volume, split the application providers for sales and sales content onto separate nodes via the export/import process to offload the sales activity onto a dedicated Portal server. The page that the user

Remote Node Name and the Trusted Database User
Enter the name of the remote node. The node name uniquely identifies an Oracle Portal installation. Enter a trusted database user and the users' password where Oracle Portal is installed. The database user name and password are used to create the database link and are not saved. Optionally, enter the name for the database link.

Remote Node Name	nyc_node
Oracle Portal Database User	PORTAL30
Oracle Portal Database Password	
Database Link Name	nyc_node.MONUMENTAL.COM

Hint: If the remote database enforces global naming, then the database link name must match the remote database's global database name. If this field is left blank, then the node's name will be used for the link name.

Remote Database Information
Enter either the TNS name for the database or the host address, the service name, and the host port number.

    ◯ Enter the TNS name for the database link

TNS Name	ORCL.DOMAIN

    ◯ Specify the database link by entering the host address, the service name, and port number.

Host Address	
Host Service Name	
Host Port	

Host Listener Settings
Enter the remote listener's Oracle Portal DAD, the host URL, and port number. If the host url or port number are not entered, then the local node's listener settings are used.

Remote Oracle Portal DAD	portal30
Remote Listener URL	exyz:7777/pls/

FIGURE 12-4. *Adding a remote node in Oracle Portal*

interacts with will then pull all sales information from the remote node, not the local node—thus reducing the load on the local database server.

In this way, you may distribute the process of building content on a page across multiple Portal database instances and reduce the load on the database to retrieve content and information. In order to do this, you need to follow the instructions to centralize the login server so that users will login centrally and then draw page content from distributed nodes. When you have set up the architecture properly, use the Monitor tab to view statistics on the most frequently used pages and applications to determine a game plan for the proper distribution approach.

To set up this distributed environment, each Portal node instance must have its own DAD, one created from the Portal install process or using the Oracle 9iAS Portal Configuration Assistant. More than one DAD, and thus more than one instance of Portal, may be installed in the same Oracle database instance. Since only one DAD is created during the Portal install process, you must create subsequent DADs using the Administer tab | Services | Listener Gateway Settings link.

Additionally, all nodes must be registered among each other so if node A registers and recognizes node B, node B must also register and recognize node A in a distributed application. If more than one Apache server is utilized, a single cookie domain must be created, and then it must be recognized in the DAD configuration for all Portal nodes. Refer to the *Oracle 9iAS Portal Configuration Guide* for the procedures required to set up multiple Apache servers and a single cookie domain.

Centralizing the Login Server in a Distributed Portal Mode

If you distribute your application at the database level and have multiple nodes, you are required to centralize your login server to ensure that there is one place for all users to log in and to consolidate the administration process. You may centralize the Login server by installing it on one of the Oracle Portal node instances. For optimum load balancing, you may have two machines running the Oracle database version 8.1.7 or above. In this scenario, one server supports the Portal applications and content, and the other database server supports user authentication, login, and login administration exclusively, as shown in Figure 12-5. To do this, you must first ensure that the host you intend to use as the login server is defined in the `TNSNAMES.ORA` file in your `IAS_HOME/network/admin` directory. If it is not, use the Net8 Configuration Assistant found in the Oracle – `ISuites | Network | Admin` menu to configure the connection.

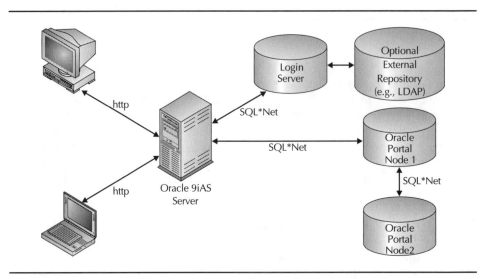

FIGURE 12-5. *The Portal architecture using a separate login server for authentication*

Next you will need to install the login server on the new login server host machine by running the `linstall` login script found in the `<IAS_HOME>portal30/ admin/plsql` directory, where `IAS_HOME` in our case is `iSuites`.

Creating a Separate Login Server

1. Go to the Windows command prompt, navigate to the `plsql` directory we just discussed, and type `linstall` to view the format for executing the script.

2. Execute the script using the parameters identified. The script will take approximately 45 minutes to run, and it will create the login server IDs and DADs to support the new login server.

3. When the script is completed, access the new DAD via your Web browser by linking to `HTTP://<new login server name:port`. You should see the Access Partner Applications page, as shown in Figure 12-6.

4. Click on the Login link and log in to the login server as PORTAL30_SSO.

5. Click on the Login Server Administration link, click on the Administer Partner Applications link, and then click on Add Partner Application.

6. Type your Portal Node name (example: exyz_login_server) in the Name field.

7. In the Home URL field, type `HTTP://<new login server name or IP address>:<Port>/pls/portal30/portal30.home`.

8. In the Success URL field, type `http://exyz_server.com:<Port>/ pls/portal30/portal30.wwsec_app_priv.process_signon`.

9. Leave the Valid Login Timeframe blank.

10. Fill in the Administrator Email address and the Administrator Information address of the primary point of contact for login administration duties.

You will see the Portal Node application added in as a partner application when this completes. Additionally, you will note that an ID, a token, and an encryption key are generated upon the successful completion of this process, as shown in Figure 12-6. Write down each of these numbers as you will use them in the next step, which identifies the login server machine and DADs to the original Portal installation.

Go back to the command prompt that you were in before to the `<IAS_ HOME>portal30/admin/plsql` directory where you will run the `ssodatax` script. Type in `ssodatax` at the command line to view the parameter syntax before

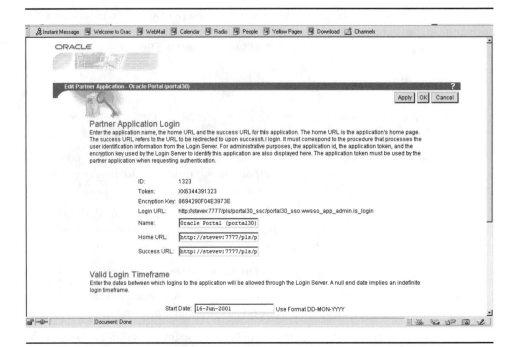

FIGURE 12-6. *The ID, site token, and encryption key identify and secure the login server*

executing the procedure. By running this script, you will identify the login server machine and DADs to the Portal. When an end user logs into the Portal application, they will be routed to the new login server for authentication.

Portal Security

Security is of paramount importance in the development and deployment of the working Portal. We have discussed in prior chapters how user and group privileges work within Portal to control user access to pages, content areas, applications, and the Portal application itself. In this section we will extend that discussion to identify how to ensure proper user authentication using the default lightweight single sign-on authentication mechanisms within Portal. We will discuss LDAP and SSL security mechanisms that enable a significantly reduced total cost of ownership for user account maintenance and integration with other enterprise systems and security procedures. In this chapter, we will discuss:

- An overview of Oracle Portal security
- Password administration

- LDAP authentication

- SSL security

- Other security considerations including firewall support

- Login server administration

An Overview of Oracle Portal Security

As we have discussed throughout the book, Oracle Portal employs a lightweight authentication process known as single sign-on to register users within Portal and to authenticate users and determine privileges for those users to access applications and content. Oracle Portal itself is registered as a partner application to the login server, as we saw in Figure 12-6, and by virtue of this subordinate relationship it requires user authentication from the login server for its use like any other application. The login server authenticates the user and then returns control to the user and to the portal itself. Having established that a user has the authority to access Portal with any associated individual privileges, the portal then provides single sign-on access to external applications that have been registered with the login server and exposed in the Portal's External Application's portlet.

It is important to understand the actual registration process of a user in single sign-on. When the user directs their browser to a Portal page or content area, a PL/SQL database procedure is invoked in Portal. If the page or content has public privileges, the page is returned back to the user's browser and the session will continue. If the object requested requires authentication, the process depicted in Figure 12-7 is invoked.

First the `WWSEC_APP_PRIV.CHECK_PRIVILEGE` function is called; the function checks to ensure that the user is logged on. If the page requested is not public and the user has insufficient privileges, the authentication process begins and a session *cookie* is established that remains a unique session identifier throughout the individual user's Portal session. Portal will pass the user on to the Login Server where parameters will be passed to the `WWSSO_APP_ADMIN.ls_login` procedure that include a token that represents the requested application and check for the login cookie that is granted every authenticated user who successfully gains access to Portal. If it is present, it means the user logged in previously and they will be granted access to the page based on the privileges they have been granted within Portal. If the cookie is not present, the user will be presented with the login screen.

When the user is requested to authenticate for the first time, they will key in their userid and password that they were assigned by the Portal administrator. If they successfully log in, they will be assigned a login cookie. The login cookie validates that the user successfully performed a login through the login server and will uniquely identify the user's login session. The URL requested will be converted to a success URL using the `WWSEC_APP_PRIV.process_signon` procedure and the `WWSEC_APP_PRIV.check_privilege` procedure will be checked one more time to ensure that the user has the proper privileges to view everything on the requested page.

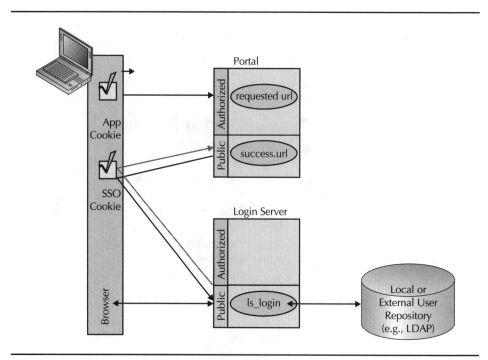

FIGURE 12-7. *The user authentication process in Oracle Portal*

If everything has checked out, the user will view the page they requested. As the authenticated user continues to browse pages, all requests for new content or applications will invoke the `WWSEC_APP_PRIV.check_privilege` procedure but the login cookie passed to the procedure will identify the user as authenticated and the procedure will only check for proper privileges on each page until the user logs out and the session is over.

Single sign-on also extends to external applications, including Oracle's suite of Web-based development tools such as Oracle Forms, Reports, graphics, the Discoverer browser tool, Express, and Oracle applications. Single sign-on can extend to almost any other external Web-based source and support one login to the Portal in order to access any application. We saw in Chapter 3 how to supply a userid and password and connect to a registered external application, using Hotmail as an example. Let's see how this works with the login server in a little more detail.

Portal must make the login server aware of external applications in order for them to be authenticated by the login server. This is done by registering the external application within Portal from the Portal home page Administer tab | Administer External Applications link. Once this registration has taken place, the application will be registered within the External Applications portlet in the Portlet Repository and it is available for inclusion on a page within Oracle Portal.

There are three ways to register an external application within Portal from the Add External Application link (see Figure 12-8). The choice of which one to use depends on how the external application expects to receive the user credentials. All options send the user ID and password directly to the external application for authentication. The login server attempts the login, and if the external application accepts the credentials, the user will be able to view the external page. The only difference between POST and GET is the method by which the credentials are passed; POST sends the credentials in the body of the request, and GET sends them in the URL query string. The BASIC AUTHENTICATION method is used for applications that normally prompt the user with an HTTP authentication request. Instead of showing the prompt to the user, the Login Server sends the stored credentials in the same format that a browser would use in response to an authentication request. All methods are as secure as the underlying protocol and are subject to eavesdropping if not encrypted over HTTPS. The GET method has security concern of displaying the user ID and password in the query string of the URL. There is currently a downloadable patch to encrypt the GET username and password in the URL.

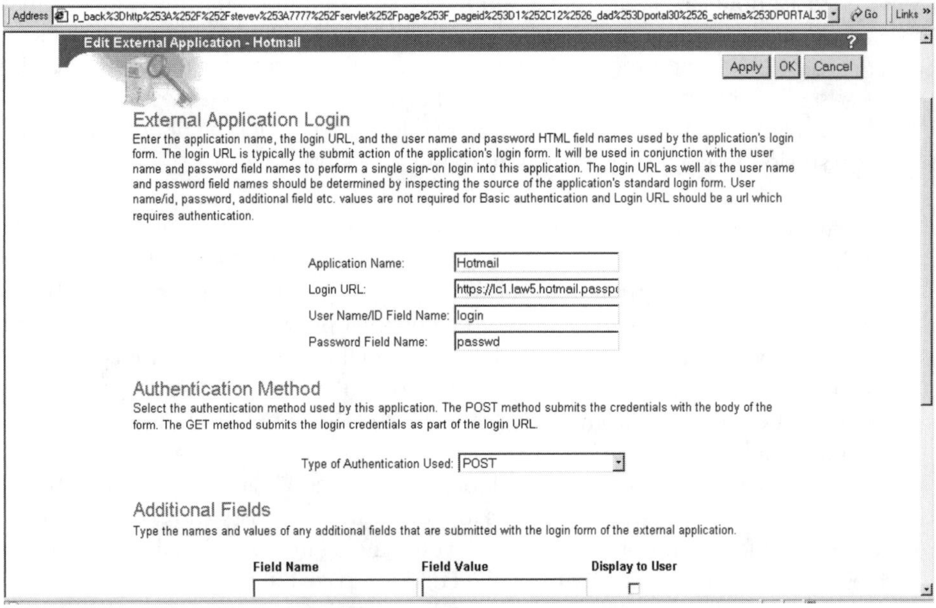

FIGURE 12-8. *The External Application login form using the POST command*

Password Administration

Password administration is an important function in any corporation. Typically, user passwords are changed on a recurring basis as a normal security measure. It is a good practice to enforce some kind of standard for passwords to ensure that a certain degree of complexity is ingrained into the structure of the password. This is enforced by navigating to the Home Page Administer tab, clicking the Edit Login Server Configuration link, and modifying the Edit Login Server dialogue screen, as shown in Figure 12-9.

The Password Policy section allows you to set policies for user password administration. You should generally follow these rules for password administration:

1. Password Life should be set to 120 days or fewer in an intranet application.

2. Minimum Password Length field should be set to at least 5.

3. Check the check box on each of the following to enforce password standards: do not allow password to be the same as username, do not allow new password to be the same as current password, and require password to contain at least one numeric digit.

4. In the Account Lock Policy field, change the single sign-on session duration to 12 hours (or less). The account lock session duration is the duration that an account remains locked after an unauthorized login attempt. It does not control session timeout. The timeout specified here is for the single sign-on session, but this has no bearing on the validity of the Portal session. The only way to terminate Portal sessions now is to logout or close your browser. Portal session timeout will be included in future releases.

Password expiration policies are set from the Login Server Configuration page. The user will be notified when their password is about to expire. We left the "Number of days before password expiration to show warning" field at 7 days, signifying that the user has a week to key in a new password when their password expires after 90 days. If a user at a specific IP address fails to log in within the number of attempts specified in the "Number of login failures allowed from one IP address" field, any user at that address will be prevented from logging back in for the amount of time specified in the "Global lockout duration" field.

Now that we have enforced some global password and login server standards for our users, we have a range of options to work with daily password administration issues. If a user forgets his or her password, you may log in as the Portal administrator and reset the password manually using the Edit User page found under the Portal home page Administer tab. The administrator must log in under the administrator ID, edit and find the specific user, and then key in their own password in the Edit User dialog box

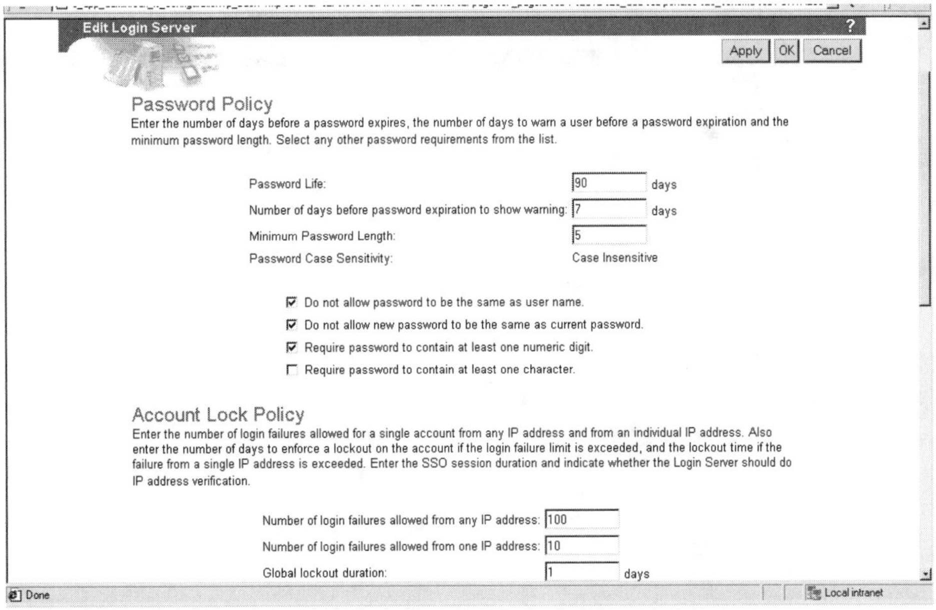

FIGURE 12-9. *The Login Server Configuration screen sets security policy*

to authenticate that they have permissions to reset the user's password. Then the administrator can key in a new password, confirm it, and save and register the new password with the login server. The user has the option of keying in a new password of their own choosing at any time following the login server standard once they are able to successfully log back into the Portal. Note also that the administrator has the option to delete the user, as shown in Figure 12-10.

External Authentication with LDAP

Corporate IT departments are increasingly implementing *Lightweight Directory Access Protocol (LDAP)* directories. LDAP is a standards-based protocol that centralizes the hosting of user accounts and allows external products and applications to leverage user account information contained in this central directory. Oracle Portal can utilize this technology to take advantage of this preexisting user repository for single sign-on authentication. If you have an existing Oracle or other implementation in place and you want to migrate those Oracle users into Portal without creating each user individually in Portal, you can do so with LDAP authentication.

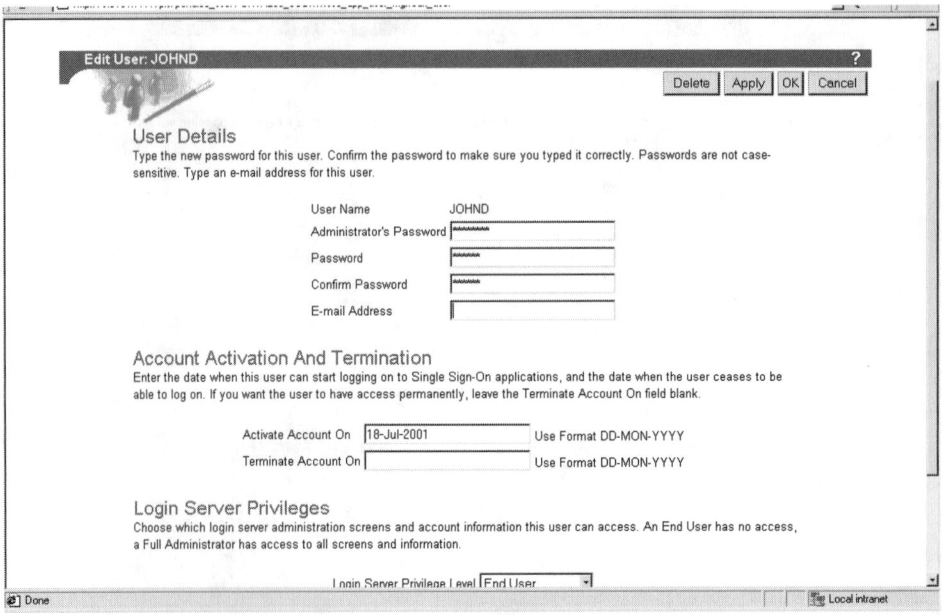

FIGURE 12-10. *The Edit User page can be used for forgotten passwords or to delete users*

Currently, corporations have many user account directories for their business enterprise systems. This is not unlike the problem we have discussed with information overload throughout the book. As an example, in a typical Oracle deployment, each instance of the Oracle server running in the enterprise has its own "directory" of user names. Multiple directories translate into a high cost of ownership, since administrators must input and maintain information about the same accounts in multiple places. As a result, account information can be out of synch.

Corporations must also have the ability to deploy Internet-ready applications and ensure their security. Companies may also desire to make some of the information stored in company directories accessible to business partners and others on a controlled basis. LDAP is the current solution to both of these problems, because LDAP centralizes management of directory information. A desirable feature of the LDAP standard is that it requires a minimal amount of networking software on the client side, which is perfect for Internet-based "thin client" applications.

The need for customers to have interoperability between directory services and client applications has driven LDAP as a de facto standard in the vendor community for centralized directory support. Virtually every hardware and software systems vendor has developed an LDAP support strategy in recent months. Oracle's answer to the

LDAP demand is the *Oracle Internet Directory (OID)*, an LDAP v3-compliant directory. Oracle 9iAS Portal can be integrated with OID to support centralized administration of user accounts. Portal works with OID so preexisting users can readily become Oracle 9iAS Portal users.

This integration was created to utilize a preexisting LDAP directory information tree (DIT), which hosts user accounts and then authenticates those user accounts as valid Portal accounts. In the 9iAS v1 release, integration of the login server/portal with LDAP is limited to authentication. In the 9iAS v2 release, the SSO server will no longer authenticate users against a local table of credentials as is the default with the current published version of Portal. All authentication requests will be verified against OID based on all entities within OID that can be authenticated.

The Portal and login server are stored as separate schemas in a common database instance whether in a single or distributed installation environment. The login server can be configured to use an external LDAP directory as its authentication repository. In this configuration, the Web browser communicates with the Oracle9i application server using either HTTP or HTTPS (Secure Sockets Layer, SSL). The Oracle9i application server communicates with the Oracle8i database through the `mod_plsql` module using the Net8 protocol. Then, within the Oracle8i database, the login server uses PL/SQL code to make an external procedure call to a dynamically linked library, which makes LDAP API calls to the Oracle Internet Directory to do the authentication check. The user is authenticated, the login server creates a login server cookie based on a successful authentication on the LDAP server, and then Portal takes over the session with the user from that point on.

Directory Information Tree

The LDAP directory hosts user accounts in a directory information tree (DIT). By using this DIT, the login server and Portal can leverage the existing user accounts. Let's look at an example directory information tree as shown in Figure 12-11.

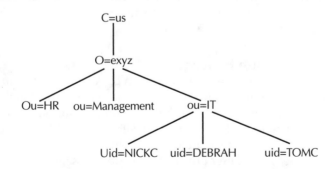

FIGURE 12-11.   *The LDAP directory information tree*

In this example, we have organized eXYZ Corporation in the directory structure within their organizational departments and users are listed under their respective departments. By looking at this tree, we can assume that all users will be found under the node identified by "o=exyz, c=us", which will be called the search base for the DIT. Let's assume the object class representing NICKC, DEBRAH, and TOMC, is the inetOrgPerson class. In this class, uid is known as the relative distinguished name (RDN). It is necessary for user accounts to always be unique within the search base so that only one unique node is returned from a search of the DIT.

In order for the Portal login server to use this LDAP DIT and allow users within the LDAP structure to log on to Portal with their LDAP account, the `ssoldap.sql` script must be run with similar to the following:

```
Host:  ldap.exyz.com
Port:  389
Search Base: o=exyz, c=us
Unique Attribute:  uid
Bind DN:  cn=orcladmin
Bind Password:  exyz
```

The LDAP hostname and port, as well as the bind DN and password are dependent on the LDAP installation on your server. In this respect, the bind DN specified should be the account that has the access control privileges necessary to modify a user's userPassword attribute. If the reset password feature is not used, the account only requires the privileges to search the DIT from the search base and below.

Adding Administrative Accounts for Portal

Once you have configured the login server for the LDAP directory to allow users to log into Oracle9iAS Portal, you will want to create the administrator accounts defined in Portal in the LDAP directory. This will allow the administrator accounts to log on and transfer access privileges to the users that have been predefined in the LDAP server. First, create an account within OID for PORTAL30, since that is our Portal schema name and master user account. Log on as Portal30 and assign administrative privileges to others using the Portal administrative screens.

LDAP Authentication Process

Let's look at how a Portal connection works with LDAP in order to complete an authentication request. A user provides a username and password in the login page or portlet and then the login server calls the external authentication module for LDAP, which attempts to bind to the LDAP directory with the bind DN that we specified in the `ssoldap.sql` script. If the module cannot bind to the directory, either because of the location or because of user privileges, an error message indicating a setup problem is displayed. If the bind is successful, the login server searches the DIT, starting from the search base, for the node with "uid=username", where uid is specified as the username/password submitted in the login form. If a node is not found, indicating the user is not in the LDAP directory, it is considered an authentication failure. If the node is found, the login server obtains binds to the DN, with the password provided. If the bind is successful, the login server considers it a successful connection and the server will authenticate the user for their session.

There is a set of sample scripts delivered with Portal under the `<ORACLE_HOME> iSuites/LDAP/DEMO` directory that provide a simplistic LDAP schema. With the configuration options of Oracle Portal, it is possible to create more complex directory information trees than the ones in the samples. Look through the documentation in the LDAP directory listed above for a more thorough treatment of OID and LDAP authentication. With the 9iAS v2.0 release of Oracle Portal, LDAP authentication will become an automatic process fully integrated in with the login server authentication. We recommend going to `technet.oracle.com`, and following the steps in the white paper, *Configuring Oracle9iAS Portal for LDAP Authentication*, for a more thorough treatment of LDAP authentication at this time.

Secure Sockets Layer (SSL) Security

The Secure Sockets Layer (SSL) security option is a secure protocol for sending and receiving information over the Internet. SSL was developed and made popular by Netscape. Netscape developed SSL with the idea of stimulating the sales of the company's Web servers by distributing a free client that implemented a public-key encryption protocol to ensure a secure connection between two parties. SSL encrypts all HTTP requests, server responses, and all authentication sessions, including userids and passwords. SSL provides authentication, encryption, and data integrity using a public-key infrastructure (PKI).

This public-key code structure is a method for a server to communicate with a client using a unique key that only the server and client can read. The server passes a public key to the client to use to encrypt information that in turn is sent back to the server in the encrypted format. The server recognizes the public key that is sent back with the encrypted request and uses its own unique private key to decrypt the information and act on it. Since its inception, SSL security has become a standard option for most Web servers and browsers, including Oracle 9iAS.

The SSL protocol exists between the raw TCP/IP protocol and the application layer in the standard network architecture. It is possible to use SSL in one of three authentication modes. You can require one server to authenticate itself to the client, both client and server to authenticate themselves to each other, and/or you can turn off authentication and neither the client nor the server will authenticate itself to the other. The recommended option for confirming SSL is mixed-mode SSL. This means that SSL is used from browser to mid-tier; but then HTTP is used from the middle-tier PPE calls to portlets. This is thoroughly described under "Ports Use HTTPs When Needed" in the configuration guide.

SSL secures Web HTTP communication between a browser and a Web server in plain HTTP over SSL (HTTPS). In order to enable SSL to work with the Oracle 9iAS, you must use the `mod_ssl` package provided by the Apache Web server. It uses the URL scheme HTTPS instead of HTTP.

Oracle Portal and the login server can be configured to run in HTTPS mode if your portal requires increased security. You can also choose to have Oracle Portal run in HTTP mode and the login server run in HTTPS mode, for better performance. You can obtain a valid server certificate from a licensed certificate provider including Verisign (http://www.verisign.com/) and Thawte (http://www.thawte.com/). The certificate that actually ships with Oracle 9i application server will not work for Oracle Portal.

Setting Up SSL to Work with Oracle Portal

Let's look at the steps required to configure SSL on both Oracle Portal and the login server:

1. Generate the certificate request by going to the following location:

   ```
   cd IAS_HOME\Apache\open_ssl\bin
   ```

2. Edit the `openssl.cnf` file and find the following line:

   ```
   RANDFILE = $ENV::HOME/ .rnd
   ```

3. Add the following line just above the line you found in step 2, so it appears as follows:

   ```
   HOME = .
   RANDFILE = $ENV::HOME/ .rnd
   ```

4. Now run the following commands from DOS:

   ```
   openssl md5 * >rand.dat
   openssl genrsa -rand rand.dat -des3 1024>key.pem
   openssl req -new -key key.pem -out csr.pem -config openssl.cnf
   ```

5. The last command will prompt you to provide the common name. At this point, enter the name of your server, including the domain—for example, www.exyz.com.

You will now have a `key.pem` and a `csr.pem` file. At this point, you will send the `csr.pem` file to the certificate authority to obtain the certificate. Let's step through the process of obtaining the certificate online at www.verisign.com:

1. Navigate to http://www.verisign.com, and request a trial certificate by clicking on "Secure Your Website."

2. In the form field, locate the CSR field. Copy the contents of the `csr.pem` file that was generated and paste it in the field.

3. You will receive an email with the trial certificate attached (we'll call it `portalcert.crt`), as well as some further instructions.

4. Export the certificate from your browser into a file that you can later install on Oracle HTTP Server Apache listener.

5. Save the certificate as a "Base-64 encoded X.509" certificate. Save it as `trialcacert.crt` for this example. In order to do the export from Internet Explorer, go to Tools | Internet Options | Content | Certificates | Trusted Root | Certificate Authorities | Export. It now important to remove the password from `key.pem` in order to work on NT:

```
copy key.pem key.pem-orig
openssl rsa -in key.pem-orig -out key.pem
```

6. Copy the certificates to the appropriate locations:

```
Copy portalcert.crt to Apache\Apache\conf\ssl.crt\
Copy trialcacert.crt to Apache\Apache\conf\ssl.crt\
Copy key.pem to Apache\Apache\conf\ssl.key\
Copy key.pem-orig to Apache\Apache\conf\ssl.key\
```

We have now successfully configured SSL on Oracle Portal and the login server. We now need to enable SSL for the Oracle HTTP server powered by Apache, which includes modifying the `httpd.conf` file. Make the following changes to the `httpd.conf` file found in the `<IAS_HOME>/apache/apache/config/` directory:

```
...
#
# Port: The port to which the standalone server listens.
#
Port 7777
Listen 7777
Listen 443

<IfDefine SSL>
Port 7777
</IfDefine>

##
## SSL Support
##
## When we also provide SSL we have to listen to the
## standard HTTP port (see above) and to the HTTPS port
##
<IfDefine SSL>
Listen 7777
Listen 443
</IfDefine>

...
##
## SSL Virtual Host Context
##
```

```
<VirtualHost _default_:443>

# General setup for the virtual host
DocumentRoot "D:\isuites\Portal\apache\apache"
ServerName eXYZ.com
ServerAdmin PATM@eXYZ.com
ErrorLog logs/error_log
TransferLog logs/access_log

Port 443

# SSL Engine Switch:
# Enable/Disable SSL for this virtual host.
SSLEngine on

# Server Certificate:
# Point SSLCertificateFile at a PEM encoded certificate. If
# the certificate is encrypted, then you will be prompted
for a
# pass phrase. Note that a kill -HUP will prompt again. A
test
# certificate can be generated with `make certificate' under
# built time. Keep in mind that if you've both a RSA and a
DSA
# certificate you can configure both in parallel (to also
allow
# the use of DSA ciphers, etc.)
SSLCertificateFile
D:\isuites\apache\apache\conf\ssl.crt\portalcert.crt

# Server Private Key:
# If the key is not combined with the certificate, use this
# directive to point at the key file. Keep in mind that if
# you've both a RSA and a DSA private key you can configure

# both in parallel (to also allow the use of DSA ciphers,
etc.)
SSLCertificateKeyFile
D:\isuites\apache\apache\conf\ssl.key\key.pem

# Server Certificate Chain:
# Point SSLCertificateChainFile at a file containing the
# concatenation of PEM encoded CA certificates which form
the
# certificate chain for the server certificate.
Alternatively
# the referenced file can be the same as SSLCertificateFile
# when the CA certificates are directly appended to the
server
# certificate for convinience.
SSLCertificateChainFile
D:\isuites\apache\apache\conf\ssl.crt\trialcacert.crt

If you want IE browsers to work, comment out the following
line
#SetEnvIf User-Agent ".*MSIE.*" nokeepalive
ssl-unclean-shutdown
```

Stop and start the HTTP server in order for the configurations to take effect. In order to use HTTPS, you must ensure JServ recognizes the secure port. In order to do this, we need to edit the `zone.properties` file, found in `IAS_HOME\Apache\Jserv\servlets` directory.

Add the following lines at the bottom of the file:

```
servlet.page.initArgs=httpsports=443
servlet.page.initArgs=requesttime=30
```

This specifies the port to be used for all HTTPS requests. You can list multiple ports, but you must have a certificate created on the Oracle HTTP server on that port and configured in the `http.conf` file. We want to configure Oracle Portal to use HTTPS. After configuring the server to support HTTPS ports, run the `ssodatan` or `ssodatax` script(s), specifying the appropriate protocol and ports to use the HTTPS URLs.

```
Ssodatan -w https://exyz.com/pls/portal30/ -1
https://exyz.com/pls/portal_sso/ -s portal30 -o portal30_sso
```

Stop and start the HTTP server. From this point on, you want to access the URL with the HTTPS, as opposed to the HTTP URL, because the login was registered on the HTTPS URL, not the HTTP URL.

Now let's log in to Oracle Portal as PORTAL30. Click on the Administer tab, then Global Settings. Scroll down to the Login Server section, and update the Query Path URL Prefix so that it points to an HTTP (not HTTPS) URL—for example, `http://exyz.com/pls/portal30_sso/`. The current code has the portal making HTTP requests to certain login server URLs for some information needs, and is currently not coded to support HTTPS over this interface. In an Oracle environment, the user will initiate a Net8 connection to the server using the HTTPS SSL connection. SSL then performs the handshake between the client and server by first verifying the server certificate. If the handshake is successful, the server verifies that the user has the appropriate authorization to access the database and then all Portal security options take over for userid, password, and privilege access.

Other Security Considerations

Nothing is 100 percent hack-proof on the Internet. Experts agree the best you can do is reduce your risk factors and stay vigilant for potential entry points into your system that malicious users could exploit. We have discussed the most important issue in Portal security, and that is user authentication. SSL goes a long way toward ensuring that communications between client and server are encrypted and tamperproof. Yet, it is a virtual imperative that if you wish to ensure the security of your Web-based systems, you must have a firewall.

Portal Firewall Support

Firewalls are network software devices installed on a dedicated or shared server that act as a barrier between an enterprise network and users outside of the network. It is important to know how to set up the Oracle 9iAS Web server with the configurations you may consider for your firewall. There are three common architectures for deploying a firewall. The most common for intranet support is locating the Web server inside the firewall so that any outside connections are rebuffed by the firewall and all connections to the Web server are made on an internal basis. While this secures the intranet, it prevents extranet or Internet access to your Portal unless a hole is poked in the firewall for designated IP addresses to have access, as shown in Figure 12-12.

If the Portal is inside a firewall in an intranet setting, you may set up the Portal architecture strictly for performance and ignore the impact of the firewall from a configuration/architecture standpoint. This is the best firewall option if you intend for your Portal to work on an intranet basis only or on a limited extranet basis where you will identify and allow access to specific partner-owned external IP addresses. This option could be frustrating for partners that must request access for designated machines or IP ranges, but does supply the security you will need.

A second option is to set up the Apache 9iAS Web server on a stand-alone machine outside of the firewall and open up access through the firewall to the IP address of the database server to gain access to the Portal. Although this restricts hackers to the

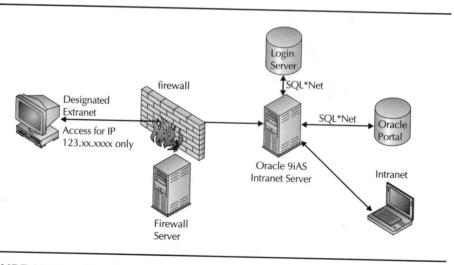

FIGURE 12-12. *The Oracle 9i application server in a secure intranet/extranet environment*

HTTP server machine and prevents access to other machines you may have inside the network, it also potentially opens up access to the database server machine through the hole you have created for Portal access. This could potentially allow a hacker to gain access to your entire network if they were persistent enough. This is probably not the best solution for your firewall.

A third solution is to create a *proxy server* firewall. A proxy server is a machine that serves as an intermediary between the client machine and the server that makes requests to one or more remote servers for the client. A proxy allows clients and servers essentially to act independently from one another, with the intermediary proxy server handling all requests. In an Internet context, a proxy server handles calls going out from the client on the network to outside server sources or within the network to a server. A *reverse proxy server* handles calls from sources outside the network on the Internet that are seeking to gain access to the intranet content on your internal protected portal. The reverse proxy will determine whether access to content is allowable and deliver content to the specific individual outside the network if they are authorized. Employees working from home would need a reverse proxy server to access the corporate intranet through a firewall.

A proxy server firewall resides on a server that acts as a broker to determine whether internal access should be given to an outside user. The firewall server will have two network cards and thus two IP addresses. One IP is for external connection and access and one IP will be for internal access only. The Apache server in this scenario sits inside the proxy server firewall. The proxy server firewall will view a request to the external NIC IP address that will have a domain name of `www.exyz.com` as an individual seeking to gain access to the intranet, and will control all access and requests to the Oracle 9i application server inside the firewall for that individual. The external port open to the user would be port 80 or some other open port, but all communication to the application server will be through the default install port 7777—or whatever port you designated on install. All internal communications to the Portal via the Apache server continue to go through Port 7777 via the internal NIC IP address on the proxy server firewall machine using a designated domain server name such as `exyz.intranet.com`.

To set up this type of firewall requires some reconfiguration in the Portal architecture to allow Portal to recognize the two hostnames `www.exyz.com` and `exyz.intranet.com`. To do this, you must access the Apache configuration file and create virtual hosts for both IP addresses. Specify the IP address of the host server in each of the VitualHost definitions but use the ServerName directive to identify the host to the outside or inside client user as `www.exyz.com` or `exyz.intranet.com`, as shown in Figure 12-13.

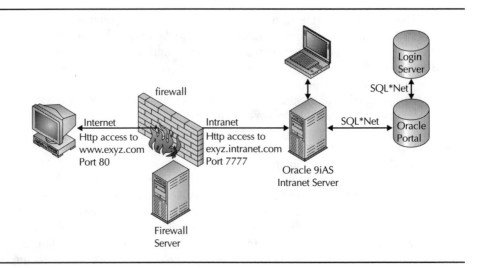

FIGURE 12-13. *The Oracle 9iAS Apache server in a virtual host environment*

Setting VirtualHost Definitions for a Proxy Server Firewall

1. Edit the `<IAS_HOME>/apache/apache/conf/httpd` conf file.

2. Search for: `Section 3: Virtual Hosts`.

3. Make sure your Virtual Hosts section looks like the following for our example:

```
NameVirtualHost 127.0.0.1:80
<VirtualHost 127.0.0.1:7777>
     ServerAdmin youremail@exyz.com
     ServerName www.exyz.com
 </VirtualHost>
<VirtualHost 127.0.0.1:7777>
     ServerAdmin youremail@exyz.com
     ServerName exyz.intranet.com
</VirtualHost>
```

Note that the listener setting should be set to both ports 7777 and 443 if SSL is enabled. In our example above for eXYZ Corp., add in a VirtualHost definition for port 443 if you are using SSL. The external server port should be set to recognize port 80. Additionally, you must change the Windows NT `HOSTS` file located on the same machine as your Apache server on the `C:\WINNT\system32\`

drivers\ETC\ directory to recognize the new virtual hosts. Ensure that it displays the following:

```
# Copyright (c) 1993-1995 Microsoft Corp.
# This is a sample HOSTS file used by Microsoft TCP/IP for Windows NT.
# This file contains the mappings of IP addresses to host names. Each
# entry should be kept on an individual line. The IP address should
# be placed in the first column followed by the corresponding host
name.
# The IP address and the host name should be separated by at least one
# space.
#
# Additionally, comments (such as these) may be inserted on individual
# lines or following the machine name denoted by a '#' symbol.
#
# For example:
#
#      102.54.94.97     rhino.acme.com          # source server
#       38.25.63.10     x.acme.com              # x client host
127.0.0.1      localhost
127.0.0.1      www.exyz.com
127.0.0.1      exyz.intranet.com
```

In our case, the IP address 127.0.0.1 is the IP for a localhost machine such as a laptop. You will use the same IP each time denoting the server machine and then subsequently identify the virtual hostname on the same line. Addresses for all Portal components must be recognized across the network when using a virtual host scheme. You will need to specify the IP address of the database component on the 9iAS server machine, and also edit and configure the HOSTS file on the database server to recognize the 9iAS server machine in return.

Last, you must register both virtual hosts and the login server as partner applications, as described earlier in the procedures for centralizing the login server. Click on the Login Server Administration link, click on the Administer Partner Applications link, and then click on Add Partner Application from the Portal Home page and use the procedures we described earlier. The ssodatax and the ssodatan scripts must be run to recognize the new external virtual hostnames so that external clients accessing www.exyz.com will be recognized by the login server and by Portal.

If you have not registered the new external domain on the Internet, you must do so at this time by requesting that service from your local Web provider, or by requesting one directly by navigating to http://www.networksolutions.com. Keep in mind that too many virtual paths on one listener can cause excessive CPU utilization and degradation in system performance. Consider multiple Web servers in this instance to balance the load—one each to handle the requests from external and internal sources. This will further enhance the security of the system by directing external users to a Web server devoted only to external requests.

Reports Server Security

Portal installation includes integration with Oracle Reports. You may or may not have noticed the Oracle Reports Security link at the bottom of the Administer tab from the Oracle home page. If you didn't notice it, it is because it was installed as a hidden link on the initial Portal install. If it is missing, click on the Edit Page Link from the Administer tab and check the check box next to Oracle Reports security and also click the Show button.

If you click on the Oracle Reports Security link, you will note several portlets, each supporting a component of the Reports server and delivery process, as shown in Figure 12-14. The Create Reports Server Access page configures the Reports server for integrated access within Portal. By identifying all Reports servers within the

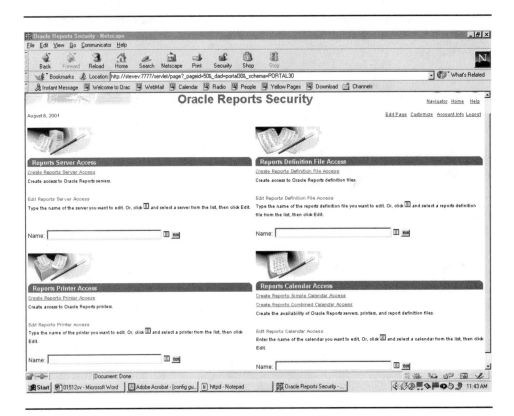

FIGURE 12-14. *The Oracle Reports Security page integrates Oracle Reports with Portal*

enterprise, Oracle Reports can be seamlessly scheduled and executed from within Oracle Portal. The Reports Printer Access allows you to set up named printers within Portal, so that you can use Portal to control access to the printers. You must have already configured the Reports Server, available as part of the Oracle 9iAS Enterprise Edition, to use any of the Portal reports features. From the Create Reports Definition File Access link, you can link a Reports RDF file to a Portal application with its attendant Portal security restrictions.

Lastly, the Create Reports Simple Calendar Access Wizard's dialog box allows the user to set restrictions and time frames for when the Oracle Reports servers and corresponding reports are available for Portal users. For instance, if the Reports server is down for Christmas and the Independence Day holiday, setting the calendar can prevent access to Reports and the Reports server on those days. In the Create Reports Combined Calendar Access section, multiple calendars can be combined with all restrictions applied to Reports' use. If one calendar prevents use of the Reports server for all holidays and another calendar sets restricted use for weekends, the two can be combined so that the Reports server is not available on either holidays or weekends.

Oracle Portal Database Administration

The Oracle relational database requires a great deal of care and feeding once it has been created, to facilitate continuous smooth operation and maintenance. The database administration functions within Oracle Portal are focused on schema manipulation, creation of database objects, and database role creation and maintenance. Portal provides a number of reports that are available for the DBA to use to monitor the configuration and performance of the database. These reports include sizing characteristics and proactive reports that identify chokepoints, bottlenecks, and sizing constraints that could affect the smooth operation of a database.

Portal Navigator's Database Objects tab provides a way to work with database schemas. Schemas are repository structures where all objects in the database are stored. Schemas own the objects that are stored in them. All database objects including tables, views, and stored procedures, as well as the Oracle Portal application components, are stored in Oracle schemas. Schema objects include tables that store data in rows with defined column fields for each element of a record. Schemas can also contain *procedures*—PL/SQL code routines that can read data input from the database or other sources and produce one or more output items that are used in an application. Stored procedures are compiled PL/SQL code stored in the database and are very efficient. *Functions* are PL/SQL program units that perform one or more activities and then return a value. *Packages* are made up of a group of related procedures and functions that are grouped together to form a focused program unit that performs a defined type of work. Each of these objects may be managed using the Portal Navigator's Database Objects tab. Portal application components such as forms, reports, charts, and calendars are nothing more than Oracle PL/SQL packages.

Portal database administrators can work with database *roles* using the Portal interface. Roles are assigned specific system or object privileges including SELECT, INSERT, UPDATE, DELETE, and EXECUTE. These privileges are given to specific users or groups of users using database grants. You may create a role with object privileges for a specific table and then assign users to that role. Since users can be given Portal user accounts but are not required to have actual database accounts, roles in Portal apply more to applications than to schema objects. Portal users are associated with a public schema by default, but they can be configured to access and/or update any schema available to the Portal, including schema tables, data, and objects.

Create and Edit schemas

You can create, edit, or modify schemas from the Administer Database tab of the Portal home page or from the Navigator Database Objects tab. Functions, tables, procedures, packages, Java objects, or any other database object can be created, edited, or made available to Portal developers and end users through developed portlets. You must have DBA or Portal administrator privileges in order to perform schema administration

In most cases you would not create a schema using Oracle Portal, you would use a design tool like Oracle Designer to generate the schema. In order to create a schema, log on as the Portal DBA, access the Database Objects tab from the Navigaor, and click on the Create New Schema link. You will name the schema in the Schema field, identify a default tablespace (USERS for our application), a default Temporary tablespace (TEMP), and create a password. Place a check in the checkbox for Use this Schema for Portal Users. This will allow the DBA to associate a Portal user with this schema in the Portal User Profile on the Administer tab of the Portal home page. You may edit any schema immediately after you have created it and create grants, roles, and privileges for all objects that will be resident in the schema you created.

Database Tables

Once you have now created and edited a schema and given the schema appropriate working privileges you can use Portal to give the schema some user functionality by creating tables, views, procedures, triggers, and other objects that will be used by the applications we will create. We begin creating these functions by using the Database Objects tab from the Navigator and choosing the Create Table link. In the Table Name field you will type the name of the table to be created while leaving the Schema Name as it is. Begin by choosing column names, identifying the Datatype (NUMBER, VARCHAR2, etc.), Precision (number of decimals), Default Value, Allow Null, and Primary Key as shown in Figure 12-15. The Check Constraint page allows constraints to be placed on table fields to ensure consistency. If in an employee table, gender can only be M or F, and a constraint should be listed that ensures any data inserted into the Gender column is either M or F. A foreign-key constraint ensures that any data entered for a particular field has a corresponding primary key value in the master table. The Storage Parameters dialog box identifies the default tablespace and storage and growth parameters for the table you are creating.

If you Click on Modify Rows and we you can add in some data to the table. You will see a Format Mask field that is used to ensure that any displayed field is shown with the proper format. Oracle uses a global standard format for numeric masks where in the following format mask, 999G999D99, the uppercase G's stand for commas and the D represents the decimal point. If you wish to round to the nearest whole figure, D99 should be represented as D00. You may ensure that the queries you execute against the table are case sensitive by checking the Case Sensitive check box. In the Where Clause area, you may choose to write a condition to query a subset of rows in the table. The Row Order option controls the sequence of rows returned in a query, and the General Options dialog area controls how the retrieved rows will be displayed on the screen. You can experiment with these options and use the Query button at the top of the page to get the look and feel you want as you browse through database tables. Lastly, you may utilize the Drop Table link action to delete the table and its

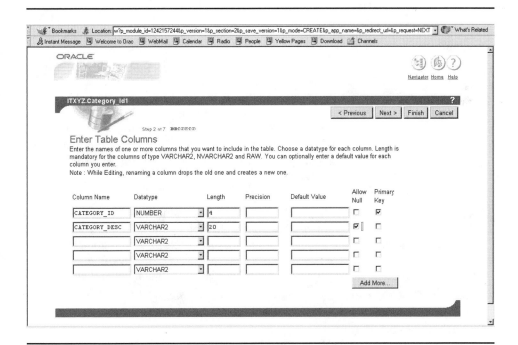

FIGURE 12-15. *Entry fields for the table columns of the CATEGORY table*

information from the schema. You can also rename the table if you don't like the table name.

The Export function uses an Oracle utility to transfer the table and all of its information to an Oracle-formatted file that can be used to save information in the table as of the time the export is performed. The export file can be used with the Oracle Import utility to restore the table and its information from the export file. It is a good practice to perform a full export of all tables on a recurring basis in order to guard against a case of database corruption or failure. The advantage of using Portal for this function is that the export can be initiated from a Web browser.

Database Views

Views, as the name implies, are SQL structures that combine columns from one or more tables together in a way that the end user can see selected portions of the database structure as if it were a table itself. This combining of selected data into a single view can serve to simplify and offer more secure database by limiting the ways a user can access tables. In the case of the eXYZ CORP_SITE schema, we might want to create a view that joins the EMPLOYEE table with the TITLES table to give only descriptive information about employees to most users. Then we can give full access on the EMPLOYEES table to members of the HR department, for view or modification. You may set up a view clicking on Create View, choosing "View using the Query Wizard" on the next page, keying in the name of the view in the Name field, and then choosing the table(s) from the pop up list that is presented in the Search dialog window. If you were to select from the EMPLOYEES and TITLES tables for your view, you might choose EMPLOYEE_ID, LAST_NAME, FIRST_NAME, USER_ID, PHONE, SUPERVISOR_ID, and HIRE_DATE from the EMPLOYEES table and TITLE_DESC from the TITLES table for your view. The Column Aliases window offers a shorter nickname for the column name listed. Choose the fields to join the two tables in Join Conditions and in the Advanced Options dialog box you may choose Read Only for a view that will contain a read-only constraint and not be used for updates.

Create Synonyms

Just as you can create a column alias in a view to shorten the names of your columns, you can also create table synonyms to abbreviate table names. To do this, click on the Create Synonym link at the top of the Database Objects page from the Navigator. In the Synonym Name field of the Schema type the name of the Synonym, choose the table you wish to create a synonym for in the Object Name field, and click finish to establish the synonym.

Database Procedures

Oracle procedures are PL/SQL programs that carry out actions in the database. They often accept user-defined input parameters that are read into the application and used to perform a series of defined tasks. Procedures can be combined collectively to form packages. Procedures can be created within Portal from the Procedures link of the Database Objects tab. Create a Procedure named ECHO using the CORP_SITE schema with the following code:

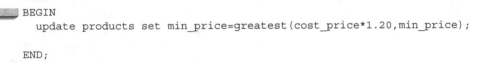

```
is
BEGIN
  HTP.print ('You entered '||p_input);

END;
```

Test out the procedure by clicking the Execute link next to the ECHO procedure listed under the CORP_SITE schema objects. Key in any text to test out the procedure. Click the Navigator link to go back to the Database Objects tab.

Database Triggers

Database triggers are blocks of PL/SQL that enforce the standards and integrity of the data in the database from a transactional application. A trigger can convert all characters to uppercase before a record is stored in the database or ensure that specific business rules within the organization are enforced. A trigger can ensure that only customers with no history of default payments can order services by check. Triggers enforce business rules and anything else that a constraint validation does not offer. Create a trigger to be executed After Each Row using the CORP_SITE.PRODUCTS table entitled AIUR_PROD_MIN_PRICE using the following code:

```
BEGIN
  update products set min_price=greatest(cost_price*1.20,min_price);

END;
```

Database Links

Database links allow a direct connection between two databases to form in essence one distributed database formed from one or more databases distributed across multiple platforms. An Oracle database in New York linked to another in Chicago and to a third in Portland via database links will allow the New York database to recognize and update all three database instances, assuming proper UPDATE permissions are granted to the user on all machines. The link is actually a direct connection between instances. You must have the proper DBA or Portal administrator account privileges to set up a database link. In order to set up a database link you must know the proper passwords and know the SQL*Net connection information for the remote database you are linking to. Ensure that you are connected to the network where your other databases are located and create the database link.

Database Reports

Portal has an extensive library of database reports that are available for the Portal DBA to use to monitor database performance. At a large organization, the DBA will likely use the Oracle Enterprise Manager (OEM) and DBA Studio to monitor and proactively manage the database. Portal provides basic database information, including information about control logs, initialization parameters, natural language support parameters, and parameter reports. Additional reports that are specific to Portal include Database Memory Consumption, Transactions, and Locks reports that support daily Portal execution reports where memory problems or transaction locks must be identified and resolved. Pay particular attention to the Find and Kill Sessions report that allows the DBA to identify users that have potentially runaway sessions that they have not logged out from. This report identifies long-running sessions and gives the DBA the ability to kill sessions that are not being used. The database storage reports show table storage statistics, including datafile tablespace utilization, datafile size and activity reports, redo log file activity, and statistics about object utilization and space they require. You may add your own reports to each of these database categories or add in a new category and subordinate reports.

Monitoring and Maintaining the Portal

You've deployed your Portal and now you want to sit back, relax, and enjoy the fruits of your labor. The first thing to understand with a portal is that once it is deployed, you have only begun the job. The job of keeping content fresh, monitoring performance, ensuring applications are adequate, and that the throughput to the Portal is controlled and reliable is paramount to the continued success of the site. We will discuss in this section the function of the Administer Services portlet, the role and function of the PL/SQL gateway settings, and how to set and monitor the log registry to ensure that maintenance of the portal is a proactive service and not reactive.

Portal Services

Portal Services set development, use, monitoring, and search criteria for all users of the portal. The global settings function sets the global home page for all users, default page styles, proxy server settings that are used for access to outside applications through the firewall, and log file maintenance. Listener gateway settings allow the administrator to set up or edit data access descriptors and to edit Portal cache settings. The log registry supports the configuration of the data collected by log registry tables within Portal.

Global Settings

The Portal Services Global Settings form adjusts settings within the portal for all users of the portal, as shown in Figure 12-16. It is here in the Default Home Page Name field that you will identify the default home page for all authenticated users of the

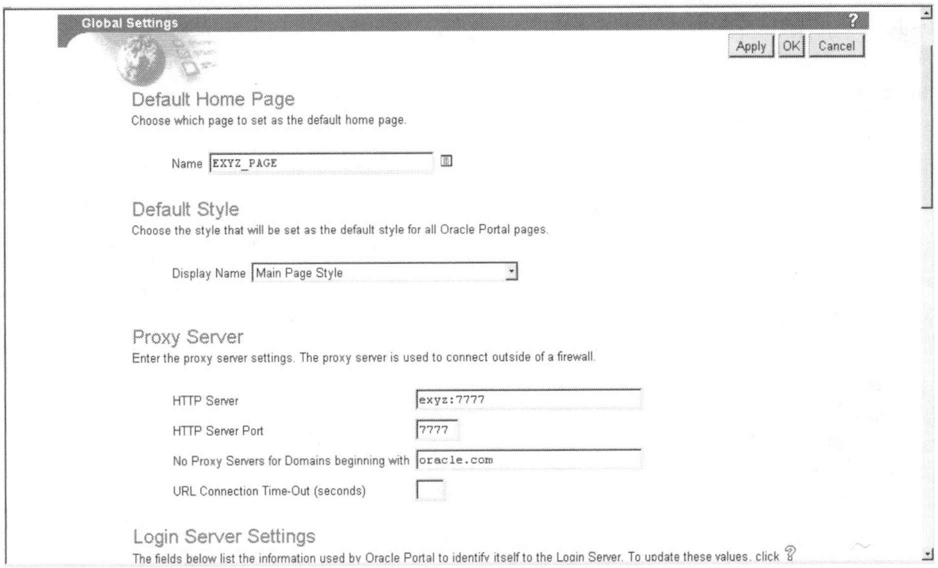

FIGURE 12-16. *The Portal Global Settings page*

portal. Individuals may override this option in their personal preferences by choosing an alternate home page. The Default Style is chosen on this page as well in the Display Name field, and it has the same override characteristics as the default home page. If you are using a proxy server or reverse proxy server in conjunction with a firewall, you will set the address and name of the proxy server in the Proxy Server settings dialog area.

The HTTP server address (IP address or server name on the network), without the HTTP prefix, will go in the HTTP Server field. The server port will go in the HTTP Server Port field (for example, 80). Any domain names that are unrestricted for the proxy server so that users can directly connect to local domain names can be listed in the "No Proxy Servers for Domains beginning with" field. The URL Connection Time-out field should be set to an acceptable limit to ensure that the proxy server can establish a connection to Portal.

The Login Server Settings field is set upon installation of the Portal on the server. If you decide to move the login server to another machine, you will need to reset the Query Path URL Prefix parameter to point to the new schema and corresponding URL. Follow the instructions earlier in the chapter for centralizing the login server in a distributed Portal mode. Portlet Show Timing can be checked when the Portal is in debug mode for developers. This check box allows developers to see how long it takes a portlet to run within the application on the screen. This should be turned off when the portal is ready for deployment. The Temporary Directory setting defines the directory on the application server machine where all temporary files will be located. All exports, imports, and any file manipulation done through Portal will take place on this temporary directory. It's a good idea to set this parameter before the Portal goes to production, particularly if you plan to allow table exports from within Portal.

If you set up a personal tab for users you will check the Create Personal Folders for New Users check box. This will create a personal folder for checking in and maintaining content on an individual basis and to share with others. The folder will automatically be created using the Portal username. The folder will be located under Personal Folders in the Navigator Content Area under the letter corresponding to the letter of the username. Lastly, the Logout Behavior field determines whether the user will log out from Portal, including single sign-on and all internal and external applications or only from the Portal session but leaving the SSO session available. You will typically want to keep this set to logout both the Portal and SSO sessions.

Listener Gateway Settings

The HTTP listener gateway is set up at installation time and includes all the information about the data access descriptors (DADs) used by mod_plsql to interact between the Apache server and the Oracle database instance where Portal resides. The configuration menu is accessed from the Listener Gateway Settings link on the Administer tab. The Gateway Configuration Menu contains links for Gateway Global Settings, Gateway Database Access Descriptor Settings, and Cache Settings.

Gateway global settings define the default database access descriptor that will be used if the end user accesses the Portal without specifying a DAD. Each DAD created represents a single instance of Oracle Portal installed in the database. More than one instance of Portal, and thus more than one DAD, may be installed in the same Oracle database instance. The default DAD is important if multiple instances of Portal reside in the same database and a default is not specified. The default database access descriptor will resolve and automatically modify the URL to access the default DAD.

The Administer DAD Entries screen allows the Portal administrator to configure existing DAD settings and also to set up new DADs within the same Oracle instance. You will note that the initial links on this page allow you to add a DAD for a Portal 3.x configuration with some initial settings preconfigured, set up a WebDB 2.x configuration, or, lastly, to set up a default configuration that can be controlled completely by the administrator with no preconfigured settings.

The Portal installation routine creates the PORTAL30 and PORTAL30_SSO DADs that can be edited.

Log Registry Administration

You can set log registry settings within Portal that will capture information from the Portal as it is used and store statistics about the way Portal is used in the database. This information is displayed using the charts and components that are available on the Monitor tab of the Portal home page. Log monitoring can be done by object or event, or specifically by thresholds that have been reached or by a specific metric. All reports are based on the log registry events that you choose, and that is done using the Log Registry Administration link on the Administer tab.

The log registry settings are initially set to monitor all Portal activities. All logged events are captured by using the Oracle % wildcard query option that captures information for all logging categories. You will notice that there are entries to be made for the Domain, Sub Domain, Name, User Name, Action, Browser, and Language. The domain relates to procedures that are prefixed by wwv, wws, and wwc that control applications, content areas, and Portal pages and portlets, respectively. The subdomain includes options to capture information about applications, calendars, charts, components, dynamic pages, forms, frames, hierarchies, links and LOVs.

The Name field can include all objects that begin with a specific name, such as exyz%, that would pull all content areas, pages, forms, reports, and other objects if the first Domain and Sub Domain fields were left open with a % wildcard in the first field. If you wish to track specific users, you can place the user name(s) in the User Name field. You may log a specific action or combination of actions using the Action field. These actions include access_control, add_to_page, checkin, checkout, copy, create, customize, debug, delete, and delete_from_page. The browser type can be logged using the Browser field. The Language field allows a choice of languages to be monitored. You may control the proliferation of log files by adjusting the Global Settings | Log Switch Interval (days) field. As always, you must have administration privileges to set these or any log parameters.

The Monitor Tab

The Monitor tab on the Oracle Portal home page provides execution reports from the Portal log files concerning the results from daily operation of the portal. Information includes Portal Pages, Portlets, and Documents, Content Area Folders, Items, Searches, Categories, and Perspectives, and Application components that can be charted and monitored by object, user, IP address, date and time, browser type, language, and other criteria. Each of these monitoring items relate to the way that the log files are set up.

The Monitor tab has a robust search capability using the content area search criteria and also supplies custom reports that include frequently asked questions. These custom reports include answers to questions such as "What are the most popular pages," "Who are the most frequent content contributors," and "What content area searches have failed to find any results?" All of these types of questions can be utilized to improve the performance and usability of the portal.

Conclusion

In this chapter you learned the principles of Apache Web server administration, Portal tuning and scaling methods, Portal security, Portal's database administration capabilities, and Portal's monitoring functions. It is important to continuously monitor your portal to ensure that all the technologies that encompass this product from the Web server to the database are finely tuned and provide consistent performance and results for your users. If you remain vigilant and proactive with content, performance, and scalability issues, your portal will be a success.

APPENDIX
A

Resources

Oracle Resources

technet.oracle.com An invaluable resource for developers. Find documentation, product announcements, software to download, sample code libraries, and discussion forums monitored by Oracle product developers. See especially the following white papers and others found at:

http://technet.oracle.com/products/iportal/

- Oracle Portal Security Overview by Paul Encarnacion
- Techniques for Creating User-Friendly Enterprise Portals by Pantanjali Venkatacharya

portalstudio.oracle.com Specifically devoted to Portal (and mostly to the PDK), this site contains downloads, specifications, and examples for custom portlet development. A new release of the PDK is published monthly. Find third-party providers for Portal-based applications here as well.

my.oracle.com A Portal site similar in nature to My Yahoo, but with the added advantage of a customizable mobile portal component. It contains some interesting portlets, including a foreign language translator. You can use your Technet user account to log in. Find fresh ideas for your own Portal site.

portal.oracle.com A hosted Portal site for small businesses and non-profit organizations. Save yourself money and time by letting Oracle handle site deployment and administration. Currently offered on a trial basis, it will eventually go to a subscription model—most likely based on usage. For a small site, this could be significantly less expensive than purchasing the 9iAS software, and you have access to a few of the custom portlets seen on my.oracle.com (some require additional fees).

www.oracle.com/metalink The support page for all Oracle products. Use this site to report or investigate technical issues, and to download patches as required. Includes a substantial database of previously reported bugs and technical bulletins, and notes.

User Groups

www.ioug.org (Portal SIG) The International Oracle Users Group-Americas home page. Significant technical resources, including a database of all IOUG-A and Oracle Open World conference papers from the past few years. Technical tips, book reviews, and more. The Portal SIG is developing an online Portal site for exchange of ideas, tips, and code related to Portal implementations. IOUG-A sponsors an annual conference each spring, and offers the University Masters' Class series, given by recognized experts in their respective fields.

www.odtug.com   The Oracle Development Tools User Group. Another excellent resource for tips, discussions, and conference papers. ODTUG has its own conference, usually in early summer, dedicated entirely to Oracle developers.

www.maop.org   The Mid-Atlantic Association of Oracle Professionals. An excellent regional Oracle user group dedicated to seminar-style Oracle presentations that include Oracle Web Development including Portal, Designer, Developer, Oracle Applications, data warehousing, and DBA issues. Conferences are typically held in May and November.

www.rmoug.org   The Rocky Mountain Oracle Users Group. Based in Denver Colorado, RMOUG is the largest regional user group in the country. The yearly Training Days conference held for one week in February is an outstanding Oracle resource and a great conference to plan a skiing vacation around!

www.voug.org   We include this local resource because their Web site is built entirely in Portal, and because they are a terrific resource for current topics. The (free) membership is not restricted to Virginians.

Examples of Production Portal Sites

www.kids123.com (US)

www.agrifusion.com/partners.html   Agrifusion develops and hosts Portal sites for its agriculture community clients. An interesting concept, because they can make similar, but personalized, content available to each organization.

www.tomatoland.com (International)

www.autoexide.com (India)

www.ixam.com (B2B, multiple languages)

www.crmexpert.nl (Dutch)

www.bisnis.com (Indonesian)

Portal Partners

Oracle encourages partner corporations to team with Oracle in a formal manner and provide Portal products and services using Oracle Portal. You can find out more about this program by visiting the Portal Community 9iAS Web site at portalstudio.oracle.com, and clicking the Portal Catalog tab.

Information Services

YellowBrix   www.yellowbrix.com
                 portal.yellowbrix.com

Factiva   www.factiva.com/oracle

Hoovers   www.hoovers.com/products/0,2960,7_3722,00.html

iSyndicate   www.isyndicate.com

Northern Light   www.northernlight.com/oracle

ScreamingMedia   www.screamingmedia.com

Search Engines

Alta Vista   www.altavista.com
              solutions.altavista.com/partners/oracle

Inktomi   www.inktomi.com/products/search/oracle.html

Verity   www.verity.com/products/portal/portlet/index.html

Business Intelligence

Business Objects   www.businessobjects.com/oracle

Cognos   www.cognos.com/partners/strategic/oracle/oracle_oppi.html

Oracle   www.oracle.com

Knowledge Management and Collaboration

Open Text Corporation   www.opentext.com/mylivelink/oracle/

Saffron Technology   www.saffrontech.com/partner/oracle.html

SiteScape   www.sitescape.com/next/oracleportlet.html

Zaplet   zaplet.com/special/oracle/splashpage.html

eCal   www.ecal.com/company.asp?action=oracle

WebEx   oracleportal.webex.com/mymeeting/landingpad.html

PL/SQL Development Tools

When you are working in Portal, particularly PDK-PL/SQL, you may find yourself writing large quantities of PL/SQL code. A good PL/SQL Integrated Development Environment (IDE) is essential to manage this code and to encourage good development practices. We have listed a few of the major PL/SQL IDEs for your convenience.

PL/SQL Developer   www.allroundautomations.nl/plsqldev.html

SQL Navigator and TOAD   www.quest.com/solutions/oracle.asp

TOAD   www.quest.com/solutions/oracle.asp

Rapid SQL   www.embarcadero.com/products/products.htm

RevealNet   http://revealnet.com/

References

Oracle Portal incorporates a host of technologies and it is impossible to do each one of them justice in this book. You may find these reference books and papers helpful, depending on the type of application you will be building, to extend your knowledge of the listed subject areas.

Web Development

JavaScript : The Definitive Guide (3rd Edition) by David Flanagan   O'Reilly & Associates, 1998

Oracle8i Web Development by Bradley D. Brown   Oracle Press, 1999

Building Oracle XML Applications by Steve Muench   O'Reilly & Associates, 2000

HTML: The Complete Reference by Thomas Powell (3rd Edition)   Osborne McGraw-Hill, 2001

Techniques for Creating User-Friendly Enterprise Portals by Pantanjali Venkatacharya   Technet.oracle.com

Oracle Database Development

Professional Oracle 8i Application Programming with Java, PL/SQL and XML by Michael Awai, et al   Wrox Press, 2000

Oracle DBA 101 by Marlene Theriault, Rachel Carmichael, and James Vescussi   Oracle Press, 2000

Oracle8i: Java Components (with CD-ROM) by Nirva Morisseau-Leroy, Martin K. Solomon, Julie Basu   Oracle Press, 2000

Oracle JDeveloper 3 Handbook by Peter Koletzke and Paul Dorsey   Oracle Press, 2001

Oracle Designer Generation by Kenneth Atkins, Paul Dirksen, and Zikri Askin Ince   Oracle Press, 1999

Oracle PL/SQL Best Practices by Steven Feuerstein   O'Reilly & Associates, 2001

Oracle Advanced PL/SQL Programming (with CD-ROM) by Scott Urman   Oracle Press, 1997

Oracle PL/SQL Tips and Techniques by Joseph Trezzo   Oracle Press, 1999

Oracle Administration and Security

Oracle Security Handbook by Marlene Theriault and Aaron Newman   Oracle Press, 2001

Oracle DBA 101 by Marlene Theriault, Rachel Carmichael, and James Vescussi
Oracle Press, 2000

Apache and Security

Professional Apache by Peter Wainwright   Wrox Press, Inc., 1999

Apache: The Definitive Guide by Ben Laurie and Peter Laurie   O'Reilly and Associates, 1999

Oracle Security Handbook by Marlene Theriault and Aaron Newman   Oracle Press, 2001

Oracle Portal Security Overview by Paul Encarnacion   Technet.Oracle.com

Index

F

N

O

T

INTERNATIONAL CONTACT INFORMATION

AUSTRALIA
McGraw-Hill Book Company Australia Pty. Ltd.
TEL +61-2-9417-9899
FAX +61-2-9417-5687
http://www.mcgraw-hill.com.au
books-it_sydney@mcgraw-hill.com

CANADA
McGraw-Hill Ryerson Ltd.
TEL +905-430-5000
FAX +905-430-5020
http://www.mcgrawhill.ca

**GREECE, MIDDLE EAST,
NORTHERN AFRICA**
McGraw-Hill Hellas
TEL +30-1-656-0990-3-4
FAX +30-1-654-5525

MEXICO (Also serving Latin America)
McGraw-Hill Interamericana Editores S.A. de C.V.
TEL +525-117-1583
FAX +525-117-1589
http://www.mcgraw-hill.com.mx
fernando_castellanos@mcgraw-hill.com

SINGAPORE (Serving Asia)
McGraw-Hill Book Company
TEL +65-863-1580
FAX +65-862-3354
http://www.mcgraw-hill.com.sg
mghasia@mcgraw-hill.com

SOUTH AFRICA
McGraw-Hill South Africa
TEL +27-11-622-7512
FAX +27-11-622-9045
robyn_swanepoel@mcgraw-hill.com

**UNITED KINGDOM & EUROPE
(Excluding Southern Europe)**
McGraw-Hill Education Europe
TEL +44-1-628-502500
FAX +44-1-628-770224
http://www.mcgraw-hill.co.uk
computing_neurope@mcgraw-hill.com

ALL OTHER INQUIRIES Contact:
Osborne/McGraw-Hill
TEL +1-510-549-6600
FAX +1-510-883-7600
http://www.osborne.com
omg_international@mcgraw-hill.com

Get Your FREE Subscription to *Oracle Magazine*

Oracle Magazine is essential gear for today's information technology professionals. Stay informed and increase your productivity with every issue of *Oracle Magazine*. Inside each **FREE,** bimonthly issue you'll get:

- Up-to-date information on Oracle Database Server, Oracle Applications, Internet Computing, and tools
- Third-party news and announcements
- Technical articles on Oracle products and operating environments
- Development and administration tips
- Real-world customer stories

Three easy ways to subscribe:

1. Web **Visit our Web site at www.oracle.com/oramag/. You'll find a subscription form there, plus much more!**

2. Fax Complete the questionnaire on the back of this card and fax the questionnaire side only to **+1.847.647.9735.**

3. Mail Complete the questionnaire on the back of this card and mail it to P.O. Box 1263, Skokie, IL 60076-8263.

If there are other Oracle users at your location who would like to receive their own subscription to *Oracle Magazine*, please photocopy this form and pass it along.

☐ YES! Please send me a FREE subscription to *Oracle Magazine*.

To receive a free bimonthly subscription to *Oracle Magazine*, you must fill out the entire card, sign it, and date it (incomplete cards cannot be processed or acknowledged). You can also fax your application to **+1.847.647.9735**. Or subscribe at our Web site at www.oracle.com/oramag

SIGNATURE (REQUIRED) X _____   **DATE** _____

What is the primary business activity of your firm at this location? *(check only one)*
- ☐ 03 Communications
- ☐ 04 Consulting, Training
- ☐ 06 Data Processing
- ☐ 07 Education
- ☐ 08 Engineering
- ☐ 09 Financial Services
- ☐ 10 Government—Federal, Local, State, Other
- ☐ 11 Government—Military
- ☐ 12 Health Care
- ☐ 13 Manufacturing—Aerospace, Defense
- ☐ 14 Manufacturing—Computer Hardware
- ☐ 15 Manufacturing—Noncomputer Products
- ☐ 17 Research & Development
- ☐ 19 Retailing, Wholesaling, Distribution
- ☐ 20 Software Development
- ☐ 21 Systems Integration, VAR, VAD, OEM
- ☐ 22 Transportation
- ☐ 23 Utilities (Electric, Gas, Sanitation)
- ☐ 98 Other Business and Services
  _____

Which of the following best describes your job function? *(check only one)*

CORPORATE MANAGEMENT/STAFF
- ☐ 01 Executive Management (President, Chair, CEO, CFO, Owner, Partner, Principal)
- ☐ 02 Finance/Administrative Management (VP/Director/ Manager/Controller, Purchasing, Administration)
- ☐ 03 Sales/Marketing Management (VP/Director/Manager)
- ☐ 04 Computer Systems/Operations Management (CIO/VP/Director/ Manager MIS, Operations)

IS/IT STAFF
- ☐ 07 Systems Development/ Programming Management
- ☐ 08 Systems Development/ Programming Staff
- ☐ 09 Consulting
- ☐ 10 DBA/Systems Administrator
- ☐ 11 Education/Training
- ☐ 14 Technical Support Director/ Manager
- ☐ 16 Other Technical Management/Staff
- ☐ 98 Other _____

What is your current primary operating platform? *(check all that apply)*
- ☐ 01 DEC UNIX
- ☐ 02 DEC VAX VMS
- ☐ 03 Java
- ☐ 04 HP UNIX
- ☐ 05 IBM AIX
- ☐ 06 IBM UNIX
- ☐ 07 Macintosh
- ☐ 09 MS-DOS
- ☐ 10 MVS
- ☐ 11 NetWare
- ☐ 12 Network Computing
- ☐ 13 OpenVMS
- ☐ 14 SCO UNIX
- ☐ 24 Sequent DYNIX/ptx
- ☐ 15 Sun Solaris/SunOS
- ☐ 16 SVR4
- ☐ 18 UnixWare
- ☐ 20 Windows
- ☐ 21 Windows NT
- ☐ 23 Other UNIX _____
- ☐ 98 Other _____
- 99 ☐ **None of the above**

Do you evaluate, specify, recommend, or authorize the purchase of any of the following? *(check all that apply)*
- ☐ 01 Hardware
- ☐ 02 Software
- ☐ 03 Application Development Tools
- ☐ 04 Database Products
- ☐ 05 Internet or Intranet Products
- 99 ☐ **None of the above**

In your job, do you use or plan to purchase any of the following products or services? *(check all that apply)*

SOFTWARE
- ☐ 01 Business Graphics
- ☐ 02 CAD/CAE/CAM
- ☐ 03 CASE
- ☐ 05 Communications
- ☐ 06 Database Management
- ☐ 07 File Management
- ☐ 08 Finance
- ☐ 09 Java
- ☐ 10 Materials Resource Planning
- ☐ 11 Multimedia Authoring
- ☐ 12 Networking
- ☐ 13 Office Automation
- ☐ 14 Order Entry/Inventory Control
- ☐ 15 Programming
- ☐ 16 Project Management

- ☐ 17 Scientific and Engineering
- ☐ 18 Spreadsheets
- ☐ 19 Systems Management
- ☐ 20 Workflow

HARDWARE
- ☐ 21 Macintosh
- ☐ 22 Mainframe
- ☐ 23 Massively Parallel Processing
- ☐ 24 Minicomputer
- ☐ 25 PC
- ☐ 26 Network Computer
- ☐ 28 Symmetric Multiprocessing
- ☐ 29 Workstation

PERIPHERALS
- ☐ 30 Bridges/Routers/Hubs/Gateways
- ☐ 31 CD-ROM Drives
- ☐ 32 Disk Drives/Subsystems
- ☐ 33 Modems
- ☐ 34 Tape Drives/Subsystems
- ☐ 35 Video Boards/Multimedia

SERVICES
- ☐ 37 Consulting
- ☐ 38 Education/Training
- ☐ 39 Maintenance
- ☐ 40 Online Database Services
- ☐ 41 Support
- ☐ 36 Technology-Based Training
- ☐ 98 Other _____
- 99 ☐ **None of the above**

What Oracle products are in use at your site? *(check all that apply)*

SERVER/SOFTWARE
- ☐ 01 Oracle8
- ☐ 30 Oracle8*i*
- ☐ 31 Oracle8*i* Lite
- ☐ 02 Oracle7
- ☐ 03 Oracle Application Server
- ☐ 04 Oracle Data Mart Suites
- ☐ 05 Oracle Internet Commerce Server
- ☐ 32 Oracle *inter*Media
- ☐ 33 Oracle JServer
- ☐ 07 Oracle Lite
- ☐ 08 Oracle Payment Server
- ☐ 11 Oracle Video Server

TOOLS
- ☐ 13 Oracle Designer
- ☐ 14 Oracle Developer
- ☐ 54 Oracle Discoverer
- ☐ 53 Oracle Express
- ☐ 51 Oracle JDeveloper
- ☐ 52 Oracle Reports
- ☐ 50 Oracle WebDB
- ☐ 55 Oracle Workflow

ORACLE APPLICATIONS
- ☐ 17 Oracle Automotive

- ☐ 35 Oracle Business Intelligence Syste
- ☐ 19 Oracle Consumer Packaged Goods
- ☐ 39 Oracle E-Commerce
- ☐ 18 Oracle Energy
- ☐ 20 Oracle Financials
- ☐ 28 Oracle Front Office
- ☐ 21 Oracle Human Resources
- ☐ 37 Oracle Internet Procurement
- ☐ 22 Oracle Manufacturing
- ☐ 40 Oracle Process Manufacturing
- ☐ 23 Oracle Projects
- ☐ 34 Oracle Retail
- ☐ 29 Oracle Self-Service Web Application
- ☐ 38 Oracle Strategic Enterprise Management
- ☐ 25 Oracle Supply Chain Management
- ☐ 36 Oracle Tutor
- ☐ 41 Oracle Travel Management

ORACLE SERVICES
- ☐ 61 Oracle Consulting
- ☐ 62 Oracle Education
- ☐ 60 Oracle Support
- ☐ 98 Other _____
- 99 ☐ **None of the above**

What other database products are in use a your site? *(check all that apply)*
- ☐ 01 Access
- ☐ 02 Baan
- ☐ 03 dbase
- ☐ 04 Gupta
- ☐ 05 IBM DB2
- ☐ 06 Informix
- ☐ 07 Ingres
- ☐ 08 Microsoft Access
- ☐ 09 Microsoft SQL Server
- ☐ 10 PeopleSoft
- ☐ 11 Progress
- ☐ 12 SAP
- ☐ 13 Sybase
- ☐ 14 VSAM
- ☐ 98 Other _____
- 99 ☐ **None of the above**

During the next 12 months, how much do you anticipate your organization will spend on computer hardware, software, peripherals, and services for your location? *(check only one)*
- ☐ 01 Less than $10,000
- ☐ 02 $10,000 to $49,999
- ☐ 03 $50,000 to $99,999
- ☐ 04 $100,000 to $499,999
- ☐ 05 $500,000 to $999,999
- ☐ 06 $1,000,000 and over

If there are other Oracle users at your location who would like to receive a free subscription to *Oracle Magazine*, please photocopy this form and pass it along, or contact Customer Service at **+1.847.647.9630**

Knowledge is power. To which we say,

crank up the power.

Are you ready for a power surge?

Accelerate your career—become an **Oracle Certified Professional** (OCP). With Oracle's cutting-edge *Instructor-Led Training*, *Technology-Based Training*, and this *guide*, you can prepare for certification faster than ever. Set your own trajectory by logging your personal training plan with us. Go to **http://education.oracle.com/tpb**, where we'll help you pick a training path, select your courses, and track your progress. We'll even send you an email when your courses are offered in your area. If you don't have access to the Web, call us at 1-800-441-3541 (Outside the U.S. call +1-310-335-2403).

Power learning has never been easier.

Oracle Technology Network

The definitive source of information
for the software that powers the internet

You know everything, right? If you are a developer, DBA or IT professional, you are expected to build the right foundation for a 24x7 e-business while keeping ahead of every new technology change that can keep it successful.

Oracle software powers the world's top e-businesses today and is leading the way for thousands of the dot-coms of tomorrow. That is why we have the fastest growing developer community in the world that you can join for FREE, and get immediate access to all the inside information, downloads, training, code samples and professional forums for the software that powers the internet.

Activate your free membership today at: http://otn.oracle.com.
Now you know everything.

ORACLE SOFTWARE LICENSE AGREEMENT

YOU SHOULD CAREFULLY READ THE FOLLOWING TERMS AND CONDITIONS BEFORE BREAKING THE SEAL ON THE DISC ENVELOPE. AMONG OTHER THINGS, THIS AGREEMENT LICENSES THE ENCLOSED SOFTWARE TO YOU AND CONTAINS WARRANTY AND LIABILITY DISCLAIMERS. BY USING THE DISC AND/OR INSTALLING THE SOFTWARE, YOU ARE ACCEPTING AND AGREEING TO THE TERMS AND CONDITIONS OF THIS AGREEMENT. IF YOU DO NOT AGREE TO THE TERMS OF THIS AGREEMENT, DO NOT BREAK THE SEAL OR USE THE DISC. YOU SHOULD PROMPTLY RETURN THE PACKAGE UNOPENED.

LICENSE: ORACLE CORPORATION ("ORACLE") GRANTS END USER ("YOU" OR "YOUR") A NON-EXCLUSIVE, NON-TRANSFERABLE DEVELOPMENT ONLY LIMITED USE LICENSE TO USE THE ENCLOSED SOFTWARE AND DOCUMENTATION ("SOFTWARE") SUBJECT TO THE TERMS AND CONDITIONS, INCLUDING USE RESTRICTIONS, SPECIFIED BELOW.

You shall have the right to use the Software (a) only in object code form, (b) for development purposes only in the indicated operating environment for a single developer (one person) on a single computer, (c) solely with the publication with which the Software is included, and (d) solely for Your personal use and as a single user.

You are prohibited from and shall not (a) transfer, sell, sublicense, assign or otherwise convey the Software, (b) timeshare, rent or market the Software, (c) use the Software for or as part of a service bureau, and/or (d) distribute the Software in whole or in part. Any attempt to transfer, sell, sublicense, assign or otherwise convey any of the rights, duties or obligations hereunder is void. You are prohibited from and shall not use the Software for internal data processing operations, processing data of a third party or for any commercial or production use. If You desire to use the Software for any use other than the development use allowed under this Agreement, You must contact Oracle, or an authorized Oracle reseller, to obtain the appropriate licenses. You are prohibited from and shall not cause or permit the reverse engineering, disassembly, decompilation, modification or creation of derivative works based on the Software. You are prohibited from and shall not copy or duplicate the Software except as follows: You may make one copy of the Software in machine readable form solely for back-up purposes. No other copies shall be made without Oracle's prior written consent. You are prohibited from and shall not: (a) remove any product identification, copyright notices, or other notices or proprietary restrictions from the Software, or (b) run any benchmark tests with or of the Software. This Agreement does not authorize You to use any Oracle name, trademark or logo.

COPYRIGHT/OWNERSHIP OF SOFTWARE: The Software is the confidential and proprietary product of Oracle and is protected by copyright and other intellectual property laws. You acquire only the right to use the Software and do not acquire any rights, express or implied, in the Software or media containing the Software other than those specified in this Agreement. Oracle, or its licensor, shall at all times, including but not limited to after termination of this Agreement, retain all rights, title, interest, including intellectual property rights, in the Software and media.

WARRANTY DISCLAIMER: THE SOFTWARE IS PROVIDED "AS IS" AND ORACLE SPECIFICALLY DISCLAIMS ALL WARRANTIES OF ANY KIND, EITHER EXPRESS OR IMPLIED, INCLUDING, BUT NOT LIMITED TO, THE IMPLIED WARRANTIES OF MERCHANTABILITY, SATISFACTORY QUALITY AND FITNESS FOR A PARTICULAR PURPOSE. ORACLE DOES NOT WARRANT, GUARANTEE OR MAKE ANY REPRESENTATIONS REGARDING THE USE, OR THE RESULTS OF THE USE, OF THE SOFTWARE IN TERMS OF CORRECTNESS, ACCURACY, RELIABILITY, CURRENTNESS OR OTHERWISE, AND DOES NOT WARRANT THAT THE OPERATION OF THE SOFTWARE WILL BE UNINTERRUPTED OR ERROR FREE. ORACLE EXPRESSLY DISCLAIMS ALL WARRANTIES NOT STATED HEREIN, NO ORAL OR WRITTEN INFORMATION OR ADVICE GIVEN BY ORACLE OR OTHERS SHALL CREATE A WARRANTY OR IN ANY WAY INCREASE THE SCOPE OF THIS LICENSE, AND YOU MAY NOT RELY ON ANY SUCH INFORMATION OR ADVICE.

LIMITATION OF LIABILITY: IN NO EVENT SHALL ORACLE OR ITS LICENSORS BE LIABLE FOR ANY DIRECT, INDIRECT, INCIDENTAL, SPECIAL OR CONSEQUENTIAL DAMAGES, OR DAMAGES FOR LOSS OF PROFITS, REVENUE, DATA OR DATA USE, INCURRED BY YOU OR ANY THIRD PARTY, WHETHER IN AN ACTION IN CONTRACT OR TORT, EVEN IF ORACLE AND/OR ITS LICENSORS HAVE BEEN ADVISED OF THE POSSIBILITY OF SUCH DAMAGES. SOME JURISDICTIONS DO NOT ALLOW THE EXCLUSION OF IMPLIED WARRANTIES OR LIMITATION OR EXCLUSION OF LIABILITY FOR INCIDENTAL OR CONSEQUENTIAL DAMAGES SO THE ABOVE EXCLUSIONS AND LIMITATION MAY NOT APPLY TO YOU.

TERMINATION: You may terminate this license at any time by discontinuing use of and destroying the Software together with any copies in any form. This license will also terminate if You fail to comply with any term or condition of this Agreement. Upon termination of the license, You agree to discontinue use of and destroy the Software together with any copies in any form. The Warranty Disclaimer, Limitation of Liability, and Export Administration sections of this Agreement shall survive termination of this Agreement.

NO TECHNICAL SUPPORT: Oracle is not obligated to provide and this Agreement does not entitle You to any updates or upgrades to, or any technical support or phone support for, the Software.

EXPORT ADMINISTRATION: You acknowledge that the Software, including technical data, is subject to United States export control laws, including the United States Export Administration Act and its associated regulations, and may be subject to export or import regulations in other countries. You agree to comply fully with all laws and regulations of the United States and other countries ("Export Laws") to assure that neither the Software, nor any direct products thereof, are (a) exported, directly or indirectly, in violation of Export Laws, either to countries or nationals that are subject to United States export restrictions or to any end user who has been prohibited from participating in the Unites States export transactions by any federal agency of the United States government; or (b) intended to be used for any purposes prohibited by the Export Laws, including, without limitation, nuclear, chemical or biological weapons proliferation. You acknowledge that the Software may include technical data subject to export and re-export restrictions imposed by United States law.

RESTRICTED RIGHTS: The Software is provided with Restricted Rights. Use, duplication or disclosure of the Software by the United State government is subject to the restrictions set forth in the Rights in Technical Data and Computer Software Clauses in DFARS 252.227-7013(c)(1)(ii) and FAR 52.227-19(c)(2) as applicable. Manufacturer is Oracle Corporation, 500 Oracle Parkway, Redwood City, CA 94065.

MISCELLANEOUS: This Agreement and all related actions thereto shall be governed by California law. Oracle may audit Your use of the Software. If any provision of this Agreement is held to be invalid or unenforceable, the remaining provisions of this Agreement will remain in full force.

YOU ACKNOWLEDGE THAT YOU HAVE READ THIS AGREEMENT, UNDERSTAND IT, AND AGREE TO BE BOUND BY ITS TERMS AND CONDITIONS. YOU FURTHER AGREE THAT IT IS THE COMPLETE AND EXCLUSIVE STATEMENT OF THE AGREEMENT BETWEEN ORACLE AND YOU.

Oracle is a registered trademark of Oracle Corporation.

Register for the *Oracle Technology Network* (OTN)

Oracle Technology Network ("OTN") is the primary technical source for developers building Oracle-based applications. As an OTN member, you will be part of an online community with access to technical papers, code samples, product documentation, self-service technical support, free software, OTN-sponsored Internet developer conferences, and discussion groups on up-to-date Oracle technology. Membership is FREE! Register for OTN on the World Wide Web at

```
http://www.oracle.com/books/.
```